MUSIC OF THREE

SEASONS: 1974–1977

MUSIC OF THREE
SEASONS: 1974–1977

ANDREW PORTER

Farrar Straus Giroux

NEW YORK

Library of Congress Cataloging in Publication Data
Porter, Andrew. Music of three seasons, 1974–1977.
Includes index.
1.   Music—Addresses, essays, lectures.   2.   Music—New York (City)
I.   The New Yorker (New York, 1925–   )   II.   Title.
ML60.P895M88   780′.8   78-1669

To the memory of

ERNEST NEWMAN (1868–1959)

RICHARD CAPELL (1885–1954)

FRANK HOWES (1891–1974)

three music critics who encouraged me

and guided my first steps

Contents

An Autobiographical Preamble

In the spring of 1972, I came home one day from the offices of *The Financial Times*, the London daily newspaper whose music critic I had been for nineteen years, ruffled by a row. I forget now whether it was over a missing comma, a misplaced paragraph, or something even more serious. The telephone was ringing. It was the editor of *The New Yorker*, inviting me to become the music critic of his magazine. I said "Mmm" and "Er" and "Do you think I would be happy?" He said, "Well, would you like to try it for a season? Could you come to lunch at the Algonquin next week and have a look at us?" I came; it was eight years since I had been in America. I liked what I saw. And the consequence was that over that lunch the "no" that had been forming in my mind changed to a "yes." It could be only a trial season; I had already accepted an invitation to be a visiting fellow of All Souls College, Oxford, in 1973–74.

So far, I repeat in the main the foreword to an English edition of *A Musical Season*, a collection of the *New Yorker* pieces that I wrote in 1972–73. When that season was over, I went back to England, to All Souls. What was to come after that was still unsure. I spent an academic year in Oxford working on Verdi, teaching a little, and enjoying a life that made a return to the conditions of daily journalism seem unattractive, even under so generous and tolerant an employer as *The Financial Times*. In England, a line between musicology and musical journalism is not strictly drawn. Jack Westrup, Heather Professor of Music in the Oxford of my undergraduate days, had worked for some years as a music critic for *The Daily Telegraph*. Gerald Abraham, on retiring from the chair of music of Liverpool University, had joined the *Telegraph* team of critics. And although Sir George Grove was by training an engineer (appropriately enough, he built lighthouses), the successive editions of *Grove's Dictionary of Music and Musicians* have been prepared by music critics of *The Times* or of *The Observer*. I was tempted to seek an academic post but decided at last that I wanted to write, not to teach—and to continue writing music criticism. And so in September 1974 I returned to New York and to *The New Yorker*.

Leaving London was not easy. Not only is London's own musical life the fullest and most adventurous to be found in the world; Aldeburgh, Bath, Canterbury, Cardiff, Chichester, York, and a hundred other places rich in history and rich in musical events are easily reached from it. I miss them. Moreover, as the jet flies, London is not far from Paris, Parma, and Prague, Berlin, Bonn, and Bayreuth, Dresden and Darmstadt, Munich and Milan, and the other places where Western musical history was made—places which a European critic is required to visit in the course of his work. Attending performances at night in those cities, by day I could walk the streets where the composers I was writing about lived, see the sights that inspired much of their music (can one feel *The Ring* fully without having been stirred by the Rhine landscapes, or *Peter Grimes* without the Suffolk sea?), and work in the libraries where their manuscripts are housed. In the preface to his Weber biography, John Warrack thanks the editor of *The Sunday Telegraph*, "as music critic of which I was enabled to undertake essential journeys to Germany, Czechoslovakia, and Russia." For most of what in the following pages is the result of travel—observations of buildings and landscapes, or on manuscripts that reveal more than any microfilm of them can—I thank the editors of *The Financial Times* and *The New Yorker*, who sent me to work in cities where there were things I wanted to see and study besides performances that deserved a review. A critic is lucky: he can keep lists of documents he wants to consult in Lisbon and Leningrad, Champaign and Chicago; sooner or later his job will send him there. It was while I was in Paris reviewing a series of Bolshoy performances at the Opéra for *The Financial Times* that I found the "new" passages of Verdi's *Don Carlos*; attendance at a Curtis Institute production for *The New Yorker* provided a chance of studying Wagner's manuscript instructions for the staging of *Lohengrin*. In return, of course, a critic will first publish any findings in his paper. Gerald Abraham and Peter Stadlen have embedded much of musicological importance in *Telegraph* daily reviews. The *Don Carlos* news was first announced in the columns of *The Financial Times*, in a review of a Covent Garden production of that opera.

"No, Sir; when a man is tired of London, he is tired of life; for there is in London all that life can afford." With respect, Dr. Johnson, "No, Sir" to you! Probably not in the 1770s, when you said that; certainly not in the 1970s. After twenty years in the same London job, I found that a New World beckoned—not only New York but Boston, Berkeley, and Bloomington, St. Paul, St. Louis, San Antonio, and San Diego, "the varied and ample land, the South and the North in the light, Ohio's shores and flashing Missouri." Anyone who has sung in a British choral society is seized early by the Whitmanesque vision, and there are passages in this book that show, I hope, that the romance of this land is still strong with me. Moreover, and perhaps more important, in the pages of *The New Yorker* I was invited, encouraged, to attempt a kind of criticism for which the British press had ever less space—part descriptive chronicle, part essay in which a particular performance may be viewed as the latest addition to the long history of a work and, more personally, to a critic's experience of it.

Often I am asked, "What should a music critic try to do?" and "What are the qualifications for being a music critic?" The second question is the easier to answer—by referring the asker to Theodore Meyer Greene's *The Arts and the Art of Criticism* (Princeton, 1940) for a long clear answer and to Winton Dean's essay on criticism in the fifth edition of *Grove* for a short clear answer. Dean's final section, "The Critic's Qualifications," makes daunting reading for anyone who actually is a critic. He goes through them as he might a list of the Deadly Sins, relieved if there are any he has not that day committed, if there are perhaps a few qualities he may claim in some measure to possess. The section begins, "The qualities required of the ideal music critic today are so multifarious as almost to place him among the mythical beasts," and the eight heads of the "formidable catalogue of qualifications" are: "a knowledge of the technical and theoretical principles of music . . . a knowledge of musical history and scholarship . . . a wide general education, covering as many as possible of the subjects with which music can be shown to have a point of direct contact . . . the ability to think straight and to write in a clear and stimulating manner . . . an insight into the workings of the creative imagination (this presupposes a touch of the same quality in the critic) . . . an integrated philosophy of life of his own . . . an enduring inquisitiveness and willingness to learn . . . an acceptance of his own limitations, both individual and generic." Implicit in the second and third, but perhaps worth specifying as a necessary qualification, is some command of the languages spoken and set by the composers a critic writes about.

To that first question, however—"What should a music critic try to do?"—my answer is always an evasive "It all depends." It depends on who and what he is, what his strengths and his interests are, what he is writing about, and where he is writing. For some two decades of my own critical career, I was employed for the most part as a chronicler on a daily newspaper, setting down day-by-day incidents in the continuing history of music. "How did you begin?" While I was an undergraduate—reading English but, as organ scholar of my college, playing for services, conducting a college choir and orchestra, composing incidental music for college plays—I reviewed some Oxford musical events for *The Manchester Guardian*. I had written to the editor of that paper suggesting that his readers might be interested to learn about a local revival of Arne's *Judith*. He replied, "Send me something, and if I like it, I'll print it"; and he did print it. On graduating, I spent two apprentice years in London as a part-time assistant in turn to Desmond Shawe-Taylor on *The New Statesman* (he visited America when the Scala company first came to England, so I had exciting material—*Otello, Falstaff*, and the Verdi Requiem under Victor De Sabata—with which to make a "London début"); to Frank Howes on *The Times* (during the Festival of Britain, when every quarter of the city rang with music, and *The Times* heard it all; the reviews were later collected in a volume);

and to Richard Capell on *The Daily Telegraph*. Capell invited me to write for *Music and Letters*, and Alec Robertson to broadcast for the BBC and to review records for *The Gramophone*. With a generosity that, I like to feel, is a mark of music critics—another quality to add to Dean's list?—these men taught and encouraged me. To their names I would add those of Ernest Newman of *The Sunday Times*, the doyen of English critics when I began, who, when I first visited the book-filled country barn where he worked, pointed to his shelves with volumes of literary criticism and advised me to take the best writing about writing as a model; and of William Mann, now the first critic of *The Times* (and then the second critic, scooped up fresh from Cambridge by Howes so that there would be a young, challenging, and un-Oxonian note in the collective, anonymous *vox Temporum*), who put in my way the useful assignment of writing, for *London Musical Events*, a monthly essay on some new composition. Alan Pryce-Jones of *The Times Literary Supplement*, J. R. Ackerley of *The Listener*, and T. C. Worsley of *The New Statesman* gave me books to review. In those days, *TLS* and *Listener* reviews were unsigned, and so Ackerley could entrust Newman's *Wagner Nights* to a beginner and either print, not needing a name, or reject the result.

In New York I am now often approached by young people who want to be music critics—"How can one get a start here?"—and find it hard to advise even the most promising of them. Back in 1953, in a city with ten daily newspapers (two of them employing teams of full-time critics, and the rest at least one or two), five or six weekly magazines with music critics, and several monthly and quarterly music periodicals, I had found it very easy to get a start. At one time or another, when their regular critics were on holiday, away at festivals, or ill, I wrote occasional pieces for just about all of those publications. *The News Chronicle*, *The Daily Herald*, and *Time and Tide*, in which as a student I used to read Scott Goddard, Martin Cooper, and Philip Hope-Wallace, disappeared, but in 1955 another daily paper opened its pages to music, when *The Financial Times* invited me to become its first music critic. It welcomed music so wholeheartedly that in time I had a team of five full-time staff critics in London, regular correspondents abroad to report on events that one of us did not fly out to attend, and five or six other people to call on when a specialist's knowledge was needed or on nights when, say, there was a new opera in Hamburg, a new symphony in Glasgow, festivals in Glyndebourne, Budapest, and Royan, and four London concerts that deserved a review. On such nights, promising newcomers could also be given a chance to show their paces. Because *The Financial Times* had never had a music critic before, I was allowed —to an extent which I don't think Gordon Newton and Garrett Drogheda, my editor and managing director, quite realized—to write the rules by which we worked. I aimed to unite what I had found best in the practices of the other papers I had written for (on *The Daily Express*, for example, that remarkable editor Arthur Christiansen had ruled that his critics' reviews should never be cut or altered without consultation) and to ban such things as snappy headlines (a plain statement of place and name is still *FT* style) and deadlines that allowed too little time to think and write (the critics of *The Guardian* and *The Telegraph* seldom saw the last act of a long opera). *FT* notices often appeared a day later than those of other papers.

When I am asked, "How did you get established?" I answer, "By intransigence," and recall the night when I tipped a tray of loose type— a review of mine that, in early *FT* days, *had* been cut—onto the floor rather than let it appear in a mutilated form. Early on, too, I decided that, since critics write most interestingly about events that interest them, I would try to assemble for the *FT* a team of colleagues whose particular interests were complementary to mine; no one would be directed to go to an event he or she didn't positively want to attend, since, sooner or later, such direction produces bored, routine reporting. So sometimes it happened that when other papers told of, say, Rubinstein's playing the Brahms Second Concerto for the umpteenth time, the *FT* told of an amateur performance of Alessandro Scarlatti's *Rosaura* in a suburban church hall. And sometimes the editor was cross. But as the team grew, it usually included someone who would leap at the chance of hearing Rubinstein. No one, I repeat, should go to and write about concerts night after night unless he wants to; otherwise, music critics are produced who seem to have stopped enjoying music. Having read them, I resolved to try not to become one or to create any more of them. An eager apprenticeship served by months of assessing début recitals and standard concerts can be useful training (though it is hard on the débutants, who deserve to be assessed by experienced ears). And a wide knowledge of all music, and of all the ways in which it is practiced, is essential to a critic. But such an apprenticeship should not last long if the critic is to keep any freshness.

One further observation, before leaving daily newspapers and crossing the Atlantic. It seems to me that a newspaper critic, if he is not to become stale, needs some other outlet, some other format to work in, than the columns of his paper. "What should it be?" "It all depends." Some critics—Newman, Capell, Cooper, Mann—write scholarly books. Most of them in Britain broadcast for the BBC and also contribute learned articles on their special subjects to the learned press. I became an assistant editor of the monthly magazine *Opera*, where Harold Rosenthal showed me how to edit and how in practical terms, with galleys, scissors, and paste, to put a magazine together. Then Messrs. Novello gave me a free hand to refashion their venerable monthly, *The Musical Times*, which I edited for seven years, from 1960 to 1967. *The Musical Times* is a periodical in which musicologists who want to be read by a wider public than other musicologists like to publish their articles; it is on sale in London's concert halls and opera houses. It gave me a chance to develop and test my belief in what Busoni, not quite in the same sense, called *der Einheit der Musik*—a belief that composers, executants, impresarios, managers, publishers, historians, musicologists, critics, and audiences are engaged in branches of the same activity, and that the critic should in some way be a bridge between the others. That belief forms a ground bass to the pages that follow. It was strengthened during years of serving on the music advisory panels of the Arts Council of Great Britain and of the British Council (the bodies that provide the main funds for British music making, and whose panels are made up of composers, publishers, executants, critics, etc.) and underlies my own chosen sideline, translating operas into English, which brings me into contact with singers, conductors, directors, publishers—and audiences.

That is the background against which what follows was written. These *New Yorker* reviews are not—at any rate, not in any systematic or comprehensive way—a week-by-week chronicle of musical life in New York, with excursions elsewhere. Nor, on the other hand, are they based *solely* on a personal, quirky selection among the thousands of events that claim a New York critic's attention. To return to that question, "What should a music critic try to do?": the critic of a New York weekly magazine, it seems to me, should attend a wide variety of events, not only within the city, and attempt to reconcile the claims of "duty" and inclination. Most weeks I heard twice or thrice as much music as ever I wrote about. For reasons set out above, and equally because a single critic cannot pretend to be any kind of comprehensive chronicler, I chose to concentrate on the things that struck me as most important or the things that interested me most. Happily, they were often coincident. Most of the large new works that appeared in New York concert programs receive extended treatment. So do the many new operas, all over the country, commissioned for the Bicentennial season. To see interesting operas of the past, I often had to travel long distances: to Portland, Oregon, for Ernst Krenek's *Leben des Orest*, to San Diego for *Rienzi*, to Berkeley for Alessandro Scarlatti's *Griselda*. Nearer home, Sarah Caldwell's Opera Company of Boston provided several adventures. I wish there had been more occasions to write about Handel, Rameau, Gluck, and Janáček, about Boulez as a composer. There would be something about Jommelli, something about Haydn's operas, something about Franz Schreker had there been "musical events" concerning those composers to review. There would be far more about Bach and about what gets lumped together as "early music" were Bach and early music more satisfactorily performed in New York than they generally are. There is more about Massenet than I would have written had not Massenet loomed so large during these three years. The reviews follow no consistent pattern. "It all depends." Often I took the chance of bringing together observations by others as well as by me on a work that I had been studying on and off since student days. When writing about new works, I tried to include as much straightforward fact—forces, duration—as possible.

My particular preoccupations will soon appear: above all, the relationship between Milton's blest pair of sirens, Voice and Verse, who wed their divine sounds "and mixt power employ/Dead things with inbreath'd sense able to pierce." I discovered music as a choirboy, was brought up in a European tradition where the concert hall and recital room are by-products of the choir loft and the opera house, and reached America too late to conform to any idea that music without words is not merely "purer" but in some way inherently more estimable than music that employs words. As Tovey said (I excerpt phrases, not quite fairly, from his defense of the choral finale to Beethoven's Ninth Symphony), "All instruments and all harmonic and contrapuntal arts imitate, on the one hand, voices, and on the other hand, dance rhythms and pulse rhythms . . . The voice is the most natural as well as the most perfect of instruments . . . The introduction of voices normally means the introduction of words, since that is how the human race uses its voice . . . It follows from this that the music must concern itself (conventionally or realistically or how you please) with the fit expression of the words." Hence my repeated insistence that when music with words is performed, those words should be comprehended; that when operas are sung in a foreign tongue, librettos with translations should be available in advance; that in the concert hall texts, translations, and light to read them by should be provided. A concern for the whole meaning of a composition, not just voice fancying, is at the base of this. When Bernard Shaw collected his weekly reviews, he introduced them by saying, "There are people who will read about music and nothing else. To them dead prima donnas are more interesting than saints, and extinct tenors than mighty conquerors. They are presumably the only people who will read these volumes." It is not so, of course; musicians of every kind read Shaw's volumes, and they remain the delight and despair of anyone who tries himself to write about music. But people whose first care is for living prima donnas and active tenors tend to find my reviews as unsatisfactory as do those whose first and perhaps only love is, say, chamber music. From readers I receive complaints of two somewhat contradictory kinds: "Too much about singing" and "Three columns about the opera and then only one paragraph about the singers." Let me attempt a defense. To the first charge: in any large city, one can take it for granted that there is a regular provision of the standard instrumental repertory of the past executed on a high level, and the critic who is not called on to be a chronicler can take it for granted that it is so, and need write about it only when he is moved by something exceptional and feels he may have something to say. Hence the emphasis in these pages, so far as instrumental music is concerned, on contemporary compositions. To the second: my interest *is* usually in the work itself, in what it has meant and what it can mean, and then in the details of individual performances insofar as they illumine or fail to illumine the composer's intention and meaning.

"The composer's intention" is another King Charles's Head. I believe that, with very few exceptions, the music of any age speaks to listeners most clearly, most directly, with the tones and accents and in the forms that its creator intended. Hence the emphasis on accuracy and integrity of editions, on aptness of instruments, acoustics, and performing style, on the circumstances of the original performances, on documents of all kinds (including phonograph records) that can shed light on a composer's intentions. Hence the concern with the performing history of a composition, with what past as well as present performances can tell us about it. Hence the repeated assertion that the discoveries of musicology become valuable only when they are put into practice.

When I came to New York, I found that the move sharpened an already quick feeling for *place*, in every sense of the word: the place on the map of a work's composition and the place, the building, of its first performance; the historical, social, political, and, for that matter, acoustical considerations that may have determined the form it took; its place within a composer's oeuvre; the place it can hold today within a particular society and culture; and the physical place—whether suitable or unsuitable in sound, in "atmosphere," in associations—of the performance I am reviewing. Those are some of the things I tried to write about, whether the composition concerned was European or American, medieval or modern. The sense of the past playing upon, shaping, and providing ways of understanding the present, and the awareness of minds and works of the past—above all, those of Homer, Shakespeare, Goethe, and Beethoven—as constant influences on the musicians of the later centuries became more acute. In an account of revisiting Munich (pp. 214–16), this sense of place and of the past acting upon a musician's present imagination finds its fullest statement. (Each summer I spent in Europe, and I wrote for *The New Yorker* about some of what I heard there.) The sense of place and past playing upon an exciting present also finds some expression in the reviews of Leon Kirchner's *Lily* (pp. 569–77) and of Elliott Carter's *Symphony of Three Orchestras* (pp. 527–32). It underlies the account of Busoni's *Doktor Faust* in Bloomington (pp. 55–8) and of Krenek's *Leben des Orest* in Oregon (pp. 245–50). It influences much of what I write.

I toyed with various "thematic" arrangements of these reviews but found that none of them worked. (Should the piece about *Doktor Faust* be classified under "Goethe and Music" or "Twentieth-Century Opera"? Would it be sensible to divide a review in which one train of thought passes through music of different centuries?) So the arrangement is chronological. Lillian McClintock's careful index will direct a reader to any composer, performer, or place that especially interests him. However, the book may fall into the hands of someone, one of whose special concerns coincides with one of mine; so here is a partial "thematic index" to direct him to the main statements of some of those concerns.

Place and "Ambience": Adelaide (332–7), Batignano (211, 401), Charleston and Spoleto (606–12), Glyndebourne (205–8), Messiaen (47–9), Munich (214–16), St. Louis (612–18), Vancouver (625–7).

Halls and Theatres: Avery Fisher Hall (419–23), Town Hall (148–9), Baltimore (628), Minneapolis (117–20), Vancouver (625–7).

Authentic Editions and Instruments: Berg's *Lulu* (550–8), Frescobaldi (386–8), Handel's *Imeneo* (154–6), *Messiah* (472–4), and *Rinaldo* (225–8); Monteverdi's *Ulisse* (310–16); Mozart's *Idomeneo* (121–6); Schubert (298–301); 102–3; 470.

Orchestra Placing: 450–2.

Words, Music, and Translation: 152–3; *Pierrot lunaire* (31–4), Schubert's *Schöne Mullerin* (523–7).

Seventeenth-century Opera: Monteverdi's *Ulisse* (310–16); Cavalli's *Giasone* (487–90).

Eighteenth-century Opera: Caldara's *Ifigenia* (403–5); Cherubini's *Lodoiska* and *Les Deux Journées* (407–10); Handel's *Rinaldo* (225–8); Mozart's *Idomeneo* (121–6) and *Figaro* (250–5); A. Scarlatti's *Griselda* (363–9).

Nineteenth-century Opera: Bellini's *I Capuleti e i Montecchi* (175–9) and *I Puritani* (328–31), Chabrier's *Le Roi malgré lui* (456–8), Glinka's *Russlan and Lyudmila* (546–9); Massenet's *Esclarmonde* (454–6; Meyerbeer's *Le Prophète* (499–504); Mussorgsky's *Boris Godunov* (60–3, 192–5); Tchaikovsky's *Eugene Onegin* (198–201); Ambroise Thomas's *Mignon* (50–4); Verdi (see main index); Wagner's *Rienzi* (508–15) and *Lohengrin* (438–45).

Twentieth-century Opera (American): Dominic Argento's *A Water Bird Talk* (602–4) and *Voyage of Edgar Allan Poe* (359–62); Samuel Barber's *Antony and Cleopatra* (97–102); Carlisle Floyd's *Bilby's Doll* (319–21); Philip Glass's *Einstein on the Beach* (460–3); Alva Henderson's *Last of the Mohicans* (389–93); Leon Kirchner's *Lily* (569–77); Gian Carlo Menotti's *The Hero* (377–9); Douglas Moore's *Ballad of Baby Doe* (354–6); Thomas Pasatieri's *Ines de Castro* (348–

9); Roger Sessions's *Montezuma* (337–43); Conrad Susa's *Transformations* (376–7); Virgil Thomson's Lord Byron (482–6); Hugo Weisgall's *The Hundred Nights* (356–8).

Twentieth-century Opera (European): Berg's *Lulu* (550–8); Britten's *Paul Bunyan* (569–77) and *Death in Venice* (14–19); Busoni's *Doktor Faust* (55–8); Henze's *We Come to the River* (431–7); Krenek's *Leben des Orest* (245–50); Prokofiev's *The Gambler* (195–8) and *War and Peace* (65–8); Viktor Ullmann's *Kaiser von Atlantis* (604–6).

Nineteenth-century Symphonic Composers: Bruckner (267–9); Mahler (425–9).

Twentieth-century Composers (apart from opera): Argento's *From the Diary of Virginia Woolf* (292–3); Harrison Birtwistle's *Nenia* (265); William Bolcom's *Open House* (290–2); Elliott Carter's Duo (127–9); *Mirror on Which to Dwell* (306–9), *Symphony of Three Orchestras* (527–32), and Brass Quintet (63); George Crumb's *Makrokosmos II* (36–9), *Makrokosmos III* (74–9, and *Star Child* (591–4); Peter Maxwell Davies's *Stone Litany* (324–5); David Del Tredici's *Final Alice* (559–63); Jacob Druckman's *Dark Upon the Harp* (90–1), *Lamia* (219–21), *Windows* (90–2), and *Valentine* (91–2); Messiaen's *Des Canyons aux étoiles* (47–9); Thea Musgrave's Clarinet Concerto (235–7) and *Space Play* (222–3); Schoenberg's *Gurrelieder* (170–4); Sessions's *When Lilacs Last in the Dooryard Bloom'd* (584–91); Charles Wuorinen's *On Alligators* (93), *Hyperion* (335), and Second Piano Concerto (92–3).

Performers: conductors, Bernstein (474–6), Giulini (267–8), Karajan (39–40, 451–3), and Solti (595–9); pianists, Dickran Atamian (298–301), Lazar Berman (300–1), Alfred Brendel (599–601), Horowitz (41–2), and Radu Lupu (299–301); singers in recital, Janet Baker (293), Klara Barlow (151), Evelyn Mandac (44–5), Catherine Malfitano (149–51), Joan Morris (540–1), Elisabeth Söderström (264), Theodor Uppman (44–5); string quartets, the Juilliard and the LaSalle (138–40).

I have taken the opportunity to add some cross-references, notes about books, articles, and phonograph records that readers may like to pursue, and a few second thoughts, indicated as such. Some repetitions I have removed; others I have allowed to stand, either so that each piece may be complete in itself or as deliberate restatements of a "rondo theme" expressing some belief.

When I wrote an overnight notice for *The Financial Times*, the piece would be taken from me paragraph by paragraph, as each was done, and fed by conveyor belt to the composing room. In later editions it was possible to make some corrections and improvements, but one edition had already gone out to the world with all its imperfections untouched. Anything written for *The New Yorker* is read by many attentive eyes before it sees public print, and then it is carefully printed. A pianist who, after years of struggling with instruments where some notes are out of tune and some notes stick, is offered a well-tuned, well-regulated instrument, precise and responsive, may feel as I did when I came to write for *The New Yorker*. The simile should be extended: it is as if that pianist, before playing his pieces in public, can play them before a small, critical audience of experts attentive to each aspect of his art. I am deeply grateful to William Shawn, the inspiring editor of *The New Yorker*; to my particular editors, Rogers Whitaker and latterly Susan Moritz, whose weekly "tutorials" make me feel—in the most stimulating and enjoyable way—that I might be back at Oxford again; to Eleanor Gould Packard, whose nice marginal comments on galley proofs give one the feeling of having a personal Fowler focused upon one's writing; to Sara Spencer and her team of checkers—Martin Baron, Evan Cornog, Patti Hagan, Anne Mortimer-Maddox, Richard Sacks, Thomas Teal—one of whom saves me each week from misnaming, misdating, miscounting, and misquoting; to the make-up department, which somehow finds space when I have written twice as much as I said I would; to Natasha Turi, who keeps intrusive promoters and publicists at bay; to Joseph Cooper, who saves me from libel; to Sheila McGrath, Dorothy Morrison, Helen Ruttencutter, Harriet Walden, and others too many to name—proofreaders, collators, messengers, the Chicago printers—all of whom I would acknowledge as active contributors to the reviews that appear over my name. At Farrar, Straus and Giroux, Aaron Asher, who invited me to collect these pieces, has been ever encouraging, and wondrously patient with an author who, accustomed to meeting a weekly deadline, failed to keep any other; Carmen Gomezplata and Lynn Warshow watched over their assemblage between covers with a *New Yorker*-like attention to detail.

A final note, on dating: issues of *The New Yorker* bear a Monday date but appear during the preceding week, and one writes as if the magazine were being read during that week. So when in a piece dated March 8, 1976, I refer to the première of Elliott Carter's *A Mirror on Which to Dwell* as having been given "on Tuesday of last week," February 24, not March 2, is meant.

New York, July 1978

1974–1975

VISSI D'AMORE

The way that opera composers have handled their women is a subject that the fiftieth anniversary of Puccini's death is bound to throw into prominence. The operatic stage has its high, shining heroines, notably Leonore and Brünnhilde, and its potent, dominant villainesses, among them Medea, Semiramis, Abigail in *Nabucco*, and Lady Macbeth. Verdi treated his women as equals, and most of them initiate action. In Wagner's gallery, only Elsa and perhaps Gutrune are weak. But in an age when Sarastro is seldom allowed his remark to Monostatos, "Your soul is as black as your face"—an age, that is, not yet ready to hear *idées* once, but no longer, *reçues* as part of history—there may be new objections to Puccini's operas beside the old charges of emotional opportunism and instant pathos. The works tell us that the composer would have agreed, largely, with Maupassant that "Woman was placed on this earth to play two distinct and delightful roles: love and maternity." The agreement is incomplete only because in Puccini motherhood is not invariably delightful. Though in Cio-Cio-San and Sister Angelica we find two mothers who love their little sons dearly, Mosco Carner was surely right in arguing that Angelica's Aunt and the Princess Turandot are in fact two redoubtable Mother Figures, authoritative and unforgiving. During his attempt to modulate Turandot's severity into tender submission to her masterful lover, Puccini died.

Maupassant's remark comes from a preface he wrote, in 1899, to the Abbé Prévost's *L'Histoire du Chevalier des Grieux et de Manon Lescaut*. He began by noting that, without exception, Woman throughout the ages has proved herself incapable of truly artistic or scientific work. Then he described four loving women in literature who "haunt and move our souls, live ever in men's hearts, and ever trouble all artists, all dreamers, all who yearn after and pursue a glimpsed, intangible form." They are the mature, ardent Dido, the adolescent Juliet brought to life by love, the candid Virginie, who awakens no brutal desires, and—"more truly feminine than all the others, frankly licentious, perfidious, loving, disturbing, *spirituelle*, formidable, and charming"—Manon Lescaut. For in Manon, "so filled with seductiveness and instinctive perfidy, the author seems to have embodied all that is most pleasing, most attractive, and most infamous in the creature Woman. . . . Woman as she has been, is, and ever shall be . . . Eve, the eternal, cunning, naïve temptress who never tells good from evil and by the mere power of her mouth and eyes leads strong men and weak astray." All four have given rise to many operas (as have Hamlet, Faust, Don Juan, and Don Quixote, four type-figures of aspirant Man). Virginie no longer treads the stage (though in their day both Rodolphe Kreutzer's and Victor Massé's *Paul et Virginie* operas were popular); Manon, particularly in Puccini's setting, is newly ubiquitous this year. The first novelty of the City Opera season was a production of the piece.

Puccini, who in *Edgar* had written an opera about a man torn between the charms of the faithful Fidelia and the tigerish Tigrana (another Micaëla and Carmen), at first desired Tosca for his next conquest, after seeing Sarah Bernhardt play her in 1889. It was six years before he possessed her; meanwhile, he had fallen for Manon, "a heroine I believe in and therefore one who cannot fail to win the hearts of the public." The making of *Manon Lescaut* was long and hard. Five librettists were employed. The scenario was often altered: first, to avoid parallels too close to Massenet's *Manon* (1884); later, and more interestingly, because in Manon herself Puccini compounded several different heroines while passing through several different manners that in his later works are more clearly defined. As a result, *Manon Lescaut* is the most copious and the least precisely cut of his operas. Theatrically it is a less successful piece than are *La Bohème*, *Tosca*, and *Madama Butterfly*, but it is fresh and attractive. In it we meet not a finished master, certain of all his effects, but an enthusiast, prolific and ambitious, striving to find his individual style. While Massenet's Manon has delightful variety, Puccini's Manon is inconsistent, and so is his score. Act I, it has often been noted, is a kind of symphony. But the composer's first request to his librettists was for something in opéra-comique vein, and much of Act II is like opéra comique: the heroine's scene with her hairdresser; her minuet with the dancing master; the little madrigal (the Agnus Dei of Puccini's Mass refashioned as an amorous pastoral); most of all, the final trio that in both situation—an elopement fatally delayed by song—and its soprano-tenor-baritone disposition repeats *The Barber of Seville*. Geronte's accents are often those of Dr. Bartolo. But at the center of the act are Manon's passionate aria "In quelle trine morbide," her duet with des Grieux, and his despairing "Ah! Manon, mi tradisce"; these, like the intermezzo between Acts II and III, borrow freely from *Tristan*. Whereas Massenet, Puccini had announced, "felt *Manon* like a Frenchman, with the powder and the minuets, I shall feel it as an Italian, with desperate passion." The passion finds its fullest outlet at the end of Act III, in des Grieux's "Guardate, pazzo son." The opera could end there—but Puccini, already eager to revel in a woman's suffering, added, in Act IV, a prolonged Liebestod, without action. It is not a success. The composer often cut the central aria, "Sola, perduta, abbandonata," but he reinstated it, revised (in part by Toscanini), at the thirtieth-anniversary performances of *Manon Lescaut* at La Scala.

Des Grieux, the protagonist of Prévost's tale, is the first in a line of lovers—Don José, Alfredo, Rodolfo, and Pinkerton are successors—who live on, matured by their experience, after the heroine has died.

Puccini gave him a great deal of music. He could dominate the opera. At the State Theater, he did not, because, although Michele Molese sang the role in strong, secure tones, he failed to enact it or give it much expression. The voice of Manon, like her characterization, presents problems; it must be light, youthful, and delicate—yet capable of rising to full-throated climax. At La Scala, the first Manons were Olga Olghina ("a clever little Russian lady with chiselled features and a somewhat courtly fastidiousness of manner, just a little too ladylike for Manon"— Bernard Shaw) and then Hariclea Darclée: a Nannetta followed by a Tosca. Puccini's favorite, it seems, was Lucrezia Bori, whose voice, although small, was so true that it sounded out over the heavy orchestra; but he also admired Lotte Lehmann, deficient in coquetry at the start but marvelously affecting in the final scene. Maralin Niska, the City Opera's heroine, tackles dramatic roles; her Manon alternates with a Metropolitan Tosca, and Salome is in preparation. But she lacked what a Tosca-weight Manon most needs—glamour, passion, in the actual timbre of the voice. Too often, at climaxes, there were not "real notes," with the core of firm, lustrous tone that, as Puccini said, "sways an audience." We heard the semblance of a fine singer, not the sound of one.

Frank Corsaro's direction was unhelpful. Never one to remain content with fulfilling a creator's requests, at the start he altered Edmond (a Mercutio to des Grieux's moody Romeo) from fellow-student to waiter, and confused the careful exposition of the Chevalier's character before Manon entered his life. In Act II, Manon's toilette and levée took place in an improbable lobby setting, and the *musici* who should sing the madrigal became housemaids. Act III Mr. Corsaro embellished with a prominent though mute role for Geronte. The words were not easy to follow; anyone who had not read the Italian libretto in advance may soon have become muddled.

By contrast, the Metropolitan Opera's staging of *Tosca*, devised in 1968 by Otto Schenk and directed now by Bodo Igesz, is a model of Puccini presentation. Rudolf Heinrich's settings, large, handsome, and realistic, but without ostentation, perfectly contain and enhance the composer's action. In the first performance of the season, small things were wrong, dramatically: Angelotti (Louis Sgarro) broke from the chapel and then stood stock-still, eyes fixed on the prompt box, to pick up his cue; Russell Christopher had worked up an elaborate, rounded portrayal of Sciarrone that was cleverly executed but far too eye-catching. The long line was right; moves were surely placed and timed; and within a style historically true to the creator's purpose there was ample scope for the three principals to give individual interpretations.

Miss Niska and Peter Glossop seized all their chances. In the large house, the soprano's loud singing sounded more substantial than it had in *Manon Lescaut*. In particular, the A's, B-flats, and C of the "Ah! Non posso più!" outbursts in Act II did have the full, firm brillance that sways an audience. Many soft, delicate passages were beautiful. She gave a subtle and stirring account of the role. So did Mr. Glossop of Scarpia. The menace of the man glowered through his bluff, burly stance. Lust seemed to throb in and thicken him without blunting the finesse of his phrasing; he became credibly but not unmusically violent. The acting of these two, and of Charles Anthony's vivid little Spoletta, in so strong a production, gave to *Tosca* its more than melodramatic dimension, created a drama of social unrest, judiciary powers perverted, and artists forced into political action. Franco Tagliavini's Cavaradossi, his first in New York, looked young and "artistic." The voice is not large or rich, but the sound was clear, the projection clean. When not singing, Mr. Tagliavini acted plausibly enough; in full cry, he tended to strike an unfortunate series of willowy, mannerist poses. Fernando Corena's Sacristan has acquired rather too cozy an assurance of being a public pet. Alberto Erede, back at the Metropolitan after twenty-two years, conducted an able, unhurried performance, and the orchestra played very well.

The second new offering at the City Opera was Johann Strauss's *Die Fledermaus*, in English, in a coarse, blunt production directed by Gerald Freedman—a production ugly to look at, tasteless and insensitive in style (in each act people put their feet on the furniture), with charm only in the person of Ruth Welting as Adele. Yet even the delightful, wide-eyed Miss Welting, who soared to a sweetly sustained G *in altissimo* at the close of "Spiel' ich die Unschuld vom Lande," and played with her coloratura so prettily, was not untouched by the surrounding brassiness. She should study Elisabeth Schumann's dainty, twinkling, naughty way of inflecting the songs. Orlofsky, a captivating role intended for a witty mezzo, was assigned to a man, David Rae Smith, who managed to make the Prince boring as well as bored. The dialogue dragged. Mario Bernardi's conducting had energy but lacked grace.

Miss Welting was more happily heard in *Lucia di Lammermoor*, as a Lucy in the Toti dal Monte or Lina Pagliughi tradition—limpid, tender, and touching through the sweet precision of her song and her supple, gentle way with the phrases. The house hung intently on her mad scene. Gene Bullard, her Edgar, has a strong, forthright tenor; he made a good sound, with the bright ring of emotion in it, though his playing was stolid. Odd things still happen in Tito Capobianco's staging. The prelude is mimed. Edgar sits down comfortably while hurling his angry defiance, "Sulla tomba," at the house of Ashton. Alice is a confidante sadly neglectful of traditional duties. Lucy fumbles for her brother's dirk at the close of Act II, although in Act III Bide-the-Bent clearly reports that

6

Arthur's is used for the murder (in the words of the old translation: "There she stood, a weapon grasping, / Even his who lay there gasping"). At the close, during Edgar's "Tu che a Dio," when all eyes should be on him, Lucy's corpse is borne on for precipitate and inappropriate burial in the Ravenswood vaults. The list could easily be prolonged. What it amounts to is another of those perverse and consequently ineffective stagings favored at the City Opera.

There is plenty of unstylish nonsense, too, in Mr. Corsaro's direction of Cherubini's *Médée* (done in Italian translation, with additions to the score by Franz Lachner and revisions by Vito Frazzi and Tullio Serafin). The revival was given distinction by Marisa Galvany, who, assuming the title role for the first time, showed the same temperament and powerful command—classical breadth of phrase fired by intense, passionate delivery of the phrases—that won her triumph as that other Medea, Giovanni Simone Mayr's, five years ago. Single-handed, she carried the piece to success. In all four City Opera shows, there was maladroitness in some of the supporting—and, indeed, in some of the major—roles. Chorus and orchestra often sounded scrawny and under-rehearsed. The conducting of Luigi Martelli (*Manon Lescaut, Lucia*) and of Giuseppe Morelli (*Médée*) was unimpressive.

October 7, 1974

I later revised my view of Elsa (see "Rhapsody in Blue," pp. 438–45). Mayr's Medea in Corinto *with Marisa Galvany as the "potent, dominant villainess" is recorded on Vanguard 10087–9.*

SCHOLARSHIP, SCENERY, AND SINGERS

In New York, the Metropolitan Opera season began with a revival of *Les Vêpres siciliennes*; in Chicago, the Lyric Opera season began with a new production of Verdi's next work, *Simon Boccanegra*. The latter coincided with the Fourth International Congress of the Institute of Verdi Studies, to which the Lyric Opera played generous host. Must I be deemed an ungrateful guest for suggesting that the scholarly discourse in the little Civic Theater and the swagger staging in the large Opera House next door had too little in common? When Mario Medici, the dedicated director of the Verdi Institute, set out its aims, nearly fifteen years ago, he began, "Honoring Verdi means more than just playing his

7

operas. . . . It means studying, understanding, *revealing* him," and he looked forward to exemplary, revelatory productions in which the results of research and analysis were embodied in performance. Over the years, the Institute has amassed much new evidence about the composer's aims. Verdi, like Wagner, composed not just musical scores but "musical actions," in which the sounds, the stage pictures, the movements of the singers, and the lighting effects were conceived together. He wanted the look of an opera to match its music.

About *Simon Boccanegra* he wrote, "Take great care over the staging. Although the directions are pretty precise, let me add some notes. In the first scene, if the Fieschi Palace is to one side, it must be in full view of the public, since it is essential that everyone should see Simone when he enters the house, and when he comes out onto the balcony and takes down the lantern; here, I believe, I have achieved a musical effect that I do not want ruined by the staging." For the next scene, he prescribed the curtains and gauzes required to portray moonlight shimmering on the sea (seconding the soft ripple and sparkle that accompany Amelia's aria); "if I were a painter, I should certainly make a fine picture, simple and vastly effective." The final scene is particularly important; on a distant backcloth the illuminations of Genoa *en fête* must be clear and brilliant, and then go out one by one, until at the death of the Doge all is dark—"a powerfully effective moment, I believe, and it would be a disaster if the staging were not good."

Well, the Chicago staging, directed by Giorgio De Lullo in décor by Pier Luigi Pizzi and lit by Gil Wechsler, was not good. None of those directions was observed. Moreover, during Fiesco's "Il lacerato spirito," the corpse of Amelia's mother (a blond slip of a girl, unlikely parent for the large Martina Arroyo) was borne across the stage. The ducal study of Act II—which should be a closed, private scene between two public settings—became an open atrium, dominated by a gilded, gaudy, baroque statue of a mounted St. George, at least three centuries out of period; on a column base, the pitcher and cup required by the plot stood ready; on another, the Doge perched uncomfortably to take his nap. Three of the principals—Miss Arroyo as Amelia, Piero Cappuccilli in the title role, and Ruggero Raimondi as Fiesco—were singers with very fine voices who give of their best only when stage and musical directors have inspired them; on this occasion they merely produced imposing and beautiful sounds. The fourth, Carlo Cossutta, as the inflammable Gabriele, passionate in expression, noble in timbre, enlivened both his music and his share in the action. He made far more of the role than is usual. David Clatworthy, a stolid Paolo, made far less than usual of his; in a vivid interpretation this embryonic Iago can begin to steal the show.

At the congress, much was said about musical structures and harmonic progressions. In the performance, the structure was often shattered and the progress halted by big, open bids for applause. Mid-act applause after a closed number such as Gabriele's aria (even when less well sung than it was by Mr. Cossutta) is forgivable and even welcome; an interruption is allowed for, even implicit, in the tension patterns of the score. But when the conductor and the singers froze after the central section of the Amelia-Simone duet instead of urging on to the great recognition climax, they showed less feeling for Verdi than did an audience that stayed quiet until it became plain what was expected of it. By normal international standards, this was a handsome enough *Boccanegra* —strongly cast, amply sung, ably conducted by Bruno Bartoletti, and decently played. But the assembled Verdiani wanted more—a more diligent and conscientious attempt to *reveal* the work as Verdi conceived it.

Boccanegra, a somber and awkwardly shaped drama, is admittedly not easy to bring off. Twice it marked a transition in Verdi's development: the earlier edition (1857) was his first attempt to ennoble Italian *melodramma* with the richness, solemnity, and lofty subject matter of *grand opéra*; the revision (1881, when *Otello* had already started to grow) embodies the new ideas about "Italianized *grand opéra*" that found fulfillment only in *Otello*, his personal and perfect transformation of the genre. *Les Vêpres siciliennes* is less problematical—a straightforward and substantial essay in the Meyerbeer manner, surpassing its models in melodic vitality and emotional directness. The Metropolitan version, directed by John Dexter and designed by Josef Svoboda, uses an abridgment of Verdi's score (its text being a poor Italian translation devised to slip past mid-nineteenth-century Italian censors; touchwood words like "liberté" are quenched) but otherwise bears little relation to the "musical action" conceived by the composer. The production book of his première survives, complete with detailed stage plans and a move-by-move, sometimes almost measure-by-measure description of the action. Verdi said that it was excellent, that after reading it attentively a child could produce the opera, and that it should be followed.

But—unlike the Chicago *Boccanegra*, which was essentially a traditional production (enfeebled by some bad new notions)—the New York *Vêpres* is a serious and ambitious attempt to trim and sharpen a long, leisurely drama, to fashion from it "a modern theatrical experience." In an age of *Werktreue* and of audiences educated to accept works of the past "in the original," so to speak, this is an old-fashioned aim. But then, theater people, with their championing of "what the author would have done if he were alive today," lag behind musicians, who have outgrown Gluck-Mottl, Handel-Harty, and Bach-Stokowski. To say this is not to deny that a twentieth-century reinterpretation can enhance understanding of an opera and even provide a thrilling experience. Wieland

Wagner's, Götz Friedrich's, Joachim Herz's work is not to be written off lightly. But "modern" productions need dapper, dynamic executions—the result of long, careful, and costly rehearsals not easily achieved by the shifting casts of an unstable international company.

Mr. Svoboda sets *Les Vêpres* on yet another of his giant staircases, a favorite device of his since, in 1963, he spanned the pit and the stage of the Smetana Theater, in Prague, with a single, immense flight of steps for Sophocles' *Oedipus*. (His latest model carries Covent Garden's new *Ring*.) In Hamburg, where Messrs. Dexter and Svoboda first mounted their *Vêpres*, this stark architecture was simply the frame for a décor achieved by light; in the designer's words, "The main element was a diffuse light that created a kind of foggy ambience for the steamy Sicilian scene, the broiling sun and sweltering climate. The effect was that of light as a substance, light materialized, resulting from the special new lighting instruments that we designed." (Mr. Svoboda has refined a technique that requires low-voltage lamps playing on and through "curtains" and "columns" of tiny droplets sprayed from an aerosol, held in place by electrostatic charges.) There was no magical light décor in the Metropolitan revival, only the drab steps, the Sicilians all in black, the French all in gray, and spotlights aimed none too precisely at the faces of the principals.

Most of these had changed since the first night of the production, last season. Cristina Deutekom, the new Duchess Hélène, as ever a puzzling and uneven singer, was excellently accomplished at her best (in the Act IV romance and the Act V trio) and did nothing thoughtless. She held herself with steady dignity and registered little emotion. Placido Domingo, the new Henri, registered truculence by slouching; though got up as a handsome, greasy ruffian, he sang like an aristocrat. (His second air was omitted, and the less interesting alternative was chosen for the first.) Paul Plishka was a temperate Procida, deprived of his patriotic cabaletta. Sherrill Milnes, from the original cast, sang Montfort's music with aplomb; at climaxes in his air the Italian translation gave him some unhappy *ee* vowels ("figlio," "vicino") where the original provides a rounder *ô*. James Levine, conducting, dispatched the score as if the sooner it were over the better.

October 14, 1974

Photostats of the production books for Les Vêpres siciliennes *and* Simon Boccanegra *are in the archives of the American Institute for Verdi Studies, housed in the Bobst Library of New York University.*

10

HIVE OF IVES

Last week, the Philharmonic and the Chamber Music Society of Lincoln Center joined to give a series of five concerts clustered under the title "Mini-Festival Around Ives." This week and next, Brooklyn College's Institute for Studies in American Music and Yale University's School of Music join to present a five-day "Charles Ives Centennial Festival-Conference"—and after that will be the time to try to say something coherent about the music of Charles Ives (see pp. 20–6). But meanwhile, without delay, centennial considerations apart, the concerts of the Mini-Festival, held alternately in Avery Fisher Hall and in the Juilliard Theater, can be praised as models of attractive, intelligent program planning, of execution on a high level, and, also, as events significant for the future of the Philharmonic's—and hence New York's—musical life. Pierre Boulez, when he came here as the Philharmonic's music director three years ago, made no secret of his wish to diversify the old pattern of the weekly symphony concerts. There were the Prospective Encounters and the Informal Evenings; then the Rug Concerts; and now the Mini-Festivals (a second, of similar scale, "Around Schubert," is scheduled for March). The last venture should be the most successful of all at bringing together the regular subscription audiences and the eager young—and, incidentally, at making life and work more interesting for the players. From a slim start, the attendances around Ives grew until on the last night Fisher Hall was full. (And how different its feel was on that occasion; slip some popular bars and buffets into those formal foyers, perhaps invite up the jolly venders who enliven Lincoln Plaza in summer, keep the houselights up during the music—and in atmosphere the place might rival the Albert Hall at Prom time.)

At each concert there was both chamber and orchestral music (bands thirty-five strong in the Theater, seventy strong in the Hall, conducted by Mr. Boulez), and at some there were also solos. Around the pieces by Ives had been grouped key works of the pioneer European composers who were more or less his contemporaries (among them Schoenberg, Berg, and Webern, Janáček and Bartók, Stravinsky and Prokofiev, Debussy and Ravel), and also music by American pioneers Carl Ruggles, Henry Cowell, Ruth Crawford, Aaron Copland) whose work resembles Ives's in vitality and enterprise. (There were also two pieces by Edgard Varèse, that independent genius who resists easy location on either side of the Atlantic.) So Mr. Boulez explained, in setting out the Mini-Festival's manifesto. In his brief, brilliant essay, he drew a distinction between the eponymous hero, rooted in a cultural (but not musical) tradition and fighting in his own inventive ways to find for it a musical expression for which there were no precedents, and the Europeans,

11

similarly rooted, generally rebellious, but able to draw on, even while extending, their traditions. With the latter, "you can see, especially in retrospect, the evolution of the musical experience throughout their works and establish a continuity in their efforts," but "it is impossible to establish Ives's *evolution*." Mr. Boulez's four paragraphs stated the theme of the celebration. The program notes, a patchwork miscellany, failed to develop it. The event and its audiences deserved better: a substantial program book containing essays, cross-references, correlative studies, a bibliography, a discography, and a less summary chronology.

Highlights of the ambience: Ursula Oppens's cogent, controlled, yet warmhearted account of Schoenberg's Five Pieces for piano; Paula Robison's passionate eloquence in Varèse's *Density 21.5*; Stanley Drucker's spry delivery of Stravinsky's Three Pieces for solo clarinet; Jaime Laredo's protean, spirited playing in Bartók's First Sonata for violin and piano (with Richard Goode as pianist) and Ravel's Sonata for violin and cello (with Leslie Parnas as cellist); Jerome Lowenthal's subtly romantic tinting of some Janáček piano music generally rendered in sharper, simpler colors. Revelation: Ruggles's *Portals* for string orchestra, a powerful, striking composition that merits a permanent place in the Philharmonic repertory. (Ruggles could well be the protagonist of a future mini-festival; the centenary of his birth falls in 1976; all his surviving works could be included.) Some Boulez specialties that fitted uneasily into conventional "full-symphony" concerts of recent seasons reappeared happily in this context: Webern's Six Pieces for Orchestra (carefully, delicately, and intently played), Stravinsky's *Soldier's Tale* suite (but in a dull, zestless execution—the one failure of the series).

Other New York events, bringing forward more music by the same composers, cast crosslights on the festival fare. The Metropolitan Opera mounted an excellent *Wozzeck*, securely conducted by James Levine, intelligently staged by Patrick Libby in the traditional Caspar Neher designs that have housed so many productions of the opera since its première, in 1925. Peter Glossop was very moving in the title role. There were small miscalculations (for example, in the second crescendo of the interlude between Scenes 2 and 3 of Act III, Mr. Levine brought up the drummed cymbal too fast, so that it drowned instead of supporting the fundamental B); the first-night balance was sometimes unfair to the singers; but nothing was seriously wrong, nothing that the run of performances should not right. A company that takes *Wozzeck* so capably in its repertory stride can be forgiven its evenings of ill-kempt routine. Whereas the City Opera cannot lightly be forgiven the *Don Giovanni* newly staged in the deplorable 1972 scenery; on the first night, in Act I—Julius Rudel's purposive conducting was not inducement enough to stay on for Act II—the singing was mediocre and Stephen Porter's direction lifeless.

Attendance on Ives precluded more than a sampling of the Los Angeles Philharmonic, in town for three Carnegie Hall concerts. But the sample confirmed the reputation for spick-and-span, top-league proficiency won under Zubin Mehta. Schoenberg's Five Pieces had a strong, colorful presentation, and Mahler's Rückert songs were marvelously well sung by Jessye Norman. When this noble soprano appeared at one of Charles Wadsworth's *concerti di camera* at the Spoleto Festival four years ago, her voice broke over the audience in waves of rich sound, a flood of vocal splendor unheard since Flagstad retired. Since then Miss Norman has on occasion, and particularly in the theater, been disappointing, but on Saturday all the first splendor was there, and a new majesty. Singing so steady, sound so grand, beautiful, and affecting, are very rare. The voice lacked speed in "Blicke mir nicht in die Lieder." It has the range, the deep, full organ tones, to make her the Erda of one's dreams.

Mahler is a composer most relevant to any consideration of Ives, and there has been plenty of his music to be heard. The Philharmonic's first concert in the regular series included his Fourth Symphony, and the second his Ninth—a performance that showed the orchestra, and especially the strings, during the finale, in glowing form. Both concerts were conducted by Mr. Boulez. His third in the series was less happy. Rameau was misrepresented by a suite of dances hacked from *Les Indes galantes*; a complete *entrée* would have been more representative, but the players (and their conductor?) need coaching in French eighteenth-century performing practices. In Mendelssohn's Italian Symphony, the fast movements were charmless, beaten too fast and too strictly for lithe, graceful articulation of the melodies to be possible, while the slow movement lacked weight and sentiment. Jeffrey Siegel was an efficient soloist in Prokofiev's Third Piano Concerto. Earlier in the week, Tedd Joselson, with the Philadelphia Orchestra under Eugene Ormandy, had made something tremendous of his Second. Both Philadelphia and Philharmonic concerts included a local première. The Philadelphians brought Nicholas Maw's *Scenes and Arias*, a work commissioned twelve years ago by the BBC for performance at the Proms by Heather Harper, Josephine Veasey, and Janet Baker. Inspiring trio—and difficult to match. Maw has written more arresting scores since. The Philharmonic played Bernd Alois Zimmermann's *Photoptosis* ("light in decline"?—the program note offered no explanation of the title), a work commissioned six years ago by the Gelsenkirchen Municipal Savings Bank to celebrate its centenary. Zimmermann wrote more impressive scores than this "prelude for large orchestra," which begins in soft, rather interesting confusion, has a collage middle section involving snatches of Beethoven, Scriabin, Wagner, Bach, and Tchaikovsky, and ends in long, loud, horrid confusion.

October 21, 1974

DEATH IN VENICE

Thomas Mann's novella *Der Tod in Venedig* is a highly wrought composition that lends itself to musical setting. It employs a technique of motivic repetition, variation, and cross-reference probably suggested by the musicians' leitmotiv system. It is rich in recurrent and developing imagery and in allusions: Plato, Platen, and Plutarch, Socrates and Schiller, Homer, Virgil, and Nietzsche all play upon it. At moments, the chiseled German prose even moves into classical meters. Benjamin Britten's latest opera, first performed at the Aldeburgh Festival last year, and at the Metropolitan Opera last week, is *Death in Venice*, to a libretto skillfully drawn from Mann by Myfanwy Piper. If Mann had written his work especially to inspire Britten, he could hardly have made it more apt for Britten's music. Uncannily, its images are those that the composer has been using throughout his career. In Mann's first chapter, his protagonist, Gustav von Aschenbach, has a vision of the exotic, menacing East (birthplace both of Dionysus and of the cholera that between them are to destroy him) and of a tiger's eyes gleaming through the steamy forest; we recall the tiger that lurked in the forest of Lucretia's dreams in Britten's *The Rape of Lucretia*, and burned bright in his Blake settings. The sea is another symbol important in Mann's tale and in many of Britten's works. Aschenbach's "love of the ocean had profound sources: the hard-worked artist's longing for rest, his yearning to seek refuge from the manifold shapes of his fancy in the bosom of the simple and the vast; and another yearning—for the unorganized, the immeasurable, the eternal." This theme Britten had already sounded, before his *Death in Venice*, in *Peter Grimes* and *Billy Budd*. The beauty and innocence of childhood have long attracted Britten, who has written the finest children's music of our day. The children in *Death in Venice* do not sing but they dance to a bright percussion patter and iridescent gamelan timbres that recall *The Prince of the Pagodas* and the child-fairy consort of *A Midsummer Night's Dream*. And Mann's central image, of a youth who seems to embody the world's grace and beauty, is one that has long troubled and inspired the composer of the *Michelangelo Sonnets, Les Illuminations, Billy Budd,* and the *Nocturne*.

14

For the mysterious, prowling menace, for the limitless sea, for the innocent children, and for Tadzio, the lovely youth, Britten has found themes, timbres, rhythms, and harmonies that can play upon one another. Through a clear rising octave followed by a chain of thirds, triad-accompanied, we behold the sea itself. Death, Dionysus, and the sweet, sultry threat from the East stalk through the stricken city, and through the stricken Aschenbach's increasingly fevered fancies, in thirds no longer open but clogged and sinister. Often enough, Mann himself seems to have prescribed the musical treatment—when, for example, Aschenbach sits contemplating the sea, "dreaming deep, deep into the void" as Britten and his heroes have so often done, and suddenly a human form disturbs the horizon; "he withdrew his gaze from the illimitable, and lo!, it was the lovely youth who crossed his vision." In the opera, Aschenbach spins serene melismas around the "sea" motif, and then, across the quiet-glowing calm, the "Tadzio" motif, radiant on the vibraphone, casts not a shadow but a different, more shimmering, immediate kind of light. At the close of both book and opera, there is a transformation and reconciliation of images. Hitherto, the attendant figures urging Aschenbach along each stage of his journey have borne the attributes of Hermes, conductor of souls; but now, in a passage that draws on the *Symposium*, Tadzio himself is seen as the young Hermes. Aschenbach's last sight as he dies is of the boy at the edge of the water, of the "lovely psychogogue" beckoning him toward Plato's "vast sea of beauty"—on whose shore the man whose love of the beautiful has transcended the particular "will create many fair and noble thoughts, grow and wax strong." In the score, the "Tadzio" motif, as heard here, seems to provide the answer to Peter Grimes's question, "What harbor shelters peace?" (A similar musical shape, a recurrent Britten motif, accompanied the inflamed Tarquin when he plunged into the cooling waters of the Tiber, and Billy Budd in his dream of long ocean sleep.) Sir Frederick Ashton, in his sensitive choreography for *Death in Venice*, mirrors the classical allusion by basing this final sequence on the Giovanni Bologna Mercury.

In his work notes for the novella (as we learn from T. J. Reed's careful, perceptive edition), Mann transcribed the *Symposium* passage and underlined the phrase "an die Ufer des grossen Meeres der Schönheit." His reference to it in *Der Tod in Venedig* is oblique, but then much about the tale, and particularly its close, is by intention ambiguous. The author's first impulse was to make of his real-life experience (what purports to be the real-life Tadzio's account of the event was published in 1965) an "intoxicate song"—in which, presumably, Aschenbach would have found new inspiration beneath the touch of Dionysus. But then, when the Apollonian pressures of thought, study, reason, and careful craftsmanship were brought to bear upon the emotional adventure, the intoxicate song became, as its author somewhat ruefully confessed, a "moral fable." Although homosexuality, he said, was a way of feeling that he honored, and although there could be more essential *Geist*, or inspiration, in it than in "normality," in the novella it had finally been rejected, not hymned, because the moral and social responsibilities of the novelist should outweigh an individual's lyrical, private enthusiasm. Within *Der Tod in Venedig* lie the preoccupations and unresolved paradoxes of Mann's unfinished essay on "*Geist und Kunst*." The work itself, though much admired, he deemed a "secret failure." Its author had shown himself not a *Dichter* but a *Schriftsteller*; the self-conscious, calculating artificer had conquered the aspirant poet.

But Mann was wrong, and Britten's opera shows it. Opera is the medium in which music can answer questions and resolve paradoxes when words must fail. Consider the closing scene of *The Ring*. Consider the penultimate scene of *Death in Venice*, when a passage from *Phaedrus* —Socrates' reflections on the path, from beauty appreciated by the senses, that may lead to wisdom, or to the abyss—is quoted by Aschenbach. In Mann, the sentences are "shaped in a disordered brain," murmured and muttered from "a rouged and flabby mouth." So, too, in the opera—but they are set to one of the most limpid, tenderly beautiful melodies that Britten has composed and are followed by a brave, splendid paean built from the "limitless sea" motif. The essential, dithyrambic quality that the author feared had been lost during the "sobering, corrective process" of his writing has by the composer been revealed.

Aschenbach, of course, is not a simple mask for Mann, any more than he is for Britten (or, *pace* the Visconti film version, for Gustav Mahler, who lent only his forename and physical appearance to Mann's hero). Though *Der Tod in Venedig* is one in the series of tales in which Mann explored the techniques by which life is made into art, here the thirty-six-year-old author projected himself forward, imagining the plight of an established, honored author whose rigorous dedication to purity of form has been extreme. One who has followed only Apollo is destroyed at the end by Dionysus. Britten approached the experience from, so to speak, the other side. Older than Aschenbach, established and honored, author of a recent opera, *Owen Wingrave*, whose musical manners and gestures, timbres, and tricks of utterance were commonly judged masterly but disappointingly familiar, he may well have been struck by some sentences in Mann's account of Aschenbach: "His later style gave up the old sheer audacities, the fresh and subtle nuances; it became fixed and exemplary, conservative, formal, even formulated. . . . Not that he was doing bad work. So much, at least, the years had brought him, that at any moment he might feel tranquilly assured of mastery. But he got no joy out of it—not though a nation paid him homage. To him, it seemed that his work had ceased to be marked by that fiery play of

16

fancy which is the product of joy and which, more potently than any intrinsic content, forms in turn the joy of the receiving world." Most creators pass through such dark hours. (Mann imagined Schiller's in another of his tales, *Schwere Stunde.*) It would be impertinent to impute any such reflections to Britten did not his *Death in Venice* make it plain that audacity, freshness, and the fiery play of fancy have not left him, were not the opera a product of joy in which the receiving world can rejoice. Dionysus and Tadzio are here not rejected. The opera embraces at once fidelity to the events of the printed tale, a marvelous musical realization of its intricate, delicate facture, and that lyrical, "hymnic" celebration of beauty leading to "many fair and noble thoughts" which Mann reproached himself for not having sung.

After that has been said, some details of the technical mastery can be noted. There is perhaps a slight naughtiness in the opening phrases: Aschenbach climbs a twelve-note row and then limps down its inversion to voice the sterility ("unyielding, unproductive") he is experiencing. His line moves with dragging, painful gait, leaping only once, from B to E. The note row does not recur, but proud declamation on and around E characterizes Aschenbach in his aspect as the famous writer. B and E underpin his involuntary avowal at the end of Act I, "I love you," and form the long pedal point of the Act II prelude, through which the notes of "love you" ("hackneyed words . . . ridiculous but sacred too and no, not dishonorable even in these circumstances"), like dancing, teasing points of light, dissolve each attempt at a resolute, connected phrase into confusion. The main themes of the music are distinct and memorable. Broad, picturesque strains conjure up a vision of Venice, the fabulous city rising from the sea. Lulling barcarolles accompany passages between the Lido and the Piazza; the gondoliers' strange, ringing cries later insinuate themselves into Aschenbach's musings. In piano-accompanied recitative—as if thinking aloud, or jotting down his reflections in a diary or writer's notebook—Aschenbach voices observations that on the page the novelist can tell us. It is a successful musical device for keeping the narrative levels apart, although as a result Mrs. Piper's and Britten's Aschenbach becomes an even more self-conscious creative artist than Mann's; Mann can preserve the distinction between his own and his protagonist's accounts of events and appearances. (Music, however, is an even better medium than Mann's prose for communicating the emotions that fill his hero during the approach to Venice, on his first glimpse of the sea, at his first sight of Tadzio.) Another device in Mrs. Piper's skillful libretto—casting Tadzio, his family, and his friends as dancers—reflects the fact that, in Mann, Aschenbach never speaks with them.

The opera is in two acts, the first lasting about eighty minutes and the second about an hour. Formally the score is divided into seventeen scenes, but several of them are "scenes" of shifting location. The ninth, for example, begins in a gondola, traverses the Piazza, settles for a while in a café, moves into St. Mark's, then down the Merceria, across to the Lido by gondola, into the hotel, to the door of Tadzio's bedroom (in the words of Plutarch's *Erotikos*, the lover whose quest of beauty has not transcended passion for a particular person "pursues by day and haunts the door by night"), and finally to Aschenbach's own room.

The Metropolitan production is a re-creation, differing only in some details of action and grouping, of the Aldeburgh original, conducted by Steuart Bedford, directed by Colin Graham, choreographed by Ashton, designed by John Piper, and lit by John B. Read. (It has also been given in Brussels, Edinburgh, Covent Garden, and Venice itself.) Having been at the Aldeburgh première, I can affirm what must anyway have been pretty evident to anyone encountering *Death in Venice* for the first time in New York: that the house here is too large for it. Its marvels can still be clearly heard, and valued. It was well worth doing, and by the first-night audience it was warmly received. But the scoring is too light, the forces Britten employs are too slender, and in general the drawing is too fine for the music to fill the place. In The Maltings, Aldeburgh's wonderfully resonant auditorium, the echoing spaces of St. Mark's were evoked, simply but grandly, by a small choir singing the same chants at two different speeds. In the Metropolitan, something on the scale of the first finale of *Tosca* is needed to create that effect. An attempt to set the place sounding by piping some of the choruses into the auditorium was spoiled by the poor quality of the reproduction; from the loud-speakers the singing emerged tinny and distorted. Scenically, too, the scale was too small for the stage. John Piper's backcloths are beautiful. His contrasting visions of Venice—enchanted city rising from the waves, and teeming, oppressive, beautiful slum—and his burning seascape play as positive a part in the opera as do Mann's atmospheric descriptions in the novella. But they were reproduced far too small. What at Aldeburgh had spanned the stage shrank here to peepshow proportions.

The opera is very nearly a monodrama for Aschenbach, a tenor. He is seldom off the stage. It is a very taxing role. The other important singing part is for a baritone, who in multiple incarnations plays all the figures conducting Aschenbach on his journey, and sounds the Voice of Dionysus in his Act II nightmare. The offstage Voice of Apollo is a countertenor or (as here) high tenor. Otherwise there are just the dancers, and a large group of soloists with small roles who combine to form the chorus. The tenor and baritone were those of the Aldeburgh production—Peter Pears and John Shirley-Quirk. Andrea Velis, his voice borne aloft by amplification, sang Apollo. The other singers were drawn from the Metropolitan Opera Studio, and were good. The bright bellhop of Jon Garrison deserves special mention.

The opera was composed for Mr. Pears, who created Peter Grimes in 1945 and has taken leading roles in Britten's operas ever since. At the age of sixty-four, the tenor made his Metropolitan début last week with brilliant success. Let me repeat what I wrote after the Aldeburgh première. "As Aschenbach, Peter Pears is beyond praise. His voice seems tireless. It can be full and proud, sweet, tender, sorrowful, ringing, angry. His placing of tone and word and his control of accent and timing are as affectingly precise as in a performance of *Die Winterreise*. His singing carries at all dynamic levels. His acting of the part is superb. It is a great performance of a great role." All that is equally true of his Metropolitan performances, and it needs qualification only in that the impact of his tone is less in the larger house. What he does can be clearly heard; but the "Phaedrus" aria, for example, should sound fuller than it did. Mr. Shirley-Quirk, in his various linked roles, is again very subtle, very deft. Careful not to exaggerate, he brilliantly reflects the ambiguity between separate veristic personages and recurrent symbol that is a feature of Mann's story. Tadzio, that "mortal child with more than mortal grace," proves difficult to cast. Bryan Pitts, from the New York City Ballet, seemed, like his Aldeburgh predecessor, a shade too old, a shade too much physically developed, and not really quite beautiful enough. But his performance was accomplished; the soft, tender glance, the "speaking, winning, captivating smile, unabashed and friendly," were nicely judged.

In this Metropolitan production, the main change is in the presentation of the "Apollonian games"—children's sports seen through the fond, classicizing eyes of Aschenbach—in Act I. The lighting now gives to the attendant, commenting chorus a more formal, less naturalistic aspect, and Aschenbach's movements during the episode are effective. (Before, he just sat and looked on, rather like an infatuated prep-school master watching his favorite on sports day.) One of the introductory choruses, the Apollo and Hyacinth episode, has been cut, but the sequence of choral dances nevertheless remains dangerously long.

The natural home for *Death in Venice* is not the Metropolitan. (Nor, for that matter, is it Covent Garden, which also proved too large a house for it.) The Aldeburgh performance is now available on disc. This should be heard as a complement to the Metropolitan's fine production. The richness and passion of this beautiful, detailed score are most fully enjoyed in a closeup.

October 28, 1974

Death in Venice *is recorded on London 13109 (three discs). T. J. Reed's edition of* Der Tod in Venedig *(Mann's text in German, Reed's introduc-*

tion and notes in English) is published by the Oxford University Press (1969). The anonymous "Ich war Thomas Manns Tadzio" appeared in the German teenager magazine Twen, 7 (1965), no. 8, p. 10.

SONGS HIS FATHER TAUGHT HIM

A composer's centenary is traditionally the time for celebration, for plentiful performances of his work, and for new study of it—a time possibly for re-evaluation and at least for checking received opinion. Charles Edward Ives, who was born on October 20, 1874, hardly needs champions now. In the 1972–73 *BMI Orchestral Survey* of works played by American symphony orchestras his total of 467 surpasses not only those of all compatriots but also of Bartók, Prokofiev, and Shostakovich. The centenary concerts (especially those of the Lincoln Center "Mini-Festival Around Ives" and the Festival-Conference organized by the City University of New York and Yale University), new books (*Charles Ives Remembered*, an "oral history" compiled and edited by Vivian Perlis, from Yale University Press; *Charles Ives and the American Mind*, by Rosalie Sandra Perry, from Kent State University Press), new records (notably a five-disc centenary album from Columbia; a Fourth Symphony from RCA; the Violin and Piano Sonatas from Nonesuch), and two exhibitions ("Ivesiana," at the National Institute of Arts and Letters; "Ives the Great Commoner," at the Lincoln Center Library and Museum of the Performing Arts, which also has a large collection of Ives autographs in facsimile)—all these proved complementary. What follows is based on a few score interlocking impressions gained from a "retrospective" that ranged from the Dvořákian First Symphony, of the Yale years (played by the Yale Philharmonia, under Robert Shaw), and the Three Choirsy cantata *The Celestial Country*, first done at Central Presbyterian Church in 1902 (in the Columbia album), through band music (the Brooklyn College Symphonic Band, under Dorothy Klotzman, was particularly spirited and well tuned), chamber music, and songs, to the Fourth Symphony (Boulez and the Philharmonic) and the two Piano Sonatas (done by their original interpreters, William Masselos of the First and John Kirkpatrick of *Concord*).

The Ives "legend" is quickly stated: insurance man by day, composer by night; experimenter with twelve-note systems and tone clusters, polyrhythms and polytonalities, long before these things became European commonplace; deviser of aleatory effects, chance combinations and collisions of musics from many sources in ways that anticipated Stockhausen's *Hymnen* and *Sternklang*; crusty eccentric who cared nothing about performance or what the world thought of his work; contemner of famous conductors ("Toss the ninny"), celebrated performers ("Rachnotmanenough"), critics, and any composers who were not Bach, Beethoven, Brahms, or—strongest and greatest of all, "because B., B., and B. have too much of the sugarplum for soft-ears"—Carl Ruggles; champion of Gospel hymns and patriotic or popular ditties as matter meet for serious compositions; pioneer, America's First and Greatest Composer, discovered as such by the *Herald Tribune* and then *Time*, when Mr. Kirkpatrick played the *Concord* Sonata in Town Hall in 1939, re-endorsed as such when in 1965 Stokowski did the Fourth Symphony in Carnegie Hall.

The legend crossed the Atlantic. But as Europeans listened to Ives's music (during the last decade performances were not uncommon, and recordings abundant) and read his writings (the *Essays Before a Sonata* and then, two years ago, the *Memos*), a rather—if not entirely—different Ives from that of the legend began to take shape: a late-Romantic composer, his thought formed by nineteenth-century thinkers, his music rooted in nineteenth-century popular melody, his backgrounds drawn from nostalgic memories of nineteenth-century New England scenes, and his emotions arrested at boyhood admiration of his father. In short, not so much a pioneer as a man tied to the remembrance of things past— even in his most audacious technical innovations, since, as Henry and Sidney Cowell had already noted in their study and the *Memos* amply confirmed, "The germ of every new type of musical behavior that Charles Ives developed or organized can be found in the suggestions and experiments of his father." Moreover, behind the bluster and the emphatic assertions of tough, masculine independence there was plainly someone vulnerable, wounded by the world's neglect, and protesting too much. His father died while he was an undergraduate; after "looking for some man to sort of help fill up that awful vacuum," but in vain, he spent the next quarter century building his father's memorial, working out his ideas, and setting down the sounds of the Danbury where Father had been town musician. During Ives's creative years, he was, as a musician, alone. His wife "never once said or suggested or looked or thought that there must be something wrong with me—a thing implied, if not expressed, by most everybody else." The younger men drawn into friendship by his unconventional music pursued interests that Ives, conventional in all else, could not approve. Mrs. Ives was surely mistaken and most everybody else was right: there must have been something wrong with Charles Ives. In Elliott Carter's phrase, "he cut himself off from music's reality." There was more than stubborn conceit and eccentricity in his rejection of all music but his own and what he had heard as a boy; in his shunning of, his inability to find any merit in, fellow composers with aims close to his; in his refusal to learn from others. His whacks at the sissies, softies, "lilypads," and old ladies of both sexes who made up the musical world (Mozart was emasculate; Chopin wore a skirt) are reiterant to a point that suggests insecurity. No one strong and sure of himself could need to carry on quite so much.

Suddenly, toward the end of his *Memos*, Ives gives a clue to what may have been wrong. He confesses that among the Danbury boys a liking for music was deemed sissy. Music—except for the sound of a band or a rousing gospel hymn—was something for girls and nice old ladies. But Charles Ives liked music. It meant much to him. And—despite Father—he was "partially ashamed" of it; he didn't want to be thought a sissy. Could it be this early conflict that led to his identification of dissonance, vernacular melody, and defiance of rules as "strong" and masculine; of consonance, grace, finished technique, and shapely form as effeminate, and contemptible? (The idea that a woman could be strong does not seem to have struck him, and he is one of the few composers—who else but Bach comes readily to mind?—in whose works romantic love is a theme unsung.)

Frank Rossiter took up this very question in a Princeton dissertation, "Charles Ives and American Culture" (revised and published as *Charles Ives and His America*, Liveright, 1975), which he summarized in one of the most striking sessions of the Festival-Conference. His researches (from which I have borrowed freely), his thorough study of Ives against his background, gave substance to and documented this hunch, and he carried the argument forward. Ives, Mr. Rossiter concluded, was "crippled" by his capitulations in turn to the social assumptions of Danbury, the philistinism of Yale, and the aesthetic conformity of the New York business world. In order to be thought one of the fellows, he hugged his instinctive rebellions and his serious music to himself and "retreated from the existing system back into his own private musical world, where he could keep his anachronistic values pure." Eventually, seconded in them by his devoted wife, he began to play two roles—incorrigible naughty boy and peppery old New England seer—that enabled him, as an artist, to evade the responsibilities of adult manhood.

That is persuasive. It explains much: Ives's isolation from the vanguard thinkers and creators of his time; his obsession with the past; his reluctance to bring works to a point where they could pass into the hands of performers; the mingled self-deprecatory nervousness and braggadocio with which *Concord* and the *114 Songs* were introduced to the world; his mulling over the same handful of musical ideas, transcribing them from medium to medium, from work to work. It may even explain why he ceased to compose: the old material was wrung dry at last, and he had shunned the experience that could have provided new.

During the composing years in New York, weekdays were spent in the insurance office, and Ives became rich. Sundays (but only until 1902) brought some contact with "live" music, and performances of his own sacred pieces in the Central Presbyterian Church. Otherwise, when work was done, he gave himself up to visions of the past and sought to capture in music the incidents and emotions that in boyhood had brought the Wordsworthian "flashes of transcendent beauty" described in the *Essays*:

In the early morning of a Memorial Day, a boy is awakened by martial music—a village band is marching down the street—and as the strains of Reeves' majestic "Seventh Regiment March" come nearer and nearer—he seems of a sudden translated—a moment of vivid power comes, a consciousness of material nobility—an exultant something gleaming with the possibilities of this life. . . .

Later in life, the same boy hears the Sabbath morning bell ringing out from the white steeple at the "Center," and as it draws him to it, through the autumn fields of sumach and asters, a gospel hymn of simple devotion comes out to him—"There's a Wideness in God's Mercy"—an instant suggestion of that Memorial Day morning comes—but the moment is of deeper import—there is no personal exultation—no intimate world vision—no magnified personal hope—and in their place a profound sense of a spiritual truth.

Just about all Ives's music, except for a few "ear-stretching" experiments such as *Chromâtimelôdtune* (incidentally, three different realizations of the *Chromâtimelôdtune* sketches made a most interesting conference event), is program music. It has that—and more—in common with Janáček's and Mahler's. The epigraph that Janáček wrote on the first page of his Dostoyevsky opera, *From the House of the Dead*—"In every creature, a spark of the divine"—chimes with Ives's transcendentalist beliefs. On occasion Mahler, in the endeavor to communicate a transcendental vision, would, like Ives, juxtapose brass-band and other popular strains, and create sound-pictures in space. Mahler once declared that a symphony should contain all the world; Ives contemplated (but did not complete) a "Universe" Symphony. The Mini-Festival sought to put Ives in his place in relation to his European contemporaries. Round Europe's rim, composers not German were working, as Ives was, to create a music with national and not German roots. Granados and Falla, Janáček and Bartók, Sibelius and Carl Nielsen, Holst and Vaughan Williams—they all had rich indigenous folk music to draw on. Ives had things like "Hail, Columbia," "Yankee Doodle," and "In the Sweet Bye and Bye." They could draw on and develop an idiom, a musical "language," related to the speech inflections of their native tongues and create new, personal melodies inspired by it. Ives occasionally attempted something of the kind (the first movement of the Second Orchestral Set, played last week by the Yale Symphony under John Mauceri, uses a melody that "is no particular one of Foster's but just a kind of remembrance of his music in general"), but most of the time he relied on direct quotation and, often enough, the force of verbal allusion.

The verbal allusion is lost on British ears that hear "God Save the Queen," "The British Grenadiers," and "Britannia, the Pride of the Ocean" cited in score after score. That is unimportant—the translation is easily made—but it suggests more important points. First, what Oscar Thompson, in his 1939 review of *Concord*, called "this question of association, which may be largely extra-musical in its promptings." He asked what a listener from abroad who knew nothing of Emerson, Hawthorne, the Alcotts, or Thoreau would make of the sonata. That leads to the question of what the music can express to a modern American who has lost its composer's points of reference, to whom many of the old tunes now mean nothing and the old writers little. Linked to this is the doubt whether Ives's direct vernacular quotations are from music strong enough to bear the weight with which he charged them. (In the ambitious Fourth Symphony, his student contrapuntal exercise on "From Greenland's Icy Mountains" and "All Hail the Power of Jesus' Name" is inadequate to serve as an "expression of the reaction of life into formalism and ritualism.") Elliott Carter has written often and perceptively about Ives, and though his views have changed many times since high-school years, the doubt mentioned remains. In 1939, in a frank essay about *Concord* (after which he never had the heart to see Ives again), he wrote, "The aesthetic is naïve, often too naïve to express serious thoughts, frequently depending on quotation of well-known American tunes with little comment, possibly charming but certainly trivial." And today, in Mrs. Perlis's oral history, he says, "It is, to me, disappointing that Ives too frequently was unable or unwilling to invent musical material that expressed his own vision authentically, instead of relying on the material of others."

Ives liked to distinguish "substance" from "manner." Turner/Botticelli, Titian/Carpaccio, Homer/Virgil, Emerson/Poe, an inspired imagination/an artistic care are among his exemplary antitheses. Fair enough—but when it came to music, it was surely what most men deem "manner" that Ives took for "substance." Two juxtaposed quotations can make the point. First, Horatio Parker, Ives's teacher, in a *Yale Review* of 1918:

It is indeed stirring to hear a great mass of people, including a seven-foot policeman, singing "Brighten the Corner" at Billy Sunday's. The policeman's eyes and attitude show sincerity and devotion beyond any chance of doubt. He is moved by his vocal efforts and enjoys his emotion and his singing. So do I, but I wish the music were such as I could swallow without gagging.

24

Then, Ives, in his *Memos*:

Once a nice young man (his musical sense having been limited by three years' intensive study at the Boston Conservatory) said to Father, "How can you stand it to hear old John Bell (the best stone-mason in town) sing?" (as he used to at Camp Meetings) Father said, "He is a supreme musician." The young man (nice and educated) was horrified—"Why, he sings off the key, the wrong notes and everything—and that horrible, raucous voice—and he bellows out and hits notes no one else does—it's awful!" Father said, "Watch him closely and reverently, look into his face and hear the music of the ages. Don't pay too much attention to the sounds—for if you do, you may miss the music."

In other words, it's not what a man sings, not even the way he sings it, but the look in his face that can make the music. Or as Ives put it in the *Essays*: "My God! What has sound got to do with music! . . . That music must be heard is not essential—what it *sounds* like may not be what it *is*."

But since sound has almost everything to do with music, it is on those movements where Ives discovered precise sounds and shaped them into disciplined forms—some of the works for chamber orchestra, the slow movement of *Concord*—that his reputation as more than an exuberant, exhilarating illustrator of localized nineteenth-century scenes and emotions, and as more than a fascinating original, will most surely rest. Knowing nothing of the Alcotts or Orchard House, identifying no quotations except the start of Beethoven's Fifth Symphony—international reference point—and its gentle Schubertian transformation (does not the B-flat Impromptu underlie the opening strains?), an Austrian listener, say, will surely respond to the "Alcotts" movement of *Concord* in essentially the same way that an American does. But in "Emerson," "Hawthorne," and "Thoreau" he is likely, even while admiring the bold, improvisatorial invention, to wish that the composer had been less self-indulgent, more securely in command of his chosen form. As Carter said, "Behind all this confused texture there is a lack of logic." The same is true of the finale of the Fourth Symphony.

Yet behind the dense, exciting, illogical, kaleidoscopic confusion is also Ives the man, contradictory, still puzzling after all his own and others' attempts to explain him. A great composer? great in a few works? potentially great but "crippled"? Does it matter? Ives the illustrator, Ives the collagist of musical fragments from the past, Ives the ear-stretcher, Ives the campus entertainer and prankster, Ives the aspirant visionary, and Ives the pure musician who can speak so warmly and directly—all must claim the attention of anyone who cares about the ways in which thought and feeling become sound. And all have something to say.

November 4, 1974

25

The Horatio Parker quotation comes from his "Our Taste in Music," in Yale Review, *7 (July 1918), pp. 777–88. Oscar Thompson's review of* Concord *appeared in the* Sun *(New York), February 25, 1939, p. 28. Elliott Carter's essay "The Case of Mr. Ives" appeared in* Modern Music, *16 (March–April 1939), pp. 172–6. Other Carter pieces about Ives are: "Ives Today: His Vision and Challenge," in* Modern Music, *21 (May–June 1944), pp. 199–202; "An American Destiny,"* Listen, *9, No. 1 (November 1946), pp. 4–7; and "Shop Talk by an American Composer," in* The Musical Quarterly, *46 (1960), pp. 189–201, reprinted in* Problems of Modern Music, *ed. Paul Henry Lang (Norton Library, 1962). They are collected in* The Writings of Elliott Carter, *ed. Else and Kurt Stone (Indiana University Press, 1977).*

On Ives's use of quotations, see Dennis Marshall's "Charles Ives' Quotations: Manner or Substance?" in Perspectives of New Music *(Spring–Summer 1968), pp. 45–56, reprinted in* Perspectives on American Composers, *ed. Benjamin Boretz and Edward T. Cone (Norton Library, 1971).*

Ives's Memos *are published by Norton, and there are Norton Library editions of his* Essays Before a Sonata *and of Vivian Perlis's* Charles Ives Remembered.

MARVELOUS PERFORMERS

The second-floor gallery of the Whitney Museum was packed—elbow to elbow, knee to knee, most of the audience on the floor, and many standing—for the first Composers' Showcase concert of the season, on Wednesday last week. The composer shown was Elliott Carter, the program his Sonata for cello and piano (1948), Third String Quartet (1971), and Double Concerto for harpsichord and piano with two chamber orchestras (1961).

Ears learn fast. Music of merit that when it first appears is hard to play and hard to follow may need only a few years to become readily approachable. Stravinsky's *Agon* is an example—perhaps not in this country, where from the start the score had, in Balanchine, its lucid interpreter, but certainly in Europe, where in concert halls both players and listeners grappled with it at first and then about five years later took it in their stride. Similarly with Carter's Double Concerto. In 1961, it looked—well, not exactly unplayable, since it was played, with Ralph Kirkpatrick and Charles Rosen as its apparently confident harpsichord and piano soloists, but very nearly so. At any rate, the London première in many places offered no more than an approximation of the rhythmic and dynamic complexities prescribed with such precision in Carter's score. How accurate last week's Whitney performance was I cannot say; since the main lights were turned out, anyone who might have wanted to use a score could not have done so. But there was no doubt that the players of the Speculum Musicae, conducted by Gerard Schwarz, with Paul Jacobs as harpsichordist and Ursula Oppens as piano soloist, sounded confident, masterly. Everyone was plainly on top of the music, not hanging on by the skin of his teeth. "Marvelous performers," Mr. Carter had murmured as he left the platform after a few introductory remarks. They were. The shape of the composition in time, balanced around its central adagio, and its disposition in space, with the location or movement of each musical idea precisely plotted in a score that is also a ground plan, became clear. One difficulty that listeners often have with "modern" music is, to put it very simply, uncertainty about the speed it is supposed to be moving at. A slow movement decked with rapid filigree may sound much like a scherzo; is that sudden skitter of darting fragments a change of tempo or merely a decorative gesture? Then there comes such a performance as this of the Double Concerto, and everything falls into place.

Speed, modulating meters, and particularly the interplay of lines that move against one another at different speeds are things that have long fascinated Elliott Carter. In the first movement of the early Cello Sonata, he set the cello's quasi-rubato line ranging freely over a 4/4 tempo giusto from the keyboard. At the Whitney performance, Miss Oppens was a decisive pianist. Michael Rudiakov, the excellent cellist of the Composers String Quartet, was perhaps not quite bold or rhapsodical enough; maybe he was just a shade daunted by the difficulties that awaited him in the next piece, the Third String Quartet. In that work, Carter pushed rhythmic and tempo complexities to extremes. I described some of them when reviewing the first performance, by the Juilliard Quartet, last year [see *A Musical Season*, pp. 140–6]. The four players divide into two duos—violin and cello, violin and viola—who pursue discourses rhythmically and thematically independent yet laid out (most of the time) between the same bar lines. The composer requires that "the two duos should perform as two groups as separated from each other as is conveniently possible, so that the listener can not only perceive them as two separate sound sources but also be aware of the combinations they form with each other." In the original Juilliard performance, spatial separation on the platform was not essayed; it would have added considerably to the hair-raising difficulties of first turning this score into sound. In the Juilliard recording (Columbia M 32738), however, separation was introduced by the engineers, channeling the duos left and right. The Composers String Quartet, who gave the Whitney performance, have found a way of bringing electronic aid to a live interpretation. Each player hears (though the audience cannot) a "click track," a tape recording that feeds, through a small earplug, precise information about what measure has been reached and where the beats fall. The device may sound inhibiting; in the event, it evidently gave the Quartet the security to make possible a full, free, and uncommonly lyrical interpretation. The tape, first prepared with mathematical exactitude, was then adjusted during rehearsals until it could serve but not straitjacket the players' interpretation. Freedom is an essential part of the composition; Duo I is instructed to play quasi-rubato throughout. It is easier to move freely when there is no danger of straying too far. Moreover, with the click track as lifeline, the two duos could risk a wide platform spacing and not lose touch.

As a whole, the evening showed New York music making at its best. Though the place was hot and uncomfortably crowded, and though a two-hour squat on the floor can be a strain, the atmosphere of communal enthusiasm was exhilarating. The performers were superb, the listeners attentive and appreciative, and the compositions among the most cogent of our time. How eagerly one awaits the local première of Carter's new Brass Quintet, given its first performance, in London, last month, broadcast on Ives's birthday. The next concert in the Showcase series, in January, will be devoted to George Crumb.

Two days earlier, coincident flute recitals at the Carnegie Recital Hall and the Avery Fisher Hall both drew decent houses. I divided the evening between them. At the former, Doriot Anthony Dwyer, first flute of the Boston Symphony, introduced to New York Oliver Knussen's *Masks* (1969), for solo flute accompanied by an occasional pretty tinkle of glass chimes offstage. *Masks* is a dramatic, arresting, and ingenious composition in which the soloist's positions and perambulations as well as his notes are indicated; during a central episode, the monologue becomes a duologue, changes of "speaker" being marked by a swiveling of stance. But Miss Dwyer missed the wit and sharp characterization; she did not "act" the music or bring it to life; and she let go of the long notes too soon. Everything was uttered in a fat, full tone "enriched" by a slow, heavy vibrato. The same vibrato was applied, inappropriately, to a C. P. E. Bach sonata, and then to Ingolf Dahl's elegant, entertaining *Variations on an Air by Couperin*, for flute and piano. Karl Kraber, in Fisher Hall, was a flutist more various. Basically, his tone is light, clear, and steady; his musical manners are alert, lively, and protean—in contrast to Miss Dwyer's comfortable assurance. His program comprised Italian, American, and German groups. In the American group, Mario Davidovsky's *Synchronisms No. 1* (1961), for flute and electronic sounds, held the ear, as ever, with its imaginative inventions. Robert Moevs's *Pan* (1951) showed how hard it is to write an unattractive piece for solo flute—and also, perhaps, how hard it is to write one with the strength and distinction of Debussy's *Syrinx* or Varèse's *Density 21.5.*

The City Opera scheduled only two performances of its *Pelléas et Mélisande* this season. I attended the second—the best thing I have ever heard the company do. Richard Stilwell, the world's leading Pelléas, appears to especial advantage in this production, where Frank Corsaro has given the characters physical identity. Patricia Brooks's sensitive, delicate Mélisande is no fey waif, nor the sly, self-aware little thing of some productions, but a touching and credible young woman. Michael Devlin's Golaud, strong yet easily bruised, is no rough blusterer. All three sang well, and they declaimed the text clearly and with feeling. Though *Pelléas* is a *symboliste* drama, Debussy's setting is forceful, and feelings are passionately expressed. The City Opera version is not wispy; without crudeness, and equally without any attempt at prettifying, Mr. Corsaro presents the action and Julius Rudel presents the music "unveiled," as it were. Even if one questions details of Mr. Corsaro's staging —particularly his decision to play the first scene of Act IV in "a chapel in the castle" (Arkel's long address to Mélisande should not be a public sermon)—in sum this is probably the most gripping *Pelléas* to be seen today. Pierre Boulez, at Covent Garden, gives an uncommonly lucid account of the score, but in New York the drama as a whole is more direct, more precise, and more moving. The eloquent orchestra under Mr. Rudel was scarcely recognizable as the body that, two days earlier, provided such lackluster, underpowered accompaniment for *Un ballo in maschera*, conducted by Giuseppe Morelli.

This *Ballo* was newly directed, by David Hicks, in the 1971 décor. His handling is intelligent, pointed, and particularly striking in solemn, momentous passages: the drawing of lots to decide who shall be the assassin, the murderous gathering of conspirators around the king. The masked ball itself lacks gaiety, but then Eoin Sprott's scenery hampers any festive action. (The production is set not in Verdi's Pomerania, or in the Boston of the published score, but back in the Stockholm of Scribe's *Gustave III*, the *grand-opéra* libretto that Antonio Somma translated and abridged for Verdi's use.) Michele Molese scarcely did justice to what, Othello apart, is the composer's richest tenor role; in middle ranges the lines were smoothly sung, but when they climbed he seemed to gargle them. Richard Fredericks was a passable Renato and Glenys Fowles an acceptable Oscar, though it was unenterprising of her to sing the second verse of "Saper vorreste" quite straight, without adornments. Marisa Galvany, the Amelia, might have come from another and superior league: a singer of temperament and passion, not always securely in control of her shining, powerful voice but always arresting and musical in her intentions. Her chief fault was to break long, arching phrases—"Consentimi, o Signore" in the Act I trio, "Che ti resta, perduto l'amor" in the Act II aria—into separate notes instead of linking them in seamless spans. The performance nearly foundered on Mr. Morelli's dim, undervitalized conducting. (What prompts Mr. Rudel's choice of staff conductors—when America seems to be filled with able young musicians who surely deserve a chance? Must they first make a name—as James Levine once did, as John Mauceri is doing now—with the Welsh National Opera, in Cardiff?) Both chorus and orchestra often lacked the strength to fill the theater. Or so it seemed up in the first ring. But at Sunday's *Faust*, heard from Row F of the orchestra seats, both chorus and orchestra sounded strong. Christopher Keene (a young American who *has* made an international name) conducted securely and deftly. Mr. Stilwell's Valentin provided further evidence of his vocal, artistic, and dramatic prowess. He sang phrases in a way to make one listen. So did Miss Brooks, who was a Marguerite sometimes peaky in tone, but attractive and interesting.

At the Metropolitan Opera, Renata Scotto has taken over the role of Hélène in *Les Vêpres siciliennes*. She should not really be doing parts as heavy as this, and already they have exacted a toll on her limpid lyric soprano. But so far the voice has lasted pretty well, and she was certainly an impassioned and rousing Hélène. The patriotic cabaletta of the first air was fiery, far more so than in Cristina Deutekom's staid interpretation, and it fired a response from the chorus. The "expression" she added to the *romance* set into the Act IV duet ("Ami, le coeur d'Hélène," or, in Italian, "Arrigo! ah parli a un core") was overdone; though the number brought the house down, it arrested the dramatic motion of the duet. But generally Miss Scotto's art and instinct combined most tellingly. If Mr. Levine, who conducted, was listening to her, he may have learned much about how to mold a Verdi phrase on the breath, and on the words, so that it communicates the emotion the composer intended. There were other cast changes. Lawrence Shadur was a reliable but unremarkable Montfort. Although William Lewis tended to shout his way through Henri's music without grace of manner or charm of timbre, his intensity of delivery held the attention. In many ways, this production must be deemed an insensitive and deplorable account of *Les Vêpres*—rudely cut, directed by John Dexter with small regard for Verdi's instructions, drably clad, and brashly conducted—and yet, all the same, it is easy to enjoy it, on the simple level of stirring tunes sung with a good deal of spirit.

November 11, 1974

MUNCHING A BEANSTALK

Earlier this year, David Hamilton wrote of his eagerness to hear Schoenberg's *Pierrot Lunaire* sung in an English translation:

> . . . and not only because it would increase the work's immediacy for most of the audience. Few American performers of *Pierrot*—not even the admirable Miss DeGaetani—focus and shape the poetic lines as sharply, as dramatically as do native Germans; they follow Schoenberg's inflections, of course, but they do not add to these the myriad tiny refinements that the native German, drawing upon a lifetime of experience and associations, will automatically, often unconsciously, practice. In an English-language performance our singers would exercise similar skills, and their responsiveness would be further heightened by the knowledge that every inflection is conveying something to the audience.

Last month, in Carnegie Recital Hall, Valorie Goodall, with the Rutgers University Chamber Ensemble, conducted by Daniel Schuman, brought us a performance in English of *Moony Pete*. The translation of Ingolf Dahl and Carl Beier was used. If Mr. Hamilton's hopes for the outcome remained unfulfilled, the fault was not any flaw in his argument (which, while true of almost all vocal music, applies with especial force to so carefully nuanced a composition as Schoenberg's). Nor was it Miss Goodall's—but, rather, that of a translation which did not fit the music closely enough. In particular, over and over again Dahl and Beier had chosen an English spondee ("pale lips," "sharp nail") or bacchius ("the dank fumes") to represent feet that in Otto Erich Hartleben's German, and Schoenberg's setting of it, are trochees ("Lippen," "Nagel") or anapaests ("aus dem Qualm"). The difficulties of pitching and projecting *Pierrot* are formidable enough; in addition, Miss Goodall was set the further task of uttering long syllables to short notes and trying to make sense of the result.

In the best book ever written about the relation of words and music, Harry Plunket Greene's *Interpretation in Song* (essential reading not only for singers but for all who essay, or pronounce upon, translation), the great Irish bass-baritone had much to say about the niceties of length, stress, speed, and sense that constitute so much of the art of song. This Rutgers *Pierrot* sent me back to his chapters. The matter of sung spondees was meanwhile raised again by Harold C. Schonberg's Sunday *Times* article about Britten's *Death in Venice*. Britten has long seemed to me one of three composers—the others being Purcell and Virgil Thomson—who set English words with so delicate an understanding of musical values that even the most familiar lines, once heard conjoined to their music, are thereafter remembered inseparably from it. And so I was surprised to read that Britten

tries to be scrupulous in matters of accent. Yet a fingerprint of his style involves the constant use of spondees, and words come out with equally stressed syllables. But there are no spondees in the English language, and thus Britten's settings often sound mannered and unnatural.

I quote this not to quarrel with a colleague but because Mr. Schonberg has brought up a point about Britten's musical prosody worth investigation. It can sound mannered, I agree; but would disagree that in English there are no spondees, or that Britten uses them constantly. Try setting the lines "A blackbird is a black bird" or "A redcap wears a red cap" to music, and the spondaic values emerge at once. English spondees are generally made of monosyllabic adjectives and nouns, as in the schoolboy mnemonic for a classical hexameter ("Down in a deep dark hole / sat an old cow munching a beanstalk"), and occasionally of monosyllabic nouns and verbs, as in Tennyson's *Leonine Elegiacs*: "Winds creep; dews fall chilly: in her first sleep earth breathes stilly."

But Mr. Schonberg is referring, I imagine, to Britten's habit of setting iambic or anapaestic lines to notes of equal length. This he has often done. In *Peter Grimes*, Ellen Orford sings, "The life at school to me seem'd bleak and empty / But soon I found a way of knowing children" in spans of equal quarter-notes. In *The Rape of Lucretia*, the Female Chorus's "Their spinning wheel unwinds / Dreams which desire has spun" flows in equal unbroken quarter-notes. In *A Midsummer Night's Dream*, the fairies sing "Over hill, over dale, thorough bush, thorough briar, / Over park, over pale, thorough flood, thorough fire, / We do wander everywhere" with a quarter-note to each syllable. In these and similar passages there is often motion up and down the scale, and the "beats" of the verse are often displaced from the strong beats of the musical measure. It does constitute a fingerprint, a mannerism. But I find little of it in *Death in Venice*, and where it is most noticeable, in Aschenbach's aria at the close of the penultimate scene, it seems, like so much else in the score, to be a favorite device of Britten's past used freshly—to anyone who knows his music doubly poignant, since the familar idea takes a new turn (reflecting, incidentally, the theme of the opera). Although the lines "Does beauty lead to wisdom, Phaedrus? . . . For senses lead to passion, Phaedrus" are set, in the main, to descending scale passages in equal eighth-notes, the slight lingering on the first syllable and the little catch, in both rhythm and melody, across the utterance of the proper name give distinction to the phrases and make them memorable. In any case, equal notes need not mean equally stressed syllables, any more with Britten than in, say, Schubert's "Der Leiermann," which is set very largely in even eighth-notes. As Plunket Greene says, discussing trochees or iambics that in a score appear to be spondees:

Why should those two crotchets, *written* of equal value, be *sung* with even values? He does not *speak* them with even values. He may give them (though even that is not always necessary) equal *time*-values, but surely there is no necessity for equal *pressure*-values? He would not speak the words "pebble," "comma," "faster," as "pebb-url," "com-mah," "fast-ur," any more than he would say "re-new," "ay-gain," "pree-tend," unless he were a prig. Yet in any song he may meet any of those words written to two equal crotchets or quavers. He has simply got to use his common sense and sing them with the same pressure-values as he speaks them . . . always on the understanding that, if ever there is a dispute in the matter between text and music, the music should have the preference.

Amplifying the parenthesis in that quotation, Plunket Greene then sets out "Der Leiermann" (in Paul England's English translation as "The Hurdy-Gurdy Man") in first a typographical and then a musical notation that attempt to show the "myriad tiny refinements" that a singer, drawing upon a lifetime of experience and associations, might practice. For

if he sang those opening words with their full quaver pressure-values or even time-values, he would be monotonous with a vengeance . . . the very negation of interpretation.

Two related observations, before getting back to *Pierrot*. First, contradictions between musical and verbal ictus can often have charm and point. Measured by the bar lines, the opening words of Stravinsky's *The Rake's Progress* must be scanned: "THE woods ARE green AND bird and BEAST-at-play;" but when the phrase is sung with natural accents, independent of the 2/4 accompaniment meter, it acquires a lilting, vernal grace. Translators must beware of making the words and the musical beats fit too closely when in the original, by design or perhaps by happy chance, they may not. The German translator of *The Rake's Progress* did not err in this way. Nor the translators of Britten phrases mentioned above; the Erzählerin of *Der Raub der Lukrezia* and the Elfenchor of *Ein Sommernachtstraum* do preserve the cross-accents that, if ignored, would correspond to ". . . unwind dreams WHICH desire has spun," and "over hill, over dale" with "o-" and not "hill . . . dale" in arsis. Singers must exercise a similar care. Banging down on the first beat of the measure in, say, "LA donna è mobile" is a fault heard often from English-speaking tenors; Italians—and students of Plunket Greene—tend to give equal "pressure-values" to the first two syllables of the aria.

Second, "unnatural" setting may be dictated by thematic or motivic considerations. In the first scene of *Death in Venice*, Aschenbach sings, "Should I go too beyond the mounTAINS?," leaping a sixth to a sustained note on "-tains" (whereas a spoken inflection would give a falling close to a weak note—as it were, "MOUN-t'ns"). Two factors may have determined the odd setting. The rising close is Britten's regular way of asking a question in music; it echoes the Junius-Tarquinius duet of *Lucretia,* where the interrogative phrases "What makes the Nubian / Disturb his heavy MOUNTAIN? . . . What drives the Roman / Beyond his river TIBER?" trace a similar pattern. More important, a stepwise descent followed by a leap to a sustained note is a basic motif of *Death in Venice*, associated with the promptings of the mysterious Stranger, on which Aschenbach is musing. So the musical point overrides strict fidelity to natural declamation.

No one could call the flighty, fantastic declamation of *Pierrot Lunaire* natural, but it has its starting point in German speech inflections, and the closer an English version gets to these the more vivid an English-speaking declaimer can be. Cleo Laine has recorded the work in English, using a different translation, Cecil Gray's (RCA LRL 1-5058). Gray avoids the awkward Dahl-Beier spondees and bacchius cited in my first paragraph; "lip of," "gimlet," and "From the mists" are his fitting solutions of "Lippen," "Nagel," and "Aus dem Qualm." Like Dahl-Beier, he uses "BALD pate OF Cassander" to render "BLANken KOPF Cassanders" (Miss Goodall changed it to "bald head"—not happier, since that also carries the spondaic stress of "red head" rather than "redhead"). Miss Laine, by a skillful adjustment of accents, gets round that one, but "giant BLACKmoths" for "Riesenfalter" defeats her; Miss Goodall was better served by the Dahl-Beier "giant mothwings."

Details could be multiplied. One more, and I have done. The opening lines of No. 10, "Raub," are "Rote, fürstliche Rubine, / Blutge Tropfen alten Ruhmes," and Schoenberg has marked them to be sung in strict tempo. Line two presents no problem; Gray has "Bloody drops of antique glory" and Dahl-Beier "Bloody drops of ancient glory." But how are we to fit "red" into the first line? Gray has "Ancient royalty's red rubies" and Dahl-Beier "Princely, luminous red rubies." "Princely" gives the better consonantal attack but a poor vowel. Both versions set "red" to an unstressed sixteenth-note, the final "e" of "fürstliche"—with the result that both Miss Goodall and Miss Laine are compelled to something like "r'drubies." Shifting Schoenberg's first comma, we might try something like "Red, imperial, gleaming rubies, / Bleeding drops of ancient glory." Not much good; the first two notes should join—but not in the manner of "re-dimperial." (If only rubies were crimson or scarlet!) So we can try reversing the lines; try starting with "rubies"; try playing with "fiery . . . fabled," "red . . . royal . . . radiant . . . rubies" in an endeavor to mirror Hartleben's alliterative patterns; then try again to match the open "o," closed "o," and sustained "uh" that color the peaks of Schoenberg's phrase.

From all this, three simple conclusions. (1) Translating verse for singing is a very tricky business. (2) Singers must be masters of prosody. Recommended reading, besides Plunket Greene: Edith Sitwell's studies of word values and letter values. Recommended listening: Plunket Greene's and John McCormack's records. (3) When, in the old arguments for and against vernacular performance, someone says, "But it sounds so awful in English," be sure that it is not just the particular ill-fitting English translation that sounds awful.

It should be possible to give a thoroughly satisfying account of a Mozart piano concerto in Avery Fisher Hall, but I have yet to hear one. It would call for a more careful attention to platform placing, orchestral tally, and dynamic balance than was evident at last week's Philharmonic concert, when Radu Lupu played the C major, K. 467, and James Conlon made his début with the orchestra. It would need, too, an instrument that Mozart would have recognized—or at least a more "Mozartian" handling of the modern Steinway. Mr. Lupu was neat but unremarkable. The hushed romance of the slow movement escaped him. The finale was a scamper.

Mr. Conlon's program ranged widely. Once again, he impressed me as an able and promising young conductor who knows his scores but does not yet give to each its due color and character. The *Flying Dutchman* overture required broader, solider sound—more string tone to support the violent brass. The solo oboe in two *Gymnopédies* (Satie scored by Debussy) was not thin enough for music that, as Henri Sauguet said, "seems to come from very far and very high." *Printemps* (Debussy scored by Henri Büsser) went best. The play of color effects was prettily managed; the rhythms were lilting. Bartók's *Miraculous Mandarin* suite needed harder, more incisive playing.

November 18, 1974

David Hamilton's "Moonlighting" appeared in The New Yorker *of April 8, 1974. Jan DeGaetani's recording of* Pierrot *is on Nonesuch H-71251. The 1940 recording conducted by Schoenberg himself, with Erika Stiedry as speaker-singer, has been reissued on Columbia Odyssey Y 33791.*

My own "basic training" as a translator for English singing versions was daily chanting, throughout school years, of the Psalms, which soon teaches one which English syllables can bear sustained tone and which not, and daily exposure to the sounds and rhythms of the Book of Common Prayer. Passages in Edith Sitwell's The Pleasures of Poetry, Alexander Pope, *and* A Poet's Notebook *deal with specific effects of weight, speed, and color.*

35

STARS

The music of George Crumb is so instantly attractive that stern, sober minds may resist it almost on principle—as if contemporary music had no business to sound so pretty, and can't be any good if it does! Finding it irresistible, I surrender to its seductions happily, without qualm, and delight in all the trick effects, the strange, small, delicate noises (rustle and patter, whisper and whinny, aeolian-harp shimmer), the "pale tunes irresolute, and traceries of old sounds," the sweet harmonic stases pierced by sudden clarion or cry. And while listening I remember the things Crumb's titles and subtitles tell of—mysterious ocean deeps melodious with the songs of the humpback whale, or dark druidical rites at Stonehenge (not that there were druids there; nevertheless, the image is powerful). When he calls a piece *The Phantom Gondolier* and asks that it be played "eerily, with a sense of malignant evil," or heads a section "Prayer-Wheel" with the indications "very slow (thirty-second note= 76); like a vision; as if suspended in endless time" and "*ppppppp* (incredibly soft, on threshold of silence)," the words can, and should, influence the way the piece is heard. There is nothing inherently inferior about music that is "impure"—music that invites its listeners to add literary and pictorial associations to their understanding of its sounds. Composers, it is true, have a habit of withdrawing their initial programs and asking later audiences to appreciate works "purely as music"; Berlioz did so with his Fantastic Symphony and Mahler with his First. Yet he would be a cold fish whose imagination was not kindled to a keener experience of the Fantastic and "Titan" by a knowledge of Berlioz's and Mahler's romantic scenarios. Crumb's compositions are not for cold fish but for people who can be moved by beautiful sounds to share in mystical visions, who set their thoughts roaming the starry skies in transcendental rapture, who can feel blood, sand, and proud, black despair compounded in a single line of Lorca. . . .

But before I get quite carried away, some facts. In 1962, Crumb composed Five Pieces for Piano (without added trigger titles), in which he began to explore the sonorities obtainable from the instrument by stroking, striking, or plucking its strings, with fingertips or a bent paperclip, and stopping them lightly to produce harmonics. These new sounds were combined with notes played in the usual way from the keyboard, while the two sustaining pedals, general and selective, of the Steinway added their veils of carefully graded resonance. Electrical amplification (except at performances in a very small hall) was recommended, so that fragile, finely distinguished sounds could be heard clearly. (These Five Pieces are recorded by their dedicatee, David Burge, on Advance 3.)

In 1972, Crumb embarked on two larger piano compositions—

Makrokosmos, Volumes I and II. The first volume, written for Mr. Burge and completed in 1972, is recorded by him on Nonesuch H-71293. The second, written for Robert Miller and completed in 1973, was given its first performance during Mr. Miller's Alice Tully Hall recital last week. [In 1976, Mr. Miller's recording of it appeared, on Columbia Odyssey Y 34135.] Each volume of *Makrokosmos* is subtitled "Twelve Fantasy-Pieces After the Zodiac for Amplified Piano." Each piece bears a title, a zodiacal ascription, an evocative expression and a precise tempo indication, and, at the end, a dedication to a person born under the sign concerned; for example, "Ghost-Nocturne: for the Druids of Stonehenge (Night-Spell II); Virgo; Dark, fantastic, subliminal (half note=40) . . . (A.B. ♍)." The heading of the whole recalls Bartók's *Mikrokosmos*. The format, twice twelve piano pieces with poetic titles, brings to mind Debussy's two volumes of Preludes. But, Crumb remarks in a foreword, "these are purely external associations, and I suspect that the 'spiritual impulse' of my music is more akin to the darker side of Chopin and even to the child-like fantasy of early Schumann." In the verbal-*cum*-musical imagery of *Makrokosmos*, there are some recurrent obsessive figures, and the composer has described how,

at times quite vivid, at times vague and almost subliminal, these images seemed to coalesce around the following several ideas . . . : the "magical properties" of music; the problem of the origin of evil; the "timelessness" of time; a sense of the profound ironies of life (so beautifully expressed in the music of Mozart and Mahler); the haunting words of Pascal: "Le silence éternel des espaces infinis m'effraie" ("The eternal silence of infinite space terrifies me"); and these few lines of Rilke: "Und in den Nächten fällt die schwere Erde aus allen Sternen in die Einsamkeit. Wir alle fallen. Und doch ist Einer, welcher dieses Fallen unendlich sanft in seinen Händen hält" ("And in the nights the heavy earth is falling from all the stars down into loneliness. We all are falling. And yet there is One who holds this falling endlessly gently in his hands").

What can one usefully add? Any detailed description of the extraneous technical devices—the strip of paper or thin metal chain laid on the strings, the glass tumblers gently pressed against and slid along them, the occasional phrases sung, shouted, chanted, or whispered by the pianist— would merely confirm the fears of anyone who thinks that *Makrokosmos* may be no more than a bag of clever tricks, an assemblage of artful sounds. Many children have played with the strange, attractive, fascinating noises that can be drawn from the complicated mechanism of a piano by placing foreign objects on the strings, twanging them, thumping them, whistling, singing, or screaming into them with the pedal down. Crumb has carried such experiments much further, and from the happier results has assembled a personal repertory of precise, picturesque, and

captivating sounds. He is willing to employ any device he deems evocative. His music is at once exuberantly adventurous and yet fastidious in
factute, very bold and yet reticent, not emphatic. Without raising his
voice but in tones of quiet intensity, where timbres and inflections are
so nicely graded that a tiny shift of emphasis can be of mighty import,
he makes profound, unpompous statements in little room.

Although the structure of his compositions usually defies traditional
methods of analysis, their shapeliness is apparent to the listening ear,
and to the eye as it scans the printed page. (His works are published by
C. F. Peters.) In each volume of *Makrokosmos*, three of the pieces are
written out in "symbolic" forms: cross, circle, spiral, etc. Such "eye
music" devices as inscribing a love song on staves bent into a heart
shape (a medieval example by Baude Cordier appears in the new edition
of Donald Grout's *A History of Western Music*) were denounced by
Thurston Dart (in *Grove*) as "descending to symbolism of the most
automatic kind." The fourth piece of *Makrokosmos II*—"Twin Suns
(Doppelgänger aus der Ewigkeit); Gemini"—appears as a pair of twin
circles. Only the player can tell us whether this quirky notation helps to
inspire an interpretation or is simply a tiresome conceit. Either way, the
device pleases the eye and the fancy. And in a program note Mr. Miller
pointed out that, whatever the symbolic intention, as a practical result
he was compelled to play *Makrokosmos II* from memory.

He is a pianist of uncommon distinction, technically adept, intellectually cogent, persuasive in all he does. His recital—the first of three
devoted to American piano music, a series that promises to be a major
event of the season—embraced many manners, entered many musical
worlds, in each of which he proved to be a sure and committed interpreter. Henry Cowell's *The Banshee* (1925), a minute or two of unearthly,
undulant howls coaxed directly from the strings, and a favorite item at
lighthearted student concerts, is not in the least "important" but a diverting pioneer specimen of sonic raw material such as Crumb refines,
polishes, and adapts to expressive use. Each of Ruth Crawford's Preludes
(1924–28) seems to have a starting point in a piquant structural notion,
which is then worked out with uncompromising yet elegant finesse. Mr.
Miller played five of them, including two still unpublished—spare, carefully fashioned works in which grace, technical resource, and exploratory
zest are happily combined. Stefan Wolpe's *Form* (1959) and *Form IV:
Broken Sequences* (1969) are strong, dramatic, and colorful; Wolpe is
at last receiving the recognition and the assured performances that were
rare in his lifetime. (Let me in passing pay belated tribute to the
Speculum Musicae's brilliantly defined account of Wolpe's *Piece in Two
Parts* at a Hunter College concert last month.) Arthur Berger's Five
Pieces for Piano (1968) are even more arresting, tough, and tense in

structure. Those works made up the first half of the recital and showed Mr. Miller to be a superlatively well-equipped pianist, quick to render the individual sense of each composition with a precise control of timing and tone color. *Makrokosmos II* formed the second half. More glamorously pianistic, it gave fuller scope to his romantic mastery of timbres put at the service of sense. His performance of it was luminous, incantatory, exquisite.

For some time, perhaps a decade or two, Herbert von Karajan has seldom been esteemed among musicians as a musical interpreter of the highest rank—a man whose readings of Beethoven, Brahms, Wagner, or Richard Strauss can be ranked beside or even preferred to any other's. Unreserved, wholehearted critical approval has been most readily accorded him in the role of accompanist to someone or something very strong—Maria Callas's Lucia di Lammermoor or her Leonora in *Il trovatore*, Franco Zeffirelli's production of *La Bohème* at La Scala. In Karajan's own operatic productions, in Vienna and Salzburg, the accompaniment has tended to be the main thing. Up on the stage, often behind a heavy gauze, the singers and the scenery provide a series of large, beautiful illustrations subordinate, even at their most spectacular, to a drama conceived principally in instrumental timbres; in much of his casting, Karajan has favored light, lyrical voices in heroic roles, and personalities that are not dominant. Yet his performances with the Berlin Philharmonic, whether in the theater, with vocal and scenic obbligato, or in the concert hall, are treated as musical wonders of our age. And so they are. The public throngs his very expensive Easter Festival in Salzburg. His records sell and his concerts sell out. And the mob adulation with which the orchestra's recent Carnegie Hall concerts were received may have been uncritical, but it was not unmerited. In his twenty years with the Berlin Philharmonic, Karajan has made of it an instrument unmatched in beauty, breadth, and homogeneity of tone.

Kobe bullocks, they say, are massaged daily so that their muscles, when consumed, may be of even consistency, flawless, without trace of fiber or gristle. Karajan has kneaded the sound of his players until it has a similar texture, firm yet succulent. The Berlin Philharmonic playing is, like Kobe beef, a luxury product. The metaphors customarily used of it are mechanical, not culinary, and even the Carnegie Hall program book praised the conductor as "the artistic prototype of our technology-oriented century and its worship of perfection." Karajan always gives the audience a smooth ride. In the two Brahms symphonies—the Fourth followed by the Second—that made up his first program, all of the bumps were ironed out. The machine started at a touch; a slight leaning on that first B from the violins and the serene, cushioned progress began

—over hill, over dale; now fast, now slow; all gradients effortlessly mounted; plentiful power in reserve; never a jarring gear shift; smooth brakes; perfect road-holding. And no direct feeling, you might say, of the road traveled. That's what was wrong. "No one experienced in great music could fail to see that the long, quiet opening sentence is the beginning of a great tragic work," said Donald Francis Tovey in his essay on Brahms's Fourth Symphony. Such a failure would have been easy on this occasion. When all sense of physical stress has been removed from the playing, when nothing sounds difficult, then the tensions of the music disappear. For Toscanini, for Szell, the Fourth Symphony was a struggle. So it is today for, say, Bernard Haitink. When Furtwängler conducted, it became a new adventure—for him, for his players, for the audience. Unexpected and wonderful things might happen in the course of it, and usually they did. In Karajan's performance, the music never took one by surprise; astonishments were limited to the nonesuch instrumental sound. Some works are particularly well suited to his supremely confident, unperturbed, equilibrate approach (the *Meistersinger* prelude is one), but Brahms calls for a trace of grit. One should be aware of the composer's "gear shifts" in the form of harmonic wrench. Even in his halcyon movements, there are apt to be moments of flurry. The episode in the finale of the sunlit Symphony marked "tranquillo . . . sempre più tranquillo" should surely be a disturbing passage, despite the indication, because each harmonic haven proves illusory. Between manner and matter there is a Brahmsian paradox, which Karajan resolved too comfortably, settling for manner. The Berliners' playing of the pages was, emotionally, easy-osy. Technically, their wind/string balance during the exchanges was a marvel.

Technically, everything throughout the evening was faultless, except some woodwind chording not quite purely in tune. (The first flute seemed to be the offender; but then fine-mettled orchestras, like highly strung pianos, are easily shaken out of tune by travel.) String tone so suave, solid, and sumptuous (pizzicatos, whether *forte*, in the first movement of the Fourth Symphony, or *pianissimo*, in the andante, plumped with a sweet kernel of ripe sound); horns so mellifluous, and well knit in chorus; full-orchestra texture so coherent, combined with luminous detail in solo work—these are Berlin glories, heard from no other band today. The *music* may have lacked force, but the playing was great. Anyone who swooned at the sound of the cellos as they began the adagio of the Second Symphony need not be thought affected; it was the kind of tone to dissolve a listener into ecstasies. The first horn, later in the movement, should be praised by name—and would be, had the program book not failed to include a personnel register.

November 25, 1974

A recording of Makrokosmos II *played by Robert Miller appeared in 1976, on Columbia Odyssey Y 43135. Mr. Miller plays Wolpe's* Form *and* Form IV *on CRI S–306, and Cowell's* The Banshee *in "Sound Forms for Piano," a recital of experimental piano music on New World Records NW 203.*

> Pale tunes irresolute,
> and traceries of old sounds,
> blown from a rotted flute,
> mingle with the noise of cymbals
> rouged with rust

are lines by Enoch Soames, the dilettante poet who is one of Max Beerbohm's Seven Men. *They are quoted, apparently in all seriousness, in the Mompou entry of* Grove's Dictionary, *fifth edition—an entry that connoisseurs of "fine writing" about music will enjoy. Since my next sentence includes a reference to "ocean deeps melodious with the songs of the humpback whale," I was much tempted to leave the reading that appeared on the first proof of the piece: "pale tunas irresolute."*

PIANO, AND VOICES

Vladimir Horowitz's recital in the Metropolitan Opera House two Sundays ago was an occasion both stimulating and disconcerting. The old familiar bravura was there. He began with a Clementi sonata, Opus 26 No. 2, sharply etched, incisively sounded, quirkily phrased as he bent the music into shapes that were captivating and thoroughly "musical." Then came Schumann's *Kinderscenen.* Impetuous pieces composed by "Florestan"—"Blindman's Buff," "Knight of the Hobbyhorse"—came off perfectly, but the flow of "Eusebius's" dreamy contentment was rudely disturbed; "Perfect Happiness" is surely not such a boisterous state of mind as Mr. Horowitz now conceives it to be. (His old recording was more serene.) Who sits "At the Fireside" jerking and jittery? When the main melody of "Träumerei" is drowned by an inner voice, willfulness has conquered musical sense. Mr. Horowitz lacked simple, easy, domestic warmth (which is what the *Kinderscenen* need) but not arc-light heat, dazzle, and flare; they were abundant in Scriabin's Fifth Sonata. In the Chopin group that formed the second half, boldness often became what must simply be termed banging, and elegance eccentricity. On a Steinway of aggressive timbre when struck hard in the octave below middle C, he sometimes generated a displeasing clatter. Of course, one was excited to encounter again this coruscant wizard of the keyboard—but memory suggested, and recordings confirm, that Horowitz's genius has hardened. His capricious commentary on Chopin's music once was more gently poetic and more persuasive.

In a program note for the Metropolitan Opera's new production of *Jenůfa*, David Hamilton remarks that the postwar decades have added the name of Leoš Janáček to those of Dvořák and Smetana, to form a Czechoslovak nationalist trio. Meanwhile, in the international operatic repertory, Janáček is beginning to take his place beside Puccini and Richard Strauss. In giving direct musical expression to human emotions honestly and quickly felt, he is their superior. The Metropolitan first did *Jenůfa* fifty years ago. Despite Jeritza in the title role and Matzenauer as the Sextoness, the production was dropped after its first season. Ernest Newman, guest critic of the *Evening Post* at the time, wrote a review that later he would gladly have forgotten (but Seltsam's *Annals* keeps it in pickle): "A more complete collection of undesirables and incredibles has never previously appeared in opera. . . . The work of a man who . . . is only a cut above the amateur." Today, *Jenůfa* is much loved, often performed, almost a repertory piece. Chicago and San Francisco are among the American houses that have mounted it, and there have been two productions in New York this season.

The first was put on for a single night, on the stage of Avery Fisher Hall, by Thomas Scherman's Little Orchestra Society. There was no décor, but otherwise there was a completely acted presentation, directed with uncommon finesse by Vlado Habunek. Indeed, three of the characters—Alexandra Hunt's Jenůfa, Naděžda Kniplová's Sextoness, and Gary Glaze's Števa—were more compellingly and completely portrayed than I have ever seen before. Miss Hunt came to international attention when she played another Janáček heroine, Kat'a Kabanová, at the Wexford Festival two years ago, and she has been invited to sing the role in Prague. The young American soprano seems to have a natural affinity with the composer's utterance; each brings out the best in the other, and although Miss Hunt's voice is "useful" rather than especially beautiful, she communicates beautifully, most touchingly and truly, the sense of each phrase. Above the staff, Miss Kniplová's tones are strident, ugly, and insecure; within it, puissant and commanding. Despite the addled climaxes, both the formidable public dignity of the Sextoness and the intensity of her private despair were potently conveyed. Mr. Glaze's Števa, cocky and confident on the surface, part hangdog and part blusterer when taxed, at once charmer and cad, was a keen interpretation. All three acted with voice, gesture, and glance in a way to make vivid the drama between them. Ivo Žídek's Laca was a capable but more routine portrayal. The instrumental timbres were bright, and Mr. Scherman let the music move at its natural speeds.

The Metropolitan version was less successful. The production, directed by Günther Rennert and designed by Günther Schneider-Siemssen, was based on Munich's. (Mr. Chapin might have done better to go shopping in Stockholm for the Götz Friedrich and Reinhardt Zimmermann staging.) "Reality" was missing—not so much realistic detail as truthfully observed behavior. One little example: When Janáček's curtain first rises, the old Buryjovka should be sitting at one side, preparing potatoes, while Jenůfa gazes into the distance. After fifty-seven bars, during which Jenůfa voices her fears, the old woman then chides her granddaughter for not helping her. But at the Metropolitan she came onstage and set to work just before singing the reproach—which, as a consequence, seemed quite unjustified. On a deeper level, the domestic background of the tragedy had not been established. Act I was a *Ring* set—craggy cleft beneath a lowering sky—decked with two tiny buildings. The scene for Acts II and III, the Sextoness's living room, might have been the Gibichung palace—a huge space that dispelled the emotional force of the drama. At the close of Act II, not one casement but three crashed open, and handfuls of paper snow were chucked in, as if to make sure we realized that it warn't a fit night out for man nor beast. Botanical detail was peculiar: Does rosemary ever bear carnation-size pink blossoms?

In the title role, Teresa Kubiak had some very touching moments, mingled with others in which her interpretation became merely stagey. The work was sung in the English translation of Otakar Kraus and Edward Downes (slightly revised, not always for the better); Miss Kubiak's command of English is imperfect, so direct, idiomatic utterance of the lines often eluded her. The voice, however, was lustrous. The Sextoness is a role for a dramatic soprano in her mature prime; Astrid Varnay brought the ruins of a once brilliant (though never wholly secure) heroic soprano to bear on it. Moreover, the character escaped her—as it did at Covent Garden nearly seven years ago. It is curious, and distressing, that someone who has been the most exciting Isolde, the most powerful Ortrud, the most passionate Brünnhilde of our day should fail here, and have so little theatrical presence. When Miss Varnay enacted Ortrud in Act I of *Lohengrin*, she used to dominate the stage though having only a line or two to sing. When the Sextoness steps forward, in Act I of *Jenůfa*, to quell the merry-making, one would expect electric charges to radiate from Miss Varnay, silencing the chorus, setting scalps atingle throughout the house. Instead, nothing much happened. Nor in the last act, where all other Sextonesses of my experience have advanced with tragic dignity, again stilling the turbulent crowd by simple majesty of gait and by force of personality. Miss Kniplová had been tremendous here. But Miss Varnay lurched and lunged into her confession in a hammy, melodramatic manner. Jon Vickers, the Laca, affected a similar lurching deportment. He sang, as always, with forceful expression, but he pushed things to the point of exaggeration. William Lewis was a lean, dapper Števa, looking like a wicked young squire from pantomime rather than a Moravian Turiddu. John Nelson's conducting altogether missed the definition of accent and color that give to Janáček's score its "speaking" quality, and his pacing of the final duet made it an anticlimax, not an apotheosis.

All in all, a disappointing attempt at an opera that usually inspires love and enthusiasm in all who hear it. Maybe in future seasons a Kubelik or a Mackerras can bring the production to life. As for the score, the 1969 edition by Joannes Martin Dürr was used. This embodies cuts and reorchestration by Karel Kovařovic, who conducted the Prague première (1916). The Sextoness's Act I narration, removed by Janáček himself when he revised the opera in preparation for the first vocal score (1908), and recovered by Dürr, was not reinstated. A good case can be made for its inclusion: it does much to explain the Sextoness's character, tells us of her passionate youth, and motivates her determination to save Jenůfa from a marriage such as hers (to Števa's uncle) had been.

Both to the ear and to the eye Town Hall remains unrivaled among New York's auditoriums. Artists singing or playing there start with an advantage—heard at their best, seen at their best, and in close, easy contact with an audience predisposed to enjoyment by the pleasant ambience. Last week's joint recital by Evelyn Mandac and Theodor Uppman, in Town Hall's "Encore" series on Tuesday evenings at six, was a happy event.

Miss Mandac is a singer so sensitive, so musical, and potentially so bewitching that it is worth trying to discern just why the promise of that Inès, in Meyerbeer's *L'Africaine*, described two years ago [see *A Musical Season*, p. 54], remains—well, promise still and not really fulfillment of all that one had hoped for. I think it is partly a matter of words and partly one of temperament. To each syllable of the line "Let us wander not unseen" (the recital began with a set of duets arranged from Purcell), Miss Mandac gave much the same weight, length, and emphasis. In "Sound the Trumpet," she pronounced "glories" as if it were just another workaday word among many. Singing not keenly responsive to the force and color and speed and stress of language can never be wholly satisfying. But instead of spurring that hobbyhorse around the familiar track, I will simply commend once again the precepts in Plunket Greene's *Interpretation in Song* and the practice to be heard in his and John McCormack's records. To those exemplars may be added: for French songs, Claire Croiza; for German, Elisabeth Schumann; for songs in just about any language, Alma Gluck. And, as a more recent, more readily available, and wholly captivating demonstration of words perfectly valued, weighted, and timed, Joan Morris's Nonesuch album *After the Ball*. (How beautifully, in pronouncing the word "elephants," Miss Morris reconciles the dactylic stress and the cretic syllable lengths.) Character is created by the use of words. Miss Mandac has the timbres and technique for Susanna, Zerlina, and Rossini's Rosina, but in singing their music she uttered the lines in the less piquant accents of Pamina and Mozart's Rosina. If I were writing in England, I could describe her as a Jill Gomez without quite the sparkle of personality. But since Miss Gomez (one of England's two most vivid sopranos; the other is Josephine Barstow—and both can be heard in the recording of Tippett's *The Knot Garden*) is not yet well known here, let me praise quite simply a fluent, flexible, and surely formed voice of distinct and most agreeable quality, and an attractive young artist who does nothing wrong and may blossom into an interpreter doing everything exquisitely right. Two songs from Miss Mandac's native Philippines; pure, finely spun cadenzas in the *Zauberflöte* duet "Bei Männern"; and a glamorous, creamy "Vilia" (a *Merry Widow* medley was the encore) were exquisite already.

Mr. Uppman's talents are familiar. Lively words and a lively, winning personality mark his performances. In "Dunque io son," the Rosina-Figaro duet from *Il barbiere*, his divisions were less exact than Miss Mandac's—but then he had already pleaded some throat trouble. Both Miss Mandac and Mr. Uppman are fair to look upon; all the same, there may have been people wanting to spare a glance at texts in that song lover's vade mecum Philip Miller's *The Ring of Words*—so it was unkind to switch off the lights in the hall.

The *Turandot* put on recently by the New Jersey State Opera in Newark's Symphony Hall for a single night represented a kind of opera performance that is now rare even in Italy, its natural home—a special event at which the enthusiasm of the audience, largely local but swelled to capacity by eager pilgrims (my PATH train to Newark took on the aspect of an Opera Special), becomes a positive element in the drama of the evening, and where, around a visiting celebrity, local talent fills the stage. (Nearly everyone seems to have a cousin in the chorus, or at least a friend carrying a spear.) A *Lucia* of the kind was recalled by E. M. Forster in *Where Angels Fear to Tread*. ("Italians don't love music silently, like the beastly Germans. The audience takes its share— sometimes more.") A few years ago, I encountered such a *Mefistofele* in Piacenza. But the New Jersey *Turandot* was exceptional in having, in all three principal roles, stars of international renown: Birgit Nilsson as the ice-girt Princess, Licia Albanese as Liù, and Placido Domingo as the Unknown Prince. The décor, by Anthony Stivanello, was bright and colorful and, within the limits of the modestly equipped stage in Symphony Hall, fulfilled Puccini's requirements. The chorus, directed by James Lucas, acted and reacted like billy-ho; such B-movie intensity of gesture and expression as theirs is preferable any day to tired routine. The orchestra, under Alfredo Silipigni, played with spirit. It was a show with never a dull moment. When Calaf struck the gong, the audience broke into cheers. I intend nothing patronizing in the account. The style of presentation is not what one would enjoin on the Metropolitan; nor is it "what opera is all about." But an excited, participant audience is at least one of the things that opera of this kind is "about," and in *Turandot* even those overzealous fans who would rather make their own appreciative noises than listen to all the composer's music prove less infuriating than usual. The social and sexual premises of the drama do not bear dwelling on today; the score has marvels of musical skill but was calculated to bear interruptions.

Miss Nilsson, as is her wont, omitted Turandot's second aria, "Del primo pianto," and this spoiled the shape of the last act. Her presence was grand, her singing very powerful. Even though the nonpareil voice showed some signs of wear (some notes were mispitched, and some unsteady), that decisive, keenly projected tone remained thrilling. To the lingering "L'amor?" that answers Liù's brave "Principessa, l'amor" she gave a poignant, self-doubting, almost wistful expression; there were many such subtleties in her interpretation. Miss Albanese's Liù was honest, direct, and most affecting; I am glad to have seen it. Mr. Domingo was in full, free voice. Harry Dworchak was a sound Timur, and Ping, Pang, and Pong—Russell Christopher, Gregory Isaac, and Modesto Crisci—sang their charming trio without fussiness, as if they meant it. A pleasure, too, to see what is rare in New York—an operatic production not lit from first to last with follow spots on the principals.

December 2, 1974

In 1975–76, Horowitz made a tour of fifteen American cities—his first tour of the kind for nearly a quarter of a century. His recitals were taped, and a recording of Scriabin's Fifth Sonata (coupled with Schumann's Concerto without Orchestra) was published on RCA ARL–1 1766.

Josephine Barstow made her Met début in March 1977; see p. 565. Philip Miller's The Ring of Words, *an anthology of song texts, with literal English translations, is published in the Norton Library. More about Joan Morris on pp. 540–1.*

GRAC'D WITH BIRDS

Peter Mennin's Eighth Symphony, completed last year, was given its
first performance on November 21, at a Philharmonic concert conducted
by Daniel Barenboim. I heard it that morning in rehearsal, with a
score before me but without the help of the composer's program notes.
The first movement, it was clear enough, was an *In principio*—not St.
John's but that of Genesis: musical depiction of a world so far without
form but rich with inchoate wonders awaiting a disponent hand. Then
came a scherzo, in which I heard burrs and blurtings of vague menace.
The adagio was plainly a *De profundis*—a long, tragic sequence of
melodies welling up from grief. After that, I felt that something like an
extended passacaglia was needed, a final movement of powerful, patent
structure and cogent argument to "clinch" the symphony. Instead, there
was a series of apparently preludial paragraphs—making fragmentary
reference to the earlier movements—which reached a climax and then
came to a close. That evening, the program notes revealed that this
finale is intended as a *Laudate*. The sounds of the trumpet, of the
stringed instruments (but no harp, timbrel, or organ), and of the high-
sounding cymbals are praising the Lord in a brisk procession of jubilant
verses. The scherzo is a *Dies irae*. The first and third movements are
indeed an *In principio* and a *De profundis*. The symphony lasts nearly
twenty-eight minutes. It is soundly planned and solidly wrought, the
product not of fiery genius but of a skillful, thorough craftsman with a
vein of poetry.

The previous day, Olivier Messiaen's *From the Canyons to the Stars*,
commissioned by Miss Alice Tully for Frederic Waldman's Musica
Aeterna Orchestra, had its first performance, in Alice Tully Hall. A long
composition in twelve movements—two of them for solo piano, one for
solo horn, and the rest for piano and orchestra—it was composed during
the last four years, after a visit to Utah. The score is a synthesis of the
familiar Messiaen materials—birdcalls in bright instrumental styliza-
tions; intense "colors" correlated with modes and harmonies; themes
associated with landscape and with devotional concepts; classical meters
and Oriental rhythmic patterns—and the new device, underlying the
recent *Méditations sur le mystère de la Sainte Trinité* for organ, of
spelling out sacred exclamations in a musical cipher. In *From the
Canyons*, "MENE TEKEL UPHARSIN" and "ἅγιος ὁ θεός" are "said" by the
instruments, in notes, "by means of an alphabet of sounds and durations." The birds are mainly those of North America, joined by some
exotics from Africa, Australia, and the Far East. The colors are a
kaleidoscope, settling into a blue A major for two movements, Nos. 8

and 12. (As in the *Lohengrin* prelude, A major is the color of an intense blue sky.) The landscapes are those of Cedar Breaks, Bryce Canyon, and Zion National Park. Colors mingle as the birds pass across them:

Bryce Canyon is the greatest wonder of Utah [Messiaen observes in his program note for the work]. It is a gigantic natural amphitheatre, with fantastic red-orange, purple rock formations, shaped like castles, square towers, bulging towers, natural windows, bridges, statues, columns, entire cities. . . . Here comes a superb bird: the Steller's Jay. His belly, his wings, and his long tail are blue; his head and his lapwing are black. When he flies over the Canyon, the blue of his flight and red of the rocks take on the splendor of gothic stained-glass windows.

Messiaen has already written a work inspired by the windows of Chartres and entitled *Colors of the Celestial City*. The symbolism of Zion National Park, with its "pink, white, mauve, red, black walls, the green trees, and the limpid river," was readymade for him by those who named it, and his last movement is "Zion Park and the Celestial City." The Wood Thrush, which is "reddish, with a white chest spotted with black," sings a major arpeggio "with a clear, gay, sunny pitch." And "for me, the song of the Wood Thrush stands as a symbol of that archetype God intended for us in his predestination, which we more or less misrepresent, in the course of our worldly life, and is fully realized only in our celestial life, after Resurrection." Messiaen goes through mortal life listening to the birds—every parakeet a paraclete—in country after country; admiring the wonders of nature and the nobler works that man has raised to divine glory (Chartres, the temple on Miyajima); rapt in a color-bright vision in which all things are but an adumbration of the Celestial City we shall one day inhabit. Then he sets it down in music. His scores can certainly bear formal analysis (the young Boulez and Stockhausen would not have sat at the feet of a man whose rhapsodies lacked structure), and the intricate rhythmic procedures of his earlier pieces have been influential. But, oh dear me, he does pile on the ecstasy!:

Cedar Breaks is one of the wonders of Utah . . . a vast amphitheatre, sliding down toward a deep abyss of which the orange, yellow, brown and red rocks stand up like walls, columns, towers, turrets, dungeons. The birches, the firs, a trace of snow, the wind which blows violently, add even more to the majesty of the site. All these features inspired in me a feeling very close to that of Awe. "The Gift of Awe" is one of the seven gifts from the Holy Spirit. . . . After the Redshafted Flicker's powerful cries follow the deep borborygmuses of the Blue Grouse (in French: "Tétras obscur") given to the bass trombone. . . .

Hard to tell whether this is genuine Messiaen (it is) or an unkind parody. Hard, while listening to his later compositions, to stop phrases like "voluble visionary," "instant ecstasy," "automatic awe," from forming. The recipe for converting transcendental joy into sonic patterns is now all too familiar. Another high-heaped serving of the avian calls, the abyss, the primeval wind, the dazzling colors, the devotional fervor, stirred together and sweetened with chords of the added sixth. There is one new ingredient in *From the Canyons*—the long horn solo, "Interstellar Call." "He telleth the number of the stars; he calleth them all by their names": the cries go breaking out into the stillness, becoming more and more intense, and there is no answer. This movement, employing the instrument in a variety of virtuoso ways, has an independent future as a recital piece. It was passionately and poignantly played by Sharon Moe. The two piano solos are "The White-Browed Robin" and "The Mockingbird." Unlike the entries in his *Bird Catalogue*, which seek to evoke habitat and habit, and to portray effects of climate and season around each songster, they are made of pure birdsong. The second, in particular, is a brilliant piece. Yvonne Loriod was the pianist, marvelously precise as she scattered glittering, joyful, and never ugly timbres from all over the keyboard. The orchestra consists of thirteen strings, each with an individual part; quadruple flutes and clarinets; triple oboes, bassoons, and brass; and plentiful percussion (eight players). Mr. Waldman had scheduled twelve three-hour rehearsal sessions, which must be more than most New York concerts receive; the playing was bright and assured. *From the Canyons*, like most of Messiaen's music, would be best suited by exceptionally resonant acoustics. The music sounded richer at a morning rehearsal, in the empty hall, than at the concert, when the place was full. (Those in side seats discovered that Tully Hall could add wind noises of its own, whistling low and wailing through the doors, to the whoosh of the wind machine on the platform.)

By comparison with the *Exotic Birds, Seven Haïkaï*, and *Colors of the Celestial City, From the Canyons* seems to me a self-indulgent piece. "Generous" would be a kinder word—but generous to a fault. There is much sweetness in it—sweetness of timbre, of temper, of harmony—but sweetness whereof a little more than a little can be by much too much. Musica Aeterna expected a composition about twenty minutes long; this one lasted ninety-six. (It was given with an intermission.) There is no movement I would not gladly hear again, but the performance of the whole brought surfeit.

December 19, 1974

TRAVELS WITH MIGNON

The inability of most modern singers to sing and speak idiomatic French, the move from small opera houses to large, the replacement of spoken dialogue by sung recitatives and of French texts by Italian translations, general aggrandizement—these things conspired to destroy opéra comique. When the Théâtre de l'Opéra-Comique in Paris closed, three years ago, the genre lost its last metropolitan stronghold. It survives precariously in the French provinces and on the French radio. But, otherwise, to discover what opéra comique is like one must read the librettos and produce in the mind's theater those plays of wit and sentiment that start with a chorus and proceed rapidly in spoken dialogue so designed that the actors can often break into song. Recasting the works in grand-opera format, even when the job was done by the composer himself, seldom improved them. By elevated grand-opera standards, *Faust* is judged trivial (though attractive) and *Benvenuto Cellini* a sorry muddle (though touched by genius). By their librettists, both pieces were initially intended as entertainments in a genre whose limitations were clearly understood and appreciated. It could compass tragedy, comedy, and romance. Great works of literature and fashionable novelettes alike passed under the fingers of seasoned professional librettists, often working in pairs, to be trimmed and furbished for the taste of a bourgeois public that liked to laugh a little and cry a little, to be diverted by spectacles exotic or picturesque (fairs, gypsies, and Oriental dances abound), and to go away with some graceful, pretty tunes to remember. Composers, for their part, knew exactly what to provide, and theater directors were ever at hand to advise, meddle, insist on alterations, and insure that the accepted rules were observed. An opéra comique, like a modern musical, reached its first night through a trail of discarded numbers, revisions, rewrites, and alternative endings. The debris survives in Paris's rich archives, and it rewards study. Often enough, there is no case to be made for reviving in actual performance the music that was rejected or replaced. Sometimes there is, especially when there is evidence that changes were imposed on a composer against his will, to placate a vain artist, lighten the task of a weak one, or meet an early curtain time. And even when last thoughts are obviously best thoughts, a knowledge of first thoughts can illumine things obscured by the alterations.

Ambroise Thomas's *Mignon*, first performed at the Opéra-Comique in November 1866 (while Verdi's *Don Carlos* was in preparation at the Paris Opera), and a Metropolitan staple from 1927 to 1944, has just been given two performances by the Dallas Civic Opera. The large State Fair Music Hall, handsomely and comfortably refitted in its public areas since I was last there, is no place for an opéra comique, and the piece was done in the familiar grand-opera version with recitatives that Thomas prepared for the London première in 1870. It was sung more or less in French by a cast of Americans and Italians—very few of whose words could be understood. It was enjoyable, because the score contains so many tunes that are skillfully and gracefully fashioned. Mignon's "Connais-tu," Philine's polonaise "Je suis Titania," Frederick's gavotte "Me voici dans son boudoir" (an addition for the London première), and Wilhelm's "Adieu, Mignon!" and "Elle ne croyait pas" are justly celebrated. Record collectors also know Mignon's styrienne (Lotte Lehmann), the Harper's berceuse (Gerhard Hüsch), and the Swallow Duet (Supervia and Bettoni). The ensembles and choruses prove to be packed with catchy strains. Many numbers are in lilting dance rhythms. The instrumentation is slight but cunning. *Mignon* is a collection of deft, delightful melodies, and must be accepted (or rejected) as such—as a typical opéra comique. *Carmen*, the masterpiece that lifted the genre to a higher level and made it a medium of music drama, was still in the future.

In 1859, the librettist team of Jules Barbier and Michel Carré had carved an opéra comique from Goethe's *Faust*. With his *Wilhelm Meisters Lehrjahre* they had a harder task, since, as Carlyle remarked in the preface to his famous translation, "of romance interest there is next to none in *Meister*; the characters are samples to judge of, rather than persons to love and hate; the incidents are contrived for other objects than moving or affrighting us; the hero is a milksop, whom, with all his gifts, it takes an effort to avoid despising." Although the types represented range widely, "from the gay material vivacity of Philine to the severe moral grandeur of the Uncle and the splendid accomplishment of Lothario," the main matter is "everlasting disquisitions about plays and players, and politeness and activity, and art and nature." However, though a *Wilhelm Meister* opera was clearly impossible, a *Mignon* could be made, since

the history of Mignon runs like a thread of gold through the tissue of the narrative, connecting with the heart much that were else addressed only to the head. . . . This mysterious child, at first neglected by the reader, gradually forced on his attention, at length overpowers him with an emotion more deep and thrilling than any poet since the days of Shakespeare has succeeded in producing. . . . She is of the earth, but not earthly. When she glides before us through the light mazes of her fairy dance, or twangs her cithern to the notes of her homesick verses, or whirls her tambourine and hurries round us like an antique Maenad, we could almost fancy her a spirit; so pure is she, so full of fervour, so disengaged from the clay of this world. . . . It is not tears which her fate calls forth; but a feeling far too deep for tears. The

51

very fire of heaven seems miserably quenched among the obstructions of this earth. Her little heart, so noble and helpless, perishes before the smallest of its many beauties is unfolded.

This Mignon was given her meetest music in Hugo Wolf's settings of songs from the novel. Something of her, I imagine, appeared in Lucrezia Bori, who played Thomas's heroine at the Metropolitan for ten consecutive seasons. She can be discerned in Jennie Tourel, whose Metropolitan début, as Mignon, in 1937, can still be heard on a pirate recording of the occasion. Thomas's first Mignon, Galli-Marié, was a mezzo, but he adjusted the role for soprano interpreters, and a lyric-soprano voice possibly suits the character best. Christine Nilsson—a Marguérite, Juliette, and Ophélie, and "helped by a certain naïvety of look and manner which was thought very charming"—introduced the opera to London and to New York; the sopranos Marie van Zandt and Geraldine Farrar were among her successors at the Metropolitan. After Bori's long incumbency, the mezzos took over there—Gladys Swarthout, Tourel, Risë Stevens. But whether soprano or mezzo, a Mignon needs limpid tones and simple, unaffected charm of delivery. Marilyn Horne, who undertook the part in Dallas, was not really suited to it, for she is a heroic coloratura mezzo, robust in temperament, in voice, and in physical presence. Being also a versatile and intelligent artist, she did her best, by timbre and demeanor, to suggest an androgynous waif. But neither the voice nor the appearance was ethereal, and so much of the fragile, delicate pathos of the piece was lost. Words like "bien" and "lointain" Miss Horne nasalized, instead of keeping them forward, and then the finespun sound became a snarl. The set pieces were sung slowly, with much artful virtuoso detail, which was very impressive, if less touching than "candeur naïve" might have been.

When Barbier and Carré drew the "thread of gold" that is Mignon's history from Goethe's book, they ingeniously conflated other characters and incidents to provide an opéra-comique setting around it. (At resourceful transference they were adept; their *Hamlet*, also written for Thomas, ends with the Ghost's ordering Gertrude to get her to a nunnery, and proclaiming Hamlet king.) In their first plan for *Mignon* (the draft libretto of which survives in the Bibliothèque Nationale), there were four acts. The Baron and Baroness, owners of the château where the present Act II is set, are among the principal characters; the former flirts with the actress Philine, the latter with Wilhelm. There are lively French-farce scenes—of concealments, eavesdroppings, and inopportune entrances—constructed around Philine and her three admirers and Wilhelm and his three. There is lively theatrical patter, based on the book, for a large cast of subsidiary characters. Mignon gives the private performance of her "egg dance," accompanied by her song and castanets (the librettists of *Carmen* took up the idea). The troupe plays not *A Midsummer Night's Dream* but *Romeo and Juliet*; Mignon, moved to despair by the ardor that Philine and Wilhelm bring to the bedroom scene, interrupts it. At the end of Act III, the Harper strides onto the burning stage, whence all but he have fled, to declaim "Wer sich der Einsamkeit ergibt" in noble ecstasy. *Wilhelm Meister* is a fecund book. (Incidentally, it also adumbrates the Marschallin's levée, and some of the *Ring* mythology.) Most of the incident in this first *Mignon* libretto can be found in it somewhere or other, but the authors left Goethe behind at the end, when they prepared the marriage of Mignon and Wilhelm. In this draft version, the celebrations turn to lament when Mignon expires in an excess of rapture. But in Thomas's score for the Opéra-Comique the death is omitted, and all ends in jollity. Then, for Germany, the composer devised an alternative unhappy dénouement by removing the final scene and making Mignon die, not merely swoon, on hearing the voice of Philine, her former rival. Next, he ended with a trio in which she revives—and this is the close published in modern scores. Dallas retained it . . . but then allowed Mignon to die after all in the final bars. (Clara Louise Kellogg hit on a similar solution for the version she published in 1874.)

Sarah Caldwell was both musical and stage director of the Dallas production. With her own company she would doubtless have done something closer to the original opéra comique, and perhaps have included some of the alternative music turned up in her researches (among it a stranger, bleaker setting of "Connais-tu"; a cabaletta to Mignon's "Elle est aimée"; a dashing trio for Mignon, Wilhelm, and the Harper when Mignon wakes to find herself in the land where the lemons bloom). As it was, she restored some of the passages traditionally cut, and invested the crowd scenes with liveliness. Nothing Miss Caldwell does is routine. Presenting the last act as a dream fantasy of the dying Mignon was a foible that proved harmless, since it made no effective difference to the staging. Only when reading the program note, after the performance, did I realize that this had been Miss Caldwell's intention. True, Wilhelm did not react to Philine's offstage voice (if he was part of Mignon's dream, surely he should have done so?), but throughout the evening Renzo Casellato had been acting so dully that his apathy here made no special point. His voice, a bright lyric tenor, is pleasant enough, but there was no romance in his musical or dramatic manners.

Ruth Welting played a cutesy-pie Philine, a pretty little ingénue rather than the chic, glittering actress implied by her music. Her voice, usually so sweet and true, she pushed to squealiness at high climaxes. Nancy Williams was a plump, not a sparky, Frederick. Nicola Zaccaria lacked the fine, forward focus that good French basses bring to the Harper's music. With this cast (Piero de Palma sang Laertes, and Enrico Campi

Jarno—both in execrable French) it might have been wiser to use the Italian translation. French, purely and distinctly pronounced, is one of the most beautiful and vivid of singing languages, but what these singers made of it was horrid. As conductor, Miss Caldwell began slowly, inflecting the overture with more expression than it can easily bear; later, she showed her wonted grace in lyrical moments, and verve in brilliant passages. The décor, by Peter J. Hall, was painted canvas that had already seen hard labor in Italy.

Dallas does four operas and twelve performances (plus four student *Toscas*) this season. Over in Houston, the Houston Grand Opera does six operas and thirty-nine performances. In the local telephone directory ("Some Interesting Facts About Houston") one is told that the company is the fourth-largest in the country. (There is also a spring festival, and a junior touring company, the Texas Opera Theater.) It plays in Jesse Jones Hall, a strikingly handsome, well-planned modern auditorium downtown, close to restaurants and other theaters. (Dallas's Music Hall is out in a deserted park.) The foyer is a picturesque, inviting space, rising the full height of the building, wrapped in a curve around the horseshoe. Terraces cascade downward, linked by a romantic stair that hugs the outer wall like an Inca trail climbing a gorge. The feel of the place—its shapes and colors, a huge Lippold rod sculpture glinting overhead—is exhilarating, and so was the feel of the company, and its audiences, at the two performances I attended.

Both were of *Il trovatore*. Each production in Houston is given in an "international series" and again by a "national" cast, in English translation, at lower prices (on subscription, all six operas can be seen for a dollar each). The English *Trovatore* was by far the more exciting. Patricia Wells may not have the weight or metal in her voice to be a complete Leonora, but she was perfectly audible in the large house— true, accurate, and musical. Mario Fusco, making his opera début, was a bright-voiced, slightly raw Manrico. Brent Ellis was by any reckoning an admirable Luna—swift in attack; keen in utterance; lyrical, passionate, and forceful in the ways that a Verdian baritone should be. Carolyne James's very dramatic Azucena was marred by a slow, wide vibrato. A sensible, singable new translation by Ross Yockey gave fresh life to the drama. In the Italian version, Lucine Amara (deputizing for an injured Martina Arroyo) and Barry Morell were a Leonora and Manrico of routine mediocrity, and Kostas Paskalis, as Luna, was something worse—a sprawly, self-centered, self-indulgent performer. Lili Chookasian was a gusty Azucena. In both casts, John Mount made a strong Ferrando. He looked very young, but since Manrico, according to the libretto, is just turned fifteen, a twenty-five-year-old Ferrando, say, might well remember the face of a child-stealing gypsy he saw when he was ten.

Chris Nance conducted the English performance, and Charles Rosekrans the Italian, both ably. The scenery, by Sally Jacobs (the designer of Peter Brook's *A Midsummer Night's Dream*), looked like Ludwig Sievert décor of the thirties—clean, simple, and effective. There was nonsense in Gordon Davidson's direction; he introduced (in his own words) "a 'family' of *timeless gypsies*—rootless souls who seem to be in touch with the inexplicable forces which even today turn rational behavior into passionate excesses." Unrelated to the singing gypsies of Verdi's drama, they sat about in or wandered through *every s*cene, and in some way they were supposed to make manifest Azucena's desire for vengeance, which "in this context . . . becomes the spine upon which the human and social drama, Verdi's own passionate theatrical cry against oppression and fascism, is constructed." Muddled thinking! But these mute "timeless gypsies" could be ignored, and for the rest Mr. Davidson's work was clear, except when, during the last few bars of Act I, he essayed a scurried mime of the action later narrated in "Mal reggendo"—with predictably ludicrous result.

December 16, 1974

FAUST IS ALIVE AND WELL IN INDIANA

Gounod's *Faust* has been dead for decades, although its obsequies continue to be celebrated in style and its pretty tunes to be enjoyed. Busoni's *Doktor Faust* awaits adoption by the great opera companies of the world. (The German Opera in Berlin is the only house where it thrived for several seasons on end.) Like Pfitzner's *Palestrina* and Szymanowski's *King Roger, Doktor Faust* is an opera of high spiritual enterprise and uncommon musical richness. Enthusiasts will travel hundreds, thousands, of miles to attend the rare performances of these works. *Palestrina* may never become popular, for it is long and wordy and calls for special patience. Nothing bars the wider acceptance of *King Roger*, a glittering, voluptuous score, or of *Doktor Faust*—except, perhaps, the public's reluctance to try what is not already familiar. Yet the City Opera, which has played *The Makropulos Affair* and *A Village Romeo and Juliet* with success, might well dare them and not regret it.

The Indiana University Opera Theater, in Bloomington, did *Doktor*

55

Faust this season, and did it well. The conductor was Tibor Kozma, precise and persuasive. The prowess of the Bloomington student orchestra is well known; there was eloquent playing (even if the Cortège calls for something like the Chicagoans under Solti to invest it with full glamour). The choirs were strong. The décor was by Max Röthlisberger —a giant astrolabe overhead, and beneath it clean, simple scenes that caught the mood of each episode and shifted swiftly. Hans Busch and Mr. Röthlisberger shared the direction. The former is the son of Fritz Busch, who conducted the first performance of the opera, in Dresden, in 1925 (the same year that *Wozzeck* appeared). By a pleasant piece of symbolic casting, the role of the Youth, Faust's son, charged with continuing the hero's work, was played by Hans Busch's son, another Fritz. *Doktor Faust* is an opera about the continuity of human endeavor, about claiming the best of what the past can offer, mastering it, adding what one can, and bequeathing the sum to the future. It is likely to mean most to someone who lives habitually amid the landscapes, historical and imagined, of classical/Christian civilization; who is conversant with Helen and Hamlet, Goliath, Guinevere, and Goethe; whose imagination is stirred by Leonardo, Laura, and Luther, by Nausicaä, Nebuchadnezzar, Newton, and Neil Armstrong; and who enjoys ordering such romantic richness.

Faust is a tale continued in each age. The scholar-magician himself practiced in the early sixteenth century. The *Historia von D. Iohañ Fausten* was published in 1587, in Frankfort on the Main, and a little later in London, as *The Historie of the Damnable Life, and Deserued Death of Doctor Iohn Faustus*. Marlowe first shaped the matter into art. The English play crossed the Channel, and the Faust-stuff passed into the hands of German puppeteers. As a youth, Goethe saw a puppet performance—and in time he gave to the legend its greatest and grandest working. Busoni—as he rhymes out in a spoken prologue to *Doktor Faust*—for a while considered Goethe's *Faust* as a libretto for the opera that was to be his testament, but then "took more modest aim,/and to the play of puppets back I came." Loose references to "the old puppet play" have led to some confusion about his source; the other day, someone even wrote that "he went back to the Italian medieval puppet plays about Faust." Busoni said that he "inspected several versions." So did I. (They were published by German professors from 1823 onward.) Two things became clear: that by the time the puppet scripts reached print they had been influenced by the Goethe drama they once gave rise to; and that Busoni's chief source was the version published by Simrock in 1846, described by one scholar as "the most literary and least reliable." (On Simrock's own admission, "the dialogue and, generally speaking, the arrangement, are for the most part mine.")

Every serious reworking of *Faust* is to some extent autobiographical.

An artist who ponders on impulses toward good and evil, on the limits to human knowledge, understanding, and achievement, on the oft opposed claims of benefaction and personal gratification is likely to be drawn to the subject. Then in writing—or painting, or composing—his *Faust*, he joins his autobiography to others'. Behind Busoni's *Doktor Faust* stand Marlowe, Lessing, the anonymous puppeteers and the learned professors, Delacroix—and, above all, Goethe. In the future are Thomas Mann's *Doktor Faustus* and other *Fausts* still to come. Destiny seems to have directed the six-year-old Busoni toward the subject when, "one unforgettable evening," he was taken to see a puppet play (shades of Wilhelm Meister, of Goethe himself) and on the way home from it encountered an imposing Signor (accompanied by a poodle—another Faustian touch), who proved to be his errant father. "My life changed completely after that evening." His father forthwith made a musician of him.

While experiencing *Doktor Faust*, the listener has a sense of "everything coming together" (Britten's *Death in Venice* provides it, too)—the author's life, his thought, his discovery of the past, and his personal inventions. In Busoni's words—from a passage about his hope for the future of opera, but plainly indicative of his own venture—"a composer, a creator, brings to a single opera all that moves him, all that swims before his eyes, all that is within his powers to achieve; he becomes a musical Dante, and his work a Divine Comedy." This inclusiveness is disciplined, given bounds and form, by Busoni's strict notions of what the lyric theater—which demands "purer and more absolute music" than the concert hall or chamber—can decently treat of. Having found his subject and sketched his libretto, he then had "to mold musically independent forms that at the same time suited the words and the scenic events." There is calculation in this—*Doktor Faust*, like many great works of art, is rigorously planned—but in the score there is also inspiration. Busoni's beliefs in melody as the main element of composition, and in the human voice as a sound more eloquent than any instrument, combine with his mastery of form and his sure, individual orchestration to create a series of marvelous sound pictures, filling the stage and at the same time making audible the unseen backgrounds of the action.

His music is hard to describe. We can find autobiographical overtones, perhaps, in his obituary of Boito, a deeply serious composer who died—as did Busoni—with his long-contemplated major work unfinished (Philipp Jarnach completed *Doktor Faust*, most skillfully), who studied Bach and late Beethoven yet strove to remain Italian, who wished "to play his trumps against Richard Wagner, and hold up a great example to the young" but was outstripped by them even while he was leaving his own once vanguard ideas behind. Early in the century, Busoni investigated new scales, and new divisions of the octave into third tones and sixth tones. His little book, *Sketch of a New Esthetic of Music*, was influential. In the twenties, he felt that its ideas had been distorted: "By 'freedom of form' I did not mean formlessness; by 'oneness in music,' not illogical and vagrant harmony; by 'freedom of the individual,' not the noisy self-expression of any blunderer. . . . A seed of corn, however strong and fruitful, takes time to produce a harvest." More important than his prose is the practice in *Doktor Faust*. Both subject matter and score exemplify "the shifting and the turning to account of all the gains of previous experiments and their inclusion in strong and beautiful forms." The harmonies and scoring are new; they spring from his belief that each instrumental line, whether leading or subordinate, should be a statement ("This is not only more beautiful but it sounds better") and that each motif carries within itself its own proper development. *Doktor Faust* is contrapuntally spun, from melodies. In sum, the listener is— to quote Edward Sackville-West—"enthralled by an intellectual power, a spiritual magnificence, and an austere yet luminous beauty that are found together only in Bach and the great polyphonic masters of the sixteenth century"; by an opera that—to quote Edward Dent—"moves on a plane of spiritual experience far beyond that of even the greatest of musical works for the stage."

In Bloomington, there were alternate casts. In mine, Roy Samuelsen (a former student, now faculty) sang Faust in firm, lyrical tones; his acting lacked subtlety. All the others were students. Michael Ballam was an alert, dapper little gnome of a Mephistopheles. (The fiend's incarnations, as monk, herald, chaplain, courier, and, finally, nightwatchman, recall the strange messengers in Mann's *Death in Venice*; they are among Busoni's additions to the traditional Faust matter, and may have been suggested by Mann's story.) Ken Haering produced a brave, romantic baritone in the role of Gretchen's brother. The directors had been more successful in laying out the lines of the action to potent effect than in inspiring individuals, in the Parma scene, to a deportment convincingly aristocratic; and the bearing of Faust's scholars was more modern Hoosier than medieval Saxon. But they sang well. The Musical Arts Center, seating 1,460, is the ideal size for an opera house. Dent's English translation was very clear.

The Opera House of the Kennedy Center for the Performing Arts, in Washington, is a little larger, seating about two thousand—two hundred more than Bayreuth—when the pit is extended to house a full Wagnerian orchestra. But it is not too large to inhibit vivid, direct experience of a Wagnerian music drama. The Opera Society of Washington began its season with a very successful performance of *Die Walküre*, the latest installment in the *Ring* production—directed by George London, designed by John Naccarato, and (let me declare this partial interest at once) on occasion sung in my English translation—which several companies across the country have arranged to share. The Washington *Walküre* opened in German. Eszter Kovacs, from the Budapest Opera, was a clear, young, bright Brünnhilde, not yet heroic, not majestic in the Annunciation of Death, but talented and true. Noël Tyl, a young American giant (just an inch under seven feet), has the noble, forceful tones of a Wotan but not yet the nobility of bearing and gesture to make the most of his stature. Bozena Ruk-Focic's Sieglinde was a shade ladylike, more genteel than spontaneous, but carefully studied and sensitively sung. Helge Brilioth's Siegmund lacked romance but his voice flowed free and strong. Less able singers than these can often be heard at Bayreuth. Gwendolyn Killebrew was a magnificent Fricka—tall, imperious, and beautiful, keen in conveying the sense of each utterance, more sharply focused of tone than I have ever heard her before. And Peter Lagger was a Hunding whose voice was big and beautiful; he conveyed the man's harshness by incisive words and rhythm, not rough singing.

Mr. London's direction underlines no single, special aspect of the boundlessly rich work. The ram-drawn chariot, the patient steed of Act II, and the flying horses of Act III are banished, but otherwise Wagner's stage directions are largely observed. Sieglinde serves supper, and Hunding eats it. The Valkyries wear byrnies, and winged helmets over streamy, curly manes. Mr. Naccarato has forgotten to provide the great door that should fly open in Act I, when spring moonlight floods the room. Nothing happens, nothing moves (even though there is a hanging that could easily fall), and the effect is spoiled. Otherwise his crags, clefts, and knarred, knurled tree roots deck the drama very successfully, and once again we can enjoy a *Ring* whose staging has color in it and the essential sense of the natural world. In the heat of the Act II battle, the lighting men evidently lost their heads, for both Brünnhilde and Wotan intervened in darkness. In Act III, Sieglinde implored a weaponless Brünnhilde to use her sword. But in general this production, not limited to a particular political or psychological "interpretation" of the action, served the opera uncommonly well and inspired fresh responses to its greatness. As Busoni once said, an opera audience should do half the interpretative work for itself. Antal Dorati's conducting was eventful, stirring, often brisk but never glibly routined. The playing of the National Symphony was dramatic.

Die Walküre was followed, two days later, by a *Valkyrie* in my English. So it would be improper for me to try to describe the effect of this. But I must at least hail a new Siegmund, a promising Heldentenor, Robert Rue. His voice is fresh and full, at once lyrical and powerful, poured out in an easy, unforced flow. His musical manner was still a trifle summary, but his direct, honest delivery and (especially to the translator) his strongly formed words were an uncommon pleasure. The American pronunciation of short *o* ("bond") is rounder than the English; of short *i* ("sister") fuller; of the *a* in a word like "command" fuller. The metamorphosis of final *t* into *d* before a vowel ("O voice thaddenchants me") makes for smooth phrasing.

December 23, 1974

BORIS REDIVIVUS

The Metropolitan Opera's new production of *Boris Godunov* is a serious, carefully studied, imaginative, and admirable presentation of the great work, and a landmark in its long stage history. The opera broke on the astonished West in 1908, when Diaghilev brought it to the Paris Opera, and from that production derive an audience's first expectations of *Boris*—large, exotic spectacle; a coronation in the Kremlin square with bells pealing and costumes gleaming; the elaborate mantle of Chaliapin falling heavy on the shoulders of whoever tackles the title role. The idea of *Boris* as a colorful Russian pageant centered on its tremendous hero persists; it was given dazzling expression in the Salzburg production of 1965, by Karajan and Schneider-Siemssen. It is not an untrue idea, but less than the whole truth. The whole truth about *Boris* is not to be contained in any single staging, but the Metropolitan version compasses much of it.

No other opera—not even *Don Carlos*—calls for so many preliminary decisions about what should be performed. The composer himself left two distinct scores and then a final revision in vocal score. Rimsky-Korsakov reorchestrated and revised the opera in his own brilliant vein, freely amending what he deemed clumsy harmonies and rhythms, and later revised and amplified his own edition. That is what Diaghilev used. It held sway until, in 1928, Leningrad (followed, in 1935, by the Old Vic) returned to Mussorgsky. For the Metropolitan, in 1953, Karol Rathaus produced a new edition. Ippolitov-Ivanov scored the scene outside St. Basil's Cathedral (omitted by Rimsky) with Rimskian panache, and the Bolshoy added it to its Rimsky presentation. Then Shostakovich rescored the whole thing anew from Mussorgsky's vocal score, retaining his rhythms and harmonies; the Metropolitan adopted this in 1960. For the new staging, it uses a conflation of Mussorgsky's own scores, thus achieving a longer *Boris* than ever the composer intended. It is nearly as full as the version Rafael Kubelik conducted at Covent Garden in 1958 (when Boris Christoff, for the first time in his career, sang the Mussorgsky lines). That lasted four and a half hours; the Metropolitan's lasts four. It is sung in Russian.

Since 1948, when Peter Brook staged the work there, Covent Garden has given *Boris* in just about every possible way: with Mussorgsky's scoring, with Rimsky's, with alternation between them to accommodate a visiting protagonist; in English, in Russian, even macaronically in English and Russian (when Christoff first came), and in English and German (to house Ludwig Weber's noble performance); with and without the St. Basil scene, with the death of Boris last, with the scene in Kromy Forest last; with the Polish act complete, or slightly cut, or cut to the bone (but never completely omitted; that bold step was left to Scottish Opera, and in this country to Boston). The experience of different musical texts applied to the same production provided a fine chance of comparing scores but prompted no hard, unqualified conclusions. Mussorgsky without Rimsky would undoubtedly be the score to prefer in an either/or choice—but it would be sad never to hear again the latter's heady orchestration. *Boris* without the Polish act is undoubtedly a stronger drama, and *Boris* with either St. Basil or Kromy, but not both, a more shapely one—but the act dominated by Marina's mezzo-soprano brings contrast in an otherwise nearly all-male opera and, after the tedious stretches in mazurka and polonaise rhythms, a melting love duet; and St. Basil and Kromy are both great music. Even in the matter of language, all decisions can be defended. The Russian-English biglot performances proved particularly successful, since the phonograph had made the Tsar's great monologues familiar, while elsewhere the translation revealed the sense of the music.

Boris is an opera focused on Boris himself; *Boris* is an opera whose real hero is the Russian people. The truth lies somewhere between these views. The new Metropolitan production, directed by August Everding, is uncommonly successful at finding it and, by many strong, subtle strokes, emphasizing the relationship between the ruled and their rulers; for once, the popular and the personal scenes cohere. Ming Cho Lee's very beautiful scenery plays a part in this. Backdrop and front gauze, patterned in rectangles, hint at an iconostasis. At the close of a scene, the light gathers on a single character; then on the darkling stage the locality shifts. (The Metropolitan's huge side-stage wagons are used to dramatic effect.) The house curtain falls only to close the acts. Prologue and Acts I and II are played without intermission. For Act III, set in Poland, the iconostasis is broken into an airy Cubist evocation of trees. This act, inserted by Mussorgsky to perk things up, could with advantage be illumined more brightly—romantic moonlight in the Sandomir park rather than spotlights fumbling along in the darkness after the principals. At the close of Act IV, a striking image is lost. While the Simpleton sings his lament for riven Russia, the fireglow specified in Mussorgsky's score fails to appear. Otherwise, nothing but praise for the scenic realization of the piece. No doubt it will one day be revived in English, when a majestic native Boris is forthcoming, and tried on occasion without the intrusive and musically inferior Polish act. The staging, free from eccentricity, yet imaginative and distinguished, should bear repetition well.

The current Boris is Martti Talvela, who gives a thoughtful, sober interpretation of the role. Nevertheless, on the first night he was less arresting than one had hoped. Deliberately eschewing, it seems, the rhetorical manner of the Borises who base their interpretation on Chaliapin's (yet what better model?), he allowed restraint to become something close to grayness. The huge voice was seldom used at full power. There were histrionic moments in the acting—the heavy table overturned in the clock scene, the curtains clawed down, and in the death scene a spectacular tumble down steps, which Sarah Bernhardt might have envied—but they were obvious, applied effects, foreseeable, and extrinsic to what had gone before. Mr. Talvela has the stature and the voice to be a tremendous Boris, though not yet the variety of nuance or intensity of phrasing. It was rather as if a grave Pimen had donned the Tsar's robes. Pimen was sung by Paul Plishka, Varlaam by Donald Gramm; both were decent, not remarkable. Robert Nagy was a trenchant Shuisky. The outstanding member of the surrounding cast was Lenus Carlson, in the small role of Shchelkalov, secretary of the boyars' council. His lyrical baritone was forward and beautiful, his phrasing was smooth, and he used his words as if they meant something. In the monastery and inn scenes, Harry Theyard gave a keen, intelligent portrayal of the ambitious novice Grigory; the Polish act needed more romantic tones than he could provide. Mignon Dunn's Marina looked glamorous but sounded ordinary. The conductor, Thomas Schippers, set steady rhythms—too steady in phrases that come to life when they are freely and emotionally molded. He adopted so fast and so regular a tempo for the Simpleton's lament (the marking is andantino) that Andrea Velis could not express its full poignancy. Mr. Schippers's intention, plainly, was to avoid a sentimental close; fearing effusiveness, he missed the poetry of the episode. But on the whole he gave an impressive reading of the score, well paced and carefully knit. The orchestral playing was deep-toned and eloquent. The chorus looked numerous enough but did not always sound it. The language difficulty—having to make what must for many of the cast be meaningless noises, learnt parrot-fashion, rather than communicating with an audience that can follow what is said— may have inhibited full-throated and sharply characterized singing. In general, the first-night performance was a shade cautious; with increasing confidence, things should become freer and more vivid.

Elliott Carter's new Brass Quintet, composed for the American Brass Quintet, broadcast by them from London on Ives's hundredth birthday, and by them introduced to New York at a Chamber Music Society of Lincoln Center concert on December 15, is sixteen minutes of lively incident ordered into a shapely form. The score appears to spring from fruitful interaction between what brass instruments naturally do best—soft, swelling harmonies in chords long sustained and, on the other hand, incisive fanfare patterns—and the composer's own more "abstract" concerns with multilayered music flowing in lapped levels, each distinct in pace and in character, each a statement in its own right, but in combination amounting to a discourse that holds the mind and delights the ear. The abstract concerns take concrete shape when to each of the five instruments—two trumpets, horn, tenor and bass trombones—Carter assigns an individual melodic "repertory" of intervals and gestures. The basic form is a slow movement, a serene chorale punctuated by brief quodlibets to which each player contributes parts of his own repertory, and further interrupted or accompanied in its progress by animated, well-varied duos and trios, each for a different combination of instruments. During these dialogues, the instruments essay one another's motifs. Long pedal tones are superimposed on quick, darting exchanges. The virtuosity of the players incites the composer to try the result, on brass, of the kind of *scorrevole* passagework he writes for strings. The sounds are produced in traditional fashion, without fancy mutes or any freak effects. (In two horn calls, half-stopped echo tone is romantically employed.) The Quintet is a major addition to the brass chamber literature.

The weekend before last there were at least fifteen different operas to be heard in New York. Two of them—and possibly others, but who can be everywhere?—were among the most moving and intense operatic experiences of the season so far, not because they were well acted (they weren't) but because they were well sung, and very well played, by dedicated young performers in intimate surroundings where every word and every musical nuance could be heard to maximum effect. In the parish-house theater of the Madison Avenue Baptist Church, on Thirty-first Street, Bel Canto Opera did Britten's *The Rape of Lucretia*. John Miner, praised last year for his conducting of Heinrich Graun's *Montezuma*, in Boston, conducted a sensitive, cunningly paced and balanced performance. Lee Winston, as the Male Chorus, was decisive in diction and subtle in phrasing; his tenor is forthright and steady. Harvey Phillips's direction was sensibly conceived, but clumsily executed by a cast that did not move well. Nevertheless the grace and the physical impact of the musical realization made the evening memorable.

Holst wanted a very simple setting for his *Savitri,* and no more was possible in the Manhattan Theater Club, on East Seventy-third Street. This is an opera with very little action and great spiritual beauty. Holst's economy of means is so finely judged that small strokes—one unaccompanied voice breaking in on another—cut deep. Joy Blackett sang the title role with tender passion. Michael Harrison was a romantic, assured young Satyavan. Harlan Foss was properly grave but not quite even enough in timbre as Death. Peter Leonard's conducting was precise. If a conclusion may be drawn from two performances, it is that well-trained voices, used with musical intelligence, are abundant in New York, and so are first-rate instrumentalists, but that the levels of acting and direction, of stage presence, demeanor, even the ability to wear costumes convincingly and not look gawky are lower. (On one of the simplest levels, why did David Shookhoff, the director of *Savitri,* not persuade Miss Blackett not to wave her arms about while she sang?)

Savitri was given on a double bill with Thomas Pasatieri's *Signor Deluso,* an *opera buffa* to his own libretto, drawn from Molière's *Sganarelle.* Like Robert Baksa's comic opera *Red Carnations,* given in St. Luke's Chapel, in the Village, earlier this season, Mr. Pasatieri's piece is a slight anecdote set to harmless, agreeable, unmemorable music. Neither comedy *needs* music. Mr. Baksa's Straussian ariosi went in one ear and out the other; Mr. Pasatieri's neat neoclassical or neo-Romantic inventions were short-breathed. Strauss himself showed one successful way to treat such subject matter in his *Intermezzo,* by allowing the orchestra to take over from time to time; Rossini another, by protracting situations in comely arias or ensembles. (The Opera Buffa Company of New York gave a fairly diverting but feebly directed account of Rossini's *La cambiale di matrimonio* in Finch College Auditorium early in the season.) The moral seems to be that vivacity is not incompatible with, is perhaps dependent on, a rather full musical working. Probably the answer to modern operatic comedy lies in spoken dialogue that breaks into fully developed songs—a revival of *Singspiel.* But the dialogue must be good. Wisely, Jens Nygaard scrapped the silly dialogue that Albert Stadler provided for Schubert's *Singspiel* operetta *Fernando* and conducted just the musical numbers at a Sunday-afternoon concert up at the Washington Heights and Inwood Y Auditorium, well attended even on one of those opera-filled days. Grayson Hirst, who should have taken the title role, had been stricken with laryngitis; Richard Frisch undertook both tenor and bass parts, transposing octaves nimbly or slipping into head voice for the former. Despite this, the quality of Schubert's music came through. Why was so fertile and fluent a great composer so insecure and unsuccessful a musical dramatist? (The same question can be asked about Haydn.) The answer can wait, since Mr. Nygaard has more Schubert operas in prospect.

December 30, 1974

The answer is still waiting; Mr. Nygaard's plans were not realized. The Bronx Opera produced Die Verschworenen *(see p. 84)—but that is the one Schubert opera that has been staged with some frequency.*

CALDWELL IN COMMAND

For the City Opera, Sarah Caldwell has directed Hans Werner Henze's *The Young Lord* and Richard Strauss's *Ariadne on Naxos*. Last week she made her Carnegie Hall début, presenting, in concert form, large excerpts from Prokofiev's *War and Peace*. The concert was a kind of parergon to the production of the opera that she both directed and conducted in Boston last May, and repeated last summer on Wolf Trap Farm. Its success was a measure of her musico-dramatic flair. *War and Peace* is an opera whose effect might be thought to depend quite largely on its vast choruses, its two extended ballroom scenes, and cunning inscenation of the kaleidoscopic episodes that make up the second part. Sans décor, sans action, and sans chorus except that provided by massing her fourteen soloists, Miss Caldwell revealed the power and richness of Prokofiev's score. She has a born opera director's genius for ordering the resources at hand—maybe a mixed batch of enthusiasts playing in a gym, maybe a cast of seasoned pros assembled rather too late for detailed ensemble rehearsal, and here a group of admirable singers ranged on a concert platform before an orchestra—to catch the essential spirit of a music drama. Although a composer's full requirements (say, the huge multiple choruses and deep-stage spectacle of Verdi's *Don Carlos*, which Miss Caldwell put on in Boston last year) may not always be attainable, whatever forces she can muster she puts to maximum use, so as to communicate, clearly and vividly, what the composer was about. In rehearsal, she has reminded me in some ways of Peter Brook: there is the same fiercely accelerating intensity of concentration toward the first performance, which can be tough on a cast and yet lift it to fresh achievement; the same gift for disconcerting last-minute improvisations that suddenly refine the expression of a long-held, long-pondered idea. In the work of both directors, preliminary research to the deepest foundations of a piece does not preclude spontaneity in its execution. There is a kind of theater—heady, exhilarating, and hazardous to professional routine—that seems to combine decisions made on a bedrock of belief and decisions taken even while the audience assembles. Miss Caldwell provides it.

A few days before the *War and Peace* concert, one of her singers told an interviewer that the choice of excerpts was still undecided. Those eventually chosen (a little under two hours of music was done, without intermission) brilliantly reflected the proportions of the work, the manner of its dramatic progress, the balance between epic tableaux and the personal adventures of the principals. Of course, the scenes must have meant most to listeners who knew the whole score (and, for that matter, the opera means most to listeners who know the whole of Tolstoy's novel; the libretto is itself a selection of scenes from something much larger). But even someone unable to place all the characters or fill in the gaps of the narrative must have felt the fire and force of the piece.

I missed Miss Caldwell's Boston production of *War and Peace*, but two other productions encountered last season, in Sydney and in London, convinced me that it is one of the large modern operas most deserving of a place in the international repertory. It was widely seen in the Western world when NBC produced an abridged but impressive television version; that was in 1957, two years before the work had reached the Bolshoy. The early history of the opera is even more tangled than that of *Boris Godunov*. In summary: 1942—a first version completed in piano score. 1944—a concert performance in Moscow of a second version. 1946—the first eight scenes of a third version staged at the Maly Theater, Leningrad, and a concert performance at the Soviet Embassy, London. 1953—Prokofiev dies, after continuing to elaborate the heroic and patriotic aspects of his work; a Florence production. 1955—a Maly production. 1957—a production at the Stanislavsky Theater, Moscow. 1959—the Bolshoy production. The opera was taken up in East Germany and Czechoslovakia. All the stagings after 1953 used as text a selection from the very long score that the composer had built up over the years. Then in 1972 the Sadler's Wells—now English National —Opera presented the fullest version yet given. Last year, Sydney chose *War and Peace* to inaugurate its new opera house. The Bolshoy brought it to Montreal in 1967, and plan to bring it to the Metropolitan this summer. Miss Caldwell has now mounted the American première. The Bolshoy recording has just achieved domestic publication, on the Columbia / Melodiya label.

And with increasing familiarity has come revaluation, a truer appraisal. Prokofiev himself prepared the way for a misunderstanding when, to Western friends, he declared that all the patriotic stuff had been put in just to please the authorities. And as a result, it has often been underrated. There is no reason to doubt Prokofiev's statement; the history of the opera's genesis supports him. On rereading the novel in 1941, he was drawn to set it when he suddenly perceived, in the reunion of Natasha and the wounded Prince Andrey, "the perfect operatic scene." His first version was turned down by the Committee on the Arts because too much attention had been paid to the aristocratic lovers, too little to the Russian people. His revisions and amplifications were largely concerned with patriotic choruses and new, noble ariosi and arias for the people's general, Field Marshal Kutuzov. Yet although the additions may have been officially motivated, that should not blind one to the merits of the extra music Prokofiev composed. There are plenty of operas that deal, subtly and stirringly, with love awakened, love betrayed, love finally triumphant. (The themes in *War and Peace* that express the love of Natasha and Andrey were borrowed from Prokofiev's incidental music to *Eugene Onegin*, composed in 1936). *War and Peace* belongs to the small band of operas that give voice to exalted popular resolve in music that is stirring but not crude. *Fidelio* does so; so do the last act of *Die Meistersinger*, several of Verdi's operas, some of Kurt Weill's. *War and Peace* was certainly a "relevant" subject at the time of its composition. The Germans invaded Russia in June of 1941, just before Prokofiev began his score; they moved toward Moscow by way of Smolensk, as Napoleon had done in 1812. As "Epigraph" to the opera, Prokofiev sets a shattering chorus: "This invasion kindled in the heart of every Russian such a deep sense of outrage and of wounded pride that their fury burst forth into sacred flame. Forth to battle went the Russian people in defense of their land: they rose in all their terrible might against the invader. Who could stand against them in the splendor of their wrath when they rose against their enemies?" The music transcends the particular occasion, gives international voice to feelings of heroic resistance to wrong, prompts emotions that can bind men as brothers. (Rather similarly, Giuseppe Giusti in a famous poem tells how Verdi's chorus "O Signore, dal tetto natio" flooded both the Milanese patriots and the occupying forces in one common wave of yearning—to a point where the poet almost flung his arms around a stiff Austrian corporal.) It is one of the glories of opera that it can provide such transcendental experiences. (Afterward, of course, the emotions must be examined; and the Brussels performance of Auber's *La Muette de Portici* in 1830 is the only recorded instance of an opera that led directly to a popular rising.) It is for the splendor of its hitherto underrated "public" music, I believe, that *War and Peace* will one day be most highly valued—for that, and for the skill with which Prokofiev follows his principals, Andrey, Pierre, and Natasha, through the events of war.

This sense of individual destinies as part of a larger history, and the musical realization of private cares against a vaster perspective, raise *War and Peace* far above the common run of operatic romances and at the same time save it from being a tub-thumping patriotic pageant.

All this Miss Caldwell understands well. The "Epigraph" she had to omit; without a large chorus it is impossible to perform. But by skillful selection, brilliant theatrical pacing, and a rare command of atmosphere created through the molding of a phrase, the lilt of a rhythm, or the intensity of a timbre, she led the work securely from the lyricism of the spring garden, in peace, through Petersburg and Moscow intrigues and amorous escapades on the eve of invasion, to the series of brilliant, affecting, and finally triumphant war scenes. Kutuzov carried the burden of the opera; his music was sung gravely, eloquently, and warmly by Donald Gramm. Natasha calls for a purer tone than Joann Yockey's, but her characterization was touching and true. I was sorry not to hear more of Pierre, partly because the single monologue left him was so well sung by William Neill, partly because I hoped Miss Caldwell might convince me that his music in the later scenes is not—well, something of a letdown. The playing of the American Symphony was glittering, enthusiastic, and powerful.

There are many good reasons for giving concert performances of opera —particularly in a country with no broadcasting system regularly producing its own performances of rare pieces and relaying the best from the rest of the world. And there are many ways of giving them—from a completely acted, if décorless, presentation such as the Little Orchestra Society mounted of Janáček's *Jenůfa*, through "semi-staging," to a perfectly straight studio-type performance. There was a touch of theater in the way Sarah Caldwell directed operations in *War and Peace* from a rostrum massively built up into a redoubt; and Natasha and Andrey waltzed a few steps together.

Four days earlier, at a concert performance of *Salome* in the same hall, Birgit Nilsson did not waltz during the Dance of the Seven Veils, even though Sir George Solti conducted it with the most alluring lilt. (She did take the chance it afforded of powdering her nose.) Norman Bailey, as John the Baptist, stood behind the orchestra when he was notionally in the cistern, up front when he was not. The gaggle of chatering Jews (characterized by Strauss as such) was clustered to one side of the stage; the soldiers and Nazarenes were on the other. It would be even more welcome to hear, from Solti, one of the extra-repertory operas at which he excels (such as Britten's *Billy Budd*, or Schoenberg's *Moses and Aaron*, which he did here in concert some years ago) or would surely excel (Busoni's *Doktor Faust*, Szymanowski's *King Roger*, Hindemith's *Mathis der Maler*), but a *Salome* from him and Miss Nilsson needs no justification. True, they have recorded the work together, memorably well; nevertheless, the pull of the live event is strong—and the performance was of superlative quality. Drawing on several productions, memory might assemble a cast with a more grandly resonant Prophet than Mr. Bailey, a more imposing Herodias than Ruth Hesse, but hardly a better Herod than Ragnar Ulfung. On a single occasion, such a team as we heard could hardly be bettered. And no other heroine of my experience, not even Ljuba Welitch, has been so subtle, delicate, and radiantly powerful as Miss Nilsson. It was as if Strauss's score, the Chicago Symphony, Solti, and Miss Nilsson had all been made for one another—and here they all were together at last.

January 6, 1975

A HUNDRED, NOT OUT

Last year saw the hundredth birthdays of Schoenberg and Ives; of Gustav Holst, Josef Suk, and Franz Schmidt; of Hugo von Hofmannsthal and Gertrude Stein. This year, the centennial names are mainly French. Bizet, the greatest of them, will no doubt be much performed. A more lasting memorial would be a decent edition of his works; today not one of the stage pieces can be bought in an unadulterate score. In 1875, the year of Bizet's death, Ravel, Reynaldo Hahn, Henri Février, and Jean Nouguès were born. Ravel is hardly in need of promotion. Hahn's songs—in particular, the delicately chased *Chansons latines*—deserve to be more widely known. Stage revivals of Février's *Monna Vanna* and Nouguès' *Quo vadis* are unlikely outside France, but perhaps some radio station will give us studio performances of those two operas, which were once widely admired. Two centuries ago, François Rébel died (the Juilliard School's admirable baroque performers should be doing something about that), and the rival composers Adrien Boieldieu and Nicolo Isouard were born (the latter in Malta, but it was in Paris that he made his name). Boieldieu is a good composer who bears revival. Who has heard more of Isouard than the air from *Le Billet de loterie* recorded by Frieda Hempel?

Compiling centenary catalogues is little more than a harmless pastime. No deep conclusions can be drawn from the fact that *Carmen*, Anton Rubinstein's *The Demon*, Sullivan's "new and original cantata" *Trial by Jury*, Goldmark's *Die Königin von Saba*, and Ignaz Brüll's all but forgotten *Das goldene Kreuz* were the new operas of 1875; or that Corot,

69

Millet, and Mörike died in that year and Rilke and Thomas Mann were born. But it is a little more than a pastime since, by tradition, each hundred years after an artist's birth and death his work is re-examined and revalued. The first concert of the New Year in New York was devoted to chamber music by Donald Francis Tovey, born in 1875. In CAMI Hall, Jens Nygaard presented the Trio for clarinet, horn, and piano, Opus 8, and the Sonata for cello and piano, Opus 4. His concert was "gratefully and lovingly dedicated to the greatest of all my teachers. . . . I wish that I could have known him personally."

Tovey deserves tribute. On all English-speaking musicians his thought has left its mark—either the direct impress of the *Essays in Musical Analysis* or ways of thinking and writing about music passed on by teachers trained on their Tovey. He established our orthodoxy. The great articles he wrote for the the great edition of the Encyclopædia Britannica, the eleventh, were surpassed only by his own revision of them for the fourteenth. (So it is not altogether fair to say that since 1911 the Encyclopædia has been in steady decline.) It is easy to disagree with Tovey in detail. Time has disturbed some of his dicta. ("Mozart's *Idomeneo* is the grave of some of his greatest music, including many genuinely dramatic strokes," he wrote in the Encyclopædia; but today *Idomeneo* is a living repertory work.) Perspectives have shifted and horizons are wider than even he, who ranged so widely, could have foreseen. Modern executants have a nicer sense of historical style, when playing music of periods before their own, than had Tovey and his friends and colleagues—Joseph Joachim, Adolf and Fritz Busch, Casals (who deemed Tovey "the greatest musician we had"). In his British Academy lecture "The Main Stream of Music" Tovey charted its course from the fifteenth century to his own. Today, we paddle or wade through higher reaches of the stream than he thought worth much exploration, and strange new channels have been cut since 1938, when he delivered the lecture. But, essentially, what he says about the making and meaning of Western music remains true. Our new methods of measurement have added only details to his map. To read Tovey is to be stimulated and tested by contact with a superior mind, that kind of "Eton and Balliol mind" (Tovey didn't go to Eton, but his father, the editor of Thomson and Gray, was an assistant classics master there) which, happily, still survives—and is still apt to provide reactions similar to Tovey's on reading Herodotus: "It is very revolting to realize what a wonderful writer Herodotus is,—in the same process in which one realizes that one's own work is abominably hasty and superficial."

His writing was often hasty (quotations, he declared, were better left unchecked when checking might destroy the point he wished to make) but never superficial. His mind flowered early. The ideas formulated in the essays, written from 1900 onward, are adumbrated in undergraduate letters from Balliol. From the start it was a musical mind: "I have (this sounds like fantastic nonsense, but it isn't) frequently caught myself positively *solving* some problem (of a more or less philosophical nature) in, say, the key of A minor, where I had utterly failed to reason it out in words." The compositions began early, too. On holiday in Scotland, during the first long vac, in 1895, he writes: "Agamemnon, Bray, Oxford in general, Durness, the Firth of Forth, the delightfully quiet and gay and intellectual Cornishes and their absurd live seagulls and cormorants, and the pompous Chester and the sea-fog with the glassy water, and the clear ring of cold gray sky with a perspective of cold gray clouds seven layers deep, have suddenly turned into an extremely gay and jovial cello sonata in F major, and a very romantic and melancholy and prehistoric trio in C minor for pfte., clarinet and horn. . . . The romantic and utterly unearthly effect of the mere combination of instruments (pfte., clar. and horn) has gripped me strongly, and I think I can ensure that it does not pall." Three years later, there was more work on the Trio, again in Scotland. A dozen years later, both the Sonata and the Trio were published by Schott of Mainz. (Unknown to Tovey, his patroness, Sophie Weisse, had paid for their publication.)

Anyone who came upon the Trio and the Sonata in CAMI Hall without knowledge of their author may have found it hard to place or date the compositions. Brahms is the immediate point of reference; the piano textures, the balance of periods, the pace and carefully directed progress of the harmonic shifts, and the general shaping of the themes suggest him. And yet an individual voice, not an imitator, is speaking. "Voice" is perhaps not the just word; it implies melody, and Tovey did not have the heaven-sent (i.e., inexplicable) gift of creating inspired melodies which distinguishes the great composers from the good. (A melody can be a theme, but a good theme is not necessarily an inspired melody.) What we hear, rather, is the thinking of a superb musical mind, a mind thinking aloud and "solving some problem" in C minor or F major. Yet poetry and romance are not missing. "Dry" and "academic" are not epithets to apply. The performances were, aptly, romantic. Mr. Nygaard is a warm and persuasive pianist. In the Trio, he was joined by Jean Kopperud, clarinet, and Dave Jolley, horn. The cellist in the Sonata was Joel Krosnick; in his playing, physical rapture in the sound of the instrument and a firm grasp of form were tellingly combined.

It is easy to echo the conventional judgments on Tovey's music— that of the London *Times*, for instance, after the 1932 performance of his only opera: "*The Bride of Dionysus* is a remarkable work from every point of view save one—that of sheer musical invention. . . . The actual substance of Tovey's music bears on it no distinctive mark of its author or of its time. . . . If only his themes were in themselves as significant as his use of them is psychologically right." But the critic also wrote, "Yet, as though this were but a small thing, the opera grips and holds the attention through the whole of its course of four hours." E. M. Forster said that the opera was most beautiful in total effect, "most certainly not the dull academic stuff which certain critics have been pleased to find it," and "something that is delightful to listen to, interesting to think about, and impressive emotionally." Perusal of the vocal score suggests as much, but only a performance could show it. (Who could deduce from the vocal score of, say, *Pénélope* that Fauré's opera proves so dramatically potent in the theater?) Fritz Busch planned to do *The Bride of Dionysus* at Glyndebourne in 1940, but the war put a stop to that. A revival is long overdue; may the centenary year provide one. And also full publication of Tovey's voluminous correspondence with his librettist, R. C. Trevelyan. The excerpts printed in Mary Grierson's life of Tovey are an exciting sample. They show that keen intelligence ranging over all the problems of opera—subject matter, diction, word setting, pacing, scoring, form. Trashy or at best unnecessary books on music pour from the presses; this one—whatever the merits of *The Bride of Dionysus* itself prove to be—would be something worth having.

Giovanni Battista Sammartini died two hundred years ago come Wednesday, and Clarion Concerts will be marking the occasion. The Clarion season began last month, however, with a Marian Vesper sequence newly assembled by James Moore from Francesco Cavalli's *Musiche Sacre* of 1656. As an opera composer, Cavalli is now in fashion all over the world. His sacred music has received less attention. Three Magnificats from his 1675 Vesper collection were published in 1960 by Giuseppe Piccioli. In 1950, Bruno Stäblein published four Marian pieces from the *Musiche Sacre*, and in 1966 Raymond Leppard (the man who put Cavalli on the modern operatic map) produced his realization of the Messa Concertata from the same collection. Until the rest of it is put into score (it survives in separate partbooks), and performed, we can hardly shape any very clear ideas about Cavalli in church. Any fool can hear that, whether in sacred or secular vein, he was no Monteverdi. But while in the theater he had distinguishing excellences of his own—a melodic fluency; a flair for pathetic, affecting utterance; a rare command of contrast, theatrical pace, and striking dramatic effect—in concerted church music there is less scope for their deployment. In the Vesper sequence, the solo motet *O quam suavis* provided one opportunity; it might have been a moving aria from one of his operas. And in the four-part *Salve Regina* there was a beautiful quasi-dramatic effect when the alto, rather like an offstage character or echo, repeated an unchanging call of "ostende" through shifting harmonies from the three other voices over a bass that slowly descended. These movements were incandescent. For the rest, although there were several striking and felicitous ideas, they were set amid a good deal of what seemed, at this first encounter, to be sound, well-wrought, but fairly conventional stuff.

To complete the "service," Mr. Moore provided chanted antiphons. The *Domine ad adjuvandum*, the one Vesper psalm missing in Cavalli's *Musiche Sacre*, he borrowed from Alessandro Grandi's *Salmi* of 1629. The orchestration was that called for in the continuo part (strings, cornetts, trombones, varied continuo instruments) and in addition a trio of recorders and bassoon. The vocal disposition is double choir and double solo quartet. Two of the eight soloists were exceptional in style, in timbre, in fluency: the tenor Robert White and the countertenor Daniel Collins. Mr. Collins can be an uneven artist. At a pleasant Christmas Eve recital by the Ensemble for Early Music, in the Cathedral of St. John the Divine, he sang some carols as if his mind were elsewhere and others (notably Attey's "Sweet was the song the Virgin sung") with marvelous beauty and intensity of expression. Cavalli evidently brings out the best in him. In the opera *Erismena*, at last year's Holland Festival, and again in these Vespers, his free, bold handling of the lines, his clearly projected tones, and his fleetness and delicacy in adornment were model. Newell Jenkins conducted with conviction but on occasion allowed simple speed to take the place of rhythmic vitality. In any case, Alice Tully Hall is not the place for such music. It is of conventional design, and therefore unsuited to music of the seventeenth or of the twentieth century which needs more than one sound source. Instead of being separated, the antiphonal choirs and bands were ranged side by side on the small platform. There must be many churches in New York that, both spatially and acoustically, would serve the music better. Nevertheless, this Cavalli revival was a notable event, another feather in Clarion's bright cap of new-preened plumes.

January 13, 1975

The BBC rose to the occasion of Bizet's centenary by performing all his operas, some of them (including La Jolie Fille de Perth *and* Ivan le terrible*) for the first time in editions representing the composer's intentions. In America, I miss the BBC, which initiates important musical performances on every scale, commissions new works and new editions of old works (the* Ivan *contained nearly an hour of previously unperformed music), regularly relays the best of British—and European—music making, and, in its illustrated talks, keeps its listeners abreast of the discoveries of musical scholarship.*

NOTES ON NOTES ON NOTES

The Composers' Showcase concerts at the Whitney Museum, put on in conjunction with the Fromm Music Foundation at Harvard, continue to draw full houses. The museum itself is oddly inhospitable—its galleries and restaurant remain closed to these new guests—but for the George Crumb concert last Thursday the line for admission stretched down Madison Avenue, and the large room on the second floor was then packed to overflowing by an eager audience, some of it on chairs and most of it on the floor. The small corps of familiar faithful who follow contemporary music at Carnegie Recital Hall was swelled by cohorts of the young. Such events are exhilarating, provided the music is good. Crumb's music is. Three works were played—*Madrigals*, Book I, *Lux Aeterna*, and, for the first time in New York, *Music for a Summer Evening (Makrokosmos III)*—and then the composer, not very audibly, answered questions from the floor. The compositions span a decade: the *Madrigals* are dated 1965, and the *Music for a Summer Evening* was completed last year.

In lieu of program notes, there was an essay by Paul Fromm entitled "How Useful Are Program Notes?" The question is perhaps in the "How ripe are strawberries?" class, and Mr. Fromm's answer is like that of someone who throughout his life has encountered only tart and tasteless fruit. After "a lifetime attending concerts," and as "a connoisseur of sorts of program notes," he concludes that those for concerts of contemporary music, "even those written by the composers involved, rarely offer any aid for the listener." My experience has been different. In defense of program notes, let me simply adduce some that I believe to be useful, to have helped people to listen to new music in ways that its composer intended: Elliott Carter's introduction to his first two String Quartets, and Crumb's to his *Ancient Voices of Children* and to his *Makrokosmos*, Volume I. Those notes appear on the covers of Nonesuch recordings; I have deliberately chosen checkable examples, in a format less ephemeral than that of the leaflets given away at, and often thrown away after, concerts. They place the works concerned in time and in relation to other pieces by the same composer. They cite any extramusical sources of inspiration and, in terms easily understood, limn particular musical problems tackled and methods essayed. They describe the form of the works. (Of course, after playing the discs repeatedly a listener can discover this for himself, but it is usually helpful to consult a map before setting out into new territory. At a concert, where the listener is given but one chance to find his way to the heart of a work, the map is even more necessary.) They tell whether the art of a particular interpreter influenced the creation of the music. Additional information is appended: the publishers of the scores; notes on the artists who perform; pointers to other chances of hearing them, and of hearing more music by the same composer.

If all program notes were of this quality, and all concert promoters could afford the space for them, then I imagine that Mr. Fromm would answer his question differently. With his main thesis, that "clarity of context in programming and active involvement in listening . . . are the concert-goers' true aids," there can be no disagreement. The concert was admirably planned, and was listened to in a silence so intense that a few invasive sounds from the world outside cut in with shock effect. The works were mutually illuminant. I regret only Mr. Fromm's rejection of the subsidiary aid that a few wise and informative words in advance can afford—regret the lost chances of making the music a little more vivid still to listeners encountering the pieces for the first time, of helping them to enter Crumb's imaginative world, and of directing them toward the further adventures there that the phonograph can so readily provide.

I tried to say something about Crumb's world of sounds and images after the première of *Makrokosmos*, Volume II, in November (see pp. 36–9). In brief, his music found its first images in lines of Lorca: proud, prime, hard earth imagery, forceful equine evocations, gentle yet pungent lament, and sweetly sensual tenderness often associated with children. A black horse with wounded legs, frozen mane, and a silver dagger in its eyes; sleeping branches oblivious of rain that falls on them; a child's yearning for the warm touch of a mother's garment—these are among the Lorca images that Crumb took up and set. In later works, his gaze moved to contemplation of the stars, as symbols of immense, eternal silence, and this contemplation mingled with mystic, romantic dreams: of unplumbed ocean depths melodious with the song of the whale, or of strange Druid rites enacted softly behind veils of awe and antiquity. Anyone who walks easily and willingly amid the dream imagery of Western art is likely to be drawn to Crumb's music; anyone who finds reflected and intensified in both *Beowulf* and *Pelléas* his own feeling that we move in a small, lit area ringed by unknowable darkness; anyone who, when he hears Nannetta's attendants in the last act of Verdi's *Falstaff* liken the dense, scented air of Windsor Forest to some green haven far below the waves, senses both the soft incense and embalmèd darkness of Keats's "Ode to a Nightingale" and the flowers so sweet which, in Shelley's "Ode to the West Wind," quiver within the wave's intenser day. ("Dull . . . Lethe-wards . . . ease," in the "Nightingale," and the "oozy woods" and "sapless foliage" of the "West Wind" then come together to suggest the Ghost's lines in *Hamlet*—"And duller shouldst thou be than the fat weed / That rots itself in ease on Lethe wharf." Boito, Verdi's librettist, may unwittingly have revealed a common source. It has now just struck me that, unconsciously, I drew on

Keats's ode to find words for an English translation of that scene in *Falstaff*, and that Boito may have used it, too.)

This gets us away from Crumb—but not too far, for a similar clustering of related images goes into the making of his music. In *Ancient Voices* he quotes from "Bist du bei mir" (now ascribed to G. H. Stölzel, but emotionally charged for us by its inclusion in Anna Magdalena Bach's *Notebook*) and from the Abschied of Mahler's *Lied von der Erde*; in *Makrokosmos II* from Beethoven's *Hammerklavier* Sonata; in *Music for a Summer Evening* from the D-sharp-minor Fugue in the Second Book of the Forty-eight. By alterations of timbre and tempo, and because of the different lights thrown by the new contexts, Crumb makes the images his own. Moreover, someone ignorant of *Das Lied* should still understand the sense of that plangent oboe cry as it pierces the final movement of *Ancient Voices*; similarly with the soft rapture of the Beethoven and the tight-woven Bach threads. Nevertheless, these quotations are obviously meant to sound larger resonances, drawn from the listeners' whole understanding of music. A particular performance of a particular work or group of related works is not—and should not, I believe, be regarded as—an event in itself. This particular Crumb concert forms part of a musical experience that ranges from *Madama Butterfly* at the Metropolitan to audio-visual high jinks at The Kitchen, on Wooster Street—and then out through time and through space to comprehend everything that its listeners may have heard, read, gazed at, dreamed of, and been moved by. I respond to Crumb's music, as I respond to Michael Tippett's, because it draws life from and gives new life to sounds, sights, ideas, emotions, poems dear to me, and at the same time reveals others, unfamiliar, which the composer is eager to share. Tippett works by addition, and his large compositions would be a fine old jumble if his genius did not give them order and form. Crumb works by distillation, finding small, precise, quintessential symbols, created by an ear that can distinguish, as it were, between five different qualities of pianissimo on a single note, and make listeners aware of them, too. On his scale, an outburst from four players can be as shattering as another man's *ffff* from a thousand.

Book I of *Madrigals* opens a series of four, each containing three brief pieces based on a fragment of a Lorca poem. By strict musical definition, madrigals are compositions for two or more voices. In Crumb's madrigals there is only one voice, a soprano, joined by two accompanying players in the first three books and by four in the fourth. But the instruments often "sing" and "utter," and the singer is often treated "instrumentally," ticking and tocking, humming, huffing, without words. At the Whitney concert, Jan DeGaetani, to whose "enormous technical and timbral flexibility" Crumb has paid tribute, Glenn Steele (vibraphone), and James Freeman (double-bass) gave a performance of great beauty and delicacy, on which the audience hung hushed, intent, and—given the incantatory nature of Crumb's music, one is tempted to say "literally"— spellbound. During *Lux Aeterna* (1971), for soprano and four players, a single candle burned on the dimly lit stage. Flutist (bass flute and soprano recorder) and sitar player sat in the lotus position; they, two percussionists, Miss DeGaetani, and the conductor, Richard Wernick, all wore half masks (as do the players of Crumb's *Vox Balaenae*). At question time afterward, Miss DeGaetani said that the masking not only helped an impersonal interpretation of music that is ritual in quality but also physically imposed stillness and concentration; a turn of the head, and eyes would miss the next entry. In Crumb's fanciful requirements, picturesque elements and sound, practical musicianship are usually combined.

The first two volumes of *Makrokosmos*, for solo piano, amplified, paid tribute to Bartók in their title. *Music for a Summer Evening (Makrokosmos III)*, commissioned by the Fromm Foundation, employs the forces of Bartók's Sonata for Two Pianos and Percussion, and will no doubt become a companion piece to it in recitals. The pianos are gently amplified, and a far larger percussion battery than Bartók's is called for. There are five movements: "Nocturnal Sounds (The Awakening)"; "Wanderer-Fantasy"; "The Advent" (a very slow, majestic introduction, "like a larger rhythm of nature," reaches a climax and leads to a "Hymn for the Nativity of the Star-Child"); "Myth"; and "Music of the Starry Night" (a "fantastic, oracular" introduction leads to a "Song of Reconciliation," marked "Joyous, ecstatic; with a sense of cosmic time"). The work lasts about forty minutes. In "Wanderer-Fantasy," the percussionists play slide whistles over the undamped piano strings. "Myth" is mainly for the percussionists; the first pianist conducts, striking a crotale and striking the strings and crossbeam of his piano with it or its beater, while the second pianist interjects bursts from an African thumb piano, held against the crossbeam of his large instrument to stimulate its resonances. The third and fifth movements are headed, respectively, by the Pascal and Rilke quotations that provided inspiration for *Makrokosmos I* and *II*. There are direct musical links between *Makrokosmos III* and its predecessors; for example, the "Hymn for the Nativity of the Star-Child" is a transposition of the "Hymn for the Advent of the Star-Child" in *Makrokosmos II*. Instructions like "as from afar, gently wafting" or "like a sound of nature" (a Mahlerian echo) are frequent. Directions for performance are both precise ("A 'Vibraslap' may be substituted for the Quijada") and stimulant ("a groaning sound . . . deep in the throat: eerie, uncanny").

All that may help to suggest the kind of music that *Music for a Summer Evening* is. Only hearing it can reveal its eloquence. The work sinks at last to silence from a deep G-flat pedal that underlies most of the last movement. Throughout the final "Song of Reconciliation" there murmurs an "Out of the cradle endlessly rocking" figure that many composers have used to evoke the sea, the sea's lullaby, the sea as symbol of limitless immensity and of cradling peace. The Nirvana waves into which the passions of *Tristan* subside, Gustav von Aschenbach's embarkation on Plato's "vast sea of beauty" at the close of Mann's *Death in Venice*, the dream visions of the deep in Crumb's *Vox Balaenae* are aspects of the same dream—each of them distinct yet related.

The instrumentalists in the first two pieces were Penn Contemporary Players. James Freeman, double-bass in the first and sitar in the second, then joined Gilbert Kalish as pianist in the *Music for a Summer Evening*; the percussionists were Raymond DesRoches and Richard Fitz. All the performances were very beautiful.

The next day, at the Chamber Music Society of Lincoln Center concert in Alice Tully Hall, Earl Kim's "*Earthlight*—Romanza for violin, high soprano, piano, and lights" was given its first New York performance, flanked by Brahms's Clarinet Quintet and Mendelssohn's C-minor Piano Trio. On the Brahms and the Mendelssohn there were fairly long program notes; information about the Kim was limited to its date (1973), its composer's birth date (January 6, 1920), its commissioner (the Serge Koussevitzky Foundation in the Library of Congress, for the Society), the titles of the Beckett works from which the texts are taken, and the fact that the violin is "con sordini" (no further explanation; here it means that the fiddler alters his tone between paragraphs by using five different kinds of mute). Since the writer, Harris Goldsmith, can hardly believe that Kim is a household name to an audience whose main fare is classical and romantic, he must subscribe to the Fromm theory that when new works are in question listeners can be thrown in at the deep end and left unaided. By those lights I cheated, glancing through a score before the performance (and then spending rather longer with it afterward).

The forces and the setting of fragmentary texts may suggest a comparison with Crumb's *Madrigals* but nothing can be made of it. *Earthlight*, which lasts about sixteen minutes, seems to me to be made of a handful of dull, simple ideas dully and finically assembled. Six people—the composer and three operators, and a consultant and a technical assistant of the Harvard Electronics Design Center—were given credit for the lighting; during the performance three spotlights shone with varying degrees of brightness on the three executants while they played or sang, and were switched off when they were silent. The effect was that of a "visual aid," kin to the gray screen in the Norton scores which lets only the main musical lines through. The sudden blackouts certainly emphasized the stop-and-start progress of the music; that may have been the composer's intention.

The work could pass unchronicled if the astonishing prowess of the soprano did not deserve a note. Merja Sargon (or Saragon; the program used both forms) is a young virtuosa who combines the velocity of a Rosalia Chalia or Marisa Galvany with the altitude of a Meliza Korjus or Mado Robin; and since her timbre is more delicate, less whistly in altissimo than was theirs, the name of Maria Ivogün can be thrown in as well to suggest the charm of the sounds produced by this swift, sweet Circe. Kim has written a vocal line stretching from the B flat below the staff to the C *two* octaves above it (a full fifth above the Queen of Night's summit). Miss Sar(a)gon in fact avoided that topmost C, but the A below it held no terrors for her. She hit it spot on, and then ran down a two-octave chromatic scale, defining each note along the way. She oscillated in portamento between the A on the staff and the C-sharp above it, swinging pendulum-true. She matched the violinist, Itzhak Perlman, in rapidity and precision of spiccato and saltato sallies. When someone wants to revive Meyerbeer's *Pardon de Ploërmel*, a Dinorah is at hand.

January 20, 1975

Crumb's four books of Madrigals *are recorded on Turnabout TV-S 34523, with Elisabeth Suderberg as soloist. At the time of the concert reviewed above, the same performers recorded* Lux Aeterna *(for Columbia; not yet published) and* Makrokosmos III *(Nonesuch H-71311).*

Excellent program notes, edited by David Hamilton, were prepared for the inaugural festival of the Celebration of Contemporary Music (see p. 327). When Michael Steinberg assumed the editorship of the program books of the Boston Symphony Orchestra, at the start of the 1976–77 season, they became (except typographically) models of what program books should be.

BOTHERING WITH BYWAYS

Giovanni Battista Sammartini, to whom we pay lip service as an influence upon the symphonic form brought to perfection by Haydn and Mozart, is unmentioned in Charles Rosen's *The Classical Style* (Norton)—even in the chapter on that style's origins. That is because Mr. Rosen's concern—to our profit—is with Haydn, Mozart, and

Beethoven, in whose works alone "all the contemporary elements . . . work coherently together." Johann Stamitz, another steppingstone toward them, does rate a passing mention, but only as an example of a composer in whom the old baroque and the new classical elements diffuse the effect of, instead of reinforcing, one another. If Sammartini figures at all in Mr. Rosen's argument it must be as one among "the mass of minor composers, many of them very fine, who understood only imperfectly the direction in which they were going, holding on to habits of the past which no longer made complete sense in the new context, experimenting with ideas they had not quite the power to render coherent." Sammartini is a steppingstone between the baroque and the classical on which many trod. Vivaldi conducted a work of his in Amsterdam in 1738. He taught Gluck. Mozart met him. He may have influenced the early Haydn (although in later life Haydn indignantly denied it). Last Wednesday was the two-hundredth anniversary of his death, and Clarion Concerts marked the occasion with a commemorative program in Alice Tully Hall.

"Martin of Milan" (distinguished thus from his brother Giuseppe Sammartini, who was "Martin of London," and deemed by Hawkins the greatest of all oboists) is undoubtedly an Interesting Historical Figure. Though he stayed put in Milan, he was performed and published in Paris and London and known throughout Europe. In *A Sentimental Journey*, Sterne can remark casually "I was going one evening to Martini's concert at Milan" and expect his readers to follow. The nineteenth century forgot him. Early in the twentieth, a few Italian patriots restaked his claims. But his St. Martin's Summer did not really begin until Bathia Churgin and Newell Jenkins, in the last decade, started to bring his music to light again. Miss Churgin is editing volumes of symphonies for the Harvard University Press. Mr. Jenkins, music director of Clarion, performs and has recorded him. Together they have compiled a Sammartini catalogue [published by the Harvard University Press in 1977], assigning their "JC" numbers to the authentic compositions.

The Clarion concert raised two questions: How interesting, to us, is the music of this I.H.F.?, and is it sensible to roam foothills while peaks remain unexplored? (To put the second personally, Why do I spend an evening listening to Sammartini when there are symphonies and string quartets by Haydn I have never heard?) The first question is, on the strength of the concert and of the recital of Sammartini chamber music that Clarion presented in Town Hall the week before, easily answered. Sammartini's music does have the virtues allotted it by Giuseppe Carpani in *Le Haydine* (a copy of which lies open in the Sammartini exhibition in the Library and Museum of the Performing Arts at Lincoln

Center). It has "abundance, fire, and novelty"; it has "certain beautiful eccentricities"; second violins and violas do lead more independent lives than in the scores of his predecessors. It is also true, as Carpani said, that Sammartini lacked harmonic science. He was an adventurer, and the first movement of his G-minor Symphony, JC 57, proved to be full of surprises—strange harmonic drifts, unpredictable turns, suddenness of a kind we associate with Haydn's piano sonatas. The adventures do not lead anywhere—except, often, to a da capo. The member of the audience who left Town Hall exclaiming that the man couldn't compose—couldn't put things together properly—had a point. Haydn called him *ein Schmierer*, a dauber; Carpani said that, in contrast to the contrapuntal and rational Haydn, he "rashly followed the impulses of his fervid imagination." But the boldness, the "fire and vivacity" (Carpani), the "fire and invention" (Burney) that excited his contemporaries can excite us still, and his melodies can still charm us. There were further astonishments in the outer movements of his late E-flat String Quintet (three violins, viola, and cello); in its central andantino and in a Notturno for flute there was lyric beauty. Those were the highlights, but none of the eight works done at these two concerts was just musical wallpaper; none settled into commonplace. Something kept happening to engage the attention. Sammartini evidently brings out the best in Mr. Jenkins, and of the G-minor Symphony he conducted an inspired performance. One small criticism: ears suggested, and tallies of Milanese eighteenth-century orchestras confirm, that his band, founded on a single double-bass, was top-heavy.

The second part of the Tully Hall concert was the 1751 Lenten cantata, *The Tears of the Magdalen at the Sepulcher*—arias for Mary Cleophas (soprano), Mary Magdalen (alto), and the Angel (tenor), and a final coro using the three voices, all framed in masses of recitative that now and again rises to highly eloquent accompagnato. The words are emotional. The first Mary sings "I go between tears and shudders to press a thousand kisses on the beloved but lifeless Body of my Lord," and the second "I pant, I burn, I freeze. Father . . . Husband . . . I seek." But the music is not like that of mid-century opera; it harks back to the jagged Passion figures, the baroque musical symbols of sighs and tears and trembling hearts, and the entwined solo-voice and solo-oboe textures of earlier decades. Then, suddenly, a phrase that starts out like Bach cadences in Mozartian fashion, and Sammartini surprises us again. The cantata does go on, rather. It needed better singing than it had—yet even the best singers might not banish memories of Burney's comment after hearing a Sammartini Mass in Milan in 1770: "It might, however, sometimes be wished that he would ride his *Pegasus* with a curb-bridle; for he seems absolutely to run away with him." Nevertheless, I look forward to hearing more—and more has been promised by Clarion before the bicentennial year has run.

That second question—should we say "Bother the byways!" or "Byways can be worth the bother"?—is frequently clarioned by Mr. Jenkins's programs. For example, Niccolò Piccinni and J. M. Kraus figure in his next concerts. Although I own to being an Elephant's Child, there are better reasons than just 'satiable curiosity for wanting to hear an opera by Gluck's rival (Piccinni's *Didon*, announced by Clarion, is counted his masterpiece, and held the Paris Opera boards for over half a century) or more music by Gustaf III's *Kapellmästare* (the scraps of Kraus I have heard reveal a distinct and engaging personality). Pierre Boulez once said that only works that rise like peaks above sea level are worth attention, that nice determination of how many fathoms below the surface Verdi or Britten may lie is so much waste of time. This makes him a different kind of conductor from say, Beecham, who delighted to share with audiences his enthusiasm for small trouvailles of no consequence and much charm. Consistently, when introducing his first Prospective Encounter in the Great Hall of Cooper Union last Friday, Mr. Boulez brushed aside as of no concern the historical resonances of the place. It meant nothing to him that he was treading where Abraham Lincoln and Dickens had trod. His loss—and our gain, since his brisk no-nonsense focus on work in hand can reveal things complementary to those discovered by more generously romantic, more comprehensive interpreters sensitive to extra-musical incidentals. For his purposes Mr. Boulez was right. For his purpose of defining classical style Mr. Rosen was right to concentrate on those composers who commanded it completely, to find in three exceptions his norm. In his preface Mr. Rosen writes:

There is a belief, which I do not share, that the greatest artists make their effect only when seen against a background of the mediocrity that surrounded them: in other words, the dramatic qualities of Haydn, Mozart, and Beethoven are due to their violation of the patterns to which the public was conditioned by their contemporaries.

Put that way, particularly in those tendentious "other words," the article of faith is easily demolished. But let us try a less restrictive formulation without the "only." There is a belief, which I do share, that the greatest artists make their effects in many different ways and for many different reasons, some intrinsic and observable in isolation, others more readily understood when they are viewed against their backgrounds. Mr. Rosen sets up three standards for judging a work of art: coherence, power, and richness of allusion. The third of them calls for a knowledge of history—and not just musical history. To borrow an example from *The Classical Style* itself: the ringing C-major cries of "Viva la libertà!" that fill the central episode of the first-act finale in *Don Giovanni* can well be interpreted in purely musical terms—"which . . . is not to deny the importance of the extra-musical significance" of such an outburst in the revolutionary atmosphere of 1787.

So there are several good reasons for exploring byways. A few may prove to be forgotten highways worth reopening. Many of them provide both pleasures in themselves and new routes to, new aspects of, the great monuments; and along the way we often find, in raw state, the materials from which the monuments are built. Paths *from* peaks can also be rewarding—backward glances as if through another's eyes. It is always instructive to hear one composer through another's ears—whether the view is forward, backward, upward, downward, or from one eminence to another. Listening to and studying what men as different as Stravinsky, Bartók, Schoenberg, and Puccini heard in *Pelléas* tells us much both about them and about Debussy's opera. Hearing the aria Wagner wrote for insertion into *Norma* tells us what Bellini sounded like to him. The echoes from the first-act finale of *Il barbiere di Siviglia* in Schubert's Great C-major Symphony are more than amusing aftertraces of the Rossini fever that broke out in Vienna in 1817 and was rampant by the 1820s (even Beethoven had a mild attack); Rossini is needed to explain late Schubert. Their names are not often coupled, except in connection with Schubert's two overtures "in the Italian Style." (But Mr. Rosen links them as reintroducers of a dotted rhythm almost unknown in the latter half of the eighteenth century.) That a change came over Schubert between his early quartets and first six symphonies, and the large-scale compositions of his late years is generally agreed. Mr. Rosen calls it an unexpected return to a more thoroughly classical spirit. Elizabeth Norman McKay has plausibly linked it to Schubert's work in and for the theater during the early 1820s. (Her paper appears in the 1966–67 Proceedings of the Royal Musical Association.) The stage forced him "to temper his genius for lyrical expansion," and to work with motifs that could be powerfully and pithily developed. His operas were failures, but he returned to the concert hall master of a new kind of thematic material and new ways of handling it.

Schubert's operas form another kind of byway—unfamiliar paths amid the works of an otherwise known composer. They are trodden from time to time, it is true; the European radio stations mount studio performances, and presumably pirated tapes of those circulate here. *Alfonso und Estrella* and *Fierrabras* contain marvelous music. They are deemed unstageable because of their silly plots and faulty dramatic timing, but I believe the second of them, at least, might successfully be revived in the theater. Only one of Schubert's operas, the one-act *Singspiel* called *Die Verschworenen*, or *The Conspirators*, is done with any frequency (nineteen well-spaced performances during the six seasons covered by the Central Opera Service's "Opera Repertory U.S.A. 1966–72"). It was composed in 1823. It was most recently produced by the Bronx Opera Company in the auditorium of the Bronx High School of Science, and then brought to Hunter College for two Manhattan performances. If Tully Hall or the Juilliard Theater is free for a couple of hours during the impending Schubert Mini-Festival, Mr. Boulez should invite the Bronx troupe to repeat *The Conspirators* there, for Philharmonic audiences. Because this aspect of Schubert is otherwise unrepresented in his programs. Because the score does indeed fill a gap between early and late instrumental pieces that do figure there. Because the metamorphosis of Rossini into pure Schubert can be observed and enjoyed. And because the Bronx performance is deft and delightful.

It was done in simple scenery (by Jim Steere), handsomely costumed (by Dona Granata), lit (by Stephen Ommerle) with blessed steadiness doubly welcome after the perky, distracting spotlights favored by the big Manhattan companies. Michael Spierman conducted buoyantly, and sensitively molded such things as the woodwind obbligati to Helen's romance. The orchestra required is not small. Schubert planned his piece for the Kärntnertortheater, and the instrumental forces are those of the Unfinished and the Great C-major (but are used all at once only in the conjuration chorus). They were all there, barring the second trumpet and the second and third trombones, which are needed in one number only. Although the high-school auditorium has no pit, the balance of singers and players was good. Best of all, perhaps, Louis Galterio staged the comedy (a *Lysistrata* shifted to medieval Austria) with style and accomplishment. All things conspired to provide a fresh and exhilarating experience.

The Conspirators was done on a double bill with Offenbach's *Ba-Ta-Clan*, of 1855, the year of *Les Vêpres siciliennes*. This high-spirited score could provide more texts for reflection upon musical reflections: Offenbach affectionately mocks Meyerbeer, and Verdi, and the performing-practice of great prima donnas. But there is no need to be solemn about it. Enough to say that the Mozart of the Boulevards is a very good composer who deserves to have theses and dissertations written about him. The production, by the same team, had the same merits. Among the talented young casts, Kate Hurney's sparkling heroine, Neil Rosenshein's debonair hero, and George Mirabella's witty master of ceremonies in the Offenbach, and Robert Vega's bright Ben in the Schubert, deserve special mention. Operatic comedy needs a delicate touch. A week before, Bel Canto Opera had been horribly ham-fisted over Donizetti's *Le convenienze ed inconvenienze teatrali*. The Bronx style was neat, witty, and much funnier. George Barker's and Humphry Trevelyan's edition of the Schubert and Ian Strasfogel's of the Offenbach were used.

January 27, 1975

DESTINY RIDES AGAIN

The Metropolitan Opera has brought back Verdi's *La forza del destino* in a new production, directed by John Dexter and Patrick Tavernia. The scenery is Eugene Berman's, of 1952; the costumes, by Peter Hall, are new. Although the show is not altogether successful, it has some points of interest, and starts a new chapter in the long New York history of *La forza del destino*. This is probably the city where the opera has been done most steadily. It came to the Academy of Music in 1865, little more than two years after its première, in St. Petersburg. (Before that, only Rome, Madrid, Reggio Emilia, and Trieste had heard it.) It reached the Metropolitan in 1918, when the cast was led by a young débutante, Rosa Ponselle, and Caruso and Giuseppe De Luca. For seventeen seasons (which must be a record) that production held the bills, seldom absent; and in 1943 it was revived with Zinka Milanov. Many celebrated singers appeared in it. (Their names do not appear in the shoddy, uninformative little program book; does the house have no pride in its past, no memory?) The current revival stars Martina Arroyo, Jon Vickers, and Cornell MacNeil, as Leonora, Alvaro, and Carlo, and it is conducted by James Levine. But since the leading roles of the opera, Verdi once wrote, are, from one point of view, Preziosilla and Fra Melitone, let us start with them.

Preziosilla, the gypsy *vivandière*, is a descendant of Rossini's Isabella (the heroine of *L'italiana in Algeri*) in her tessitura and her high-spirited, sparky patriotism, and of Donizetti's Daughter of the Regiment. In 1865, for a projected Paris production, Verdi thought of recasting the role at soprano pitch. Emile Perrin, the director of the Opéra, asked him to let it be, since he had just acquired a dazzling new young mezzo fresh from the Conservatoire, Rosine Bloch. Verdi replied that the idea of débutantes scared him, especially in this role "où il faut un air très dégagé, une grande vivacité, et *una disinvoltura scenica* extraordinaire," and that a débutante as Leonora would be a less alarm-

85

ing prospect. At the Metropolitan, we have Nedda Casei, who is assured, vivacious, and resourceful and graceful onstage. The voice is a shade peaky but nimble and bright. Her rataplan would make more effect if the directors allowed her to dominate it; instead, an elaborate, silly piece of business, a mock-religious procession, catches the eye throughout the number. There is, fortunately, none of the modern nonsense about Preziosilla's being a sinister character who furthers the cause of war. To read *Forza* in this way (Sam Wanamaker tried it in an interesting but disastrous Covent Garden production in 1962) is to mis-hear the music and misunderstand Verdi's intentions. "Death to the Germans!" (the line is altered to "Death to the foe!" in my 1944 Ricordi print of the libretto) and "Long live a united Italy!" are cries that should be taken in a historical context. Melitone, the grumbly, bumbly old monk, is played with zest and dexterity by Gabriel Bacquier. (He has illustrious predecessors: Jean de Reszke, not yet a tenor, made his Paris début as Melitone; Lawrence Tibbett sang the role at the Metropolitan in 1926.) Melitone is often considered an ancestor of Falstaff. Mr. Bacquier is an accomplished Falstaff, but his Melitone is even better—less elaborated and more sharply focused. He was in firm, clear voice, and his projection of both the character and the music in the soup kitchen scene of Act IV made him the star of the show. A monkish habit far too short for him added a needless and stock comic touch to a performance so delightfully individual.

Preziosilla and Melitone are prominent among the large band of "ordinary men and women" (in all their extraordinary variety) among whom the self-absorbed trio of Donna Leonora, Don Alvaro, and Don Carlo act out their tragedy. In this opera, the chorus is also very important, absent only in the first scene and in the last (and in Verdi's first version of *Forza* it sings there, too). At the Metropolitan, David Stivender's chorus sang well: crisply in its contribution to the rataplan, affectingly in the brief entreaty that opens the last act, merrily in the soup-kitchen mêlée that follows. Verdi's libretto (which he constructed himself; Piave was but the versifier) is far from being a well-made play, but it does have a shape. The composer simplified on his original, the Duke of Rivas's play *Don Alvaro, o la fuerza del sino*, by conflating the roles of the vengeful Calatrava brothers, Carlo and Alfonso. (In Rivas, Alvaro kills Carlo in the first duel, and Alfonso in the second.) He complicated it by adding, from Schiller's *Wallensteins Lager*, the genre scenes of camp life in Act III, and in the same process increased the tally of coincidences. (Destiny must have worked overtime to bring together, in one Italian camp, Alvaro, Carlo, Preziosilla, Trabucco, and Melitone, converging from different points in Spain.) He obscured the plot by suppressing Rivas's introduction, in which Alvaro's supposedly murky origins and his courtship of Leonora are discussed by the popu-

86

lace. (The basic information was added, as an afterthought, and rather too late, in the form of Alvaro's recitative before his aria in Act III.) But what he was aiming at is not hard to discern. *Forza* is a step on the road from *Les Vêpres siciliennes* to *Otello*—an attempt to combine the largeness, variety, and splendor of Meyerbeerian *grand opéra* with the keen passions of a piece like *Il trovatore*. It has a theme—or related themes: the predicament of a hero compelled by a series of mischances to just those actions against which his noble spirit rebels; the vanity of hoping to find peace by retiring from the world into a cloister; in Verdi's next opera, *Don Carlos*, the Monk-Emperor gives precise expression to this sentiment. The passionate personal drama is played out against a background of martial and monastic life across two countries. Verdi was dissatisfied with the result, and particularly with his original ending, which followed Rivas. In this version, *Forza I*, Alvaro and Carlo fight their last duel onstage. After it, Alvaro and Leonora are allowed an excited outburst of reunion (reminiscent of the *Trovatore* Act II finale), to which Carlo adds his wrong conclusion that they have been living together in conventual sin. As Carlo and Leonora die, a thunderstorm that has been raging increases its force and all the monks, led by the Father Guardian, troop on singing "Miserere." Addressed by his monastic name of Father Raphael, Alvaro replies, "Imbecile . . . to look for Father Raphael . . . I am an envoy of Hell." ("I always said so," remarks Melitone.) "Open, O Earth! Swallow me, Hell! Let the heavens fall, and the human race perish!" And he flings himself over a precipice. This is a meet ending to the drama, and true to its nature—but Verdi objected to so many bodies. For years he tried to think of a different finale, and begged his friends for suggestions. Perrin's idea for a happy ending, with the families reconciled, he quickly rejected. Eventually, not without misgivings, he adopted Antonio Ghislanzoni's proposal—for an offstage duel and a final trio during which, in Manzonian vein, Leonora and the Father Guardian urge Alvaro to submit to Destiny in a spirit of Christian resignation. This closes the revised version of the opera, *Forza II*, which had its first performance at La Scala, in 1869. The trio is such fine music that it is always done, but there is much to be said for the wild, romantic finale of the earlier version. Perhaps Sarah Caldwell, ever adventurous in her choice of editions, will stage it for us.

The other large difference between *Forza I* and *Forza II* (apart from the amplification of the prelude as a full-scale overture) is in the structure of Act III, Scene 2. (At the Metropolitan, the acts are misnumbered; Acts I and II are played without interval, and then III is called II, etc.) In Petersburg, the sequence was: camp scenes ending in the rataplan; second duet of Alvaro and Carlo; and aria-finale for Alvaro (a stirring piece in the vein of Manrico's "Ah si, ben mio . . . Di quella pira," in *Il trovatore*, ending on a ringing high C). To discover Verdi's next thoughts, we must turn to those largely unexamined Paris archives that contain so much material important to any present-day production of an opera that had its première or a composer-supervised revival in Paris. (I have written about changes that the formerly accepted texts of *Carmen, Les Contes d'Hoffmann, L'Africaine,* and *Don Carlos* have undergone as a result of Paris researches [see *A Musical Season*]; the Metropolitan's forthcoming *Siège de Corinthe* and the Opera Company of Boston's *Benvenuto Cellini* will also be affected by them.) The Opéra's *Forza*, as noted above, did not come off, but plenty of planning was done. Verdi decided to end Act III with the rataplan and to cut what followed as "quite unnecessary"; the gist of it he summarized in a new recitative for Act IV. From *Forza II*, however, he eventually removed only the final aria; the Alvaro-Carlo duet was kept after all, but moved to an earlier position, before the camp scenes. And to mark it off from the previous scene, which is also concerned with Alvaro and Carlo, he wrote a new little *ronda*, or "dawn patrol"—a delicate piece of music omitted at the Metropolitan. I go into this detail to support an assertion that the reversal of camp scenes and duet, as practiced in the new Metropolitan staging, is unfortunate. In all Verdi's projects for improving *Forza*, the rataplan figures as the third-act finale. The duet ends the act ineffectively, and in the wrong key. (In both of Verdi's versions, Act III opens and closes in C major.) Incidentally, the curtain was made more ineffective by Mr. Vickers's avoidance of the high B in the final cadence. (Verdi insisted on Alvaros with full, powerful high notes.)

The Messrs. Levine, Dexter, and Tavernia are by no means the first to have attempted to revise Verdi's revision. The German Verdi revival began in 1913, with a *Macht des Schicksals*, in Hamburg, in which Georg Göhler "solved" the expository problem by lifting out a chunk of Alvaro's recitative in Act III and dropping it into the first scene— thus wrecking the musical forms of two carefully constructed numbers. Franz Werfel, in a 1925 arrangement (which Bruno Walter introduced to the Metropolitan in 1943), tinkered with Act III much as the Metropolitan team has done. Fritz Stiedry and Herbert Graf, for the 1952 production, concocted an abridged *Forza*, without the inn scene; the overture was played as an entr'acte. The current revival is at least an improvement on that. But a study of *Forza* in all its versions (there are others, unmentioned here) suggests, and my experience of the piece in the theater has confirmed, that the opera is best performed as Verdi wrote it, unshuffled and unshortened. All the objections still made to it were long ago considered by him (for example, he played with the idea of an introductory chorus, to clarify the plot), and he came up with the best answers he could find. The piece proved intractable, and he could not get things quite the way he wanted them, any more than he could when reworking *Simon Boccanegra* and *Don Carlos*. In *Forza II*, two duets for Alvaro and Carlo do come awkwardly close together (even though there is a scene change between them—unobserved in the Metropolitan staging). Verdi knew it, and he knew, too, that nothing better could be done—short of composing the opera all over again.

As Leonora, Miss Arroyo made some sweet, full sounds, but her performance did not have much character. Verdi wanted "an animated soprano" in the role; Miss Arroyo, soft-grained in timbre and unincisive of phrase, hardly filled the bill. *Forza* singers, Verdi said, need not so much bravura technique as "spirit, and the ability to understand and express the *words*." Mr. Vickers, as Alvaro, had those qualities. Indeed, the intensity he brought to his aria almost tore it to tatters—but then he often begins by overexpressing a role and settles later into a more disciplined interpretation. In the second and third duets with Carlo he was magnificent. Mr. MacNeil, the Carlo, was in powerful and impressive voice. His acting was—well, traditional; his delivery was firm; his intonation was not always true. Bonaldo Giaiotti was a dull Father Guardian. In the tiny part of the Surgeon, Arthur Thompson registered sharply.

The Berman scenery is at once too square, too sober, to match the romantic moods of the work—Act III is supposed to open in a wood, at blackest night, and the last scene should be "a valley amid inaccessible rocks, traversed by a stream"—and too emphatic to allow the imagination, or an imaginative director, free rein. One understands the Metropolitan's reluctance to incur the expense of new décor, but that is no reason for praising the old. The stage direction is not imaginative but basically plain, with some unnecessary "glosses." (It does not make the plot any clearer to introduce the mute figure of Carlo into the first scene; anyone unfamiliar with the story will merely wonder who he is.) The military maneuvers provided some unintended and inappropriate comedy, and the camp scenes, that marvelous sequence of changing moods, were not laid out as clearly as they should be. Mr. Levine heffalumped through the score, crashing into the overture at a speed that turned the "destiny" motif into a smudge, and failing to "breathe" the second subject. The tarantella was slow and heavy. In Alvaro's aria, the first clarinet, who is just about equal soloist with the tenor, made a poor showing.

February 3, 1975

"GETTING TO KNOW YOU"

Pierre Boulez may well be reviving in Philharmonic audiences a healthy nineteenth-century appetite for and curiosity about contemporary music. Earlier in the season's programs, there were Bernd Alois Zimmermann's *Photoptosis* and Peter Mennin's Eighth Symphony. Then came Charles Wuorinen's Second Piano Concerto. And then, at three consecutive Thursday concerts, Mr. Boulez introduced in turn Harrison Birtwistle's *The Triumph of Time*, Jacob Druckman's *Windows*, and Carman Moore's *Wildfires and Field Songs*. The last, commissioned by the Philharmonic in association with the New York State Council on the Arts, was a première. It is a confused "third-stream" composition, an overextended, loosely rhapsodic sequence of procedures from traditional black and modern white musics. Moore's ideas could probably have been worked out more sharply with smaller forces. The two other pieces are big-orchestra compositions of proven merit. Birtwistle's *Triumph* has been widely played since it first appeared in 1972. Druckman's *Windows* had its première, from the Chicago Symphony Orchestra, in 1972; later that year it was played at Tanglewood, and it won the 1972 Pulitzer Prize for Music; the Cleveland Orchestra played it last October. Chance brought up more Druckman and more Wuorinen around the time of the Philharmonic concerts, and in other concerts Mr. Boulez himself brought up more Druckman and more Birtwistle.

Jacob Druckman, born in Philadelphia in 1928, is a composer whose music is always carefully worked out and set down. There is nothing slapdash, nothing shoddy or imprecise, in the facture. His fancy is fertile and exuberant; his natural accents are dramatic. The ideas can be extravagant, exciting, and entertaining. The themes often sound like the musical embodiment of gestures; they have a "graphic" quality, such as is often admired in Handel. These gestures are expressive of emotions keenly felt, which the composer is eager to share. His scores call for responsive and imaginative executants. Uninterpreted, played through straight, a Druckman work can be dull hearing. Not that the composer expects his performers to cover up any inadequacies of his, or to order notions set down in disarray. On the contrary, it is clear that Druckman, before handing over a score to performers and audiences, has "heard" its possibilities and made sure that his ideas will work.

Dark Upon the Harp, which closed a concert given by the Light Fantastic Players in Columbia University's Horace Mann Auditorium last week, is a fairly early piece (1961), a cycle of six psalm texts set for soprano, brass quintet, and percussion. The words are vivid, a progression from fierceness in adversity ("Strong bulls of Bashan have beset me round. They open wide their mouths against me" . . . "Break their teeth, O God, in their mouth; break out the cheek-teeth of the young lions"), through rejoicing, to serenity ("The lines are fallen unto me in pleasant places. . . . I shall not be moved"). Not only a reference to "precious oil," in the fifth song, gave new life to the sense of psalms whose words had been dulled for me by years of blameless Anglican chant. Druckman's setting is vivid, too, and the close is particularly beautiful. By various mutes, the range of brass colors is skillfully extended. By delicate attention to balance, the voice remains unobscured. The soloist, Judith Bettina, sang rather too plainly; the players were admirable. Texts were provided, but the lights in the hall were turned out.

Druckman's *Valentine* (1969) is a virtuoso comic turn for double-bass—a duo, really, for the player and the bulky instrument that he assaults, slaps, caresses, and coaxes into song. Introducing the piece, at Mr. Boulez's first Prospective Encounters concert in the Great Hall of Cooper Union, the composer spoke of the ribald sexual play that his work is intended to suggest. On a Nonesuch recording, and in the Joffrey ballet that Gerald Arpino has made of *Valentine*, the soloist is Alvin Brehm. At Cooper, he was Jon Deak, of the Philharmonic—also high-spirited and brilliant. Of *Animus III*, a piece for clarinet and tape, and *Valentine* Druckman wrote:

The works are involved with the actual presence of the performer theatrically as well as musically, limiting their focus to a particular area of human affections as well as a limited body of musical materials. Each work presumes that the theatrical and musical elements are inseparable; that the ideal performance of the music already embodies the performance of the drama.

That appears on the sleeve of the disc (where *Valentine* is preceded by its electronic avant-propos, *Synapse*; this was omitted at the Encounter). *Animus II*, for a mezzo-soprano seductress and two percussionists stimulated by her, is another work of the kind, enjoyable just as sound, heady and exciting when enacted as music theater. A record cannot do full justice to the pieces. But whoever stage-managed the Cooper *Valentine* made rather a feeble job of it. Mr. Deak, poorly lit, was not up on the platform but tucked down at its foot. In Avery Fisher Hall, cunningly amplified and in a spotlight, he might well be a big success at a Philharmonic concert.

Windows at its New York première was given so spiritless, so lack-luster a performance that it was easy to miss its quality altogether. But a conviction that Druckman simply could not have written so turgid and inchoate a work as the one I heard brought me back to hear it again (the Philharmonic gave four performances in all). Confidence in the composer was restored; the orchestra had begun to get the measure of a large, arresting, and imaginative composition. I say "begun," because even this second performance was a gray, clumsily formed thing compared with the glinting, variegated, shapely, and sharply colored account of *Windows* that the Berkshire Music Center Orchestra, under Bruno Maderna, had given at Tanglewood. (This I heard later, on a tape.) The composer offers this description of the work:

The "Windows" of the title are windows inward. They are points of light which appear as the thick orchestral textures part, allowing us to hear, fleetingly, moments out of time—memories, not of any music that ever existed before, but memories of memories, shadows of ghosts. The imagery is as though, having looked at an unpeopled wall of windows, one looks away and senses the afterimage of a face.

The piece demands both very careful balance and individual playing of exceptional brilliance and brio. Long passages are built of a free-for-all counterpoint in which much is left to the invention and musicality of the instrumentalists, invited to devise—within carefully defined limits—their own figures in their own time, while being constantly alert to what their colleagues are up to. "Thick orchestral textures" thus woven are a commonplace of much contemporary music. They can be clotted and clogged, to a point where the ear, assailed by a murky muddle, simply stops listening. They can be an alluring mosaic, lively in general effect, sparkling in elusive detail. Properly played, large sections of *Windows* prove to be such mosaics. The fragments of "old music"—galant dances, wisps of chorale, hints of waltz—are cunningly placed. *Windows* is a deft, romantic, and expertly crafted composition. The score, and that of *Valentine*, are published by MCA Music.

Charles Wuorinen, born in New York in 1938, is an audacious, prolific, and uneven composer. His Second Piano Concerto (for amplified piano and orchestra) didn't stand a chance at its première; it was sabotaged by the mechanical equipment that should have been the making of it. Mr. Wuorinen was the soloist, and Erich Leinsdorf conducted. The idea of the piece is fine: a concerto in which the soloist initiates all the material while the orchestra picks it up, bit by bit. The orchestra doublings and embellishments become less and less synchronous, until some sort of dialogue results. In order that the piano may have dominion over a large orchestra, even when the percussion section is crashing away *tutta forza*, no ordinary solo instrument is used but, instead, a Baldwin ED–1 Concert Electropiano, which has no soundboard. "The string vibrations are picked up by ferroelectric cantilever transducers," fed through "electronic circuits for timbre control," and then emitted through three loudspeaker systems—one out in the body of the hall, one on the platform but far from the piano, and one by the piano itself. By using these systems separately and in different combinations, various interesting effects can be achieved; however, the "antiphonal deployment" of the music, says the composer, is ornamental and may be dispensed with; all that is essential is the powerful amplification.

Brahms played his concertos with the Meiningen Orchestra, a band of modest size, forty-eight strong. Pianos and orchestras have both become noisier since then, and concert halls have become larger. Instead of balancing his orchestral forces against what an ordinary Steinway can achieve, Wuorinen has turned his instrument into an electric monster. With ten fingers, his soloist has the power that before only organists had—that of drowning a hundred men banging, blowing, and scraping with all their might. With care, the result might have been spectacular. In the event, the Electropiano made pungent, painful, and horribly distorted noises. The piano tone, traduced, blared and battered at listeners from whichever loudspeaker was nearest. Somewhere in the distance, the orchestra could be heard as a kind of background tinkle. And this was a pity, for the score of the concerto reveals many striking and potent musical inventions.

Wuorinen's verve and fluency were heard to better effect at the Light Fantastic concert, in his *On Alligators* (1972), a seventeen-minute octet (string and woodwind quartets combined). His music can sound undisciplined. He takes chances. When the recklessness pays off it does so handsomely—given performers as dexterous as Daniel Shulman's Light Fantastic Players; but I should hardly like to hear *On Alligators* snap and crackle from any ensemble less spirited. The program had a satisfying build. As prelude to each of the three principal pieces, a contrapunctus from *The Art of Fugue* was played in an instrumental transcription related to the forces of what followed: string quartet before the Wuorinen, brass quintet before the Druckman, and woodwind quartet before what should have been Donald Martino's Concerto (but this fell out of the program, and Mozart's Quintet for Piano and Winds took its place). Thus, the audience's ears were "tuned" to the expressive possibilities of each medium by a few minutes of pure discourse in related tone colors.

At the second of his three recitals of contemporary American piano music, in Alice Tully Hall, Robert Miller played Wuorinen's Piano Variations (1963), a dashing piece that is carefully and compactly organized. Once again, in a wide-ranging program, Mr. Miller demonstrated his rare combination of grace, beauty of tone, elegance of phrasing, and powerful intellectual control. No première this time (a work by Bülent Arel was not ready), but many captivating pieces. Mario Davidovsky's *Synchronisms No. 6*, for piano and electronic sounds, makes striking and delicate use of the combination.

93

For such a recital, Tully Hall is a shade large. It functions best as an orchestra hall. Here, with the full-size Juilliard Orchestra, Mr. Boulez gave the second of his Two Special Concerts of New Music. There were just three works, all by Juilliard doctoral candidates. They were well rehearsed, sharply and brightly played. Paul Alan Levi's *Symphonic Movement* and Ellen Taaffe Zwilich's *Symposium* are both coherent, soundly planned structures that hold the attention. Ira Taxin's *Saba* (the West Indian island, not the Arabian kingdom) is a musical travelogue with no harm in it and a good deal of pretty, colorful sound. Even more nourishing was the earlier concert, at which Mr. Boulez conducted the Juilliard Chamber Ensemble in the Juilliard Theater. This program included works by Bruno Maderna and Luciano Berio; Birtwistle's dramatic *Tragoedia* (but in far too careful and poker-faced a reading); George Balch Wilson's *Concatenations*, which is a stimulating and beautiful work (it is available on a CRI recording); and Boulez's own *Éclat*, glistening, sparkling, and seductive in two separate realizations. (Donald Martino's Piano Concerto was originally billed, but for the second time last week a Martino work was dropped.)

Any conclusions to be drawn from all this? Most of them are obvious enough. Young players bring more "éclat" to the performance of contemporary music than does the Philharmonic. Boulez is at his most dazzling when conducting his own music—and he should be urged to present his *Pli selon pli* as an annual staple at Fisher Hall. When the Philharmonic players can manage that formidable piece to his satisfaction, they should be able to take things like *Windows* in their stride. Contemporary music on the chamber and solo scale is well served in New York, but the Philharmonic programs should probably include a recent work in each concert as a matter of course. For a start, there are big-orchestra compositions by Boulez and Stockhausen, Elliott Carter and Michael Tippett, and Roger Sessions and Roberto Gerhard that deserve to be in the repertory.

February 10, 1975

A MANON OF GREAT PRICE

It could be argued that two productions of Puccini's *Manon Lescaut* playing in one city are two too many. But in a season marking the fiftieth anniversary of the composer's death that argument would be unkind. One too many, then, this year; and since the Metropolitan Opera already had a workable *Manon Lescaut* in stock, it can be gently regretted that the City Opera chose to mount another, also in Italian, instead of venturing into *Edgar* (an extraordinary and exciting piece) if Puccini commemoration was the intention, or Auber's or Henze's handling of the Manon story if the heroine herself was deemed to be the draw. The City Opera's *Manon Lescaut*, which opened last September, is an animated, overingenious, and unfaithful presentation. The Metropolitan's, which was revived last week, is the oldest staging in its repertory. It was born in 1949, directed by Herbert Graf and designed by H. M. Crayon. Dorothy Kirsten as Manon and Jussi Bjoerling as des Grieux led the cast. The show still looks good, staged now by Patrick Tavernia, under sensitive and stylish lighting, by Rudolph Kuntner, that matches the manner of the décor and catches the expression of the singers' faces. It is presented frankly as a period piece—not so much a drama as a pretty diversion with emotional outbursts. Criticism is disarmed. The inconsistency of the score can be forgiven when we are not expected to take it very seriously. We can enjoy it as the most copious and least narrowly calculated of Puccini's works. Four heroines are billed to appear: Leontyne Price, Miss Kirsten, Montserrat Caballé, and Teresa Kubiak.

Miss Price is the first. Three Manons form her sole contribution to the season, and this is her first new role here since Samuel Barber's Cleopatra, in 1966. It is not one to which she is especially well suited. Miss Price—Renata Tebaldi was a singer of the same kind—is always herself, a delightful and distinctive self that can assume, memorably, the emotions and demeanor of Aida, of Leonora in *Il trovatore*, even of Cio-Cio-San, but has trouble turning into Manon. Directness, unaffected simplicity of utterance, noble naturalness are her virtues; a warm and beautiful voice, lustrous, powerful, and never glaring, is her glory. But, as John Steane puts it in *The Grand Tradition*, there is also "a certain absence of flexibility in characterization." Puccini's Manon demands more sophisticated resources and a protean vocal personality. The writing of the role itself is inconsistent; Act II is close to opéra comique, but Act IV is a Liebestod. At La Scala (as I noted when reviewing the City Opera production; see p. 5), the first Manon was a Nannetta and the second a Tosca—Olga Olghina followed by Hariclea Darclée. Three Manons whom Puccini admired were Lina Cavalieri, at the Met première, in 1907 ("I was really struck by her temperament, especially in the moments of exaltation and of emotion"); Lucrezia Bori, heroine when the Met company, under Toscanini, introduced the opera to Paris, in 1910 ("Little Bori was exquisite and her voice, which had seemed a shade immature and small, achieved such expansion in the theater that it rode the powerful Act III ensemble"); and Lotte Lehmann, in Vienna, in 1923 (a lack of coquetry in Act II, but "I have never heard an Act IV Manon like her"). Those three very different sopranos all made records of "In quelle trine morbide," the Act II aria.

In Act I of the Metropolitan revival, Miss Price was content to open her eyes and her mouth wide and sing straight out to the audience, without bothering much about characterization. In what Puccini called the "powdered scenes" of Act II, she was very funny and charming—a plump, pretty kitten got up in crinoline and white wig. The audience's laughter was a little uneasy at first, but when it became confident Miss Price responded to it and romped through the remaining episodes for comedy. The scenes of the eunuchs warbling a madrigal (the Agnus Dei of Puccini's Mass, reworded), of Manon learning the minuet while ancient roués and foppish abbés ogle her ravenously, and of Manon caroling her pastoral "L'ora, o Tirsi" are meant to be entertaining—though Puccini must have intended a more finely pointed, less downright kind of humor. Miss Price was not so much Manon as someone enjoying the absurdity of pretending to be that dainty heroine. Her sense of fun proved infectious. She also sang "L'ora, o Tirsi" very prettily; true, the trills and grace notes were not clean, but the little arching line that opens its phrases was delicately shaped and the held G that acts as springboard to the reprise was timed to perfection. Connoisseurs of operatic laughter were offered a new prize for their collections. What Puccini wrote simply as "Ah! ah!," *ridendo*, and two headless eighth-note stems, Miss Price turned into a quick, upward pitched "Haha!" of glee, melting into a delicious portamento gurgle of mirth deftly tuned to the version of the *Manon* motif from the orchestra. This was something to set beside Galli-Curci's sparkling peals in the laughing song from Auber's *Manon Lescaut*, or the arpeggio of amusement that Lehmann threw into Mistress Ford's aria in Nicolai's *Merry Wives*.

I have never seen Miss Price look more beautiful than she did in her plain, dark prison dress of Act III—long hair falling simply and abundantly down her back, demeanor purged of civetishness, penitent yet still passionate. At the close of the act, when, "with features irradiated with supreme joy, from the top of the gangplank Manon extends her arms to des Grieux," she rather overdid things. In Act IV she was affecting, but not in her best vocal state. "Smoky" is a word often applied, with approval, to Miss Price's tone, but the sound in "Sola, perduta, abbandonata" could more properly be described as foggy.

In a serious, dramatic, balanced performance of *Manon Lescaut*, the emotional weight of the piece is carried by des Grieux, who has most of the numbers. At Spoleto, last year, Luchino Visconti directed a production in which the principals looked their parts, a production in which, by all reports, des Grieux (played by Harry Theyard) was indeed at the center—and could plausibly ask the Captain, in the ardent

96

apostrophe that closes Act III, to be taken on as a cabin boy. (From Caruso, the request must have sounded odd.) At the Metropolitan, John Alexander looked suitably aristocratic. I like his keen, sharply focused tone. His phrasing was elegant. But neither the stage personality nor the sheer sound of his voice in climaxes was romantic enough to fill the passions of the role. William Walker's Lescaut was robust and vigorous; vocally, however, he was a good *comprimario* in a role that used to be cast at Scotti, Sammarco, or Amato strength. Fernando Corena's Geronte was expertly played—a rounded, unexaggerated, uncaricatured impersonation. (In passing, Mr. Corena's Don Pasquale, earlier in the season, can be praised in much the same terms; it was humorous, human, and unclowned.)

Peter Herman Adler conducted. The orchestral opening, marked allegro brillante, was hectic; the intermezzo, whose main section is marked andante calmo, was bumpy. Too much striving for instrumental effect. But once singers began, the conductor provided a lively and not unduly prominent accompaniment.

February 17, 1975

ANTONY'S SECOND CHANCE

When Samuel Barber undertook to compose an *Antony and Cleopatra*, to words by William Shakespeare, for the inaugural performance of the new Metropolitan Opera House, in 1966, he set himself a triple hurdle. First, of all the operas whose librettos are taken word for word from Shakespeare, only one—Britten's *A Midsummer Night's Dream*—has ever been successful. Second, none of the operas based on the Roman tragedies has been successful at all; *Julius Caesar* and *Antony*, in particular, are built in a way that has resisted operatic treatment. And, third, misfortune has often, though not invariably, attended large new works premièred in untried houses (for example, Bellini's *Zaira*, which opened the Teatro Nuovo in Parma) or before audiences attracted as much by the event as by the music (for example, Britten's *Gloriana*, composed for the 1953 Coronation; at the première, in Covent Garden, the new Elizabeth was the star of the show and the opera about her predecessor—in the words of Harold Rosenthal's Covent Garden history —"was quite a secondary affair"). Barber's *Antony* did not clear the hurdles. It was not a success, and disappeared from the boards. But

97

many people believed that a score of merit had been stifled, submerged, in the abundant, expensive, and elaborate décor and ponderous, populous staging provided by Franco Zeffirelli for that first production. This struck me as unlikely, when I heard the piece. (I missed the show itself, but obtained a tape recording and a score.) The music, while containing several most agreeable lyrical passages—mellifluous, fluent, and romantic in a general way—and much able invention, simply did not rise to the size of its subject. Maybe, at the Met, it had been treated as "music to move scenery to," but then much of it seemed to do little more than go through the familiar gestures of late-Romantic grand opera. All the same, *Antony* plainly deserved a second chance, with at least the third of the three hurdles removed. (When *Gloriana* was given such a second chance, it became a public success.) And now it has received one. The Juilliard American Opera Center has just revived the work for four performances, in the Juilliard Theater. At the same time, the composer took the opportunity to revise his score, cutting a good deal, adding some new matter, pruning, and judiciously retouching.

But what of the first and second hurdles—the language, and the structure, of Shakespeare's play? The great Shakespeare operas (Verdi's *Macbeth, Otello,* and *Falstaff*) have texts written by a contemporary of the composer's. They include some passages lifted almost unaltered from the original—but any translator who tries to put Shakespeare's words to Verdi's music soon finds that, even though the syllables may fit, the tone goes disastrously wrong. Some good Shakespeare operas (Ernest Bloch's *Macbeth,* for example) set Shakespeare in a contemporary translation—and similarly reject any early-seventeenth-century verbal grafts. When Gide approached Stravinsky about making an opera from his translation of *Antony,* the composer said that, since his music would be modern, the costumes and the whole style of presentation would have to be modern, too, and the project fell through. In Barber's *Antony,* Shakespeare's verses and Barber's music are jostling bedfellows. Lines like "I shall break the cause of our expedience to the Queen" seem stilted when declaimed in Cilea-type arioso. *Antony* would probably sound better in a modern Italian translation carefully fitted to the music. A few small "glosses" (such as "gibe" altered to "jeer," or "practice on my state" to "plot against my state") merely disturb anyone who knows the play well. Much of the syntax and vocabulary jars against the manner of the music, and inhibits the performers from an easy, communicative dramatic utterance. Moreover, Barber's word setting can be cavalier, at odds with the natural speeds and stresses of the lines. Perhaps he intended a deliberate stiffness in the exchanges of the Antony-Caesar encounter ("I learn *you* take things ill. . . . I wrote *to* you"). This scherzo-duettino—a Hindemithian two-part invention over a perky bass in steady eighth-notes—followed by a passacaglia begun on

Agrippa's "Thou hast a sister, admired Octavia" and continued as the *Verwandlungsmusik*, is one of the clearest musical structures in the score. But what intention can lie behind Cleopatra's "tawny-finn'd fishes" set with the "ny" and "fi" syllables extended, or her question "Hast thou the *pretty* [as opposed to the ugly?] worm of Nilus there?" Octavia's name is given four full syllables ("Oc-tay-vee-aah"), and the last syllable of the hero's name is sometimes prolonged with a rising inflection. As a result, much of *Antony* sounded as if it were being sung in a clumsy translation. The fault may have lain partly with the singers, who did not give the impression that they would command the poetry to any great effect in a spoken performance of the play; and partly with the publisher, who, in the blunt modern manner, has tied together the tails of eighth- and shorter notes, as if voices were no more than wordless instruments. This procedure regularly prompts singers toward metrical delivery rather than an eloquent utterance in which each syllable, separately stemmed and flagged, is invested with its appropriate weight, speed, and color. Whatever the reasons for it, the lines emerged with as many false emphases as in a Royal Shakespeare Company production. Paradoxically, this would have mattered less if Barber had been bolder still and imposed such strong, independent musical rhythms on the text that we could then ignore it (rather as Peter Brook did, in another medium, in that production of the *Dream* that was all action and no verbal poetry). What proves fatal, in opera, is any effect of tagging along respectfully behind Shakespeare's lines and then every so often getting them wrong.

The structure of *Antony* is best discussed in connection with the revisions. In 1966, the title page carried the credit "The Text of William Shakespeare adapted by Franco Zeffirelli," but Zeffirelli's name has been dropped from the program of the revival. Essentially, his rearrangement of Shakespeare's scenes for the lyric stage and his mosaics of lines and part-lines ingeniously jigsawed from the text remain. There are three acts. The first closes after the Roman revelry on the galley (the scene is shifted ashore in the revision), and the second with Antony's suicide. Act III is the two Monument scenes, IV: 13 and V: 2 of the play. There can be no question of getting all of *Antony* into an opera. Its earliest musical treatment, J. C. Kaffka's *Antonius und Kleopatra* (Berlin, 1779), was in the form of a duodrama. A less obscure handling, Gian Francesco Malipiero's *Antonio e Cleopatra* (Florence, 1938), omits all the scenes outside Egypt, except that on the galley (into which the composer-librettist, like Zeffirelli, introduces Enobarbus's "The barge she sat in") and a brief Actium battle piece—no Octavia, and Caesar's contribution but a few lines. Although the imperial consequences of Antony's love are by intention not shown, "even so," as Winton Dean remarks in the operatic chapter of *Shakespeare in Music*, "what remains demands a lyrical sweep, a grandeur of characterization and a power to fascinate that only the greatest opera composers have possessed," and Malipiero's opera fails because his music is no more than attentive to the text, sensitive, intelligent, and unimpassioned.

Zeffirelli's Act I alternates between Egypt and Italy—three scenes in each, after a choral prologue. By redisposing some episodes and omitting others, Barber has now obviated two scene changes. He retains Zeffirelli's exposition, which is less dramatic—and less operatic, I would say—than Shakespeare's. In the play, hard on a short introduction, the lovers appear together: "If it be love indeed, tell me how much. / There's beggary in the love that can be reckon'd. / I'll set a bourne how far to be belov'd. / Then must thou needs find out new heaven, new earth." Four lines—and then a messenger cuts into the scene with "News, my good lord, from Rome." Zeffirelli moved those four lines to the second scene of Act II and, instead of striking the principal theme at the start, brought up his curtain on Antony in conversation with Enobarbus. Shakespeare follows with a playful scene in the luxurious Egyptian court (Charmian, Iras, sweet Alexas, the Soothsayer); Zeffirelli moved this, as well, to Act II, and there it stays.

The main cuts in the new version are of Mardian's song and Cleopatra's chatter with him, and of the stick dance and "Come, thou monarch of the vine" (set as catchy-rhythmed brindisi for Antony)—all in Act I. Otherwise it is chiefly a matter of a few bars here, a page or so there. The earlier version runs to 342 pages of vocal score, and the revised version (in a preliminary form; it is not yet published) to 294. Some of the big moments have been given broader and more effective declamation—"Eternity was in our lips and eyes," "Let Rome in Tiber melt." Minor characters—Octavia, Mardian, Maecenas, Lepidus—have been muted, or removed altogether. A new love duet has been added, sung in Antony's tent on the dawn of Actium; its words are "Oh take, oh take those lips away" (not the *Measure for Measure* version but the two strophes in Fletcher's *The Bloody Brother*). It is an agreeable piece of music, in a vein that suggests Franz Lehár, or perhaps Victor Herbert. Other moments of love music have been expanded. The "concert close" of Cleopatra's final monologue, "Give me my robe," as heard in Leontyne Price's recording of the number, has been taken into the opera. The heroine no longer dies in mid-question ("What should I stay—") but adds Charmian's completion, "In this wild [Barber reads "vile"] world?"; and where Charmian once sang, "So, fare thee well. / Now boast thee, Death, in thy possession lies / A lass unparallel'd. Downy windows, close; / And golden Phoebus never be [Barber omitted to set the "be"] beheld / Of eyes again so royal! / Your crown's awry! / I'll mend it, and then play," Cleopatra now survives to sing, "Now I feed myself with most delicious poison, that I might sleep out this great gap of time. My man of men!"—lines adapted from the "Give me to drink mandragora" dialogue of I: 5. The entry of Caesar's guardsman is cut. Two other numbers that appear in the interim revised score were not performed at the Juilliard: Barber's 1969 choral setting of Louise Bogan's poem "To Be Sung on the Water," at the start of the galley scene, and a funeral-march prelude to Act III, based on the music of the final monologue.

Only someone who has seen both productions of *Antony* in the theater can properly assess the effect of the changes. The original music did not strike me as too long. Some of the scenes in the new version do strike me as a shade skimpy for so vast a drama. (The three acts play for roughly thirty-six, thirty-eight, and thirty minutes.) I suspect that if the opera is revived a century or so hence, directors of the future will want to combine both scores in new arrangements (as directors of today do with Gluck's *Orfeo / Orphée, Idomeneo, Don Carlos, Boris Godunov,* and *Carmen*), reinstating valued passages which the composer himself cut but retaining passages he strengthened by recomposition. My own view is that *Antony* (even though it may not show "a grandeur of characterization . . . that only the greatest opera composers have possessed") deserves a third chance: a large-scale production given preferably in France, Italy, or Germany, where the first hurdle—the dependence on Shakespeare's verbal poetry—could also be removed, and in a house the size of Hamburg's or West Berlin's, where the stage can hold big spectacle and the auditorium is small enough for the voices to tell strongly. The little Juilliard Theater, though generally admired, I find essentially unfriendly to operas. The acoustics, except when the stage is adjusted for concerts, with the pit floor raised, are dry. Voices do not set it ringing. The physical impact of a piece like *Antony* (or of Virgil Thomson's *Lord Byron,* a subtle and interesting opera that evaporated in the Juilliard, and most certainly deserves a second chance, too) is lost. The most striking scenes in this production of *Antony* were two that do not depend on full-throated lyricism: soldiers' conversation during the mysterious "music i'th'air" (hautboys under the stage in Shakespeare; the ondes Martenot in Barber) that tells of the god Hercules, whom Antony loved, leaving him; and the last conversation of Antony and his page, Eros, over a kettledrum ostinato. Elsewhere, during what should have been the music of rapture, of love for whose splendor the world was well lost, it was easier to perceive what effect the composer had aimed at than to be exalted by a surge of sound.

Cleopatra was Esther Hinds; the voice is soft-focus, not keenly projected, but of pleasant quality in the middle ranges. Ronald Hedlund, as Antony, seemed rather tired and worn. Joseph McKee was a slight Enobarbus. In a more sympathetic theater, all three would probably have sounded much better. Enoch Sherman declaimed Caesar's lines clearly enough but adopted the demeanor of Lady Blanche (Professor of Abstract Science at Princess Ida's Castle Adamant) and so was more funny than formidable. The Eros of Rainer Lokken and the Charmian of Faith Esham were both touching performances. Gian Carlo Menotti's production, in simple, effective scenery by Pasquale Grossi, moved easily. James Conlon's conducting was first-rate—poised, passionate, sensitive, masterly in its dramatic timing.

February 24, 1975

Winton Dean's long study "Shakespeare and Opera," in Shakespeare in Music *(ed. Phyllis Hartnoll; St. Martin's Press, 1964) is required reading for all who take opera seriously.*

THREE BOWS TO HIS STRINGS

There is something winning about a performer who feels it necessary to confess to his audience, ruefully, that he has not examined the autograph of the next piece he's going to play. Sergiu Luca, who did so at his recital of eighteenth- and twentieth-century music for violin and keyboard, in Alice Tully Hall, is a "modern" interpreter of the best kind. That's to say, he likes to play on appropriate instruments, from correct texts. He played his Bach (the G-major Sonata) on a 1740 "Peter of Venice" Guarnerius—gut strings, slackened tension, low pitch—with a 1720 bow; and he played his Mozart (the D-major Sonata, K. 306) on the same instrument but with a late-eighteenth-century bow by John Betts. Busoni's Second Sonata, William Bolcom's *Duo Fantasy*, and Ravel's *Tzigane* he played on his 1733 Carlo Bergonzi with a standard modern rig—metal strings, pitch screwed up, and a late-Peccate bow. In the Bach and Mozart duos, Albert Fuller played the harpsichord, a William Hyman copy of an early-eighteenth-century Blanchet. In the Busoni and the Ravel, David Golub played the piano (the only instrument whose date and maker remained unidentified). In the Bolcom, authenticity was further assured by the presence of the composer himself as pianist.

Care about instruments and care about texts in themselves provide no guarantee of musical merit, but they certainly enhance the achievement of as lively an interpreter and as spirited a fiddler as Mr. Luca is. An exceptionally dashing, even reckless performance of the *Tzigane*

102

(this was the piece on which he admitted having done no musicological research) was the proof of his virtuosity and his temperament. In earlier works, said Mr. Luca (who spoke his informal program notes), the different bows, by defining what could not be done and suggesting what could be, gave the performer a sense of freedom. The Bach was a gentle, poised dialogue. The Mozart was slightly out of balance—the treble of Mr. Fuller's harpsichord never quite let the first subject break clear of its jangling Alberti bass—but both performers brought grace and wit to the molding of their phrases, shaped the andantino cantabile as if it were a lyrical rhapsody invented while it went along, and sparkled in the surprises of the finale. The Busoni, a noble composition, received a moving performance—grave, powerfully articulated, and also sounded with a sensuous, affecting beauty of tone missed by performers intent only on its rigorously controlled structure. Mr. Golub is an admirable pianist. So is Mr. Bolcom. His *Duo Fantasy* (commissioned for the Portland Summer Concerts, 1973, and on this occasion given its New York première) is a kaleidoscope assembled with elegance and charm. It includes a parlor waltz and a fast rag; nimble ideas fall deftly into a series of teasing, entertaining—and coherent—patterns. The textures are limpid, and the rhythms chipper; the tone is light, the musical thought dapper and distinguished. A happy addition to the repertory. And, all in all, an exceptionally cultivated and satisfactory recital. Mr. Luca's nice sense of period styles faltered only in a late-Romantic encore, Josef Suk's *Love Song*. Suk himself would certainly have played the piece with a good deal more "soupy" portamento.

Last week's major first performance was of George Perle's *Songs of Praise and Lamentation*, an extended choral composition dedicated to the late Noah Greenberg. The first part is twelve verses of Psalm 18, set in Hebrew for four-part chorus with large orchestra. The second is four of Rilke's "Orpheus" sonnets set in the original German, two for single and two for double chorus, unaccompanied. The third, specifically an elegy for Mr. Greenberg, includes quotations from Ockeghem's lament on the death of Binchois, Josquin's on the death of Ockeghem, and Vinders's on the death of Josquin. Quatrains by John Hollander grow from them, with the refrain "Timor mortis conturbat me" (as in Dunbar's *Lament for the Makaris*). There is a salute to Auden, Greenberg's collaborator, "the best shaper of words"; and, finally, the opening verses of Psalm 1 are refashioned: "His ever-fruitful life shall stand, A tree in a well-watered land; Winds through unwithered leaves will play; Laus musicae componet me." This movement is for soloists, double chorus, a smaller orchestra, and, in the Renaissance *déplorations*, Renaissance instruments such as used to play in Mr. Greenberg's New York Pro Musica. It is a difficult work to hold together, and at its first performance—given, in Carnegie Hall, by the Dessoff Choirs, members of the Concordia Choir from Bronxville, and the National Orchestral Association, conducted by Michael Hammond—it fell to pieces. In fact, what reached the ear was but a dim, feeble approximation to the music the eye could perceive in Perle's vocal score. The composer had evidently overrated the abilities of the amateur choristers. They sang Hebrew, German, Latin, and English without feeling for words. The colorful sonorities were reduced to one drab hue. Phrases that were meant to leap proudly and phrases planned to flow in soft, supple curves became one plod. The only effect that succeeded was that of Perle's new music, on modern instruments, flowering from the Renaissance cadences —a fine image of the stimulus that Noah Greenberg's work brought to New York's musical life. It would be good to hear a performance of the *Songs* with a crack choir; the Chicago or the Cleveland orchestra, each of which maintains an adept chorus, might take up the work.

In Carnegie Hall, Eve Queler, with her Opera Orchestra of New York, conducted a whizzing concert performance of Verdi's *I masnadieri*. Three Metropolitan singers—William Lewis, Matteo Manuguerra, and Paul Plishka (as Karl, Franz, and Maximilian Moor)—sounded twice as ringing there as ever they do in the big theater. There was a new soprano, Giuliana Trombìn, who arrived fresh from a series of *Masnadieri* performances in Parma. "No great shakes" is a phrase applicable in the literal sense—and Amalia is a role composed to display Jenny Lind's great shakes in profusion (seventeen of them in "Carlo vive?" alone, the last seven beats long, on the G above the staff, sustained through an orchestral tutti). Miss Trombìn did not trill properly, but in other ways she was pleasing. The voice, although heavy and powerful, is wieldy. She has a sense of line. Her timbre is full and lustrous. A soft phrase or two was delicately floated; most of her effects were made by an ample, well-disciplined swell of excellent sound.

Schiller, whose *Die Räuber* provided the plot of *I masnadieri*, was once better known, throughout Europe, than he is now. When Jane Eyre approached Moor House, and peeped through the kitchen window, she heard a speech of Franz from Act V of that play, read by Mary Rivers, Diana's repetition of a line from it, and her comment "Good! good! There you have a dim and mighty archangel, fitly set before you! The line is worth a hundred pages of fustian." "My God, Southey," Coleridge once exclaimed, "who is this Schiller, this convulser of the heart? . . . Why have we ever called Milton sublime?" To understand Verdi's four Schiller operas (and the Schiller episode in *La forza del destino*), we should remember how popular Schiller was and how deep a print he left on the Romantic imagination. Among modern authors, says an editor of his "Collected Plays," done into Italian by Andrea Maffei and Carlo Rusconi, only Scott and Byron have been so widely translated and copied. *I masnadieri* marks Verdi's first close encounter with the poet (since *Giovanna d'Arco* is a long, long way after *Die Jungfrau von Orleans*). There are affinities between the two men. Of each it could be said that he "made his appearance as a man endowed with all the qualifications necessary to produce a strong effect on the multitude as well as on nobler minds," and that "although a genius independent and boldly daring, he was nevertheless influenced in various ways by the models which he saw" (A. W. Schlegel on Schiller). Then comes a second period, in which "we can observe a greater depth in the delineation of character; the old timid extravagance is not altogether lost, but merely clothed with choicer forms." Finally, in the late masterpieces, there is complete control but no waning of inventive fire. Of course, Verdi did not work through Schiller chronologically. *Die Räuber*, Schiller's first play, is ardent, impassioned, extravagant, wild; like Victor Hugo's *Hernani*, fifty years later, it aroused immense enthusiasm among the young. *I masnadieri*, Verdi's eleventh opera, and his first to a foreign commission, has ardor and passion, but, unlike his *Ernani*, three years earlier, it did not arouse immense enthusiasm. (Had London, where it was first performed, liked it better, and had the composer not found the British climate intolerable, we might have had a string of London operas from Verdi; he was offered a ten-year contract at Her Majesty's as house conductor and composer.) *Die Räuber* lives in its language, but Verdi received Schiller's "material sublime" tailored by the temperate Maffei, who, in a preface to the libretto, defined his task as "presenting to the maestro little more than a skeleton awaiting forms, warmth, and life from the notes, rather than from the words." Forms, warmth, and life it received. *I masnadieri*, contemporary with *Macbeth*, shows Verdi moving from his first toward his second period. Two acts composed before *Macbeth* present him in bracing and brilliant or in tender, affecting veins; the last two, composed after it, are more ambitious, darker, more complicated in forms and in orchestration. They include the Meyerbeerian oath that ends Act III, and, at the start of Act IV, the speech that Mary and Diana so much admired, treated as a narrative aria—a bridge between Macbeth's "dagger" soliloquy and Rigoletto's "Pari siamo." Mr. Manuguerra, at this Carnegie performance, made much of it. A strict judge would note that a good deal of the singing, from all the principals, was louder than it need have been; nevertheless, such spirited singing, and Miss Queler's fiery conducting, were enough to turn the strictest of judges into an enthusiast, his scruples swept away by the surge of the music. The Schola Cantorum was good. The anonymous solo cellist was eloquent in the overture, composed for Alfredo Piatti, who led the section at Her Majesty's. The score was not mutilated by cuts. No libretto was on sale at the hall.

Massenet's *Thaïs* seems to be becoming a vogue opera. New Orleans inaugurated its new opera house with it, two years ago; an unhappy recording is being widely advertised at the moment; several productions are announced. As a music drama, the piece is pretty rubbishy, and even distasteful—accomplished courtesan who becomes a saintly nun, handsome, sexy monk whose asceticism is worn like a hairshirt over his lust. Vincent d'Indy called Massenet's music "discreet and semireligious eroticism," but in *Thaïs* there is little discretion. The "Méditation" symbolizes the workings of divine grace. Glamorous sopranos—Sibyl Sanderson (the creator), Mary Garden, Lina Cavalieri, Maria Jeritza— once made *Thaïs* live. Good, solid singers, such as Helen Jepson and Marjorie Lawrence, at the Metropolitan, had less success. Only at the Paris Opera—where I first encountered *Thaïs,* with Géori-Boué as a shrill but assured and even convincing heroine—did it survive. Yet, Massenet's music is so damnably attractive that at almost any encounter with it one simply stops thinking, and is content to enjoy it.

In Baltimore's Lyric Theater, a place with admirable acoustics, the name Gluck, prominent in a composers' frieze that decks the hall, prompted reflections on the public taste that ignores the noblest products of the Paris Opera. Not one of the *Iphigénies*, nor *Armide*, but *Thaïs* was done there last week, by the Baltimore Opera Company. It was a pretty production, in simple but striking décor by Allen Charles Klein, carefully lit by Robert Brand, and intelligently staged by Bliss Hebert. Incense rolling from the stage tickled Protestant nostrils with a whiff of wickedness and glamour. The Baltimore Symphony's playing was colorful. The chorus was strong. Emerson Buckley's conducting was dramatic. The opera was sung in French, which is surely not a tongue of common converse in Maryland—but perhaps everyone in the audience had studied the libretto in advance. The singers, however, did not have that forwardness of focus and pure, distinct projection of the words that are the special pleasures of sung French. Otherwise, Carol Neblett made an alluring heroine. Thaïs's mirror air, "Dis-moi que je suis belle," defeated her, as it does most sopranos (Sybil Sanderson must have been able with uncommon ease to fly to an exposed G, A-flat, or B-flat above the staff, on any vowel and at any dynamics); in the more comfortably written "Qui te fait si sévère" and "L'amour est une vertu rare" Miss Neblett's tone was smooth, rich, and beautiful. In the New Orleans production, she achieved notoriety by taking all her clothes off to the high C that ends Act I; in Baltimore, a delicate suggestion proved sufficient. Her portrayal of both courtesan and nun was sensitively achieved (but surely the former would not have walked through the streets of Alexandria in bare feet). Ryan Edwards's baritone was not keen and bright enough to project Athanaël's fanaticism and passion; his timbre sounded "enriched"

106

rather than naturally forceful and forward. Nicias, the young sybaritic philosopher, has the catchiest tune in all the opera, his "Ne t'offense pas" in the Act I quartet; it was liltingly sung by Robert Johnson.

March 3, 1975

Every critic has unsettled areas of judgment. Massenet is one of mine— as later reviews of Esclarmonde *(pp. 279 and 454–6) and of* Marie-Magdeleine *(pp. 277–9) will show. I came to admire* Thaïs *more highly than appears above when I reviewed that "unhappy recording" (RCA, with Anna Moffo), together with a happier one (a Westminster reissue, with Renée Doria) for* High Fidelity, *XXV (May 1975).*

Angel Records later invited me to write an introduction to the opera for its Thaïs *with Beverly Sills. "The duty of the writer of programme notes," said Tovey, "is that of counsel for the defence"; I did not find it a difficult duty.*

VARIETIES OF OPERATIC EXPERIENCE

The lack of a Piccolo Met—dormant since its first season, in 1973— matters less when the Juilliard Opera Training Department can, within the context of its regular activity, offer to the public a presentation as sensitive and accomplished as its workshop production last week of Britten's *The Turn of the Screw*. Conducted by Martin Isepp, directed by Emile Renan, designed by Robert Yodice, and lit by Joe Pacitti, this was one of the most satisfactory evenings of opera I have encountered in New York. The Juilliard School is the heart of the Lincoln Center complex. One looks to it to maintain the standards of careful preparation, scholarship, and dedication sometimes unattained amid the hurly-burly of professional life in the large institutions on the plaza. An evening like this *Turn of the Screw*—or Albert Fuller's Rameau program two years ago—is worth a dozen vociferous *Turandots*.

Bonnie Lee Leys, the Governess in the first of the alternate casts, gave a delicate, intelligent, and beautifully poised performance. Her voice is narrow in timbre (so was that of Jennifer Vyvyan, for whom the role was written) but was skillfully used, and she is a subtle, distinguished actress. The double role for tenor was divided between John Aler (Prologue in the first cast, Peter Quint in the second) and Steven Pearlston (vice versa). Mr. Aler, who reminded me of a young McCormack when first I heard him (in Haydn's *Philemon und Baucis*),

107

has a fresh, forward, lyrical tenor and a feeling for words which make him an ideal exponent of Peter Pears roles; Mr. Pearlston had both the stage presence and the command of eerie cantilena to be a striking Quint. Miles was cunningly and powerfully played by a young lady, Penny Orloff, who looked, sounded, and acted convincingly like a boy. Some little things were wrong: Mrs. Grose exclaimed about Flora's pinafore, but Flora did not wear one; the game of cat's cradle, instead of matching the words, never got beyond first position. (However, the anachronistic pronunciation of "*malo*" to rhyme with "Barlow" rather than "halo" is sanctioned by the composer; it provides a better vowel for the melismatic refrain.) The large problems of the work—getting the atmosphere right, fleshing the ghosts, catching the precise tone in the scenes between the Governess and Miles—were perceptively and persuasively solved. Under Mr. Isepp, the student instrumentalists were eloquent, and his control of the music's paces was masterly. Everyone was responsive to the high-tension charges of this score, in which every detail tells—everyone, that is, except those members of the audience who sought to obliterate the interludes by their applause. And by Act II even they were silent and attentive.

The Metropolitan's and the City Opera's plugging of Puccini—*Manon Lescaut, La Bohème, Tosca, Madama Butterfly*, and *Turandot* are in both repertories, and last week they were playing *Manon Lescaut* on the same day—matters less while Eve Queler and her Opera Orchestra of New York are at hand to expand our experience of grand opera with such things as their *I masnadieri*, reviewed last week, and now, again in Carnegie Hall, *La Favorite*. The latter is not to be reckoned among Donizetti's top ten, or perhaps even top twenty, operas, but it is worth hearing from time to time, and New York had not heard it properly since 1905, when Edyth Walker, Caruso, Scotti, and Plançon sang it at the Met. *La Favorite* is a fascinating product of those last five busy years (1840–44), when Donizetti, based in Paris, dominated the lyric theaters of Europe as decisively as Rossini before and Verdi after him—the years in which he produced a dozen operas, revived (often with considerable recomposition) half a dozen more, and somehow found time to direct the Italian and Viennese premières of Rossini's *Stabat mater* and to introduce Verdi's *Nabucco* to Vienna. *La Fille du régiment* and *Don Pasquale* date from this time. *La Favorite* is the third of his four *grands opéras* (that simple phrase could be qualified by thousands of words, sorting out a tangled chronology). Like *Dom Sébastien*, the last of them, it was composed for a mezzo-soprano, the odious Rosine Stoltz, the *favorite* of Léon Pillet, who directed the Opéra. Italian mezzos—Stignani, in a famous 1934 revival at La Scala; Barbieri; Simionato; currently Fiorenza Cossotto—have kept it alive, but like Spontini's *Fernand Cortez*, Cherubini's *Médée*, Rossini's *Le Siège de Corinthe*, Meyerbeer's *Les Huguenots*, Verdi's *Les Vêpres siciliennes*, and several other pieces (Rameau and Berlioz apart, the principal composers of French grand opera are foreign), it awaits a major revival in the high French manner and in the original language. Miss Queler wanted to do it in French, but various difficulties arose, and in the end the usual Italian translation was employed. Yet there is no reason the cast could not have sung in the original while the orchestra played from "Italian" parts. The crude translation may blunt the rhythms and make nonsense of the plot, but the instrumental score of *La favorita* (unlike that of *Lucie de Lammermoor*, *La figlia del reggimento*, or *Le Trouvère*) is quite compatible with the original vocal lines.

Never mind. Anyone wishing to perform a Paris grand opera from a freshly studied text has an arduous task. (Last summer, some light spadework on the *Dom Sébastien* material, which is divided between four Paris libraries, turned up six unpublished numbers for that opera, and a glance at the *Favorite* autograph—there is a microfilm of it in the Library of the Performing Arts—will show the sort of problems that arise there.) Using the standard text, Miss Queler made a splendid job of it. Her Léonor and Fernand were the best to be had: Shirley Verrett and Alfredo Kraus. Miss Verrett was intense, brilliant, lustrous, electric—more varied, less monotonously ample, than Miss Cossotto is in the role. An artist of uncommon caliber, she obviated applause after an "O mon Fernand" that could have brought the house down by catching the ensuant recitative on her next breath—before the rapt listeners could draw theirs—and thus joined air and cabaletta in one exciting number. She could be more impressive still if there were moments of calm in her singing. The tension was so constantly maintained that to increase it, for special effects, she resorted to noisy breaths, fierce attacks that were almost grunts, and cutoffs that were nearly snarls.

Mr. Kraus had no inhibitions about accepting applause. "Ange si pur" (he sang it as the familiar "Spirto gentil," but the alternative translation, "Angiol d'amor," is much closer to the sense of the original) elicited the longest mid-scene ovation I have ever heard any singer receive anywhere, and Mr. Kraus made no attempt to get on with the opera until what seemed like ten minutes had passed. An ovation was in order, for in this repertory he is peerless. (Luciano Pavarotti, his nearest rival, has a lovely, easy tone, but no such fine-drawn distinction of style.) Fernand is one of Mr. Kraus's finest roles, and in the warm Carnegie acoustics he sounded better than ever. Pablo Elvira, the Alphonse, has a potent baritone of excellent quality—very forward, very even—but he used it without much imagination. Barbara Hendricks, the Inez, sang her pretty air in the prettiest fashion, with dainty, bewitching graces and cadences. James Morris, as Balthazar, was clear and precise, although ideally the Prior needs a heavier, more magisterial voice for thundering anathema. Miss Queler's command of dramatic pace and her feeling for the natural surge or settle of a vocal line were sure. The Brooklyn College Chorus sounded light, and unskilled in Italian. Mr. Kraus made his usual cuts, including a verse of "Un ange, une femme" and the whole of the air that should end Act I (it is a poor piece, unregretted except from a formal point of view); the ballet was omitted; and further cuts brought the work down to a little under two and a half hours of music.

La Favorite is a stiffer, less romantic, and less fluent work than Donizetti's Italian dramas of the 1830s. The shadows of Meyerbeer and Scribe fall on it. To, say, his *Pia de' Tolomei*, it is as Rossini's *Guillaume Tell* is to his *Elisabetta*. On Italian composers the Opéra regularly imposed an odd mixture of ambition and conventionality. Instead of being effortlessly true to themselves and their earlier styles, they adopted Paris formulas, strove for (and often achieved) grandeur, and constructed musical edifices in which numbers could be shifted from act to act (as happened in *Les Vêpres*), at the expense of direct, natural characterization. *Dom Sébastien* is probably Donizetti's best *grand opéra*; there the composer treated Scribe in cavalier fashion (the cross poet obtained depositions to that effect, which survive among his papers). *La Favorite* may be only second-best, but it still flowers in an execution as warm as the one Miss Queler gave us.

Meanwhile, at the City Opera, the spring season has brought new productions of *Turandot* and *Salome*. The Metropolitan is engaged on *Ring* operas—too widely spaced to be experienced as a cycle. More of all that later. In Alice Tully Hall, Newell Jenkins's Clarion Concerts staged (in modern dress) another example of an opera composed by an Italian working in Paris—Niccolò Piccinni's *Didon* (1783). Had Piccinni never crossed the Alps, he would be remembered as the merry composer of *La buona figliuola*. Instead, he survives in the histories as the unfortunate whom the Parisians, ever eager to promote an operatic squabble, set up as Gluck's rival. On the page, *Didon* looks very much like Gluck—the same strong, square cut to the phrases, plain harmonies, and ostinato accompaniment figures. We turn on, and find a D-major chorus, "Dieux des Troyens," surprisingly like the finale of *Idomeneo*. (But *Didon* came three years after *Idomeneo*; Mozart's and Piccinni's paths crossed several times, and Mozart owned some Piccinni scores.) Singers who command the grand classic style, in which passion and majesty are combined, could make something noble of *Didon*, I feel sure, but the singers of the Clarion performance could do no more than suggest what the work might be. The synopsis went astray and had Aeneas killed on the Carthaginian shore. So no Rome? But, in fact, Marmontel's libretto does follow Virgil faithfully. The 1785 print of this libretto has thirty-two pages (sixteen "openings") and cost twelve sous; would a simple modern reproduction have cost more than the enthusiasts who attend this kind of event would care to pay?

Shoestring opera was represented by Bel Canto Opera's production of Alessandro Scarlatti's *Mitridate Eupatore*. Of the handful of Scarlatti dramas that get done nowadays, *Mitridate*—his ninety-first opera, and the first he composed for Venice—is the noblest and most interesting. The plot is an *Electra* shifted to Pontus, in which the Orestes (here called Mitridate) has a wife and the Electra (here Laodice) a husband, and Stratonica and Farnace (the Clytemnestra and Aegisthus of this version) are killed onstage. The score represents Scarlatti in his broadest and grandest vein. The great numbers are an air for Laodice beside her father's tomb; one for Stratonica in which she hesitates to ordain the murder of her son; the entry of the disguised Mitridate, at the start of Act IV, bearing an urn supposed to contain his own head; and, most wonderful of all, Laodice's lament over this urn, "Cara tomba del mio diletto," which Edward Dent, who knew Scarlatti's music well, deemed the finest air in all his operas.

Mitridate cannot fail to make a considerable effect in the theater, but it deserved an ampler American première than Bel Canto's brave effort. The Madison Avenue Baptist Church Hall is a poky place. Scarlatti's orchestra, which includes trumpets and drums in the pit echoed by stage trumpets and drums, was reduced to string quartet and oboe, directed from the harpsichord. (Gerard Reuter was the stylish and tireless oboist.) The cast tried to sing the piece in Italian, which involved their plodding doggedly through yards of recitative that went for nothing. (A neat English translation, by Jack Westrup, is available, and in any case there are usually only two good reasons for staging an opera in a language not that of the audience: the work is very familiar, or the original is a convenient lingua franca for an international cast. Neither applied here.) Keith King's stage direction was summary, and lapsed into comedy when character after character plucked at a pair of sacrificial (paper) pigeons, or Stratonica, ending her big air and about to strike a dagger into her breast, had to keep it poised in midair while we applauded. The musical director, Louise Basbas, although credited with "extensive experience with baroque music," allowed her cast to stub out blunt repeated notes—instead of appoggiaturas—at the close of almost every recitative phrase.

Nevertheless, the work came through, for the principal singers were accomplished. Elizabeth Hynes's impassioned yet disciplined delivery of "Cara tomba" would have been enough in itself to make the evening worthwhile. Her lyric soprano is as sweet, firm, and round as a filbert.

111

Her breath is well managed. She draws long lines. And the planes of her attractive features, her clear brow and large eyes, tell strongly on the stage. Carole Walters, the Stratonica, has a rich, commanding, and steady mezzo and a dignified mien. Since Jonathan Rigg is not a castrato, he had to sing the hero's music an octave too low, but he did so in a bold and keenly projected tenor, and he has a good appearance.

If I were a rich man, I would find a small New York theater and equip it with the basic scenes needed for eighteenth-century opera—a palace, a public square, a quayside, a garden, a "pleasant place," a "smiling grove," and a "horrid wood"—and also an Appia-type kit of rostra, steps, and columns; and then open it to the Piccolo Met, Bel Canto, Clarion, the Eastern Opera Theatre, the Handel Society, the Metropolitan Opera Studio, the Light Opera of Manhattan, etc., as well as to out-of-town troupes that wanted a Manhattan showcase. There is certainly enough operatic activity in New York to keep a small opera house busy on a regular basis (and plenty of dance companies would be glad to fill any gaps). This activity is at present scattered, and usually ill-housed; audiences are divided; publicity is hit-or-miss; sharable resources are not shared. Would such a scheme be impossibly expensive?

March 10, 1975

In the summer of 1977, the elegant little Harkness Theater, a 1,300-seater across the road from Lincoln Center, well suited to opera and dance, was sold to a private developer for a million dollars, and demolished.

THE FANTASY AND THE FACT

Any music lover's spirits should leap at the prospect of five days of concerts, presented by a city's major orchestra and chamber-music society, billed as a "Mini-Festival Around Schubert." What would he expect? Programs carefully chosen to show Schubert's music in its close context and in distant perspectives; an introduction to some wonderful songs that have so far not entered the standard repertory; some unfamiliar chamber and choral music; some familiar chamber and orchestral and piano music lovingly performed; one concert, at least, sounded on the instruments of Schubert's day or on modern copies of them; introductory talks, or lecture-recitals, presenting the latest fruits of Schubert scholarship and linking these to the programs of the week. What else? A program book that might include, say, an essay by Charles Rosen expanding the splendid aperçus about Schubert in the epilogue of his *The Classical Style*; full notes, of course, on all the works performed, with sufficient background to define the position of each in the total picture composed by the programs; a timetable of any other Schubert concerts and of any Schubert opera productions in or near the city; a note about when any Schubert Masses were to be sung in any of the city's churches; an account of the best books about Schubert (latest among them a Vienna House reprint of his enchanting letters), a guide to the best editions of his music available, and a discography of the most desirable records. And in the lobbies of the halls where the concerts were given, a Schubert exhibition, and, naturally, the books, the scores, and the records on sale.

In any musical center except New York such expectations would probably be fulfilled. Here, the "Mini-Festival Around Schubert," presented last week by the Philharmonic in collaboration with the Chamber Music Society of Lincoln Center, proved to be a flabby, half-baked affair. There may have been some loving performances (though there were none in the concerts I attended). There was a performance of the cantata *Lazarus*. But nothing else along the lines suggested above. It is true that several good works were played. Half a page of platitudes from Pierre Boulez ("His imprint can be found in the works of many later composers"; "To know Schubert only through his symphonic works is to know him insufficiently") scarcely helped to explain the structure of the haphazard programs, and his was the only "general" essay. The notes by Harris Goldsmith did not add perspective. To contrast Schubert's Octet with the Beethoven Septet is to discover much about him; the Septet opened the celebration (the Octet did not figure in it). This is all that Mr. Goldsmith had to say about the relation of it and the Schubert work:

Granted the popularity of the Septet, it hardly need be added that Spohr, Hummel, and others took their heed of the piece. The "others" included one Franz Schubert who penned an Octet that owes its very existence to Beethoven's precursor.

Another program opened with Antonio Salieri's *Axur, Re d'Ormus* overture (last played by the Philharmonic in 1965). Mr. Goldsmith noted that Beethoven was proud to style himself a Salieri pupil, quoted the Grove entry in one paragraph, and paraphrased it in the next. It would have been more to the point to tell the audience that Schubert was for a time a Salieri pupil.

113

No Schubert songs were billed—which may have been deliberate, though the omission was unexplained—but in the event (illness brought a change of vocalist and of program) three were sung. They were "Die junge Nonne," "Der Lindenbaum," and "Erlkönig." There must be half a dozen talented Juilliard students (to look no further) with less hackneyed Schubert songs ready at performance pitch—and, for that matter, a keener sense of Schubert style than was shown by Betty Allen.

There are to be four new productions in the City Opera's spring season. One is of Mozart's *Idomeneo*, an important addition to the New York repertory. Another is of a curiosity—*Die tote Stadt*, composed in 1920 by the young Erich Korngold, and chosen by Jeritza for her Metropolitan début the following year. Those two are still to come. The others—of Puccini's *Turandot* and Richard Strauss's *Salome*—double the Metropolitan fare without even the distinction of being English-language performances.

There are two reasons for reviving *Salome* today—as an "audiovisual concerto" for a remarkable soprano (another Welitch, Varnay, or Anja Silja), or as a vehicle for a virtuoso orchestra and its star conductor (such as the Chicago Symphony under Solti, who gave a tremendous performance, with the added attraction of Birgit Nilsson as heroine, in Carnegie Hall earlier this season). There seems to be no good reason for the City Opera's having tackled *Salome*. Maralin Niska gets through the title role in competent house-soprano fashion, but there is no special force or allure in either her singing or her acting of the part. And the orchestra is reduced. Strauss composed his opera for about a hundred players (and so, even in houses of Covent Garden size, they sometimes spill over into the stage boxes). To make the work accessible to theaters of more modest means, he prepared alternative versions, one for regular large orchestra (with triple instead of fourfold and fivefold woodwinds) and another still further reduced. *Salome* comes in the middle size at the State Theater, but this is a big place, with notoriously dead acoustics, and so the edge of the music was blunted. A good deal of the individual playing was of high quality, and Julius Rudel, conducting, drew the best from his forces. It was not enough. *Salome* can seem to be at once a repellent opera and a score of blazing genius. But on this occasion it provided a dull evening.

For his heroine, Strauss wanted "a sixteen-year-old princess with the voice of an Isolde." (We can hear one in the London recording, made in 1961; *seeing* Nilsson enact the role might be another matter.) He also remarked that "anyone who has observed the decorum with which Eastern women behave will understand that Salome, being a chaste virgin and an Oriental princess, must be played with the simplest and most restrained of gestures, unless her defeat by the powerful, hostile world is to excite, instead of compassion, only disgust and terror." So the composer said—yet it must be owned that the three notable stage Salomes mentioned above (Welitch, Varnay, and Silja) were far from simple and restrained. Miss Niska shimmied about slinkily in the early scenes, stripped to display a shapely body during the Dance of the Seven Veils, and rolled around with the head of the Baptist in the finale, but seemed to have no clear ideas about the character and its development. Ian Strasfogel, who directed, and Douglas W. Schmidt, who designed the set, gave no indication that they did not consider the piece a load of old rubbish. They may be right—except in respect of the virtuoso score—but then why bother with it? The effect was tacky B movie, "A Night in Old Galilee." The set was a kind of debased Bakst, in murky colors. The costumes, designed by Randy Barcelo, were caricatures— Herodias as the Duchess, Herod as the Red King (but Salome not at all like Alice). Hans Sondheimer's lighting tended to fall on the characters' shoulders and leave their eyes in pools of shadow. There was a lively, entertaining, and pungent Herod, Alan Crofoot. Frances Bible was an imposing Herodias. Miss Niska—any account of a *Salome* performance returns constantly to its heroine—had some good, shining notes, but her voice was uneven and unreliable; often there was no firm core of pure, easy tone. Neither her words nor those of the dullish Jokanaan, William Justus, told strongly. Herod's did. So did those of two soldiers, Willard White and Irwin Densen, whose strong, forthright declamation was a pleasure.

Turandot is another opera that might as well have been left unperformed at the State Theater—left to the Metropolitan—since the City Opera could not muster a suitable cast for it. The title role is a killer, except to a soprano with lungs of leather and vocal cords of steel. Rachel Mathes (who sang Gerhilde, a Valkyrie, at the Met *Walküre* the night before *Turandot*) will surely have no voice left if she goes on forcing it as hard as she did here. Already there was an unhealthy wobble in the sound. As an actress she was puddingy. Perhaps, intent on making a big noise, and keeping her balance the while on the steep staircase that fills most of the sets, she had little attention left for niceties of interpretation. Calaf was Ermanno Mauro, formerly a Covent Garden lyric tenor (Pinkerton, etc.), who bawled his way through the heavy music. In its gaudy fashion, Beni Montresor's décor is rather prettier than Cecil Beaton's, at the Met, but Beaton at least provided a staircase from whose treads the soprano can sing in safety; Montresor's is a constant invitation to a tumble. Dino Yannopoulos's direction has no strong character but is perfectly acceptable. Mr. Rudel drew good sound from the orchestra and chorus. His cuts are curious (there was a sudden bump in the Ping-Pang-Pong scene), but he did include Turandot's aria

"Del primo pianto," which, although it falls into the section completed by Alfano, is an essential part of Puccini's design. If only Miss Mathes could have sung it more affectingly!

Figaro, revived during the early days of the City Opera's season, was a happier occasion. There was nothing especially distinguished about it, except the crisp, elegant Figaro of Samuel Ramey, projected with a clarity of voice and a definition of phrasing that could take him straight to Glyndebourne. There was nothing especially wrong, except an Almaviva, John Darrenkamp, whose manner was more that of a foot-man than of a count. Patricia Wells's Countess Almaviva, now laid out on more traditional lines than those set for her by Götz Friedrich at last year's Holland Festival, has grown in dignity and charm. Sandra Walker's Marcellina is a delightfully ripe, warm, uncaricatured im-personation. David Hicks's direction is neat and unfussy. Christopher Keene, conducting, sometimes got out of time with his singers, but not often. The opera was sung in the very clear English of Ruth and Thomas Martin (until Glenys Fowles, the Susanna, broke into the Dent version for "Deh vieni"). Some improvements have been made to the Martins' printed text—it is tribute to the enunciation that one could hear this—and more still could be made ("That's the only solution whereby our man . . . can be forced to accede to all her dictates" and "With this complication they cannot contend" are needlessly stilted phrases). The Moberly-Raeburn refashioning of Act III, by which the Countess's aria follows hard on the Count's, was adopted. Both dramatically and musically, this reconstruction of Mozart's presumed first plan is con-vincing.

A *Puritani* on a Sunday evening—and thus this company's fourth per-formance in a space of two days—found the orchestra and the chorus in ragged form. The production, by Tito Capobianco, is handsome. Carl Toms's heraldic décor is fine. Beverly Sills, as Elvira, looked wonderful, acted enchantingly, and expressed the music with great eloquence, so far as her voice would allow. But that voice, unlike her person, was in very poor shape, and developed a flutter on almost every sustained note. Nevertheless, she was commanding. Sir Richard and Sir George (Rich-ard Fredricks and Robert Hale) were almost comical in their failure to grasp how Bellini should be sung. Can they speak Italian, or just pronounce it? Enrico Di Giuseppe, the Arthur, was a stick.

March 17, 1975

Samuel Ramey sang Figaro at Glyndebourne in 1976. For more about the Moberly-Raeburn refashioning of Act III of Figaro, *see pp. 252–3.*

116

MINNEAPOLIS

Minneapolis has a new Orchestra Hall, the home of the Minnesota (formerly Minneapolis Symphony) Orchestra. It opened in October, but that was an inaugural gala, with an uncharacteristic program, and the players were still unused to their surroundings. So I waited for the orchestra and its audiences to settle, and then visited the place in mid-season, for a regular concert in the subscription series. I was impressed by what I heard and saw.

Orchestra Hall stands downtown, in an open space that next season will be a park. Nicollet Mall, Minneapolis's central shopping street, free of all motor traffic except buses and taxis, extends to within a block of it, and will soon reach it; a new spur of "greenway" will lead to another park, across which are the Guthrie Theater and the Walker Art Center. The hall cost $7,200,000 to build; the land, fees, furnishings, etc., brought the cost to $10,073,000. It seats 2,573 people, 1,590 of them in the orchestra and the others in three balcony tiers. The principal architect was Hugh Hardy, of Hardy, Holzman, Pfeiffer Associates, working with Curtis Green, of the St. Paul firm Hammel, Green and Abrahamson, who has designed several performing-arts centers in the state. The acoustical consultant was Cyril Harris, who has the Metropolitan Opera House, Washington's Kennedy Center [and the rebuilt Avery Fisher Hall] to his credit. Their Minneapolis auditorium is dramatic in appearance. Essentially, its shape is that traditionally associated with good acoustics: a rectangle comfortably wide (not long and thin), a coffered ceiling, narrow balconies along three sides, and plenty of space above the orchestral platform. (Modern halls built in fan or funnel shape, with reflectors swooping down over the players, have often run into acoustical trouble.) But "coffered" is not exactly the word for the Minneapolis ceiling. Apparently embedded in it is a series of giant cubes, of different sizes, set in edge-on, to various depths and at various angles. They are scattered symmetrically on either side of the central line (except for one, an odd cube out, which can catch and tease the eye when a listener's attention strays from the music). More giant cubes seem to have tumbled from on high and been caught in the wall behind the players (and again there is just one so set that its planes break mirror symmetry). The projecting cubes (which turn out to be in fact polyhedrons, of rock-crystal formation, when they are viewed from the platform end of the hall) are white. The ceiling and the wall behind them are pale blue-gray. The other walls and the floor are of oak; the seats and the tier fronts are of a color that might be called rose-persimmon. The first effect is of an explosion that drove the cubes into the building; it yields to one of serenity, of repose after violence. I was reminded of the great column drums of the Temple of Zeus at Olympia, roughly thrown about by an earthquake centuries ago, and now at rest. The hall is very picturesque. The orchestral players, wearing the black-and-white uniform that is still standard in America, looked rather out of place against so theatrical a décor. One felt that their costumes had still to be designed.

The sound is marvelous, and can bear comparison with the best music halls in the world—with, say, Vienna's Musikvereinssaal, Boston's Symphony Hall, Amsterdam's Concertgebouw, or, to take two modern buildings that have turned out well, Adelaide's Festival Theatre and Aldeburgh's The Maltings. As I write that list, I realize that each place has its distinct acoustical qualities, not easily described until one has heard many kinds of music in it. I first entered the Minneapolis hall the afternoon of the concert, on the top tier, at the point farthest from the stage, and conversed in low tones, easily, with someone at the very back of the platform. This is a place, like Epidaurus, where one can literally hear a pin drop. Not a sound, not a noise—a footfall, a chair scraped back—is lost. None of the other halls mentioned have, I think, quite so keen and sharp a response to very small sounds. Morton Feldman's *The Prince of Denmark* (which is the quietest composition I know, after John Cage's completely silent *4'33"*) could well be performed there. The program that evening consisted of a new work by Eric Stokes, *The Continental Harp and Band Report*, for all the instruments of the orchestra except the strings; César Franck's Symphonic Variations and Liszt's *Totentanz*, both with André Watts as the capable soloist; and Rimsky-Korsakov's *Spanish Capriccio*. One of the Stokes movements used the full cohort of brasses and woodwinds in broad, swelling chords, underpinned by drummed gong and cymbal, and this showed the hall's capacity for grand, big sound that could make a noble blaze without becoming a racket. Another was a "toccata" in which the instruments were only touched by the fingers, not blown into, and its dainty patterns of pit-a-pat could be heard clearly. The fortissimo string octaves that open the Franck were crisp. The pyrotechnics of the Liszt, its clarinet solo against a soft octave oscillation from the piano, the dry rap of fortissimo strings *col legno*—all made a vivid effect. So did the glitter, jingle, and brave, quick pageantry of Rimsky's *Capriccio*.

Untested by this fare were the hall's responses to a singer, to a chorus, and to string-saturated late-Romantic orchestral textures. But I believe that all these would come across well, for the acoustics appear to be happily even through all dynamic and pitch ranges. Mid-orchestra and first tier proved to be equally good locations for listening from. The instrumental sound was fresh and immediate, not fierce, not dry. The place seems to behave as if it were a musical instrument itself, a resonant box snug within its brick outer shell. That extraordinary ceiling (I climbed into its recesses) hangs from hundreds of tense wires, like a giant soundboard shaped by some modern Amati. Clustered around the brick shell, not quite touching it (there is an inch gap), are the offices and the foyers and lobbies. The last are of open, airy construction; glass outer walls and exposed girders and ducts form a lighthearted, unpompous, and interesting pattern of bridges, landings, and staircases, painted in bright colors. But there is not enough space for a full audience, during intermissions, to walk and talk, meet, eat and drink, and buy their scores and phonograph records without jostle.

Eric Stokes, born in 1930, teaches at the University of Minnesota. He has written a piece for the Minnesota Opera, incidental music for a Guthrie Theater production, and various works for the orchestras of St. Paul and Minneapolis. *The Continental Harp and Band Report*, commissioned by the Minnesota Orchestra for this inaugural season in the new hall, is a set of nine pieces, most of them reflecting aspects of Americana. "Cindy," for example, is a set of variations on the mountain tune. "Watergate Galop"—a dance "executed with many changes of steps and with hopping movements"—recalls Shostakovich's satirical *The Golden Age*. One "Contrapunctus" is an Ivesian quodlibet on American popular tunes; another, subtitled "A Shopping Center Xmas Eve," is a merry piece of music theater in the manner of Mauricio Kagel. The first and last movements, "Brooklyn Bridge" and "The Triumph of Time," are tone poems, both of which I found moving. The former, prefaced by a line from Hart Crane, prefigures a setting of the whole Crane poem which has occupied Mr. Stokes for some years; the other was inspired by the Bruegel engraving that also gave its title to a piece by Harrison Birtwistle. Time passes with Mahlerian tread in Mr. Stokes's piece; a distant trumpeter, slowly drawing nearer, provides another Ivesian touch. The *Report* is an album of scenes in many moods, an anthology whose items can be offered singly or in various groups. In all, it lasted about forty minutes, and was a stimulating sequence of entertainment, ingenuity, and poetic musing. The forces were deftly employed in many different manners. Any or all of its parts I would gladly hear again.

The orchestra, founded in 1903, has a distinguished history. The last four of its conductors have been Ormandy, Mitropoulos, Dorati, and, since 1960, Stanislaw Skrowaczewski. It plays well, and has moved into a hall that can only make an orchestra play better. Its prowess can be heard in the new four-disc set of Ravel's orchestral works, recorded in that hall and just published by Vox. Most of its concerts are broadcast, so that the whole community can share in them. Its program book, a publication that covers all the events in the busy hall, has long, thorough notes and is attractively printed.

119

In fact, Minneapolis, on this brief visit, struck me as in all ways an uncommonly civilized city. The buildings—both new things, like the Orchestra Hall, Philip Johnson's IDS tower, springing from a bustling city piazza, and Minoru Yamasaki's graceful temple for the Northwestern National Life Insurance Company, whose portico closes the vista down Nicollet Mall; and grand old things, like Harry Jones's Butler warehouse (an Arnolfo di Cambio palace reclaimed for modern use)—are exhilarating. Walking there is a pleasure—down the carless mall, or through a glazed "skyway" system if snow starts to fall. The orchestra's concerts are fully subscribed, and there is contemporary music on twelve of the twenty bills in the regular series. The famous Children's Theater was thronged. The two main art collections are housed in fine buildings—the Walker, by Edward Larabee Barnes, and the Institute of Arts, by McKim, Mead & White, now elegantly extended by Kenzo Tange. I wish I could have stayed longer, to get out to see Marcel Breuer's Benedictine abbey in Collegeville, and to attend some of the campus concerts and workshop opera productions that were imminent.

At the Guthrie Theater, the Minnesota Opera Company presented Opera Today's production of an adventurous new work, *Gulliver*. Two librettists (Robert Karmon and Louis Phillips), three composers (Elliot Kaplan, Frank Lewin, and Easley Blackwood), and the ensemble talents of this troupe long celebrated for its enterprise were concerned in the creation. *Gulliver* is not a show for children, or one for voice fanciers, but a highly intelligent, fast-moving piece of music theater for an audience with honed wits and alert consciences.

There is some reference to Brobdingnag, but the first part of the opera is a voyage out, and most of the second is set in "that unknown Tract of America, Westward of California, and North to the Pacifick Ocean," whose metropolis is Lagado, with its Grand Academy, and on the islands of Luggnagg and Glubbdubdrib. The piece is shaped as an odyssey. Gulliver's wife is the Penelope, and her lyrical arias, sung back in England while Gulliver dreams of home, punctuate the fantastic adventures. But his homecoming is horror. The beautiful songs of the Houyhnhnms (gentle haiku from an invisible chorus, stealing through the theater) sound in his ears, but, with coarse sexual imagery, his family and friends force their and his Yahooism upon him. The use of Swift is largely allusive. There is no clear narrative structure. The listener needs a close knowledge of the *Travels* but must recognize that ideas from the book have been no more than starting points; they are dissolved into new scenes, which make sense only in terms of theatrical and musical imagery. Although Swift's account of eighteenth-century political and commercial morality hardly needs alteration today (on Glubbdubdrib, Gulliver discovered "How many Villains had been exalted to the highest Places of Trust, Power, Dignity, and Profit"), it is not the main concern of the opera, whose subject is not so much the world as an individual's journey through it. The libretto contains a certain amount of facile doggerel, which seems to me slightly imprecise stuff. *Gulliver* is admittedly a work in progress; some episodes need polish, and others a sharper focus. But the whole—created by sounds, lights (Patricia Collins), powerful costumes (Robert Israel), film, singing, speaking, music on tape, music from the orchestra, keen stage direction (H. Wesley Balk)—was wonderfully gripping. Just twelve singers, all of them accomplished, spirited, and physically agile, and twelve players, under expert musical direction by Herbert Kaplan, achieved an extraordinarily rich kaleidoscope. Swift said that his aim in the *Travels* was "to vex the world rather than divert it." Some people found this *Gulliver* vexing. Not I.

March 24, 1975

A SERIOUS MATTER

Idomeneo is the opera that caught the first full fire of Mozart's dramatic genius. The circumstances of its creation were propitious. In Mannheim, in the winter of 1777–78, Mozart formed an ardent desire to compose an opera for the Elector Carl Theodor's excellent troupe and celebrated orchestra—a serious rather than a comic opera, in French rather than in German, but, best of all, in Italian. Some years before, he had composed two *opere serie* for the great theater in Milan; a few months later, in a Paris divided between Gluckistes and Piccinnistes, he shared the bill at the Opéra (as composer of the ballet *Les Petits Riens*) with Piccinni. Meanwhile, Carl Theodor succeeded to the Bavarian throne and took his musicians with him to Munich. Sometime in mid-1780, Mozart was commissioned to write the principal work, an *opera seria*, for the Munich carnival season. All had fallen together as he wanted it. Working closely with a Salzburg librettist (of whom he was greatly demanding), working for, and later with, singers and instrumentalists whom he knew, working in a theater admirably equipped, intelligently directed, and maintained by a duke devoted to the arts, Mozart could expend on *Idomeneo* all that he had learned about *opera seria*, and do all that he had dreamed of doing. The score is as elaborately wrought as that of *Die Entführung*, his next major commission; the combination of youthful freshness and patent ambition, the sense of his rising in every paragraph to produce the very best of which he was capable, gives to

121

these two works a special place in the affection of Mozartians. *Idomeneo* is an *opera seria* of uncommon force, grandeur, and intensity. The matter is classical. The libretto is adapted from a Racinian *tragédie lyrique* (Antoine Danchet's *Idoménée*, set to music by André Campra and performed at the Opéra in 1712). Among Mozart's models, plainly, were Gluck's *Alceste* and *Iphigénie en Aulide*. Gluck sought a noble simplicity. *Idomeneo* is noble, but it is not simple. It contains networks of motivic allusion, tonal structures on a very large scale, and great sequences in which texture, instrumental coloring, harmonic and rhythmic motion, stage action, and scenic device work together to one dramatic end. Fierce storms, at once marine and in the characters' hearts, may remind us that *Idomeneo* and Schiller's *Die Räuber* (first performed on Carl Theodor's Mannheim stage) were written in the same year. If *Idomeneo* fails to arouse extraordinary enthusiasm in audiences, the fault is with them or with the performance—and not with the work.

From Fritz Busch's revival at Glyndebourne, in 1951, with Sena Jurinac as Ilia and Birgit Nilsson as Electra, the work spread through Europe and increased the Mozartian canon from five operas to six. (Today, a new appreciation of *La clemenza di Tito* has pretty well raised that number to seven.) Last year, there were five productions of *Idomeneo* in Britain alone, three of them by major companies. The Salzburg Festival mounted the piece. The fourth complete (or nearly complete) recording was published. And there was a staging at the Kennedy Center in Washington. This production, considerably revised, has now come to the New York State Theater, and it is most welcome. All is not yet right with it, but it can be made into something. What it needs—besides more precisely focused singing, which later casts may well provide—is a closer attention to Mozart's aims and greater confidence in his stagecraft.

Last year's bumper crop of *Idomeneo* was fertilized by Daniel Heartz's important new edition of the score, dated 1972 and published (at a high price) in the *Neue Mozart-Ausgabe*. Back in the 1967–68 *Mozart Jahrbuch*, Mr. Heartz had deplored the practice of putting on *Idomeneo* "without taking the trouble to penetrate its true nature, or even ascertain the form in which Mozart left it," and he had added, "No wonder that performances of the work rarely allow more than an inkling of its greatness, a proper understanding of which seems as remote as ever." His score then, for the first time, established the text of the opera as Mozart did it in Munich and made available its careful scenic directions. The previously received text, from which earlier performing editions were quarried, is a compilation of all the music that at one time or another Mozart composed for his opera. Let us call it *Idomeneo I*, and remember that it contains material that Mozart jettisoned, and in part replaced, during the last weeks of composition.

122

From Munich, the composer reported home that a rehearsal of Act III went splendidly but that "the text, and consequently the music as well, is far too long, as I have always maintained." So the act was much shortened. Two prayers—the chorus's very powerful "O voto tremendo," and "Accogli, oh re del mar," for Idomeneus and the priests—were reduced to a single strophe. Three full arias were dropped: Idamantes' "No, la morte" (those who had heard the number, said Mozart, sighed at its loss—but "in any case an aria is awkward here"), Idomeneus' "Torna la pace" (at whose loss "they sighed even more—but one must make a virtue of necessity"), and Electra's outburst of spitfire despair "D'Oreste, d'Ajace" ("Odd that everyone should hurry offstage so that Mme. Electra can be alone"). The Oracle's utterance was shortened. ("If the Ghost in *Hamlet* were not so long-winded, he would be more effective," said Mozart. *Hamlet* was being played in Munich that season.) Recitatives in Acts I and II were also abridged. And thus was created *Idomeneo II*, which carries the composer's imprimatur, as *Idomeneo I* does not. It is a drama whose acts flow continuously; there are but two conventional exit arias, inviting applause, and they are both for the minor character Arbaces, the royal counselor. *Idomeneo* is the most nearly seamless of all Mozart's operas.

The composer retouched his score for a performance by some noble Viennese amateurs in 1786. The role of Idamantes, originally written for a castrato soprano, was adjusted for a tenor. A new duet for Ilia and Idamantes, now a soprano and a tenor, replaced the former two-soprano duet near the start of Act III. But a new aria, with violin obbligato, was composed for, puzzlingly, a *soprano* Idamantes. This version can be called *Idomeneo III*.

Mr. Heartz sets out *II* and *III* as the main text of his score. The recitative measures and the three arias cut from *I*, and the longer pronouncements of the Oracle are relegated to an appendix. But in the main text he does include the two prayers complete (with indications, of course, of how Mozart cut them), opining that their abridgment was due "more to the special circumstances of the Munich première than to general musico-dramatic necessity." Once the clock, local circumstances, or weaknesses and strengths of the original performers—rather than the composer's wish—are held responsible for aspects of an abridgment, the way is open for anyone to propose his own edition compiled from the surviving materials. *Idomeneo* is in the category of *Carmen*, the first version of *Don Carlos*, and Donizetti's *Dom Sébastien*. (In a different category are Gluck's *Orfeo / Orphée*, Rossini's *Maometto II / Le Siège de Corinthe*, and Mussorgsky's *Boris Godunov*, where a mixture of two versions, each prepared by the composer and each with its own integrity, is harder—though not impossible—to defend. And in yet another category are, say, *Leonore / Fidelio*, *Falstaff*, and *Madama*

Butterfly, where the composers' final thoughts are not in doubt, although their first thoughts, found in early scores, can still be interesting, and even effective, in performance.) In the preparation of a performing edition, documentary evidence, stylistic perception, and present-day possibilities must be nicely and imaginatively pondered. Establishing a text for a particular occasion—and, for that matter, staging it and sounding it appropriately—often calls for a collaboration between scholars and executants which is too rarely practiced. (This is true not only of operas, but the problems there tend to be greatest.) The City Opera was generally pasted for its version of Monteverdi's *Poppea*. Both London's Royal Opera and the Met took a trouncing over their latest *Carmen* texts. The Met received another, in advance, from Philip Gossett— lecturing last week in the Lincoln Center Library, under the auspices of the Toscanini Memorial Archives—for the edition of *Le Siège de Corinthe* it plans to perform next month. (That leaves time enough, perhaps, for some righting of the things Mr. Gossett declared and demonstrated to be unacceptable.) When the world's Verdi scholars gathered for a congress in Chicago last September on the subject of *Simon Boccanegra*, and the Lyric Opera performed the piece, the gulf between research and theatrical practice yawned wide. (The production moves to San Francisco next season; it will be interesting to learn if it is modified to accord with what the *congressisti* revealed of Verdi's own ideas about his work.)

The *Idomeneo* now on show at the State Theater has, as I said, been modified since it left Washington. The Kabuki elements noted by the Washington reviewers have disappeared. The setting, by Ming Cho Lee, is now a plain arrangement of platforms and broken columns, dull but not unworkable, behind which landscapes and seascapes vaguely after Claude, and a temple interior, appear on painted cloths or in projection. (Why do designers of *Idomeneo* fear to create within a neoclassical convention? Glyndebourne produced circular fragments of well-known Turner paintings framed by concentric hoops; the Welsh National Opera opted for a metal construction.) But some of the faults remarked before were retained. Arbaces still rested indecorously on the royal throne. Idomeneus turned rudely aside while Ilia addressed him in "Se il padre perdei." The chorus waved palm fronds as if parodying village-hall operatics. "Edited by Daniel Heartz," it says in the program, but there was still no evidence that Gerald Freedman, the director, had conned Mr. Heartz's edition with any great attention or otherwise profited by his writings on the opera and on eighteenth-century stagecraft. Only Electra and Arbaces bore themselves well, but the former had terrible trouble with a Turandot-length cloak imposed on her in the embarkation scene. Idamantes was assigned the demeanor of a glum page boy, and Idomeneus that of a kindly sheep. Ilia glided through a series of affected

124

poses. This is no way to stage a noble and clearly defined drama. In his plight, the hero is kin to Jephthah, bound by a vow to celebrate his safe return by sacrificing whomever he first meets—and meeting his own child; and then kin to Agamemnon in the necessity of killing his child for the public weal. In legend, and in Campra's opera, the sacrifice was accomplished; in Mozart's drama, when father and son, now like Abraham and Isaac, are steeled for sacrifice, the loving Ilia runs forward to offer herself as an alternative victim, and the god relents. But Idomeneus is more human than Jephthah or Agamemnon; simple terror prompted his rash vow, and by its consequences he is also terrified. As Mr. Heartz has put it, "Idomeneus may be dilatory and vacillating in his subsequent actions, and much less of a ruler than that ruthless King of Kings Agamemnon, but he is much more of a man—tormented, helpless, sympathetic, and ultimately very noble in spirit when he gladly lays down his burden, in happy compliance with the divine decree that his son rule in his stead."

By Mozart, the dramatic pace and dramatic contrasts are superbly controlled. The characters are rounded. How touchingly and truly drawn, in arias at or near the start of each act, is Ilia's realization that her love for Idamantes has conquered grief for the destruction of her parents! How striking is the distress of Electra, daughter of Agamemnon and Clytemnestra, as she watches the daughter of Priam and Hecuba find this happiness with the man she herself loves! Electra is the reactive character, so placed that what makes others rejoice gives her pain, and (as is heard in her lyrical "Idol mio") vice versa. Dramatic irony is potently employed. Act I ends with a divertissement honoring Neptune's clemency, from a populace unaware of the scourge that the god is preparing for them. In Act III, the fanfares of victory herald the entry of Idamantes dressed in white, for sacrifice.

Little of this dramatic pattern was revealed by the City Opera staging. (The opera, incidentally, was performed in Italian; a strong case can be made for doing it in English, at least until all its details are familiar.) Julius Rudel, conducting, showed a far keener appreciation of Mozart's eloquence. The first night was a Sunday; it was the company's fourth performance in thirty hours; both the chorus and the orchestra lacked ardor and intensity. But Mr. Rudel's natural and convincing tempi, his fine control of instrumental textures, his command of transition and contrast, his concern to project the emotional sense of a progression, and not just slip through it, showed a confidence in and understanding of Mozart's dramatic methods which his stage director lacked. Individual phrases were expressively molded. The singers were sensitively supported. (Harpsichord continuo, however, was not employed in accompanied recitatives or during the numbers—not even in the discriminating way suggested by Mr. Heartz in his preface.) The actual singing was less successful. Veronica Tyler's handling of Ilia's music was gentle, supple, and pretty, but her tone was soft-focus, not limpid and forward. Maralin Niska's feeling for line and her projection of Electra's emotions were vivid, but the voice was unreliable and many notes lacked a core of pure, firm tone. Gary Glaze's notes, as a tenor Idamantes, were admirably definite, but he lacked expression. (A soprano Idamantes, I feel sure, is preferable to a tenor; in a long experience of the opera, I have heard such excellent tenors as Léopold Simoneau and Luciano Pavarotti in the role, but none has sounded more heroic and ardent than the soprano Kiri Te Kanawa.) Richard Taylor essayed the virtuoso version of Idomeneus' principal aria and came a cropper; the piece is just about unsingable today—but Mozart did provide a more manageable alternative.

The full version of the two prayers and, naturally, the soprano-tenor duet in Act III were used. Electra reclaimed her final aria, but neither Idamantes nor Idomeneus his. Both of Arbaces' arias were skipped, and the Idamantes aria of *Idomeneo III* was not added. Some recitatives were cut back even beyond the bare bones of *Idomeneo II*. (When good performers are available, it would make more sense to amplify certain scenes. Mozart shortened Idomeneus' first speech and the crucial meeting between father and son only because the original interpreters, he said, "sing recitative so utterly without spirit and fire, so utterly monotonously—and are the most wretched actors that ever trod the stage.") The final ballet, highly prized by both its composer and Mr. Heartz, was omitted. It would be hard to bring off. Modern audiences are thought to have little taste for formal dance as an essential ingredient of a musical drama. But how can that taste be acquired—and *Idomeneo*, Rameau, and Gluck be played as they were planned—if companies always take the easy way out and cut the dances? All in all, this was a play-safe rather than an adventurous text. When the City Opera rethinks its approach to the staging, it may well need revision. Meanwhile, the important thing is that *Idomeneo* has arrived here.

March 31, 1975

DUO

Elliott Carter's latest composition, a Duo for Violin and Piano, commissioned by the Library of Congress, was given its first performance at the Philharmonic's Prospective Encounters concert, in the Great Hall of Cooper Union, on March 21. The players were Paul Zukofsky, violin, and Gilbert Kalish, piano. The Duo lasts a little under twenty minutes and is written as a single, unbroken span of music. Like Carter's previous work, the Brass Quintet, it is a new development of his ideas about "musics" that proceed simultaneously but not synchronously. In three string quartets these ideas were explored, refined, and elaborated. The two later chamber pieces are not simply, or even complicatedly, just more of the same thing, for each takes a specific color and a distinct character from the nature of the instruments concerned in it. The Quintet is inspired by the kinds of sound and musical motion inherent in and traditionally appropriate to ensemble and solo brass; the Duo springs from contemplation of a fundamental contrast in the sound-producing methods of the violin and of the piano. A note played on the violin is a living thing, and dependent for each moment of its life on the muscles of the player; volume, pitch, tone, and intensity can be controlled by the will and the techniques of the interpreter. But the note from a piano string, once struck, can only die away into silence or be cut short by the fall of the damper—unless the string's vibrations are reactivated by a second stroke from the hammer, or sympathetically stirred by the sounding of other strings with which it shares harmonics. (Which is true, of course, only when the piano is played in the usual way, from the keyboard. Once the pianist reaches into the body of his instrument to stroke or harp directly on its strings all sorts of other effects become possible. But such devices are not employed in Carter's Duo.) That sounds obvious enough. One of the things that make Carter's music substantial and, even at its most intricate, accessible is its foundation on such simple musical "truths," on obvious, fundamental taken-for-granted things that he has not taken for granted but considered anew with his alert, questioning musical intelligence. The violin recitative that opens the Duo is like an exposition of the instrument, a demonstration of its abilities string by string: first, a D long sustained; then G and D, and other intervals between the two lowest strings, shaped as a motif; next, the A string brought into play while the motif grows and flowers; and then the E string drawn into the discourse as well. For a hundred measures the long recitative continues, a passionate utterance mounting in intensity, reaching higher and higher, leaping boldly, suddenly whispering, sighing, shouting, breaking off as if for breath, resuming fortissimo with an attack across all four strings, coming to rest at last on concords—a fifth, and then a major third, long sustained, on G and B. The meter is a regular 4/4 but its beats are a springboard from which the player projects free, exuberant rhythmic patterns. It is as if the Duo began with an accompanied cadenza—a cadenza not gathering up but introducing the basic material of the work.

The accompaniment is unemphatic—a background of shifting, lapped chords from the piano, hazed over by the sustaining pedal. These chords are sometimes struck at once and sometimes built up note after note. Chosen parts of a chord are often kept sounding—the player's fingers hold the notes down—while the dampers are gently lowered to quench the other parts; then new elements can be added to the attenuated chords that remain. Notes depressed silently quiver into faint life as they pick up sympathetic vibrations. And thus the violin's brave song is heard in company with a dreamy drift of resonances. The note G is recurrent, not as home base in the old diatonic sense but at any rate as an identifiable fixed point, emergent from time to time and catching the ear as a rock, intermittently revealed by a swirl of waters, may catch an eye that contemplates the moving patterns of a sea- or riverscape. G is the fundamental note of the violin; its tuning leaps by fifths from that note—another "truth" that every schoolboy knows, and it may underlie the role of G in the Duo; the natural chordmaking propensities of the violin strings may have prompted the use of the traditional consonances—fifths, fourths, thirds, sixths, and tenths—far more frequently than in Carter's other works. The last notes of the Duo are three G's, sounded together with the F-sharp below; in the penultimate measure, a long trill on F-sharp and G has urged the listener to interpret them as leading note and tonic. But before the final point is reached there are many adventures.

About fifteen measures before the violin's opening recitative has run its course, the accompaniment grows restive, as if eager for an active rather than a contemplative role; and while the violinist holds his G and B, the pianist breaks out into lines of busy counterpoint. A later episode is a *scorrevole* scherzo. Another is a flight of high harmonics, in double-stops from the violin, over piano pedal notes and pedal chords that recall the opening but allude more insistently to familiar triads. One brief interlude is as punchily laconic as a late-Beethoven bagatelle. Finally, the violin again plays a long, singing recitative, but this time the piano accompaniment is *secco*, and its short chords grow more and more infrequent until the violin is left to sing the last five measures solo.

The two players were stationed far from one another, at opposite ends of the platform. Each has his own kinds of music to play. No more than a flowing river and the wind-stirred forest on its bank do they share or exchange identities—but the beholder perceives both at once, and also broken reflections of trees in the water and rippled light cast upward on the boughs, and he makes of it all a single "picture." Analogies from the natural world cannot be pressed, but that they come to mind at all is perhaps a measure of the richness in Carter's music. On paper, it may look formidably cerebral, calculated to the nicest subdivision of a sixteenth-note septuplet; in performance it is warming, inspiring. Starting from home truths, the composer invites us to follow him on flights of the most daring fancy. The density of his incidents can be daunting. Both his performers and his listeners find their abilities tested to the utmost. At first, they may have to take some of his utterances on trust; later, when understanding comes with familiarity, he proves to have been a guide and seer in whom confidence was not misplaced.

At the concert, a double encounter was possible, for the Duo was done twice. Mr. Kalish's playing seemed to be ideal. Mr. Zukofsky's was not quite that, for there are melodies in the work that cry for the warm, emotional tones of a Kreisler, and his tone tended to be thin and keen. Moreover, his observance of time values was not always precise, especially in the final page, where long notes were shortened beyond any point that the composer's instruction to "play somewhat freely" might sanction. (I own that without a score I would not have noticed this; but since Carter is a composer who takes pains to write exactly what he means, it is always worth doing just what he asks.)

Another world première was billed for the occasion, Lucia Dlugozewski's *Abyss and Caress*. But Pierre Boulez announced that, since this had turned out to be a far longer score than he expected, he had decided to postpone its performance and devote the ensemble-rehearsal time available to the other large work on the bill, Peter Lieberson's Cello Concerto —to give one orchestral piece well prepared rather than two badly. So in place of the Dlugoszewski, two chamber compositions were done: Webern's Quartet for violin, clarinet, tenor saxophone, and piano, and Berg's Four Pieces for clarinet and piano (exquisitely, memorably played by Stanley Drucker and Paul Jacobs). Of the Lieberson Concerto, however, the ensemble then gave a performance so inaccurate that during the final discussion, which is a feature of Prospective Encounters, the composer was moved to tell a questioner that it was not worth talking about his work until it had been properly heard. (Again, I had a score, and so could see and hear what Mr. Lieberson meant.) The Concerto is formidably difficult to play, metrically pernickety beyond the point, surely, of artistic necessity. Even when I heard it more accurately and persuasively executed (last November, with Fred Sherry, for whom it was written, as soloist, and the Group for Contemporary Music under the composer) it seemed to me rather scrappy both in sound and in structure, a work of lively, interesting ideas—three different trios clustered round the soloist, each reflecting an aspect of his

129

protean character—not yet given a convincing and apprehensible form.

One last word. Although the Great Hall is in many ways an apt setting for such concerts, it has a voice of its own. A low, steady hum—perhaps from the air conditioning—added its faint but disturbing pedal point to very quiet passages.

April 7, 1975

The score of Carter's Duo is published by Associated Music Publishers, and a recording of it, made by the original interpreters, appears on Nonesuch H-71314.

A TALE OF TWO CITIES

The eponymous dead city of Erich Korngold's *Die tote Stadt*, the latest work to join the City Opera repertory, is Bruges. *Bruges-la-morte* is the novel, by Georges Rodenbach, from which the plot is drawn. At its close, Hugues Viane, Rodenbach's hero, murmurs "Morte . . . morte . . . Bruges-la-morte" over the body of the mistress he has strangled with a long plait of his dead wife's hair. The town, says the author, is no mere backdrop to his tale but "comme un personnage essentiel, associé aux états d'âme"; the phrase chimes with his friend Mallarmé's account of Symbolism—evoking an object, little by little, to reveal "un état d'âme." The text is interleaved with gray illustrations of Bruges—her "quays, deserted streets, old dwellings, canals, Beguine houses, churches, precious reliquaries, belfry"—so that those who read "may also submit to the presence and the influence of the town." In low-keyed, muted prose, Rodenbach tells how the sounds and colors of Bruges mingle in the air; the tolling of her bells turns gray and glides like a tangible substance along the gray water of her canals. Here Hugues, five years widowed, starts each day by paying tribute to the relics of his wife, visiting them "comme les stations du chemin de la croix de l'amour." Prominent among them, the shining tress he cut from her corpse lies in a glass reliquary on his piano. The latest station of this rite has become Jane Scott, a dancer who resembles the dead woman. At the Bruges Opera, Jane plays the ballerina role in Meyerbeer's *Robert le Diable*, rising from her tomb at Bertram's command "Nonnes, qui reposez . . . quittez votre lit funéraire"; Hugues seems to witness the resurrection of his wife, in a décor of moonlit enchantment. The symbolism thickens.

130

Hugues fancies that Death, whom he has tried to cheat, is stalking him through the streets. In St. John's Hospital, he gazes at Memling's "Martyrdom of St. Ursula and Her Virgin Companions": their blood flows like roses; their wounds are petals. On one of the canals, a swan breaks into sweet song. Jane insists on spending the night in his house. The next morning, while a religious procession goes by, Hugues sees in it the figures of Memling and van Eyck brought to life, approaching him. Profaning the shrine, Jane seizes the hallowed tress and taunts him with it; and he kills her, while the bells of Bruges ring in at the window.

Cunning choice of material for a successful 1920s opera, combining as it does erotic verismo—the violence of *Pagliacci* and *Tosca*—with a cachet of Symbolism to make it artistically respectable in a Vienna which knew Debussy's *Pelléas et Mélisande* and Dukas's *Ariane et Barbe-Bleue*, both drawn from Maeterlinck. In this Vienna, in the second decade of the century, the leading composers were Richard Strauss and Franz Schreker and the Wunderkind was Erich Korngold. Korngold was thirteen when his *Der Schneemann* was acclaimed at the Hofoper, eighteen when, in 1916, Bruno Walter brought out his *Der Ring des Polykrates* and *Violanta*, in Munich. Schreker had the backing of the influential Berlin critic Paul Bekker. (And in his otherwise pretty comprehensive study *The Changing Opera*, Bekker does not so much as mention Korngold.) Korngold had the backing of the influential Viennese critic Julius Korngold, his father, who had succeeded the powerful Eduard Hanslick on the *Neue Freie Presse*. There were other, greater composers in Vienna at the time—Schoenberg, Berg, and Webern. Dr. Korngold did not care for their music. Berg's biographer Willi Reich, sued for libel by Dr. Korngold, declared in court that "the plaintiff in his critical appraisal of musicians had been influenced by the attitude of these musicians towards the compositions of his son." The old Viennese feuds are recalled by Hans Heinsheimer in his model introductory essay to *Die tote Stadt* which appears in the State Theater program.

But there is another sense in which the opera evokes a past Vienna as well as a dead Bruges. Bruno Walter wrote an essay shortly before his death—it forms the preface to Luzi Korngold's biography of the composer—in which he describes how, hearing Marietta's Lute Song from *Die tote Stadt* over the radio, he was plunged into nostalgic dreams of a Vienna that found her fulfillment in this music—a Vienna where "the social life of the time, the beauty of sound, indeed the reveling in beautiful sound that marked music making then in concert-halls and opera-houses, the general delight in song, the beautiful voices and the musical culture of the Hofoper, and the music making of the Philharmonic had filled the ear and soul of the highly gifted youth." Before the City Opera revival, all that *Die tote Stadt* meant to most listeners was its hit number, Marietta's Lute Song, on a phonograph record, sung in its original duet form by Lotte Lehmann and Richard Tauber or as a solo by Maria Nemeth. (The Jane of the book becomes Marietta in the opera.) The melody flows like treacle—and is similarly adhesive. Those twelve diatonic measures, simply and sweetly harmonized, metrically ingenious, are a kind of inspiration. Once heard, Marietta's Lute Song clings to the mind's ear for days. But it is not quite enough to be the making of a whole opera.

Rodenbach fashioned a play, *Le Mirage*, from his novel, and it was put into German as *Das Trugbild*. From both play and book, Julius and Erich Korngold made the libretto of *Die tote Stadt*, ascribing its authorship to an imaginary "Paul Schott"—a pseudonym combining the names of the opera's hero (Rodenbach's Hugues is now called Paul) and its publisher, the house of Schott. A foreword to the first American print of the libretto, however, issued here when the Metropolitan did *Die tote Stadt* in 1921, is signed "Dr. J.K." Korngold was an eclectic. His *Violanta*—which was given a shoestring piano-accompanied production earlier this season by the Bel Canto Opera—combines Debussyan harmony, verismo emotionalism, and the fashion for Renaissance costume drama. *Die tote Stadt* borrows freely from successes of the time. The prelude to Act II, an atmospheric tone poem about bell-filled Bruges, is a tribute to the prelude to Act III of *Tosca*. Marietta's divertissement with her admirers, in Act II, owes much to Zerbinetta's with hers, in Strauss's *Ariadne auf Naxos*. The portrait that comes to life and sings, at the close of Act I, and the key to Marietta's room that Paul sees in the hand of a rival, in Act II, are from *The Tales of Hoffmann*. In each act there is one "surreal" episode: in Act I, there is the incarnation of the portrait just mentioned (Paul's wife, Marie, steps from the frame, to tell him that a living woman now lures him); in Act II, the resurrection scene from *Robert le Diable* is played out in jest on a Bruges quay (the naturalistic townscape turns to an enchanted décor; the Beguines—lay sisters—appear in white nightdresses at the windows of their house; storm clouds cross the sky; midnight strikes, and clockwork figures in a belfry start to move); and in Act III, the religious procession in the street below seems to enter Paul's room, bathed in lurid light, glaring at him, threatening him. These scenes gain their theatrical effect by being magic transformations of the naturalistic settings carefully specified in the score. At the State Theater, for reasons suggested below, they are less striking than they were meant to be.

The murder of a mistress is not a pretty tale. (Berg dealt with it in *Wozzeck*, a work contemporary with *Die tote Stadt*—and *his* opera did not reach the Vienna stage until 1930.) But "Paul Schott" found a way of removing all offense from the story. After Marietta has been strangled, there is another scene. Marietta comes back, charming and insouciant, to fetch the umbrella she left behind at the end of Act I. So it was all just a dream! Paul sings another strophe of the Lute Song, "very slowly, and with the deepest sentiment," draws a curtain across the portrait of the dead Marie, and sets out to rebuild his life. So it *is* a pretty tale after all; the eroticism and violence are spices, not substance. An oblique comment on this: When the Austrian *Tabakregie* named its imitation-American cigarette Jonny, after Krenek's jazz opera *Jonny spielt auf*, and its luxury brand Heliane, after Korngold's next opera, *Das Wunder der Heliane* (Mr. Heinsheimer tells us that a dark-red rose petal covered its mouthpiece), Berg proposed that "a cheap—the cheapest—people's cigarette should carry the name Wozzeck."

Die tote Stadt was a success. In December 1920, simultaneous premières were given in Hamburg, conducted by Egon Polak, and Cologne, conducted by Otto Klemperer. A few weeks later, the lovely Maria Jeritza and the handsome Karl Oestvig introduced the opera to Vienna. Jeritza chose the piece for her Metropolitan début, in 1921. Hans Knappertsbusch conducted it in Munich, and Georg Szell in Berlin. We need not suppose that all these men were concerned simply to be in Julius Korngold's good graces. German audiences were then, as they are now, eager to hear the latest operatic sensation, and *Die tote Stadt* is an alluring vehicle for a glamorous soprano whose voice and manner have the quality described as *strahlend* (the warm radiance of timbre and personality that characterized Jeritza and Lotte Lehmann in full flight—a Viennese attribute, different in sentiment from the noble shine and passions of, say, a Rosa Ponselle). But the last line of the opera is "Hier gibt es kein Auferstehn"; there can be no resurrection of *Die tote Stadt* without a Marietta and a Paul who bewitch and beguile us, for the drama is a synthetic confection, and most of the music is tawdry—Strauss and Puccini, plus dashes of Mahler and Debussy, served in syrup. The operatic historian curious about *Die tote Stadt* will welcome the opportunity of catching it in the theater—and then wonder, when he has heard it, why the City Opera did not spend the care, time, and money that have gone into its production on something more worthwhile. If the intention was to strengthen the German twentieth-century wing, then Hindemith's *Cardillac* and *Mathis der Maler,* Busoni's *Doktor Faust,* and Kurt Weill's *Mahagonny* and *Die Bürgschaft* are works with a superior claim to be heard. Or—if Frank Corsaro wanted to direct something erotic—then Franz Schreker's *Der ferne Klang* or his *Die Gezeichneten*; Schreker is a far more substantial and interesting composer than Korngold.

If—questions of musical quality apart—*Die tote Stadt* makes for a dull evening in the State Theater, it is for two distinct reasons, one concerned with the singing and the other with the staging. Neither of the principals—Carol Neblett as Marietta and John Alexander as Paul—has a voice and manner that could be described as *strahlend*. Although Miss Neblett can be a seductive Thaïs, Marietta eluded her; her playing

133

of the dancer was curiously gauche. There are pretty notes in her voice, but they were seldom joined into a glowing stream of sensuously beautiful sound. Loud high notes tended to be strident. Mr. Alexander reliably, efficiently, and intelligently "stated" the music and the character, but there was no charm in his delivery and no romance in his timbre. The other tune in *Die tote Stadt* besides the Lute Song is an irrelevant "spot" for a baritone during the divertissement of Act II—a rather gooey but catchy waltz, the Pierrotlied. In Vienna, Richard Mayr used to stop the show with it; here Dominic Cossa made it sound protracted and doleful.

The production, "conceived by Frank Corsaro and Ronald Chase," is directed by the former, with films and projections by the latter. Their idea was to pack the show and its action with images of Bruges as insistently as did Rodenbach his novel. Unfortunately, this does not suit the style of the opera. The phantasmagoria is assembled and put through its paces with great technical resource—and Korngold's calculated effects of naturalistic décor suddenly turning surreal and assuming a symbolic quality are lost amid the continuous scenic dissolution. The potency of a dream, or of a nightmare, depends on its seeming real while it lasts; in this staging, Paul's dream has no such "reality." The charm of the prelude to Act III of *Tosca* lies in its aural depiction of a whole city waking, stirring into life around the actual scene that we look at; it would not be enhanced by adding a movie travelogue of Roman campaniles or by bringing the shepherd boy and his flock across the stage. The corresponding prelude in *Die tote Stadt* is diminished by being treated as a sound track for Mr. Chase's photographs and movies. Staged frankly as a period piece, an evocation as much of Vienna as of Bruges, the opera would have a better chance. Despite the skill and care that have been lavished on this ambitious production, and despite Imre Pallo's warm, stylish conducting, *Die tote Stadt* stays dead. *Hier gibt es kein Auferstehn!* Acts I and II were run together—a procedure sanctioned by the composer but not a happy one; an hour and a half of Korngold uninterrupted is hard to swallow. A new English translation of the piece, by Ruth and Thomas Martin, made with the support of a National Endowment for the Arts Composer-Librettist-Translator Fellowship Grant, is published by Schott, but it is not used; the all-American cast sings the opera in German.

April 14, 1975

A Bavarian Radio performance of Die tote Stadt, *with Miss Neblett as its heroine and René Kollo as Paul, conductor Erich Leinsdorf, is published on RCA ARL3–1199.*

RING *REFLECTION*

In many respects the Metropolitan *Ring* was just about as good as could be, given the circumstances of its performance. It would have been unrealistic to expect a first-rate presentation. The Met season and its finances are not so organized that for perhaps six weeks the theater can devote all its resources—orchestra, singers, coaches, stage crews, lighting team—to the preparation and performance of the work, and to nothing else. The three "cycles" that the company gave this season—the first since 1961–62—were not so much real cycles as discrete individual performances dropped into a busy repertory. The continuity of adventure that is important both for the executants and for the audience was impossible. Nearly six weeks divided the first *Das Rheingold* from the first *Götterdämmerung*. The final *Götterdämmerung* was given on a day when the orchestra had already played *Falstaff*; and the day before that it had played both a public dress rehearsal of *The Siege of Corinth* and then *Don Pasquale*. Such things are inevitable in the present Metropolitan scheme of things. One may wish that it were a different kind of company, with different priorities; that it could give to the *Ring* the kind of attention that the two London companies and Scottish Opera do; and that it would perform the cycle within a week, as the Seattle Opera plans to do in July. The English National prepared each *Ring* opera for a year before assembling its cycle. The orchestra was rehearsed section by section. Every singer was coached individually by the conductor. Since that conductor was Reginald Goodall—increasingly recognized as the greatest Wagnerian of our day—the result was a performance in which in every bar the instruments seemed to be "speaking," while the whole had a coherence, dramatic power, and eloquence unheard since the deaths of Furtwängler and Knappertsbusch. (Associated, as translator, with the venture, I must in decency add a "declaration of interest"; but I am talking now only of musical matters and ways they were tackled.) Such preparation is possible only with a stable resident company; the City Opera might manage it, once it has the necessary singers on the force.

Another approach was Karajan's at the Salzburg Easter Festival. In a Berlin studio, with the forthcoming Salzburg cast and orchestra, he recorded each opera, achieving the detailed musical polish possible in such circumstances, and then at Salzburg, in a great theater entirely at his disposal, he gave it scenic form. The Met *Ring* was planned as a pendant to Salzburg's, and for two seasons—*Die Walküre* was mounted in 1967, and *Das Rheingold* in 1968—Karajan himself shaped it; but from the start it was bedeviled by four things: big-city bustle instead of a quiet town in which, for audiences who have come as pilgrims, the opera is the only fixed point of the day; a theater of traditional design for which the Salzburg scenery had to be distorted; the employment of singers other than those whom Karajan had rehearsed; and an orchestra not the Berlin Philharmonic—those players who bow and breathe as if by his will alone they exist. At its best, the Met *Ring* could be no more than a reflection. Without Karajan, as it has been since 1972, it is but a reflection of a reflection. Wolfgang Weber, the stage director, has set out the moves of Karajan's production, more or less, but their motivation is gone. Günther Schneider-Siemssen's scenery was planned as a series of huge, dim-lit illustrations to the drama that Karajan unfolded in the pit; their gloom was tiresome, and finally depressing, even in Salzburg, and to Sixten Ehrling's less broodingly poetic interpretation they are not a fit accompaniment. But, plainly, the company is stuck with this scenery for a while. If Karajan cannot be coaxed back, the question is: Is an inevitably unsatisfactory *Ring* better than no *Ring* at all? Answering yes, I will confine harsh criticism to what was needlessly wrong. This report is on the first three operas of the first cycle and the *Götterdämmerung* of the third.

The start was unpromising, for the orchestral playing in *Das Rheingold* was both drab and untidy, and there was no glow in the instrumental sound of Act I of *Die Walküre*. Things came to life—at any rate, for me—in one particular measure of Act II, at the moment when, after Brünnhilde had sung "Weh! mein Wälsung!," the bass clarinet struck in with the Dejection motif. Dozens of times, during Wotan's monologue, this motif has sounded; but now Vincent Abato sounded it with a *meaning* to suggest that he, too, was concerned at the crumbling of all the god's hopes. The concern was contagious; the other instruments followed suit. Later in the act, during what Wagner calls a "long silence" while Siegmund bends to kiss the sleeping Sieglinde, the "silence" is in fact a bass clarinet solo, continued by the lower strings. Mr. Abato charged it with a rapt intensity that inspired the cellos, in turn, to tender, loving tone. From Act II of *Die Walküre* onward, there was much color and plenty of keen, incisive solo and ensemble work in Mr. Ehrling's interpretation. What the reading lacked was breadth, grandeur, a sense of "organic" growth from one dramatic paragraph, one act, one opera to the next, and that long-breathed orchestral sound, massive yet luminous, which few can achieve. There are but three great *Ring* conductors active today—Goodall, Karajan, and Solti. Since the Metropolitan would not be able to meet their rehearsal requirements, in practical terms it could not have done much better than engage Mr. Ehrling, a thoroughly reliable conductor, who nothing uncommon did but nothing mean.

Heroic singers are in even shorter supply. Neither Thomas Stewart, the Wotan, nor Jess Thomas, the Siegfried, has a voice of limitless power, lyricism, and romance. One can note that, and regret that it should be so; but since each is still among the finest current interpreters of his role, the Met's casting can hardly be criticized on that score. In fact, I found both men's complete understanding of their roles one of the most dependable and satisfying features of the cycle, but did wish that Mr. Stewart, in *Siegfried*, had not chuckled and chortled quite so often. (In *Siegfried*, most of the Wotan-Siegfried encounter was omitted. The cut is not uncommon, but is unwelcome; the meeting of the old order and the new is a climax in the drama. Moreover, Wagner himself —as we learned when excerpts from Cosima's diary were published— described it as "the most beautiful scene he has written" [entry for October 20, 1870].)

Similar considerations apply to Berit Lindholm, who, as Brünnhilde, made her Metropolitan début, and who is generally considered heiress-apparent to Birgit Nilsson (who sang Brünnhilde in the second cycle). The voice is not generous in timbre but narrow and bright. For two operas, it seemed that she had increased its projectile force at the expense of expression; she was a plucky and incisive heroine but not affecting. Then in the final *Götterdämmerung*—the end of her long stint in sight—she sang with majesty and amplitude, achieving in the large house the vividness and intensity for which, in smaller theaters, she has often been admired. Miss Nilsson was Sieglinde. Her "Siegmund, so nenn' ich dich!" was stentorian; her powerful "O hehrstes Wunder!" shot out of tune; otherwise, she scaled her goddess voice down in an intelligent but not quite convincing attempt to suggest the tender, impulsive maiden. Once Jon Vickers had settled some differences of tempo with the conductor, he was, as ever, a notable Siegmund. In *Das Rheingold*, three Met débutants came to grief: Maureen Forrester was a feeble Erda; Glade Peterson barked his way through Loge's witty, elegant music; Kolbjörn Höiseth broke Froh's lyrical effusion into short segments. Ragnar Ulfung was a keen, lively Mime, with not quite enough tone in his voice. Bengt Rundgren was a touching Fasolt, a rather tame Hunding, and a striking, clever Hagen—one of the few basses who get the point of the joke Wagner intended with his trill imitative of terrified sheep (at "dass gute Ehe sie ge - - - be"). The Three Norns—Lili Chookasian, Mignon Dunn, and Nell Rankin—were impressive. Miss Dunn was less effective as Fricka and Waltraute. Miss Rankin was a poignant Gutrune. Donald McIntyre, the Gunther (and the Wotan of the second cycle), has a commanding baritone, but it did not focus precisely on the notes. Marius Rintzler's Alberich wanted force.

In sum, it was a cast of mixed quality, and one such as might be encountered in any major house today. What the production as a whole lacked was the stamp of a directing hand and a sense of ensemble endeavor. A director intent on "making a statement" about the *Ring* can, of course, dreadfully diminish the audience's experience of the many-layered work even while illuminating some special aspect of it. In a city that has no other *Ring* cycles within easy reach, a conventional staging is probably preferable. But it need not be as characterless as the Met's. Possibly some young director and conductor team, knowing the scenery and prepared to work with it, will come to Schuyler Chapin with their ideas and, if they are approved, begin at once to choose and coach their cast for the next revival, so far unannounced. All over the country, *Ring* operas are now performed; discoveries are to be made. But New York's *Ring* should be more than an ad-hoc assembly of various international celebrities supported by local talent.

There were specific things wrong in the performance that should have been put right before curtain rise: inept effects (Rhinemaidens employed six at a time, three popping out at moments to sing, alternating with three ballet girls mugging to loudspeaker sound); major strokes of dramatic symbolism missed (in *Die Walküre*, Nothung, the sword, made no contact with Wotan's spear); above all, the encircling gloom, not lifted even when a fiery glare should fill the stage, or when Brünnhilde wakes to hail the bright sun. During the *Ring* I do ask to see the distant scene; one spotlight not enough for me. It was a mishap that Nothung, drawn from the tree, came to pieces in Siegmund's hand, and that in *Siegfried* the anvil refused to break under its stroke. It is probably a mercy when the horse, to whom the last twenty lines of the cycle are addressed, is left to our imagination. But it is simply a mistake when Siegfried, singing specifically of the shield Brünnhilde has given him, carries none.

I am sometimes charged with the neglect, in these pages, of chamber-music concerts. It is true that, as a rule, I prefer to hear chamber music in a chamber rather than at a public concert in a large, cheerless, and sometimes distractingly drafty hall. A music lover's day ends well in a comfortable chair, with a decanter at his elbow and a Haydn quartet sounding from the loudspeakers. A phonograph record may not be the real thing, but it can come closer to it than even the finest performance heard in unsuitable surroundings. Although the pull of the live event remains strong, the attractions of intimacy, of having choice listening companions, or none, and of being able to turn the pages of a well-lit score without compunction about disturbing other listeners may prove stronger still. Nevertheless, let me declare next that the purest pleasure of the New York season so far was brought me by the Juilliard String Quartet's recital in Alice Tully Hall last week. It was the first of two devoted to Schoenberg's quartets; Nos. 3 and 1 were played. (Nos. 2 and 4 and the early, unnumbered D-major Quartet are due later.) Twenty years ago, the Juilliard taught me to love these compositions; their performances were revelatory in the way that Hans Rosbaud's of Schoenberg's orchestral music were. Once, this music had seemed forbidding, baffling; suddenly there shined a light, and there fell from my ears as there had been scales. The Juilliard recorded the quartets then, and it is announced that they are to record them again. Welcome news, for their performances are peerless.

The best modern recording at the moment is that of the LaSalle Quartet, in a splendid Deutsche Grammophon album that contains all the string-quartet music of Schoenberg, Berg, and Webern. This Second Vienna School "cycle" the LaSalle have given live in many cities and are now giving in New York for the first time, also in Alice Tully Hall. The Juilliard Quartet and the LaSalle—both, incidentally, of Juilliard School origin—make an interesting contrast. The timbre of the LaSalle Quartet is exquisite—so sweet, pure, clear, and homogeneous that a listener is tempted to revel in the sounds and forget the sense. At the first of their four concerts, Berg's Quartet, Webern's Six Bagatelles, and Schoenberg's First Quartet were played. The Webern was bewitching; the players knew how (in the words of Schoenberg's foreword to his colleague's score) "to express a novel in a single gesture, a joy in a single breath." In the more robustly romantic Berg and Schoenberg, they drew fine, nervous lines but reduced the power of both pieces by working within a somewhat limited dynamic range; the Berg, which has *fff* and *ppp* markings in consecutive measures, calls for more violent contrasts. The LaSalle are aristocrats of this repertory (when four expert Viennese players banded as the Alban Berg Quartet, they traveled to Cincinnati to study with the LaSalle), and they perform it with all the delicacy, sensitivity, and polish of manner that the term implies. In Schoenberg, they to the Juilliard are rather what, in Beethoven, the Léner Quartet was to the Busch. The Juilliard interpretation of Schoenberg's First was bigger, stronger, and, I believe, deeper. "What wonderful playing!" one could exclaim after both performances, but it was Juilliard's that would more forcefully prompt the addition "And what wonderful music!"

The Juilliard have a new cellist—Joel Krosnick. He is a noble player, at once definite and subtle. If a single episode is to be pointed out, it might be the famous E-major melody of the adagio section, deemed by Schoenberg himself an "inspiration," delivered by Samuel Rhodes, the violist, and accompanied by the others (Mr. Krosnick holding a pedal point; Robert Mann and Earl Carlyss, the violinists, lulling in triplets) with a beauty that dissolved a listener into ecstasies. In control of colors, in cogency of discourse, in the balance of voices and the balance of form, in the molding of melodies, in the pacing of rhythms, in the carefully graded emphases given to harmonic events—in every way, to cut short the catalogue of merits, this was a performance that approached not merely the humanly attainable but the ideal. If I say "approached" rather than "achieved," it is only because toward the end of the long, sustained, and terribly demanding composition Mr. Mann seemed to be tiring a little, and then not all his contributions were quite true.

The protagonist of Rossini's *Le Siège de Corinthe* is the chorus, which takes part in every number of the opera except one (a trio in Act III). This choral dominance is obscured in the new Metropolitan production of the opera, which has been mounted for the début there of Beverly Sills—as a vehicle for a remarkable soprano, supported by coloratura mezzo-soprano, tenor, and bass. It serves this purpose, but can hardly be said to serve the composer well. Rossini's opera becomes a decorative showcase for the prima donna. Sandro Sequi, who has staged it, handles the choirs as if they were part of the décor. Decoration of another kind has been plastered all over the vocal lines, often appropriately, in ways that Rossini would expect, but sometimes with ludicrous result. (When the heroine rushes in and sees an executioner's sword poised over her father, she adds to Rossini's tense exclamations a cascade of pretty twiddles.) The tenor of the show is on record as saying that with Rossini "You check your logic as you come in the door." He is wrong, but the particular Met edition of *Le Siège* bears him out; it has been assembled, by anonymous hands, with scant regard for either dramatic or musical logic.

Rossini composed his *Maometto II* (concerned with Mahomet the Conqueror, the captor of Constantinople in 1453) for Naples in 1820; it is an adventurous piece, with some remarkable innovations in form. Three years later, he refashioned it for Venice, adding some new music, and some old music from earlier operas, and providing a happy ending. Three years after that, he reworked *Maometto* as the lyric tragedy *Le Siège de Corinthe*, the first of his three French *grands opéras*. The action was shifted from the shores of the Bosporus to Corinth a few years later; the besieged Venetian garrison became Greek; the young officer to whom the heroine is plighted, originally a contralto role, was rewritten for a tenor; the orchestration was amplified and the vocal lines simplified; new numbers were composed, old numbers were reordered in new forms, and some bravura arias for the soloists were dropped. The subject was topical. Two new Mahomets, the Sultan Mahmud II and the Pasha Mehmet Ali, now threatened Greece; at the time of *Le Siège*, Athens itself was besieged. Two years earlier, Byron had died at Missolonghi. (Byron's *The Siege of Corinth*, published in 1816, although dealing with the eighteenth-century sack of the town, shares with the opera not only its title but also the situation of the Corinthian governor's daughter being in love with the infidel captain; it may have been a contributory source to the plot of *Maometto II*.) Today, it would be easy for a director of *Le Siège* to shove modern "relevance in our faces by projecting scenes from present-day Cyprus, and film clips of helicopters lifting the survivors from a city about to fall. Such things are not needed. They would smash the stylistic mold of the opera. But what is needed—what was plainly intended by Rossini—is that the audience should be sympathetically stirred by the plight of a populace facing death and destruction, by heroic defiance, and despair, and the anguish of personal happiness destroyed by the disasters of war. The principals have no inner life but are mouthpieces for such emotions. A colleague describes the character of Pamira, the heroine, as "one-dimensional (not even that, really)"—which pretty well reduces it to vanishing point. But the music has substance—romantic, emotional, and dramatic substance. As the Victorian critic Henry Chorley once wrote, "*Le Siège de Corinthe* contains music too noble to be forgotten."

In Italian translation, as *L'assedio di Corinto*, it has been revived in our day with success. The young Renata Tebaldi headed a cast in Florence in 1949, and in Rome two years later; Beverly Sills led the cast of a Scala production, in 1969, which marked her European début. The Metropolitan staging is an elaborated reconstruction of that performance; in addition to Miss Sills, it has the same conductor (Thomas Schippers), director (Sandro Sequi), designer (Nicola Benois), and Mahomet (Justino Díaz). Shirley Verrett has succeeded Marilyn Horne as Néoclès, the young officer (this tenor role is reclaimed, as it often was in the nineteenth century, by a mezzo-soprano), and Harry Theyard is the new governor, Cléomène (played by Franco Bonisolli at La Scala). The Met edition, still sung in Italian, is a mixture of *Maometto II*, in both its Neapolitan and Venetian versions, and *Le Siège*, together with a trivial Act II cabaletta for the heroine lifted from Rossini's early opera *Ciro in Babilonia*, and a final cabaletta for her (by Mercadante? Pacini?) that Giuditta Grisi inserted into an 1829 performance. The principle of creating, for a Rossini revival, a performing text matched to the talents of the particular cast and to the circumstances of its production is unassailable. But in its practice the Met has erred, mainly on two counts. First, large cuts have been made that destroy carefully balanced forms and harmonic structures. For example, in the introduzione of Act I and the duet of Act II the second support of what was originally a symmetrical tonal arch has been kicked away. And a listener need not know the original score to feel that Mahomet makes his first entry with impossible abruptness; in fact, his opening recitative, the first section of his aria, and the orchestral introduction to his cabaletta have all been excised. Second, numbers have been introduced that weaken the musical and dramatic shape. The Grisi cabaletta, already mentioned, is one of them (in any case, it was written for the start of Act II, and so is doubly unwelcome in the Act III finale at a moment when, after Pamira's noble prayer, the action should rush to its close).

Another such number is a trio from the Venice *Maometto*; redundant in *Le Siège*, which already has four trios of its own, it clogs the progress of the third act, and is, moreover, a dramatic absurdity.

That said, one can praise the zest, enthusiasm, and, from the two ladies, high accomplishment with which the singers tackled their fancy-work. Miss Sills looked beautiful, bore herself with dignity and pathos, and rippled through her roulades with a facility that set the audience cheering. In the delivery of Rossini's simple, limpid melodies—such of them as remained—she was a shade less poignant than at La Scala, and some ill-judged final *acuti* were strident and untrue. But, all in all, this was a magnetic, virtuoso performance, vocally and dramatically of uncommon merit. Miss Verrett, sporting a Clark Gable mustache, looked rather silly, but she was dashing, lustrous in tone, fleet, energetic, and powerful in divisions. (Nevertheless, it was hard to banish memories of Miss Horne, who was vocally so astounding in the role; her performance of Néoclès' big scene—in a much longer version than Miss Verrett is allotted—is preserved on a London Records recital.) Mr. Theyard's tone was strained and disagreeable. Mr. Díaz's tone was commanding, but his coloratura was often no more than a blurry sketch of the notes. Much of *Le Siège* is ensemble—those five trios!—and of the four principals only Miss Verrett produced firm-focus, every-note-hit-plumb-in-the-center phrases (and she not always; vibrancy crept in under emotional pressure). So, especially in the "canonic" passages, the chording was not always pure, nor did one hear one line moving against another with each interval beautifully defined. Since the opera was put on as a vocal (and scenic) display, not as a musical drama, only the highest vocal standards should be applied to any assessment.

Scenically, it looked very handsome. Mr. Benois's sets are in the "romantically neoclassical" manner of Alessandro Sanquirico, who designed the Scala première of the opera, in 1828. For the Met, Mr. Benois has provided a new Act II, which suggests the Sanquirico décor done over by Bakst. Mahomet's ships still form the backdrop to the piazza of the second scene. (Were they drawn there on the Diolcus? Although Nero began cutting the Corinth canal in A.D. 67, it opened to shipping only in 1893.) Mr. Schippers's conducting was lively and colorful. His only failing was to push some fast passages, including the allegro assai of the overture, at a speed faster than the players and singers could cleanly articulate them—almost as if daring his performers to get through at his tempi. The natural vigor of Rossini's music was thereby diminished, not enhanced.

The show is a success. Given Miss Sills and Miss Verrett, it could not fail to be. But it is not quite a worthy representation of the heroic opera that Rossini composed.

April 21, 1975

Le Siège de Corinthe, with the Metropolitan principals, is recorded on Angel SCLX 3819; for more details about the edition used, see my review of the album in High Fidelity *for June 1975. Miss Horne's dashing account of the* Maometto-*plus*-Siège *scene is on London OS 26305.*

KING OF INSTRUMENTS

Organists—I speak from experience, having spent undergraduate years as organ scholar of my college, and some later years editing a magazine, *The Musical Times*, that was, among other things, the monthly "organ" of the Royal College of Organists—tend to be a rum breed, with passions and prejudices distinct from those of ordinary musicians. The audiences for organ recitals are also rather special. In New York, there are several series of recitals that cater for them but receive little general publicity. One day, I hope to make the rounds of the more celebrated instruments, and report. But today, just a preliminary account of an important instrument that is at the center of the city's musical life—the organ given to Lincoln Center by Miss Alice Tully, which stands in the hall that bears her name. It has been inaugurated by a series of four concerts: two solo recitals, given by André Marchal and Karl Richter, and two orchestral programs featuring works in which the organ has a large role. The account can be but tentative, for Mr. Marchal is a veteran (he won the Guilmant Prize at the Paris Conservatoire in 1913) who commands our affection and respect but no longer commands the techniques that once were his, while Mr. Richter's registration, in his all-Bach program, too often presented the instrument as a box of painfully shrill, strident whistles. There were stretches of noisily insistent, even brutal, playing of the kind that gets organists and their followers a bad name among lay musicians. Who but a tin-eared organ fancier, they ask, can bear to listen to elaborate contrapuntal textures sounded in consecutive fifths—the result of drawing stops that make the first and second harmonics of a note nearly as prominent as the fundamental tone? Let us suppose that Mr. Richter did not have time to study the sound of the organ in the hall—and postpone consideration of its merits as a solo instrument until it has been heard to better advantage.

The hall must have caused problems. The commission was for a pretty big and versatile organ, such as might be built for an abbey or large church (it is a four-manual job, with sixty-one stops), and so in Tully Hall everything had to be scaled down if listeners were not to be blown out of their seats by the Trompettes and Clairons in full cry, or by the *Grand Jeu*. Moreover, what was planned was the kind of instrument that is generally to be found in resonant buildings, where space and echo take the edge off the sound and, like Silas Wegg's meaty jelly, are "mellering to the organ," while the maker holds things in balance and maintains distinctness by devising stops with a clean attack and well-defined timbres. Tully Hall is unresonant. Pipework that in a reverberant church might sound admirably clear would there sound clinically precise. So everything had to be newly thought, if music written by Couperin, Bach, César Franck, and Olivier Messiaen was to make the kind of effect that the composers had in mind. The initial "chiff" that marks the more extreme products of the baroque revival has been avoided. On the whole, the problems seem to have been solved well. But the precision of the hall's acoustics created an odd effect in pedal solos, when the line hopped from one side of the platform to the other, from one to the other of the two flanking towers that contain the pedal pipes.

The organ was built by the firm of Theodore Kuhn, in Männedorf, Switzerland. (There are some older Kuhn organs in America, but this is the only modern example of the firm's work here.) "The tonal design was developed by Lawrence Phelps" (I quote Lincoln Center's official handout), and the stop-control and combination systems are by Lawrence Phelps & Associates, of Erie, Pennsylvania. (There is little chauvinism in the organ world; the new organ in Hexham Abbey, Northumberland, is a Phelps, shipped over from Erie—a two-manual tracker with thirty-four stops.) Voicing the instrument seems to have been the joint responsibility of Kurt Baumann, of the Kuhn company, and Mr. Phelps. The keyboard action is "tracker" (i.e., there is direct mechanical linkage between the keys and the valves that admit air to the corresponding pipes), but the stops are shifted by electricity. (They are controlled by little rocking tablets, not those hefty drawstops linked directly to sliders that bring the ranks of pipes into play.) A rough analogy from the motoring world might be an automobile that had rack-and-pinion steering, which gives one the precise feel of the road under one's fingers, but an electrically operated gearshift. The pedal board is concave and radiating, not straight. Wind is supplied by motors, at the touch of a switch. (My college organ, with its straight pedals, needed a pair of strong arms to pump it—a dependable system on days when the power supply was erratic.) Tracker action is once again in favor. It was standard in the days before Charles Barker introduced his Barker-Lever Action to the great French organ builder Cavaillé-Coll (1837), and Henry Willis equipped the St. Paul's Cathedral with tubular pneumatic action (1872), and Robert Hope-Jones, later in the century, devised his delicate electric actions. Playing a big tracker needs strong fingers (as I discovered in Haarlem last summer, when playing the big Mulder organ that Mozart once played). Indiscriminately applied, tracker action can spoil instruments that were never meant to have it. (A fine, romantic Hill in Adelaide Town Hall became hard to play when the assistance provided by its Barker-Lever Action was withdrawn recently, in a misguided attempt at "barockification.") Fashions in the organ world change fast, and the postwar "back to baroque" movement has already been succeeded, or at least joined, by another: to save, unaltered, the noblest organs of Victorian and Edwardian times, the threatened Willises and Hills and early Walkers, the Hope-Joneses, Skinners, Austins, Aeolians, and Casavants. (What has happened to their giant successors? Is the monster in the Atlantic City Auditorium, with its seven-manual console and its stops on a hundred-inch wind pressure, still the largest organ in the world, and what shape is it in? Does the six-manual organ in the Wanamaker store in Philadelphia still sound? Any active organ enthusiast can answer these questions. I am drawing on schoolboy memories of the American marvels I once read of, and have not yet begun to explore.)

The Tully Hall organ represents a return to eighteenth-century sound ideals and to crisp eighteenth-century touch, combined with every modern convenience for the player. It has sixty-four combination pistons (buttons, set below the keyboards, that automatically bring on any chosen combination of stops)—eight for each of the four manuals, eight for the pedals, and twenty-four more affecting the whole organ. Twenty of this array are duplicated by toe pistons (for use when the hands are busy but a foot is unoccupied). In addition, further pistons can bring on or silence the mixtures, the reeds, the *Plein Jeu*, the *Grand Jeu*, and "Tutti." All this is temptation for the player. When changing the stops of an organ requires physical effort, and hands must be lifted from the keyboard to push them in or pull them out, there is less provocation to indulge in fidgety, unstylish shifts of registration. (Similarly, when manpower provides the wind pressure, the player is less likely to use the organ at full force for long periods.) But the temptation can be resisted. The gadgetry is not needed for Bach, but it will be useful in the modern repertory, which the instrument is also designed to serve.

There is always a danger that a versatile instrument may prove to have no distinctive character of its own. The Tully organ was put through such protean paces during the inaugural concerts that it has been hard to form more than a generally favorable but unparticularized opinion. The organ is said to combine French, German, and Italian characteristics (in proper Swiss fashion). So far, it seems to me more classical French than anything else. The Great (or *Grand Orgue*; the organ is titled in French) chorus is founded not on any noble Anglo-Saxon Diapason but on an unassertive, even somewhat featureless, Montre that takes fire and color from the ranks of pipes, sounding upper harmonics, that can be added to it. The Swell (or *Récit*) has a good array of full, sweet flutes, and a silvery *Plein Jeu*. The Choir (or *Positif*) has a lively chorus with a character nicely distinct from the Great's. The fourth keyboard controls a *Positif de Chambre*, a little chamber organ planned especially for continuo use, which can also be played from the Choir manual. What is apparent at once is how good the instrument looks. The auditorium, which was architecturally a shade dull while the tall wooden ribs ran unbroken all around it, has now received its focus. The *Werkprinzip* scheme of construction, musically, mechanically, and aesthetically sound, has been followed; that is to say, each of the organ's five departments is defined by its case. Directly over the player's head is the little *Positif de Chambre*, in a box whose doors can be opened and shut by a pedal. Above that, the gleaming *Grand Orgue*. Above that, projecting in a case of its own, the *Positif*. The tall *Pédale* towers close the scheme on either side. The *Récit* is in mysterious darkness, behind the louvres of the box that encloses it. The visual design is by Jacob Schmidt, of Lucerne; and even when the organ is not being played its appearance will enhance any recital given on the platform below it.

The first orchestral concert, by the Juilliard Orchestra conducted by Sixten Ehrling, brought Hindemith's Organ Concerto, a rather dry, schematic late work, composed for the new Aeolian-Skinner instrument in Philharmonic (now Avery Fisher) Hall, in 1963. Organ and orchestra did not sound good together (in anything but gentle music they seldom do), but the fault is the composer's. In Saint-Saëns's Third Symphony, "for orchestra with organ," the organ is used for much of the time as a quiet, sweet continuo, and John Schuder, the organist, made it sound very beautiful. He is a sensitive player. How often, at the end of this symphony, or of Elgar's *Enigma* variations, or of his *Cockaigne* overture, the listener quails before rude blasts from an organ that overpowers the orchestra! But Mr. Schuder did not confuse majesty with bombast; organ and orchestra were in balance, and the C-major of this life rang out grandly, not grossly.

Three organists appeared at the second orchestral concert, given by the Musica Aeterna Orchestra, conducted by Frederic Waldman. E. Power Biggs (whose name, according to the program note, "is literally synonymous . . . with the instrument he plays") was the soloist in the Sinfonia to Bach's Cantata No. 29, *Wir danken dir*, and Haydn's Second Organ Concerto in C. Fortunately, his playing was neither powerful nor big. It was slight and unassuming. But he did show that the new instrument could provide bright, pretty, delicately dancing sounds, much like those still to be heard in the Bergkirche in Eisenstadt, where Haydn played. A pity, though, that Mr. Biggs did not also provide a continuo part (this was supplied by a harpsichord). Catharine Crozier was the organist in Samuel Barber's *Toccata Festiva*, composed for the inauguration of the new organ in the Philadelphia Academy of Music, in 1960. Her playing was brilliant. The Toccata was done without the "percussion crashes and bursts of brass" and "slashing scales and triad figures of brilliant . . . woodwinds" mentioned in the program note; a version for string orchestra, with trumpet, was used. This is a more acceptable and more pleasing combination of forces than full orchestra and full organ in competition or conjunction. Poulenc used something similar in his Concerto for Organ, String Orchestra, and Timpani. Thomas Schippers was the trim soloist in this dapper, beguiling little composition.

The organ repertory is large, and not all of it is only for organ fanciers. Other cities have found that the general public welcomes a well-planned, coherent series of short organ recitals—an hour of the instrument is enough for most people—which can conveniently be given between, say, six and seven. The hall is then freed for the main concert of the evening, and the audience can go on to its theaters, concerts, or dinners. I hope that Lincoln Center will consider such a series, based in Tully Hall but perhaps moving into Fisher Hall for programs to which the Aeolian-Skinner is better suited. (In fact, there are now organs by three notable builders under the roof of the Juilliard School: the new Kuhn-Phelps in Tully Hall, a forty-four-rank Holtkamp in Paul Hall, and a Flentrop in the Organ Studio. Paul Hall seats only 278 and is in regular student use, but perhaps, if timetables allow, it could also be brought into the series. The Organ Studio can seat only fifty or so.) The Philharmonic's thematic program planning—when, say, Mendelssohn, Brahms, Liszt, or Schoenberg is the chosen composer—could be amplified by reference to these recitals. The players are at hand, for they have to participate in the various recital series of the city's churches. And so—to judge by the house-full sign that went up for the inaugural concerts—is the audience.

April 28, 1975

Lincoln Center did not try embarking on a series of short six-o'clock organ recitals, like those on London's South Bank (where some recitals are played on the large, versatile instrument in the Festival Hall and others on the Flentrop tracker in the Queen Elizabeth Hall), which bring organ music into the regular run of concert life. Except when the Alice Tully organ was being played, it was hidden away again, out of sight, behind tall wooden shutters, and the hall reverted to its former plain, dull aspect. Repeatedly—as readers will discover—I regretted that this should be so. It was not, I was told, a matter of acoustics.

When Avery Fisher Hall was rebuilt, in 1976, the Aeolian-Skinner instrument was taken out, and no provision was made to house an organ; when one is heard there now, it is either a small portable instrument standing on the platform or an electronic device sounding through loudspeakers. The Atlantic City organ, I learned, still survives, though no longer in its former majesty, having been damaged by a storm; and the Wanamaker instrument in Philadelphia is still going strong.

147

THREE HALLS, THREE SOPRANOS

Town Hall needs money. It needs, to be precise, $365,000 to underwrite its programs for the next three years, and has announced that unless the sum can be found it will close on August 31. Most cultural institutions need money. The reason for raising Town Hall's plight in these critical columns is that—when the tricky equations of acoustics, accessibility, atmosphere, sight lines, performers-and-audience contact, and comfort have been made—Town Hall seems to me the best of New York's homes for solo, chamber, and chamber-orchestra music making. It seats fifteen hundred people—four hundred more than Alice Tully Hall does—and it lacks Tully Hall's spacious lobby. But the back rows at Town Hall are closer to the platform than the back rows at Tully Hall, and in general the sound of the place is warmer. Since Town Hall opened, in 1921, it has housed many great interpreters. Mary Garden, Povla Frijsh, Jennie Tourel, Lotte Lehmann, Elisabeth Schumann, Rosa Ponselle, Kirsten Flagstad, Elisabeth Schwarzkopf, and Joan Sutherland; Kreisler, Szigeti, and Heifetz; Wanda Landowska; Casals; Paderewski, Rachmaninoff, Gieseking, Schnabel, and Guiomar Novaës; Bartók, Strauss, and Stravinsky are but a few names chosen at random from the long list of musicians who have appeared there. (The lecturers include Eve Curie, Galsworthy, Maeterlinck, and Winston Churchill. In fact, Town Hall was built, by the League for Political Education, as a lecture hall, and its musical excellence was a chance by-product of the League's insistence that its auditorium should be designed on "democratic principles" that allowed speakers to be seen well and heard well from every seat.) History is a good reason for saving a building; an even better reason the fact that there is no other building to serve a particular purpose quite so well. (What would New York's orchestral life be if Carnegie Hall had been torn down?) Town Hall slumped when Tully Hall opened—and the increasing sordidness of Times Square did not help. But since I have been in New York I have watched Town Hall activities grow, have often enjoyed its conveniently timed five-forty-five or six-o'clock recitals, and have noted the lively attendance at other events—the series of travel films; the appearances of Bette Davis, Joan Crawford, Lana Turner, and Myrna Loy; the al-fresco excursions from Town Hall into Bryant Park and Grace Plaza for jazz concerts—beyond a music critic's sober brief. Only the musical celebrities seem to have forgotten a place their predecessors favored. If I were an established artist—a Janet Baker, Rostropovich, or Segovia—I would insist, as Julian Bream does, on giving at least one Town Hall recital on every New York visit. Although in a larger auditorium I could earn more money and reach more people, Town Hall serves the music better.

Klara Barlow, who appeared as a coloratura soprano at Carnegie Recital Hall twenty-one years ago, chose Town Hall for her New York début recital, last week, as a dramatic soprano. The first part of her program was arias, ranging from "O Hoffnung! O komm'!," from Beethoven's *Leonore* (a more elaborately florid piece than the familiar "Komm', Hoffnung" in the revised *Fidelio*), to "Al dolce guidami" and "Coppia iniqua," from Donizetti's *Anna Bolena*. The second part began with songs by Brahms and Richard Strauss; then Miss Barlow changed into a black robe and boldly essayed a full dramatic enactment of the heroine's first monologue in *Elektra*. Miss Barlow, who has sung Leonore, Isolde, and Marina (in *Boris Godunov*) at the Metropolitan and has been engaged there for Elektra next season, has a secure, powerful, and well-schooled soprano. She is the kind of honest, solidly reliable singer, definite in intention and definite about the actual notes, that is becoming increasingly rare. (Florence Easton, a Turandot and Isolde versatile enough to be Puccini's first Lauretta, in *Gianni Schicchi*, was an exemplar of the breed.) There is not much sensuous allure in Miss Barlow's firm, strong tone, and no trace of dainty charm in her heroic manner. Yet I feel that I could go to hear her even in so apparently inappropriate a role as Verdi's Violetta or Puccini's Mimì with the assurance that nothing would be fudged or shirked. She drew long, clear lines. She plainly knew the meaning of everything she sang, and how to express it. The Donizetti, its coloratura sounded and not fluttered through, revealed an agility that most sopranos lose when they have graduated to Isolde and Brünnhilde. Town Hall gave its usual acoustic welcome to both soft-breathed, shapely confidences, in Brahms's "Von ewiger Liebe" and the full-throated, passionate outbursts of the *Elektra* monologue.

Catherine Malfitano's recital in Tully Hall, the next day, was a family affair. Her father (and teacher), Joseph, played violin obbligatos in Mozart's "Schon lacht der holde Frühling" (done in an unattributed arrangement for voice, violin, and piano) and Adam's "Ah, vous dirai-je" variations, and the accompaniment in voice-and-violin songs by Vaughan Williams, Alan Hovhaness, and Villa-Lobos. Her sister Elena, an active little modern dancer, danced to the Bach Chaconne, played by her father and choreographed, not happily, by Elena herself and her mother, Maria. The event could be dismissed as a cozy domestic celebration—were it not that Miss Malfitano, a City Opera Mimi and Liù, may have in her the makings of an important singer. She came on like a little girl dressed for a party, in a hoop dress of ivory and rose, with rosebuds in her hair, and sang her first numbers—the Mozart, Adèle's air from Rossini's *Le Comte Ory*, and "Ah, non credea" and "Ah, non giunge," from *La sonnambula*—like party pieces carefully learned. There was no sense of character or of situation (the elegant plaint of Rossini's Countess was delivered in the heartbroken accents of Mozart's), no rhythmic vitality in the long spans or supple molding of small rhythmic displacements within a phrase. But the sound of the voice was very attractive, clear, and sweet, with soft notes "like the sighing of a zephyr, yet all heard" (as Queen Victoria once wrote of Jenny Lind's "Ah, non credea") and ample, healthy loud notes. I felt that she could with profit study Patti's record of "Ah, non credea" and Tetrazzini's of "Ah, non giunge" to learn from the first expressive rubato and from the second bounciness. And then, during her next item, the Adam Variations, I wondered whether she had perhaps been studying Beverly Sills's record of the piece, since she brought to it the charm and variety that had been missing before. In the second half—it was that kind of evening—she returned in an elaborate Sicilian-looking dress of lace and fringes, such as Lola (in *Cavalleria rusticana*) sometimes goes to Mass in. Vaughan Williams's *Along the Field* cycle, already an odd compound of A. E. Housman's fastidiously donned and V.W.'s more natural ruralism, took on a new, rich color from Miss Malfitano's lustrously Latin interpretation; the result was surprising but curiously attractive. Hovhaness's *Hercules* was stirring, and gave one a fuller idea of Miss Malfitano's powers. In the composer's words, "The soprano becomes the voice of a priestess or an oracle. . . . A feeling of wildness pervades the music." She sang the dramatic piece in consistently beautiful tones, passionately shaded. I felt that I should like to have a recording (and discovered later that there is one, on Musical Heritage Society 1976; but there Miss Malfitano gives a less vividly inflected performance). Jolly kitsch, a sort of tribute to Carmen Miranda, with both sisters dancing, Catherine singing, and Joseph fiddling—music by Villa-Lobos—ended the show. Miss Malfitano needs guidance, but she certainly has a voice.

Régine Crespin's recital of French songs, in Carnegie Hall, two days later, also turned into an act. Not in the first half, when two or three songs each from Debussy, Roussel, Chausson, Poulenc, and Duparc were done with a grace, a purity of style, and a beautiful pronunciation of the words to make one tolerant of some threadbare notes at the top of the voice. The second half began with a composite *bestiaire*. The Swan from Ravel's *Histoires naturelles* was poetic, and his Guinea Hen was appropriately perky. But then, as Chabrier's Little Ducks and Manuel Rosenthal's Elephant, Dog Fido, and English Lady-Mouse followed in procession, the singer's manner became broader and broader. Mme Crespin is an accomplished and witty diseuse, and admittedly she made me laugh; it was probably the sheer size of Carnegie Hall, and the need to signal the jokes to an audience unprovided with French texts, that led her into unseemly exaggeration. Offenbach *opérette* came next. The voice was by now flowing more freely, and the program ended with a ringing high A, the first of the evening, from the Grand Duchess of Gerolstein. Half the recital had been encore pieces. The audience wanted more. Mme Crespin returned and, with a gesture of those beautiful hands to indicate "Enough of such nonsense," she sang Wagner's "Schmerzen" with glowing intensity. She is an excellent entertainer; but I should have preferred to hear her, in the intimacy of Town Hall, singing a less motley program. I appreciate the fine acoustics and civilized atmosphere of Carnegie Hall. A single performer can command it. Earlier this season, I heard Donald Gramm hold a large audience intent on Ives's "Ich grolle nicht," Rostropovich on Britten's Third Suite for solo cello, and Galina Vishnevskaya on songs by Tchaikovsky and Mussorgsky. And it is good that large audiences were able to enjoy those artists. Nevertheless, in each case the impact of the music, and of its interpretation, was somewhat diminished by the size of the auditorium.

A program book at a song recital should provide the texts, and literal English translations where necessary. It should supply the poets' names as well as the composers'. It should indicate the context of numbers that are taken from collections or from larger works. Miss Barlow's and Mme Crespin's program leaflets contained only epitomes or translations, and no mention of the poets. (During Miss Barlow's recital, the lights were turned out, so such words as were printed were not of much use anyway.) Miss Malfitano's was a little better. It gave the composers' dates, if not those of the works, and full texts for at least the Vaughan Williams and Hovhaness compositions. The designers of Miss Barlow's and Miss Malfitano's dresses were named. So, of course, were the accompanists—and if I have not referred to them, it is only because they were unremarkable. (Of those earlier recitalists mentioned, Mme Vishnevskaya did have a remarkable accompanist, in the person of Mr. Rostropovich; and her admirable program book contained complete translations—if not the original Russian—with the poets duly named.) I have seen the program book for Elisabeth Schwarzkopf's New York farewell recital, in Carnegie Hall, later this week. It contains all the necessary information, and is almost a model of the kind of thing that audiences should be able to take for granted. "Almost" only because Walter Legge's brief, illuminating introductions to the individual songs have been bunched up at the front and not dropped in where they belong.

May 5, 1975

151

SINGERS, SINGERS, SINGERS!

Anonymous letters I throw into the wastepaper basket without a second glance. But a phrase of complaint from one of them recurs to me now: "Singers, singers, singers!" It came from a correspondent unwilling to accept that most music is vocal music, and that most writing about music reflects the fact. There was a time, earlier this century, when youth was taught to regard sung music as somehow inferior to the "real thing," the "pure" music of orchestra or string quartet. That was before Bach's cantatas, Haydn's and Handel's and Monteverdi's operas, and in general the music of the seventeenth, sixteenth, fifteenth, and earlier centuries became part of the living repertory. I dropped into a library to scan the shelves and see which famous composers, besides Beethoven, Chopin, and Brahms, had not covered most of their pages with music involving singers, singers, singers! Well, there is Stravinsky; most of his music was written for dancers, not singers. Of the eighteen volumes of Schubert's collected works, only five are instrumental and twelve are vocal (one is mixed). Schumann in thirty volumes divides equally—fifteen each of instrumental and vocal. Brahms was a surprise: of his twenty-six volumes, a full ten are vocal. Throw in Byrd, Purcell, Rameau, Alessandro Scarlatti, Gluck, all the nineteenth-century Russians and Czechs, Wagner and Verdi, Palestrina and Lassus and Josquin, make almost any list of ten or twenty great composers, and the balance in favor of vocal music is overwhelming. Varèse, Webern, Elliott Carter, Boulez, and Stockhausen are among the few major moderns who have not written prolifically for the voice; among the late-Romantics, Sibelius and Carl Nielsen. The results of the rough survey are not unexpected. Most composers of the past served their apprenticeship in the church or the opera house, or both. Most of the time and money spent on music has gone into one or the other of these institutions. Music itself is an art that developed from the combination of drumbeat (or heartbeat) patterns of time measurement with the melody of speech lifted into articulate song. (When melodious birds sing madrigals, and leviathans their sweet cantilenas of the deep, a drop of dragon's blood could no doubt provide human listeners with their texts.) The art developed far, and discovered that profound things could be "said" without words, but the human voice remained stubbornly at the center of its existence. In most European cities, the opera house is still the main focus of musical attention; the great orchestras independent of theaters—the Berlin Philharmonic, the Amsterdam Concertgebouw—are for the most part of late-nineteenth-century foundation (and they play mostly nineteenth-century music). Things are admittedly different here. In most American cities—Cleveland, Chicago, Boston, Philadelphia, Minneapolis; in fact, all except New York—the orchestra, not the opera, is the main thing. (But of New York's three large regular orchestras, two play nightly in opera houses during the season.) Demotic music continues to use words.

It happens that wordless "drum music," made by the Percussion Ensemble of the Juilliard School, provided one of the most exciting concerts of recent weeks. But that can be reviewed later, together with a companion concert by the Brooklyn College Percussion Ensemble. Bach and Handel wrote most of their greatest music for singers, and the cantatas of the one, the operas of the other, have come to be a necessary part of our musical sustenance. I regret having missed the regular Sunday series of Bach cantatas in Holy Trinity Lutheran Church, on Central Park West, and will try to make good the omission soon. A concert of four Bach cantatas, given last month in the Metropolitan Museum by the Musica Sacra Orchestra and Chorus, under Richard Westenburg, was disappointing. It looked promising. The Medieval Sculpture Court of the museum is a venue of suitable size, if not so resonant as St. Thomas's in Leipzig, or as Central Presbyterian Church on Park Avenue (where I had last heard the Musica Sacra group). But it was jam-packed with chairs to a point at which propinquity hindered enjoyment of the music. It was plunged into darkness, so that one could not follow the texts. (No texts were provided, in fact—only the opening words of each number and brief English epitomes—but wise Bachians, knowing that the matter of each cantata arises from the Gospel of the day for which it was written, and that words and music must be followed together, would have come armed with texts.) The program book gave no indication of what Gospel was being musically glossed or what season of the church year we were in. Now, even the instrumentalists in a Bach cantata must know exactly what is being said before they can invest their melodies with due expression. If these performances seemed perfunctory and pedestrian, it was because both the executants, not without accomplishment, and the listeners were gliding over the surface of the works, not coming to grips with their meaning. I urge Mr. Westenburg to obtain, for future use, Alfred Dürr's series of introductions to the cantatas. We are not eighteenth-century Lutheran Leipzigers, but Dr. Dürr's notes, while presenting the latest and often astonishing results of Bach research, can help to persuade us for a time that we are. Why gather for a concert—given, more often than not, with women singers substituted for boys, and on modern instruments—when, text in hand, we can listen to the cantatas on phonograph records, given by authentic forces? Because, with thoughtful preparation and presentation, and in apt surroundings, live performances can draw singers, players, and listeners together into the communal experience that these works were meant to provide.

An authentic sound for Bach's cantatas may be hard to achieve; an authentic sound for Handel's operas is impossible, since we no longer have castratos to take the heroic roles. An enthusiast may find an eighteenth-century theater, equip it with scenery in the eighteenth-century manner, even light it—fire regulations permitting—with lamps and candles, and hire a band playing eighteenth-century instruments or copies thereof; but Nero, Otho, Tamerlane, and Julius Caesar will still have to be played by women *en travesti* or by countertenors (unless we are prepared to hear their music growled out, an octave too low, by baritones). After two centuries of neglect, Handel's operas have returned to the theater, and performance styles for them have been found which attempt, in various ways, to reconcile the conventions of Handel's day and the practicalities of our own. There have been some curious experiments.

To attend a Handel opera this season it was necessary to travel—to Boston, where, in March, the New England Chamber Opera Group staged his *Imeneo* in the Massachusetts College of Art. I have now seen most of Handel's operas on the stage, done in manners that range from the straight verismo favored in Halle, the composer's birthplace, to the flummery with which Franco Zeffirelli decked *Alcina* (for Joan Sutherland, in Venice, Dallas, and London), but had never before seen a production acted out in quite so odd a style as that of the New England *Imeneo*. The program book cited some sentences from Manfred Bukofzer's *Music in the Baroque Era*—among them, "The arias of the *opera seria* provided the composer with only one basic affection and ruled out the detailed description of single words." The second statement, at least, is questionable, and in any case Handel's genius resists the rigid application of general rules. But Rafael de Acha, the director of *Imeneo*, evidently set out to illustrate the sentence. He asked his singers to strike fancy poses and hold them throughout the arias, singing the while with deadpan faces. They, as it happened, were too sensitive to the dramatic power of Handel's music to maintain the style with complete consistency, but were obedient enough to diminish the emotional force of a little masterpiece in which the composer, as Winton Dean has remarked, "tells us far more about human nature than we could ever guess from the libretto."

Imeneo, Handel's penultimate opera, has a small band (just oboes and bassoons with the strings and harpsichord), a small cast (five singers), no elaborate scenic requirements, and no subplot. In 1740, it was announced in the London *Daily Post* as an operetta. There are none of the high, grand, heroic aspects of the earlier operas but, instead, a directness and a naturalness that make *Imeneo* uncommonly attractive and affecting. The heroine, Rosmene, hesitates between Tirintius, who has both her love and her promise, and Hymeneus (Imeneo), who has saved her (and, with her, all the maidens of Athens) from a band of pirates and claims her hand as his reward. Torn between love and public duty, and unwilling to offend either suitor, Rosmene feigns a mad scene—a brief but powerful piece of music—in which she pretends that Fate has declared for Hymeneus. So Duty triumphs, and the final chorus points the moral: "Consulting duty, a noble soul or heart pays no attention to its desires and follows reason, banishing any love that does not conform to reason." Handel, regretting that it should be so, writes a sad chorus in the minor. For a Dublin revival, he increased the poignancy of the scene by inserting a duet, "Per le porte del tormento" (borrowed from *Sosarme*), for Rosmene and, not the titular hero, but the rejected Tirintius. In this skillful libretto—adapted, by an unidentified poet, from one that Silvio Stampiglia wrote for the composer Porpora twelve years earlier—the possibility of a happy ending is kept open until the last. The soubrette, Clomiris, who loves Hymeneus, could have been used to effect the customary double pairing. But instead of banal convention we have only one satisfied lover, Hymeneus. The Argument prefixed to the 1740 libretto tells us that, having won Rosmene, "he liv'd happy with her the rest of his Life." Whether Rosmene lived happy, too, is open to question.

There was much to commend in the Boston performance. Philip Morehead, the conductor, directed a little band of baroque instruments, and did so pleasingly, except when he treated minuet rhythms with too deliberate and even an emphasis. (Ideally, however, more strings than Mr. Morehead's seven are needed to realize Handel's textural variety.) The singers were clear and definite, true in pitch, and accomplished in divisions. Susan Larson was the Rosmene, Kimberly Daniel the Clomiris (she produced a beautiful measured trill, on the upper G, in the reprise of her aria "E si vaga"), D'Anna Fortunato the Tirintius (the castrato role), and Thomas Olsen the Hymeneus (a tenor, as Handel originally intended, though he recast the role for a bass before the first performance). The fifth character, Argenius, Clomiris's father and Rosmene's guardian, is a subaltern role with only one aria. Stanley Wexler, the Boston Argenius, appropriated a second, which should be Hymeneus's entrance aria and serves to establish his stern, stiff character. Unwarranted tinkering. In other ways the edition was even less acceptable. Handel's structure is dramatically and musically sound. But here the Act II finale was moved to the close of Act I. Act II ended with the aria that is supposed to open Act III. The delightfully ironic and humorous device of both suitors' addressing Rosmene in identical strains was omitted, and only the subsequent duettino, in which they combine in canon, was retained. Conductor and director had produced a singable English translation (with some happy pilfering from the

155

translation by Brian Trowell and Nigel Fortune, used for the opera's first modern revival, in Birmingham, England, fourteen years ago), but the somber, moving finale was quite spoiled by their textual imposition of a pointless "Give me your hands, if we be friends" envoy. James Sellers's décor was apt and simple; the scene changes were archly effected by "two blackamoors," Swami Amrit and Swami Harideva, supplied with the compliments of the Chaotic Meditation–Joy of Movement Center. In general, a mixture of silliness, perception, and admirable singing marked the presentation. There was more than enough of the last two to reward a convinced Handelian, but doubters of the ability of Handel's operas to hold the modern stage probably remained doubtful.

Mr. de Acha was also the director of a production of Mozart's *Idomeneo*, given in the hall of Jonathan Edwards College at Yale, that was dramatically so inept that it would pass unnoticed here did not the exceptionally fine conducting of C. William Harwood deserve a word. Mr. Harwood is the conductor of the Yale Symphony. He handled the miraculous score boldly, gracefully, and sensitively, and at several points molded it, I felt, even more eloquently than Julius Rudel did in the recent City Opera production. Mozart conductors who can give just the right shade of emphasis to a fleeting modulation, neither forcing it on one's attention nor letting it slide past unnoticed, and who can invest a phrase with subtle rhythmic freedom yet not distort the meter, are rare; Mr. Harwood is one of them. There was full, lyrical singing, fresh and pure in tone, delicately accomplished in phrasing, from Susan Davenny Wyner, as Ilia, and Jack Litten compassed the fiendish coloratura of Idomeneus's "Fuor del mar" more fleetly than his New York counterpart. The edition had some points of interest. Mr. Harwood took up Daniel Heartz's suggestion (in the new *Idomeneo* score) of dropping in the gavotte from the ballet music before the final chorus of Act I; it sounded fine there (though the dancing it accompanied was absurd). Despite having chosen a tenor rather than a soprano Idamantes, he used the original (two-soprano) duet of Act III, which has a wonderfully eloquent first section; but the subsequent 6/8 allegretto cannot compare with the soprano-tenor duet that Mozart later put in its place. Ilia was allowed the recitative that opens Act III (denied her by the City Opera). But she was also allowed applause after "Se il padre perdei," the Act II aria, which should not be (here, singer and conductor must between them insure that Mozart's music flows unbroken). Yale has a celebrated School of Drama, and a School of Music whose opera performances are praised. But none of their teaching seemed to have rubbed off on this staging, which, even when all allowances were made for the hall's meager theatrical resources and the amateur status of the chorus, was simply deplorable. A connoisseur of misconceived *Idomeneo* productions gained a new specimen for his collection. A lover of the music found the evening well spent.

May 12, 1975

Alfred Dürr's cantata-by-cantata notes are collected in Die Kantaten von Johann Sebastian Bach *(Bärenreiter, two paperback volumes). Even more helpful, to concert audiences, are the many cantata notes he has provided over the years for the program books of the English Bach Festival.*

THE DOUBLE DOUBLE DOUBLE BEAT
OF THE THUND'RING DRUM

There are ancient African and Far Eastern musics sounded entirely by families of percussion instruments. In the West, recitals by percussion ensembles—there were two at Lincoln Center last month—are a fairly new thing. Compositions like Pierre Boulez's *Le Marteau sans maître*, Olivier Messiaen's *Et exspecto resurrectionem mortuorum*, and Hans Werner Henze's *El Cimarrón* call for a new breed of percussion players, adepts on a dozen and more Eastern and Afro-Cuban instruments. Virtuosos of our day inspired the composers (*Et exspecto* was written with Les Batteurs de Strasbourg and the sonorities of their famous battery in mind; around Stomu Yamash'ta, who is dancer, acrobat, mime, and percussionist in one, *El Cimarrón* was created), and now the compositions that resulted inspire new performers. A few years ago, I spent two weeks in Shiraz and Persepolis, listening for hours every day to percussion from all over the world: to drummers from Africa, Iran, India, and the United States; to varieties of dulcimer (zither, santir, cimbalom) from a dozen countries. I heard a Balinese gamelan one night and the Strasbourg Battery in Iannis Xenakis's latest "stochastic" composition the next; watched the Professor of Percussion from Bloomington, Indiana, teach a group of village children, wordlessly, how to clash stones in simple and then increasingly complex rhythms; attended group improvisations in which players from different cultures picked up, exchanged, and modified one another's rhythmic patterns; and learned, in general, how vividly music could be made without melody. These were new sounds, new timbres, and new musical shapes. Debussy was fascinated by new sounds when a gamelan visited Paris for the Great

157

Exhibition of 1889. Benjamin Britten brought new sounds back from the East and put them into his ballet *The Prince of the Pagodas* and his church parables. The assimilation of exotic percussion has been a recurrent feature of Western musical history.

Percussion entered Western music as the accompaniment to action—marking rhythms to dance to, or rhythms to march to. Drum and dance go together in the Bible. After the crossing of the Red Sea, "Miriam the prophetess, the sister of Aaron, took a timbrel in her hand; and all the women went out after her with timbrels and with dances." The Psalmist tells us to praise the Lord with the timbrel and dance. The Greeks had timbrels, cymbals, and castanets, which, the authorities tell us, they banged and clashed "mostly in the orgiastic cults of Cybele and Dionysus." Kettledrums, nakers, Islam's *naqquāra* were introduced to Europe by the Crusaders. At first, their use was military. Drum calls preceded bugle calls as army signals; in Dryden's words, "The double double double beat / Of the thund'ring DRUM / Cryes, heark the Foes come; / Charge, Charge." Edward III entered Calais in 1347 to the sound of "trumpets, tabours, nakquayres & hornyes," but it was not until the late seventeenth century that Matthew Locke, in London, and Lully, in Paris, added kettledrums to the civilian orchestra. Once there, they stayed. Purcell wrote a brief solo for kettledrums in *The Fairy Queen* (1692); in 1733, Bach began his cantata *Tönet, ihr Pauken* ("Sound, Ye Kettledrums") with another; in Handel's *Semele* (1744), the solemnity of Jove's vow is underscored by a solo on two drums. By the mid-eighteenth century, Johann Melchior Molter, in his Symphony No. 99, was writing melodic lines for a set of five kettledrums, and the way was open for the kettledrum devices of Beethoven, Berlioz, and Meyerbeer.

Meanwhile, the eighteenth-century craze for "Turkish music" brought the bass drum and cymbals, the triangle, and other jingles and clashes into Western orchestras. In *Die Entführung*, Mozart used "Turkish music" for picturesque local color; Haydn claimed it for the concert hall in the "Military" Symphony; Beethoven elevated it, as an energetic expression of joy unbounded, in the finale of the Ninth. The next large wave of new percussion sounds broke over Europe only in the second decade of our own century, when—as Percy Scholes rather sniffily put it—"in the universal weakening of social conventions, Afro-American elaborations of rhythm and noise, suited to the dances of the period, were carried over the world and, under the influence of a highly commercialized sophistication, still further elaborated." The instruments soon lost their locative connotations. Stravinsky used a güira (a Latin-American gourd with a notched surface over which a stick is scraped) in *The Rite of Spring*; Prokofiev used the maracas of South and Central America in his patriotic Russian cantata *Alexander Nevsky*. Two movements of Milhaud's *Les Choëphores*, composed in 1915 and first performed in 1919, are for narrator, chorus, and percussion orchestra. Primacy of Western concert music played by percussion instruments alone is claimed for the last two of the six *Rítmicas* by the Cuban composer Amadeo Roldán; they were first performed, in Havana, in 1930. But the *Rítmicas* are no more than brief studies in Cuban dance patterns. In 1929, Edgard Varèse began, and in 1931 completed, his substantial *Ionisation*, the classic of the genre, and a work in which Eastern, Western, and Afro-Cuban instruments combine.

Ionisation was the climax of the concert given, in the Juilliard Theater, by the Percussion Ensemble of the Juilliard School, conducted by Saul Goodman. The piece was accorded a strong, steady, and very impressive performance. In Varèse's earlier *Amériques, Offrandes, Hyperprism, Intégrales*, and *Arcana*, percussion plays a very important role; in *Ionisation* it takes over completely. This is a music of timbres and rhythms that has no roots in the classical or romantic traditions, no program that can be verbalized, no links with any spoken language. When I was asked to suggest what Western music could be performed in the palace of Persepolis and neither be dwarfed in a setting that combines huge natural majesty with ancient imperial splendors nor seem exotic there, before an audience gathered from East and West, I could think only of Varèse's compositions. His music, whether for large forces (the hundred and twenty players of *Arcana*) or small (the single flutist of *Density 21.5*), would be seemly there. For it is "absolute"—untied to the vocal inflections and song-influenced instrumental melodies of the West, linked neither to place nor to period. Rhythms are not of universal significance (try teaching Balinese musicians to play in three-quarter time; the notion seems to them absurd), but Varèse's music is the most nearly universal I know. *Ionisation* can be analyzed and charted; one can note the moments when the orchestra plays only on instruments of metal, and when, in the coda, instruments of definite pitch—bells, glockenspiel, the piano treated percussively—strike in for the first time. But a Varèse chart explains little. Varèse performances prompt assertions, such as Virgil Thomson's, after hearing *Hyperprism*: "Your listener found it absorbing, convincing, beautiful, and in every way grand. . . . I know it is great music."

The Juilliard program was skillfully assembled to lead up to *Ionisation*, to avoid monotony of timbre, and to show percussion in many moods. Michael Colgrass's *Three Brothers*, which began it, is a beguiling essay of Afro-Cuban inspiration for nine drummers drumming—three soloists (bongos, snare drum, kettledrums), and six other players pattering a background. Robert Hall Lewis's Toccata for violin and two percussion revealed a richness and aptness in the combination of instruments that would have surprised me had I not, in Persepolis, admired

Betsy Jolas's concerto composed for solo violin and the Strasbourg Battery. Susan Lang was the violinist in the Lewis piece, David Fein and Scott Eddlemon were the percussionists, and all three were highly accomplished. Mr. Eddlemon then took the piano part in John Cage's *Amores*—two solos for prepared piano framing two delicate percussion trios, one of the neatest and most attractive Cage compositions. Lester Trimble's *Quadraphonics* (*Panels VI*), for four percussionists, closed the first part with inventions of many colors. The second part began with divertissements: Bach's D-minor Toccata and Fugue transcribed for marimba, his D-minor Chaconne transcribed for vibraphone, and Barber's Adagio for Strings transcribed for three marimbas, eight hands. The Juilliard students showed their skills; Mr. Eddlemon, now marimba soloist in the Toccata and Fugue, was the star. Mr. Goodman played his own "Ballad for the Dance" on kettledrums; and then the full ensemble mustered for *Ionisation*. Everything conspired to provide an enjoyable evening. The lighting was carefully planned. The "scene shifts" between numbers—moving the picturesque apparatus into new groupings—were trimly achieved. Thought had been given to what the players wore.

The Juilliard ensemble was on its home ground. When the Brooklyn College Percussion Ensemble, directed by Morris Lang, moved into Alice Tully Hall, a few days later, to present a Manhattan concert, it did not manage the extramusical trappings half so well. Percussion events are usually, and properly, something of a show. The glinting instruments would have looked good set out beneath the gleaming pipes of the new organ—but on this occasion the organ was hidden away behind shutters. The platform was used in its narrow size, unextended, which meant a clutter on the stage, not the elegant scenic effects of the Juilliard event. The lighting was ordinary. The audience was smaller. (Admission was three or five dollars, whereas the Juilliard concert was free.)

The first work of the evening—Karlheinz Stockhausen's *Kreuzspiel*, for piano, oboe, bass clarinet, and three percussionists—came off best, in a sensitive, carefully balanced performance. Jacob Druckman's *Animus II*, done later in the program, is a piece of sexy music theater for a mezzo-soprano temptress, two percussionists who work out on their instruments the feelings she arouses in them, and an electronic tape. I described a Juilliard student performance, in the Juilliard Theater, two year ago [*A Musical Season*, pp. 300–1]. The Brooklyn group had the same alluring singer, Barbara Martin; in other ways, its version was not comparable, for the players seemed more intent on their scores than on the girl, and so the drama of the action, which moves back and forth through the hall, was reduced. Mr. Lang himself played Elliott Carter's Four Pieces for Kettledrums on instruments whose tone rattled in fortissimo in the "Recitative" and whose tuning pedals creaked noisily in the

"Canto." His handling of note values in the "Improvisation" was cavalier. Three other works were for larger ensemble: David Loeb's *Nocturnes and Meditations* for nine players, Marta Ptaszynska's *Siderals* for ten, and Irwin Bazelon's *Propulsions* for seven. The Loeb consists of three fragments of mood music, vaguely Oriental in effect; in the first two, mainly the " 'phones and 'spiels" are used; drums are added to the third. The outer movements of the Ptaszynska were noisy and conventional, but in the central panel pretty sounds were stroked from musical glasses and, with bows, from cymbals and gongs, and curious sounds were coaxed from an instrument that looked like an ice bucket and lowed like a cow. In the finale there was an enthusiastic free-for-all climax, everybody crashing away; and another in the Bazelon.

Perhaps the most famous bass-drum strokes in Western music are those near the beginning of the Dies irae of Verdi's Requiem (where the player is instructed to have the strings on his drum good and tight, so that the syncopated thumps will be "dry and very loud") and then those that punctuate the bass solo, "Mors stupebit," later in the movement (where, having slackened the strings, the player produces a dull, dead thud, *ppp*). In the mezzo solo that follows, "Liber scriptus," a kettledrum fills the pauses of the vocal line with an ominously muttering figure, which Verdi had tried before, in the (subsequently discarded) duet for Elizabeth and Eboli in *Don Carlos*. These percussion details, like all the other instrumental details of the score, were realized with the utmost finesse and precision in the performance of the Requiem that Georg Solti and the Chicago Symphony Orchestra and Chorus brought to Carnegie Hall on the last day of April. Instrumentally and—apart from an occasional weakness in the bass line—chorally, it was a blazing interpretation. Gwynne Howell, the bass, was the best of the four solo singers. Luciano Pavarotti was unwontedly tight in tone. Yvonne Minton, the mezzo, was secure but not magical. Leontyne Price tended to go her own, impulsive way rather than mold her interpretation and her dynamics to the rest.

May 19, 1975

For what may be an earlier use of kettledrums in the civilian orchestra —in the intermedio The Rare Triumphs of Love and Fortune *(London, 1589)—see Robert Weaver's "Sixteenth-Century Instrumentation," in* The Musical Quarterly, *47 (1961), p. 375. For their early use in church orchestras, see R .M. Lockyear's "Some Aspects of 16th-Century Terminology and Practice," in the* Journal of the American Musicological Society, *12 (1964), pp. 197–8.*

MUSIC OF OUR MAY

May, it seems, is the most fecund month for new music in New York. First performances are busting out all over, and a conflict of concerts attractive to a listener is bound to occur at times. But when—as happened on Monday last week—programs by the Speculum Musicae, the Composers Theater, and the League of Composers/International Society for Contemporary Music (United States Section), each of the three containing premières, are coincident, planning is agley, and the result is tertiation of the potential audience at each. (The same day, there was also a pair of Composers' Showcase concerts at the Whitney Museum, devoted to the theater music of Leonard Bernstein, but their appeal was doubtless to a different crowd.) Similarly, but worse, for Tuesday this week the bills showed the Group for Contemporary Music, the Juilliard School, Richard Teitelbaum, Steve Reich, and Carla Hübner all competing for much the same contemporary-music audience. Most of the organizations concerned receive funds from the New York State Council on the Arts. So does the Center for New Music, an office set up to coordinate activities in the field. The Council would presumably like the concerts it supports to be not merely played but heard by many interested listeners. So I hope its music officers are preparing to knock the Council clients' heads together in good time to prevent wasteful clashes next season.

On busy Monday, I chose, perhaps undaringly, to go to Alice Tully Hall and hear the Composers Theater event. It proved to be devoted to music of what might be called middle-guard composers. There is a place for them in the musical life of every country—these erstwhile venturers into territories then unfamiliar, and the younger men still content to work yesterday's fields. Measured words, even appreciative words, about decent, soundly made middle-of-the-road compositions provide dull reading; a critic who feels neither enthusiasm nor wrath should at least be brief. I heard Karel Husa's Poem for Viola and Orchestra at its first performance, fifteen years ago, at the ISCM Festival in Cologne. It was a point of repose then between adventures instigated by Karlheinz Stockhausen, György Ligeti, Mauricio Kagel, Sylvano Bussotti, and Nam June Paik. At the Composers Theater concert, in its New York première, it again sounded unadventurous but completely agreeable, in its temperately romantic way. By Walter Trampler the solo part was very beautifully played. Ezra Laderman's Violin Concerto, first performed in 1951 and then, reorchestrated, over CBS Television in 1963, is a work of greater variety and distinction than were apparent in the monochrome performance given by Gerald Tarack and the Composers Festival Orchestra, conducted by Alvin Brehm. Although Laderman uses an orchestra without violins, his score need not sound, as it did here, constantly somber. Walter Ross's Trombone Concerto, which ended the concert, was colorful, and effective in an obvious sort of way; this was also a local première. The new works were John Herbert McDowell's *Practical Magic*, subtitled "A Brief Concerto for Orchestra," a cheerful assemblage of fragments in popular vein; and John Watts's *Laugharne* (the name of the little town where Dylan Thomas is buried), a memorial that sets three French poems (not by Thomas) for soprano, orchestra, and an "atmospheric" tape background such as accompanies pan shots over bleak, windswept headlands. It was not exactly an exciting event; the word "Festival," applied to this concert and another, a week later (promising a new work by Roger Hannay and old works by Wallingford Riegger, Vincent Persichetti, Otto Luening and Vladimir Ussachevsky, and Leon Kirchner), seemed inappropriate. But if the evening was not festive, it was at least respectable. The epithet has acquired damning overtones; I intend it in the precise sense of deserving respect.

Two days earlier, in Carnegie Recital Hall, the New Structures Ensemble introduced Matthias Kriesberg's setting of Dylan Thomas's *Not from This Anger*, for tenor and eight instrumentalists. The cantata, an imaginative and delicately scored piece of work, deserved its public hearing, and Steven Algie was a cogent soloist. Two other works were worth hearing, too; Krzysztof Penderecki's *Strophes* and Stefan Wolpe's Sonata for oboe and piano. But both needed more incisive execution. Charles Wuorinen's *Making Ends Meet*, for piano duet, and Maurice Wright's Chamber Symphony for seven instruments, a first performance, proved intolerably dull; were the players or the composers to blame for the monotony of texture and the absence of any compelling musical incident? Nineteen artists were engaged in the concert, and there were maybe thirty-eight auditors in the hall. Unhealthy proportion. I suspect that central Manhattan may be overstocked with events of this kind; the next week or two will show.

Jean-Philippe Rameau is the genius the Metropolitan and the City Opera do wrong to ignore. (Not that they are the only troupes at fault; Covent Garden, Glyndebourne, and, for that matter, the Paris Opera itself are equally neglectful.) As a candidate for regular exposure on the modern stage, his great predecessor Jean-Baptiste Lully is harder to champion. Lully is important. Voltaire deemed him "the father of true French music," and the line from him to those other Italian creators of French grand opera—Cherubini, Spontini, Rossini, Donizetti, and Verdi—runs unbroken. His *tragédies lyriques* proceed in a clear, noble, and spacious manner. They contain some marvelous airs (such as Cadmus's "Belle Hermione, hélas! hélas!," Charon's lively patter as he collects the

163

ferry fares in *Alceste*, "Bois épais" from *Amadis*)—airs, as Burney observed, "so easy and natural, that it is hardly possible for a lover of Music, gifted with a voice and disposition for singing, to hear them frequently performed, without remembering them." Yet, despite these bright, memorable episodes, despite the energetic rhythms of the recitatives, despite the strength of the large choruses that are the load-bearing pillars of his dramatic structures, Lully at length can be wearying. Francesco Cavalli, from whom Lully learned so much, had a directness that Lully lacked. Cavalli's characters show more personality and simple warmth in their singing, and his operas now grace our stages. Lully, for the most part, is revived only in studio productions, mounted in countries that have adult broadcasting systems, and in concert performances.

To celebrate their fiftieth anniversary, the Dessoff Choirs, in Alice Tully Hall, performed Lully's massive Te Deum and then the Prologue, Act III, and the Act V finale of his *Amadis*. (*Amadis* was first performed, at the Paris Opera, in 1684, and first performed in America, in Lowell House, Harvard, in 1951.) The sacred piece bears out Manfred Bukofzer's remark that "Lully handled his keys with striking monotony"; variety comes from ringing textural changes with *grand chœur*, *petit chœur*, and soloists in diverse combinations. *Amadís de Gaula*, a romance admired by readers as different as Francis I and Charles V, Ariosto and Montaigne, inspired many composers, and Lully claims to have tackled the subject, suggested to him by Louis XIV, with especial delight. The striking things in the excerpts presented by the Dessoff Choirs were the opening chorus of Act III, for prisoners (among them a chained Florestan) and jailers in alternation; the solemn utterance of a Specter arising reproachfully from his tomb; and the substantial Chaconne from Act V. Most of the solo singing was passable; that of David Britton, in a small tenor role, was distinguished. The chorus was assured. The anonymous orchestra was able, though perhaps a shade top-heavy; Lully's Vingt-Quatre Violons du Roi (not all violins in the modern sense, of course) were disposed, it seems, 6.4.4.4.6 along the five-part texture, while Michael Hammond, the conductor of the Dessoff Choirs, arranged his sixteen players 4.3.3.3.3, mixing violins with violas on inner parts, and using gamba, cello, and double-bass on the bottom line. He adopted an interesting and deliberately inconsistent approach to *notes inégales*, and many small details of the execution evinced an approach to the text both scholarly and imaginative. Mr. Hammond's actual conducting showed a good feeling for the driving rhythms that propel Lully's music. The new organ was brought into play for the Te Deum but was shuttered from sight again during *Amadis*. Is there an acoustical reason for hiding it? The hall looks so much more attractive when it closes the view. A pleasure to report that the program book included a libretto of the *Amadis* excerpts, with Philippe Quinault's

French and an English translation. (Beckmesser adds a line of regret that the pointing, the lineation, and the typographical distinction between lines long and short of Quinault's verses were not more carefully followed.) There were also suggestions for further reading.

In matters textual and contextual, the presentation of Bach's Ascension cantata (No. 11, *Lobet Gott in seinen Reichen*) in Holy Trinity Lutheran Church, on the Sunday after Ascension, can be lauded. The German words and a translation were provided. The pastor spoke a brief program note. The Lesson, on which the cantata text is a gloss and its music a meditation, was read (the music was performed as the center of a vesper service); the organ prelude and postlude were Bach chorale-preludes on hymns sung by the congregation-audience. Women took the boys' parts, which is regrettable but inevitable in most churches today. There were some tension-dropping gaps between recitatives and arias. If the executants, who were in the West gallery, could have listened to themselves down in the nave, they might have striven for still more precise articulation, because the church is resonant and much contrapuntal detail was lost. Nevertheless, not even in Bach's own St. Thomas's, in Leipzig, are his cantatas today performed so meetly.

May 26, 1975

THE SOUNDS OF SUMMER

This in the time of year when the Juilliard School dominates the music making of the city, when its various halls sound daily with carefully prepared recitals and concerts, open without admission charge to the public. Last week's concert in the School's Twentieth Century Music Series, given in the Juilliard Theater by the Juilliard Ensemble, conducted by Richard Dufallo, introduced several interesting pieces to New York. The most substantial was Oliver Knussen's Second Symphony, commissioned from the eighteen-year-old composer for the Windsor Festival of 1970 and first played, in a preliminary, unfinished version, in Windsor Castle that year. Completed, it was heard at Tanglewood in 1971; corrected, in Boston in 1972. Knussen, the son of a double-bass player in the London Symphony Orchestra, came before the public, in 1968, as the youthful composer of a First Symphony that showed exceptional flair and facility; he knew how to handle the materials of music, and did so with gusto. The talented youth has grown

165

into an exceptionally capable and refreshingly undoctrinaire composer. From some points of view, it may seem that the Second Symphony could have been written in Vienna any time during the last half century. It is at once an orthodox four-movement classical symphony (with the scherzo placed second); a tone poem concerned with night thoughts, sleep, and dreams that end at dawn (the final sound is a cadenza for two flutes, marked "very slow and wistful, like distant birds"); and an Expressionist setting, for high soprano, of poems by Georg Trakl and Sylvia Plath. The orchestration is quite small—double woodwind, two horns, twenty-two strings—but there is much divided and solo writing for the string players, and the score (published by G. Schirmer) reveals a fine ear for delicate, intricate, carefully distinguished yet unfussy textures. The look of the pages suggests someone who has just discovered the marvels of middle Schoenberg; the sound of the piece reveals a young man with plenty of ideas of his own and an assured technique for their communication. In Doreen DeFeis the Juilliard performance had a remarkable and sensitive young soprano, who can leap without effort to the Queen of Night's high F and sustain it with sweet, true tone.

Australian musical life is probably as stimulatingly creative as any to be found today. Barry Conyngham, born in 1944, is one among many young composers brought forward by the country's combination of inspiring teachers, prompt performances, public interest, ready official patronage, and a good broadcasting system. Conyngham's *Water . . . Footsteps . . . Time*, given its American première at this Juilliard concert but composed in 1970 and already recorded, must count as an early work of his. It contains elements of picturesque self-indulgence that he has outgrown. But it remains an attractive piece, his response to a Japanese stay and to study with Toru Takemitsu. Australian music is healthily open to winds from Europe, from America, and from the Orient. Rather as, in Sydney's botanical gardens, flora from all the world seem to have rooted and flourished amid the indigenous splendors (or, on a culinary level, the arts of France, Italy, and the East join with a bounteous nature to inspire the city's restaurants), so musical seeds from, say, Boulez, Stockhausen, Maxwell Davies have fallen on fertile ground there. Elliott Carter may lie behind Conyngham's *Dialogues for String Trio* and his *Lyric Dialogues* of 1967. Japanese sounds, Japanese dreams lie behind *Water . . . Footsteps . . . Time*, but also the cosmopolitan excitements of Expo '70 in Osaka (for which Conyngham wrote *Horizon*, performed in the Australian Pavilion). The piece is for four soloists—harp, guitar, piano, and gong—and orchestra. The large gong, used in ways that recall Stockhausen, is especially important, and it was played upon with resource and finesse by Barry Jekowsky.

166

At this concert, Charles Ives's *Chorale for Strings in Quartertones*, a "lost" work reconstructed by Alan Stout from the third of the *Quartertone Pieces for Two Pianos*, also had its New York première; defined by two keyboards, the novel harmonies are easier to hear than from a string ensemble. Orchestrated versions of Elliott Carter's early songs "Warble for Lilac-Time" and "Voyage"—the first curiously close to Michael Tippett in its ebullient springtime figuration—were also New York firsts. The piano-accompanied originals let the voice through more readily. Flagstad, or Dame Clara Butt, seemed to be needed in the new version of *Voyage*; Faith Esham, admired on other occasions as a clear and attractive soprano, had difficulty in making the vocal line dominate. The concert began with David Diamond's *Elegy in Memory of Maurice Ravel*, a strong, somber pavane for brass, harp, and percussion, composed just after Ravel's death; it was nobly played.

A first theatrical encounter with *Benvenuto Cellini*, Berlioz's first opera, tends to be a heady affair. A listener swept along by the colors and rhythms of the Roman carnival, and caught up in the surge of romance, irreverence, and passionate high spirits, does not stop to question. I first met the opera in small theaters: the Carl Rosa troupe played it up and down Britain for several seasons from 1957 onward; the Holland Festival did it, in 1961, with Nicolai Gedda as the hero. It was a larger production—John Dexter's at Covent Garden, in 1966—that then forced upon my notice how ill-constructed, inconsistent, and, by any nice dramaturgical tenets, unsatisfactory an opera it is. Thus, with *Cellini*, I moved into the customary second stage of Berlioz appreciation, when joy in the achievement is tempered by judicious regrets that the glorious music is so often poured into ramshackle molds. Some people never leave this stage (I'm still in it so far as *Béatrice et Bénédict* is concerned); "flawed, erratic genius" is the regular judgment of most nineteenth-century and much twentieth-century comment. But there are two further, alternative stages. One leads to blind, ardent championship, which proclaims as sheer mastery what others have deemed muddle and is prepared to defend even the structure of *Lélio*; the other to exhilaration undamped by a sane recognition that not every one of Berlioz's works is a faultlessly constructed masterpiece. Unreasonable advocacy can harm a man's cause as severely as his foes, but many of the newer claims made for Berlioz were just, and validated in performance: when, for example, great conductors revealed that the notorious "miscalculations" of his orchestration—the far-flung bass trombones and flutes of the Requiem, the shrill, unfounded scurry that opens *Les Troyens*—do, in fact, combine (in Wagner's phrase) "daring fantasy and strict precision." All that Berlioz required, it appeared, was excellent and appropriate performance; then there was less talk of his tumid extravagance and more of his technical mastery. The Requiem and the Te Deum sound oddly scored in a dry concert hall but magnificent in a large, resonant church such as they were meant for; the old charges against *Les Troyens* were dropped when, a century after its composition, it was at last heard complete, or very nearly so.

Cellini, Berlioz, Sarah Caldwell, and Jon Vickers were made for one another, and when these fiery spirits met in the Opera Company of Boston's latest production, of *Benvenuto Cellini*, the result was predictably exciting. After experiencing it, I am ready to assert that, despite "miscalculations" obvious to a baby, the opera's claims to performance are stronger than those of a dozen well-made pieces that hold the stages of the world—provided that it gets done with the verve and virtuosity that marked the Boston presentation. Berlioz tackled his first opera with a recklessness that long kept it from all but a few theaters. The libretto, by Léon de Wailly and Auguste Barbier, is an opéra-comique confection—a string of numbers entertaining, romantic, or picturesque. When the Opéra-Comique rejected it, Berlioz set it to music for the Opéra, where it had a few performances in 1838–39. A dozen years later, Liszt decided to mount the opera in Weimar, and Berlioz worked over the score. But after two or three performances Liszt decided that the last act was "useless" and "only wearied people and sent them to sleep," and so he set his young assistant Hans von Bülow the task of cutting the act and altering the text and music as necessary. (Bülow's contribution to *Cellini* goes generally uncredited, but is mentioned in an 1852 letter of his to his mother.) The composer gave his advice by correspondence. In Weimar, that November, he saw the result (the first of the original two acts had been divided into two) and apparently approved it, for he himself conducted *Cellini* in a similar form at Covent Garden the following year. (It was a fiasco, withdrawn after a single performance.) The story does not end there. The Théâtre-Lyrique, in Paris, planned a production with spoken dialogue in 1856. The project was abandoned, but that year *Cellini* was revived in Weimar (in a new German translation, by Peter Cornelius), and the vocal score of this version was published. In 1863, a French vocal score appeared with the Weimar numbers but cues for dialogue in place of sung recitative. Then *Cellini* disappeared until Bülow conducted a performance at Hanover, in 1879. The Carl Rosa production already mentioned, the 1966 Covent Garden revival, the Philips recording of 1973, and now the Boston presentation have all looked beyond the published scores to combine unpublished music from the original Opéra version, the best of the Weimar revisions, and some passages of spoken dialogue. There is still more music awaiting rediscovery, preserved in the 1838 performance material surviving in the library of the Opéra. The tale of

Cellini will be complete only when the critical full score is published in the New Berlioz Edition and all of it has been heard.

In Boston, Miss Caldwell returned, happily, to the two-act division and, essentially, the original order of numbers in Act II. She reinstated a delightful (unpublished) scherzo ensemble to close Act II, Scene 1. She omitted—and this I regret—all but the cabaletta of the Teresa-Cellini duet in that scene (Liszt did the same), and omitted Cellini's second air, in which he suddenly expresses a yearning to be a simple, solitary shepherd, leading his flock to pasture. The sentiment is surprising, and the air is hard to place convincingly, but the music is beautiful. Except in the awkwardly paced and not very funny divertissement of the carnival scene—Berlioz's clumsiness, not Miss Caldwell's—the Boston version ran swift and sure. Miss Caldwell, both stage and musical director of the show, had solved the main problem of *Cellini*: to reconcile delicacy with dash, and comedy with passionately serious outbursts. One moment, all is mirth, and in opera-buffa fashion a duel is begun; the next, Cellini has killed a man and is in danger of his life. The contradictions crystallize in the figure of the Pope (demoted by the Paris censors to a mere cardinal, but Clement VII once more in most modern productions); the music Berlioz wrote for His Holiness is simultaneously impudent and imposing. Miss Caldwell, in her timing of the grandly pompous entrance, and Donald Gramm, in a beautifully sung impersonation both very funny and very formidable, got the tricky tone exactly right. The hero himself is a man of extremes, musically and emotionally. So, on the stage, is Jon Vickers. He compasses the volatile inconsistency of the firebrand who can cry "To hell with my statue" and think only of elopement with his Teresa, and a few minutes later be prepared to destroy his cherished statue rather than let another hand touch it. Urgent, ardent, heroic, poetic, Mr. Vickers was a thrilling Cellini. His voice lacked suppleness for some of the tender music; the force and fire of his singing were ample compensation. The other characters scarcely break the bounds of opéra comique. Patricia Wells was a pretty Teresa. Nancy Williams was a sprightly Ascanio, Cellini's apprentice. John Reardon (Fieramosca), Gimi Beni (Balducci), Ralph Griffin (doubling as the foreman Bernardino and the bravo Pompeo), and Joseph Evans (Francesco, the other foreman, bright-voiced leader of the male-voice ensembles) were all accomplished.

In the Orpheum Theatre, with scenery by her regular designers, Helen Pond and Herbert Senn, and handsome costumes, by Beni Montresor, borrowed from Covent Garden, Miss Caldwell created a series of animated stage pictures, mounting to the great climax when the statue of Perseus, new-cast, stands triumphantly before us. (The Opéra stage direction, technically more plausible, calls only for a stream of molten metal to rush into the buried mold; the Weimar direction—under Cellini's blows the mold falls away to reveal the Perseus statue, red and incandescent—provides a dramatic resolution more telling than any mere metallurgical accuracy would be.) The very limitations of the theater seem to inspire this company. Although the Orpheum is a large house, seating nearly three thousand in an auditorium well designed to keep an audience in contact with the stage, that stage is shallow, and the wing space is constricted. Miss Pond and Mr. Senn, breaking through the proscenium arch, took the theater's Italianate boxes into the scenes, so that the action could flow outward and upward into the body of the house. On the stage proper, an ingenious and architecturally pleasing set of movable colonnades formed house, piazza, and foundry. There seemed to be plenty of space for a whirl of excitable action. Miss Caldwell's conducting was poised, eloquent, vigorous. The orchestral playing was vivid, the choral singing brave and bright. The opera was given in English—a revised version of Arthur Hammond's translation for the Carl Rosa. All conspired to provide a performance at once spirited and sensitive.

June 2, 1975

Under the impact of an exciting performance, I later found myself very nearly "prepared to defend even the structure of Lélio" *(see pp. 261–3).*

SÄNGERFEST *IN CINCINNATI*

Cincinnati is not *quite* a civilized city, for it has no streetcars any more and must therefore be ranked below such places as Amsterdam, Boston, San Francisco, and Munich. But its Dresdenesque river-girt site amid hills, its parks and trees, its rich museums, its active campus, and the great though now trainless Union Terminal can provide the extramusical rewards sought by a festival visitor. The musical fare at the start of the Cincinnati May Festival was good, too. This is not a festival in the modern European manner. There is no busy round of concerts, recitals, operas, plays, exhibitions all over the town. This year, there was not even any first performance, and the newest music on the bill, Schoenberg's *Gurre-Lieder*, was nearly seventy-five years old. The Festival is a joyous local celebration: not a *Sängerkrieg* but a *Sängerfest* during which many choirs who have been rehearsing all year join their voices

170

under the baton of a celebrated conductor. This year, there were four large choral concerts, grouped in pairs a week apart: *Tannhäuser* and *Gurre-Lieder*, then *Ernani* and *Messiah*. Also, a massed *Messiah* at which all the audience sang.

The May Festival, founded in 1873, is familiar in name at least to all who read musical history and the memoirs of famous singers. *Die Walküre, Götterdämmerung,* and *Parsifal* were very modern operas when Theodore Thomas first gave scenes from them in Cincinnati. *The Dream of Gerontius* and *The Apostles* had early performances there; Elgar came to conduct, Muriel Foster and John Coates to sing. The French composer Gabriel Pierné seems to have become a local favorite; over the years, his oratorios *The Children of Bethlehem* and *St. Francis of Assisi* were given thrice each, and *The Children's Crusade* seven times. But Wagner was always the dominant composer, and most of the celebrated Wagnerian singers made the trip to Cincinnati, from Amalie Materna (Bayreuth's first Brünnhilde, the first Kundry) and Hermann Winkelmann (the first Parsifal), through Lilli Lehmann, Emma Eames, Nordica, Fremstad, Schumann-Heink, Flagstad, and Traubel, to Birgit Nilsson in 1967. The next six Festivals were Wagnerless (apart from a *Rienzi* overture). James Levine, who became musical director last year, has both revived the old Wagnerian tradition and started a new one: the performance of complete operas—last year *Lohengrin,* and now *Tannhäuser.* But he has not been able to find singers such as his predecessors enjoyed. The *Tannhäuser* soloists were undistinguished; Nancy Tatum, Mignon Dunn, and Jon Andrew are not Wagnerian names to set beside those listed above. Miss Tatum was the best of them. Her voice is strong and shiny. The quick ardor of Elisabeth's Greeting and the quiet ardor of the Prayer were both affectingly suggested, and her phrasing was sensitive. Miss Dunn turned Venus's outbursts into strident, curdled cries. Mr. Andrew, Tannhäuser, was stolid and stentorian in a role that needs poetic sensibility. Lawrence Shadur brought coarse, strong tone and bumpy phrasing to Wolfram's music, which calls for the smooth line and eloquent portamento of a great cellist. Simon Estes has a supple, distinctive bass of beautiful quality but his musical manner lacks the authority, the *gravitas,* for the kind of roles—Sarastro, Don Pédro in Meyerbeer's *L'Africaine,* and here the Landgrave—in which he often appears. The massed choruses, however, were splendid: alluring in those first seductive phrases that drift from the depths of Venus's grotto; enthusiastic courtiers in their hailing of the Landgrave; as pilgrims, adepts at those great choral crescendos—distant chant mounting to an incandescent forte—which provide some of the most thrilling moments in the opera. Mr. Levine's handling of the score was large and impressive. Like most modern conductors, he alternated between the Dresden and the Paris versions of the piece, including the bacchanale of the latter (a vivacious and colorful performance by the Cincinnati Symphony) but also, from the former, Walther von der Vogelweide's unnecessary contribution to the *Sängerkrieg*.

Schoenberg's *Gurre-Lieder*, not *Tannhäuser*, was the great attraction of the opening days. Like Mahler's Eighth Symphony, composed some six years later, *Gurre-Lieder* was just about its composer's only large-scale triumph during his lifetime. Not long ago, few listeners could have needed more than one hand to number the times they had heard either work. Now Mahler's Eighth, despite the huge forces required, is no longer a rarity; there is even a danger that a performance of it may cease to be an "event." Of *Gurre-Lieder* there has been a crop of recent performances, prompted by the Schoenberg centenary—Tanglewood, San Francisco, Atlanta, and Milwaukee are among the places where it has been done—and there have been five recordings, from Stokowski's, of 1931, to Boulez's, just issued. But the work is still hardly repertory fare. Stokowski conducted the American première in Philadelphia in 1931. Twenty years later Thor Johnson revived the work in Cincinnati (not at the May Festival). It has only twice been given in New York. I can still count on one hand the live performances I have heard. And the most exciting of all has been Mr. Levine's at the May Festival—a real festival event.

Gurre-Lieder—an earlier work than Mahler's Fifth Symphony, earlier than *Salome* and *Elektra* (the composition and most of the orchestration date from 1900–1, although the scoring of Part III was completed only in 1911)—is an amazing achievement. The orchestra is huge (eight flutes, five oboes, seven clarinets, ten horns, etc.) and used with great clarity and delicacy. The text is a German translation of Jens Peter Jacobsen's *Songs of Gurre*. (Gurre is the castle where Tove, beloved by King Valdemar the Great of Denmark, lived, and was murdered by Valdemar's jealous queen.) There is no connected narrative. In Part I, Valdemar and Tove alternate love songs, and finally a wood dove sings of Tove's funeral. Part II is short: Valdemar's blasphemous reproach to God. He is condemned to ride the skies every night. Part III opens with the Wild Hunt of Valdemar and his men and ends with "The Wild Hunt of the Summer Wind," a transformation of the *scherzo macabre* into a paean to nature, ending with a blaze of C-major sunrise. Jacobsen (nineteenth-century botanist, translator of Darwin, novelist whose *Niels Lyhne* provided the plot of Delius's opera *Fennimore and Gerda*) charged nature imagery with the emotions of high chivalric romance and the shadows of old crimes still inexpiate. His polished writing has prompted comparisons with De Quincey and with Pater; that leaves out of account the sense of present scenes stirring the poet to his dreams which underlies the *Songs of Gurre*. The text suggests disjunct excerpts from an Idyll of the King written by Wordsworth. Schoenberg was evidently drawn to it by the opportunities for instrumental tone-painting (which he achieved with superlative strokes), by the emotional intensity of the utterances (for Valdemar and Tove he wrote some of the most loving and passionate music composed since *Tristan*), by the thematic cross-references of the poems (reflected in a score filled with thematic recurrences and developments), and by the implicit evocation of a larger order that unites apparently diverse adventures (never stated in the text, made manifest in the music). The words of *Gurre-Lieder*—the German translation is by Robert Franz Arnold—are not usually considered important, but Schoenberg thought they were. In 1950, he wrote to Thor Johnson:

ONE THING IS VERY IMPORTANT: Make the performance in *ENG-LISH* not in German. People do not understand German, neither here, nor in Australia, England, Canada and in many other places. There is an excellent translation in the Stokowski Victor Album. I possess besides a translation into English, which I myself used in my performance in London and which is also very, very good. There is no reason why it should be given in German.

Mr. Johnson used German all the same, and so did Mr. Levine, and no one can blame them for having rejected the standard translation, which is not very, very good, and begins: "Now stills the twilight ev'ry sound on land and sea, / The far-sailing clouds are anchor'd now in harbour by Heaven's lee." The Festival long ago abandoned its original ideal of doing everything in English. German and an English singing version for *Gurre-Lieder* and *Tannhäuser*, Italian and an English translation for *Ernani* were printed in parallel columns of the program book (a good piece of work, which included detailed Festival annals from 1873).

Schoenberg used the full chorus only in the last few minutes of the work, in that clinching way common in large compositions of the time (e.g., Scriabin's First Symphony, Mahler's Second, Busoni's Piano Concerto). The Cincinnati choirs greeted the sun with a brave burst of sound, excellently sustained. Earlier, the three male-voice choirs of Valdemar's men were fierce and fiery. Although the orchestra and the soloists carry the main burden of the *Gurre-Lieder*, the chorus must crown it, and here it did so nobly. The soloists, all new to their roles, were outstanding. Robert Nagy, as Valdemar, was uncommonly audible; by vivid projection and keen tonal focus, not by shouting, he made his effect, and rode the orchestral storms triumphantly. Carol Neblett was a touching, romantic Tove, and Beverly Wolff was poignant but not effusive in the Wood Dove's lament. Mr. Shadur's rough manner was better suited to the Peasant's song than it had been to Wolfram's. James Atherton, as the Royal Fool, almost stole the show, for he was lively, witty, sweet in tone, and nimble in his use of the words; what a good

David, in *Die Meistersinger*, he could be! The penultimate movement is for a speaker, accompanied by a light, transparent, iridescent orchestra. Pitched musical speech in strict tempo is always a problem. Schoenberg, in that letter to Thor Johnson, asked for "a higher voice, about tenor range or high baritone. It should, if possible, be a voice which should not be too fat, too thick, too bombastic. It should be a light voice." Schoenberg himself once used Albertine Zehme, for whom *Pierrot Lunaire* was written, and found her "very, very good." In Cincinnati, Nico Castel spoke the part with dapper precision. Mr. Levine's conducting of *Gurre-Lieder* combined the necessary virtues of rhythmic and dynamic accuracy, care over textural details, and full-hearted romantic expressiveness. His pacing of the huge work was wonderfully assured. On earlier occasions, and especially in Verdi, I have deplored his way of bouncing an allegro forward as if in an excess of exuberance. But the energy he brought to the more frenzied pages of *Gurre-Lieder* never distorted the natural shapes of Schoenberg's phrases. He did not drive singers and chorus along so much as join with them in a surge of passion. Painting the quiet background for such a phrase as Tove's simple utterance "Nun sag ich dir zum ersten Mal: 'König Volmer, ich liebe dich,' " he did so in soft, warm tints. (The passage was sung by Miss Neblett in tender, glowing tones; clarinet, solo violin, and solo cello played their complementary phrases most eloquently.) *Gurre-Lieder*, composed at the turn of the century, draws on the full array of the nineteenth century's musical resources and anticipates many of the twentieth's. Mr. Levine made bright each varied facet of the astounding work, and presented the whole as one connected and complete experience.

The venue of the Cincinnati May Festival is the Music Hall, a noble Ruskinian pile built in 1878 to house it. The hall seats thirty-six hundred people but does not seem forbiddingly large, for two tiers of deep balconies curve gracefully around three sides, holding many people in small space. The acoustics are excellent. The architecture is conducive to musical enjoyment. The foyers are ample and airy. Across the street is a pleasant park with a bandstand, and old trees. Here, remembering the initial German inspiration of the Festival, I looked to find an open-air festal beer garden—but looked in vain. Still, even if Cincinnati is not, by Bayreuth standards, *quite* civilized, it is very nearly so. And, after all, even Bayreuth has lost its streetcars.

June 9, 1975

STAR-CROSS'D IN BOSTON

"Nowadays, one hardly ever hears a really beautiful and technically perfect trill; very rarely, flawless mordents; very seldom, a rounded coloratura, a true, unaffected portamento, a perfect equalization of all the registers, and absolute maintenance of intonation through all the various nuances of crescendo and diminuendo. . . . And the public, accustomed to imperfect execution, overlooks the defects of the singer if only he is a capable actor and knows his stage routine." That lament for the passing of bel-canto glories, which might be sounded after any of the Rossini, Donizetti, and Bellini revivals of our day, was penned by Richard Wagner, in *Mein Leben*, and was prompted by his memories of hearing Wilhelmine Schröder-Devrient as Bellini's Romeo, that "daring, romantic figure of the youthful lover." Romeo was one of the great nineteenth-century roles for sopranos and mezzo-sopranos—Pasta and Malibran among them—until, in Gounod's setting of the story, it became a tenor's province. Wagner used *I Capuleti e i Montecchi*, Bellini's Romeo and Juliet opera, as a stick with which to beat Weber's *Euryanthe* and all "solid German music," and said he would never forget the impression it made on him. Berlioz was more critical, except of a passage in the first-act finale when

the lovers, forcibly separated, escape for a moment and rush into each other's arms, singing "We shall meet in heaven." The setting of these words, which is intense, passionate, and full of life and fire, is sung in unison, which, in these special circumstances, intensifies the power of the melody in the most wonderful manner. Whether it was owing to the setting of the musical phrase, to the unexpected effect of the unison, or to the actual beauty of the tune itself, I do not know; but I was completely carried away, and applauded frantically.

I had long wanted to be carried away by *I Capuleti* as Berlioz and Wagner were, but had to wait until the Opera Company of Boston's production of the piece, last week, to achieve that wish. In the late sixties, the opera was quite often given—in Milan, Rome, Amsterdam, Edinburgh, and Montreal—but always in an edition by Claudio Abbado marred by many cuts, by some reorchestration, and, most gravely, by the recasting of Romeo as a tenor. While most of the role was taken down an octave, passages in the mezzo's chalumeau register were left at the original pitch, with disastrous effect on both Bellini's melodic line and his expressive deployment of tessitura. In his earlier performances, Abbado even divided that famous unison, giving Romeo its first statement and Juliet its second, but by 1968 he allowed the voices to join in octaves. Giacomo Aragall was the usual Romeo, and Luciano Pavarotti the Tybalt. Juliets ranged from Renata Scotto to Anna Moffo. (The only other roles, Capulet and Friar Laurence, are subaltern.) As if in an excess of loving tenderness, Abbado, conducting these performances, tended to slow down allegro to andante, and andante to adagio, and put the cabalettas through dainty, moderate paces. (Lorin Maazel did much the same in a Rome radio performance of the fifties, which had Fiorenza Cossotto as its hero.) The melodies were gently and affectionately molded, but the brilliance and force of Bellini's music —the qualities that first brought him fame—were missing. Bellinians disappointed in the opera were left reflecting that it had, after all, been run up in a great hurry (to plug a gap in the Venice season of 1829–30 when Giovanni Pacini failed in a commission). Bellini used up music from his earlier pieces *Adelson e Salvini* and *Zaira*; his librettist, Felice Romani, adjusted a libretto he had made four years earlier for Nicola Vaccai.

But the strength of Ottocento operas can be judged neither from the vocal scores nor from lackluster theater performances in faulty texts. Sarah Caldwell, musical and stage director of the Boston presentation, and Tatiana Troyanos and Beverly Sills, its Romeo and Juliet, have now rewritten the *Capuleti* chapter in the twentieth century's book of Bellini criticism. Does it need stressing that Miss Caldwell's baton is a more subtle, trenchant, and precise musicological instrument than the most learned of thematic and harmonic analyses? By her control of tempo, of timbres, and of rubato within a phrase, Miss Caldwell revealed Bellini's intentions in this work. For the first time, I became aware that the melody which transported Berlioz derives its rhythmic shape from the middle section of the lovers' duet in the preceding scene. Moreover, Juliet's music has a "motto" rhythm; each of her three solos —the entrance air "O quante volte," "Morte io non temo," which opens Act II, and its cabaletta, "Ah! non poss'io partire"—begins with a rhythm that can be represented as *rum tum-ti tum tum / rum-ti tum-ti tum.* "O quante volte" is an elaborated and refined reworking of Nelly's romanza in Bellini's first opera, *Adelson e Salvini*. In the new version, a horn solo, warm and a little solemn in tone (kin to the melody of the duet "Il rival salvar tu puoi" in *I puritani*), introduces the scene. Juliet sings recitative, unaccompanied but punctuated by the orchestra. The flexible horn solo is resumed, and above it Juliet sings of the fever that burns her. She goes to the window, and cooling breaths seem to spring up from the harp. Then the romanza begins. Both the situation and some turns of phrase in the melody recall Desdemona's scene in the last act of Rossini's *Otello*. Perhaps unconsciously, Bellini transposed his *Adelson* number into Rossini's key of G minor, and remembered Desdemona's harp. The second measure of "O quante volte," lifted into a new harmonic context, becomes, note for note, the second measure of

176

"Morte io non temo"; and those same five notes are then used as the sixth measure of "Ah! non poss'io." Juliet, a role consistent in its musical characterization but not at all monotonous, was composed for the very gentle, delicate singer Maria Caradori-Allan (later the first soprano in Mendelssohn's *Elijah*), admired not for dramatic power but for her sweetness, flexibility, and faultless style. It was a lapse on Miss Sills's part to shrill out a high E flat at the end of the first finale, but otherwise she was tender, touching, and sensitive. She would not have satisfied Wagner, for we did not hear "a really beautiful and technically perfect trill" (her trills started correctly but then slipped downward into a vague oscillation) or, for that matter, "absolute maintenance of intonation" in sustained high notes. Moreover, she made rather heavy weather of, gave almost Sutherlandian overemphasis to, some recitative delivery. But a public accustomed to vocal execution far more imperfect than this could easily overlook the technical defects of a singer who delivered the phrases with so eloquent a feeling for their musical sense. Most of the soft music was sounded in exquisitely judged tone colors, and Miss Sills knows how to join note to note to make communicative music. ("Song," said Wagner, "is the language in which mankind must communicate its musical ideas," and he said it with Bellini's music in mind.) Miss Sills looked beautiful; her acting was vivid and poignant.

Juliet's keys are G minor and A major; the tempo indications of her three solos are andante sostenuto, lento, and andante; her melodies move by step. The solo music for Romeo and Tybalt is in C major and G major, and their melodies leap. It was probably Juliet's music that led a critic of the Venetian première to discern in *I Capuleti* "a completely new genre, not noisy, but pensive, harmonious, and very gentle." This is the genre for which the Bellini of *La sonnambula*, much of *Norma*, and *I puritani* is conventionally admired. But his earlier operas *Il pirata* and *La straniera* were hailed for their energy and passion of declamation. (It was from them that Donizetti learned his vigorous dramatic manner, while Bellini went on to develop a milder lyrical vein.) *I Capuleti* is the transitional work. Where Maazel and Abbado, with ears only for its lyrical side, took Tybalt's cabaletta at a snail's pace and turned Romeo's defiant allegro marziale, "La tremenda ultrice spada," into a funeral march, Miss Caldwell was fiery and fearless in her employment of Bellini's heavy brass. Her dashing approach to the spirited episodes, her almost reckless but never unjustified tempi, gave, by contrast, new depth to the romantic and the pathetic scenes, and showed *I Capuleti* to be a more various, interesting, and shapely opera than in recent years it has been held to be.

Miss Troyanos, the Romeo, has an exceptionally fine instrument, with a timbre distinctive in ways that are hard to describe. It is not one of those bright, tense, forcefully projected mezzos, but has warm, full tones that rise without audible break into the soprano range. (In their duet, Romeo and Juliet sing their solo strophes at the same pitch.) Her acting lacked bravura; her rather heavy Roman features did not flash. Wagner's niece Johanna (his first Elisabeth in *Tannhäuser*) chose Romeo for her London début, in 1856, and the impresario Benjamin Lumley recalled the occasion thus: "She appeared: tall, stately, self-possessed, clothed in glittering mail, with her fine fair hair flung in masses on her neck . . . She sang! The sonorous voice, which heralded the mission of the young warrior to his enemies, rang through the house as penetrating and as awakening as a clarion." None of this could apply to Miss Troyanos's entry, except the epithet "sonorous." By beauty of tone, easy, unforced power, smoothness of phrasing, fullness and evenness of sound, and flexibility and accuracy in divisions, she triumphed. Tybalt (who combines the roles of Shakespeare's Tybalt and Paris) was played by Boston's rising young tenor Joseph Evans. He sang his aria with charm and finesse of manner, and in fresh, clearly projected tones. In his duet with Romeo he pushed the voice slightly too hard but at least ventured all the florid writing, which Pavarotti used to simplify. The Capulet and the Laurence were unimpressive. The parts are so small that it hardly mattered.

Miss Caldwell's musical direction was consistently impressive. Who, since Tullio Serafin died, has been able to shape a Bellini score so surely and so sensitively? There was an almost miraculous feeling for the just tempi, for the small inflections within a phrase, for the relation of one movement to the next, for the control of dynamic gradients that give life to this music. The solo instrumental playing—the horn already mentioned, the cello in the prelude to Act II, the clarinet that winds through Romeo's reverie in the following scene—was all admirable. Miss Caldwell's stage direction had the same unobtrusive certainty of touch. She essayed only one questionable tour de force: setting Romeo and Tybalt to fight while they sang their duet. It was ingeniously achieved but distracting and out of style; the swords should clash only when the pair have reached their cadence on "All'armi!" Excellent scenery, by Herbert Senn and Helen Pond, turned the limitations of the Orpheum Theatre stage to positive advantage, and Yasmina Bozin's costumes were handsome. All in all, a whizzing evening in the theater—and a major contribution to Bellini studies.

June 16, 1975

In 1976, a recording of I Capuleti *with Miss Sills as Juliet, and Dame Janet Baker as Romeo, appeared (Angel SCLX 3824). It was con-*

ducted, not by Sarah Caldwell, but by Giuseppe Patanè; the performance does not have the fire and energy that, in Boston, revealed the previously unsuspected merit of Bellini's opera.

BOLOGNA QUADRILLES?

The recital entitled "Music of Medieval Jewry," given by the New World Consort in St. Stephen's Church, West Sixty-ninth Street, last week, was one of those increasingly fashionable modern entertainments at which, to put it unkindly, the ears of a twentieth-century public are tickled by old tunes and the timbres of old instruments. Because the four performers making up the Consort are accomplished artists, it was a superior example of the genre. And it was well attended: the line waiting to get into the first show stretched down the block; a second house was mustering as the first came out. "Medieval" was a catch-all description for a program of music that spanned six centuries. (By that reckoning, a program of "modern" religious music might include motets by Machaut, Mouton, Monteverdi, Mozart, Mendelssohn, and Messiaen.) Instrumental participation in synagogue music was generally banned after the destruction of the Temple, and so it was odd to hear the proceedings begin with three chants, written (or written down) by Obadiah the Proselyte in the early twelfth century, accompanied by hurdy-gurdy and bells and punctuated by lira solos. The chants were followed by that mid-fifteenth-century motet which Eric Werner published as "a sort of benevolent parody of synagogue chant" but Alfred Sendrey, in *The Music of the Jews in the Diaspora*, deems an attempt "to ridicule in a musical fashion the Jewish religion," a piece of "anti-Semitic musical comedy"—as it were, a rendering of the "*Gegurgel, Gejodel, Geklapper*" that Wagner declared Jewish music to be. Next came a new-old "liturgical drama," *The Binding of Isaac*, constructed by Judith Eisenstein by applying to a Sephardic narrative poem more or less contemporary Sephardic melodies. It made an attractive piece, not enacted but decked with the bright instrumental trappings made popular by the New York Pro Musica's performances of the medieval music drama *Herod*. The fourth item could be called a "dance suite" drawn from the music of Salamon Rossi, Monteverdi's colleague, the Jewish composer at the Gonzaga court. Sinfonie and galliards alternated with arrangements of hymns from the famous *Hashirim Asher LiSh'lomo*, or *Songs of Solomon*, published in Venice in 1623, which Rossi composed "to give thanks to the Lord and to sing to His most exalted name on all sacred occasions." The finale was his five-part *Qadish* (to use the transliteration of Fritz Rikko's edition), performed in tripping fashion by two voices and pizzicato strings. Since Rossi's hymns were written for service use, they are unaccompanied. Since there are only two singers in the New World Consort, a soprano and a baritone, instruments—recorders or viols—took the lines of the missing voices. The three-part benedicite *Bar'khu et Adōnai* became a solo song with viols—once through straight and then a reprise with decorations, over plucked strings. Finally, there was a group of very beautiful Sephardic songs. One would have liked texts and a translation for these (and light to read them by); the opening words suggested that Ladino, in which tongue they are written, is a language easily followed. ("Arboles yoran"—"The trees are weeping"— sounds like a line of Lorca.) Some of the songs were sung; one was played on a bagpipe, and another on a recorder with psaltery accompaniment.

If there are traces of criticism in this account of what was done, they are deliberate, and reflect disquietude on two counts: whether the culling of liturgical music to provide fodder for a kind of cultural cabaret is altogether seemly; and whether there is a danger of modern medieval performing practices' being applied, like some all-purpose sauce (spiced by snarling, tangy wind tone, the tap of tabors, and the ting-a-ling of little bells and finger cymbals), to a variety of musics whose flavors should be kept distinct. On the first count, it would take a new Mrs. Post to draw the line of decorum, although sometimes it is clear that a line, wherever it lies, has been crossed. London once danced to the catchy strains of a set of *Bologna Quadrilles*, but the work was withdrawn and its plates were destroyed when the publishers discovered that the tunes came from Rossini's Stabat Mater. Scarpia's libidinous descant to the Te Deum, in the first-act finale of *Tosca*, gains pungency from the holy setting—but then the coupling of sex and sanctity is a titillation often provided by late-Romantic operas—*Thaïs, Salome, The Jewels of the Madonna*. Episodes in *Tannhäuser* and *Parsifal* differ from them not so much in subject matter as in seriousness of intention. Britten has thrice used the Benedicite in dramatic compositions in ways that can hardly offend even the pious. (Offstage in Act II of *Peter Grimes*, the morning canticle punctuates the quarrel of Peter and Ellen with complicated ironic effect. In *The Turn of the Screw*, the two children, on their way to matins, produce an evil, sacrilegious parody of it. In *The Burning Fiery Furnace*, this Song of the Three Holy Children returns to its original context, shining forth amid the flames.) Music can move easily between sacred and secular settings; Monteverdi, who transformed his *Lamento d'Arianna* into a *Pianto della Madonna*, and Bach are among many who have shown it. And, to get back to the concert and

180

the Consort, Rossi's *Hashirim* certainly employ the devices of Mantuan canzonetta and madrigal; if his *Qadish* were provided with a light amorous text—some Damon recounting his Amaryllis' charms rather than "Magnified and sanctified be the name of God throughout the world"—one would hardly guess its devout origin. But it wasn't. And so the deft, easily palatable sequence of ancient chants, synagogue hymns, and frivolous dances, slipping down so agreeably, brought one uncomfortably close to the world of the *Bologna Quadrilles*.

In the matter of old instrumentation I am no expert—not a cook who has studied with scholarly care the numerous recipes (deduced from paintings, sculptures, and poems rather than specified by the musical scribes) but a taster who has begun to suspect that the sound of old instruments is sometimes indiscriminately sprinkled, like a musical monosodium glutamate, to give instant zest to works that need more detailed, individual preparation if their innate merits are to be revealed. No one doubts that medieval music was sounded in brighter colors than its look on the page would suggest. But the all-purpose medieval instrumentation of our day—uniformly applied to music in many moods, for many diverse occasions, and from scattered centuries—the fresh, quaint sounds, the color shifts as fidgety as a Monteverdi continuo part composed by Raymond Leppard are in themselves no sure mark of authenticity.

This is not criticism brought to bear specifically on the New World Consort but, rather, a general plea that the increasing public appetite for "old music" should be discriminate, not gobbling, and reject anything homogenized or synthetically flavored. Else both impropriety and opportunism will flourish. All four members of the Consort are cogent and talented players on a variety of instruments. Rosemarie Caminiti, the soprano, has a flexible voice (the Moorish arabesques of the Sephardic songs were delicately and passionately traced) with a wide range of attractive timbres. William Mount, the director, has a smooth, clear baritone. Accustomed to the fiercer attack and more open "medieval" sound of British groups—David Munrow's Early Music Consort, John Beckett's Musica Reservata—I found the tone of the New World a little bland at first, but was soon won by their charming, unaggressive approach and their cultivated yet buoyant manners.

June 23, 1975

VIOLETTA IN VIRGINIA

I have seldom seen an opera so eagerly and enthusiastically welcomed as *La traviata*, the second production of the new-founded Virginia Opera Association, was in Norfolk, the week before last. The enthusiasm was not misplaced. Three young principals—Diana Soviero, from the New York City Opera, Raymond Gibbs, from the Metropolitan, and Jake Gardner—gave talented and touching accounts of their roles. The town had evidently taken the visitors to its heart, but the local pride could be in a carefully rehearsed production, achieved not so much "around" them or "for" them as *with* them. The scenery and costumes were hired, but the chorus, orchestra, and dancers and the nine singers of the smaller roles were Virginian, and already there was the feeling of a company working together. Virginia Opera—after an all-local *Elisir d'amore* last year, which was apparently something of a false start— began operations in earnest last January with a *Bohème* based on a similar combination of visiting principals and resident support. Its success persuaded the organizers that Norfolk was hungry for "real opera"; an artistic director was appointed on a regular basis; and this *Traviata* is the result. *La Bohème* and *La traviata* were each given twice; for next season, three operas, each played thrice, are planned.

Not having witnessed much home-based small-town opera in this country—or, for that matter, Boris Goldovsky's touring productions, or the Opera Company of Boston's junior troupe that settles to work in small communities—I have no basis for comparative assessment of the Norfolk achievement. On a similar scale (and, in fact, in the same stock scenery, memorable only because a well-known portrait of Malibran hangs in Violetta's salon), the New York Grand Opera put on a *Traviata*, earlier this season, in the Harkness Theater. It was a lusty but pretty routine performance, with just two points of interest: the score was played uncut, and the heroine, Norma French, is an artist of some temperament and ability. It was hardly the necessary contribution to New York's cultural life that the Virginia Opera's *Traviata* so evidently was to Norfolk's. The latter was done with the standard "theater cuts" and in the standard reduced orchestration by Giuseppe Bamboschek (with single flute, oboe, bassoon, and trombone). The cuts mean that each of Violetta's arias is reduced to its first strophe, the tenor's and the baritone's cabalettas are dropped, the second section of the duet "Parigi, o cara" is halved, and its cabaletta is truncated; thereby about twelve minutes are gained—and then twenty or more are usually wasted on an intrusive and dramatically destructive interval between the two scenes of Act II. Regrettable—but perhaps forgivable in the case of a young company in its first season. (In any case, the cuts are built into the Bamboschek parts, so "opening" them would need a good deal of work by an orchestrator and by copyists.)

Peter Mark, the artistic director of Virginia Opera, made his début as an operatic conductor with this *Traviata*. He has sung the Shepherd Boy in *Tosca* and the Tsarevich in *Boris Godunov* at the Metropolitan; I knew him before as a viola player, admirable soloist in the fine Viola Concerto composed for him by Thea Musgrave. As conductor, he showed an easy command both of the score and of his forces, and inspired confidence. If, again and again, I felt an urge to seize the baton to set slower and more flexible tempi (an allegretto for the brindisi that would be lilting and graceful, at which the small notes had time to sparkle, like little bubbles breaking; an andantino for "Un dì felice" that ebbed and flowed and did not fetter the vocal line to a precision-beat *one*-two-three), well, that is no special criticism of Mr. Mark, since I feel it at nine of every ten modern *Traviata* performances I hear. Everyone must feel it who has studied interpretations of the piece by artists closer to Verdi's day than to ours. Listen, I want to say, to the way "Ah, fors'è lui" was sung by Gemma Bellincioni, whose Violetta Verdi himself admired, and whom Professor Edward Dent, not a man to think a singer more important than her song, deemed unforgettable in the role. Listen to "De' miei bollenti spiriti" sung by Fernando De Lucia. Listen not simply in order to copy but to discover a style of execution appropriate to the music. Listen intently, after making all due allowance for individual eccentricities. Performers of eighteenth-century music work hard to wring secrets of contemporary performing practice from written evidence; for the late nineteenth century, documents in sound exist and are all too often ignored. Young American singers, and most modern conductors, are shy of portamento and rubato, and hesitate to depart any further from the written notes than what they see printed, petrified, in the Ricci volumes of *Traditional Variations and Cadenzas,* published by Ricordi. Like most good things, portamento, rubato, and personal melodic embellishment can of course be abused; they should not therefore be eschewed. And when Verdi marks the first three notes to the words "unico raggio di bene" (in Violetta's duet with Germont) with a slurred staccato, and then draws a full slur over the next three, the soprano who does not sound the dropping, then rising, seventh of "raggio di" in one unbroken span is plainly at fault. Maybe Melba went too far, with her emphatic, lingering portamento at this point (though I don't think so). But, in Norfolk, Miss Soviero positively separated "rag-" and "-gio," not carrying the tone down from the C to the D.

Mr. Gardner, the Norfolk Germont, showed the fullest command of the rhythmic, timbral, and dynamic finesses that bring the music to life. Moreover, he has a baritone of very beautiful quality, more French than Italianate in its clarity of focus, firm on the note, and not "enriched" with vague, spreading resonances. (Most of Verdi's late baritone roles—Posa in both versions of *Don Carlos*, the revised Boccanegra, Iago, and Falstaff—were created by Frenchmen; Paul Lhérie, the first Don José in *Carmen*, as a baritone sang Posa in the première of the revised *Don Carlos* and two years later, at Covent Garden, was a successful Germont to Nordica's Violetta.) Miss Soviero, an impassioned and appealing young heroine, had both the artistry to sing phrases very softly, *estremamente piano, con un fil di voce*, wherever Verdi called for it and the ability to project these very soft lines into the house so that every detail in them could be clearly heard. (The house was the Center Theater, an eighteen-hundred-seater, initiated as a WPA project and opened in 1942 as a USO theater. Norfolk has a larger and more elegant auditorium, the Chrysler Hall Theater for the Performing Arts, beside Pier Luigi Nervi's dome; but its acoustics are reputedly poor, while those of the simple, unpretentious Center are satisfactory.) Many sopranos start "Addio del passato" well; most of them then spoil things by launching a crescendo far too early, when the A-minor music moves into C major at "l'amore d'Alfredo." But Miss Soviero sustained the pianissimo, with poignant effect, and held back the crescendo to the place where the composer asks for it, at the Schubertian tonic major on "della traviata." Mr. Gibbs, the Alfredo, has a small tenor of tight and somewhat charmless timbre, but his charm of manner and appearance and a keenly intelligent grasp of the role told in his favor. Joan Evans's Flora and Nancy Boling's Annina had character.

Directing an amateur chorus and supporting cast requires special gifts, and I have known directors who possessed it more fully than David Farrar. Neither in an *Elisir d'amore*, earlier this season, for the Bronx Opera nor in this *Traviata* did he achieve that easy matching of assignments to abilities which, in a production conceived for the forces available, can make an amateur chorus almost as convincing as professionals. His direction was a curious mixture of beginner's blunders and bright effectiveness. Alfredo came in from the garden and put his muddy boots up on the sofa. Violetta's guests began waltzing during the brindisi, making nonsense of the text (toast comes first, dancing next; "Would you not *now* like to dance?" says the hostess when, after the brindisi, the band strikes up in an adjoining room). Worse, Violetta and Alfredo were required to sing the third verse while themselves twirling and spinning. The curtain went up on Act III with Violetta and Annina *both* recumbent—a faintly comic effect (the stage directions make it clear that the servant has fallen asleep in a chair). On the other hand, the staging of the soprano-baritone duet was sensitive, and the soprano-tenor dialogue in the Act II finale—the conversation that starts "Mi chiamaste? che bramate?"—was both enacted and sung with uncommon urgency. Mr. Mark and Mr. Farrar were at one in their quick, passionate, emotionally tense approach to the work, but both made the mistake of pushing too hard. *La traviata* becomes more, not less, moving when there is time for all the nuances to be sounded. Nevertheless, it was a lively, arresting, considered performance that could grip both someone meeting the work for the first time and a connoisseur who had heard it a hundred times before. Virginia Opera has started well. I question only two things: its commitment to stock repertory (a choice of three from *Tosca, Rigoletto, Lucia*, and *Il barbiere* is announced for next season—though *La sonnambula* is also being discussed, and that would be just a shade more adventurous), and its use of Italian. Opera performed in a tongue not that of the audience and executants can never be the real thing, or put down roots, but remains "an exotic and irrational entertainment" (Dr. Johnson's definition, not of opera, but of opera played in Italian to Englishmen).

The Bronx company is rightly committed to opera in English, but its *Elisir*—which I saw as the inaugural performance in the auditorium of the Harry S. Truman High School, in Co-op City—was, for mingled reasons of economy and convenience, played not in the best existing translation but in the one most readily and inexpensively available and most widely known to singers in this country. Its infelicitous jingles are the kind of thing that brings opera in English into disrepute. The second production of the New York Grand Opera, a *Nabucco*, again in the Harkness Theater, was put on in a manner that brings opera itself into disrepute among serious musicians. The gap between the fully equipped productions of the Metropolitan, the City Opera, and the Juilliard and brave enterprise in a tiny hall seems unbridgeable—though the Bronx Opera is a promising development, and I remember with pleasure Brooklyn College Opera Theater's thoroughly adept presentation of Robert Starer's *Pantagleize*, two years ago. In New York, presumably only in a pipe dream could some adventurous young company afford to hire an opera house, the Philharmonic or the Philadelphia Orchestra, Lorin Maazel to conduct, John Dexter to direct, and Ming Cho Lee to design, and mount in style two performances of Szymanowski's *King Roger*, but in poverty-stricken London the New Opera Company has just managed something roughly equivalent. Over there, the music society of John Lewis, a large department store, promotes an opera each season, professionally conducted, directed, and designed (materials from the stockrooms), orchestrally accompanied, and cast with a mixture of guests and store personnel; and in that way works like Bizet's *Don Procopio*, Boieldieu's *La Dame blanche*, Dvořák's *The Peasant Rogue*, Wolf-Ferrari's *Le donne curiose*, and Weber's *The Three Pintos* can reach the stage in deft performances. What about it, Macy's, Bloomingdale's, Lord & Taylor?

185

But enough of possibly odious comparisons. From the New York season's mass of shoestring operatic endeavor so far unrecorded in these pages, let me single out, and register mild gratitude for: Verdi's *I due Foscari* put on in an enthusiastic concert performance, in Town Hall, by the Riverside Orchestra; the American première of *Garni Sands*, a clumsy but energetic Australian opera by George Dreyfus, clumsily and energetically performed by Bel Canto Opera in the parish hall of Madison Avenue Baptist Church; and Wolf-Ferrari's *The Jewels of the Madonna*, done with piano accompaniment, in the hall of the Church of the Covenant, by the Stuyvesant Opera Company. The last had a soprano and a tenor, Alice Kolb and R. Mack Miller, with the ability to bring the drama to life despite the rudimentary presentation. Something came through. One could enjoy the fine workings of Wolf-Ferrari's mind, even when applied to this lurid subject matter. New Yorkers got a chance to see and hear, after a fashion, an opera that left the boards of the Metropolitan in 1927. Two talented young singers got a chance to perform. But they, the audience, the work itself all deserved more than this hole-and-corner, pinch-penny show. What about it, Gimbels, B. Altman, Bonwit Teller?

June 30, 1975

I am happy to add that the Virginia Opera has announced, for 1978, the American première of Thea Musgrave's new opera, Mary, Queen of Scots.

OPPORTUNITIES

The Philharmonic's Rug Concerts, now in their third year, are a promising development. The seats are removed from the floor of Avery Fisher Hall, carpet (if not the rich rugs suggested by the title) is laid there, and squares of foam rubber are scattered about. The players are stationed where the front rows of seats usually are, and some of the audience sits behind them, on the platform. Admission to floor and platform costs four dollars; regular seating remains in the loge and the terraces, and tickets there cost from three to five dollars. The lighting, alas, is gloomy. Good houses have attended the concerts, whose programs are drawn largely from the twentieth century and mainly from the Philharmonic repertory. The achievement should not be overrated. The Rugs are a modest little venture, not yet to be compared with the London Proms that are presumably their inspiration: eight summer weeks of music orchestral, choral, chamber, and operatic, including new commissioned works, whole operas, and reprises of the season's major events, filling the vast Albert Hall and, in live broadcasts nightly, reaching a wider audience still. But the Rugs made a small, good start in 1973, and this year there has been some progress: ten concerts instead of six, and the invitation to a visiting ensemble, Peter Serkin's Tashi, to join in the proceedings (it played Messiaen's *Quartet for the End of Time*) and slightly lighten the rehearsal load on the Philharmonic players. Rehearsal time seems to have been inadequate; execution at the concerts I attended varied from the first-rate to the deplorable.

"The critic who is grateful is lost." Shaw said so, refusing to thank Sir Augustus Harris for producing *Otello* and reviving *Fidelio* at Covent Garden but asking instead why he had not done *Siegfried*; threatening that when *Siegfried* was done he would ask about *Die Walküre* and when *Die Walküre* was done about *Tristan*.

After that, I can fall back on *Das Rheingold*, *Götterdämmerung*, and *Parsifal*; but by that time, at the present rate of progress, I shall be celebrating my hundred and fiftieth birthday. If even then I say that I am satisfied, let there be an end of me at once; for I shall be of no further use as a critic.

I won't be quite so severe as Shaw, won't "purposely refrain from saying anything about the praiseworthy points," but before praising them I will ask why Pierre Boulez settled for play-safe programs and missed so many chances. Only one work by a living American composer, and that Aaron Copland's Orchestral Variations, an instrumental reworking of a 1930 composition (an excellent piece, but an early one). Of postwar compositions only three, and those pretty well established favorites: Luciano Berio's *Circles*, Peter Maxwell Davies's *Eight Songs for a Mad King*, and György Ligeti's *Lontano*. Ravel in his centenary year represented only by the Mallarmé songs. Well, perhaps we've had enough familiar Ravel lately, but why not bring to a wide audience, in world deuxièmes, some of the unknown Ravel works given world premières at Queens College in February? Or invite Beveridge Webster, a Ravel pupil, to play a piano piece or two? Bartók's Sonata for Two Pianos and Percussion, fine—but why not George Crumb's new *Music for a Summer Evening*? Where was Jacob Druckman's *Windows*, an excellent orchestral piece that, earlier this season, the Philharmonic hashed at first but then learned to play? On the same bill, Jon Deak, Philharmonic bassist, could have repeated his virtuoso turn with Druckman's *Valentine*, admired at a Prospective Encounters concert. Six of the seven works that

Mr. Boulez and the orchestra are billed to take to the Edinburgh Festival next month (works by Bartók, Beethoven, Berlioz, Ligeti, Mahler, and Stravinsky) figured in Rug programs; why not the seventh, Elliott Carter's Concerto for Orchestra? There are possibly good answers to these questions. Behind them lies a charge that Mr. Boulez and the Philharmonic management underrate the curiosity, adventurous appetite, and receptiveness of the young audiences who attend the Rugs, and another, that the organization is inward-looking, unresponsive to music making outside its orbit. The invitation to Tashi was a move in the right direction. When the Rugs resume—there may be a hiatus next year, for in summer the interior of Avery Fisher Hall is to be rebuilt—I hope there will be guest evenings from, say, Speculum Musicae and the Light Fantastic Players. (In fact, the Bartók Sonata and the Berio did use several Speculum artists, though uncredited as such.) Some of the orchestras from other towns which visit Carnegie Hall in high season and do not fill it might be able to reschedule, and play their boldest programs to an assured and appreciative Rug audience. The City Opera or the Minnesota Opera might like to give a concert showing to one of its new productions. Ensembles medieval as well as modern might take part. And soloists—when was Schoenberg's *Variations on a Recitative* last heard from the Fisher Hall organ? The events that could give New York a great summer season exist already. Imaginative planning could bring them together and insure that they were more widely heard.

Plainly, the Philharmonic cannot carry the full burden. Even by this year's ten concerts it was taxed beyond its abilities. In a performance of the *Siegfried Idyll* (at chamber strength, with single strings), its playing touched bottom. Frank Gullino was a thin and insecure first violin; pitch and balance generally were errant. The program that evening closed with an account of Stravinsky's *Pulcinella* suite that was very promising, brilliant by intention, crisply and wittily conducted by Mr. Boulez. But it needed much more rehearsal for his intentions to be realized. The concert began with a miserable Schubert's Fifth Symphony. Usually it is possible to hear what a conductor is trying to achieve, to "tune in" to his conception of a work rather than match and measure it against one's own ideal conception or great interpretations of the past. But what Mr. Boulez thought he was up to in this Schubert, or in Mozart's E-flat Symphony, K. 543, a day or two earlier, eluded me. He plowed his way regardless through both works, showing no feeling for their melodic and harmonic incident, and left me sighing for Beecham or Bruno Walter, men who understood the essence of this music. Is it because Mr. Boulez has so little response to the individual shape of a "singing" instrumental phrase and so little concern for charm of instrumental timbre that of classical and romantic music he can be so insensitive and depressingly dull an interpreter? Dvořák's Serenade for Strings is better un-played than gracelessly and unsmilingly delivered, as it was, with scrawny string tone, at the start of another concert. Mozart's C-minor Wind Serenade, K. 388, followed; if the eight players had been invited to rehearse by themselves and do it as chamber music, rather than to the conductor's beat, they would surely have given a more flexible, more eloquent performance.

On the other hand, at each of these concerts there were also superb things. After the Mozart Serenade, Varèse's *Octandre* was given as power-ful and cogent a performance as I have heard. (Not so his *Offrandes*, the next day; there dynamic distinctions were blurred, and Jan DeGaetani tended to coo a vocal line that should be brilliant and forward.) After the Mozart symphony, Gerard Schwarz was a dazzling soloist in Haydn's Trumpet Concerto. He played the work earlier this season, in the regular Philharmonic series, but not with the merry, mischievous virtuosity that made his Rug performance so keenly delightful. A ca-denza of his own composition in the first movement was outrageously brilliant. Reprises in the andante were graced and decorated with the aplomb and artistry of a great singer. The finale was taken at a lick that left the string players unable to articulate, but who could mind when the limelight was on the nimble, coruscating soloist? After the *Siegfried Idyll*, Phyllis Bryn-Julson was a beautiful soloist in Webern's Opus 8 and Opus 13 songs, and between the two song groups Mr. Boulez and the orchestra gave an ideally accomplished, delicately shaped, and ex-quisitely balanced account of Webern's Five Pieces.

A performance on a level that would have graced the Rugs was that of Holst's First Suite for military band, done at one of the free-admission end-of-term concerts of the Juilliard School, in Alice Tully Hall, at lunchtime. Mr. Schwarz conducted it, and showed Holst's inventions to be heady stuff. James Chambers conducted Strauss's Second Sonatina for winds, "From a Happy Workshop"—a protracted but endearing work. At a formal concert, one might become impatient at the winding bouts of linked sweetness long drawn out, but they whiled away forty-five minutes or so of the early afternoon most agreeably. These Juilliard School concerts deserve to be better known. They are more carefully rehearsed than much of what we hear professionally, and add variety to the Lincoln Center repertory. At a choral concert, also lunchtime, in Tully Hall, Ravel's *Trois Chansons* were deftly done. At an evening con-cert in the Juilliard Theater, Paul Dowling gave the American première of Hans Werner Henze's *Prison Song*, for tape and a solo percussionist who must also declaim the Ho Chi Minh poem on which it is based. The work was written for Stomu Yamash'ta, a flamboyant, beautiful acrobat-

189

actor-percussionist. Mr. Dowling's version was a trifle restrained, but confident and compelling; Rug audiences would probably have enjoyed it. On the same bill, Richard Reid's limpid, poised playing of the piano part in Stravinsky's Duo Concertante was impressive.

The Tycho ensemble's claim to be "the American counterpart to the Fires of London" is unfounded. The London group is formed of seasoned, spirited young professionals, among the most brilliant players of their instruments in the country; their nearest New York counterparts are the Speculum Musicae, the Contemporary Chamber Ensemble, and the Light Fantastic Players. The Fires are stoked by a composer-conductor of international renown, Peter Maxwell Davies; the Group for Contemporary Music, founded by the composers Harvey Sollberger and Charles Wuorinen, and the Composers Ensemble have something of that composer/executants relationship, though neither has yet built up a repertory or a following to compare with that of the Fires. (Rug appearances would help to swell the public; catchier titles might also help.) What Tycho and the Fires do have in common is a starting point in Schoenberg's *Pierrot Lunaire*. The Fires began life as the Pierrot Players and consisted of the vocalist and five instrumentalists needed for Schoenberg's work, plus a percussionist. Tycho, named for the lunar landmark, is twelve strong, but looks similarly to *Pierrot* as its inspiratory composition. (In *The New Yorker*, last year, David Hamilton praised a Tycho performance of *Pierrot*.) Two concerts the ensemble gave a few weeks ago, in Washington Square Church, contained some dross but also some first performances worth brief mention. Andrew Thomas's "Music of the Wind Road," a virtuoso piece composed for Barry Jekowsky, an alert Juilliard —and Tycho's—percussionist, and tape (there was also a dancer moving about while it happened, but her contribution was best ignored), is an orderly and colorful work. Lawrence Widdoes's "Love Song" is a dialogue for voice and pianist, again with tape. It is built from slight materials, often incoherent banalities of amorous pleading ("Touch me" is the refrain), to which the pianist responds unfeelingly with sounds and a spoken word or two, but is cunningly organized. Whenever it seemed to be going on too long, something new and arresting happened. And the singer, Nadine Herman, is a magnetic performer. "Love Song" made an impression that has remained unexpectedly strong. Claus Adam's *Herbstgesänge*, a cycle for soprano and piano to poems by Georg Trakl, is an endearing work, not distinguished but honestly felt and lovingly composed. As the season draws to its close, from a mass of new-music events I remember with pleasure these two modest but enterprising concerts—even though only the two performers mentioned above were in any way exceptional. The bare, shabby church makes a very agreeable, informal, but somewhat over-reverberant recital hall. There were six members of the public at the first concert, and about sixty at the second.

July 7, 1975

The Rug Concerts were resumed in June 1977, after Boulez's departure as music director of the Philharmonic. The programs were unadventurous, and none of the exciting events of what had been rather a good Philharmonic season were taken into them. No guest ensembles were invited to take part, and the Philharmonic playing in all the performances I heard was below its best level. I began to write a review with the title "Opportunities Missed" but did not have the heart to finish it.

AURORA BOREALIS

The Bolshoy Opera, now at the Metropolitan Opera House on its first visit to this country, brings to New York audiences a revelation of what grand opera can be when it is done by a company that is solidly founded and securely funded, a company whose artists are accustomed to performing in their own language to an audience that understands them, whose whole concern is for the work in hand and not the greater glory of particular interpreters. Graved in bronze, on a tablet overlooking the pool at Lincoln Center, are some fine words by John D. Rockefeller III:

The arts are not for the privileged few, but for the many. Their place is not on the periphery of daily life, but at its center. They should function not merely as another form of entertainment but, rather, should contribute significantly to our well being and happiness.

The Bolshoy productions are conceived in this spirit. The jungle world of Western opera has bred some rare, wonderful monsters, and I am glad they exist. Only one of the Bolshoy performers—and he a conductor—would I rank among the handful of the world's greatest operatic artists. In Europe and America, we can encounter some grand performances that reach the level of the Bolshoy offerings in integrity of purpose and surpass it in imaginative power and splendor of individual executions. And there are still some companies—though ever fewer in

these days of jet travel and of instant, instantly exploited reputations—
that are steady, true ensembles. But a company quite like the Bolshoy
is not to be found. I should not want it as my only troupe. The repertory
is not unadventurous—of the six operas brought to New York, three
(Prokofiev's *The Gambler* and *War and Peace*, and Kiril Molchanov's
The Dawns Are Quiet Here) are from the twentieth century, and three
(Mussorgsky's *Boris Godunov*, and Tchaikovsky's *Eugene Onegin* and
The Queen of Spades) from the nineteenth—but it is small. (The
company does no Wagner, for example, though it is contemplating a
Lohengrin.) I am grateful to have lived and to live in two cities that
have both an "international showcase" and a "national" opera company,
each playing a large and varied repertory. But very grateful, too, for
the chance of hearing and seeing the sure, established, consolidated
work of the Bolshoy.

The season opened with *Boris Godunov*. It was given in the Rimsky-
Korsakov version of the score, and this I regret, for the Bolshoy is a
company vocally, orchestrally, and temperamentally superbly equipped
to sound the full eloquence of Mussorgsky's original. It was shortened,
notably by the removal of the first Polish scene (the pretty cracovienne
for Marina's women, her mazurka, and the dialogue with Rangoni),
and it was lengthened by the addition of the scene outside St. Basil's
Cathedral, scored by Ippolitov-Ivanov in Rimskian manner. The scene
in Kromy Forest came not last, where Mussorgsky placed it, but before
the Death of Boris, whither Rimsky moved it. This, too, I regret; although Mussorgsky's first version of the opera did end with Boris's
death, the Kromy scene he added in 1871 is a more potent and more
affecting finale. Boris usually has the last word in productions that
"star" an exceptional performer of the title role; the Bolshoy presentation would end more fittingly with the popular scene and the Simpleton's
lament, not only because the chorus is the "star" of the show but also
because the drama enacted is above all that of the people. (For St.
Basil and Kromy, Mussorgsky's alternatives, to be done consecutively
is also unfortunate, but the Bolshoy got over this difficulty, in part, by
doing St. Basil before the last intermission; there, it joined with the
surviving Polish scene to make a new Act III.)
    No one denies that in its own right the Rimsky recension is a splendid
and powerful opera. The Bolshoy performance of it is traditional in
the best sense of the word. Mahler is often credited with the remark
"Tradition ist Schlamperei" ("Tradition is slovenliness"). What he
really said—he was director of the Vienna Opera at the time—is "*What
you people call tradition* is mere slovenliness," and referred to practices
unthinkingly followed, to musical or dramatic observances motivated

only by the fact that others had done things that way before. There is nothing thoughtless or unmotivated in the Bolshoy's traditional presentation of *Boris*. The production dates from 1948 but makes a vivid and fresh impression—fresher, indeed, than it did when I last saw it, in Paris, five years ago. (In general, the company is more lively, less routined than it was then; the new dominance of admirable young conductors may have something to do with this, and also, of course, the challenge of a New York début.) There are at least nine-and-sixty ways of going about the opera, and although not every single one of them is right, most of them can cast light on some aspect of it. In Salzburg, Karajan directed a glittering supershow—Rimsky version, in Russian. In Glasgow, in a small theater, Michael Geliot directed a somber, intimate drama—Mussorgsky version, in English translation. Covent Garden, whose production, originally by Peter Brook, is coeval with the Bolshoy's, has over the years rung countless changes both textual and linguistic. Earlier this season, the Metropolitan Opera itself produced a large, thoughtful, and beautiful realization of the Mussorgsky score, in rote-learnt Russian. The Bolshoy handling is less distinctive than the Met's, does not bear so prominently the particular seals of its designer, director, and conductor, but it does have what, in these days of *Werktreue*, or truth to a work as its creators conceived it, would be counted the highest virtue if only the concept of *Werktreue* had been extended to the musical theater. To do—and, for that matter, to admire —a production of a nineteenth-century masterpiece in a style that its creators would recognize and approve is to be called "old-fashioned," since fickle fashion heaps its praises on the novel conception, the personal reinterpretation, the "re-creation in terms of our own day." Fashion is certainly important, and the innovators with genius have taught us much. But tradition—the dedicated exploration and interpretation of a work in its original terms, not Mahler's "What you people call tradition"—is more important still, and its results can be more deeply satisfying.

The Bolshoy *Boris*, staged in big, handsome, realistic scenery by Fyodor Fyodorevsky, looks much as *Boris* must always have looked in the nineteenth century. The production is quite uneccentric, and within it, as a viewing of successive casts made clear, there is room for individual ideas about movement, gesture, and dramatic emphasis. From first to last, the choral singing was superb—powerful, deep-toned, dramatic, and many-colored; for the sound of the Bolshoy chorus alone this performance would merit a visit. Yevgeny Nesterenko, the Boris on the first night, was a reliable and correct performer, fairly impressive but without the huge personality and compelling vocal authority of the very best Borises. Of Alexander Vedernikov, at the second performance,

193

much the same can be said. Neither did anything wrong; neither was magnificent. Mark Reshetin, the Pimen on both occasions, has a very fine, expressive bass. Boris Morozov, at the second performance, was a splendid Varlaam; not just his delivery of the Kazan song but all the colors of his voice were energetic and filled with character. Grigory was sung first by Vladimir Atlantov, a Bolshoy tenor who has made an international reputation. His timbre and, it would seem, his artistic intentions are somewhat crudely Italianate rather than characteristically Russian—as if he took Franco Corelli as his model. His successor, Vladislav Piavko, gave a keener, subtler performance. Elena Obraztsova, Marina both times, brought the house down with her big, cantabile solo at the close of the fountain duet, in the Polish scene. If there was some vinegar in her tone, there was honey in her phrasing. This was the way I have long waited to hear the passage done—each note glued to the next, the tempo slow, flexible, yet amorously urgent, the whole sequence irresistibly seductive in utterance. Other performers of note were Nina Grigorieva, the Nurse one night and the Hostess of the Inn the other, with a big, solid, bouncy contralto; Mikhail Shkaptsov, as Mitiukha, the peasant who sings a few solo lines; and, above all, Yury Mazurok, as Shchelkalov. At his best, Mr. Mazurok seems to me to have the most beautiful baritone voice in the world, and as Shchelkalov, on the first night, he was at that best. Every operagoer must recall phrases the sound of which moved him to ecstasy. Not since the young Fischer-Dieskau, as Wolfram in a Bayreuth *Tannhäuser*, turned my heart over with his singing of the words "Bleib' bei Elisabeth!" have I been so transported by lyric baritone sound as during Mr. Mazurok's delivery of Shchelkalov's brief address, in the first scene. Both Xenias— Tamara Sorokina and Lidia Kovalyova—were edgy, impure, unpleasant sopranos, but they were the only singers in the large casts who seriously let down the side. The numerous basses, baritones, and tenors maintained a good level.

But a simple report sheet, artist by artist, cannot give much idea of the whole or convey the sense one gained of an ideal performance, existing in the imagination of all, toward which each was striving to contribute his share. Very beautiful, very clear enunciation of the text was a general virtue. When Stanislavsky prepared this opera for performance by his Opera Studio, he told his cast that

the whole of *Boris Godunov* needs to be based on dazzling diction. You need to know how to speak Pushkin's lines. There is very little staging involved. Everything is based on the words in the phrases! You are to pronounce the text in such a musical way that Pushkin's verse will be preserved. That is your main objective. . . . In contrast to all the former productions you have been in here, you will be concerned not with action but with conveying all the charm of Pushkin's poetry.

(Stanislavsky's direction of *Boris*, and of *Eugene Onegin, The Queen of Spades*, and several other operas, is described in detail in *Stanislavsky on Opera*, by Constantin Stanislavsky and Pavel Rumyantsev, published by Theatre Arts Books.) "All the charm of Pushkin's poetry" must elude anyone not versed in Russian, but the charm of words distinctly, purely, and expressively uttered is universal, and the Bolshoy's "dazzling diction" made me feel that, if only I knew more than a few words of Russian, I would understand all that these singers say. Russian-speakers in the audience confirm that almost every line is intelligible. The artists must be praised for it. Also the conductor, Yury Simonov, who let the words through without in any way reducing the expressive power or dimming the colors of his orchestra. Verbal audibility is partly a matter of instrumental rehearsal, of achieving (as Karajan does) a balance so precise and intonation so true that the orchestral sound is transparent, a support for and not a barrier to or a veil over the voices. This transparency was not Mr. Simonov's only merit. In every way he persuaded me, during *Boris*, that he is one of the world's great operatic conductors, with a perfect sense of timing and timbre, a pacing that leads the listener from phrase to phrase, a sense of form that spans the whole of a scene. He covered a huge dynamic range, without ever inviting attention to stray from the music drama and dwell simply on its stunning execution. He has an immaculate, very precise and communicative, unflashy technique. Responsive, cooperative and not dictatorial, he seems to breathe and bow along with his singers and players, to inspire and draw inspiration from them. Still in his thirties, he is now the Bolshoy Opera's principal conductor. Conductors who combine virtuoso command, unobtrusiveness, and profound interpretative powers in so high a degree are most rare.

The second opera of the visit was *The Gambler*, an uneven but exhilarating product of Prokofiev's impetuous youth. In about 1914 he began it, at a time when stage adaptations of Dostoyevsky were being tried. The ballets for Diaghilev—*Ala and Lolly* and *The Buffoon*—intervened. (The first never reached the stage, but was converted into the *Scythian Suite*; war delayed production of the second to 1921.) Spurred by the Diaghilev successes abroad, the Maryinsky Theater began to think about new works. One of its conductors, Albert Coates, said to Prokofiev, "Write your *Gambler*, and we'll produce it." Prokofiev wrote it. ("Encouraged by the interest aroused by the *Scythian Suite*, I chose the most radical language possible.") A read-through for the Maryinsky opera committee was arranged on a day when the conservative Glazunov and Cui could not be present; *The Gambler* was accepted, put into rehearsal, and announced for 1917. But soon after the February Revolution work on it was dropped; the singers could not cope with the "cacophony of sounds, with its incredible intervals and discordant notes." Not until 1929, in Brussels, was *The Gambler* performed; Prokofiev revised his score for the occasion. It disappeared again until performances were given in Naples in 1955, in Darmstadt the following year, and in New York (in the Eighty-fifth Street Playhouse, with two-piano accompaniment) the year after that. Since then there has been a trickle of productions, and last year the Bolshoy took *The Gambler* into its repertory. The standard Soviet work on Prokofiev—Israel Nesteyev's, of 1957—disapproves of the opera:

Despite its satirical note, the libretto of *The Gambler* is on the whole very pessimistic, and lacking in morality and faith in man. The music accentuates these qualities. . . . The continuous recitative, for the most part high-strung and unrelieved by a single arioso passage, inevitably becomes monotonous.

But the line on Prokofiev has changed since then; several pieces of his once scorned have entered the Soviet repertory, and Boris Pokrovsky, the director of the Bolshoy production, can find in *The Gambler* one "positive character"—the composer himself, whose music "exposes, denounces, and passes a merciless verdict" on "the world of material gain" and its contemptible inhabitants, by whom Alexei and Polina, "the poor tutor and the dowerless young woman," are destroyed. "Therein lies the moral message of the opera and its humanism: the lyrical sympathy with which the composer depicts the victims of this warped and ugly environment."

I don't believe Prokofiev intended any such moral message. Dostoyevsky's autobiographical tale, from which the composer drew his own libretto, is of two self-destructive and mutually destructive lovers who move in a "mist of egoistical preoccupations." (The phrase is John Updike's, from his review, in *The New Yorker*, of the University of Chicago Press volume that gathers Dostoyevsky's *The Gambler*, related letters, the diary of the real-life Polina, and *her* story, *The Stranger and Her Lover*.) Prokofiev discerned in it, I believe, no more than some dramatic confrontations lending themselves to music of high emotional tension, a well-varied supporting cast who, with touches of caricature, could be made vivid, and the chance for a virtuoso divertissement round the roulette tables. Characteristically, the enfant terrible began his composition by setting Alexei's satirical account of Russian family life. In adapting the book for the stage, he encountered two problems. First, it is written as Alexei's journal; we learn about the other characters, their relationships, and past events only as the narrator learns about them, and see them only through his eyes. Second, the principal theme is a troubled, undefined relationship between two people who cannot themselves comprehend or formulate their feelings. (In Prokofiev's next opera but one, *The Fiery Angel*, based on Valery Bryusov's autobiographical allegory, both difficulties recur in exactly the same form.) Prokofiev solves the second problem by writing, so to speak, eloquently unspecific love music that can prompt a listener to feel intensely with Polina and Alexei without quite understanding—any more than they do—just what is being felt, or why. The first problem—transforming a first-person narrative into a dramatic action—is often quite gauchely tackled; there are lines and incidents in the libretto that make no sense unless one has read the book. (That is true of almost all Prokofiev's operas.)

What *The Gambler* shows abundantly—Nesteyev admits it, Pokrovsky delights in it—is Prokofiev's flair for brilliantly theatrical music. In a well-known passage, the composer analyzed four strains in his creative personality at the time of *The Gambler*: neoclassical; toccata-like ("this perhaps the least important"); lyrical; and "the modern trend . . . the search for a language in which to express powerful emotions." A possible fifth, an element that some termed grotesque, he preferred to regard as an intensification of the others, and rejected the word "grotesque" in favor of "scherzo-ish—or else the three words describing the various degrees of the scherzo: whimsicality, laughter, mockery." Examples of all five strains may be found in almost any of his works. Lyricism dominates in *The Ugly Duckling* and in the Akhmatova song settings, Opus 27, composed around *Gambler* time; but in *The Gambler* the fourth and fifth strains are uppermost. The performances of the opera I have enjoyed most have been crisp, "scherzo-ish" readings in which the drama of the characters has seemed less important than the exuberant quality of the music and its torrents of headlong invention. The Bolshoy performance disturbed me because of its imprecision—not orchestrally (for under the young Alexander Lazarev the playing was bright and keen) but vocally. The singers were seldom exactly on the beat; they tended to utter the lines with the kind of freedom from strict tempo that Richard Strauss asks for in his conversation piece *Intermezzo*—parlando and rubato. Such expressive freedom is in many works welcome, but cannot be right for this score, in which the voices are so often an element in elaborate scherzo patterns. Not understanding Russian, I may have missed compensating verbal inflections that give life to the characters; the imprecision may have been deliberate, or it may have arisen from a stage/pit acoustic relationship different from that of the Bolshoy Theater. In a few cases—notably in lines sung by the important characters of the General and the Grandmother, played by Alexander Ognivtsev and Larissa Avdeyeva—it extended to cavalier pitch definition of the notes. Mr. Pokrovsky and his designer, Valery Leventhal, had devised an animated production that was, appropriately, conceived in the "modern" manner of the twenties, and set on a revolving turntable. The show had plenty of spirit.

July 14, 1975

LYRIC SCENES

Tchaikovsky, who wrote his *Eugene Onegin* "in love with the image of Tatyana, under the spell of Pushkin's verses, and drawn to compose the music as it were by some irresistible attraction," feared what might happen to his opera when it reached the solid unrealities of the stage:

Where shall I find the Tatyana whom Pushkin imagined and whom I have tried to picture in music? Where is the artist who can even approach the ideal Onegin, that cold dandy penetrated to the marrow with worldly *bon ton*? Where is there a Lensky, an eighteen-year-old youth with the thick curls and impetuous and original ways of a young poet *à la* Schiller? How Pushkin's charming and original picture will be vulgarized when it is transferred to the stage, with its routine, its senseless traditions, its veterans of both sexes who . . . shamelessly take on the roles of sixteen-year-old girls and beardless youths.

Twice I have seen Tchaikovsky's Tatyana plain—once in the theater (when she was the Rumanian soprano Ileana Cotrubas, in a production by Peter Hall), and once at the movies (when the voice was Galina Vishnevskaya's; the actress was Ariadna Shengelaya). But more often than that I have *heard* her—and, through the sympathetic magic that can shape characters by sound, have then *seen* her, too, with eyes that the ear has directed. Leonid Sobinov was twenty-six when he sang his first, all-conquering Lensky at the Bolshoy, in 1898, and by his naturalism (he studied the role with Nemirovich-Danchenko) broke with the tradition established by Nikolai Figner, the great Lensky of Tchaikovsky's day. (Figner sang the role sporting his beard and waxed mustaches.) Sobinov, Dmitri Smirnov, Ivan Kozlovsky, and Sergei Lemeshev are prominent in the line of great Russian Lenskys. The Bolshoy's leading interpreter of the role today, Vladimir Atlantov, breaks the line. He can be heard in the Melodiya-Angel recording of the opera, published in 1970, and he sang in the first *Onegin* of the Bolshoy season at the Met. As J. B. Steane remarks in his book *The Grand Tradition*, Mr. Atlantov's Lensky is "an ardent, big, rather simple fellow, his voice strong and with a touch of baritone about it, unusual in Russian tenors. . . . In the finale of the second act of *Eugene Onegin* he has the grief at his command but not the grace. The poetic, lingering essence of a Smirnov is not his, nor is the lyrical gentleness of his own predecessor in the role, Sergei Lemeshev." That finale begins with Lensky singing, in a low register and in free recitative time, "В вашем доме!" ("In your house!"), repeating it a third higher, and then moving into the slow, tender, 12/8 sequences that lead into the ensemble. It is one of the most poignant moments in all opera. Russian tenors traditionally make much of it. They linger, caressing the notes, voicing the phrases in a tone of piercing sweetness, along a line as unbroken as a stream of poured honey. Mr. Atlantov took part in the "musically re-studied" *Onegin* prepared by Mstislav Rostropovich (who conducts the Melodiya recording, and conducted the Bolshoy performances of the opera in Paris in 1970), and it may have been then that he decided to eschew sentiment and deliver both this passage and the aria in a more "manly," less mannered, more straightforward way than his predecessors had done. But he is wrong to do so. Even Stanislavsky, no upholder of hallowed tradition, had this to say to his Lensky about "В вашем доме!" while he was rehearsing *Eugene Onegin*:

This is where you must see with strong impact an inner picture of what these words mean to you. At this moment, all your life in this house must pass before your inner vision. . . . How many memories surge into your mind now! The more of them you see in your imagination the truer will be your expression. As you pronounce these words, more significance, a fresher color will go into your voice. . . . Your voice must be pregnant with drama. You must win me not by the power of your voice but by the expressiveness of the way you say those words, by the emotional coloration you give to them.

And then, after the words "In your house!" had been sung, and Lensky drew breath to launch the ensemble, Stanislavsky cried:

Wait! Wait! Now all this is in the hands of your emotions. Make use of the fact, do not hurry, give us a chance to concentrate on the thoughts in your mind. Do not be in a rush to *sing*, hold on to your emotions.

Stanislavsky also told his tenor to listen to Sobinov's records; and Sobinov was a very distinctive, tenderly poetic, not at all straightforward singer. At the Bolshoy's second performance of *Onegin* in New York, Denis Korolyov sang both "In your house!" and Lensky's aria with the traditional inflections and in the traditional sweet, "sentimental" tone. And he was far more moving than Mr. Atlantov had been.

Stanislavsky's direction of *Onegin* is described in detail in *Stanislavsky on Opera* (see p. 195). His production was first performed in 1922, with piano accompaniment and without costumes, in the studio/ballroom of the Moscow house where he lived and had his Opera Studio, and later that year was transferred to the Novy Theater, where it was accompanied by the Bolshoy Orchestra. It was very influential. I wonder whether the influence is not still felt in Moscow, even in small scenic details. Bolshoy designers love columns, and columns played an important part in every scene of Stanislavsky's *Onegin*. They had to, being immovably there in the studio/ballroom. The Bolshoy's current production of *Onegin*, by Boris Pokrovsky dates from 1944 but has no staleness in it, and with different casts its details are differently enacted. On the first night in New York, Yevgeny Nesterenko, as Prince Gremin, followed the "Stanislavsky scenario":

Just before the middle of the aria, when the tempo is heightened, Gremin makes a sign to Onegin inviting him to sit down. They seat themselves in armchairs at either side of a small table and Gremin finishes his aria in that position. This gives a quality of intimacy to the whole episode. . . . After the aria there is a long pause, during which the two men sit, each deep in his own thoughts.

During this long pause, the audience did not sit deep in thoughts, too, but applauded with enthusiasm. Mr. Nesterenko had sung the piece smoothly, nobly, inwardly, with beautiful utterance of the words, giving no impression that he was simply enjoying the sounds of his own voice. At the second performance, Alexander Ognivtsev remained standing— stood and delivered, in fact, addressing the audience rather than Onegin.

Makvala Kasrashvili, the second Tatyana, played the Letter Scene in much the way that Stanislavsky had suggested. (Twenty pages of *Stanislavsky on Opera* are devoted to his work on this episode.) She began it lying down, sang her first words without raising her head from her pillow, and did not move from her bed ("though the fact that you have now risen to a kneeling position is tantamount to a real move") until the end of the scene. Tamara Milashkina, in the first cast, moved about the set in much the way that the stage directions prescribe, and she wore diamond clips in her ears. Vishnevskaya's departure has left her more or less the Bolshoy's prima donna, insofar as an ensemble company can have one. She is a correct, careful, steady, and reliable singer, clear-cut in her intentions, with a voice that can be called useful rather than particularly attractive or exciting. In the final scene, for the sustained F that starts the phrase "Ах, Счастье было так возможно" ("Ah, happiness was so nearly possible") she found an exquisite tone of sad, keen regret for what might have been. (This is another famous moment in the opera; Vishnevskaya also excels in it.) Miss Kasrashvili, who likewise has a steady, assured, and adequate rather than remarkable soprano and a clean, definite style, looked younger, sounded younger, seemed more impetuous, and so in the earlier scenes was rather more touching. Both ladies were satisfactory; neither was outstanding.

The first-cast Onegin was Yury Mazurok. As I remarked last week, at his best his baritone is possibly the most beautiful to be heard today. The finest note in this performance was his (unwritten) high F at the end of his aria—soft, clearly projected, and perfectly formed. There were many admirable, smoothly produced sounds, some gentle, some ringing. He looked elegant, well-mannered, supercilious, just as Onegin should. And yet the interpretation did not come to life. Vladimir Malchenko, the next Onegin, and one of the youngest soloists of the company, also has a very fine lyric baritone. His broad, handsome features remained set in a heavy expression of sulky pride. He sang the musical lines correctly but did not act subtly; the aria was just an aria, and he presented it to the audience as if he had forgotten about Tatyana. But he has a voice we should be hearing more of.

A Bolshoy production, as I noted after its *Boris Godunov*, is more than the sum of its constituents. We may weigh specific pros and cons: debate the merits of two strong, merry Olgas (Tamara Sinyavskaya and Galina Borisova); one night enjoy a Mme Larina and a Nurse (Tatyana Tugarinova and Larissa Avdeyeva) of fine accomplishment and the next night regret that their successors, though also good singers, are apt to keep an eye cocked on the conductor or the prompter. But the strongest impression is of a whole performance established over the years and built up from the best of what everyone has contributed to it. Since no one is perfect, any particular manifestation of this ideal, collaborative interpretation is bound to have its imperfections. Despite them, what we see and hear *is Eugene Onegin*, the opera that the Bolshoy has been performing ever since it mounted the professional première of the piece in 1881—the opera that Tchaikovsky conceived, and not anyone else's commentary on it. Peter Williams's settings, in manner, color, and size, are exactly what is needed. (For the intimate scenes, the stage is cunningly scaled down.) Although Mr. Pokrovsky's staging departs at times—as did Stanislavsky's—from the written letter of the score, and was criticized for that in 1944, there is now nothing willful and nothing merely personal about it. It contains more of Pushkin than any other version I have seen—but never at Tchaikovsky's expense. (The composer's tone, and his treatment of the characters, are far more emotional than the poet's.) Its progress is so sure, its spirit so right, that there is room in it for the individual variations noted above. When a style is grasped, freedoms within it can be memorably achieved. Just one small miscalculation breaks the realistic idiom. Since, during the St. Petersburg ball, Onegin asks about "the lady with the red beret,"

Tatyana wears one, but she is the *only* lady present wearing headgear, and it looks odd. And one large failing flaws the show: the lighting is terribly crude. It consists mainly of spotlights pointed at the principals. Fuat Mansurov conducts an eloquent reading—not sluggish, not over-vitalized, but ardent, ample. First cello, first oboe, and first horn are named along with the cast, and deserve to be, for they have important "singing" to do, and do it very well.

July 21, 1975

1975–1976

GOLDEN EVENINGS

The Glyndebourne Festival Opera, from its first season, in 1934, has shown that a combination of careful casting, first-rate musical and dramatic direction, and ample rehearsal time in a rural setting free of big-city tensions can provide opera on a superior level, and different in kind from even the starriest productions of the big companies. "Ensemble opera" is not there a euphemism for second-rate singing. The Festival has not lacked eminent artists: Sena Jurinac was in effect the resident diva of the postwar decade, and Elisabeth Söderström is that now (sustaining the position, this season, as the heroine of Richard Strauss's *Intermezzo*). Birgit Nilsson, Régine Crespin, Montserrat Caballé, and Ileana Cotrubas are among the sopranos who chose or were chosen by Glyndebourne for a British début; Teresa Berganza, Mirella Freni, and Luciano Pavarotti made early appearances there; Erich Kunz and Peter Pears rose from its chorus. This season brought Donald Gramm's triumphant British début, as Nick Shadow, in a new production of Stravinsky's *The Rake's Progress*. (Next year, he is due to return as Falstaff.) In fact, three of the four principals in that *Rake*, and three of the six singers in the first cast of *Così fan tutte*, another new production of the season, were American (stretching the term to include the Philippine Evelyn Mandac). So was the protagonist of *Eugene Onegin*, Richard Stilwell. There is nothing like Glyndebourne anywhere else; in America, perhaps in Santa Fe or at Caramoor, some of its elements may be found, but nowhere the same combination of a small opera house thoroughly equipped (with good workshops, rehearsal rooms, etc.), a long season during which productions can grow (Glyndebourne's runs for eleven weeks), and a leading metropolitan orchestra (Glyndebourne employs the London Philharmonic, currently deemed London's best).

Glyndebourne is fifty-four miles south-southeast of London—about two hours' drive, or an hour and a half by train from Victoria Station and then by connecting motor coach. Performances begin at five-fifteen or five-thirty, and Londoners get home about midnight. There is a long dinner intermission; a restaurant; and gardens, lawns, and lakeside meadows to picnic in. The excursion can be expensive; most of the seats cost £11.90 or £10.80 ($25 or $23); the train-and-motor-coach fare is £3.55 first class and £2.60 second; the celebrated wine list, which has twice been the subject of essays in the Festival program book, can run up the bill still further. The theater, attached to the country house of George Christie (the son of John Christie and the soprano Audrey Mildmay, who founded the Festival), seats eight hundred. About 80 percent of the budget comes from ticket sales, the rest from individuals, trusts, and firms. (The government, through the Arts Council, supports

Glyndebourne Touring Opera, a company of young singers that, on an autumn tour, takes the productions up and down the country.) Live broadcasts, full-length television performances (including Peter Hall's memorable productions of *Le nozze di Figaro* and of Monteverdi's *Il ritorno d'Ulisse*), and semi-staged concert versions played to a large audience at the Albert Hall Proms and broadcast to one still larger make Glyndebourne's work more generally available.

A few—but very few—of the hundred and more visits I have paid to Glyndebourne have been duds, but the chief memory is of golden evenings, either with familiar Mozart enjoyed in the detail that only a small auditorium can make vivid, or with other Glyndebourne specialties: revivals of unfamiliar operas that then have often gone out to join the international repertory. Mozart's own *Idomeneo* was one; others were the Rossini comedies produced while Vittorio Gui was musical director; now, the waves of seventeenth-century Venetian opera that sweep Europe and America rise from Glyndebourne. Operas of our day make not too bad a showing in the annals: the world première of Nicholas Maw's *The Rising of the Moon*, the British premières of Hans Werner Henze's *Elegy for Young Lovers*, of Poulenc's *La Voix humaine*, of Gottfried von Einem's *The Visit of the Old Lady*, and of *The Rake's Progress*. That first *Rake*, designed by Osbert Lancaster and directed by Carl Ebert, produced in 1953, lasted a decade. The new production is even more successful. It has been designed by David Hockney in his most elegant, delightful, and cunning manner. The scenes and costumes are crosshatched, in homage to the Hogarth prints that inspired the fable, but the general effect is light and clear, as lucid and unemphatic as Stravinsky's score. John Cox, Glyndebourne's director of production, has directed with a similar transparency and imposed no heavy interpretation on a work that needs only to be perceived, not explained. Best of all, Bernard Haitink's conducting combines all the diverse virtues that other conductors have brought to the score. By and large, Mr. Haitink must be the conductor most solidly esteemed in Europe today. Solti and Karajan may generate more heat; they are more extravagantly acclaimed, but often with reservations, while Haitink is simply and unanimously praised for his excellence. His *Rake* was at once precise yet lyrical, pungent in timbre yet delicate, purposive in gait yet never stiff. The London Philharmonic woodwinds played like angels.

Donald Gramm's Nick Shadow is a wonderful piece of work, infinite in faculty, in form and in moving admirable, in action like an exquisitely polished and courteous devil. Such impeccable command of notes and words is rare; rare such wit, such finesse of timing. Leo Goeke's Tom Rakewell was young, attractively vulnerable, and clearly projected except when some of the shorter notes and unaccented words disappeared. Rosalind Elias made an alluring Baba the Turk. Jill Gomez, who has been so tender and touching an Anne Trulove in other productions of the opera, was tender and touching again but not in her very best voice.

Glyndebourne's other brand-new production was of Janáček's *The Cunning Little Vixen*. Its *Così fan tutte* was newly directed, by Adrian Slack, in Emanuele Luzzati's scenery of 1969, which predicates a certain plainness in the spectacle. By a Polish Fiordiligi, Bozena Betley, a Bulgarian Dorabella, Reni Penkova, and an American Ferrando, Robert Johnson, making his British début, it was fairly well sung; and admirably sung by the Philippine Despina, Miss Mandac, a Norwegian Guglielmo, Knut Skram, and an American Alfonso, Michael Devlin, whose commanding presence and clear articulation dominated the evening. Glyndebourne's plainness was preferable to Covent Garden's frippery; in London, the Royal Opera was also playing *Così*, and John Copley, the director, had larded what was once a poised and elegant production with many crude jests. The international cast included three Covent Garden débutants: Anna Tomowa-Sintow, from Bulgaria, a bright but uneven Fiordiligi; Judith Blegen, from the Metropolitan, a lively Despina but somewhat peaky in timbre; and Rüdiger Wohlers, a moderately accomplished young Mozart tenor from Germany. At Glyndebourne, John Pritchard conducted the opera with easy mastery. At Covent Garden, I struck Colin Davis on one of the nights when he seemed determined to "bounce" everything along.

Mr. Davis's merits—his vigor, his determination that everything should sound and sing—were more apparent in *Peter Grimes*, the last new production of the Royal Opera's 1974–75 season. The piece has been much played in Britain: two productions by the Sadler's Wells—now English National—Opera; others by the Welsh National Opera and by the Scottish Opera; and the previous Covent Garden version, which lasted from 1947 to 1971. To refurbish the last (which had, essentially, the same Tanya Moiseiwitsch décor as the Metropolitan's version) would apparently have cost little less than the new, low-budget show has done. Timothy O'Brien and Tazeena Firth have designed a simple, versatile, well-proportioned plain box of a setting—boardwalks, a strip of shingle, not much else—that throws the action forward. A talented young director, Elijah Moshinsky, made his Covent Garden début with a tough, punchy staging, based on character vividly observed. (Asked where he got his training, Mr. Moshinsky replied, "By writing an Oxford thesis on Alexander Herzen, for Sir Isaiah Berlin.") The cast, led by the violent, visionary Grimes of Jon Vickers and the mild, placatory Ellen Orford of Heather Harper (this staging implied that a stronger character than Ellen's might have averted the tragedy), was first-rate, with Heather Begg's venomous and trenchant Mrs. Sedley especially vivid.

The Rake's Progress and *Peter Grimes* are the two postwar operas that have kept the longest hold on the international repertory. Glynde-bourne's *Rake* was ideal. Covent Garden's *Grimes* lacked only the ro-mantic depth that links it to the traditions of grand opera. Everything was unremittingly front-stage. Britten's "sea interludes" are meant to be played with the curtain down while the orchestra alone evokes Suffolk scenes and stirs the imagination of the audience; these interludes were played with the curtain up, as accompaniment to a pantomime, and the music was impoverished. Similar troubles beset most "modern" stagings in anachronistic theatrical manners of works that in their creators' minds were both seen and heard. Romantic operas such as Wagner's *Lohengrin* and Verdi's *Les Vêpres siciliennes* can be as much diminished by the absence of romantic scenery as Shakespeare's plays can be cumbered by its presence.

October 13, 1975

HERE AND THERE IN ITALY

Opera performances in the Roman Arena of Verona began in 1913. *Aida* was played that year, *Carmen* the next. The season grew, and now, for six summer weeks, the huge place is filled almost nightly. The Arena holds twenty-two thousand people. The acoustics are remarkable; the old Roman engineers evidently knew secrets unguessed by modern experts, who resort to amplification when audiences run into tens of thousands. Sometimes Arena opera can be a bawling match under the stars, but I have enjoyed delicate things there: Maria Callas's Violetta, the young Giuseppe Di Stefano's Nadir in *Les Pêcheurs de perles*, Montserrat Caballé's Elizabeth in *Don Carlos*. Three operas and a ballet are the usual fare; this year, the operas were *Carmen, Turandot*, and *La forza del destino*, and the ballet was Beethoven's Ninth Symphony, set to movement by Maurice Béjart. Over the years, *Aida* has been the most popular piece, with a hundred and forty performances listed in the annals; *Carmen*, with fifty-six, comes second.

Things are quieter now, but the 1968–69 season was a troubled time for Italian opera. Eggs were thrown at elegant first-night audiences; the very existence of opera companies became a matter of political polemics: was public money justifiably spent on their support? And in 1969 "arena opera" was put forward as an unexceptionable, non-élitist form of the art. In Verona, Jean Vilar, a master of serious-minded open-air spectacle after his years with France's Théâtre National Populaire, staged a strong and simple *Don Carlos*; *Turandot* was done in a way to suggest that the audience and the chorus were all one mob, gathered outside the great wall of the Peking palace, just before moonrise, to learn the fate of the latest candidate for the Princess's hand; Luciano Damiani devised a stark, non-spectacular *Aida* (whereas in 1953, in G. W. Pabst's Arena production of the opera, elaboration had been carried to a point at which Amneris's barque, taking her to the Temple of Isis, beside the Nile, was afloat in real water). Instead of sporting massive scenery by the ton, the Arena was treated as, in Peter Brook's sense, an Open Space for dramatic action—and a magnificent one. Since then, Verona opera has been sometimes a conventional big show for the tourists, and sometimes a stern and striking "statement of belief" in opera as a social experience as salutary to modern audiences as Attic drama was to the ancients. From this year's offerings I chose *Forza*, but I chose badly. True, there were impressive moments. The little dawn patrol in Act III, which on regular stages must either, like the troops of Midian, prowl and prowl around, or else enter, come to attention to sing, and then march off, here had space enough to keep up a convincing reconnaissance until its chorus was done. And the big finale of Act II—one of Verdi's recurrent attempts to rival the coronation scene of Meyerbeer's *Le Prophète* (he added it himself to the Rivas play on which *Forza* is based)—came off splendidly: monks by the hundred, bearing tapers, filed from a monastery façade, set high on the Arena steps, to circle the huge stage, thunder their *maledizione*, and float "La Vergine degli Angeli" into the night sky. But for the most part it was a routine, unimaginative presentation, conducted without distinction by Francesco Molinari-Pradelli, and directed by an old Verona hand, Carlo Maestrini, who made his Arena début in 1955, long before the new ideas about "arena opera" were hatched. Chance after chance was missed in the genre scenes, which Verdi deemed much the most important part of his opera. He once wrote severely about a performance in which the soloists had been superb and the solos and duets magnificently executed, but not "the varied, ampler scenes that fill half the opera"; as a result, "the work itself—the *opera*, the *dramma scenico-musicale*—was but imperfectly realized." The Verona cast, not exactly superb, was mainly good. Ileana Meriggioli, the Leonora, is a well-schooled, useful young soprano who sang her music truly and purely, without strain or stridency. Garbis Boyagian, the Carlo, has a dark, easy, effortless, and smooth baritone that we shall probably hear more of. But Carlo Bergonzi, the only big name of the evening, turned Alvaro into a vulgar caricature of a Famous Italian Tenor concerned only with the sound of his voice and not at all with what might be taking place around him. On the simple level of a large show and a full-throated sing, it all made for a jolly enough evening, and I had a good time. But recent Arena developments had raised hopes of something more adventurous—and more Verdian.

Opera itself began in Florence, and its origins are graphically explored in an important exhibition, "Il luogo teatrale a Firenze," set out in the Palazzo Medici-Riccardi. The show begins with fifteenth-century religious dramas, for which the churches of the city were equipped with elaborate aerial machinery (among the most celebrated, Brunelleschi's for an Annunciation play in San Felice—a skyful of singing cherubs, elaborate lighting effects, and an angel descending in a mandorla from the dome to the floor of the church). It continues with Medici pastorals, intermezzos, and Machiavelli comedies. Then, in 1586, Bernardo Buontalenti designed the great Teatro Mediceo, in the Uffizi. It opened with *L'amico fido*—words by Giovanni Bardi, music by Bardi, Cristofano Malvezzi, and Alessandro Striggio. Jacopo Peri's *Euridice* was the first real opera, in 1600, at the Pitti Palace. Three days later, Peri's rival, Giulio Caccini, brought out his *Il rapimento di Cefalo* in the Uffizi theater. And so the procession continues, to close in the mid-seventeenth century with sumptuous equine ballets in the amphitheater of the Boboli Gardens. It is at once a show that brings textbook names, learned theses, and scholarly scores to life and a feast for any theatrical person who enjoys early solutions of problems that are with us still. Back in 1589, we find Bardi (whose claim to be the principal begetter of opera has ample support here), as author of the intermezzos in an opulent new production of Giroloma Bargagli's play *La pellegrina*, "striving with all his might" (in the words of a contemporary chronicler) "to ensure that whatever happens does so naturally; that, for example, if in an intermezzo people dance, or sing, the story should demand that they do so." We find Buontalenti, in his scenes for *Il rapimento di Cefalo*, seeking, like a modern Arena designer, to bridge stage and auditorium and make the spectators feel that they and the action inhabit one space. Pabst may have flooded a section of the Verona stage for his 1953 *Aida*; in 1589, Buontalenti flooded the whole courtyard of the Pitti Palace to stage a naval battle between Christians and Turks. That courtyard is used today for concerts; in the exhibition, one finds an account of how its acoustics were first tested by a singer in 1637. Large model reconstructions of the machinery and the lost theaters, librettos, stage designs, engravings, plans, old chronicles, portraits, scores, and musical instruments of the time are brought together in a rich display. The exhibition lasts till the end of October.

Florence's Maggio Musicale extends into June. For the rest of the summer there is music all over Tuscany. Arezzo, the birthplace of

Guido, the great choir trainer, has its annual Polyphonic Competition, and there are related choral concerts throughout the province. In Siena, there is the Settimana Musicale. In Montepulciano, an improbable triumvirate of the tenor Mario Del Monaco, his son, and the composer Hans Werner Henze is starting up a "festival." Lucca already has one, inspired by the many-faceted musician Herbert Handt. Barga, a small town in the Apennine foothills, boasts a Festival Lirico Internazionale in connection with its summer school of opera, and this year put on *Don Pasquale*, Alessandro Scarlatti's *Il trionfo dell'onore*, and a Ravel-Satie evening. Outside Grosseto, at Batignano, in an abandoned convent now being restored by the British designer Adam Pollock, there has been a week of Musica nel Chiostro. The principal event was Francesco Cavalli's opera *Ormindo*, in the edition prepared for Glyndebourne—with an inventive hand—by Raymond Leppard, here rescored for a smaller band by Henry Ward, who conducted. (It is high time people started to look at what Cavalli actually wrote; and to perform an arrangement of an arrangement is doubly odd.) The cast—all British except for the Erisbe, Silvia Baleani, a clear, attractive soprano from the Teatro Colón, Buenos Aires—consisted mainly of young singers associated with Glyndebourne and Wexford; John Wakefield, who "created" the Cavalli-Leppard title role in 1967, undertook it once more. I was glad to hear again two rising singers who have been lately winning golden reviews in England, and impressed by the Sicle of Eiddwen Harrhy, who has become a more passionate and intense artist; less so by the Amida of Peter Knapp (he sang Szymanowski's King Roger in London earlier this year), whose voice had some beautiful notes but others that sounded artificial. Still, it is not fair to judge any baritone in an alto role transposed down; no baritone sounds good, either, as Otho in the Leppard transposition of Monteverdi's *Poppea*. Malcolm King, as the old King Ariadeno, a bass, was the best singer of all. Mr. Pollock designed and Patrick Libby directed an attractive production, which, along with the audience, moved from the cloister into the monastic barn for the Conjuration Scene. The feeling was of country-house opera got up by a party of talented professionals for their own and their friends' enjoyment. The fact that it was altogether a very pleasant excursion and evening pass-time—drinks served in the walled monastery garden during the interval—must not stop a critic from complaining that Mr. Ward had not coached his singers and players into that command of Cavalli's lines which should make his own role as conductor almost superfluous. Properly, a libretto was provided, and for some of the British Italian it was needed.

Siena's Musical Week, organized by the Academia Chigiana, comes at the close of the Academy's celebrated summer courses. The town is filled with an international throng of young musicians. Simultaneously, the Academy and Siena University cosponsor a musicological congress; this year's theme was "Italian Musical and Theatrical Culture in Enlightenment Paris," chiming with two of the opera performances—*Iphigénie en Tauride* by Gluck, and *Iphigénie en Tauride* by Niccolò Piccinni. The Paris Opera, cashing in on the famous feud between Gluckists and Piccinnists that gave Parisians something to talk about in the late eighteenth century, commissioned both works. Piccinni didn't get a fair chance then, for he was assigned the inferior libretto; and he didn't in Siena, either, for while Gluck's opera was staged, his was done in excerpt and in concert performance. Nevertheless, enough of his *Iphigénie* was heard to confirm the impressions left by his *Didon* in Alice Tully Hall earlier this year: that, after the lapse of centuries, the similarities between contemporary composers are apt to be more striking than the differences (will Schoenberg and Stravinsky sound much the same to the general public of two hundred years hence?); that Piccinni has Gluck's solidity and noble gravity but not his genius; that, no more than Bononcini to Handel, can Piccinni to his erstwhile rival hold a candle. The Gluck production, though clumsily staged (in décor derived from Piranesi prints) and not grandly cast, was powerfully affecting—largely because the conductor, Gabriele Ferro, adopted several unwontedly slow tempi. Anyone who has heard Alice Raveau's record of "J'ai perdu mon Eurydice," from *Orphée*, will know the Gluckian eloquence that only at a slow tempo can be achieved. Many conductors, fearing that modern audiences may find Gluck's music dull, try to "inject vitality" by driving it along—with the result that it does indeed sound dull. Not so Mr. Ferro. His interpretation, unhurried and intense, made vivid a masterpiece often accorded lip service rather than loving appreciation from rapt audiences. Lynne Strow, the Iphigenia, has a large voice and a large, passionate style. Lajos Miller was a ringing, virile Orestes. As Thoas, Mr. Boyagian confirmed the good impression he made in the Verona *Forza*.

But the most promising singer heard in Siena was another baritone, Alessandro Corbelli, Thoas of the Piccinni *Iphigénie*, and the Paolino in the third operatic offering of the week, *La villanella rapita*. He provided that sudden, instantly recognizable, and not common pleasure of discovering a voice that hits every note plumb-center, with sharply focused tone and quick, bright, forward attack. *La villanella rapita*, composed by Francesco Bianchi in Venice, 1783, shed some of its numbers and acquired others as it made its way around the opera houses of Europe. By the time it reached Paris, in 1789, there were additional or alternative pieces by Mozart (a quartet and a trio composed for a Burgtheater performance in 1785), Giacomo Ferrari (the chief architect of the Paris score), Giovanni Paisiello, Pietro Guglielmi, Giuseppe

Sarti, and Johann Paul Martini. Contributions from all these composers figured in the composite Siena edition, prepared by Mario Salerno and given in concert form. The result was like a quick tour of some eighteenth-century minor masters grouped around a genius. The listener registered snap judgments (Bianchi, a pretty melodist; Paisiello, a thorough professional, with some Rossinian zip; Ferrari, someone who thought about his orchestra as well as his singers; Guglielmi, a man apt to overwork his attractive inventions; etc.), and then at Mozart's first chords heard a sonority, and in his first clauses a richness of musical incident, that made the rest seem thin stuff. Cecilia Valdenassi was the pretty heroine, most successful in her sentimental, slightly serious moments, for she seems to be a lyric soprano rather than a soubrette— more a young Elvira than a Zerlina. The conducting was shared between four members of Franco Ferrara's conducting course. Lorenzo Muti, who made his Broadway début, in 1958, as Trottolò, in Menotti's *Maria Golovin*, was the most talented of them.

As usual, Siena was concerned with not only the eighteenth century (further represented by a chamber concert of Sammartini works brought to light by Newell Jenkins and Bathia Churgin) but the twentieth. The composer Luigi Dallapiccola, who died earlier this year, was a vivid presence at earlier Siena festivals. A memorial exhibition stressed his links with Schoenberg and Berg; with writers such as Thomas Mann, Eugenio Montale, and Carlo Emilio Gadda; with art that is at once adventurous, serious, and attentive to tradition. He was further commemorated in a concert at which eight compositions in his honor, by eight Italian composers, had their first performances. In this cross-section of contemporary Italian composition, the richest veins were struck in Franco Donatoni's *Lumen*, a brief and delicately wrought chamber work for six players, and Carlo Prosperi's rhapsodic *Chant* for violin and piano. The long evening ended with Dallapiccola's last completed composition, the elegiac *Commiato*. The performers were the Musicus Concentus, directed by Massimo De Bernart—an adept ensemble, which, I am told, has brought new life to the musical scene in Florence, where it is based.

Like all good festivals, Siena's has coherence and continuity. This was stressed by the publication, during the Musical Week, of the latest number of *Chigiana*, the Chigi Academy's annual collection of musicological studies. The volume includes the talk on Schoenberg that Dallapiccola gave there in 1973, and many important papers on Gluck, who—on that occasion, in relation to the Italian culture in the Vienna of his day—was the subject of the 1973 congress, and represented in performance by his opera *Paride ed Elena* and his ballets *Don Juan* and *Semiramide*.

October 20 1975

THRICE CARLOS

Munich is the city where the continuity of opera is most strongly felt. At this year's Opera Festival—three and a half summer weeks with one performance, sometimes two, every night—*Idomeneo* could be seen in the theater of its first performance. And so could *Die Walküre*. The Kurfürsten created the baroque and rococo city; Max Joseph the Well-Beloved built the Cuvilliés-Theater, and Carl Theodor commissioned *Idomeneo* to be performed there. But essentially Munich is a neoclassical metropolis, shaped as such by its nineteenth-century kings, and rebuilt as such after the last war: an affirmation of classical architecture, sculpture, and drama as the perennial font of Western art. The visitor who sees the Aegina marbles and the Barberini faun housed again in Leo von Klenze's Roman-vaulted Glyptothek, who enters the National Theater beneath Karl von Fischer's majestic portico, is drawn at once into the Northerner's romantic dream of noble antiquity—Goethe's, Kleist's, Hölderlin's, Thomas Mann's. The nineteenth-century evocations of Renaissance Florence—the Pitti Palace as Königsbau, the Loggia dei Lanzi as Feldherrnhalle—serve to remind him that it is not only a Northern dream; that Donatello and Bernini strove consciously to emulate antique greatness and technical skills; that art itself has been a series of renascences. Opera began as an endeavor to recapture the effects of Attic tragedy. When things went wrong, Gluck and Wagner initiated their reforms by looking back to that source. The Munich composer Carl Orff is one of the latest to return to first principles, and his *Antigonae*, one of the new productions at the Munich Festival, brought into focus the scattered musings about art, history, and (in a city where road signs point to Dachau) human behavior that throng the Munich visitor's mind.

Orff's *Antigonae* is Sophocles twice interpreted: by Hölderlin, in his ardent translation, and then by Orff, in his powerful, passionate declamation of the Hölderlin text. But in performance the spectator is aware only of the great play and its great issues. Consideration of the means comes later. Orff uses many kinds of declamation: straight speech; monotone; stichomythia on one note, across octaves, or with varied intervals; chant whose strong outline makes each step or leap an "event"; sudden garlands of diatonic or chromatic melisma. The six grand choral odes that punctuate the work are diverse and expressive. The scoring calls for six each of pianos, flutes, oboes, and muted trumpets; four harps; nine double-basses; seven or eight timpani; and percussion to keep from ten to fifteen players busy. (In practice, the forces are usually reduced.) Orff works through words, rhythms, and sounds. There are no symphonic developments. Counterpoint is confined to simple imitations. The harmony is uncomplicated affirmation or contradiction. "Primitivism," cry those who scorn Orff's music—but his techniques, though direct, are far from simple. I agree with Andreas Liess's comment, in his monograph on the composer, that Orff's primitivism "touches the deepest, most secret centers of spirits and senses at once. . . . When he summons the vital powers by gesture, dance, word, image, and, not least, the rhythm of urgently insistent repetition, he advances toward that center of human experience where vital excitement arouses spiritual emotion."

The first performance of *Antigonae*, at the 1949 Salzburg Festival, before Bayreuth had reopened and before Stravinsky's *Oedipus Rex* became regular operatic fare, was influential. The director was Oscar Fritz Schuh. Wieland Wagner, who worked on it with him, owed, and owned, his debt to the production. The chorus was still, in a semicircle; the actors strode the stage of the Rocky Riding School in buskins and masks. A thunderstorm rolling through the Salzkammergut added an unplanned but appropriately numinous commentary. Munich's first production of the work, in 1951, in the Prinzregententheater, conducted by Solti, again used a static chorus, but this time ranged in front of the stage platform. In the new version, Günther Rennert has essayed a more plastic interpretation, with big, bold gestures and much variety in choral groups not quite symmetrical but balanced. Rudolf Heinrich has designed a kind of classical chapterhouse with benches down the sides and light streaming in from a circular opening above—a room in which important matters can be debated, and strong theatrical architecture. The performance, dominated by Colette Lorand as Antigone and William Murray as Creon, was superbly accomplished. This *Antigonae* showed the Munich company at its best.

Busts of Mozart, Wagner, and Richard Strauss grace the main foyer of the National Theater, and their works form the foundation of the Festival bill. Busts of Weber and Orff at one end, Verdi and Puccini at the other, close the long prospect through the marble halls on the second floor. Verdi's *Don Carlos* was another new production of the Festival, and it showed a less admirable aspect of the company—Munich as just another stop on the international opera circuit, with an audience come to shout for the stars, applaud the scenery through the music, and dismember the drama into a series of showstopping solo numbers. Brigitte Fassbaender, who belted out Eboli's two airs, and Ruggero Raimondi, who, as Philip, did big, obvious things in a big, obvious way, were applauded beyond their deserts. Katia Ricciarelli deserved praise for her efforts to mold an unwieldy but eloquent voice to the needs of Elizabeth's music, but prolonged plaudits, in this opera, should sound when the curtain is down; the beautiful coda to Elizabeth's Act II romance was played to the sound of an ovation, and the solemnity of the final scene was shattered by another, after her "Toi qui sus le néant." Eberhard Wächter, the Posa, was mercilessly booed, and did not deserve to be. So was the conductor, Georges Prêtre, who did.

Munich announced that it had acquired "the first-performance rights of an important new edition of Verdi's opera *Don Carlos*—the five-act *Originalfassung*." This is Ursula Günther's careful edition of the very long opera, which was cut before its first performance, in 1867, and it includes the unpublished passages that David Rosen and I brought to light, a few years ago, from the archives of the Paris Opera. Munich may have acquired those rights, but it did not use them. It performed, in the bad old Italian translation, not the *Originalfassung* but the familiar second version of 1883, preceded by Act I from 1867 (which Verdi dropped in his revision). The only "new" passage done was the Prélude et Introduction to this act. A large and important section of the first duet for Elizabeth and Carlos was cut; so, in Act II, Scene 2, was most of the Chœur des Dames d'Honneur, "Sous ces bois," and a verse of Posa's ballade, "L'Infant Carlos." On the credit side, two passages commonly omitted—the second verse of Elizabeth's romance and the *marziale* episode of the final duet—were retained. Rudolf Heinrich's sets were conventional in style, and there is no harm in that, but they were also dully and poorly painted. The principal innovation in Otto Schenk's stage direction was to open the auto-da-fé of Act III as a *Bauernfest*, with a very jolly crowd dressed in light, pastoral colors, some of them wearing straw hats. It did not fit the ceremonial mood of the music. The visual inspiration of this scene, a grim engraving of the 1559 auto-da-fé in Valladolid, ascribed to the Flemish artist Franz Hogenbergh, survives. So does the production book of the first performance; its moves are calculated to bring the right voices forward at the right moments. Both should be studied by modern directors.

A *Don Carlos* directed and conducted by Herbert von Karajan was the big event of the Salzburg Festival. Otherwise, the opera productions were revivals from previous years, and orchestral concerts were prominent (the Vienna Philharmonic conducted by Claudio Abbado, Riccardo Muti, Karl Böhm, Karajan, and Leonard Bernstein; the London Symphony by Seiji Ozawa, Böhm, Bernstein, and James Levine; the Israel Philharmonic by Zubin Mehta; the Berlin Philharmonic by Karajan). Salzburg is an expensive festival. Most tickets for the operas cost fifteen hundred Austrian schillings (about $83), and ten times that price was the reported black-market rate for the first night of *Don Carlos*. In terms of music played, the *Carlos* audience hardly got its money's worth. Karajan served, in Italian translation, an abridgment of the four-act version, shortened by, in the second scene, two thirds of "Sous ces bois," a verse of the Veil Song, a verse of Posa's romance, a section of the Elizabeth-Carlos duet, and a verse of Elizabeth's romance; in the auto-da-fé by a stretch of processional music; in the last act by not just the usual brutal cut in the final duet but also—incredibly—some of Elizabeth's and Carlos's solemn, tender farewell.

In somber, symmetrical scenery by Günther Schneider-Siemssen, Karajan laid out the action with formal, stately precision. The emphasis was on beauty of tone, not on dramatic delivery. The playing of the Vienna Philharmonic was an enchantment throughout the evening. The Viennese choirs sang nobly. Mirella Freni's Elizabeth was a limpid flow of exquisite sound. Piero Cappuccilli, as Posa, and Nicolai Ghiaurov, as Philip, voiced their roles in full, commanding tones. Placido Domingo, as Carlos, was not at his freshest or most even—he took on the assignment between some open-air Calafs in Verona and his first Othellos, in Hamburg—but was still pretty impressive. Christa Ludwig, the billed Eboli, retired after the first night; I heard Eva Randova, Bayreuth's new Kundry, a forceful but not quite polished singer. Karajan cast even the smallest roles at strength: Robert Kerns and Anna Tomowa-Sintow, who the month before had been the Guglielmo and Fiordiligi of Covent Garden's *Così*, were the Herald and the Heavenly Voice. The performance was finely calculated. There was no hint of spontaneity. Except by Miss Freni's tender, delicate phrasing, the emotions were untouched. But it was magnificent.

In London, while the Royal Opera devoted the first four weeks of its season to a new *Siegfried* and then three turns of its three-quarters-completed *Ring*, the English National Opera played yet another *Don Carlos*. This was also done in translation—my English translation, as it happens, so I must declare an interest, even though I have no intention of praising the performance. The Fontainebleau act, with its prelude and most of the introductory chorus, was included. The cuts were small: "Sous ces bois" was shortened; a verse of Elizabeth's romance, some of the processional music, and the *marziale* section of the final duet were omitted. But the execution was not good enough—the production was drab, the scenery monotonous, and the singing (apart from some touches in Rita Hunter's Elizabeth and the gay, sparkly Eboli of Elizabeth Connell) unremarkable—to sustain so much music.

Encounter with these three very different *Carlos* productions, in quick succession, prompted the following conclusions. For general use, Verdi's four-act score of 1883 is to be preferred. Two cuts in it are unexceptionable—the tawdriest section of the processional music and the insurrection at the close of Act III. (Verdi included the latter in his revised version only at his librettist's insistence, and the episode is too much of a scurry to make any great theatrical effect.) No other cuts should be made: "Sous ces bois" should be heard in full, Posa's and Elizabeth's romances need both verses, and the final duet needs the *marziale*. A large, colorful staging can safely be introduced by the

Fontainebleau act, when singers and scenery are on the grand scale, but the act should be added only when there is time enough to give the rest of the opera unshredded. This unrevised act more aptly introduces the unrevised and expansive score of 1867, and a performance of that 1867 score in extenso (such as Sarah Caldwell mounted in Boston, two years ago), further extended by the "new" passages, proves mightily impressive, but can be done only by a company, and for an audience, prepared to devote five hours to the enterprise. Music that Verdi jettisoned should not be reinstated at the expense of music he chose to retain.

A more general conclusion is that most companies are not equipped to tackle French grand opera, while those that are hesitate to devote to it the kind of attention they willingly give to Wagner. In Salzburg, Karajan had the resources for a full-scale *Don Carlos* but chose not to use them. Usually the works are trimmed down (*Les Troyens* in London and New York, that Boston *Carlos*, and an uncut *Guillaume Tell* in Florence a few years ago have been notable and acclaimed exceptions) toward the dimensions of the more easily manageable verismo repertory, and lose their character in the process. A production as intelligently conceived as San Francisco's of Meyerbeer's *L'Africaine*, three years ago —grand in effect, though the forces were far smaller than those of the 1865 première—is rare. It is no use looking to the Paris Opera for a lead. There, *Les Vêpres siciliennes* and *Don Carlos* are now performed in Italian translation, and shortened. The imposing French manner that inspired Gluck, Cherubini, Spontini, Rossini, Donizetti, and Verdi is no longer practiced; Paris has become yet another stop on the international round, an importer, no longer a producer, of great singers.

In New York, the Metropolitan opened its season last week with Rossini's *Le Siège de Corinthe*, a key work in the history of grand opera, but played it in Italian translation and reduced it to an evening of decorative twiddles. The shortcomings of that unhappy edition were widely remarked last season, when the show was new. None of them have been righted. *Le Siège* is a less silly and scrappy piece than it here appears.

New Orleans was once a bastion of French grand opera. Meyerbeer's *Les Huguenots* had its American première there, in 1839 (it was then a modern opera, just three years old), and the Louisiana company introduced it to New York six years later. In the Théâtre d'Orléans and then the French Opera House, *Les Huguenots* played regularly until the latter house burned down, in 1919. Who knows what those old performances were like? At any rate, according to the local *Bee*, in 1839 "thousands of dollars were liberally lavished in bringing forward the piece in a style of perfection and magnificence unequalled, it is said, in America"; six new sets were prepared; an orchestra "well known as the largest and best organized in the country" was further enlarged; and, since the show lasted five hours, most of the music must have been heard. This month *Les Huguenots* opened the current New Orleans season in an abridged version that, with two intervals, lasted less than three and a half hours. The staging was summary, and the chorus was too small and too uncertain for anything like justice to be done to the work. It was sung in French, but not very good French; the pleasure of hearing that language purely and powerfully declaimed becomes increasingly rare. (Régine Crespin and Robert Massard are among the few singers left who provide it.) Two of the New Orleans cast had some command of the necessary manner: Marisa Galvany, the Valentine, is a vivid soprano in whom temperament and an exciting timbre are combined, and Paul Plishka sang the music of the blunt, honest Marcel robustly and accurately. The others seemed unable to phrase or bear themselves or even wear their clothes as aristocrats; wanting elegance, charm, finesse, and vocal prowess, they afforded no more than a rude sketch of the work.

I had seen *Les Huguenots* twice before: in the Scala Theater, London, on a tiny scale, by a band of devoted revivalists, and in the Scala Theater, Milan, done grandly, with a cast led by Giulietta Simionato and Joan Sutherland. The New Orleans version fell between stools. It was more than a brave little effort by enthusiasts deserving of indulgence, but a good deal less than an adequate representation of a very demanding work. Meyerbeer's music is not strong in itself. The composer "built in" the supports of fine singing, spectacular staging, abundant forces, and sheer repetition. The result can be overwhelming. But when the supports are removed, his structure collapses. On the professional stage *Les Huguenots* is not a good enough opera to be worth doing badly.

October 27, 1975

ENCHANTRESS

Jacob Druckman's *Lamia*, a concert scena for soprano and orchestra, was the first new work of the Philharmonic concert season. The title refers neither to the seductive serpent-maid of Philostratus, Burton, and Keats nor to a blood-sucking she-devil; this Lamia is a sorceress, cousin to those tragic heroines—Handel's Alcina, Gluck's Armida, Cherubini's Medea, Wagner's Kundry among them—who have often inspired composers. "Devil's-flower! Herodias wast thou, and what more? Gundryggia

219

there, Kundry here," says Klingsor as he summons Kundry to work the pure Parsifal's destruction. His "What more?" is easily answered: woman as a predatory serpent and vampire—Lilith, Lamia, Mélusine—and woman as a lovely witch—Circe, Alcina—whose charms can transform rational man into a beast but who loses her power when she herself falls in love with a strong man are deep-entrenched in male mythology. The texts of *Lamia* are old conjectures, cries of Medea in words by Ovid and by Giacinto Andrea Cicognini (the librettist of Francesco Cavalli's *Giasone*), a magic spell from Malaysia, and Isolde's fierce apostrophe to winds and wave. And, specifically, *Lamia* is a celebration of the incantatory powers of Jan DeGaetani, the singer for whom it was composed. In a program note, Mr. Druckman recalls an account of his *Animus II*, at the 1972 Aspen Music Festival, when Miss DeGaetani "gave a particularly magical performance . . . in which everything that sounded and befell seemed to be the direct result of her will and her powers." *Animus II* Mr. Druckman has described as "the celebration of a sybaritic ritual." It is a piece of music theater for a woman whose siren song leads, lures, cajoles, and excites two percussionists into eloquent pursuit of her through a concert hall. Miss DeGaetani is an astonishing singer to whom very little seems impossible. She can produce notes that come, like the lament of Keats's Lamia, "as through bubbling honey, for Love's sake." She can sound like a mischievous, merry, untainted child. Except when she clouds it by expressive intention, the timbre is limpid; she can project a pianissimo murmur and make it audible, and sing high C with steady shine. Awkward intervals give her no pitch problems; with chamois certainty she negotiates the trickiest vocal path. At rapid, flickering ornaments, flashing phosphor and sharp sparks, she is adept—also at melting melodies, luting soft.

Lamia begins with a spell, "Ramuc ✠ Malin ✠ Fora consummatum est. . . ." The instruments rise like summoned wraiths around the voice, and crash into tutti climax when it cries "In te confeto Satana." The scene in which Ovid's Medea owns that she is passion's slave is divided by three pretty little prayers, by girls of Poitiers, for dreams of their future husbands. Against a misty background, small, bright musical images form and disappear. The dainty, pattering Malaysian charm that follows—a conjuration to call back a human soul that has darted from its body like a little bird—was newly composed for the New York performance; *Lamia* was commissioned by Carl Touhey and the Albany Symphony Orchestra, and when, with Miss DeGaetani, they gave the first performance, last year, the work went straight on to its final section: after a vocalise on magic syllables, brass and organ sound the celebrated E-minor chords of Medea's invocation, "Dell'antro magico," from Cavalli's *Giasone*. Soon this is "intercut" with Isolde's exclamations, "Entartet Geschlecht! Unwert der Ahnen!"—words by Wagner, but music newly composed by Mr. Druckman. Isolde, of course, was no sorceress. Winds and wave refused to obey her. Rather as in Handel's *Alcina* the lovelorn heroine's convocation of "Ombre pallide" meets with silence, so in *Lamia* the orchestral climax of Isolde's call collapses into a troubled pianissimo, accompaniment to a muttered spell, and then dies into silence. Although it may suit the dramatic program of the piece that this final Medea-Isolde outburst requires powers that even Miss DeGaetani does not command, it can hardly have been the composer's intention to display by that means the impotence of a sorceress foiled. Nevertheless, the heavy majesty of Medea's "Dell'antro magico," as here scored, seems to call for a Callas or a Nilsson, for a more grandly heroic voice than Miss DeGaetani's, and her cries of Isolde's "Heran zu Kampf und Wettergetös'! Zu tobender Stürme wütendem Wirbel!" did not match the orchestral tempest. Miss DeGaetani was the inspiration of the piece, and it would be hard to match the charm, variety, and subtle virtuosity that she brings to its performance. All the same, it would be interesting to hear Mme Nilsson or Mme Caballé essay it. (For Mme Callas it is probably too late; the only "new" piece she has ever taken part in was Haydn's opera *Orfeo*, at its world première. Today's prima donnas, unlike their predecessors, are not eager to interpret, nor are their audiences avid to hear them in, brand-new music.) Mr. Druckman uses a large orchestra divided into two groups, each with its separate conductor. (They were Pierre Boulez and David Gilbert.) The singer's role is dominant, and is meant to be; the orchestra provides background, color, atmosphere, illustration, support, and some interludes. A keen, cruel, perceant, stinging eye, such as, in Keats's poem, discerned that Lamia's pleasure dome was but an insubstantial pageant, might find in the score little beyond a series of striking effects. But striking and effective they are. The work lasts about twenty minutes.

On its summer tour of Europe, the playing of the Philharmonic won some glowing reviews. In the October *Musical Times* one reads of "warm, rich string tone (a cello section to rank with Berlin's), full-bodied, articulate winds (even the E-flat clarinet made lovely noises), brilliant brass (the horn trills in the first ländler [of Mahler's Ninth Symphony] would be the envy of any coloratura soprano) and timpani." It is good to know that the orchestra can sound like this. Perhaps it will in Carnegie Hall, later this season—or next season, in the rebuilt Fisher Hall. But the performance of Stravinsky's *Pulcinella* suite that preceded *Lamia* was ill-balanced and unpolished. Two days later, the violin-and-piano version of the suite was played by Pavel Kogan and Elizaveta Ginsburg, in the dreary auditorium of Hunter College, a place depressing to eye and spirits. At this his New York début, Mr. Kogan, the son of Leonid Kogan, showed himself to be a highly trained and technically accomplished violinist, but there was no charm or fancy in his

221

account of the Stravinsky, and little emotion in his reading of Shostako-vich's somber, resolute Sonata. That he seemed to regard his partner as the merest accompanist, while accepting applause or when walking off in front of her, was merely a matter of platform manners; but during music in which the piano is as important as the violin it amounted to artistic insensitivity.

Thea Musgrave's *Space Play*, a chamber concerto, was introduced to New York at the first concert of the Chamber Music Society of Lincoln Center season, in Alice Tully Hall. It is a musical game for nine players. Flute, oboe, clarinet, and bassoon are stationed round the platform; violin, viola, cello, and double-bass cluster at the center; just behind them, as a kind of referee and genial master of ceremonies, is the horn. The wind players have most of the fun. The oboe stands up to lead the first episode, *andante espressivo, con molto rubato*. Then the horn takes charge, rises, invites the others to emulate his cadenzalike flourishes, and sets the new tempo for a *più mosso* section, in which the flute and the bassoon play leading roles. The clarinet, silent on the sidelines dur-ing these exchanges, comes forward at the close of this, musing on a two-note figure, and proposes a *calmo* episode under his direction. This ends with some skyrockets from the instrument and leads to an alterca-tion with the horn. The latter enlists the flute and the bassoon as his followers; at his summons, they imitate his calls. He turns to the clarinet next, "as if about to lead him in"; the clarinet is stubbornly silent, so the horn "turns pointedly away . . . and toward [the] oboe," who proves more biddable. The clarinet interrupts *furioso*, but the argument is won by the horn, who celebrates victory in a big *declamando* melody. There is an amicable coda, in which the violin is allowed a say of his own.

In a series of recent works—notably the Clarinet, Horn, and Viola Concertos—Miss Musgrave has explored the play of music through space, and dramatic dialogue involving mimicry, parody, and what sounds like straightforward conversation, or quarrel, between instruments. There is a moment in the Viola Concerto when the soloist seems to be giving a master class to the viola section of the orchestra. The soloist of the Clarinet Concerto moves about through the orchestra. *Space Play*, which lasts about twenty minutes, is slighter than those works—a happy diver-sion in which the composer holds an adroit balance between letting the players do what they like and making sure that they do so within bounds that define the piece she has devised. The rules for each stage of the game are cunningly framed. Many of the moves—though not always the speed or volume or pitch level at which they must be exe-cuted—are obligatory. The shape of a musical gesture, and often the precise note on which it begins or ends, may be indicated, while inflec-tions are left to the individual's fancy. Only three measures are strictly metered; for the rest, the ensemble takes its cues from whoever happens to be leader at the moment. There is a good deal of twiddle and twirl and flourish, but also—and this, perhaps, is what gives the work its endearing character—a recurrent vein of lyricism, in the form of fully composed melodies. *Space Play*, commissioned by the Serge Koussevitzky Music Foundation in the Library of Congress, was first played by the virtuosi of the London Sinfonietta, a year ago. The virtuosi of the Chamber Music Society gave a musically deft performance, just a little inhibited on the "acting" side, which should reinforce the scenario of the score. The "independent musical personalities" that the composer had in mind did not emerge very strongly. *Space Play* is a game that could become popular with ensembles, and their audiences. The score is published by Novello.

For the second half of this concert, at which two of Mozart's "Bible" sonatas for organ and strings were played, the tall screens that usually close off the new organ had been opened. How the position of the screens affects the acoustics I have not been able to determine; but the sound of Dvořák's Piano Quintet, played after the Mozart, did not suggest that anything sonic is lost when the organ stands revealed. Visually, a great deal is gained. The sight of that instrument, with its admirably designed cases and rows of glinting pipes as background to the players on the platform, makes Tully Hall a place cheering to the eye and spirits; it was a rather plain wooden box before the organ arrived.

In the old box formation, the hall welcomed the first of a new series of Saturday "Coffee Concerts," some at noon and some at four in the afternoon. (Free coffee and doughnuts, in paper cups and on paper plates, are served in the foyer afterward, while the performers mingle with the audience.) The series looks attractive, and the first concert was certainly enjoyable. The most enduring product of the Ravel centenary junket is plainly Arbie Orenstein's thorough, if rather pedestrian, study *Ravel: Man and Musician*, just published by the Columbia University Press; the most bewitching performance of his music I have encountered this year was the Tokyo Quartet's of his String Quartet, at the Coffee Concert. The violins of this ensemble are in perfect accord. They play octaves as if on a single instrument. In the first paragraph of the Ravel, when they switch roles, their successive statements of the same phrase were almost too much alike. But a more exquisitely wrought account of the work is hard to imagine. The lines of Mozart's D-major Quartet, K. 575, the other piece on the program, were finely drawn. It was not a robust performance, and so not a complete account of the work, but it had a truth of intonation, a supple precision, and a consistent purity of timbre that more passionate interpreters often miss.

Carnegie Hall is a civilized place, once the scrum in the narrow lobby has been breached. Its ushers are courteous, smartly caparisoned, and often comely. It serves coffee in cups, with saucers under them. It pleases both the eye and the ear. The hall was packed, last week, for the recital at which Dietrich Fischer-Dieskau and Alfred Brendel performed Schubert's *Winterreise*. Mr. Fischer-Dieskau is a superlatively efficient singer of lieder, with an anaconda appetite. It is hard not to be prejudiced by the knowledge that he tackles so much. He stars in perhaps thirty opera recordings, from Gluck's *Orfeo* to Busoni's *Doktor Faust* and Berg's *Wozzeck*, and six of Wagner's, six of Verdi's. Working through collected editions from first page to last, omitting only pieces, such as "Die junge Nonne," unsuited to a male interpreter, he has put on record the complete songs of Schubert, Brahms, and Richard Strauss, most of those by Mozart and Mendelssohn and Wolf, much Schumann, substantial servings of Carl Loewe, Othmar Schoeck, and (most recently) Meyerbeer. Bach, Telemann, Haydn, Fauré, Carl Orff, and Hans Werner Henze fall into his domain. The wonder is that he never gives a perfunctory performance. Most of what he does—everything, perhaps, except the Italian operas—he does better than anyone else around. The words are clearly pronounced and subtly expressed. His timbre is beautiful. His only vice—and in this *Winterreise* he succumbed to it rarely—is a touch of boisterousness, a sudden bang on an accented note, a bouncy marcato, or a crescendo so violent that it can break the scale of a song. And yet, and yet . . . Why is it that what seems to be perfection, what by any standards must be counted near-perfection, can leave one admiring but unmoved? Is there something lacking, something that Gérard Souzay, Peter Pears, and (to judge by the eight songs from *Winterreise* that she recorded) Elena Gerhardt have brought to performances of the cycle? I leave it as a question, and, if the answer is yes, cannot suggest what that something missing might be. In the detailed song-by-song comparison made possible by the phonograph, Mr. Fischer-Dieskau's insight into the work is at least equal, or often superior, to any other's, and his tonal resources are usually greater. Near the start of his recital, in the third strophe of the first song, he moved me deeply by the beauty of tone and word he brought to the phrase "Die Liebe liebt das Wandern." But by the end of it I hardly felt that, with the poet and the composer, I had made that winter journey; rather, I had noted a hundred exquisite details of execution. In his book *The Grand Tradition*, that eloquent and indispensable guide to the singers of our century, J. B. Steane remarks, of Mr. Fischer-Dieskau's later recordings of works he has recorded before, "that, while they generally preserve and develop the earlier insights, they also tend to reduce emphasis, increase the smoothness and beauty of singing, and thus absorb the individual points into the body of the music." The same is true

224

of his live performances. But song can follow upon song almost too effortlessly. Mr. Brendel's perfectly controlled, nearly but not quite understated interpretation of the piano part, sensitive to each shift of harmony, delicately, not obtrusively, pictorial (when the cocks crow, the dogs bark, wind sets the weathervane whirling, or frost lays a leafy tracery on the windowpane), was ideally matched to the singer's interpretation.

November 3, 1975

A FAMOUS VICTORY

Grand Handel productions in America have been few. There was *Alcina* in Dallas, *Giulio Cesare* at the State Theater, and *Ariodante* in Washington. Now *Rinaldo*, the first of Handel's London operas and the first Italian opera written especially for London, has had its American full-scale première, as the opening production of the Houston Grand Opera season. The performance was a success. Marilyn Horne, in the title role, was its commanding hero; Noelle Rogers, Evelyn Mandac, and Samuel Ramey were in strong support. Frank Corsaro and Franco Colavecchia, the director and designer of the show, put on an attractive spectacle with decorative dragons and other fabulous beasts, large chariots, athletic armies, and monstrous engines of war. A wrongheaded declaration of Mr. Corsaro's in the program—that "Handel's tongue was in his cheek during much of the writing"—made one fear the worst, but in the event the director did not poke fun at the opera; instead, and rightly, he made the magic transformation scenes, the pitched battles, the enchanted bark gliding through siren-infested waves fun to watch, while encouraging his audience to take seriously the accomplished singing and the sentiments it expressed. All this was aptly in the spirit of the opera's originator, Aaron Hill, the young director of the Queen's Theatre, where *Rinaldo* had its first performance, in 1711. In dedicating the libretto to Queen Anne, Hill told how he had "resolv'd to frame some Dramma that, by different Incidents and Passions, might afford the Musick Scope to vary and display its Excellence, and fill the Eye with . . . delightful Prospects, so at once to give two Senses equal Pleasure." At London productions of *Rinaldo* in 1961 and 1965, the audiences were on occasion moved to ripples of mirth. The fact that the piece was sung there in English translation may have had something to do with it; in Houston, the original Italian of Giacomo Rossi, who versified Hill's

225

drama, was used, and that left some of the plot's less plausible turns in decent obscurity. (But there are, as always, two sides to the translation question. Unless an audience has pretty good Italian, it may find the sense of lines like "Sibillar gli angui d'Aletto, / E latrar vorace Scilla" and "Il Tricerbero humiliato / Al mio brando renderò, / E d'Alcide l'alto fato / Colà giù rinoverò" hard to follow when they are sung, and that sense is necessary to full appreciation of the aria concerned; for example, the angry hissing of Alecto's serpents is what the violins portray when the first lines quoted are sung. Addison, a stern critic of *Rinaldo*, was right when he declared that going to an opera without understanding the language in which it is performed is "an absurdity that shews itself at first sight." And Dr. Burney was right when he declared that "the vocal Music of Italy can only be heard in perfection when sung to its own language and by its own natives, who give both the language and Music their true accents and expressions." Best, therefore, to leave the houselights up and provide bilingual librettos; that's what Handel himself did. The Houston audiences did not laugh at or mock *Rinaldo*; they smiled happily at its diverting extravagances—and they behaved badly only when they applauded what pleased or entertained the sight while fine music was still sounding.

Handel was serious when he wrote *Rinaldo*—not in the manner that prompted later, finer operas more carefully constructed and more interesting in their dramatic lineaments (*Giulio Cesare, Tamerlano, Alcina*, to name but three), but in his intention of showing mastery of dramatic music in all its variety. He borrowed hit numbers and successful ideas from earlier compositions. He used a large orchestra. He brought the first act to a close with an aria di bravura for his hero, a solo violin, and a solo bassoon in concert, and the second with an aria for Armida that he himself embellished with brilliant improvisations at the keyboard. Act III comes to a climax in "Or la tromba," "an excellent air of spirit" (Burney), in which Rinaldo alternates with four-trumpet fanfares or vies in duet with the first trumpet. Miss Horne sang Rinaldo's virtuoso music in flexible, dashing, exhilarating fashion, and his pathetic numbers with a fine and imaginative control of tone and phrase. Casting a heroic castrato role is no problem when there is a singer like this to astonish us with her ringing, accurate divisions and move us by her expressions of tender grief. Handel's first Armida, Elisabetta Pilotti-Schiavonetti, was a coloratura whose voice ran to the high C; in Houston, Miss Rogers went even higher, to D. She made a lively and appealing sorceress. Miss Mandac, as Almirena, caroled sweetly to the pretty, warbling choir of birds in the aria "Augelletti" (represented in Houston by a piccolo and two flutes, in place of Handel's recorders), and phrased the celebrated "Lascia ch'io pianga" in full and moving tones. Mr. Ramey, as Argante, the pagan King of Jerusalem, sang definitely and fluently. As Godfrey, the Crusader general, John Walker lacked effectiveness, but the role in its tenor form is unrewarding—and that brings us to the question of the new edition that Martin Katz compiled for this Houston production.

In the first version of *Rinaldo*, Godfrey was a part composed for a woman. Twenty years later, Handel recast it for a tenor. But this 1731 *Rinaldo* is, in Winton Dean's words, "a monumental example of the artistic vandalism Handel often practised on his own works after the ardour of composition had cooled," and we should have nothing to do with it—beyond, perhaps, welcoming the elimination of the irrelevant character Eustazio and his five arias. In 1711, there was only one low voice, the bass Argante, among the principals; in 1731, there was again only one, the tenor Godfrey, since in this version Argante becomes an alto. But Mr. Katz combined 1711 and 1731 to obtain both a tenor and a bass in the cast. And he did worse things. The finales of Acts I and II both consist of paired arias; before the arie di bravura already mentioned, there are arias of tender sentiment—one in the relative and the other in the tonic minor; the effect is kin to that of cavatina-plus-cabaletta. But Mr. Katz severed Rinaldo's "Cara sposa" from its bravura companion piece, at the close of Act I, and placed it as a finale to Act II. In Act II he cut altogether the poignant accompanied recitative that should introduce Armida's finale, moved its fast section to an earlier position in the act, and—unforgivably—broke the heart of it, "Ah! crudel!," into two separate numbers inserted into Act III. This kind of tinkering with Handel's carefully planned sequences is monstrous. It was also ineffective: Mr. Katz's crosscutting between Rinaldo's trumpet aria and the battle music was more acceptable, for aria-plus-battle did come off as a tremendous set piece; Miss Horne directed operations from aloft while, below, Mr. Corsaro and his choreographer, Eugene Collins, provided a whirlwind fight in which dancers and local gymnasts were joined. (Blunt, monosyllabic names like Brad, Steve, Jeff, and Beau made a surprising appearance in an opera-seria program.) It was perverse of Mr. Katz to substitute, for Rinaldo's "Il Tricerbero humiliato" (a piece that would have suited Miss Horne very well, and one of Rinaldo's hit tunes), an air from *Partenope*, and to add a duet from *Admeto* to Act III. In the October issue of the magazine *Opera*, Winton Dean, celebrating the twenty years during which the Handel Opera Society and other small companies have brought back thirty of Handel's forty operas to the British stage, castigates the New York *Cesare* and the Washington *Ariodante* for "a new form of barbarity . . . shifting arias or duets from their proper contexts to positions where they make total nonsense." A pity that Houston should have followed suit: just about everything else was so stylishly achieved. Except, perhaps, some adornments to the vocal lines which, instead of enhancing their original

227

expressiveness, amounted to new composition. Miss Mandac turned the reprise of the unison aria "Bel piacere" (also displaced, incidentally, from Act III to Act I) into a two-part invention, and she obscured the lovely melody of "Lascia ch'io pianga" during the repeat. The British productions that Mr. Dean mentions have "in one respect nearly all . . . been defective: they have found no equivalent for the baroque love of elaborate spectacle." And the campaign for Handel "will not be finally won . . . until our professional opera houses at last get down to tackling his operas in productions that do justice to their large-scale design, involving music, drama, scenic spectacle, and sometimes ballet in a comprehensive unity." Editing apart, this full-scale Houston *Rinaldo*, ably conducted by Lawrence Foster, represents a notable victory in that campaign.

At the Juilliard School, last week, a production of *Dardanus*, by Rameau, Handel's contemporary, filled the Juilliard Theater. A devoted *ramoneur*, I delighted in this opportunity of seeing and hearing the score, or at least large parts of it, take shape in sight and sound. It was done not complete but in substantial excerpt, with a linking narration. The scenes, by Robert Yodice, and the costumes were drawn mainly from Juilliard stock, and were sensitively lit by Peter Earhardt. It was a simple but attractive production. A special feature, which set it aside from the few other Rameau stagings that have come my way, was Wendy Hilton's choreography, built from eighteenth-century steps. Rameau has been called the greatest ballet composer of all time, and dance is an essential element of his lyric dramas. His dance music vividly suggests physical movement, and, conversely, Albert Fuller, who directed *Dardanus*, said that his instrumentalists had been inspired to stylish articulation and phrasing by watching Miss Hilton's dancers in authentic action. In the earlier of its two versions (which the Juilliard used), *Dardanus* has a weak plot but a wealth of enchanting music; the revised version is tougher, but we lose the tender, flexible, and entertaining dream sequences of Act IV. The singers, all students of Beverley Johnson or Oren Brown, at the Juilliard, failed (with the partial exception of John Aler, in the title role) to declaim the text distinctly, with lively consonants and pure, forward vowels, and so something was missing. The show was a special project of the Juilliard's Dance Division and Mr. Fuller's baroque class. Enjoyable in itself, it could be a pilot to the full presentation of a Rameau opera for which the Juilliard is well equipped.

The first new staging of the Metropolitan season—Patrick Libby's of *Così fan tutte*—was successful. By all the rules, the house should be too large for effective Mozart, and yet well-balanced productions of

Don Giovanni, Die Zauberflöte, and now *Così* have provided some of my happiest evenings there. This *Così* was pleasing less for any individual vocal prowess than for being the kind of performance that makes one aware all over again what a beautiful opera it is. Kazimierz Kord, conducting, set some uncommonly slow tempi, and did so persuasively; a welcome chance of hearing in detail exactly what the music was doing —how the harmony moves, how line plays against line, color against color—was offered. The scenery is not new but Rolf Gérard's for the Alfred Lunt staging of 1951; it is slight, and has the merits of being uncluttered and unemphatic and of seeming to reduce the Met stage to a Glyndebourne shape and size. Mr. Libby's staging has the great merit of being lyrical and unclowned—a polished study of credible human behavior, not a romp; the drama was diverting, as *Così* should be, but also poignant. Four in the cast of six were Met débutants. Elizabeth Harwood's Fiordiligi was gentle, lyrical, and unexaggerated—"Viennese," sometimes, in the mannered way of sacrificing distinctness to a melting phrase, and always in the admirable way of voicing everything as beautifully as possible. Anne Howells's Dorabella had character and finesse. Neither her voice nor that of her husband, Ryland Davies, the Ferrando, sounded quite first-rate, but she sang her two arias, and he his two (a third for Ferrando, "Ah lo veggio," was omitted), with style and subtlety. Guglielmo was Richard Stilwell. His baritone is uncommonly steady and definite, and in his performances there is always a hint of patrician reserve that is attractive. In this *Così* Guglielmo was the more earnestly romantic of the officers, Ferrando the more twinkly. The cast was completed by Colette Boky's lively Despina and a Don Alfonso, from Renato Capecchi, with very little voice (except in the trio "Soave sia il vento," which he seemed to regard as a bass solo while two voices murmured above) but prodigies of virtuoso inflection. This Alfonso suggested a Falstaff seasoned with a dash of Scarpia.

Un ballo in maschera, the next day, was disappointing. There was a new cast. Teresa Kubiak has a voice for Amelia, but she sang the upward span of "Consentimi, o Signore" as disjunct notes, and elsewhere often failed again to join notes into a smooth phrase. Except in a delicately turned "È scherzo od è follia," Nicolai Gedda, as Gustavus III (alias Riccardo—but the Met uses a royal Stockholm and not the Boston Colonial setting), gave the impression of trying to sing loudly and merely achieved monochrome timbre as a result. Never much of an actor, he affected a curious waddle rather than romantically striding the stage; it may have been a halfhearted gesture in the direction of Goeran Gentele's Stockholm production of the opera, in which Gustavus (very much against the spirit of Verdi's score) was played as a flittery queen. Louis Quilico's Anckarström was solid of voice but also solid in manner. Maureen Forrester did not carry the guns for Ulrica. Roberta

Peters's sparky, dapper Oscar was the bright spot of the show. The prompter was in good, strong voice. The production is an old one, by Günther Rennert, of 1962; Fabrizio Melano, who directed the revival, had not licked the new cast into a coherent shape, and Henry Lewis, who conducted, let fall to pieces a score usually notable for its unbroken progress.

These comments are based on the first night. *Ballo* probably became better. Opera performances generally do, and it is an unfortunate convention that makes the first night the review night. Had I seen the Met's new staging of *La Gioconda* only when it opened, I should have written about it more coolly than I can now, after having returned to it last week. Martina Arroyo's first Gioconda was mild and rather undramatic; her fourth was passionate, both amply and powerfully sung. She lacks a strong, incisive low register, which is precisely where a Gioconda is expected to make many of her most telling effects, but only in that respect is there now any serious failing. Giorgio Casellato-Lamberti, the Enzo, is a handsome tenor with a voice that on the first night was serviceable but unremarkable and on the fourth night rang out fully and freely. Matteo Manuguerra's keen Barnaba became more imposing. From the start, Mignon Dunn was a striking Laura. Opera criticism has other variables that must be taken into account. I should add that at my second visit I had a seat where both sight and sound were better. (On what quicksand foundations assertion and assessment can rest! An interpreter of genius may reverse long-accepted judgments overnight; a performance ineffective in one part of a theater can prove overwhelming to listeners seated elsewhere.) At any rate, the sum of these gains made into a dramatic event what had previously seemed a ponderous, creaky old vehicle inadequately occupied. John Dexter has restaged the work in Beni Montresor's opulent scenery of 1966, and has evidently essayed no more than minimal direction ("You move here, then you move there; in this scene, chorus, you all have fans, and you stand round the sides and fan yourselves"). *La Gioconda* calls for traditional staging. This is an undistinguished example of it, but at least preferable to a positive, resolute inscenation that—like Mr. Dexter's of *Les Vêpres siciliennes*—swears at the style of the opera in question. It allows scope to the singers instead of straitjacketing them. The lighting, based on head-and-shoulders follow-spots, is crude, and Louis Johnson's choreography for the Dance of the Hours, classroom-classical, simply evades the problem that Mr. Montresor in his décor has solved so well—presenting, to twentieth-century eyes, a nineteenth-century view of seventeenth-century Venice. David Stivender's chorus was in peak form.

The City Opera's new production of *The Mastersingers of Nuremberg* (the work is given in John Gutman's English translation) is less than a triumph. On the first night, it was not particularly well sung, staged, or conducted. Nor particularly badly. It was a fairly enjoyable presentation of a work that should be profoundly stirring. But the State Theater is a notoriously unsuitable house for opera, and especially for an opera as warm and full in tone as *The Mastersingers*. So I prefer to withhold detailed comment (see pp. 240–5) until I have a clearer idea what may be right and what wrong with its execution, and what is simply acoustic diminishment of its splendors.

November 10, 1975

TALKING THROUGH THE MUSIC

In Hunter College Playhouse, last week, there was the first of four concerts making up the Raymond Lewenthal Romantic Revival Ensemble Series. The programs, mainly from the nineteenth century but reaching into the twentieth, bring forward the music of men like Ignaz Moscheles and Ingolf Dahl, Henri Kling and Henri Herz and Heinrich von Herzogenberg. Slight stuff, most of it—but not all: some noble compositions are billed among the diversions. And it has been fashioned into shapely programs. The first opened with a strong, early work of César Franck, his First Piano Trio, and ended with a long, late work of Franck's pupil Ernest Chausson, his Piano Quartet. Between them, three melodramas—recitations to musical accompaniment—and Saint-Saëns's "Tarantelle" served as a sorbet after the second.

"Melodrama" is a word with senses unrecorded in the Oxford English Dictionary. In Italy, it began as an alternative to *dram(m)a per musica* or *dramma musicale*; the earliest *melodrama*, thus called, that I have found is the libretto Niccolò Beregani wrote for Marc'Antonio Cesti's *Tito*, in 1666. In early-nineteenth-century London, where the O.E.D. definitions of the word begin, melodramas were theatrical entertainments with songs, choruses, incidental music, and action of a kind that continued to be called melodramatic even when music no longer accompanied it. But in Italy a *melodramma* (the spelling with a double "m" soon became established) was, and is, simply an opera. It seems a matter of chance whether a Verdi libretto is termed *tragedia lirica*, *dramma lirico*, or *melodramma*; perhaps the tendency is to reserve the last term for texts that have some literary pretension.

Does this name-calling matter—except to a contributor of definitions to Grove's Dictionary? It does, I think, to anyone fascinated by the con-

231

junction of μελος and δραμα, of music and action, song and theater. For by their naming of things, creators often sought to show what they were up to. (Vittorio Alfieri termed his *Abele* a *tramelogedia*, inserting *melo-* into the heart of *tragedia* to indicate how closely the lyric and the tragic elements were knit.) Melodrama in its fundamental sense is what opera is about, and in yet another, narrower, technical sense—spoken words punctuated or accompanied by instrumental music—it provides some of opera's celebrated episodes (in *Fidelio, Der Freischütz,* Busoni's *Doktor Faust,* to name just three). Whole dramas have been written in the medium. Mozart heard one, by Jiří Benda, in 1778, and recorded his impressions of it:

There is no singing in it, only recitation, to which the music is like a sort of obbligato accompaniment to a recitative. Now and then words are spoken while the music continues, and that produces the finest effect. . . . I think that most operatic recitatives should be treated in this way, and sung only occasionally when the words can be perfectly expressed by the music.

Mozart planned a piece of his own in the same genre, *Semiramis*; he used melodramatic recitative in his opera *Zaide* and speech-against-music in his incidental music for the play *König Thamos.* Benda's *Ariadne auf Naxos* started the whole thing off. Although Jean-Jacques Rousseau's *Pigmalion* (1770) is sometimes called the first melodrama, in that *scène lyrique* speech alternates with music, *Ariadne auf Naxos* (1775) first made them coincident—not all the time but, as Mozart noted, "now and then." Mozart's admiration for *Ariadne* was not misplaced; when staged, it proves an astonishingly effective work, for Benda had a sure command of motivic development, of affecting harmonic progressions, and of theatrical timing. One of our smaller companies should mount the piece. It is quite short and employs only two actors. (A whole evening of melodrama might grow tedious; Zdeněk Fibich's *Hippodamia* trilogy, three whole evenings for actors and large orchestra, is still sometimes performed in Prague, but I have not seen it.) *Ariadne,* if I remember rightly, came into being by chance, when Benda found himself with excellent actors and a good orchestra but no decent singers at his disposal. It quickly made the European rounds and was much imitated; melodrama soon became a regular ingredient of opera and of incidental music (e.g., in Beethoven's *Egmont*), and then moved from the theater into the concert hall as well. Gradually, refinements were developed—rhythmically notated speech, speech with approximate pitch notation added, singsong, *Sprechstimme,* and all gradations between simple talking and true song. When Stravinsky was asked what he thought of the conjunction of speech and music in his *Perséphone,* he replied, "Do not ask. Sins cannot be undone, only forgiven." But, if melodrama be a sin, it is a sin oft committed. Schoenberg has been a notable offender; Jacob Druckman, in his *Lamia,* is one of the latest.

The melodramas included in Mr. Lewenthal's program belong to a subspecies of the genre—the poetry reading with musical accompaniment. And even here we can perhaps make a further distinction: between a lyric recited over a suitable background, and a declamatory ballad, often in dialogue, heightened and punctuated by theatrical musical gestures. Schubert wrote a "song" for speaker and piano, "Abschied von der Erde," in the former vein, and Wagner set Gretchen's Prayer, from *Faust,* in the same way. Schumann's "Ballade vom Haideknaben," the first of the melodramas declaimed at the concert, has dramatic words, but the rather undramatic music is spun, for the most part, from developments of a single chromatic theme. Liszt's *Lenore,* which followed, is one of the most famous "ballad" melodramas. The piano part, at first shot through with *Tristan*esque sighs, moves to soft chordal progressions that infuse a new color into each of Gottfried Bürger's lines, and ends in a wild gallop. The best of all such pieces is Richard Strauss's *Enoch Arden,* which lasts an hour, and was composed (to a German translation of Tennyson's poem) for declamation by Ernst von Possart, a powerful actor. A Columbia recording of *Enoch Arden,* by Claude Rains and Glenn Gould, does something to explain the success that Possart and Strauss once had with this piece: Mr. Gould's playing is electric; Mr. Rains's reading is sonorous, though it could with advantage, I think, be more "melodramatic"—as Tennyson's was. C. V. Stanford has left an account of Tennyson's reading:

It was a chant rather than a declamation. A voice of deep and penetrating power varied only by alteration of note and by intensity of quality. The notes were few, and he rarely read on more than two, except at the cadence of a passage, when the voice would slightly fall.

But how dramatic and how forceful that "chant" was, how violent its accent, and how sonorous the singing of its vowels, we can still hear in the poet's own recordings. Melodrama calls for flamboyant treatment. Herta Glaz, the reader at the Hunter concert, did not really let herself go. She distinguished cunningly between the different voices of the dialogues. She timed nicely. But the pieces—the third was Strauss's *Das Schloss am Meer,* also composed for Possart—seem to call for a full-throated, larger-than-life Burgtheater approach, able to dominate sharper, brighter, louder piano playing than Mr. Lewenthal provided. The recitations were in German. Is this sensible, in New York? True, there are moments in *Enoch Arden* when words and notes are plainly meant to coincide (for example, at the phrase "Sie sah dem Segel nach," which cannot be fitted to "Even to the last dip of the vanishing sail"), and the recurrent cadences of Lenore's plaint, in the Liszt piece, are probably meant to be timed precisely with the music. But, since most of the recitation is free, translation (or Tennyson) would for the most part pose no problems of inflection and accent.

Mr. Lewenthal, who plays in almost all the works in this Romantic series, is not really my idea of a Romantic pianist. He has a somewhat coarse fluency that gets him through the reams of virtuoso music he tackles. He plunges in with a sweaty enthusiasm that produces its effect. But of aristocratic charm, the sudden, lilting surprise that makes listeners catch their breath, the piece of fiendish bravura so lightly and gracefully turned that we know hours of practice have gone into the making of one magical second, the spells by which a Lhevinne or a Rosenthal transfigured whatever trifle he touched—of these there was little trace. Because Anton Rubinstein could play like a god, that stern critic Eduard Hanslick forgave him the moments when he changed, like Jupiter, into a bull; Mr. Lewenthal's godlike moments were few. In the Franck Trio he was teamed with a violinist and cellist unwilling or unable to seize the melodies, when their turn came, and shape them fully, commandingly; the pianist drove ahead like a demon coachman, rattling on, while the string players clung as best they could to the sides of the carriage. But in the Chausson Quartet they were joined by a truly Romantic player, the violist Daniel Phillips, who to everything he played, and especially to his singing of the melody that opens the slow movement, brought all the enchantment that had until then been missing.

November 17, 1975

LADIES' NIGHT

The Philharmonic played an unusually interesting program at its Pension Fund Benefit concert last week, conducted by Sarah Caldwell. Three generations, roughly, of Nadia Boulanger pupils were represented, in works by Lili Boulanger (born 1893), Grażyna Bacewicz (born 1913), and Thea Musgrave (born 1928). Lili Boulanger's cantata *Faust et Hélène* was an entry for the 1913 Prix de Rome competition, and since it won, it must be considered almost by definition an academic work—the prize is awarded by the Académie des Beaux-Arts—conforming to conservative taste of the time. (Debussy's *L'Enfant prodigue* is the only other unforgotten Prix de Rome piece.) In a game of guess-the-composer, *Faust et Hélène* would probably be placed in the ambit of Ernest Chausson's *Viviane* (1882); Boulanger wrote more distinctive music later. Yet her early cantata is a substantial and attractive product of *wagnérisme*—at once delicate, sensuous, and intellectual. The Philharmonic spared a hap'orth of tar by failing to provide a text. The romantic appeal of the music and its strong, fine working were evident, and Gwendolyn Killebrew as Helen, Joseph Evans as Faust, and Lenus Carlson as Mephisto sang sweetly. But a closely typed synopsis of Eugène Adenis's libretto proved insufficient guide to the drama of this archetypal dream encounter. The Philharmonic must do *Faust et Hélène* again—with text sheet provided.

Bacewicz's Overture for Orchestra (1943), composed during the siege of Warsaw, was announced as "a musical summary of the war," but it proved to be one of those bright, undemanding eight-minute pieces for full orchestra which make a good start to a concert—a work much in the vein of the *Capriccio burlesco* that William Walton wrote for the hundred-and-twenty-fifth anniversary of the Philharmonic. The *Capriccio*, one possible example among many, comes to my mind because it was introduced to London at the Royal Philharmonic concert in 1969 at which Thea Musgrave's Clarinet Concerto had its first performance. This concerto, which closed the Philharmonic bill and won a standing ovation, is a large and exhilarating composition. The germ of it is the moment in Musgrave's Concerto for Orchestra (1967; influenced by Charles Ives) when the first clarinet rises to challenge the conductor's authority and, with brilliantly subversive music, incites other players to join his rebellion. It is one of a group of works in which Musgrave has devised such concert-platform dramas. In her Horn Concerto (1971), the soloist summons horn calls from colleagues placed about the hall. In her Viola Concerto, the soloist enlists the orchestral violas on his side; they stand up in his cause—and then almost overwhelm him. Subscribing to a disputed etymology of "concerto"— deriving it from a root of contest rather than concord—Musgrave writes of a "struggle or conflict in the sense of balancing unequal forces." A concerto soloist in Mozart's day directed the performance; Musgrave's Clarinet Concerto has two directors: the conductor on his or her platform, and the soloist. The latter—at the Philharmonic performance it was a he, Stanley Drucker—is peripatetic. He attaches himself to different sections of the orchestra in turn, sometimes attracting from them subsidiary soloists to form a concertante group in dialogue with, or prominent against a background of, the rest of the orchestra, which remains firmly under the main conductor's control. There are free rhythms against formal, and some elaborate, many-voiced cadenzas rhapsodically uttered within a carefully plotted harmonic field. The work, which lasts twenty-two minutes, is in a single movement with defined paragraphs. The basic materials are a rat-a-tat repeated-note theme and a more lyrical curving melody, which audibly maintains its identity even while its outlines shift and stretch. Each of the paragraphs has a definite and individual character; the contrasts between them are effective but not obvious. A *sensuoso* episode launched by the clarinet, harp, and vibraphone is particularly attractive.

These devices—the spatial deployment of players, the unmeasured rhapsody freed from bar lines, the standing up for emphasis—are not new, of course, but Musgrave has made them her own. From the start of her career (which dates, effectively, from the *Cantata for a Summer's Day*, performed at the Edinburgh Festival in 1955), her music has evinced good sense, intelligence, resolution, and clarity of purpose. She has been always a thoroughly practical composer, eager to try out things that strike her as new, good, and manageable, and prompt to reject those that are new and silly, merely modish, or not for her. Ten years ago, in *The Musical Quarterly*, I wrote that "it is as if she has regarded each new discovery of our times with a coolly appraising eye, and then taken possession of such elements of it as can enhance her already considerable skills." Her very capableness may have obscured, for a while, the veins of adventure and of romance that became so evident in her compositions of the last decade. Ives helped to bring them out. His music first assumed prominence in British programs in the early sixties. The effect on Musgrave's Concerto for Orchestra I have mentioned; before that, in her Second Chamber Concerto, she cast the viola as Rollo, the personification of a musical plodder who turns up throughout Ives's *Memos*. Two instances of her borrowing good ideas, developing them, and making them her own can be documented. First: when she heard the Moscow Chamber Orchestra play, she was— she wrote—"struck by the freedom of the string tone, due in part to the fact that all the violins and violas played standing up." And "the effect of standing was interesting: not only does it highlight the solo player visually for the audience, but also one plays *differently* when standing—more freely, more solistically." She tried that effect in her Third Chamber Concerto (1966), found it good, and has often employed it since—most recently in *Space Play*, reviewed earlier this month (pp. 222–3). Second: nearly a quarter-century ago, during a performance by a Yugoslav folk-dance company in Paris, Musgrave heard a colorful duet between a clarinet and a piano accordion; the sound of it remained with her; in 1967, she used the combination in some incidental music for a television play, again found it good, and then used it prominently—with delightful consequence—in the Clarinet Concerto. Sometimes the accordion holds cluster chords; in a scherzo episode,

236

with deliciously humorous effect, it plays impudent canons with the soloist.

The protean character of the solo instruments is fully employed from the first, minatory entries, fortissimo in a low register. It cries in shrill clarion with the trumpets, spins opaline romance with vibraphone and harp, darts like a grayling through the prestissimo central section. In his musical role, Mr. Drucker was masterly. As master of the score's alternative ceremonies, as co-conductor, he was a shade less dashing and debonair than the work's dedicatee and first soloist, Gervase De Peyer. Perhaps another production rehearsal was needed. But in any case the Fisher Hall platform is a rather cramped stage for the musical drama, and the seating plan suggested in the score had been altered; the work's structure-in-space was not made ideally clear. Nevertheless, the playing and Miss Caldwell's conducting were so spirited that what resulted was an even brighter, more dramatic, more rousing performance than one that has just appeared on an Argo disc—recorded in association with the British Council—which has Mr. De Peyer in his original role. A study score of the Concerto, published by J. & W. Chester, is distributed here by G. Schirmer.

There were two other works on the program—the andante of Ruth Crawford Seeger's Quartet, and Pozzi Escot's "Sands . . ." Seeger's prophetic Quartet (1931) is familiar in its string-quartet form; the program note referred, puzzlingly, to an "original version" for string orchestra, but it is hard to imagine an orchestra's doing justice to the flexible, rhythmically difficult lines of the rubato-assai, the leggiero, and the allegro-possibile movements. For the andante there is an optional double-bass part, and the slow, urgent swell of the sonorities and the shifting dynamic balances within sustained chords lent themselves to orchestral treatment.

Escot, a Peruvian-born composer living in Cambridge, Massachusetts, is new to me, and I hope to hear more of her work. Although things she (purportedly) says in reference to it may be forbidding ("Music is a mathematical discipline"), untrue ("All music is highly rationalized, just as life is highly rationalized"), or simply hard to understand ("The title . . . has no illustrative implications but simply stands as it sounds, an integral part of the music itself"), and although a computer was called in to insure that in the second movement "the time-lapse between the entrance of one pitch and the next is never duplicated," "Sands . . ." turned out to be an arresting and accessible composition, as direct as some of Iannis Xenakis's most formidably mathematical constructions. As Messiaen once observed of Xenakis's early *Achorripsis*, "Les calculs préalables s'oublient complètement à l'audition. . . . Le résultat sonore est une agitation, delicatement poétique, ou violemment brutale." The work lasts fourteen minutes, is scored for violins and double-basses, drums, saxophones, and a drastically amplified electric guitar, was commissioned by the Venezuelan government, and was first performed, in Caracas, in 1966. [P.S. In a letter to me, after this review first appeared, Miss Escot indignantly denied having said any of the things quoted above; they were attributed to her in the program notes.]

It was not by chance that the five composers in this program were female. The concert, given in association with the magazine *Ms.*, was billed as "A Celebration of Women Composers." Gloria Steinem, an editress of that magazine, introduced the program notes with the question "Why are there no women composers?"—a question with a false premise, as the concert itself soon revealed, but in any case one that need not be asked in Australia (where Anne Boyd and Alison Bauld would be high on any list of leading musical creators), in France (Betsy Jolas, ditto), or in Britain (Elisabeth Lutyens, Thea Musgrave, Priaulx Rainier). In fact, it had not occurred to me before to distinguish composers by sex. Doing so now, I glance through the programs of the South Bank—London's "Lincoln Center"—for this month and see that the Birmingham Orchestra is introducing a large orchestral work by Nicola LeFanu, that the New Philharmonia is playing Lutyens's *Music for Orchestra II*, that Phyllis Tate has a première and Lutyens another performance in the Purcell Room. Internationally, women play so important and so unquestioned a role in music that to devote a special concert to their works must smack a little of Ladies' Nights in an Oxford college—those special occasions when women are allowed to dine in hall and enter the common room. On the other hand, since in the regular Philharmonic programs for the season I find as the only composeress Barbara Kolb, whose *Soundings* is being played next month, Miss Steinem may have a point when she says that "it will take many, many more such concerts . . . before all our human dreams and talents are set free." Such concerts will always be welcome when, like this one, they provide adventurous and excellent fare. And when they are played in so spirited a fashion. With its usual four rehearsals, the Philharmonic often has difficulty in bringing a single new piece up to a decent performance level. Here, after only three rehearsals, it did five unfamiliar pieces, and did them well. That Miss Caldwell is a genius needed no further proof. That (given players so expert as the Philharmonic's but little rehearsal time) inspiration, a swift, sure grasp of a work's particular character, and a passion to communicate it, to share insights and understanding, are a conductor's largest assets was amply demonstrated at this, her Philharmonic début. Some details were imprecise, but all that is most important about the pieces was vividly realized.

At Alice Tully Hall the day before, Mrs. H. H. A. Beach's Piano Quintet in F-sharp minor was played by the Chamber Music Society of Lincoln Center. Although it bears the opus number 67, the Quintet, published in 1909, must count as a fairly early work of hers (Her Piano Trio of 1938 is Opus 150; she died in 1944.) The adagio is distinguished by a scrumptiously Straussian melody, but otherwise the piece (available on a Turnabout record, coupled with the A-minor Piano Quintet of Arthur Foote, another New Englander who wrote blameless Germanic music) is dull. Yet Mrs. Beach has her place in history; her "Gaelic" Symphony, played by the Boston Symphony in 1896, is claimed as the first symphonic work written by an American woman. There followed at Tully Hall Benjamin Britten's *Canticle V: The Death of Saint Narcissus*, one of T. S. Eliot's *Poems Written in Early Youth* set for tenor and harp. It is drawn with a thinner pencil than are the earlier canticles. The mannerism of quirky word repetition—so noticeable in the opera *Owen Wingrave*—is sometimes disturbing. ("When he walked over the meadows, over the meadows / He was stifled and soothed, stifled and soothed by his own rhythm, own rhythm, own own rhythm.") But in point of rhythmic finesse this is one of the most fascinating and subtle things Britten has done. The central strophes, dealing with Narcissus's imagined metamorphoses (tree, fish, maiden), flicker and dart from a base of flowing eighth-notes. Sections on either side move to a slow, marked beat in quarter-notes, grouped into irregular measures that convey a sensation of walking onward with a light, graceful stride while thoughts go wheeling and images come winging in rhythms of their own. The introduction and envoy are recitatives. The more I contemplate the piece, the more it seems to me a small miracle of sensitivity to the speeds and stresses of Eliot's lines. It was performed, superbly well, by Peter Pears and Osian Ellis. At the close of the concert, Mr. Pears sang Vaughan Williams's *On Wenlock Edge*, for tenor, piano, and string quartet. And one could not hope to hear words more beautifully uttered along a musical line.

In two public master classes at the Juilliard School, Mr. Pears strove to impart some of the lore that marks his singing. Join notes into a line; carry the whole of a phrase on one seamless thread of tone; in legato phrases, sing "through" the consonants; don't spit words, except when some special effect is required; rubato, always rubato—these were the burdens of his instruction, amid the individual points brought up by each song. When singing in English, cultivate a clean, forward tone. (Mr. Pears kept indicating the forehead as a place to aim for.) Think of clear, carrying French vowels when faced with those toneless English "neutral" syllables. One class was devoted to Handel and Britten, the other to Schubert and Schumann. The students who turned up at the latter were the more accomplished—less metronomic, more responsive to the color of words. To the obvious moral—that German is on the whole a more vivid singing language—Mr. Pears by practice and precepts added another: that English can be equally vivid, and means more to English-speaking listeners, when it is handled as it should be.

November 24, 1975

VERY GOOD, CONSIDERING...

Die Meistersinger von Nürnberg is a moving and beautiful opera, a long, rich musical and dramatic poem to wit and wisdom, to ardent, impetuous young love and tender, prudent, paternal care, to dashing artistic adventure and justly cherished tradition. A world without *Die Meistersinger* would be a poorer place; it is one of the necessary operas, like *Fidelio* and *Figaro*. Fortunate the city that has two productions, to provide complementary experiences: the world's finest interpreters gathered in an original-language version, and a "company" performance rehearsed by a stable cast and played in the language of the singers and the audience. The Metropolitan and the City Opera have some repertory overlaps hard to justify on grounds of artistic necessity (*I puritani*, this season, is one), but a city the size of New York has room for two *Meistersingers*, and the City Opera's new production is welcome.

It is a difficult piece to do well. For one thing, it is one of the two longest operas regularly performed. (The other is *Götterdämmerung*; their durations are just about equal.) The 1968 *Mastersingers* at Sadler's Wells, another "national" production, complementary to the international stagings at London's Royal Opera, produced five hours and fifteen minutes of music. That, admittedly, was exceptional (and achieved an entry in the *Guinness Book of World Records*); it was led by Reginald Goodall, the most lingering and loving—and, I believe, the greatest—Wagner interpreter of our day. The longest *Meistersinger* recorded in the Bayreuth annals, Hans Knappertsbusch's in 1952, lasted four hours and forty minutes, and the shortest, Fritz Busch's in 1924, and Wilhelm Furtwängler's in 1943, both four hours and fifteen. Four and a half hours' playing time is about par for an uncut performance. Add two intermissions, and it makes a long evening. The City Opera's *Meistersinger* (billed in German, though it was sung in John Gutman's English translation) was not, in fact, integral. Nearly twenty cuts, some of them small and others more extensive, removed about forty minutes of the music. Nevertheless, for a company to have given, in the course

240

of sixteen days, seven performances of even an abridged *Meistersinger* must be a record in itself—and that without counting the eleven intervening shows of other works. Assessment is bound to hover between the views "It was very good, considering . . ." and "It's not good enough to put on *Die Meistersinger* in circumstances that allow no more than a summary account of the great opera."

For summary it was. In every house there are likely to have been people who had never seen *Die Meistersinger* before. They would have received not a false impression of the piece, only an incomplete one. But to listeners familiar with the opera the City Opera version could serve as little more than a reminder of what the work can be. Heaven knows, I have sat through some unworthy *Meistersinger* performances in my time, but never before one in which there were not phrases, colors, sudden inflections, points of timing, glances between characters, utterance of particular moments that came as a new revelation, an enrichment of earlier experiences. Of course there is a danger that a new production may be unfairly measured against not the possible but a composite ideal, unattainable on a single occasion yet built up from memories of the way one Eva sang "Euch oder keinen!," another "O Sachs! Mein Freund!," and still a third the climax of the quintet. And similarly with the other characters. If Hans Sachs is shaped for us by, say, a compound of Friedrich Schorr's incomparable recordings, Hans Hotter's poetic grandeur, and Paul Schoeffler's good sense, can any baritone add anything? Well, Norman Bailey did, when first he undertook the role at Sadler's Wells, and the unknown new singer was revealed overnight as a Wagnerian of more than local importance. (The following year, he was Bayreuth's Sachs.) One made no comparisons, merely hung intent on an individual, unusually direct, definite interpretation, with a curious touch of restraint in its romanticism. Mr. Bailey also sang Sachs in the City Opera performances, but the effect here was less remarkable. With orchestral playing less eloquent than Mr. Goodall had provided, without warm instrumental tinting of everything he said— a rapturous declamation, from the pit, of Sachs's inner world, revealing the emotions whose verbal formulation eludes him—a dimension was lost. Mr. Bailey was still excellently clear and uncommonly intelligent, but not quite poetic enough. (The British public's fervent acclaim of its Wagnerian heroes Rita Hunter, Alberto Remedios, and Mr. Bailey often seems exaggerated to those who hear them on away dates; that is because only in partnership with Mr. Goodall do they regularly rise to greatness.) Moreover, although Mr. Bailey, by now a very experienced Sachs, did not put a finger wrong, one sensed a lack of intense involvement with the particular Eva, Walther, and David around him.

I know that memory can play tricks, and shed a golden glow on what is past. The greatest *Meistersinger* cast of my experience was Beecham's, at Covent Garden nearly a quarter-century ago: Elisabeth Grümmer, Peter Anders, Hotter, Benno Kusche as Beckmesser, and Ludwig Weber as Pogner. But this was a performance that Beecham himself, a few years later, described as "inferior . . . poor singers and an indifferent orchestra." I vividly recall the choral singing, splendid as the sun, at a 1968 Bayreuth *Meistersinger* and forget—until I consult my notes—how poor the orchestral playing was. Memory retains what is right and beautiful about performances witnessed, blots out the after-image of the final scene as Wieland Wagner first staged it in Bayreuth (stiffly suggesting the wrong sort of Nuremberg rally) but holds forever the vision that began Act II in the same production: the soft, dense, luminous blue air, Nuremberg's houses gently glimmering, the elder blossom shining overhead—all the magic of Midsummer Eve in an unspoiled old city. That was right, and Carl Toms's prosaic set at the City Opera is wrong—or, if not exactly wrong, at any rate inadequate. All four of his scenes are built to stage plans that lead to awkwardness in the action. The style of his designs is workaday conventional; brown and gray, for two acts against a black backcloth and wings, are the dominant colors. The scenes are not particularly attractive to look at, and their departures from Wagner's carefully planned scenario are unhelpful. The mastersinger meeting of Act I is held in the nave of the church, in the fixed pews; the marker ensconces himself in the pulpit. There is no space, and during the finale the masters can only stand in a line, addressing the conductor like members of a choral society.

John Cox directed. His successes—among them Richard Strauss's *Ariadne, Capriccio*, and *Intermezzo* at Glyndebourne, his *Rosenkavalier* in Houston—have been mainly with operas dependent on delicacy and finesse of individual characterization, operas in which the passing moment counts for more than a long, broad line of dramatic development. His successes in this *Meistersinger* are again with the careful definition of characters in specific situations. *Die Meistersinger* needs more—a heavier weight of emotion than Mr. Cox brought to it. And even in matters of detail there were some disappointments. For example, no one seemed to have told the David, Gary Glaze, that his remark in Act III—"Ach Meister! Wollt mir verzeih'n; kann ein Lehrbub' vollkommen sein?"—is one of the most touching little utterances in all opera. He made next to nothing of it. The moment passed unremarked. On a detail like this, singer, director, conductor, and English translator must combine. The conductor must judge exactly the degree of slackening implied by Wagner's marking "Immer zurückhaltend im Zeitmass." The singer must get his timbre, inflection, and placing of the crucial F just right. The translator must find something that fits the accents and lengths of the notes a little more precisely than Mr. Gutman's "Forgive me, please, all the same; can a prentice be without blame?" ("Ein saures Amt" is his, in truth.) I do not know when the City Opera began work on *Die Meistersinger*, but a year's preparation is not too long if the singers and the instrumentalists are to learn the possibilities of the score in all its richness.

Slowness in Wagner is not inevitably a virtue, but it is often needed if the music is to rise to full majesty. On the last page of his *London Music in 1888–89*, Bernard Shaw recalls a *Meistersinger* Prelude conducted, very slowly, by Siegfried Wagner:

I felt that the overture would certainly peter out and stop from sheer inertia if he did not speed up the final section. Instead, to my amazement, he achieved the apparently impossible feat of slowing it down. And the effect was magical. The music broadened out with an effect that is beyond description. It was immense, magnificent.

I have never heard a Wagner performance that seemed altogether too slow (passages, yes: Goodall in the forging song of *Siegfried*, Knappertsbusch in the flower maidens' waltz of *Parsifal*), and often a performance that was altogether too fast (Boulez's *Parsifal*, for one). At the City Opera, Julius Rudel's tempi were not so much fast by the metronome as hurried in the effect they produced, brisk-seeming because he had not urged the singers to lean expressively on certain notes, to "stretch" gruppetti such as the recurrent turn in Walther's prize song, to sound the beauties of the music as if they had all the time in the world at their disposal. It is true that at Eva's radiant protestation— "O Sachs! Mein Freund!"—there is no indication of any tempo change from the "Sehr lebhaft" of Sachs's previous outburst, until the "Ein wenig breiter" of the central section. But, leaving memories aside, I could summon the evidence (on disc) of generations of Wagner conductors to support a claim that the marvelous passage should not be held to a strict tempo. Rushed, as Mr. Rudel rushed it, it loses half its eloquence.

Johanna Meier is a promising Eva. She has the right temperament, and the right voice. When she sings the part a little more smoothly, and makes more of its famous moments, she could be pleasing indeed. John Alexander, the Walther of the first night, was no more than efficient; he was certainly not romantic, ardent, or in any way interesting. Elliot Palay, the Walther at the last performance, was raw, not exactly efficient, but rather likable. More convincingly than Mr. Alexander, who was somewhat routine about it, he delivered the prize song as something new-mint and wonderful. James Billings's sharp-cut, alert little Beckmesser was on—but just not over—the verge of caricature. Mr. Glaze's David looked charming, but a sweeter timbre than his is needed. Richard T. Gill, a gauche Pogner, simply left a hole in scenes he should fill. David Holloway sang Kothner's roulades with admirable distinctness.

It was all "very good, considering . . ." Considering the orchestra's work load, one could hardly expect, night after night, the full-hearted, full-bowed, full-breathed, massive, magnificent tone that the climaxes of the score require. Considering the State Theater's poor acoustics, it was sonically more impressive than one might have expected. And by any standards the lighting was a cut above usual. The odious follow spots were banned.

Some of the cuts were unexceptionable. I cannot get very heated about a missing verse of the cobbling song or of Beckmesser's serenade, in Act II. I regret abridgment of the conversation between Sachs and Walther before the prize song comes to birth, for its matter lies at the artistic heart of *Die Meistersinger*. If the David has limpid tones and a lively utterance, then to hack out most of his recital of the modes, in Act I, is barbarous. The worst cut was of most of Sachs's outburst in Act III—the passage referred to above, which starts "Hat man mit dem Schuhwerk nicht seine Noth!" Sachs was allowed only ten measures before Eva broke in with her cry of "O Sachs! Mein Freund!" The portrayal of his character was thereby diminished, while her protest lost its motivation. In the last scene, both of Sachs's solos were abridged. Now, in the second of these, the passage about keeping German art pure from foreign influences is a notoriously "sensitive" one. It did not figure in Wagner's first sketch of the opera, and Cosima Wagner claimed that it was only at her insistence that it went into the final version. But I do not think it should be cut, as here it was. When Wolfgang Wagner produced a centennial *Meistersinger*, at Bayreuth in 1968, he set out on the cover of the program, as a kind of manifesto, a sentence from his grandfather's *Art and Revolution*:

Whereas the Greek work of art expressed the spirit of a splendid nation, the work of art of the future is intended to express the spirit of free people irrespective of all national boundaries; the national element in it must be no more than an ornament, an added individual charm, and not a confining boundary.

At the least, that ornament, that added individual charm, is worth preserving. More important, it sounds a theme—the local as symbol of the universal—that runs through *Die Meistersinger*, and affects so much of our lives. The passage is not bombastic; in the score, "was deutsch und echt" is marked *piano*. At that Bayreuth performance, Theo Adam sang the phrase not assertively but with an almost elegiac sweetness, beauty, and intensity of tone; these things *would* be lost if they were not kept alive (and here his voice began to glow with gentle pride) by honoring the German masters. The effect was overwhelming. And no *Meistersinger* that does not overwhelm us, at the very least, five or six times during the evening can be counted more than a limited success.

December 1, 1975

ORESTES IN OREGON

In the prospectus of the 1975–76 season published by *Opera News* in September, two major events caught the eye: the American premières of Ernst Krenek's *Leben des Orest* (first performed in Leipzig, in 1930) and of Roger Sessions's *Montezuma* (first performed in Berlin—by all accounts not well—in 1964). *Montezuma* is due in March, from the Opera Company of Boston. *Leben des Orest* has now happened; it was done, very successfully, by the Portland Opera on November 20, 22, and 24. This large, dashing, brilliant grand opera raises so many issues that one hardly knows where to begin discussing it. Perhaps on the simple level of acclaim: for an arresting, entertaining, frankly and fluently melodious, very theatrical, and powerful opera; and for the lively, dexterous Portland performance, given, as *Life of Orestes*, in the composer's own English translation.

Krenek, who attended the show, is seventy-five this year. He has always been a composer so prolific, so versatile, so adept in a variety of idioms—first atonal, then neoclassical, neo-Romantic, jazzy, Frenchified, Schoenbergian, post-Webernian, then electronic—that, as he himself has said, "it is quite possible that the unusual variety of my output has baffled observers accustomed to more homogeneous phenomena. It is my impression that this confusion has surrounded my work with an unusual obscurity—almost anonymity." But, he adds, "It may well be that at some future time its seemingly erratic aspects, which now hide whatever values it may contain, will be revealed as the very carriers of these values." In the Library of Congress, but inaccessible until fifteen years after his death, there piles up volume after volume of his autobiography. Meanwhile, there are the scores—and but scattered performances. His hit opera of the late twenties, *Jonny spielt auf*, brought him money and fame but is now seldom heard. Frankfurt revived *Leben des Orest* for his fiftieth birthday; Darmstadt and Wiesbaden revived it for his sixtieth; Munich revived *Karl V.* for his sixty-fifth. Hamburg premièred *Pallas Athene weint* in its new house in 1955, and in 1964 *Der goldene Bock*.

245

But the operas tend to be done and then dropped. In two decades of pretty heavy operagoing I encountered only *Karl V.* in the theater and *Jonny* in a radio performance. In America, where Krenek has lived for thirty-seven years, there has been, until now, no major production since the Met staged *Jonny* in 1929 (with Michael Bohnen, Rudolf Laubenthal, Friedrich Schorr, and Florence Easton in the leading roles). Krenek is admired, respected, and not much played. The reasons are complex now, but once they were simple: from 1933 until after the war his music was not performed in Germany, where he had won his greatest successes; in 1934 an appeasing Austria withdrew from rehearsal and canceled the *Karl V.* he had composed for the Vienna State Opera. In 1938 he moved to America.

The dispersal of German and Austrian composers brought about by Hitler's accession and then the Anschluss closed two brilliant, concurrent, and in part overlapping chapters of musical history. Some pages were literally consigned to the flames (Kurt Weill's publishers recalled his music and burned it); the war blurred and blotted others. One of those chapters, concerned with Schoenberg, Berg, and Webern (the Second Viennese School), has since been reconstructed; the music it produced is played and known. But the second, dealing with the music of the Weimar Republic, written largely by Franz Schreker's and Ferruccio Busoni's pupils at the Berlin Hochschule, is still unfamiliar. Although some of its achievements, notably Weill's *Dreigroschenoper* and *Aufstieg und Fall der Stadt Mahagonny*, are put on from time to time, they tend to be revived—and listened to—in a spirit of "nostalgia" for twenties Berlin, without much understanding of their composers' aims or of the context in which they were created. (The staging of Weill's *Der Jasager* in St. Luke's Chapel last month was on just about every count a wretched misrepresentation of the opera that from 1930 to 1933 was in effect a set piece in the schools of the Weimar Republic and had over a hundred productions.) The Republic was an experiment in democracy. The chief medium of its composers was musical theater. Large among their aims was the establishment of lyric drama as a moral force. But contemporary opera of all kinds flourished. In 1930 alone, Leipzig introduced *Leben des Orest* in January, *Mahagonny* in March. Frankfurt introduced Schoenberg's *Von Heute auf Morgen* in February and George Antheil's *Transatlantic* in May. That month, Berlin staged Milhaud's *Christophe Colomb*, and, in June, *Der Jasager*, Hindemith's *Wir bauen eine Stadt*, and other school operas. Together with earlier pieces such as Berg's *Wozzeck*, *Jonny*, and Schreker's *Die Gezeichneten*, the new works made their way from city to city. Klemperer was conducting *Leben des Orest* in Berlin within weeks of its Leipzig première; then Darmstadt mounted a production in which Agamemnon the Great Leader was played as Mussolini. And soon a dozen companies had given the opera.

Krenek's role during this most active time for the development of modern opera was characteristically protean. He came to the theater almost by chance, "prompted . . . by sheer curiosity, for I felt no real urge to express myself in opera. But I had written something for nearly every other medium." Two operas, *Die Zwingburg* and *Der Sprung über den Schatten*, were completed in 1923 and staged the following year. In 1926 there was *Orpheus und Eurydike*, a setting of the Kokoschka play. (All the Krenek operas mentioned here, except *Die Zwingburg* and *Orpheus*, are to his own librettos.) The critic Paul Bekker recognized a born theater composer, and when he became director of the Cassel and then of the Wiesbaden Operas he engaged Krenek as his assistant. The resultant practical knowledge of the theater, and of its audiences, produced *Jonny*, tailored for success—no longer in a difficult, advanced idiom but tonal, tuneful, and spiced with jazz. And then, after three little one-acters (two satires and a fairy tale) put on in Wiesbaden, there was the grand opera *Leben des Orest*.

In Krenek's "Self-Analysis" (published in the *New Mexico Quarterly* for Spring 1953), he detects two contradictory pulls in his nature: a concern for "everlasting values," whether they are fashionable or no, and a temptation to aim for quick success in terms of "this world." In *Jonny*, the conflict is dramatized: Jonny, the black jazz player, and Daniello, the slick virtuoso, affirmative and satirical mirror images of a success figure, are pop and classical princes of the "this world" with which Max, the spiritual, dreamy, intellectual composer, cannot come to terms. One might say that *Jonny* was composed by Krenek-Jonny, and *Karl V.* (which in twelve-note music proclaims a vision of a Europe united, as Charles V sought to unite it, in one supernational Catholic Empire) by Krenek-Max. Between them comes *Leben des Orest*, in whose composition Jonny and Max conspire, and whose hero, now existentialist, now dreamer, is finally at peace. The jangle of musical styles reflects the theme.

Krenek's first idea was for a drama in which Orestes, pursued by the Furies, wanders through time and the world until, in contemporary America, he finds Iphigenia, "and all comes right." This developed into a full-scale *Oresteia*, set not in white-marbled antiquity but partly in a polychrome South under hard, clear, violent light and partly in a tenebrous Northland (Krenek's transformation of Tauris), a country of speculation, indecision, and philosophical dreams that need to be tested by the Southern sun. Act I is (roughly) *Iphigenia in Aulis*. Act II introduces Thoas and a newly invented character, his daughter Thamar, in a scene recalling both Prospero with Miranda and Klingsor with Kundry; Iphigenia materializes as if in answer to Thoas' yearning incantations. And then there is a bustling, merry Athenian fair (kin to the genre scenes of Meyerbeer's operas) at which the lad Orestes, on his way to

Phocis, escapes from his nurse Anastasia and is carried off by a circus troupe. Act III is (roughly) an *Agamemnon* and an *Electra*, separated by a very beautiful long scena for the maturing Orestes on his wanderings. Act IV is (roughly) *Iphigenia in Tauris*—Krenek's Teutonic Tauris, where Thoas loves Iphigenia, Thamar falls in love with Orestes, and after the recognition scene North and South are united; all four set out together for Athens. Act V is (roughly) *The Eumenides*.

I repeat that "roughly" because Krenek has altered familiar events and added touches of his own. Some are decorative. (At the Athenian fair, a white ball from a cockshy—its target, to young Orestes' fury, a cardboard Troy and the prize a kiss from the floozy who impersonates his Aunt Helen—falls into Anastasia's lap. This, her only possession, she offers to Athene, with a prayer that the goddess keep watch over Orestes. In the final scene, this ball reappears as the casting vote at his trial.) Others affect psychological motivation. Father-son parallels are stressed, and there is a suggestion, as we watch Orestes' progress, that there, but for lessons learned in adversity and then the grace of the goddess, would go a second Agamemnon, brutal, ambitious, and uncontrolled. Not that Agamemnon himself remains unchanged: in this version he returns from Troy disillusioned and weary, and willingly embraces death (here proffered in a cup, not by net and ax). Yet another change emphasizes the father-son pattern: in Tauris the Euripidean roles of victim and executioner are reversed, and Orestes, like his father before him, is about to sacrifice Iphigenia. The finale, like that of the real *Oresteia*, is a reconciliation, and a recognition that tyranny is well replaced by corporate reason, even though some cases prove too hard for men alone to decide. By this ingenious libretto, Krenek insured plenty of action: two near-sacrifices, three murders, and two tremendous recognition scenes. The deft, cunning planner who wanted a theater success could be satisfied. But the visionary had a further object in mind. In an essay written for the magazine *Anbruch* at the time of the première, Krenek said:

A man in all his various aspects and embodiments, living, suffering, loving, impelled by passions, restrained by reason, now falling to the depths without hope of rescue, then raised by incomprehensible grace—that man is the theme of my piece. . . . The belief in mystery and in grace, today scorned and feeble, needs to be revived.

From this conception, he continued, the verbal and musical idiom arose of its own accord. There would be no evocation of period, whether prehistoric, classical, or Hellenic, and no specific local color, only the generalized South-North antithesis. He cited as a parallel Bruegel's "Massacre of the Innocents," taking place in a snowy Flemish village, and the Old German Masters who painted Jerusalem as another Nuremberg.

The musical idiom is Krenek's own bright compound of theater vernaculars of his day, and 1930s ears must have heard it differently from ours. Then, the jazzy syncopations of some episodes must have had a piquantly shocking effect when applied to Attic tragedy. Now, late-twenties jazz is just another historic style, inherently no more anachronistic than the heated Expressionism of Strauss's *Elektra* (1909) or the cool, lapidary precision of Stravinsky's *Oedipus Rex* (1927). (There are traces of both those works, too, in the eclectic score of *Orest*—even an echo of Strauss's famous Agamemnon motif.) But not all styles are suited to all subjects. The year before *Orest*, and doubtless with works like *Jonny* in mind, Weill had written, also in *Anbruch*, that "for the serious European musician it was out of the question to wish to imitate, let alone 'ennoble,' American dance music." The implication must be that Krenek is not serious. *Jonny* was the exemplary *Zeitoper*, cashing in on the "here and now." In *Von Heute auf Morgen*, Schoenberg satirized the genre. Weill himself imitated jazz very seldom, and always with specific critical intent. *Jonny* must be defended by someone who has seen it on the stage (vocal scores of such pieces are more than usually misleading; reading that of *Orest* left me quite unprepared for the effect it made in the theater), if it is defensible. But there are four points worth making about the "jazz" in *Orest*. First, it is very precisely placed, and always in association with vivid characters as yet untouched by grace. Second, in the perspective of the years much of it has drawn surprisingly close to the ostinatos and simple figurations of neoclassicism. Third, Krenek, like Weill, knew exactly how to use the timbre of the banjo "seriously," with poignant expressive effect. Fourth, he himself would probably own that there *was* a calculated element of naughty, titillating irreverence and modishness in his employment of foxtrots and "Tiger Rag" rhythms during the course of an *Oresteia*.

But too much can be made of the jazz. If I had to name two dominant "influences" on *Orest*, they would be Schubert and Offenbach, the latter for the verve of invention and sheer mastery of putting music together, and the former, less demonstrably, for a kind of lyric emotion given musical form. *Die Winterreise* underlies more than one of Krenek's song cycles, and the thoughts of a traveler have always been a source of inspiration to him, from the early *Reisebuch aus den österreichischen Alpen* to *The Ballad of the Railroads* and the a-cappella setting of the Santa Fe timetable. At the center of *Orest* is the hero's soliloquy in the mountains at sunset, Schubertian in spirit and also in some of its musical details. No one who hears it can doubt that Krenek has a heart as well as a formidable mind.

Leben des Orest was intended to be a very long opera. In the vocal score, the composer indicated, and recommended the observance of, several cuts "prompted by the experience of the première." (But it is perhaps significant that he has now provided an English translation even for those episodes marked for optional omission by "VI . . . DE" indications.) The cutting in Portland was even more extensive. The Meyerbeerian scale of the work was drastically reduced, and to some extent its five-act structure was obscured by collapsing it into three acts. In Act I, entrances and exits became a rather jerky sequence, more comic-strip in effect than was intended; and Act IV, in Tauris / Northland, was not set off from the rest as it should be. But the abridgment did not dim the Portland achievement. Carey Gordon Wong's strong, elegant, very practicable scenery, his inventive and colorful costumes, and Ghita Hager's crisp, stylish, and often powerfully affecting production were marked by an imaginative grasp of both the opera's glittering surface and its emotional inner themes. Stefan Minde, the general director of the Portland company, had been wanting to do *Orest* there for years (he conducted the 1961 production in Wiesbaden), and he had evidently inspired the cast, the chorus, and the orchestra with his passionate belief in the work. His handling of the score was masterly—dynamic but not driven, emotional but not sentimental. The principals were mainly American artists with German experience—good actors, accomplished singers, and accustomed to communicating. In the exceptionally demanding title role, Victor Braun was versatile, romantic, and eloquent—a notable performance. There was no weakness, and a great deal of dramatic and beautiful singing, to be heard from a cast so large and, in vocal types, so various that a roll call must here suffice: Sylvia Anderson (Clytemnestra), Barrie Smith (Iphigenia), Anita Salta (Electra), Linda Cook (Thamar), Glade Peterson (Agamemnon), Kenneth Riegel (Aegisthus), William Wildermann (Thoas), and Donald Miller (Aristobulus, president of the Athenian court). Now that so excellent a production exists, and a fine cast knows the work in English, it would be a great pity if after three performances this *Life of Orestes* were to disappear.

December 8, 1975

KEY MOMENTS IN FIGARO

If, in Act II of *Le nozze di Figaro*, the Countess has turned the key and locked the door of her dressing room, with Cherubino inside—as she does in Günther Rennert's new production of the opera at the Metropolitan—how does he get out again, once the coast is clear? There are two possible ways: Susanna has a second key and lets him out, or the lock is of a kind that can be opened, without key, from the inside. But in the Met production Susanna had no handy chatelaine, and the lock, both sides of it clearly visible at different stages of the action, looked like no eighteenth-century example I have seen that could make the page's escape possible. So what should happen? The original, 1786 libretto gives the answer when it says, "Cherubino enters the dressing room and closes the door; the Countess takes the key." She does not *turn* the key to "double-lock" the door; the lock must be of that common, click-to kind opened from one side by turning a key and from the other by turning a handle. It is a small point, but not negligible in an opera for which Mozart and his librettist, Lorenzo da Ponte, have devised things so carefully; any hitch in their smooth stage mechanism strikes a jarring note. A larger point is that directors and executants need to work from good editions reproducing all that the creators had in mind. For Acts I and II of *Figaro* such an edition—Ludwig Finscher's, in the *Neue Mozart-Ausgabe*—is available. But the autograph of Acts III and IV— all but a scrap that made its way to Stanford University—has since the war been missing from its home in the German State Library, and until it emerges from its Polish hiding place we must make do, as Professor Finscher had to, with scores that (to judge by a comparison of the earlier acts against the autograph) are far from trustworthy. We do, at least, have the original libretto. (There is a copy in the Library of Congress, and a film of the autograph score for Acts I and II in the New York Public Library.)

What should happen later, after Cherubino has got away and Susanna has taken his place? The Countess, at the words "Egli è innocente," hands her husband the key. (Some editors have placed the action later, at her "Io non son rea," but Mozart's autograph is clear.) A few measures on, with this key the Count opens the door of the dressing room, and Susanna comes out. I have never seen things happen quite that way; Susanna has always opened the door herself, from the inside. It matters little, but it would be good, for once, to see the scene enacted as Mozart imagined it. Passing to Act IV, we find (in the libretto) that Susanna and the Countess have already changed garments before they enter the garden. If the change is effected later, during the course of the act, as it is in the Met production, and if the travesty, as at the Met, is a full one, not merely a switching of distinctive mantles, then a disturbing thought of dressers conveniently at hand in the wings to help with the complicated quick change is apt to flit across the listener's mind. I prefer mantle-swapping to the full change; it allows the Countess to make her breathtaking final appearance dressed once again as a countess, allows her to unmask even as she steps forward with her "Almeno io per loro perdono otterò." The stage directions give us no help here; the preference is prompted by a belief that the stage picture should reflect the musico-dramatic climax of the opera. After the phrase just quoted, the music drops into the minor and then through troubled progressions, resolved at the Count's "Contessa, perdono!," the Countess's answer, and its sotto-voce echo by all the company. This transfigured moment, as Professor Joseph Kerman has put it, "uncovers a core of decency under all the shabbiness which the comedy has exposed and tried to rationalize in laughter. . . . The Countess has never been more lovely and true to herself." And how can she be that, fully, if she is still disguised in the soubrette skirts of Susanna? At her "Almeno io per loro" there is, in fact, a rubric, not concerned with costume but revealing of the characters of both the Count and the Countess. Everyone else, as she or he sings "Perdono! perdono!," has been directed to kneel; now, as the Countess advances into the ring of suppliants, she, too, "wishes to kneel; the Count does not permit it." I have never seen this detail observed. I think it should be. The other directions mentioned depend directly from those of Beaumarchais's original play; this one involves a significant alteration, for in Beaumarchais the Countess "se jette à genoux" and rises only after, for the third time on that *folle journée*, she has forgiven her errant husband.

Any thoughtful production of *Figaro* tends to send one back to the score to check what happened in the theater against what happens there. In Jean-Pierre Ponnelle's staging for Karajan and the Salzburg Festival, made a few years ago and revived this summer, there were some rather startling departures from tradition. After his aria in Act I, Bartolo remained onstage during the duet for Susanna and Marcellina—a bad idea, and contradicted by the "he leaves" of the libretto. At the end of the act, the Count and Basilio remained onstage during Figaro's "Non più andrai"—but for this Mr. Ponnelle has the authority of both the libretto and Mozart's autograph. (In the corresponding Beaumarchais passage— "Tu ne rôderas plus . . ."—the Count and Basilio are likewise present.) At the start of Act III, Mr. Ponnelle's Countess concealed herself at one side to observe the first exchanges between her husband and Susanna. It looked convincing, and the "she hides herself" of earlier editors may be authentic; we will know when the autograph reappears. But in that case when does the Countess leave? There is no indication, and she can hardly remain eavesdropping indefinitely. In Mr. Ponnelle's production, she left quite soon—and rightly so. The duet for Susanna and the Count is best played without an onlooker; the Countess would hardly wish to witness her husband's infidelity, and if she stayed she would learn what later in the act she says she is eager to discover: whether the Count has taken Susanna's bait.

With Act III, a director's dramaturgical problems begin, for the action does not make sense as it stands. Something has gone astray. Not only has a cavatina for Cherubino, before the Countess's aria, been lost (its words, beginning "Se così brami / Teco verro," survive in the 1786 libretto), but the Countess's aria itself must be in the wrong place. She is anxiously awaiting Susanna's return, she says, but in the previous scene Susanna has just come from her. In 1965, the Mozart scholars Robert Moberly and Christopher Raeburn proposed a revised order for Act III. Presuming a last-minute dislocation caused, shortly before the 1786 première, by the fact that one singer had to double the roles of Antonio and Bartolo, needed time for a costume change, and was therefore given the duration of the Countess's aria to achieve it, they reconstructed a hypothetical original form for the act, in which Antonio and Bartolo are played by different singers, and the Countess's aria can follow hard on the Count's. That done, everything else falls convincingly into place. Their arguments were so persuasive that the new order has been widely adopted—by, among others, Sadler's Wells, Glyndebourne, Covent Garden, Karajan at Salzburg, the City Opera, and, this season, the New Haven Opera Theater. So widely, in fact, that when the Met stuck to the old version it came as something of a shock.

As for Act IV, the autograph alone will be able to tell us whether the first three scenes (Barbarina's cavatina, the conversation between Barbarina, Marcellina, and Figaro, and Marcellina's aria) were meant to be played indoors, with a scene change to the garden only at Barbarina's second entrance—thus the libretto, and the corresponding passages of Beaumarchais's play—or whether, as custom has it, the whole act should take place in the garden. A scene change might help to mask a structural weakness: the sequence of five arias on end with which the act begins. But it might seem fussy. At the Met, the second of these arias, Marcellina's was omitted, and with its disappearance something of *Figaro*'s fullness was lost.

Every worthy production of *Figaro* has its special interest. Different elements can be made to dominate. One conductor may offer a text both complete and stylishly graced with the ornaments, variations, cadenzas, and necessary appoggiaturas that eighteenth-century artists would have added as a matter of course to the plain notes on the written page. Some productions stress the charm and vivacity of the music, and others its force in revealing character and emotion. Sometimes we see a pretty comedy of manners, and sometimes a social conflict to remind us that Beaumarchais's *Mariage de Figaro* was once a banned play, overture to the Revolution. (That formidable schoolmarm Mme Campan once told Marie Antoinette that before *Le Mariage* could be performed the Bastille would have to fall.) *Figaro* can be a divertimento and it can be a tense drama. And in the best performance it does and is all these things at once. To treat it mainly as a revolutionary study is to narrow it—yet at some point we should be shocked by the aristocrats' calm, unjustified assumption of rights, and question it, as Mozart does. (A flicker of scorn, for example, in the Countess's inflection of "Ah, questa serva.") To treat it as a costumed concert of lovely singing is to lessen it, yet the singing must be lovely if we are to respond fully to the drama of the music. The presentation must not be dryly schematic, yet we should sense the underlying structure: two parts each of two acts, the first beginning with a duet for Susanna and Figaro, leading to Figaro's "Se vuol ballare" (Figaro vs. the Count), and ending with an ensemble in which the characters are ranged in opposition; the second beginning with a duet for Susanna and the Count, leading to the Count's "Vedrò, mentr'io sospiro" (the Count vs. Figaro), and ending with an ensemble in which all the characters are united. There is something to be said for playing the piece with only one intermission. Above all, *Figaro* is a drama about love and what love can lead to; about mature profligacy, romantic, adolescent sensuality, and the innocent eroticism of a twelve-year-old girl; about love betrayed, love rewarded, tender devotion, possessiveness, suspicions, jealousy. All the characters are involved. The two arias in Act IV often omitted as superfluous are further philosophies of love: Marcellina's declaration of women's rights, contrasting the manner in which men treat them with the natural order that prevails in the animal kingdom, and Basilio's cynical dismissal of the whole business, his theory of emotional self-castration, his bachelor wooing of "Donna Flemma." Anyone who dropped into *Figaro* at this point (and understood the language it was sung in) might be startled by the bestial imagery. Goats, rams, and savage beasts, says Marcellina, are kind to their mates; only men are cruel. Don a stinking ass's hide, says Basilio, and the fierce predator turns away in disgust. In the next aria, Figaro calls women beautiful vixens, smiling she-bears, and malicious doves, deceitful and pitiless. Oh, *Figaro* would be a bitter piece if the next aria were not Susanna's "Deh vieni," suffused with the happiness that love can bring. The sex war and the class war, love and liberty—preoccupations of the eighteenth century and of ours—are its themes, but the drama is played out by human beings who win our love, and in a world where there is at least the possibility of happiness. The dramatic situation of this "Deh vieni" is revealing. Susanna sings of her love for Figaro; but when he hears it, he misunderstands, and smarts under it.

Mr. Rennert's previous Mozart productions for the Met, *Don Giovanni* and *Die Zauberflöte*, have worn well, and his *Figaro* may do so, too, for it is firmly laid out on traditional lines, in scenery, by Robert O'Hearn, which is not attractive but perfectly serviceable. Like some other recent designers, Mr. O'Hearn has aimed to show more of the palace than just the room immediately necessary; in Act I there is also a corridor, in Act II a terrace. The intention is presumably to give a sense of intrigue scuttling through all the building, but surprise entrances become impossible. The garden of Act IV is a labyrinth of trellises that look like giant fire screens, ugly but useful for darting behind. Mr. O'Hearn's Goya-based costumes are handsome. Lighting depends largely on follow spots—there is even one on Cherubino during Figaro's "Non più andrai"—which catch the screens of Act IV when characters move behind them. What the show lacked, on the first night, was any strongly defined character, musical or dramatic. The text was not quite complete, and the singers' approach was literally graceless. Justino Díaz, the Figaro, declined Mozart's invitations to a cadenza in "Non più andrai." Evelyn Lear, the Countess, left an empty hole in the middle of "Dove sono." There were some hundreds of "wrong notes" in the form of blunt phrase endings where appoggiaturas are implicit. Steuart Bedford, conducting, favored swift, unyielding, unfeeling tempi that straitjacketed the marvelous harmonic and melodic movements of the music. The social lines were fuzzily drawn, largely because the Count, Wolfgang Brendel, behaved like a young Baron Ochs. (A grown-up Octavian would be more appropriate.) There was no menace in the man, and little seigneurial command; his servants, in the Act I chorus, were quite out of hand—and therefore out of style. The emotional line went wrong when the Countess, she who has just sung the heartbroken "Porgi amor," set out to seduce Cherubino. (Beaumarchais's third Figaro play, La Mère coupable, in which the Countess, raped by Cherubino, has borne him a son, appeared only in 1792—six days after the attack on the Tuileries—and has no bearing on Mozart's opera. But a Countess subtly touched by the boy's ardor can be very moving.) Lovely singing was to be heard only from the Cherubino of Frederica von Stade, even though she lacked the delicate accompaniment that Karajan had given her in the Salzburg performance. She is apt to turn her recitatives into a meaningless pitter-patter rather than sing them as sense. Judith Blegen was a delightful Susanna, a complete character, acting with her eyes as well as her voice, alert to every inflection of the score. That voice is a little thin and narrow in timbre for the role, but she used it with great skill. In the Act II trio, she took over the Countess's coloratura, running up to the high C, and, since Miss Lear's tones were flowing with difficulty, this was rightly done. (The prompter's interventions turned the trio into a quartet.) The singing of Mr. Díaz and Mr. Brendel was passable, unremarkable. Jean Kraft was an excellent Marcellina. Andrea Velis's Basilio was incisively sung and played, but he had got himself up to look like Fagin. The audience behaved badly and preferred the sound of its own clapping to the little dialogue between oboe, bassoon, and flute with which Mozart rounds off "Deh vieni."

Not much in music matters more than Mozart, but some other Met performers deserve at least a word. Régine Crespin's Carmen was very beautifully uttered. I had not heard a Frenchwoman in the role since Solange Michel, in my student days, at the Opéra-Comique, and hearing Mme Crespin was a rare pleasure. Her interpretation was rich and subtly alluring. The voice was colorful and clear, though it sounded worn at the top; her words and her acting were telling. James McCracken's José has become nobler than ever; his powerful voice has acquired a new lyric flexibility, and nothing in the part escapes him. Henry Lewis's conducting was very poor, and the edition used is still a mess. (Is *Carmen* to be the only celebration here of Bizet's centenary? Or will some radio station borrow the tapes of the BBC's "Bizet Festival"—all his operas in sequence, including the world première, in effect, of the splendid grand opera *Ivan le Terrible*, hitherto performed only in abridgment?)

Conducting, this time Gianfranco Masini's, was also the main thing wrong with the Met *Norma*. Anyone who compared favorable reports of Rita Hunter's first Norma, in San Francisco, with accounts of her New York appearance may have been puzzled at the disparity. In a limited way, by means of a tape recording, I was able to compare the performances, and there *is* a difference. With Carlo Felice Cillario as her conductor, in San Francisco, Miss Hunter was warmer, more flexible, and consequently altogether more expressive. Mr. Masini—who for Montserrat Caballé has on occasion been a conductor permissive to the point of sluggishness—beat rigidly through the New York performance and did not allow Bellini's melodies to shape themselves naturally. Miss Hunter, in the tradition of Lilli Lehmann and Maria Callas, is a soprano who sings both Brünnhilde and Norma. She has the power and the fluency that are needed, and she struck all the notes with pleasing definition. Her assumption of majesty had a somewhat homey aspect. Miss von Stade was a lustrous Adalgisa, if lushly mezzo in a role that calls for—but is seldom assigned—a bright young soprano. John Macurdy, Oroveso, was in sonorous voice. John Alexander made next to nothing of Pollione. Since Desmond Heeley's handsome set provides its different scenes swiftly, at the revolve of a turntable, the extra intermission breaking the progress of Act II seemed quite unnecessary.

The Los Angeles Philharmonic, under Zubin Mehta, came to Carnegie Hall for three concerts. I heard the second: Act III of *Die Walküre*, from Wotan's entrance to the end of the act, preceded by a "Ride of the Valkyries" (without Valkyrie voices), and then, after the intermission, a *Götterdämmerung* sequence of "Dawn," "Rhine Journey," "Funeral March," and "Immolation" played on end. The orchestra is a powerful and polished ensemble. Its tone was full and rich in every department; the viola sound was especially impressive. Mr. Mehta's tempi seemed to be sometimes too fast and sometimes too slow. The Brünnhilde and Wotan of the evening, Ursula Schröder-Feinen and Noël Tyl, have strong, efficient voices, but both of them tended to sing in notes rather than in long, unbroken phrases.

Long, free phrasing was a glory of the Scottish National Orchestra's concert in the same hall five days earlier. As a critic who prefers warmth of interpretation to brilliance of execution, who admires the Berlin Philharmonic but loves the Czech Philharmonic, who would rather hear deeply serious music conducted by Bernard Haitink than by Karajan, I have long counted among my favorite orchestras the Scottish National, molded by its conductor, Alexander Gibson, into an eloquent and poetic if not, by Chicago standards, virtuoso ensemble. Mr. Gibson and the orchestra played Mendelssohn's *Hebrides* overture and Elgar's *Enigma* with easy, unforced ebb and flow and generous rubato. Only some shyness about using portamento—in the dropping sevenths of the Theme and the Nimrod and B.G.N. variations—could be regretted in an otherwise ideally romantic and emotionally overwhelming account of the Elgar. There was a première on the bill—Iain Hamilton's *Aurora*, commissioned by the orchestra and dedicated to its conductor. It is a short (twelve-minute) progress from darkness to light—a nocturne and scherzo, in which tricky solo writing emerges from tenebrous, close-knit textures, and which ends in a sudden, splendid blaze. It is a strongly made, gripping composition. The première of Hamilton's opera *The Royal Hunt of the Sun* has been announced by the Santa Fe Opera for next season; elsewhere on its American tour, the Scottish Orchestra played his Violin Concerto, but in New York the concerto—most New York orchestral concerts include a concerto—was the *Emperor*, with John Lill its soloist, in a sensible, healthy performance. Since the Philharmonic was playing the *Emperor* a few days later, the Hamilton would have been a more interesting choice.

December 15, 1975

In April 1977, it was announced that the Poles would return the immense hoard of musical autographs missing from the German State Library (see "The Great Music Find," Sunday Times [London], April 3, 1977, p. 17).

Robert Moberly and Christopher Raeburn proposed their new order for Act III of Figaro in "Mozart's Figaro: the plan of Act III," in Music & Letters, 46 (1965), pp. 134–6.

The Santa Fe production of Hamilton's Royal Hunt was canceled; the piece had its première at the English National Opera, on February 2, 1977.

STRANGE ENCOUNTER

Among the many attractions of San Diego is the chance it offers of meeting (in its Sea World park) gentle, intelligent, mysterious, attractive creatures coming up out of the water to establish relationships with mere mortals. And so Dvořák's *Rusalka*, whose heroine is such a creature, was a natural choice for the San Diego Opera. The performance, this month, was billed as the American professional première. Last month, the Juilliard American Opera Center, in whose productions there is often a sizable professional element, also did *Rusalka*. (The American première of the piece is recorded as taking place in Chicago's Sokal Slav Hall in 1935.) Before the world discovered Janáček, *Rusalka* was probably considered, after Smetana's *The Bartered Bride* and Jaromir Weinberger's *Švanda the Bagpiper*, the most exportable Czech opera. All the same, it was not much exported. Every record collector knew Rusalka's lovely aria, "O silver moon," but the first non-Slav production was only in 1929, in Stuttgart, nearly three decades after the Prague première. In 1939, just weeks before Hitler's invasion of Czechoslovakia, Covent Garden announced a performance to be brought there by the Czech National Opera, but after the invasion a postponement, "probably till next season," was announced. (Instead, Beecham conducted a *Bartered Bride*, in German, with a cast in which Nazi and Jew, Teuton, Slav, and Briton were mingled.) I saw the British première of *Rusalka*, given after the war by the operatic troupe of the John Lewis Partnership (that department store with so many premières, local and, on occasion, "world," to its credit), and then a Sadler's Wells production in 1959. But the opera did not catch on. My reaction was that of many people who attended the Juilliard performance—beautiful music, but an unworkable, untheatrical piece. It was a Prague production of the early sixties, designed by Josef Svoboda and directed by Vaclav Kaslik, that showed me what *Rusalka* could be. In general, operas are best staged as their composers envisaged them. Janáček's *Kat'a Kabanová* needs solid-seeming walls, and the *Ring* needs pine trees. But *Rusalka* is perhaps a special case, and Svoboda's "magical" treatment of the stage, with a free use of projections, and translucent panels that became rippling water surfaces or flashed into brilliance as the floor of a palace ballroom and then disappeared, matched Dvořák's "lyric fairy tale." The music blossomed as it had failed to do when encased in painted canvas. (Young folk who know only the later, mannered, international, and ubiquitous Svoboda, the designer of the Met's *Carmen* and *Vêpres siciliennes*, can hardly guess how delicately poetic his earlier work could be.)

Both the Juilliard and the San Diego productions were well designed (by, respectively, Robert Yodice and Santo Loquasto) and sensitively lit (Joe Pacitti and Bruce Kelley). The Juilliard staging was particularly pretty at curtain rise. The wood nymphs grouped amid the trees looked like a painting by Philipp Otto Runge; the nix, or water goblin, rose from the depths as a spiky blue cylinder and then unfurled wings like those of Blake's Lucifer. (The effect was slightly lessened when he had to refurl them tightly and carefully, like an umbrella, to get down again through his trap. At Sadler's Wells, when the strapping Joan Hammond exactly fitted into the palace well of Act II without an inch to spare, the stage magic was similarly weakened.) The nymphs were represented by dancers from the Juilliard Dance Ensemble, while their voices were piped in from an offstage choir. Such "dubbing" is seldom effective—difficult to bring off even in a large theater like Bayreuth (where Wieland Wagner on occasion used, in *Parsifal*, one team of dancing and another of singing flower maidens), and even more so in a small theater like the Juilliard's. But the chief reason that the New York *Rusalka* failed to cast a consistent spell was a lack of romance in the demeanor of the principal characters. In San Diego, there was more poetry.

The ninth of Dvořák's ten operas, *Rusalka* was composed in 1900. *Tosca, Louise, Pelléas, Jenůfa*, Rimsky-Korsakov's *The Tsar's Bride*, Richard Strauss's *Feuersnot* are among its contemporaries. The score is a work of late Romanticism, rich and full in its orchestration, with harmonic and instrumental touches that show Dvořák was alert to developments of the time. Like *Hänsel und Gretel*, which reached Prague in 1895, *Rusalka* is a reaction against the violence of verismo. The librettist, Jaroslav Kvapil (not to be confused with the composer of the same name, Janáček's pupil), was a poet with a feeling for the theater; he became a distinguished director, and died only in 1950. Drawing on La Motte Fouqué's *Undine* and on Andersen's *The Little Mermaid*, he produced his own version of the tragic incompatibility myth that underlies pieces as diverse as the ballets *La Sylphide, Swan Lake*, and *Ondine*, the various musical workings of the Mélusine story, Wagner's opera *Die Feen*, Rimsky's *Snow Maiden*, and Strauss's *Die Frau ohne Schatten*—the myth whose most profound handling is found in the Helen scenes of Goethe's *Faust*. Roughly, it's the story of a fellow who falls in love with a fairy, and she with him. (Wagner reversed the usual pattern in *Der fliegende Holländer* and *Lohengrin*, making the man the supernatural partner.) Sometimes, as in *Die Feen* and *Die Frau*, there is a happy ending, but usually the mortal cannot put on immortality, or vice versa, and union in death—at any rate, not in this world—is the best to be hoped for. The myth provides creators with a frame for exploring man's, and woman's, desire for the elusive, the unattainable, the other. But I feel unsure how far Kvapil intended a symbolist drama. His libretto is a sequence of dreamlike emotional scenes—the water nymph singing of her love to the silvery moon, the water goblin rising from the well to pour out his grief, the wood nymphs' merry sport turning to grief as they learn of Rusalka's fate. Contrast is provided by two scenes of robust Bohemian comedy for the forester and the kitchen boy (set in Dvořák's most buoyant vein), the sudden pomp and glitter of the court scene, the proud, Amnerislike scorn of the princess, Rusalka's rival, and the incantations of the witch Ježibaba. Dvořák responded to the dramatic poem with some of the most beautiful melodies he ever composed. For the characters he invented memorable motifs. His scene-painting of the moonlit forest is magical; throughout the work, his scoring ravishes the ear. Charm, tenderness, gaiety, despair, tender passion, rapt contemplation of natural beauty—the strands are drawn together in a long, lyrical song. It is an opera not so much of character as of atmosphere, and the effect is that of a symphonic poem given theatrical shape.

Theo Alcantara's handling of this music, in San Diego, was more romantic, more pliant, than Peter Herman Adler's, in New York. Both the Juilliard and the San Diego directors, Moni Yakim and Tito Capobianco, seeking to increase the dramatic interest, had hit on the idea of assigning the roles of witch and princess to a single singer. (They are designated for alto and soprano, respectively, but a mezzo can compass both.) And in San Diego, the princess, at her final phrases in Act II, specifically revealed herself as an incarnation of the witch. The identification of the two added a new and, I think, unneeded twist to the plot; Rusalka and her beloved became victims of an evil agency, rather than of their own doomed, unconsummatable love. Mr. Capobianco aimed generally to concentrate the action. He cut out altogether the forester and kitchen boy, and with them the scenes of light relief. Not a good idea. There were many other cuts, beyond the authorized VI . . . DE's of the published score—among them the moonrise interlude of Act II, the trio of wood nymphs in Act III, and a particularly luscious phrase of the final duet. (I was sorry to lose the return of the nymphs, for in Act I the trio—Elaine Pavlick, Teri Sinclair, and Melanie Sonnenberg—had pretty voices, pretty forms, and an ability to dance gracefully.) Kathryn Bouleyn, in the title role, revealed an aptly silvery voice, clear and attractive after a shaky start; she moved delicately and acted tenderly. The prince, William McDonald, had a small, accurate tenor, very clearly projected but apt to diminish as it rose. Gwendolyn Killebrew was imperious, incisive, not always quite focused in tone, as witch and princess, and Spiro Malas was sonorous, but not affecting, as the nix. The staging was elaborate and the scenery was aptly magical, though perhaps a shade fussy in detail. The sudden, hard glitter of the palace scene, which strikes across Rusalka's idyll and shows her the world she can never hope to be part of, was brilliantly evoked by Mr.

260

Capobianco's staging, Mr. Loquasto's costumes, and Elena Denda's choreography.

San Diego's Civic Theater is large, a three-thousand-seater—too large, therefore, to be a really suitable home for any but the grandest opera productions with the grandest and loudest performers. But in the close-up intimacy of the little Juilliard Theater it is probably harder to cast an enchanted scenic spell. There, Judith Haddon, as Rusalka, and David Bender, as the prince, were constricted, rather wooden actors. Her singing lacked lyrical flow and his tended to be forceful declamation of notes rather than lines of poetic tone. Willard White sang solidly as the nix, but once again the poignancy of the role proved elusive. Faith Esham, a perky kitchen boy, was the most secure performer, as singer and actress. A doggerel English translation, by Ruth and Thomas Martin, was used. San Diego used doggerel by Walter Ducloux. ("Who is calling? It's appalling!," etc.)

There has been talk of the San Diego *Rusalka* production's being taken up by the New York City Opera at the State Theater, and, provided some of the music is restored, it should succeed there. There may be Czech works with a higher claim to be heard—among them any of Janáček's mature operas still unfamiliar here; in the comic field, Smetana's *Two Widows* and Dvořák's own *The Devil and Kate*; and in the serious, Smetana's noble *Dalibor*—but this imaginative production of *Rusalka* exists, and it could bring a new, romantic ingredient to New York's operatic fare.

December 22, 1975

MUSES

Any list, however brief, of the city's notable concerts in recent seasons is likely to include some given by Eve Queler and her Opera Orchestra of New York. In Carnegie Hall, the week before last, Miss Queler showed once again her ability—already admired in performances of Verdi's *I Lombardi* and of Donizetti's *La Favorite*—to present a controversial or uneven work so persuasively that its weaknesses pale before splendors she knows how to reveal. This time, the work was Berlioz's lyric monodrama, or *mélologue, Lélio, ou Le Retour à la vie* (that sequel to the *Symphonie fantastique*), a mixed-media piece for actor and (invisible until the finale) chorus, orchestra, two pianists, one or two tenors, and baritone. The general view of *Lélio*, as a farrago, is suggested by a defensive index item in Jacques Barzun's big biography of the composer, referring to Berlioz's "SANITY (even while composing *Lélio*)." The musical numbers, composed independently, at various times and for various forces, reflect Berlioz's preoccupations: Goethe, Shakespeare, Italian banditry, daydreaming, Shakespeare again. The monologues for the link man, Lélio-Berlioz, represent an attempt to find some order and sequence in his life and in these musical manifestations of it. Three real women move through the double adventure of the *Symphonie fantastique* and *Lélio*—Estelle Dubœuf, Berlioz's first and last love; the Irish actress Harriet Smithson, who, with Shakespeare to help, inspired the *vague des passions* of the symphony; the pianist Camille Moke, who delivered him, for a while, from his obsession with Harriet. Berlioz won the Prix de Rome in 1830, performed the symphony, became engaged to Camille, and left Paris with ideas of a "great project I shall try to realize during my exile" at the French Academy in Rome. But soon he learned that Camille had married another. Project forgotten, Berlioz packed his pistols, poisons, and a disguise, and set out to kill the girl, her husband, her mother, and then himself. As he approached Nice, his resolution faltered. He felt an increasing reluctance "to say farewell to life and art . . . to leave my first symphony unfinished, to have other, greater works in my head, unwritten. . . . Life was contending with death." In Nice, life won. Berlioz wrote to Horace Vernet, the head of the French Academy in Rome, and asked to be taken back. Vernet replied kindly, pointing out that "work and art were the two sovereign remedies for a mind afflicted." On the way back to Rome, Berlioz began to sketch the *Lélio* monologues, and the substance of Vernet's letter is echoed in Lélio's speech as he moves from the sweet melancholy of "Souvenirs" to the confident assertions, the invocation of Music as a faithful and pure mistress, that introduce his *Tempest* Fantasy. But—the irony of it is characteristic—that Fantasy had been composed to the glory of Camille-Ariel, whose light, charming presence had banished the grief brought by Harriet-Ophelia.

The biographical background is worth recalling, since *Lélio*, unlike the *Symphonie fantastique*, can hardly be considered an absolute musical entity. Its unity is personal, not formal. Thoughts of the three women and his feelings for them, of an Ideal Woman, of Juliet, Ophelia, and Miranda, of Faust, Prospero, and Hamlet (whose speech to the players is parodied in Lélio's speech to the performers) go whirling through it. In the course of the monologues, the musicologist François-Joseph Fétis is chided for his tamperings with the text of Beethoven symphonies; the choristers are warned not to hold their parts in front of their faces, obstructing the flow of sound. Does it all cohere? Only if we regard it as a verbal and musical illustration of Berlioz's autobiography, a composite self-portrait dated 1827–31, with likenesses taken from many angles. The listener needs to know the *Memoirs*. When the brigands sing of drinking from the skulls of their mistresses' lovers, he may remember that Berlioz, roaming the Campagna, carried a skull in his gamebag, and filled it with stream water to soak the salt from his prosciutto. Hearing the "Chant de Bonheur," he must recall that it "came to me one day as I lay on the flat top of the thick clipped box hedge in our formal Academy garden, lulled by the soft insidious airs of my foe the south wind." (Did Berlioz forget that it also came, in large part, from his earlier cantata *La Mort d'Orphée*?) The passionate lover, the ambitious young composer, the musician with a keen eye to practical details of performance, the romantic sallying into the lovely Italian countryside, singing to his guitar strange, improvised recitatives of Pallas's death and Evander's despair, dreaming of a heroic past, reminded of his own troubled present, murmuring snatches of Shakespeare, Virgil, and Dante through a passionate fit of weeping—they are all there. But in performance *Lélio* always seemed to me a ramshackle muddle—until this Carnegie Hall presentation drew it together. It was very well "staged"—not with an invisible choir and orchestra (that would present acoustical problems) but with carefully planned lighting to suggest the stage directions of the score. Of the title role, Donald Madden gave a brilliant account. He spoke, gestured, moved, listened, looked with quick, vivid sensibility. He was neither too solemn (as concert narrators often are) nor too stagy, but entirely convincing. Miss Queler paced both the individual numbers and the piece as a whole with a sure romantic instinct. John Aler, doubling as Horatio, Lélio's friend, and Lélio's inner voice in the "Chant de Bonheur," sang sweetly. The monologues were spoken in English translation; the singing was in the original French and Italian. Almost the only criticism—it is one that can often be made when nineteenth-century music is played today—concerns the bunching together of first and second violins on the conductor's left. This modern orchestral disposition deprived us of some antiphonal effects that Berlioz must have intended in the *Tempest* Fantasy.

Lélio was the first half of the bill. After the intermission, Renata Scotto sang scenes from Spontini's *La Vestale*, Rossini's *Armida*, and—a kind of trailer for the Philadelphia production of Donizetti's opera, in which she starred last week—the finale of *Anna Bolena*. For Spontini, she did not really have the tempered-steel strength of line that is needed. Both here and in the Rossini there was a trick of letting the last note of a phrase fade into inaudibility, and her loud *acuti* were strident. But her soft phrases were ravishing, and, as ever, the personality was endearing. Between the Rossini and the Donizetti, Miss Queler conducted Richard Strauss's orchestral fantasy on *Die Frau ohne Schatten*—a performance not always quite in tune but richly felt. Then Miss Scotto returned to give a bewitching account, delicate, dexterous, and stirring, of the long Donizetti sequence: dramatic recitatives, affectingly uttered, introducing and linking the aria "Al dolce guidami," a decorated version of "Home, Sweet Home," with three other voices in accompaniment, and the vigorous cabaletta "Coppia iniqua!"

The Sunday-afternoon recitals at the Frick Collection are civilized occasions, and provide—without admission charge—a chance to listen to solo and chamber music in an intimate chamber. Elisabeth Söderström's recital last week was a delight. On the stage, her quick musical intelligence, her vivid and engaging temperament, and a protean voice not exceptionally powerful but well able to compass soubrette mirth and tragic passion have brought her triumphs in a wide variety of roles —notably by Monteverdi, Mozart, Tchaikovsky, Strauss, Debussy, Janáček, and Hans Werner Henze. In this recital, she passed through many moods—Schubert, Wolf, and Liszt, a modern Swedish group, and Mussorgsky's "Nursery"—and defined each of them precisely with the small, sure touches of a great lieder singer. Her voice was in beautiful shape, doing all she asked of it, flowing evenly through richly colored phrases. Her command of words, in five languages, was complete; in four foreign languages she sang, and in English introduced some of the songs. She reminded us that one of the composers represented, Wilhelm Peterson-Berger, was also a critic, and quoted a review by him: "Miss C. gave her second recital yesterday. During the year since her début, she has not made any progress. Nor has she stood still." During the twenty years I have been hearing Miss Söderström, she has not stood still, either, but has become an ever more alluring, picturesque, and cogent interpreter, progressing to a point at which she must be counted one of our most valuable singers. The playing of her pianist, Martin Isepp, combined boldness with subtlety.

There are some artists who can attract a public whatever they perform, but too often, in New York, advance bills and handbills vouchsafe no more details of a program than a few composers' names, and sometimes not even that—as if the singer (or instrumentalist) mattered more than the specific songs (or sonatas). It was their flyers' detailed listing of interesting programs that drew me to hear two other sopranos —Sheila Barnes at her début in Carnegie Recial Hall the day before Miss Söderström, and Janice Harsanyi in Alice Tully Hall last month. Miss Barnes has a clear, fresh, and well-formed young voice. Its range of colors is still limited, but there was liveliness in her eyes and in her rhythms. We should be hearing more of her. After a Mozart group, and Poulenc's *La Courte Paille*, she sang the first two books of George Crumb's *Madrigals*, and then Debussy, Britten arrangements, and Walton. Miss Harsanyi's program was a spectrum of twentieth-century song, ranging from Anton Webern's three Ferdinand Avenarius settings (1904) to a solo, "In the Swamp," from Roger Sessions's Whitman cantata *When Lilacs Last in the Dooryard Bloom'd* (1970—and still unheard in New York; how regrettable that the Chicago Symphony's impending performance has not been booked into Carnegie Hall). An Italian diva is apt to consider the term *artista* an insult; it implies a lack of sheer vocal glamour. Miss Harsanyi's voice is not glamorous and she *is* an artist—one who brought distinction to all she did. It was a particular pleasure to hear Luigi Dallapiccola's *Quattro liriche di Antonio Machado* so sensitively sung.

The Tully Hall audience for this cultivated recital was small. It was also small—less than two hundred—when Arthur Weisberg's Contemporary Chamber Ensemble, at its first concert of the season, played an admirable program there, with high accomplishment. Both events might perhaps have been better housed across the street, in the auditorium of the Library and Museum of the Performing Arts. Although this place, a 212-seater, has its own busy schedule of afternoon activities, to which the public is admitted free, its potential as the workshop and élite small recital hall of Lincoln Center is not yet fully realized. But as the new home of Lincoln Center's own New and Newer Music series—Tashi there last month, the St. Paul Chamber Orchestra next month—it may gain prestige. Mr. Weisberg's program included two New York premières. One, Allan Schindler's *Cirrus, and Beyond* (undated in the program notes), is an agreeable study in textures, woven by flute, cello, percussion, and tape, which held mind and ear by its shapely disposition of events. The other, Harrison Birtwistle's *Nenia: The Death of Orpheus* (1971), was written for, and has been recorded by, the able British mezzo-soprano Jane Manning. It here received, from Jan DeGaetani, the kind of performance that composers must dream about. The soloist takes three parts—narrator, Orpheus, and Eurydice—and on occasion must sing, as it were, a duet with herself, and keep two distinct vocal lines going while she hops between them. Miss DeGaetani was not merely accurate; she sang with uncommon beauty of tone and expression. *Nenia* is a striking and imaginative work (though it is difficult not to regret Mr. Birtwistle's setting of the name "Orpheus" as a trisyllable). George Rochberg's *Serenata d'Estate* (1955), a relaxed and pleasant piece, opened the program. Chou Wen-chung's *Yün* (1968), a work in which the composer "decided to replace surface complexity with an all-embracing philosophical concept," followed, and made easy listening. At the end, there was Salvatore Martirano's undemanding Octet (undated). All the playing at this concert was on a very high level.

If Miss DeGaetani is the desirable Helen of American contemporary composers, Bethany Beardslee is perhaps their Athene—a scrupulous, precise, letter-perfect, and note-perfect soprano. At the Group for Contemporary Music's concert last week, in the Manhattan School of Music, she sang Schoenberg's *Buch der hängenden Gärten* scrupulously, precisely, and (to my ears) with no trace of warmth or expressiveness in either her timbre or her interpretation. That was the first half. The second was excerpts from Charles Wuorinen's forthcoming opera *The W. of Babylon*. Its heroine was arrayed in purple and scarlet color, was decked with gold and precious stones and pearls, at one point held a golden cup in her hand, and had a mind full of abominations and filthiness of her fornication. But Wuorinen seems to have intended nothing apocalyptic. In a note on the opera he says, "Its greatest virtue may be that it is, finally, about nothing at all: its function is to entertain." Entertainment on a locker-room level! Renaud Bruce's libretto suggests a Ronald Firbank story stripped of its elegance and retold, heavily, by a smutty-minded schoolboy. Wuorinen has set it to leaping vocal lines that made the words largely inaudible. Such jokes as could be heard were concerned with anatomical dimensions.

December 29, 1975

A CONTEMPLATIVE MAGNIFICENCE OF MIND

Wagner wrote that "the surest sign of a conductor's having completely solved his task would be the ultimate experience, at the performance, that his active lead is scarcely noticeable." Admittedly, he was writing about an opera performance, and specifically of his hopes for an execution of *Tannhäuser* in which the singers, having first learned their roles in strict tempo, then gave free, "creative" play to their feelings; in which the orchestral players had been "brought to the exactest knowledge of the vocal phrasing" (and could see the vocal lines written out in their parts, of course); and in which the conductor needed only to follow the singers and "keep untorn the bond that binds the vocal rendering with the orchestral accompaniment." A symphonic performance is not quite the same thing. (A concerto performance comes closer.) It is seldom the concertmaster's or first oboe's or first cello's task to determine the tone and temper of a subject and the conductor's task simply to follow. Sometimes it is—and not only in those modern works in which a "conducting" role may be positively assigned, during certain passages, to a single player. There is a long, free oboe solo in the first movement of Berlioz's *Symphonie fantastique* (starting at measure

360) in which a player of character can take the limelight and, in effect, assume the direction of the music for a while as he leads it toward the triumphal restatement of the principal theme; and a conductor who is confident of his man will allow him to do so. (It is surprising to discover that this oboe solo was an afterthought on Berlioz's part, added to a texture already complete in itself.) Such readiness to share responsibility grows, as a rule, from long years of experience and mutual trust. Beecham and the Royal Philharmonic showed it. Karajan and the Berlin Philharmonic, Ormandy and the Philadelphia Orchestra show it now. And Carlo Maria Giulini and the Chicago Symphony showed it when they did Bruckner's Eighth Symphony in Carnegie Hall last month.

Giulini first conducted the Chicago Orchestra in 1955. Six years ago, he became its principal guest conductor. For Giulini, the Chicago Orchestra is a less high-tension and insistently virtuoso body than it is under Solti, its music director. Its tone—or so it seems to me—becomes broader and somewhat more tender. Instead of high-gloss wind playing, there is a warmer, gentler sound. The strings in this Bruckner performance did not have quite the full, deep-based, "saturated" sound of the great orchestras—Berlin's, Vienna's, Dresden's—that can count such string tone as their especial glory. But these comparisons are evoked in an attempt at definition, not to "grade" conductors or orchestras. The playing of the Chicago Symphony at this concert was just about as good as orchestral playing can be—string tone firm and singing at every dynamic level; woodwinds cohesive, perfectly balanced, exactly tuned; brass big and round but not aggressive. The Eighth Symphony does not call for passages of solo virtuoso display, but it does need players of great sensitivity—first horn and first oboe through the pianissimo E-flat hush that closes the exposition in the first movement; first flute, first oboe, first clarinet, first trumpet in the quiet dialogue of its recapitulation. And such players it had.

The Eighth Symphony is an immense work, and it becomes more and more static. After the first movement and the scherzo, the adagio is built on a theme that starts as a straight-line phrase—repeated A-flats, varied only by the semitones above and below—and is continued as a straight-line descent. Neither motif, as Robert Simpson notes in his Bruckner monograph, "has innate kinetic energy; both bear down oppressively on the spirit." The finale has more than once been likened to a cathedral; and Dr. Simpson calls it "the background, in a sense, of Bruckner's lifework, a contemplative magnificence of mind beyond the battle. This finale is not so much a victory over tribulation as a state that had to be found behind it, slowly and sometimes painfully uncovered by the adagio." As this C-minor Symphony bursts at last into the major, we may recall Browning's "I have dared and done, for my resting-place is found, / The C Major of this life." Beethoven is relevant, too—to point a difference. Bruckner's Third, Eighth, and Ninth Symphonies all begin in ways that recall Beethoven's Ninth (and the opening theme of the Eighth is even identical in rhythm with that of Beethoven's symphony). But they continue in ways that reveal, on the one hand, a forgetive composer hammering his music into shape and, on the other, a contemplative composer assembling his music block by block. The C-major attained by Beethoven's Fifth Symphony is assertive, a victory of the human will; the C-major at the end of Bruckner's Eighth is a glorious benediction, not a triumph won but a joy revealed.

Giulini unfolded the ninety-minute span as if, to paraphrase Sir Adrian Boult's precept to young conductors, the whole score lay open before him at once, its music set out on two gigantic pages. (In fact, he used no score at all.) If I describe his conducting as, in Wagner's phrase, "scarcely noticeable," that is intended as high praise—an indication that conductor, players, and listeners seemed rapt in the progress of the music, that any personality other than Bruckner's disappeared in a transcendental experience. On occasion I have heard Giulini exaggerate, and even in his specialty, the Verdi Requiem, produce an overhushed pianissimo or an inflection so daintily nuanced that one's attention was drawn away from the music to the art of the executants. But everything in this account of Bruckner's Eighth—though scrupulously prepared and minutely rehearsed, I have no doubt—was natural. This kind of conducting, free from all self-seeking, is the highest kind—provided it is accompanied by interpretative genius and the necessary technical skills. (To watch, Giulini is the most elegant and unaffectedly aristocratic of all our conductors.) Conductors as individual as Toscanini and Furtwängler were exemplars. It may seem odd to call either of those great musicians "scarcely noticeable." One could not fail to notice when Toscanini was conducting—but what one noticed was the power of the music he made.

A textual point: Giulini used the score of Bruckner's version edited by Leopold Nowak, not the score edited by Robert Haas. The former has what has been called "musicological rectitude" on its side, since it corresponds to a score that Bruckner himself passed. But ardent and scholarly Brucknerians—among them Dr. Simpson, Deryck Cooke, Hans-Hubert Schönzeler, and Erwin Doernberg—seem united in their preference for the Haas edition. Haas, in brief, accepted the large alterations that Bruckner had made to his original version (including a new ending for the first movement, a new trio in the scherzo, and considerable structural change to the adagio), but to the adagio and the finale he restored some passages that Bruckner had cut when, probably influenced by his former pupil Josef Schalk, he revised his work. Two of these

268

passages are particularly important. Haas also reinstated some of Bruckner's original instrumentation, and, in Mr. Cooke's words, "His score always seems the more Brucknerian" (more so, that is, than Nowak's). I'm also a Haas man, but own that I would probably have no informed opinion had not the BBC, some years ago, provided an opportunity of hearing, at two days' distance, the two editions of the score in performance.

January 5, 1976

AT THE RIGHT TIME, IN THE RIGHT PLACE

The Metropolitan Opera audience is generally deemed the most ill-mannered and ignorant to be found in any of the world's major houses, and often it lives up to its reputation. But it is also one of the world's most warmhearted audiences: appreciative, enthusiastic, ready—all too ready!—with noisy acclaim for whoever or whatever pleases it. Its bad habits are rooted in generosity, not indifference. And so, although a musical person may feel fury when, say, the coda of Susanna's "Deh vieni," in *Le nozze di Figaro*, is blotted out by a volley of applause for the singer, that fury is tempered by pleasure in the fact that so many people are enjoying themselves.

Applause, like puffing, is of various sorts; the principal are, the applause preliminary, the applause automatic, the applause collusive, the applause interruptive, and, highest kind of all, the applause manifested by rapt silence, tribute to a spell that must not be shattered. Examples need not be confined to the Metropolitan.

The applause preliminary greets the conductor as he advances to the rostrum. At this point, in the concert hall, some orchestras rise to their feet in respectful salute—a ceremonious observance, and one that is presumably determined in advance by the conductor and the players; many conductors prefer to cut the frills and get on with the concert. On great occasions, the whole audience may rise; I have known it happen for Toscanini, for Richard Strauss, for Stravinsky, and such spontaneous honoring of a great man is fitting. Unfitting, I think, and unnecessary, is the preliminary round of applause that, with increasing frequency, now greets the entrance of the concertmaster.

The applause automatic is that which breaks forth whenever the curtain rises in the theater and a scene is revealed. It is always an exciting

269

moment, but grownups should learn to control their excitement, to enjoy things inwardly and not make a noise—however striking the spectacle— if that noise is going to blot out several measures of a composer's music. It is a new phenomenon, this regular applause for the scenery, a bad new habit that must be stopped before it becomes an accepted part of audience behavior. It used not to happen; recordings of the old Met broadcasts are the proof. Some directors deflect the destruction of music drama it causes by raising the curtain before the music begins, thus getting the audience racket out of the way before the show starts in earnest. And some composers have thought along similar lines. Puccini planned curtain-rise on *Il tabarro* to be an applause-catching sight—a full-size barge floating on the Seine, plane trees on the quais, Notre-Dame looming behind—but he wanted his river music to be heard, and so, in capital letters, he began his score with the instruction "THE CURTAIN OPENS BEFORE THE MUSIC BEGINS."

The device is not always practicable. Curtain-rise is often written into the music, coincident with the introduction of a new harmony (as in *Götterdämmerung*) or a new theme (as in *Pelléas et Mélisande*), or with an intensified restatement of something already heard (as in *Die Entführung*, or the fourth act of *Don Carlos*). Mozart favored no break between the overture and the first scene of his operas. Belmonte's aria at the start of *Die Entführung* is also the final movement of its overture; the *Don Giovanni* overture cadences directly into the music of Leporello's "Notte e giorno faticar"; and even at the close of the *Figaro* overture, eleven measures of reiterated tonic, Mozart wrote, "Attaca subito il Duettino di Susanna e Figaro." Wagner, in *Die Meistersinger*, closes his massive prelude with the opening measure of Act I. In such cases, the composer trusts that the audience will be musical enough to follow his intentions and not break in, however delectable a surprise the scene painter may have prepared. That trust is often betrayed.

Curtain-fall is another moment for the applause automatic; and modern audience practice in this country has made impossible an effect that many composers have valued—a slow curtain, and a soft instrumental coda after the scene has vanished from our eyes. The first acts of *La Bohème* and *Madama Butterfly* are not over once the soprano (along with the tenor, if he goes up, too) has sung the high C, but it is some years, I'll wager, since the final cadences of those acts have been audible in a New York theater. One of the most daring slow curtains in opera occurs at the end of Virgil Thomson's *The Mother of Us All*. Susan B. Anthony's last monologue dies away in soft plagal cadences, serene amens, chords of F major and C major. After the penultimate chord, the curtain falls slowly during three measures of complete silence, and only then, *pp possibile*, the orchestra closes the work in C major. At Columbia University, in 1947, when *The Mother of Us All* had its première, the audience was sensitive; in a recording of that performance one can "hear" it, so to speak, holding its breath during the long silence, not applauding until the harmony has come to rest. But at a Queens College production of *Mother* last month that final C major became a lost chord. As soon as Susan B. had sung "my long life," and the curtains had started to move, din broke out and the harmony could not reach home. Again, directors sometimes find a way to remedy this automatic hailing of curtain-fall. John Cox did so in the City Opera *Mastersingers* by holding the curtain up and ending each scene with a sudden blackout after the music had finished. But not all operas lend themselves to such treatment. *Tristan* calls for a slow curtain while the final chord is sounding. (And if it is not followed by at least a moment of silence, the Isolde has failed to touch her listeners' hearts.)

By the applause collusive, I signify that planned and paid for in advance. Claqueurs are still a pest in some Italian houses but, so far as I know, they are not active here. No need for them when vociferous volunteer enthusiasts abound. These enthusiasts are responsible for the applause interruptive, which occurs at three points: at the favored one's entrance; improperly in the course of her aria; and, often properly, when that aria is done. Applause at entrance is plainly justified on very special occasions: when a Beverly Sills or a Magda Olivero makes her first-ever appearance on the Metropolitan stage, for example. Only a killjoy could take exception to the spontaneous and thunderous welcome with which those distinguished débutantes were greeted. But *regular* applause for the prima donna—or tenor or baritone—of the evening the moment she or he is glimpsed, regardless of what the music may be doing at that point, is a barbarism. Even during the Entrance of Butterfly I have heard it— that aria which starts offstage, the soprano's voice bowered by those of her maidens, and ends onstage. Not long ago, a typical dialogue heard during the first act of *Aida* might have run:

> Prompter: Dessa!
> Radamès: Dessa!
> Whisperer in the row behind: That's Leontyne Price.

Today, it is more likely that when the clarinet starts to sound the *Aida* theme and Miss Price comes on, all is drowned for a while, though the Radamès and the Amneris can be seen moving their lips.

Mid-aria applause arises from enthusiasm coupled to ignorance. Roberta Peters had to suffer it this season when she sang Oscar in *Un ballo in maschera*. Each of Oscar's arias is in two stanzas, and of each Miss Peters sang the first stanza so delightfully that her ruder admirers broke in and did not hear, or let anyone else hear, how she started the second. In *Rigoletto*, Gildas quite often find themselves interrupted after the cadenza of "Caro nome" by people unaware that there are further beautiful phrases to come. (Rule for clap-happy folk attending an opera for the first time: wait for someone else, someone who knows the piece, to begin the applause; otherwise you may deprive yourself—and deprive everyone else—of hearing something wonderful.)

Knowing when and when not to applaud after an aria needs connoisseurship. Many arias call for applause—and require it as soon as the singer has finished, even though the orchestra may still be playing. The noisy tonic-and-dominant perorations of Donizetti often serve best as accompaniment to cheers. But, well before Wagner, there were also composers who aimed to avoid mid-act applause. Mozart tried to write it out of his *Idomeneo*. To the librettist of *Il trovatore*, Verdi said, "If only the whole opera could be, so to speak, all one number, I should find that reasonable and right." I treasure the memory of a *Trovatore*, its cast led by Martina Arroyo and Shirley Verrett, in which there was no mid-scene applause—not because the artists sang badly but precisely because they sang and acted so well that no one wanted to add noises of his own. After Azucena's "Stride la vampa," the gypsies' voices stole into an electric silence; the Miserere bell tolled into an attentive hush that succeeded Leonora's "D'amor sull'ali rosee"; and after the Miserere the soprano could continue the verbal and dramatic thread unbroken into "Tu vedrai che amore in terra." Verdi may have been bowing to the inevitable when he added a full close to the end of Eboli's veil song, in *Don Carlos*; originally, his music passed without break into Elizabeth's entrance. But the veil song is the kind of aria after which applause does no harm, is even dramatically apt. On the other hand, a sensitive Elizabeth, I believe, will work with her conductor, director, and tenor to insure that there is no audience interruption after the aria in the last act of that opera. Any disturbance breaks the solemn mood. In *La Bohème*, a good Mimì and Rodolfo should be able to act and inflect and time things so that "Che gelida manina," "Mi chiamano Mimì," and "O soave fanciulla" are heard as an unbroken sequence. (At the end of his aria, Rodolfo turns to Mimì with his request "Please tell me," quickly she replies "Yes, they call me Mimì," and at the end of her reply the offstage voices break in almost as her last note is sung.) But artists with both the wish and the ability to hold an audience silent after a striking and familiar aria are rare. Maria Callas is the only Tosca of my experience whose genius has been able to keep listeners hushed and spellbound after "Vissi d'arte."

Fidelio attracts a more serious audience than *Tosca*. At the Met revival of *Fidelio*, last week, there was only one noisy brute who tried to destroy the effect Jess Thomas had made with his nobly earnest account of Florestan's aria. The sonic intruder was quickly shushed, but already the damage to Beethoven's dying fall had been done.* Do such people really think they are honoring an artist whose achievement they thus degrade? At the heart of Ernst Krenek's *Life of Orestes* there is a romantic, yearning soliloquy for the hero. In the Portland Opera performances of the work, Victor Braun sang it with deep feeling. He seemed to fill the stage, to fill all the theater, with Orestes' strong, sweet sadness. But one listener was untouched, and did not share the experience; seated prominently in the front row of the circle, at each of the performances I attended she bawled an impassioned "Bravo!" the moment Mr. Braun had sung the last note of this solo (which does not end the scene). In vain had he conjured an imaginative world for us to dwell in; his admirer had ears and eyes only for a singer on the stage.

Audiences are apt to resent being told how they should behave. (The Metropolitan has removed from its program books the little note requesting its patrons not to interrupt the music with their applause.) Back in the eighteenth century, the great castrato Gaetano Guadagni, a pupil of David Garrick, forfeited public favor when he put the claims of music drama before those of voice fanciers. For him, Gluck had written the title role of *Orfeo*. When he sang the opera in London, in 1770, then, according to Burney,

with his determined spirit of supporting the dignity and propriety of his dramatic character, by not bowing acknowledgment, when applauded, or destroying all theatrical illusion by returning to repeat an air, if encored at the termination of an interesting scene, he so much offended individuals, and the opera audience in general, that, at length, he never appeared without being hissed.

Renata Scotto is a soprano who can make listeners do her bidding. When she sings the three soprano roles in the Met *Trittico* later this month, it will be interesting to discover whether she endeavors to keep the house quiet after Suor Angelica's aria, "Senza mamma" (see p. 155). Gilda Cruz-Romo, the Angelica of the first cast, did not try to; she openly invited applause—at a moment where it is dramatically intrusive. An ovation after Lauretta's aria, "O mio babbino caro," in *Gianni Schicchi*, is another matter. A turning point early in the action, this number is meant to stop the show. If it passes in silence, there is a flatness; and

---

* The aria is different in the three versions of *Fidelio*. Joseph Röckel, the 1806 Florestan, declared that Demmer and Radichi, the 1805 and the 1814 Florestans, both craved applause after the aria, and insisted on a bravura final section; that Demmer was provided with "a conventional allegro" (it does not survive), and Radichi with the familiar F-major poco allegro, to which Beethoven then added "a new short pianissimo coda, by which means the stillness necessary for the succeeding scene would be re-established." Röckel's full statements are difficult to square with the surviving scores but suggest clearly enough that the composer himself preferred no applause.

even an encore does no musical or dramatic harm. After the première of *Il trittico*, at the Met in 1918, Gatti-Casazza sent Puccini a cable including the sentence IN SPITE OF PUBLIC NOTICE FORBIDDING ENCORES BY INSISTENCE LAURETTA'S ARIA WAS REPEATED STOP

But appropriateness, not historical precedent, should be the guide. Some old practices are better unrevived. When Beethoven's Violin Concerto was first performed, in 1806, the allegro figured in one part of the program, the slow movement and finale in the other, and among the intervening pieces was a "novelty item" played with the violin upside down. When Verdi's *La traviata* was first performed, in 1853, the composer joined Violetta and Alfredo onstage to take a bow after their brindisi, and again after their intimate duet. Such curious customs we have reformed altogether. On the other hand, I think modern concert audiences sometimes go *too* far in their observance of reverent silence between movements. There are jolly numbers in orchestral suites, and even some first movements of concertos, after which it seems positively churlish not to applaud. Nevertheless, silence is probably the better course; though stirred to express his enthusiasm, a concertgoer refrains, lest his racket shatter another's rapture. The person who maintains his "right" to applaud whenever he feels like it is cousin to him who claims a "right" to smoke wherever he chooses to. Their motives may differ; but the former, when, say, he decides to show how much he has enjoyed a scene in *Pelléas* or in *The Turn of the Screw* by adding his manual percussion to the ensuing interlude, pollutes the musical air for everyone.

So a plague on the person who drowns any measure composed by Mozart! Another on the slow-wit who is not content to laugh at a joke but claps his hands together as well—and goes on clapping them while a second joke has begun! A third on the popinjay whose pride it is to get in the first "Bravo!" while *Winterreise* or *Tristan* or *Das Lied von der Erde* should be dying into silence! And long live full-hearted, discriminate, tumultuous applause—at the right time, in the right place!

Last week's *Fidelio* was dedicated to the memory of Bruno Walter, who conducted the opera at the Metropolitan in 1941, 1945, and 1951. He would have been a hundred this year. (In the lower foyer of the house, the Bruno Walter Foundation, which contributed to the revival, has mounted a small exhibition of Walter mementos.) The performance was carefully rehearsed, earnestly conceived, and moving, and I thought it the highest achievement of the Met season so far. Gwyneth Jones, who bowled me over when she sang her first Leonore, in Cardiff, in 1964, did so again. But "bowl over" is too glib a phrase; a very beautiful and now very powerful voice, an interpretation spontaneous, intent, impassioned, and free from any taint of self-display, her clear, candid features, and naturalness, directness, honesty in all she does combine to prompt unconditional surrender to Beethoven's radiant heroine. Miss Jones does not always sing as well as this, and on Friday she did not sing all episodes equally well. Although the transitions from boyishness to loving woman were subtly and unselfconsciously achieved, she is still an imperfect actress, who tends to stand in a crouch, with elbows crooked. But her feelings shine through, and Leonore comes to life. Jess Thomas, as noted above, was a noble Florestan. He has the ability to emphasize individual words without breaking Beethoven's lines. Donald McIntyre's Pizarro was curious—no simple tyrant but a fussy, neurotic creature with fidgety gestures, Himmler-like in appearance. His intonation often strayed. John Macurdy's, as Rocco, was rock-firm; a magnificent voice was kept within the bounds of character. Judith Blegen was a captivating Marzelline, and Kenneth Riegel an alert Jaquino. Don Fernando was cast at strength; James Morris sang his elevated utterances smoothly and firmly.

John Mauceri's conducting was athletic and assured. It was a young man's *Fidelio*, not weighted with the deep eloquence that a Furtwängler or a Klemperer brought to the score. (I never heard Walter conduct it.) So the prisoners' chorus was not overwhelming—despite ardent singing from the First Prisoner of Douglas Ahlstedt. *Leonore* No. 3 was played as scene-shift music in the second act, and—a vulgar touch, though some illustrious conductors have given a precedent for it—the last chord of the prison duet was sustained as the first of that overture. (This means that the sublime opening measures accompany a battle between clappers and shushers; at this point in the drama, after the long tensions of the prison scene have been released, applause is appropriate—and *Leonore* No. 3 is not.) The dialogue, especially before the canon quartet, was too severely abridged. Otto Schenk's production, first staged here in 1970 and now freshly directed by his own hand, is powerful and unaffected. One obtrusive, eye-catching chorister—the prisoner whom Don Fernando raises from his slavish kneeling—needs toning down.

January 12, 1976

ENJOYING THE SOUND

I seldom visit Carnegie Hall without a thought of thankfulness that it is still there. Without it, New York would be for musicians a sad and sonically drabber place. Yet some fifteen years ago it was in danger of being destroyed. The Philadelphia Orchestra's Carnegie concert last week was a feast of first-rate orchestral sound. It began with Krzysztof Penderecki's *De natura sonoris* No. 1. This is modern music without tears, made of sounds high and low—often the highest and lowest notes of which the instruments are capable—of silences, and of clusters and flurries that coalesce into blocks of quivering sonority. Short, shapely, skillfully assembled, it made a good starting piece. Brahms's Fourth Symphony followed, laid out clearly, broadly, and lyrically by Eugene Ormandy, and superlatively well played. The Philadelphia Orchestra produced a warmly homogeneous sound, of peerless blend and balance. Its woodwind choir, in the andante, seemed to breathe a benison on the audience. Nothing was forced or labored. It was not a passionate performance, not tragic, but serene, majestic, Olympian. In the second half, the Mussorgsky-Ravel *Pictures at an Exhibition.* This is generally deemed an orchestral showpiece, but there was no sense of showing off on this occasion. Everything fell effortlessly into place. The colors were vivid, the phrasing was subtle, the virtuosity unselfconscious.

The next day, Itzhak Perlman and Samuel Sanders, violin and piano, gave a recital in the same hall. The most substantial piece in the program was one for violin solo, Bach's Third Sonata, in C. Before it, there was Stravinsky's *Suite italienne,* an arrangement of music from the ballet *Pulcinella* which violinists enjoy playing. The second half brought forward three works employing American themes: Dvořák's Sonatina, Op. 100, the larghetto of which Kreisler arranged as "Indian Lament"; Charles Ives's Second Sonata, which includes hymn tunes and barn dances; and Henri Vieuxtemps's *Souvenir d'Amérique,* a set of variations on "Yankee Doodle." There was also Scott Joplin's *Pineapple Rag,* arranged by Mr. Perlman, and, as encores, Kreisler's *Schön Rosmarin,* another Joplin rag, and Antonio Bazzini's *Ronde des lutins.* Curious hodge-podge of a program. But the evening was enjoyable because Mr. Perlman plays the violin so well. His tone is unfailingly beautiful—not, on the one hand, schmalzy and syrupy or, on the other, gritted and forceful. Round but not fat, sweet but not cloying, smooth but not slippery, thewy but not wiry, glittering (when glitter is needed) but not flashy—in short, everything one wants violin sound to be. The musical personality is harder to appraise. There is warmth, and exuberance. Mr. Perlman was particularly captivating in the Vieuxtemps—a violinist's counterpart to a soprano's "Ah, vous dirai-je, maman" variations by Adolphe Adam. With the delicacy of a great singer, he delivered the theme, not tongue-in-cheek, not mockingly, but with such daintily artistic inflections that the result was at once bewitching and witty. He played the long fugue of the Bach sonata with excellent intentness. The Dvořák was agreeably lyrical. But the Ives did not hang together—it sounded only half the work it can be (in, say, the masterly performance that Paul

Zukofsky and Gilbert Kalish have recorded for Nonesuch). It was as if Mr. Perlman had explored and mastered the sounds but not discovered their meaning. Mr. Sanders was a sure, efficient, and bold pianist but he seemed content to remain an accompanist; the sonata was presented as a work for violin with piano, not a dialogue between equals. I sat near the back. At the back of Carnegie Hall one is still close to the music.

There is a large repertory of sacred music worth hearing and seldom heard, and the Sacred Music Society of America, which gave its inaugural performance, in Avery Fisher Hall, the day after Epiphany, may have a valuable part to play in New York's musical life. To be sure, the work chosen for its first concert, Massenet's *Marie-Magdeleine*, described as a *drame sacré*, proved to be barely worth revival in its own right, and scarcely sacred music in any respectable sense. But the performance, with Régine Crespin in the title role, *was* worth hearing, and the piece is one about which Massenet enthusiasts—a growing band, soon to be cheered by *Le Cid* in Carnegie Hall, *Esclarmonde* at the Met next season, and *Thaïs* the season after that—have long been curious. *Marie-Magdeleine* is early Massenet, begun while he was a Prix-de-Rome winner at the Villa Medici. It was first performed at the Odéon, on Good Friday, 1873, with Pauline Viardot as the Magdalen. After her, a succession of famous singers of widely differing vocal types undertook the role—among them Pauline Gueymard (the first Eboli in *Don Carlos*), Marie Miolan-Carvalho (the first Marguerite, Juliette, and Mireille, in Gounod's operas), Gabrielle Krauss (a "Falcon," or French dramatic soprano), Marguerite Carré (a Mimì, Mélisande, and Manon), and Aïno Ackté (the heroine of London's first *Salome*).

Mme Crespin's performance was in the big dramatic line. It was announced that she had been suffering from a cold and a cough, and possibly for this reason she ventured little soft singing. But at the top of the staff, and above, her voice was in freer, more ringing form than I have heard it for some time, and as lustrous as ever below. She looked beautiful. She acted not with gestures, in this concert performance, but with touching expression in her eyes, in the carriage of her head, in the way she held her eloquent hands. Her utterance of French words is always an uncommon pleasure. The Magdalen has three airs. Mme Crespin sang all three with passionate feeling and in firmly molded, seamless lines, infusing them with the noble "classical passion"—at once sensuous, ardent, and dignified—that good French actresses can command. (To Gluck's *Iphigénie en Tauride*, Mme Crespin brings the same quality.) The central air, "O Bien-Aimé," set at the foot of the Cross, was particularly striking. Jesus is a robust tenor role, and by Louis Roney, a Samson, Don José, and Othello, it was powerfully and impressively sung. A Christ who put on gold-rimmed half-glasses to read by looked a shade odd, but otherwise Mr. Roney's demeanor suggested that in the theater, where I have not yet seen him, he should cut a heroic figure. Judas was cast at strength, in the person of Joseph Rouleau, and Sheila Nadler made a vigorous young Martha. The Sacred Music Society had assembled an able orchestra and chorus. Anthony Morss conducted with a steady beat but did not give sufficient light and shade to the music. His handling lacked charm and finesse. A libretto, printed for the occasion, with Louis Gallet's text and an English translation, was available free of charge.

The score, like those of Handel's oratorios, carries scenic indications. Act I is set beside a fountain in Magdala. Act II is the supper party given for Christ by Martha and Mary. It opens, like the last scene of *Così fan tutte*, with servants' preparations, and ends with the Lord's Prayer, launched by Christ and continued in male-voice chorus. Act III has two scenes. The first is the Crucifixion. At its close, in a big climax, Christ from the Cross cries with a loud voice "It is finished," reaching a diminished-seventh chord, fortissimo, through which the Magdalen sings "Ah!" in octave with Him. The chorus clinches things in brief, fierce C-major shouts. (At the Fisher Hall performance, all this brought the house down.) The final scene is by the Sepulcher: the Magdalen's lament, with a chorus of attendant women; a sweet *Noli me tangere* dialogue; and a final Resurrection outburst for full choir, full orchestra, and the assault of full organ. In his memoirs, Massenet speaks of a "presentiment that the work would in the end gain honors on the stage." In 1903 it was staged by the Nice Opéra, and three years later by the Opéra-Comique. Did those audiences also cheer the Crucifixion? When Vincent d'Indy, who admired some of the choral writing, congratulated Massenet on it, he was shocked by his colleague's reply: "Oh, I don't believe in all that creeping Jesus stuff . . . But the public likes it— and we must always agree with the public." *Marie-Magdeleine* had successors in the *mystère Ève*, and then the *légende sacrée La Vierge*, music from which accompanies some episodes in Kenneth MacMillan's *Manon* ballet. The public liked Eve but did not care for the Virgin; Massenet's next Biblical heroine was Salome, in the opera *Hérodiade*, and then came the secular Manon.

The prettiest number in *Marie-Magdeleine* is the first, a chorus that opens with a fragment of bright bagpipe tune (which Massenet heard in the woods of Subiaco, St. Benedict's retreat, and "noted down on a bit of paper borrowed from a Benedictine monk in a neighboring monastery") and continues in lilting pastoral vein over drone basses. This movement has the light touch of his *Scènes pittoresques*. Much of the rest is prentice work—repetitious, uninspired, and constructed sometimes in a lame "academic" style, with imitative entries, such as Berlioz parodied in the epithalamium of *Béatrice et Bénédict*. By the mention of Berlioz, at the mere thought of any passage in his *L'Enfance du Christ*, serious regard for *Marie-Magdeleine* is put to flight.

What will the Society do next? The Halévy-Bizet *Noé*? César Franck's *Ruth*? Sir Hubert Parry's *Judith*? Perhaps Sir Frederick Arthur Gore Ouseley's *The Martyrdom of St. Polycarp*? Or Schoenberg's *Jakobsleiter*?

Massenet soon became a more inventive and interesting composer. Let me pay belated tribute to the Bel Canto Opera's production, last month, of his *Esclarmonde*. It was a shoestring performance, piano-accompanied, simply but intelligently staged by Jane Judge in the hall of the Madison Avenue Baptist Church. I went expecting little—and came away with a sharp impression of what a full-scale *Esclarmonde* might be. The young soprano Marilyn Brustadt was brave and brilliant in the role Massenet devised to show off the glamorous accomplishments of Sibyl Sanderson. As Roland, Lawrence Farrar, a former baritone who has made the transition to robust tenor, broke on some high notes but was generally triumphant. Stuart Price was musical director and one-man orchestra. *Esclarmonde* proves to be an opera seria, based on enchantress-and-crusader matter such as Handel used to deal in. It is a surprising and striking piece.

January 19, 1976

VERDI AND VIOLETTAS

"She has a beautiful face, spirit, and theatrical presence—the best qualities for a Traviata." So Verdi described Rosina Penco, who he hoped might first sing the role. (Instead, it was taken by the plump, fluent Fanny Salvini-Donatelli.) Penco had been his first Leonora in *Il trovatore*, and Verdi wanted her again not only as Violetta but also as Amelia in the projected Naples première of *Un ballo in maschera*. She was not a perfect vocalist but had qualities that he valued more highly than impeccable vocal technique. Again and again in his letters we find Verdi declaring that his operas require interpreters with spirit, musical understanding, theatrical flair, and a vivid command of words, rather than consummate singers with little or no feeling for drama. The letters must not be used to condone rough and incompetent singing, however impassioned it may be. There are limits; and once we reach the phonograph era there is proof that the singers Verdi most admired knew how to sing well, and were strong technicians. (Adelina Patti wins just about the most unqualified praise to be found in Verdi's writings.) But his

279

remarks can be a corrective to the view that beautiful singing justifies everything. That view was given strong expression when Luisa Tetrazzini made her Covent Garden début, in 1907, as Violetta. She conquered most of her audience, but not one lady, who exclaimed to Henry Higgins, chairman of the Grand Opera Syndicate, about the diva's "impossible" hat. To which Higgins replied that, if Mme Tetrazzini continued to sing so well, she might undertake the role wearing a top hat if she chose. There have been occasions when I've shared Higgins's sentiment. I only wish there had been more of them. Singing of such wondrous accomplishment that it can triumph over, let us say, any or all of an appearance hopelessly at odds with the character represented, shabby décor, absence of acting and stage direction, dummies in the supporting roles, and crass orchestral accompaniment—such singing has become all too rare. In her private theater at Craig-y-Nos, the retired Patti would relive her triumphs by entertaining her guests and the tenantry to a *Traviata* in which she was still Violetta while her butler stood in as Alfredo, respectfully accepting the stage endearments lavished on him by the diva. In less remarkable circumstances, all opera lovers must have recognized and prized the vocal art that can turn a fat, plain woman into a radiant young heroine, transform a sedate, complacent tenor into an ardent, impetuous lover, and cast its glow over warehouse scenery. In a chapter of *Where Angels Fear to Tread*, E. M. Forster described the enchantment, and, in fact, Tetrazzini was the real-life model for the Lucia di Lammermoor there immortalized.

But operatic enchantments can be of many kinds. One of the *Traviatas* I remember most keenly was sung and conducted without distinction. If it had been recorded, the records would hardly bear listening to. But in the theater, as directed by Walter Felsenstein and designed by Rudolf Heinrich, it afforded a *Theatererlebnis* that could not be forgotten. By different means, other memorable *Traviatas* have been created for me by Maria Callas. I missed the famous Luchino Visconti production at La Scala, where, by all accounts, the frame was worthy of her central figure, but did see, hear, fall subject to Callas's transfiguring power in other, less eminent stagings of the opera. In most listeners' minds, there is probably an ideal *Traviata* assembled from memories of what great performers have achieved in the work. An early ingredient can be the glowing, passionate phrasing of Gemma Bellincioni, a Violetta much admired by Verdi, in her 1903 recording of "Ah fors'è lui." From a year later there are Fernando De Lucia's artful, exhilarating discs of "Un dì felice" and "De' miei bollenti spiriti." Both artists reveal that strict adherence to written rhythms is a modern practice. They phrase freely, with much life-giving rubato. Bellincioni even graces the familiar vocal line. Then, there is Nellie Melba, perhaps the only perfect vocalist since records began. Verdi himself had reservations about her, but people would travel hundreds of miles just to hear her utterance of "Dite alla giovine," the central section of the Act II duet in *La traviata*. (She would begin it facing away from the audience, then slowly turn around.) Fortunately, Melba, with her compatriot John Brownlee, recorded the piece, in 1926, and we can still hear what her admirers of the day heard —the soft yet fully cantabile line, the poignant portamento through the falling seventh on the words "un unico raggio di bene." The discography is extensive. Everyone will have his irreplaceable favorites. From even the shortest list, Tito Schipa's Alfredo, Giuseppe De Luca's Germont, and the passionate Violetta of Rosa Ponselle, preserved on pirate discs from a Metropolitan broadcast, can hardly be omitted. Or, even by someone who feels that the singers were driven too hard, Toscanini's thrilling account of the score. To this immense "documentation," reaching back to artists whom Verdi himself knew and worked with, the operagoer then adds all his live experiences, and possibly also the features and forms of Ladies of the Camellias met in other mediums: perhaps Garbo, Edwige Feuillère, and Margot Fonteyn.

And then, if the operagoer is fortunate, he encounters such a *Traviata* as was performed at the Metropolitan Opera last week: one in which all that matters is the present; one during which memories fade, comparisons are forgotten, and any critical faculties are largely suspended; one in which the heroine holds an audience rapt and intent on everything she says, does, thinks, feels.

The heroine of that Metropolitan performance was Beverly Sills. "She has a beautiful face, spirit, and theatrical presence—the best qualities for a Traviata." Like Rosina Penco, she is not a perfect vocalist. But she, and her conductor, Sarah Caldwell, know exactly what her voice cannot do—and all the eloquent things that it can do, and all the ways in which, even without full-throated, glorious sound for the climaxes, Verdi's music and his drama can be brought to life. In only one passage did I feel that Miss Sills failed us musically—in the long rise and fall that thrice punctuates the Act II finale. ("Ah perchè venni, incauta" are the words at its first appearance.) Each time, it is marked by a crescendo to its peak and then a diminuendo, and spanned by a single slur. But, each time, Miss Sills sang it not in a span. The notes were not joined. And only once did I feel that her acting was less than complete. When Germont announced his identity, she did not start forward in joyous surprise that her lover's father should have come in friendship to visit her—a moment's joy before the cruel rebuff of his next words.

When those two points are made, the rest can be a catalogue of excellences. Singing and acting can hardly be divided. The musical and the physical phrasing went hand in hand. Before "È strano," the recitative that launches the first-act finale, Miss Sills sustained an uncommonly long silence. On a record or in a broadcast it would seem surprising—as surprising as the long silences in Chaliapin's account of the Death of Boris Godunov, in Mussorgsky's opera. (Those silences were shortened when Chaliapin's record of the scene, made "live" in Covent Garden in 1928, was re-edited for a long-playing issue.) During that silence, Violetta mused; we knew what she was thinking; and her murmured "È strano" seemed to be a continuation of those thoughts, overheard. More than any Violetta I have heard before, she suggested that the voice of Alfredo, when it broke into the whirl of the cabaletta, was a voice sounding on in her mind—a memory of his ardent protestations earlier in the act, not the man himself singing outside in the street. She listened to it, dreamed for an instant of a different kind of life, and then dismissed the impossible dream with "Follie! follie!" When the memory returned, insistently, in the second verse, her brilliant coloratura became an attempt to drown its seductive call. In this passage, for the repeated-note scale down from the high C, Miss Sills, like many great sopranos before her, substituted a smoother variant; rightly, in my view, for even when it is impeccably sung it makes a slightly yapping effect. Verdi miscalculated for once.

In Act II, there was beautiful weighting of all the expressive melodies, careful avoidance of more pressure than the voice could bear, exquisite projection of lines that could always be heard. The famous outburst "Amami, Alfredo" is marked to be sung *con passione e forza*." On the first note of each of its three phrases the orchestra is fortissimo, and then it drops down to piano. Miss Sills sang the passage *con passione*; she did not really sing it *con forza*, but she and Miss Caldwell certainly conveyed the necessary force of emotion. The orchestral swell was so controlled that, after each fortissimo emphasis, the voice could shine through, and the singer avoided any stridency or unsteadiness. The soft, supple, and again clearly projected lines of the last act were equally poignant. It is a moving experience to hear a large house hanging intent on very subtle, delicate, emotionally charged singing. The aria "Addio del passato" carries no dynamic indications above pianissimo (except for piano at the oboe solos), and Miss Sills did not commit the common faults of opening up too soon or exaggerating the crescendo at the move to the major.

The precisely judged degree of "leaning" on the first note of the oboe solos in this aria was one among many fine details of Miss Caldwell's performance. Until *La traviata*, the Met season lacked first-rate conductors. Miss Caldwell's arrival there—it was her début in the house—brought a triumph for her and confirmation of her great powers to animate a score and reveal its composer's intentions. By the stopwatch, and by tradition, many of her tempi must probably be counted fast—as fast, even, as the metronome markings in Verdi's score! But there was no sense of hustle—only Verdian vitality, tension, vigor, dramatic impetus. The singers were not straitjacketed. When a phrase needed to expand, or a syllable to be dwelt on, or an attack to be delayed for an instant, Miss Caldwell was there. She also showed an uncommon command of dramatically striking timbres and of instrumental balance in support of, not in competition with, the individual voices.

Miss Sills and Miss Caldwell were the making of this memorable *Traviata*. The rest was not negligible but unremarkable. Stuart Burrows, if unromantic, was at any rate a lyrical and fluent Alfredo. William Walker, stepping in, as Germont, for an indisposed Ingvar Wixell, produced smooth tone of fine, firm quality. Annina (Constance Webber), Dr. Grenvil (Edmond Karlsrud), Baron Douphol (Robert Goodloe), and Giuseppe (Abram Morales) were all good; other small parts were less happily taken. Alfred Lunt's 1966 production, directed now by Fabrizio Melano, has its tiresome "touches"—Liszt fusses about, score under his arm, in the first scene; the Marquis d'Obigny behaves insufferably at Flora's party; the handling of the Spanish divertissement is risible— but in the main it proceeds on conventional lines that allow the principals scope to give impressive performances. I don't think Alfredo should sit down comfortably to sing an aria that begins "Of my boiling spirits," even if the sense of it is that Violetta has now brought those spirits off the boil. Certainly he should not sit down again to sing the cabaletta. (Are there *any* cabalettas that can properly be sung sitting down?) It is unveristic, I am told, for nineteenth-century consumptives to sleep lying flat, as Violetta did, rather than propped up. I prefer the first scene of Act II to be set indoors, not outside, as it is here: the emotions need containing, the arias and the duet are all pieces of "indoor" sentiment, and detailed stage directions show the kind of scene Verdi had in mind. But otherwise Cecil Beaton's décor remains serviceable, even handsome. An unfortunate interval was allowed, as so often, to break the two scenes of Act II. Three of the usual cuts were made—a verse of Violetta's "Ah fors'è lui," a verse of her "Addio del passato," and Germont's cabaletta—but Alfredo was allowed one verse of his cabaletta, and, most welcome, the stretta of the last-act duet, "Gran Dio! morir sì giovane," was done complete. The exclamations after Violetta's death, commonly omitted, were sung. In fact, the show was rehearsed without any cuts, and, once everyone is at full strength, Miss Caldwell intends to perform it that way.

January 26, 1976

JAVA SPARROWS

A Java sparrow, ornithologically "a finchlike weaverbird (*Munia oryzivora*)," is by extension anything—a rare word, a name, a piece of music—that, previously unencountered, flutters to one's attention and then within days, sometimes within hours, reappears from diverse sources again and again. The phenomenon, while not uncommon, always proves surprising; this term for it—is there another?—arose in a private circle (where, during one country weekend, references to Java sparrows cropped up on all sides) but can perhaps be generally useful. Paganini's *Centone* ("patchwork") for violin and guitar has flown into New York as a kind of Java sparrow—unheard here, probably, for years, and then featured in two separate Carnegie Hall recitals just a fortnight apart. G. W. E. Friederich's *Brass Band Journal*, published in 1853, is another. Who had heard of it—until, on two consecutive days, Sunday afternoon and Monday evening last week, in Carnegie Recital Hall, the Empire Brass Quintet and the American Brass Quintet played selections from it? These days, the solo tuba is for me a Java sparrow, of robust build: there were tuba solos at both the Empire and the American concerts; between them, on Sunday night in the same hall, J. Lesley Varner played a full recital for solo tuba, and Patrick John Mills another, on Monday evening, in Paul Hall.

Brass music sounds good in the open air—Gabrieli antiphonies ringing through the Venetian Piazza; Johann Pezel five-part sonatas played from a tower. It also sounds good inside a very large, resonant church. St. John's, Gouda, lives in my mind's eye and ear as a place at once aglow from the great windows and filled with waves of noble tone from the Brass Quartet of the Netherlands Christian Radio Union as it played Andrea and Giovanni Gabrieli and Melchior Franck; the four-hundredth anniversary of Dirck Crabeth's window of Christ in the Temple overthrowing the tables of the moneychangers and the seats of them that sold doves, presented to the church by William of Orange in 1567, was being celebrated. That Dutch memory calls up others: of evening rays pouring into the basilica of Saint-Maximin, in Provence, to add their splendor to the sounds of the great eighteenth-century organ; of St. Paul's Cathedral, in London, ablaze with Berlioz; of the cheerful Bergkirche in Eisenstadt, where Haydn's Masses were first performed; and, in a secular transposition, of the huge foyer of Washington's Kennedy Center become a nave while Haydn Masses were performed at one end of it, during last year's "Haydnfest." New York concertgivers are not always sensitive to the matching of music and surroundings which can enhance even the most accomplished executions (though some promising events in adventurous locations are due soon). As stops on the regular round, the Hunter College and Columbia University auditoriums are dreary: Abandon all hope of enjoying yourselves, ye who enter here, their approaches seem to proclaim. Even Alice Tully Hall is dull to the eye except when the organ stands revealed; then it comes to life. Carnegie Recital Hall is quite a decent little room, but the lobby and stairway that lead to it are dismal. The Empire Brass Quintet played there on a bright, sunny afternoon and deserved to be heard in bright, cheerful surroundings. (If only the Metropolitan Opera House faced west, not east, its foyers and staircase could provide an interesting many-leveled performance space for sunlit afternoon concerts.) Huddled on the Carnegie stairs during the intermission, the audience conversed in whispers, as if at a wake.

But the music was bright and brave. The Empire Brass Quintet, which was making its official New York début, is a Boston group (including three members of the Boston Symphony) some three years old. That the players were fresh and neat in appearance, pleasant to look at, and not dressed in the dreary soup-and-fish that immediately makes things formal may be of no musical importance but certainly increased the sum of enjoyment provided by their concert. (It is not only on the opera stage that musicians' looks constitute part of their offering.) The components of the Empire Quintet are two trumpets, horn, tenor trombone, and, at the bottom, a tuba—whereas the American Quintet, otherwise similar, generally has a bass trombone on the bottom line. The sound, even in the tiny hall, never hit the threshold of pain—no forcing, but well-balanced tone and carefully judged dynamics across a very wide range of timbres. The American Quintet, which has been active since 1958, has enormously increased the repertory of available chamber music for brass, by its commissions and simply by existing, as an inspiration for composers drawn to the medium. And now the Empire Quintet is extending that repertory; four of the works on the program were dedicated to it. The first of them, Ira Taxin's brief *Fanfare* (1976), which opened the concert, is not quite as masterly as Stravinsky's *Fanfare for a New Theater*, for two trumpets, which opened the second half, but is an ingenious and effective call to order. Taxin's Brass Quintet (1973) is a one-movement piece that, like his tone poem *Saba*, played at the Philharmonic earlier this season, contains much arresting and picturesque incident within a secure structure. Joyce Mekeel's *Hommages* (1973) "attempts to make a consistent statement out of three different musical styles" and does it so successfully that, without the program note to help, one might not have guessed that Ives, Webern, and Cage are the composers honored. Brian Fennelly's *Prelude and Elegy* (completed in 1973) is a moving composition that employs the funeral sound of brass, its aptness for incantation and for expressing a choral surge of grief, in an emotional but finely disciplined and indi-

285

vidual manner. Other modern works played were Gunther Schuller's *Little Brass Music* (1963) and Alvin Etler's Quintet (1964). Both gripped the attention: there seems to be something about the medium that stirs composers to adventure.

Retournons à nos moineaux. Friederich's *Brass Band Journal* is an anthology of *Gebrauchsmusik*—tunes for American waits to play at dances, weddings, funerals, and patriotic assemblies. Among the arrangements, "The Star-Spangled Banner," "Hail, Columbia," and the "Marseillaise" appear; "Yankee Doodle" and "My Old Kentucky Home" are treated straightforwardly; other melodies are worked up into quicksteps and marches. This is the sort of music that reappears in Ives's medley movements. Heard straight, it proved very attractive. Coming at the end of the concert, after two hours of contemporary music, it reaffirmed the simple force of sound diatonic harmony, classically correct part writing, and a regular beat of two, three, or four. Friederich laid out his pieces for a saxhorn family of six, with optional percussion. The Empire Quintet brought in a baritone (the instrument, not the voice), played by Jon Taylor, and a snare drum, played by Gordon Gottlieb, to complete the ensemble. The baritone, to which the solo line is often allotted, has a warm, delightfully oily tone; "oily" I intend as a compliment—smooth, golden, and fragrant, like the virgin oil pressed from Tuscan olives.

The American Brass Quintet's program was heterogeneous. It began with three "Courtly Masquing Ayres" from the collection by John Adson, Charles I's music teacher. Then came Ralph Shapey's Brass Quintet (1963), thoroughly and meticulously composed, arresting, difficult to grasp in a single hearing, and sometimes played so loudly that it hurt. In the second half, there was long, tedious exposure to David Reck's *MetaMusic for Brass Quintet, Slides, and Tape* (1968–74)—a self-indulgent, messy gallimaufry of sketches, ideas, doodles, and spoken thoughts. Reck claimed sustained attention for his workshop debris but did nothing to earn it. Finally, a Brass Sextet in harmless neo-Romantic vein by one Oskar Böhme, undated, but presumably written about the turn of the century. To make up the sextet, Harvey Phillips and his tuba joined the Quintet, both here and in the *Brass Band Journal* selection, placed at midpoint in the concert. (In the latter, the bass trombonist shifted to baritone.) The American Quintet may be the more celebrated of the two groups, but in the Friederich its playing was no match for the Empire's. There were smudged notes, errant ensemble, less careful balance, and some out-of-tune chording. And the absence of a drummer was felt.

The tuba solo at the Empire concert, played by Samuel Pilafian, was William Kraft's *Encounters II* (1966). Kraft's *Encounters* are a series of solos and duets exploiting new-found virtuoso techniques. (No. II and No. IV, "A Duel for Trombone and Percussion," are recorded on the Crystal label.) The tuba *Encounters* is a fascinating invention; it includes stretches of two-part writing—one part played, the other sung through the instrument—chords, and rapid toccata-type figures. At the American Quintet concert, the tuba solo was Ed Sauter's *Eight Random Thoughts*, played by Mr. Phillips. Hearing the legendary Mr. Phillips for the first time, I was captivated by the poetic quality of his tone, by the absence of grossness, and by phrasing that recalled that of a great singer; less happy when, between phrases, he came up noisily for air; and disturbed by the clack of the valves on his instrument. Sauter's *Thoughts*, prompted by hearing a Bach unaccompanied cello suite played on the tuba, are melodic rhapsodies, agreeable to follow but too similar in mood to add up to an effective suite.

At the second concert in the Contemporary Chamber Ensemble's series of three, in Tully Hall, there was a première, of Roger Reynolds's *The Promises of Darkness*, and an American première, of Alun Hoddinott's *Ritornelli*. Of the Reynolds piece I can merely record that it is for eleven players, disposed in four instrumental groups, and lasts about twenty-one minutes; that the density of thought is formidable; that, without a score to help me, I felt baffled by it but enjoyed many striking ideas. Which is not saying much, and I say it only because "intuition"— that sadly imprecise instrument of critical perception on which one falls back when impressed one knows not why—tells me that *The Promises of Darkness* would probably reward the effort of getting to know it. Hoddinott is a fluent, prolific Welshman, and his *Ritornelli*—a sort of extended concert scena for trombone solo, wind band, and percussion— is an easy, likable, undemanding composition. By John Swallow, the trombonist, and Arthur Weisberg's ensemble it was taken a little too soberly. The Contemporary Chamber Ensemble is made up of first-rate players, and its executions are marvelously deft, but sometimes I wonder whether, even while playing immaculately, it sufficiently reflects the individual moods and character of the works concerned. The Hoddinott needs cheeky, cheerful, almost nonchalant handling. The other works on the program were Hans Werner Henze's *Being Beauteous*, with Susan Belling the clear, sweet, accurate soprano soloist, and Aaron Copland's *Appalachian Spring* in its original, thirteen-instrument version. For the Henze, clear, sweet, accurate singing is not enough: in this cantata, a Rimbaud setting, the voice, four cellos, and harp must spin a tense, tender, erotic web, until the whole audience seems to tremble in the embrace of the "beloved body" hymned by the poet and the composer. Sexual rapture so intense that it becomes a mystical experience is the subject of the piece.

Copland performances, in this season of his seventy-fifth birthday, have been plentiful, and again and again during the celebrations I have been warmed by open-hearted, open-handed melodic turns in the vein that seems to me his special and most treasurable gift to the world—the "tan-faced prairie-boy" passages that will suddenly smile through in even his most celebrated constructions. *The Tender Land* is an opera almost entirely in this vein. It is a Midwestern idyll—not a realistic drama but a romantic, pastoral fairy tale. All productions I have seen have got the tone wrong, and the Bronx Opera Company's, given in the auditorium of the Bronx High School of Science, was no exception. Richard Getke's direction lacked the right sort of verismo (in such details as the way Sears, Roebuck might pack a mail-order graduation dress) and made heavy weather of the flimsy, sentimental close. The heroine's behavior at the end does not bear thinking about; it is as unrealistic in its way as the opera-seria convention of tying loose ends into a tidy bow, and should be played as such. And Michael Spierman's effortful conducting lacked the lilt, the easy charm, that could make the score irresistible. Sheila Barnes, as Laurie, sang most winningly.

February 2, 1976

Brian Fennelly's Prelude and Elegy *was recorded by the Empire Brass Quintet on Advance 19; the* Brass Band Journal *was recorded by the Quintet on Columbia M 31492.*

SONG FROM THE TWIN CITIES

Two song cycles from Minnesota came to New York on consecutive days: on Sunday afternoon last week, in Town Hall, William Bolcom's *Open House*, commissioned by the American Choral Society and first performed, last year, in the O'Shaughnessy Auditorium of St. Paul; the evening before, in Carnegie Hall, Dominick Argento's *From the Diary of Virginia Woolf*, commissioned by the Schubert Club of St. Paul and first performed, last year, in the new Orchestra Hall of Minneapolis. Bolcom's work, for tenor and chamber orchestra, is dedicated to Paul Sperry; Argento's, for mezzo-soprano and piano, to Janet Baker. Both were done here by their original performers: Mr. Sperry and the St. Paul Chamber Orchestra, conducted by Dennis Russell Davies; and Dame Janet and Martin Isepp.

The St. Paul orchestra is the only full-time professional chamber orchestra in this country. Its Town Hall concert—given, to a warm and appreciative audience, as one of the People's Symphony Concerts, now in their seventy-fifth season—was the last of four that it played on a New York visit. I wish I could have attended all, for they were done in four very different locations, to four very different kinds of audience, and the programs reflected the range of the orchestra's activity. In the Auditorium of the Library and Museum of the Performing Arts, as part of Lincoln Center's New and Newer Music series, there was Copland's Piano Quartet, Henry Cowell's *Persian Set*, and two works, by Minneapolis-St. Paul composers, written for the orchestra: Paul Fetler's Violin Concerto and Eric Stokes's *Five Verbs*—both New York premières. At The Kitchen, on Wooster Street, there was an adventurous evening of John Cage. A Carnegie Hall concert was classical—Handel, Mozart, and Pleyel. The Town Hall concert was classical in the first half—Haydn and Johann Melchior Molter—and the second half was Bolcom's song cycle.

There are twenty-four players: a string strength of 4.4.3.3.1; pairs of oboes, horns, and bassoons; a single flute and clarinet; harpsichord or piano. That is not enough for the larger scores of Haydn and Mozart (for them, trumpets and drums and extra woodwinds must be brought in), but it does cover a good deal of the baroque, classical, and contemporary repertory. The orchestra's classical style is gentle and unemphatic, alert but not forceful, and sometimes, to my ears, a shade lacking in incisiveness. Mr. Davies does not favor strong accents. Mozart's A-major Symphony K. 201 and Haydn's Symphony No. 98 (done without trumpets and drums) flowed easily. They were played like chamber music, with delicate phrasing and careful balance. Mr. Davies seemed not so much to impose his will on the players as to be their unobtrusive guide. The result was captivating but perhaps not quite bright enough. It may be that through gentleness of attack Mr. Davies seeks to dim the unauthentic brightness that modern instruments give to eighteenth-century music. A soft, tender glow is certainly preferable to glare. Yet I felt some lack of vigor in the executions. The other works at the Carnegie concert were concertos. Jean-Pierre Rampal, flute, and Martine Géliot, harp, were rather dull, plain soloists in Pleyel's C-major Flute Concerto, Handel's Harp Concerto (the Organ Concerto Op. 4 No. 6 in its harp version), and Mozart's Concerto for flute and harp. In Town Hall, Gerard Schwarz was the soloist in Molter's Second Trumpet Concerto, a pedestrian composition that not even his skill could enliven.

Two records on the Nonesuch label are due in spring from the St. Paul orchestra. One is devoted to galant pieces: a J. C. Bach sinfonia, "Mozart's Symphony No. 37" (which is by Michael Haydn, with a

Mozart introduction), and an early Mozart cassation. It should provide a clear idea of the orchestra's eighteenth-century manner. In music of the twentieth century, Mr. Davies's skill has long been recognized. Internationally, he has become one of the best-known American conductors, leading the orchestra on its tour of Western and Eastern Europe, and conducting for the Netherlands and Stuttgart Operas. The other record is twentieth-century; it contains two works by William Bolcom, his *Commedia*, written for the St. Paul orchestra some years ago, and the new song cycle. *Commedia* is that rare thing, a piece of instrumental music that can make one laugh aloud. It is Mahlerian in its clear instrumental colorings, its tunefulness, its sudden, drastic juxtapositions—a slight, deft piece with Mahler's charm and gaiety and none of his angst, now perky, now sentimental, and totally winning. Bolcom (born in 1938) is a composer who is always pleasing but sometimes puzzling. He can be a poet, but he is one who shrinks from too lofty a flight; in full, rhapsodic utterance he is apt to drop suddenly into a "Call me Bill" vein, as if to say "Enough of that long-haired stuff; I'm not one of those cerebral composers who write only for the critics and campus intellectuals; music should be fun; here's a tune, a rhythm, a chord sequence of a kind that we all know!" Bolcom's *Seasons*, a sixteen-minute tone poem for solo guitar, was introduced to New York last month by Michael Lorimer, at a Tully Hall recital. Most of it is magical. The small sounds of nature astir—tap and twitch and rustle, bright twitter and sleepy chirrup—can well be shaped into guitar music. But twice, in sections called "Spring and Summer Dances" and "Harvest Time," Bolcom drops into a jarring popular idiom, jolly enough in itself but not of a piece with the rest of his composition. The episodes seem contrived, self-conscious, mannered, put in merely to prove a point that needs no proving.

Open House is a setting of seven poems by Theodore Roethke, a poet to whom several American composers have been drawn. The best Roethke songs I know match his disciplined diction and meters with a disciplined vocal line, not leaping fiercely, not rhythmically extravagant, but controlled in its energy. The eponymous poem that opens Bolcom's cycle starts:

> My secrets cry aloud.
> I have no need for tongue.
> My heart keeps open house,
> My doors are widely swung.
> An epic of the eyes
> My love, with no disguise.

Bolcom sets the lines in a declamatory, melodramatic fashion, with several leaps of a seventh, and strong emphases. It is not their tone as

I hear it. The second song, "Give Way, Ye Gates," uses a more exclamatory, erratic poem; Bolcom's setting sounds almost like a parody of post-*Pierrot* expressionism, and it is hard to follow the sense ("Believe me, knot of gristle, I bleed like a tree; / I dream of nothing but boards; / I could love a duck"). The third, "The Waking," affords an interesting comparison with Ned Rorem's setting of the same text. Roethke's poem is a villanelle in regular iambic pentameters ("I wake to sleep, and take my waking slow"). Both composers have hit on exactly the same basic meter, a steady tread of quarter-notes in common time, one to a syllable—an upbeat to start with, and the last syllable of each line prolonged. Moreover, both use much stepwise motion, and this has led to some of the words being sung to the very same notes. Rorem, in a skillful and beautiful piece, maintains the pattern unbroken throughout his song, and in doing so he faithfully reflects the technical structure of the poem. Variety is provided by subtle displacements of pitch levels, by carefully plotted harmonic and dynamic contours, and by piano textures sensitive to the shifting emotional tensions. It is up to the singer to sound the poet's punctuation, within the regular march of quarter-notes, and to adjust verbal stresses so that the first syllables of the lines beginning "God bless the ground!" and "Light takes the Tree," though set to a weak beat, are given due weight. Someone reading the poem aloud would do the same. And, in this play of stress and weight against the regular meter, poem and musical setting are a match. In Bolcom's setting, the villanelle structure is less clear. His common time is soon varied by measures of three, five, and six. Stepwise motion changes to leaps, and the inflection of the words is sometimes unnatural. The fourth song, "The Serpent," is a piece of would-be comic doggerel broadly handled in "Bowery waltz tempo." The fifth, "I Knew a Woman," is set to a slow, syncopated night-club melody. The sixth, "First Meditation," from "Meditations of an Old Woman," seems to me the greatest success of the cycle, a piece in which Bolcom's various manners knit together. It starts with half-spoken recitative, and fragments of arioso, and then moves "lazily, smoothly" into a popular rhythm, rolling fluently along; Roethke's phrase "through western country" may have brought "country-and-Western" to mind. Lulled by the motion of the bus in which she imagines herself, the old woman lets her thoughts slip into the past, and the music slips into E-major, cradling the line of memories that she voices in free rhythms against the regular beat. The poem of the final song, "The Right Thing," is another villanelle, but one less strictly constructed than "The Waking." Bolcom sets it as a hymn tune in C major, with varied accompaniments. The tone is serene, affirmative. The timbre of the first tercet is beautiful: voice doubled two octaves higher by a recorder, and bassoon and viola in diatonic note-against-note counterpoint. But the word setting seems to me awkward at times—an octave leap, for example, starts the refrain "The right thing happens to the happy man."

Mixed impressions, at the end: plenty of good ideas; vitality most of the time, but also some dead patches; word setting frequently at odds with the natural rise and fall of Roethke's lines and the beat of his measures, but not so strong in itself as to subdue them to the composer's will; incoherence of the cycle as a whole, because Bolcom has not here brought poetical, finely trained William and lively, jolly Bill, the entertainer, into harmony. When that happens, he becomes one of our most attractive composers.

No reservations about Argento's song cycle, *From the Diary of Virginia Woolf*. It is a beautiful, moving, and masterly work. From *A Writer's Diary* the composer has chosen eight extracts. The first is an early entry, from 1919—"What sort of diary should I like mine to be? Something . . . so elastic that it will embrace anything, solemn, slight or beautiful that comes into my mind"—and the last is the final entry, of 1941. The second song uses a paragraph on anxiety, foreboding; the third is the fancy "Why not invent a new kind of play; as for instance: Woman thinks . . . He does. Organ plays." Then accounts of Hardy's funeral (1928) and of tea at the Caffè Greco, in Rome (1935). From June, 1940, there is war ("This, I thought yesterday, may be my last walk . . . the war—our waiting while the knives sharpen for the operation—has taken away the outer wall of security"), and from later in that year a remembrance of parents and herself as a child ("How beautiful they were, those old people—I mean father and mother"). And then that last entry: "I will go down with my colours flying. . . . Occupation is essential. And now with some pleasure I find that it's seven; and must cook dinner. Haddock and sausage meat. I think it is true that one gains a certain hold on sausage and haddock by writing them down." In the musical setting, the piano accompaniment has already strayed back to the music at the start of the cycle, and now lines from the first song are repeated—the wish that the collection of observations thus set down may have "sorted itself and refined itself and coalesced, as such deposits so mysteriously do, into a mould, transparent enough to reflect the light of our life." The text is coherent, and affecting, and proves to be marvelously apt for musical treatment. The words are, as it were, "recited" in a flexible arioso of melodic contour, uncommonly sensitive to natural weight, speed, and inflection, embracing both recitative and full-throated lyrical song. The piano part gives to each song its basic character and a firm musical structure, and on the way picks up the passing, picturesque details so sharply noted and makes motifs of them.

Song follows song in masterly sequence. "War," in C-sharp minor, is accompanied only by the notes G-sharp and C-sharp in the bass and sudden, stabbing, or fluttering repeated-note signals in the treble. At its close, the menace fades for a while before the serene E major of "Parents." The last song begins resolutely, a repeated C-sharp major clung to as if in desperate affirmation, but soon the harmony starts shifting and breaking. A tolling G-sharp in the bass and other motifs from earlier songs recur. The vocal line is expressive and very good to sing; by Dame Janet it was sung with the utmost eloquence. The piano part is vivid, many-colored, and subtle; by Mr. Isepp it was played superlatively well. The cycle is published by Boosey & Hawkes.

It was a recital in which all the writers were important. The texts were by Niccolò Minato (Cavalli's librettist; arias from his *Serse* and *Orimonte* opened the evening, and it was interesting to hear "Ombra mai fu" set not by Handel), Virginia Woolf, then, after the intermission, Schiller (five Schubert settings), and finally Verlaine (three poems, each in settings by both Debussy and Fauré). The Schubert group came to a climax with a thrilling performance of the tremendous "Gruppe aus dem Tartarus." The wretched program book gave no texts—only excerpts from the Woolf cycle, and translations of the rest. There was nothing about Schiller and Schubert, nor any notes on the songs. Anyone not knowing that "Amalia" is from *Die Räuber* and what *Die Räuber* is about can have made little sense of the piece.

I have long revered Dame Janet—in Monteverdi, Cavalli, Handel, Berlioz—as a goddess made of finer stuff than mere mortal clay. On the stage she sounds and looks so noble, so inspired, as to make other singers seem stagy; with utter directness she gives voice to the words. Not always in recital have I felt this transfiguring power, for sometimes she has exposed emotions so fearlessly, so uninhibitedly, as to break the song mold—has been too *open* both in timbre and in expression. But in this Carnegie recital she was matchless. The nineteenth-century Italian roles recently tackled—Donizetti's Mary Stuart, Bellini's Romeo in the forthcoming Angel recording—seem to have enriched and extended the glorious voice, which now ran in its full splendor from the A below the staff to the A above it more evenly and fully than ever before. The style in Schubert, in Debussy and Fauré was more certain than ever before. In the *mélodies*, she showed a new command of that Claire Croiza-like quality in which candor, clarity, passion, and, with it, a certain mysterious restraint are combined. In an encore, "My Boy Tammie," she threw her voice into every corner of the hall and set it ringing.

February 9, 1976

293

The St. Paul Chamber Orchestra's record of J. C. Bach, Michael Haydn, and Mozart is Nonesuch H-71323, and of the Bolcom pieces H-71324.

EGYPTIAN ATTITUDES

The Metropolitan Opera's new production of *Aida*, which opened last week, is a handsome affair, decked by David Reppa (scenery) and Peter J. Hall (costumes) in strong, somber colors and rich, heavy brocades. Six of the seven scenes play in variants of a single set, a tall Egyptian chamber whose battering walls bear huge reliefs that have been cracked as if by an earthquake. Only Act III, beside the Nile, suggests the out-of-doors. Within this chamber, the floor is a version of the Bayreuth "saucer," with the raised central circle ringed by two narrow tracks, around which the triumphal processions of Act II rather warily proceed. There is not much space. Gilbert Hemsley's lighting is fairly consistently tenebrous. The triumph is a torchlit nocturne. Paper flames are kept aflicker by some mechanical device noisy enough to disturb the music. Follow spots pick out the singers and spray onto the scenery of Act III. The priestesses' "sacred dance to slow, solemn strains," in the temple scene, during which Radamès, beneath a silver veil, should be led to the altar, is reassigned to a single male dancer, flapping ibis wings. Conversely, the little blackamoors of the next scene are replaced by three madcap maidens. In the triumph scene, the dance episode is done, as usual, in the padded-out Paris version, but instead of a "troop of dancing-girls bearing the treasures of the vanquished" we see a duel to the death between an Egyptian and an Ethiopian warrior. The choreography is by Louis Johnson.

Much of this is wrongheaded, in contradiction not only of what is spelled out in Verdi's careful stage directions but also—and, in an age when it has become common to disregard a creator's express intentions about staging, perhaps more importantly—of what is clearly implied by the music itself. The costumes for the first production of *Aida*, in Cairo, in 1871, were designed by the Egyptologist Auguste Mariette; they were made in Paris, and Mariette was sent there from Cairo to insure their authenticity; they were rich and colorful but light. Several details suggest that Mr. Hall studied Mariette's designs, but his costumes are hot and heavy in effect, suited to a northern clime. So perhaps it is realistic to hold the triumph by night, after the sun has set. Yet in Verdi's music for that scene I hear a blaze of brilliant light. In the Met production,

294

the contrast between this glare, blare, and splendor and the soft, starry romance of the next scene, with moonbeams winking gently on the Nile and filtering down through the palm fronds, has been removed. In the final scene, no attempt is made to suggest that other intended contrast, between the Temple of Vulcan above, "gleaming with gold and light," and the blackness of Radamès's dungeon.

With *Aida*, at its Opéra production in 1880, Verdi at last obtained the Paris success for which, since *Jérusalem* in 1847, he had striven. Before *Les Vêpres siciliennes*, he had asked Scribe to contrive for him one of those "grandiose and at the same time impassioned" spectacles, such as the coronation scene in *Le Prophète*, which were a Scribe specialty. Before *Don Carlos*, he had asked for the same thing—and obtained it in the auto-da-fé scene of Act III, which he deemed the "heart" of that opera. But a fully successful grand opera in the Meyerbeer manner continued to elude him; *Simon Boccanegra, La forza del destino*, and *Don Carlos* all underwent patching in subsequent years. In 1870, Verdi was toying with the idea of writing an opéra comique when there arrived from Cairo, via Paris, the *Aida* scenario, with an invitation to base a large new work on it, and he determined to tackle grand opera once again. (This scenario was written by Mariette, but Verdi believed it to be the work of the Khedive.) The financial rewards offered were handsome. More important, he found the scenario "well made, splendid from a scenic point of view, and containing two or three situations that, while not exactly novel, are certainly very fine."

The structure of this "well made" piece is tidier than that of *Don Carlos* but in many ways similar: first scene with the tenor aria placed early, then an assembly and a choral close; second scene in a temple, with solemn chanting; third scene the traditional women's chorus and solo; then a massive spectacle with stage band, multiple choruses, and all the principals experiencing, in public, a crisis in their private affairs. And then three "private" scenes built of monologues and duets, except when priests thunder their doom on the hero (the original *Don Carlos* contained an inquisitors' chorus in the last scene); in the last duet, hero and heroine bid farewell in this world. The parallels may not run consistently true, but, once observed, they can throw into relief the greater flexibility and compactness of *Aida*—flexible in such things as the placing of the heroine's first aria, "Ritorna vincitor!" (whose embryonic idea is Carlos's despairing cries of "O destin fatal" while a jubilant procession recedes into the distance), compact in that only three characters, not five, are tangled in the emotional web and rent by divided feelings. Moreover, in *Aida*, as not in *Don Carlos*, the plights are clear-cut and conventional, the traditional stuff of which operas had long been made—hero and heroine on opposed sides and torn between love and patriotic duty, other woman torn between jealousy and love.

Verdi's observation that the situations were "not exactly novel" was just. Amneris is a descendant of Racine's Roxane. The plot is an opera-seria libretto romanticized. Metastasio might have devised it; in his *Nitteti*, he nearly did. (That much-set libretto, of 1756, concerns an Egyptian princess and a humble beauty, who is really a princess, as rivals for the hero's love; there is a spectacular triumph scene, with stage bands, Egyptian cohorts, Ethiopian prisoners, a white elephant, and camels; the hero prefers death to marriage to the wrong princess.) But Metastasio would have effected a happy ending for *Aida*: Amneris, perhaps, would be revealed as Radamès's long-lost sister, and wed Amonasro instead. Yet another source for *Aida* is the *Medea* of Cesare Della Valle, the librettist of Rossini's *Maometto II*. In Della Valle's play, the Lord of Corinth appoints a warrior to be defender of his threatened country and win his daughter's hand as prize; Medea and Glauca are the Amneris and Aida figures. It seems obvious that Antonio Ghislanzoni, the official librettist of *Aida*, had Della Valle open before him when we compare the opening lines of the play ("Alta cagion, fidi Corinti, al vostro Signor d'intorno oggi v'aduna") with the King's opening words in *Aida* ("Alta cagion v'aduna, o fidi Egizii, al vostro Re d'intorno").

Mariette wrote the original scenario; Camille du Locle (Verdi's collaborator on *Don Carlos*) expanded it into a draft libretto, in French prose; Ghislanzoni fashioned this into Italian verse. But the controlling hand was Verdi's own, as the long series of letters to Ghislanzoni, now in the Morgan Library, makes clear. The composer who in the past had insisted upon curious, original, unhackneyed situations here turned deliberately to the clichés of Italian opera and sought to reanimate them by the power of his music and by his special care for direct, theatrically telling utterance—for strong, simple, unflowery diction. In this respect, *Aida* is an experimental work. In Joseph Kerman's phrase, there is "an almost constant disparity between the particular glib simplicity of the libretto and the alarming complexity of the musical expression—for of course Verdi's technique had never been so rich." The Metropolitan staging shows that its director, John Dexter, understood all this, but to his perceptions he has given a peculiar form. He has drilled his cast to the acting style parodied by Gilbert in *The Mikado*—which opens, you remember, on a chorus of "Japanese nobles discovered standing and sitting in attitudes suggested by native drawings." "Our attitude's queer and quaint," they sing, "You're wrong if you think it ain't, oh! If you think we are worked by strings, Like a Japanese marionette, You don't understand these things: It is simply Court etiquette." I don't understand why Mr. Dexter decided to present *Aida* as—well, I would say a grand-scale puppet show were not puppets more eloquent in their movements than any of the *Aida* cast. He has prescribed a repertory of queer and quaint Egyptian Attitudes; his actors strike one and hold it until, generally on the first beat of a measure, they move to the next one. So there is no emotional contact between the characters; rigidly and awkwardly they stand, and sing. This is not the old flowing "Egyptian plastique" that prima donnas used to practice but something stiffer and jerkier—Swedish drill by numbers, "Under the Spreading Chestnut Tree" routines. The King puts his hands on his hips to launch "Su! del Nilo." There is much pressing of palms to breasts or to tummies (at one point mass stomach ache seems to seize on the ladies of the chorus), crooking of elbows, and supination of hands. The formalized substructure of the *Aida* plot is reflected, but not the quick, keen emotions that Verdi portrayed so vividly. Of course, the actors could not keep it up consistently. Human nature, and physical response to the dramatic situations, prompted them at times to move like real people. In later performances, with different casts, the unfortunate drill will doubtless be forgotten.

James Levine conducted, cogently but with an enthusiasm that amounted to brashness and insensitivity, for he kept pushing ahead through phrases that need time—a slight yielding, broadening—to discharge their eloquence. The big ensembles—"Nume, custode e vindice," "Ma tu, Re, tu signore possente"—lacked weight and grandeur. There was plenty of energy but not much poetry or emotion. And so by both the stage direction and the conducting the individual singers were hampered, and could not give of their best. Nearly twenty years ago, I first heard Leontyne Price sing Aida. Then she was uncommonly affecting— direct, natural, fresh and instinctive in the expression she gave to each phrase. In last week's production, those epithets could no longer apply to her. Her interpretation was mannered, self-conscious, unspontaneous. She was in good vocal shape and, particularly in the Nile act, produced rich, beautiful sounds. The high C of "O patria mia" was soft and clear, and the floating B-flat of "fuggiam, fuggiam," in the first duet with Radamès, was very beautiful. The final duet was unmoving, partly because some fog crept into Miss Price's timbre, partly because it was so clumsily staged. James McCracken's Radamès was strongly sung and declaimed with intensity. It was presumably on Mr. Dexter's instructions that for stretches of the role he turned the heroic warrior into a booby, a semaphoring Boy Scout; other passages were nobly enacted. In "Celeste Aida" he eschewed a caressing portamento on the rising fourths and thirds, and thereby reduced the rapt, dreamy quality of the aria; but he did end it softly and made the soft ending sound natural and right, not a strain. Marilyn Horne's Amneris was curiously unimpressive—partly, I suspect, because in striving for a dark, dramatic tone she tended to push her vowels in the direction of "aw" instead of making each clear and distinct (not "Dai sacerdoti Radamès" but "Daw sawchaw-dawti Rawdawmes"), and partly because Mr. Levine seldom allowed her time to produce the ample, grandiose sounds that are needed in the judgment scene. Cornell MacNeil's Amonasro was simply magnificent; he has become the grandest Verdi baritone of our day. James Morris's King was majestic; Bonaldo Giaiotti's Ramfis was smooth but not quite imposing enough. Marcia Baldwin sang the High Priestess's offstage solo in strong, clear tones.

February 16, 1976

PIANISTS AND PIANOS

Dickran Atamian, the latest Naumburg Piano Competition winner, gave a pleasing recital in Alice Tully Hall the week before last. The largest work on his program was Schubert's G-major Sonata—though on this occasion not as large as it should be, since from the first two movements he omitted the repeats. He played a Baldwin instrument and it sounded beautiful, as well suited to Schubert as any modern concert grand can be. Ideally, Schubert's piano music should be heard played in a small hall on the kind of piano Schubert knew—light and clear, vigorous but not massively sonorous in fortissimo. Nevertheless, in the large recital hall, with his large instrument, Mr. Atamian created an illusion of intimacy: he never forced his tone or broke the scale of the music; he established the range of dynamics Schubert calls for, from *ppp* to *ff*, without exaggeration at either extreme, and within them achieved all the contrasts one could wish for. From a formal point of view, his interpretation reflected those features which in their combination make a progress through any of Schubert's large compositions a never-failing delight: a sense of adventure, a "What shall we do next? Where shall we go from here?" feeling, followed by advance in a direction unerring, though often unexpected, which resolves the moment of delicious doubt. Schubert seems to pause, to linger at some point reached (the music does not stop, but the harmony settles or the melody turns to expectant figuration), to survey the prospects ahead before striking out toward a goal that, once attained, we realize was implicit from the first. To put it more plainly, Mr. Atamian did not play in dull strict time but understood how a harmonic intensification may check the impetus of an episode; how a phrase may need to be shaped as if borne on a singer's breath; and how to resume, and perhaps emphasize the return to, the basic tempo. He united freedom, rhapsody, with very clear definition of Schubert's form. His recital began with Donald Keats's Piano Sonata (1964), an arresting and pianistically rewarding composition; included Chopin's A-flat Ballade, played with strength and grace; and ended with Prokofiev's Sixth Sonata. Prokofiev's piano music is probably more enjoyable to master and play than to listen to, but the Sixth Sonata, introduced by the composer himself in a radio performance, and first played in public by Sviatoslav Richter, has, in the words of Edward Sackville-West (who was both an accomplished pianist and an acute critic), "good claim to be considered Prokofiev's best work for piano solo, for it combines rhythmic energy with unusually interesting, and even deeply-felt, thematic material." (He was writing before the lyrical Ninth Sonata made its posthumous appearance in print; the Ninth, in my view, is the finest of them all.) Mr. Atamian played it with brio, and with charm in the slow waltz that is the third movement, but he spoiled things at climaxes by adding a vocal accompaniment of fierce, low growls.

Two days later, in Carnegie, an even larger hall, and on a Steinway, Radu Lupu played another Schubert sonata—the late A-major, D. 959, done complete. I have not heard Mr. Lupu much since he won the Leeds International Piano Competition in 1969—through lack not of opportunity, which has been plentiful, but of inclination, for at Leeds he seemed to me to coat Schubert (the Opus 90 Impromptus) and Beethoven (the Waldstein, the C-minor Concerto) in a thick, sticky, unappetizing emotional sauce. (Who ever agrees with competition juries? What has become of the young Russians Boris Petrushansky and Vadim Sakharov, respectively fourth and unplaced at Leeds that year, who struck me as the most remarkable pianistic talents there?) Still— to borrow a reckless metaphor from a colleague's prose—"glowing reports filtered down through the grapevine" that Mr. Lupu is playing like an angel these days. And so, at Carnegie, he was. But like an angel with *Flügel* a size too big. Haydn's F-minor Andante with Variations began things; then Beethoven's Opus 110; then the Schubert. All three pieces contain passages that are intended to be played full out— passages of clumped left-hand chords with a treble line running high above, or, inversely, of hard-struck treble chords above a heavy running bass—but cannot decently be played full out on a big modern Steinway: the texture implies the timbre of an early-nineteenth-century piano. In fact, for this particular program, of Viennese music from 1793 to 1828, Mr. Lupu was using the wrong instrument. It is too soon, perhaps, to insist that Beethoven's sonatas should be played on the kind of piano for which they were composed; we are not yet so nice about classical music as about baroque and continue to accept the former rendered on Romantic instruments. But the time will come, I believe, when audiences —and pianists—having once discovered the tone colors and clarity and alertness of wooden-framed pianos with thin strings and buckskin-covered hammers, will want to hear more of them, and new makers of such instruments will spring up, as now harpsichord builders have done. Artur Schnabel's, Wilhelm Kempff's, Wilhelm Backhaus's, Ernst Lévy's greatness will not dim, of course, but their Beethoven performances will be counted—as Edwin Fischer's and Dinu Lipatti's of Bach now are—great interpretations superbly executed on the wrong instrument.

At any rate, Mr. Lupu was stuck with a modern piano, and had to try to make the best of it. He might not put it quite that way, for under his fingers the Steinway rippled, and purled, and sang, and its notes ran—at moderate dynamic levels—in a limpid stream. There was a new, fine lucidity, both of thought and of sound, in all he did; that thick emotional sauce is evidently a thing of the past. There was fancy in the Haydn, and emotion in the Beethoven: the recitative and arioso were poignant, and the fugues began like improvisations—the themes softly sounded, not struck out, until the octave entries in the left hand brought a sense of reaching firm ground. Every music student knows that the fugue subject takes shape from the opening measures of the first movement; in Mr. Lupu's performance one seemed to hear the process of transformation. His Schubert style was less spontaneous than Mr. Atamian's but also captivating, with exquisite evenness in runs, carefully planned dynamic gradients, precise balances, and delicate rhythmic inflections. The phrasing of the andantino was tricksy, Mahlerian, but charmingly, not irritatingly, so. His playing was always gentle —which is a word of high praise. There is not enough gentleness in much of today's music making; power and brilliance are qualities more highly prized. But in those fiery passages where an early piano can be hit hard and not complain, passages where the sparks should fly, Mr. Lupu's restraint reduced the musical force of his discourse.

Lazar Berman, the Russian pianist who, amid a blaze of publicity, has been playing concertos with the Brooklyn Philharmonia and the New Jersey Symphony and recitals in the Ninety-second Street Y, has a big technique: plenty of weight and plenty of speed. He has no reservations about hitting the Steinway hard, but his tone does not become harsh. At his recital last week, the first half was Liszt (five pieces from the Italian books of the *Années de pèlerinage*), and the second Rachmaninoff (four of the *Moments musicaux*) and Prokofiev (the Eighth Sonata). Everything was dissolved into technique. In a curious way, there seemed to be no musical content in the Liszt—only various demonstrations of quick playing, loud playing, fat, luscious tone, delicate, crystalline tone, and quicksilver sparkle. In the Rachmaninoff there was more emotion, but Mr. Berman's concentration was evidently disturbed—as well it might have been—by a sustained barrage of coughs from the audience; he flinched physically under it and darted some distressed glances at the noisiest offenders. The Eighth Sonata—to quote Mr. Sackville-West again—"is possibly Prokofiev's least successful piano work. The first movement is full of skinny, two-part writing, and the Finale wearies the listener with a lengthy and exasperating episode in D-flat major." Even Emil Gilels, who gave the first performance, can hardly persuade one otherwise, though he finds more charm in the slow minuet of the second movement than Mr. Berman did. The recital reached its climax in the last encore, a thunderous, high-velocity, and physically exciting account of Falla's *Ritual Fire Dance*. But one had only to recall the lilting charm of Rubinstein in that piece, of Kempff in the Liszt, and of Rachmaninoff in his records of Rachmaninoff to feel that Mr. Berman, while being a prodigy, is no poet—a virtuoso with his arms and fingers but a dull musician. It was astonishing and exciting to hear him play, but at no point did he prompt the reflection "What beautiful music!"

Program notes on the music at Mr. Atamian's recital were limited to a single sentence ("Mr. Keats has used this opportunity to exploit the many virtuoso aspects of the piano in a contemporary idiom"). At Mr. Lupu's and Mr. Berman's recitals there were none. Is the assumption that New York audiences are so familiar with the repertory as to need no introductions, or that they are uninterested in anything except the performer?

February 23, 1976

MUSIC IN SPACE

The Church of St. Paul the Apostle, on Columbus Avenue at Fifty-ninth Street, begun by Jeremiah O'Rourke, is a large, awkward building, a heavy, clumsy attempt at a great basilica. Tucked away in its gloomy side chapels are some pieces of art worth investigation. By day, there are John LaFarge windows to look at; by night, when the lighting allows it to be seen, the roof is a blue vault spangled with stars, as the Sistine Chapel's used to be before Michelangelo got to work on it. In this church the Boston Symphony Orchestra, with the Westminster Choir, gave a performance of Berlioz's Requiem in memory of Charles Munch. (A second commemorative performance, during the orchestra's forthcoming visit to Paris, was to have been held in the church of the Invalides, where the Requiem had its first performance, in 1837, but has been shifted to the Palais des Congrès.) The Requiem is one of Berlioz's three great "architectural" works—the others being the Te Deum and the rarely heard cantata *L'Impériale*. Their inspiration goes back to Berlioz's first visit to St. Peter's as a young Prix de Rome winner. "Immense! sublime! overwhelming! Michelangelo, Raphael, Canova this side and that; underfoot, precious marbles and rare, beautiful mosaics; the solemn silence, the still, cool air . . . then a slight sound rising from some far, dim corner of the church and rolling around the great vaults like distant thunder. . . . As I thought of the glorious role my cherished art must play there, my heart began to beat with excitement." But the music Berlioz heard in St. Peter's was scrannel stuff, and it was years before he himself received the commissions to compose works that would animate—that, as he put it, would become the "soul" of—huge reverberant buildings. When Saint-Saëns heard the Requiem, he said that in the "Tuba mirum" it was "as if each separate slim column of the church became an organ pipe, and the whole edifice a vast organ." (He continued, "Even more, I admired the poignant feeling of this marvelous work, the constant and incredible elevation of style.") Berlioz believed—even then; what would he think now!—that most music was performed in spaces too large for it. Often, in the giant opera houses of this country, I am tempted to echo his complaint: "One hears, but one does not vibrate." In the score of the Requiem he asks for over a hundred strings, winds to match, and a chorus of over two hundred. In a footnote, he suggests that the chorus can go up to eight hundred in the larger movements, with the orchestra increased in proportion. Conductors employ what forces they can muster. One of Beecham's last concerts was a Berlioz Requiem in the Albert Hall. He had the full complement of ten cymbal players needed to drum up that tremendous roll into the "Tuba mirum," and in the Sanctus— where Berlioz indicates only three pairs of cymbals—he used all ten players again, ringing the platform and creating, with their very gentle clashes, a mysterious sonic apse of soft, shuddering tone. Seiji Ozawa, who conducted the Boston Symphony performance, had seven cymbal players. (In Paris, he will command the combined forces of the Boston Symphony and the Orchestre de Paris, two of Munch's former orchestras.) He stationed the four brass bands not, as Berlioz directs, "at the four corners of the large choral and instrumental mass" but at the four corners of the rectangular church, so that last trumps blew at the listeners from every side. The result was majestic, awe-inspiring. The church has the right sort of acoustics for the music, resonant enough for the silences to be "living" but not so reverberant that the strong, slow march of the harmonies clogs into confusion. In the Agnus Dei, the pedal tones of the trombones and the cluster of four flutes high above became single sounds, almost "shapes" that seemed to hover in the air. Stuart Burrows, the tenor soloist, singing from beneath the Stanford

302

White baldacchino, filled the church with a flood of warm, expansive tone—perhaps too warm and forthright, not mystical enough in a movement that should evoke a haze of thick incense smoke with the prayer winding up through it. Mr. Ozawa's direction was very clear. The Westminster Choir sang well in the softer passages but lacked force, rhythmic energy, and bright, ardent tone in the climaxes. The church, just two blocks south of Lincoln Center, and seating about two thousand, is well placed to become an ecclesiastical annex of Fisher Hall; next time the Philharmonic tackles Berlioz's Te Deum, it might move there. Old St. Patrick's, on Mott Street, is a more pleasing and the Cathedral of St. John the Divine, on Morningside Heights, a more impressive building, but both are farther from New York's musical center than the Church of St. Paul the Apostle. Thought, however, must be given to the lighting, which can do so much to create—or destroy—an apt atmosphere for musical enjoyment. (When a Francesco Cavalli Vesper sequence, drawn from his *Musiche Sacre*, had its first performance in London, in January, Brompton Oratory was lit for the occasion by hundreds of candles.) The program leaflet for the Berlioz contained the text of the Requiem and a translation, but the lights were dimmed to a point that made them illegible.

Puccini's *Il trittico* had its première at the Metropolitan Opera, in 1918. It was revived the following season, and then dismembered. *Suor Angelica* disappeared; *Il tabarro* came back only in the 1945–46 season; *Gianni Schicchi* lived on as a curtain-raiser or afterpiece to such diverse works as *Pagliacci, Salome, Elektra,* and *Hansel and Gretel.* This season, the triptych has been reassembled: a new *Tabarro* and *Suor Angelica* join the 1974 staging of *Gianni Schicchi.* All three are directed by Fabrizio Melano and designed by David Reppa. The point about *Il tabarro* and *Suor Angelica,* I believe, is that, in addition to their dramatic content, they should captivate the audience as "pictures" for the eye and the ear at once; Puccini's scores are filled with small, fine episodes of instrumental painting. The point is not made in the Metropolitan version. Under Sixten Ehrling, the orchestral playing has been efficient but not bewitching. *Il tabarro* is mounted on the right veristic lines, but neither the set nor the staging is polished in detail. *Suor Angelica* is mounted on the wrong lines. The opera had a bad press in New York from the start, and now, as if afraid to commit themselves to the composer's intentions, Messrs. Melano and Reppa have endeavored to strip the piece of all its sentimentality and prettiness. There is no delightful garden, no garden of any kind, in the cloister; it is bare. There is no bubbling spring to catch the garden rays of the evening sun. Angelica does not build a little fire to brew her poison over; she heats it at a sort of outdoor cooking range, shaking in dried herbs reached down from the kitchen shelf. The setting suggests a women's prison in the desert. There is no miracle—no Virgin, no golden-haired little boy. And if *Suor Angelica* is not played as a sweetly and richly sentimental piece it loses all its character and charm. It is the most elegantly tender of Puccini's scores, as *Gianni Schicchi* is the most elegantly inventive. The Met *Schicchi* is a low, undisciplined romp. At the end, the medieval walls fly up to reveal Brunelleschi's dome, a century and a half in the future.

In the first cast, only Cornell MacNeil, as Michele and then as Schicchi, sang with distinction. Teresa Kubiak and Gilda Cruz-Romo were an acceptable Giorgetta and Angelica. Evelyn Mandac, in her Met début, as Lauretta, was very attractive but a shade small for the enormous house. Later, Renata Scotto undertook all three heroines; though their characters are very different, the combined vocal demands hardly exceed those of a Butterfly or a Manon Lescaut. Miss Scotto's Giorgetta and Angelica, both the first of her career, were assured interpretations but mannered in their execution, as her portrayals usually are. Intended by nature to be a lyric soprano and a delicious little butterball, she has invented a grand manner of her own and built up her voice to match. One can regret it, for she has acquired force at the expense of sweetness, but at the same time must admire and enjoy her thorough command, vocal and dramatic, of the spinto roles she essays. Nevertheless, it was as young Lauretta and in an effortlessly seductive account of "O mio babbino caro" that she was most enchanting. (She managed to hold the house silent and attentive, too much moved to crash in with applause, after Angelica's "Senza mamma.") At this performance, Frank Guarrera was the admirable Schicchi.

The *Otello* that opened in Houston a few weeks ago is a production shared by the opera companies of Houston, Washington, San Diego, and Seattle. By Peter Wexler it has been designed to fit the stages and stage equipment of the four theaters concerned, and plays in a "one-truck décor" that can be transported with ease and stored in its truck when not in use. The idea is good, but Mr. Wexler's set itself is not especially distinguished, or helpful to Verdi's opera. A round central platform, thrust forward over the footlights, proves as cramping to the flow of action as such constructions on anything less than the Bayreuth scale generally do. The vertical component is a kind of large rope-strung loom, shifted about from place to place between scenes. Behind all this, a gallery traverses the stage, set too far back to be of much practical use; Desdemona walks across it to be greeted by the (in this production, invisible) chorus of Cypriots, in Act II, and Iago and Cassio cross it in the course of the "handkerchief" conversation. One scenic effect is striking: at the arrival of the Venetian envoys, in Act III, the stage fills very quickly with a mass of people costumed in brilliant red. This is the strong stroke in Fabrizio Melano's stage direction. Its weakest stroke is Othello's first entrance: he stumbles up through a hole in the stage, and after his "Esultate!" he stands about, shaking hands with the company and receiving their congratulations. "Esultate!" should be a blaze of passing glory, a pause in the warrior's progress before he enters the citadel. Mr. Melano was Franco Zeffirelli's assistant in the Met production of *Otello*, and has inherited the quaint notion that Iago was not only ensign but also librarian to Othello.

Two of the individual performances were exceptional. Desdemona is a role that evidently lies very well on Evelyn Lear's voice; her singing and acting alike were richly colored, subtly molded, and affecting. And Sherrill Milnes was a powerful, impressive Iago. The company had Othello troubles: James King was stricken shortly before the première; Jon Andrew sang that, and then he, too, was stricken; Glade Peterson, the hero of the English-language performances that Houston alternated with its original-language presentations, stepped in for the second Italian performance, singing in English—and so sang Othello three days running. I was at the third Italian performance, when Herbert Doussant undertook the role, not inadequately; Othello's quick, keen suffering was movingly portrayed. The Houston chorus, prepared by Conoley Ballard, sang with force and fervor. Julius Rudel's conducting was skillful and sure. The opera was given with two large cuts: twelve pages of vocal score were missing from the Act II ensemble, and twenty-nine from the Act III finale.

One has come to expect performances by the Opera Company of Boston, conducted and staged by Sarah Caldwell, to provide operatic adventure on a very high level; to be rough at the edges, perhaps, since the Orpheum Theatre is no opera house and the orchestra and chorus are not full-time professionals attached to the company, but always inspired by an inner force that prompts a sharper, more intense experience of the work concerned than mere professional routine, on however smoothly accomplished a level, can do. All other productions I had seen of Berlioz's *Benvenuto Cellini* and of Bellini's *I Capuleti e i Montecchi* paled before the spirited Boston presentations of those works. So I expected Miss Caldwell's *Fidelio*, last week, to be overwhelming—but it was not. On the first night, there were too many flawed performances and too many miscalculations for any grand vision of Beethoven's opera to stir and elevate mind and spirit. Perhaps it suffered from its director's divided attentions: the day before the première she was in New York, conducting *La traviata* at the Metropolitan; the staging was credited jointly to her and her associate director David Gorin. On a simple level, the Leonore, Teresa Kubiak, did not know her role securely; twice—in the first section of the aria and again in the Act II trio—she broke down.

More seriously, she gave little sign of possessing the moral, intellectual, and emotional stature of a true Leonore; there was a strong, shiny voice to admire, and not much else. Jon Vickers is the great Florestan of our day, but he needs discipline, not encouragement. Miss Caldwell allowed him to overexpress, overinflect, overact. He chewed up as much of the scenery as his chains would let him reach. In spoken dialogue, he sounded like a rhetorical Welshman in full flood. The musical phrases were distorted by the weight of passion with which he bore down on them. Don Pizarro was undercast; Richard Van Allan's bass-baritone is too light for the role, and the weakness was compounded by his being stationed, for the aria, on a rampart walk high above and toward the back of the stage. The noble Don Fernando was played as a rosy-cheeked old fuddy-duddy and had a voice to match. When the final chorus, some onstage, some in the aisles of the theater, some in the stage boxes, began to throw down rose petals, and Leonore and Florestan were hoisted up on the crowd's shoulders like football heroes, it seemed for a dreadful moment as if Miss Caldwell meant to make fun of the happy ending. Pizarro had the whole of the Harvard Glee Club in his cells; as scores of tousle-headed youths emerged, acting very badly, his prison seemed to become one for juvenile delinquents. Joseph Evans was a charming Jaquino. Donald Gramm gave a dry, cleverly pointed portrayal of Rocco. But the star of the show was the Marzelline of Magdalena Falewicz, a lyric soprano from the Berlin State Opera, whose voice is clear and bright and full, and who joined her notes into smooth, shapely, lively phrases.

March 1, 1976

REFLECTIONS

When an important composer who for years has worked only with the "abstract" imagery of instrumental music returns to words, the result is likely to be arresting. And when that composer is Elliott Carter and the words he sets are by Elizabeth Bishop, two masters of rhythm and of imagery meet. Carter's latest composition, *A Mirror on Which to Dwell*, is a setting of six poems by Miss Bishop, for soprano and an instrumental ensemble of nine players. The first performance was given on Tuesday of last week, in Hunter College Playhouse, by the Speculum Musicae, who commissioned the piece, and Susan Davenny Wyner. Carter has alternated poems of observation and description and poems founded on the affections. That Wordsworthian distinction does not mean that Miss Bishop's descriptive poems are not emotional or that her poems of troubled passion are not illumined by images of things seen; but there is a difference between "Anaphora," "Sandpiper," and "View of The Capitol from The Library of Congress," the first, third, and fifth of the poems Carter has chosen, and "Argument," "Insomnia," and "O Breath," the other three, and his music reflects the difference. Music has many abilities, and among those it may employ when brought to bear upon a poem are the heightening of emotion, the intensification of the poet's prime or incidental imagery, and the sustaining of simultaneous images in a way that mere words cannot so readily achieve. Someone who speaks, say, the line "I see the mountain peaks before me" can do so in accents of dread or of exultation, but he can hardly convey by his inflection of those words that he is at the same time thinking of a fair maiden he left behind in the valley below, several strophes back. Such communication is a musical commonplace. More: a singer with instrumental accompaniment can by his utterance of that single line let his listeners know that he not only sees the mountain peaks before him but anticipates meeting there a fearsome dragon who guards a magic ring that the singer plans to secure for the fair one left behind in the valley below. A melodic phrase, a harmony, a rhythm, an instrumental color—any and all of these can express "fearsome dragon," "magic ring," and "fair maiden." The composer who adds music to words has an invisible chorus to echo, amplify, elaborate on, perhaps even contradict the plain sense of the text. His resources are almost limitless. The singer can fall silent while the music makes explicit the course of an interior monologue. In a calm melody, he can protest that calm has re-entered his soul—while a nagging accompaniment figure proclaims that he lies. That happens in Gluck's *Iphigénie en Tauride*. In the last scene of Bellini's *I puritani*, a simple, beautiful musical reminiscence tells us—though the words do not—that Elvira is recalling the dawn of what should have been her wedding day. By unstable harmonies, Mozart can throw into question an apparently serene moment of reconciliation. Musical allusiveness— not just the plain labeling of objects or emotions but the complex play of thought upon thought, of one idea passing into another—was brought to its highest pitch of development by Wagner. The procedures involved were implicit from the moment man began to sing to accompaniment, and their application is not only operatic. All song composers use them.

"Sandpiper" is the most picturesque of the songs in Carter's *A Mirror on Which to Dwell*. When I first read the poem, I assumed that the bird had been watched on the sea-marge of Jamaica Bay, running through the ripples of the retiring waves, undisturbed by the monstrous mechanical birds roaring in and out of Kennedy Airport ("The roaring alongside he takes for granted, / and that every so often the world is bound to shake"). But perhaps simply the Atlantic breakers are meant. In any event, Carter lets the lines pass, so to speak, and builds the song on the double imagery of the quick, finical bird, intent on the observation of what lies between his toes, and the motion of the huge slow sea. (Beneath the poem there seems to lurk Blake's line "To see a World in a Grain of Sand"; the words "Blake," "sand," "world," and "grains" rise up through Miss Bishop's lines to be assembled, almost subconsciously, in the listener's mind.) The surface imagery of the song is a rapid, delicate piping on the oboe, at once onomatopoeic and evocative of the bird's movements. Double-bass, cello, and chords low on the piano evoke the long flat beach and the long slow swell of the water, a sheet unbroken except where it hisses on the sand. Carter's favorite care for investigating the results of two kinds of musical gait, simultaneous but not synchronous, illumines the poem. The prowess of the Speculum oboist, Steve Taylor, enabled the composer to use most effectively the very high notes, the color changes in the course of repeated-note calls produced by alternative fingerings, and the mysterious chords that have recently been added to the repertory of sounds achievable on the instrument. "View of The Capitol from The Library of Congress" describes a scene that I, a tree-lover, had contemplated with pleasure before ever reading the poem, and adds to it a fancy that will enliven the sight for me next time I visit Washington: that, when the Air Force Band plays hard and loud on the east steps but "the music doesn't quite come through," it's because "the trees must intervene, / catching the music in their leaves / like gold-dust, till each big leaf sags." The fancy lends itself to musical depiction: *maestoso*, the scene is set; *quasi da lontano*, piccolo, oboe, high clarinet, side drum, and big bass drum strike up, and snatches of their music, but snatches only, "come through." "Anaphora" opens the composition with a blaze of energy. I'm not sure where Miss Bishop lived at the time, that each day should begin "with birds, with bells, / with whistles from a factory," but it seems to be a New York morning light she describes, white-gold, energetic. The paean turns to lament; the declamation grows heavy; time is stretched; and Carter's music stresses the repetitions—"instantly, instantly falls . . . mortal / mortal fatigue . . . endless / endless assent"—that give the poem its title.

I include "Insomnia" among the love poems because its last words suddenly color the conceits of a looking-glass world where all is reversed, left is right, shadows are body—a world where (the final phrase, breaking the established rhyme scheme, catches one by surprise) "you love me." But the poem begins with an image, "The moon in the bureau mirror," and this has prompted Carter to a high, sustained, quiet-shining music for piccolo and violin, disturbed by a restless flickering from marimba and viola. To these two kinds of motion the voice, in rhythms determined by the verse, adds a third; for much of the time the soprano voice is the bass line of the ensemble. The composer sustains his initial imagery throughout the song; I am not quite sure whether his ending fully reflects what happens in the poem, when the carefully controlled Audenesque meter ("So wrap up care in a cobweb / and drop it down the well") collapses, and emotion is no longer to be ordered by poetic discipline.

The two kinds of movement in "Argument" are a rhythmic interchange between piano and bongos, and occasional sustained notes from the voice or sustained chords from the instruments which seem to pick up the phrases "all that land / beneath the plane" and "dim beaches deep in sand / stretching indistinguishably." The verse moves in lines long and short, rapid and then suddenly arrested; so does the music. The words "Days" and "Distance" punctuate the poem, and the music emphasizes the repetitions by setting them always to the same notes. "O Breath," the final song, is marked *tranquillo*; the instrumental music is tranquil while the vocal line moves in soft rapid steps and breaks into roulades of quiet rapture. The effect is as of intense, troubled contemplation, with observant eyes and a quivering heart, of a sleeping and beloved form.

Only the first and fifth songs use the full ensemble: flute (also piccolo and alto flute), oboe (also English horn), clarinet (B-flat, E-flat, and bass instruments), percussion (vibraphone, marimba, side drum, bass drum, bongos, suspended cymbal, triangle), piano, violin, viola, cello, and double-bass. "Argument" is for bongos and piano, flute and clarinet, and the lower strings. "Sandpiper" is for oboe, piano, and strings. "Insomnia" is for piccolo, marimba, and the upper strings. "O Breath" uses the three low wind instruments, the strings, and soft, shuddering rolls on cymbals and bass drum. The vocal line spans two octaves, from the B below the staff to the B above; it is rhythmically intricate but "grateful" to sing—or at any rate Miss Davenny Wyner made it sound so, in a performance at once intelligent, expressive, and beautiful. The playing of the Speculum Musicae, conducted by Richard Fitz, was superb. The problems of balancing voice and a large "solo" ensemble are formidable, but in the hall they were solved. (Not so by the WNYC engineers, to judge by a tape recording made from the broadcast of the performance.) The program book, twenty-four pages long, contained no program notes, but, rightly, a text sheet for the poems was provided and the lights were left up. The work lasts about twenty minutes, and I am eager to hear it again.

March 8, 1976

A SONG TO GRACE PENELOPE

Many operas have been woven around Penelope, and at least two of them merit a place in the repertory: Fauré's *Pénélope* and Monteverdi's *Il ritorno d'Ulisse in patria*. Fauré's opera still awaits an American staging. Three scenes of Monteverdi's were semi-staged at the B. de Rothschild Foundation for the Arts and Sciences, in New York, twenty years ago, and there have probably been fuller versions here since then. Last week, the piece was produced by the New York City Opera—an important presentation of a noble and beautiful composition. For *Il ritorno d'Ulisse* is at once a milestone in the history of opera and a musical drama that—provided the singers and the listeners understand the language in which it is performed—speaks directly across the centuries to modern ears. Monteverdi's expressed aim was directness, and the portrayal of human emotions in a manner that made men not just perceive but sympathetically feel them. He played a leading role in the early adventures of the new medium, opera, which set out to recapture the expressive power of Attic drama—the medium that soon dominated, and has continued to dominate, all other forms of musical composition. With the poets who provided his texts he was exigent, as Mozart, Verdi, and Richard Strauss were with theirs. Myth, romance, comedy (he wrote the first comic opera, *La finta pazza Licori*—lost, alas!), epic, and history he claimed in turn for opera. For the first two decades of its existence, opera's concern was almost entirely with Ovidian mythology: Apollo and Daphne, Orpheus and Eurydice, Cephalus and Aurora, Ariadne, and Andromeda were its dramatis personae (and Monteverdi's *La favola d'Orfeo* was its highest achievement). During the next twenty years, heroines like Ariosto's Angelica and Alcina and Tasso's Erminia and Armida joined the company. (Monteverdi's dramatic works of the time—all but *Il combattimento di Tancredi e Clorinda*—are lost.) Then, in 1641, Virgilian and Homeric subject matter appeared: Francesco Cavalli's *Didone*, Monteverdi's lost *Le nozze di Eneo con Lavinia*, and his *Il ritorno d'Ulisse*. The following year, classical history was drawn on for the first time, in Monteverdi's *L'incoronazione di Poppea*.

Like *Poppea*, *Ulisse* was composed for the Venetian public theater. The central characters are two, not four, yet the subject is larger and the scope more ambitious. A score was discovered only in the late nineteenth century, in the Vienna National Library. It was published only in 1922. (A microfilm of the Vienna manuscript is in the Juilliard Library.) The music drama, as set out in that seventeenth-century copy score, unfolds in three spacious acts. Since Giacomo Badoaro's libretto is based closely on the *Odyssey*, the gods have a large part to play; although Monteverdi's and Badoaro's chief concern is with the intensely personal scenes that surround Ulysses' homecoming, they never forget, nor can we, that this is the final episode of the Trojan adventure. By the close of Act II, the great bow has been bent and the suitors have been slain, but still there can be no rest for Ulysses and Penelope while the gods remain angry. And therefore, before the final duet of reunion, there is a divine council of Minerva, Juno, Neptune, and Jove, with a chorus sounding from the heavens and another from the sea. Then, in sharp contrast, a very human scene for Eurycleia, Ulysses' old nurse; and so the finale—where reconciliation is still impossible, on the plane of human psychology, until Penelope, who for so long has hugged hope to her that she can hardly relinquish it, even to embrace its fulfillment, learns at last to reopen a heart that for twenty years has been pent. Badoaro's adaptation and condensation of Homer for the lyric stage is a model of its kind. His chief change is to the characters of Eurymachus and Melantho: not a rude suitor and the saucy hussy who becomes his mistress but a young couple (she rather like Despina in the advice she gives her mistress) who in playful love scenes amid the graver passions provide contrast—like the Damsel and the Valet in *Poppea*. His chief expansion is of Homer's lines in which Telemachus tells his mother that in Sparta

> *Argive Helen* I beheld, whose charms
> (So Heav'n decreed) ingag'd the Great in arms.

In the opera, this becomes a full scene. Telemachus tells his mother at length, and ardently, how after one look in Helen's eyes he understood that for such a glance a ruined world was small price to pay. "Beltà troppo funesta," Penelope exclaims with a flash of sudden anger, and, remembering what Helen's beauty has cost her, she chides her son. (Very little of this scene remains in the City Opera version.)

Minerva aids both Ulysses and his son, and the gods help to determine their destiny. But Penelope is a woman alone. Only courage has sustained her. Halting Time, fickle Fortune, and importunate Love have been her adversaries, and they are symbolic personages in a prologue. After this prologue, the drama proper opens with Penelope's great lament: a long scene, the longest solo in the opera, sorrowful, reproachful, passionate, steadfast, sometimes declamatory, sometimes melodious, and punctuated by a refrain, "Torna, deh torna, Ulisse!," which leaps like a flame of longing and love. Penelope is at the heart of the opera.

In 1607, Monteverdi's court opera *Orfeo* summed up all the styles available to a composer at the time. Thirty-four years later, after much madrigal experiment and the new developments of opera as a popular entertainment, his *Ulisse* did the same, with recitative declamation, ariosi, brief arias, invention in all the madrigalesque genres, canzonettas,

311

duets, and ensembles—in every manner except the overelaborate. The mustering of these elements, the formal shaping of the scenes, is masterly, but the musical forms seem to have been molded by the dramatic pressures. (For example, a rondo is made of Penelope's steadfast refusal to her suitors' very individual pleas—until at last, driven beyond patience, she cuts short the rondo refrain and breaks into declamation.) Librettist and composer delight in bringing characters together—Ulysses and Minerva, Ulysses and the swineherd Eumaeus, Ulysses and his son —so that the confrontations may flow from dialogue into eloquent duet and then back to dialogue again. There are many characters. There is incident both supernatural and human. There are, as mentioned, scenes of lighthearted love to set off the profound emotions of heroine and hero. There is comedy at court with Irus the stuttering glutton. (He provides opera's first example of the heroic style parodied.) The gods are sharply characterized in their various utterances. There is spectacle in their aerial and submarine entrances. There is action in the scene of the bow and the slaying of the princes. Penelope's three principal suitors are vividly and distinctly etched. So are Eumaeus and Eurycleia. All this richness surrounds a steady dramatic progress. Act I is based on two great monologues, for Penelope, and then for Ulysses, newly landed on Ithaca. Each of them is near to despair, not knowing that their trials are almost done. Step by step, amid scenes of increasing tension, the long-parted husband and wife move closer, until at the very last their voices join in a duet. Musically, the symbolism of this final duet is beautiful: in successive entries one voice rises, the other descends, to the note D; in thirds, the two voices circle it, and then they close on a unison.

The City Opera uses a practical performing edition of *Ulisse* prepared by Raymond Leppard for Glyndebourne and first done there in 1972. This saves it the trouble of having to take any what might be called "creative decisions" of its own; Mr. Leppard's edition is one of proved effectiveness. Clearly written scores and tidy orchestral material showing just what is to be played and sung are available, and for a hard-pressed repertory company that is a boon. The City Opera has simply cut still further an already abridged edition of the score, and redistributed the two acts of the Leppard version as three, displacing the first Melantho/ Eurymachus exchange from its original position, after Penelope's monologue, to the start of the new second act. Any detailed discussion of what Leppard did to Monteverdi and of what the City Opera, by its cutting and shuffling, has now done to Leppard is bound to be tricky and can perhaps be most clearly set out under three heads, representing Mr. Leppard's three main editorial activities: transposition, instrumentation, and structural alteration.

TRANSPOSITION: The Glyndebourne edition was to a large extent made for (or in dance parlance "on") the Glyndebourne cast. In particular, the role of Penelope was composed—the word is hardly too strong—for Janet Baker; it was freely transposed and rewritten in order to show her voice and her art in their fullest glory. That it achieved: Miss Baker's memorable Penelope, one of the great operatic performances of our day, could be deemed a justification in itself for all that Mr. Leppard had done. At the written pitch of the manuscript, Penelope is a contralto role, ranging from the B-flat below the treble staff to the C on it, rising a tone above that only for some emotional outbursts, and settling often on or around middle C. It would be difficult to find a Penelope who, held to that tessitura, would not begin to sound dull and heavy. I understand why Janet Baker cried out, and why at the State Theater Frederica von Stade cries out, "Ecco l'arco d'Ulisse" an octave higher than shown in the original score. But then Penelope's phrase starts to climb, and Mr. Leppard gets into difficulties: in sustained octave transposition it would climb out of the mezzo range; a sudden octave drop would be awkward. So, having put those three measures up an octave, Mr. Leppard puts up what follows by just a fourth, recomposing Monteverdi's harmonic sequence. The role of Ulysses, although written in the tenor clef, centers on middle C, reaching climaxes on a few G's above it, and therefore it lies comfortably for a baritone—especially a Pelléas baritone such as Richard Stilwell, who has sung the part at Glyndebourne and sings it now at the State Theater. But if Penelope's line is lifted in the final duet, she will draw a baritone Ulysses too high. Mr. Leppard's answer there is to take Penelope up a fourth and Ulysses *down* a fifth. So their thirds become tenths, and, instead of uniting on a unison, Penelope and Ulysses remain an octave apart. The effect of two voices joined, at the last, is lost.

The principle of tactfully tailoring a role to suit some remarkable performer is unassailable. More dubious that of tailoring later casts to suit the *édition d'occasion* thus created. But in practice all is well at the State Theater, for Miss von Stade fits perfectly into Janet Baker's role. She was engaged at Glyndebourne, as Cherubino, when *Ulisse* was revived there in 1973; many inflections, and her bold, open way of crying certain phrases, suggest that she listened attentively to Miss Baker's great Penelope. At the State Theater, on the first night, the long monologue was curiously lifeless, because, I think, Miss von Stade sang it quite simply too slowly, and had not mastered the subtle tempo relations between sections that move and flow in response to Penelope's changing thoughts yet at the same time build a formal pattern. Thereafter, she was noble, eloquent, passionate, brave. Her lustrous voice rang out fearlessly, or glowed with tenderness. A slim, tall, regal figure, she stood like a Pisanello princess. She declaimed the text freely, and with fire. Mr. Stilwell made an ideal Ulysses. His timbre is distinctive yet hard to describe—not one of those richly resonated Italianate baritones of dark color, nor a big straightforward voice in the grand American tradition. The tone is forward, clean-cut, and agreeably grained; it focuses on the words, so that both words and sound are projected with uncommon vivacity. His physical presence, like his vocal, is alert.

INSTRUMENTATION: Seventeenth-century opera scores cannot just be played as they stand. The music of this particular *Ulisse* is by Monteverdi-Leppard, but that of any performance of the opera must be, to some extent, by Monteverdi-another, since the vocal lines are accompanied only by continuo instruments, and for this accompaniment the original score provides only a bass line. At the least, someone must decide whether the chords supplied above this line are to be major or minor, and there should be some prior agreement about which of the continuo instruments (harpsichord, harp, reed organ, wood organ, lute, archlute, etc.) are to play in any particular passage. Mr. Leppard has made these decisions, and then gone on to write out the continuo parts in detail. In the manuscript, fuller-textured music, in five parts, is sometimes prelude, postlude, or punctuation to the sung phrases but is never coincident with them, except in four measures when Irus cries "Son vinto" in his wrestling match, and at Ulysses' triumphant "Alle morti, alle stragi, alle ruine" at the end of Act II. (Generally, these "orchestral" passages were first set down as a bass line only; the staves for the upper parts were filled in later, in a different ink.) Mr. Leppard, like most previous editors of *Ulisse*—among them Vincent d'Indy, Luigi Dallapiccola, Nikolaus Harnoncourt, and Dennis Russell Davies, who submitted a score of Act I as his Juilliard doctoral thesis—has composed new orchestral accompaniment to a good deal of the singing, when it moves from declamation into lyrical meters. Some like it, some don't. I like some of it but think several passages too lushly Straussian to be acceptable. Beyond dispute is the fact that all this writing-out tends to stiffen the singers' declamation and straitjacket the accompanists. *Ulisse* came to Glyndebourne as the fourth in a series of seventeenth-century operas, all Leppard-adapted, and by then the performers of the company knew the style. Mr. Leppard himself conducted, and he is an adept at getting singers to declaim freely and continuo players to accompany as if moved only by the singers' breath and their emotions. Much of *Ulisse* no more needs a conductor than do a lieder singer and her accompanist. But in the State Theater production, except when Miss von Stade and Mr. Stilwell were singing, one tended to feel bar lines where they should not be felt, and to be conscious of Mario Bernardi, on the podium, keeping the performance together—most ably and sensitively, but still as a link between singers and players who should be in direct contact. In practical terms, such direct contact calls for a more

314

intimate house and for longer rehearsal than the City Opera can probably provide. Most charges made against Mr. Leppard's editions can
be defended on practical grounds. They should nevertheless continue
to be brought. Gluck-Wagner, Mozart-Strauss, and Handel-Prout were
once similarly defended. Only by bearing the ideal in mind can the
limits of the possible be progressively raised.

STRUCTURAL ALTERATION: The Vienna score is divided into three
acts. The seven manuscript librettos that survive in Venice are in five
acts, and only one division coincides with those of the score: Ulysses'
slaying of the suitors ends an act (II of the score, IV of the librettos).
Leppard's edition is in two acts, broken where the Venice Act II ends,
after the reunion of Ulysses and Telemachus. The City Opera production is divided into three acts, but not those of the Vienna score; the
slaying of the suitors, instead of bringing down the second-act curtain,
is shifted to the start of Act III, and Act II ends with—and thus throws
into prominence—a luscious aria that is not by Monteverdi at all but
was composed by Mr. Leppard to build up Penelope's role. Any further
discussion of the relation between Venice and Vienna would involve
considering crossings-out and different-colored inks—and speculation.
But, in practical terms, I believe that (outside the special conditions of
Glyndebourne, where the long dinner interval favors a two-act structure) the three acts of the Vienna score form the most shapely and
effective drama, and would urge the City Opera to adopt those divisions,
as they easily could do when *Ulisse* is revived.

Mr. Leppard dropped one scene altogether—the second encounter
of Melantho and Eurymachus—and otherwise kept something of everything and just about nothing complete except Penelope's monologue
and Irus' and Eurycleia's arias. (These arias, however, have been drastically shortened by the City Opera.) A measure-by-measure checking
of his score against the original can be revealing. In the Vienna Act II,
Scene 3 (Telemachus and Ulysses), for example, we find four measures
by Leppard, then ten of Monteverdi's measures in, six out, three in,
fifteen out, seven in, four out, four by Leppard, six of Monteverdi's in,
nine out, eight in, nineteen out, three in, twelve out—and so into the
father-and-son duet. (Mr. Leppard's own measures, it should in fair-
ness be said, are here no more than appropriate and necessary flourishes
to accompany scenic effects.) Each separate cut can perhaps be defended, but, here and elsewhere, the sum of them significantly alters the
pacing of the scenes. Some of the cuts leave rhymes hanging in midair.
Others spoil the bending-of-the-bow episode: the three suitors address
themselves to that task with three elegant invocations, respectively to
Cupid, Mars, and Beauty; Mr. Leppard retains only the third, which
refers verbally to the others. Since Glyndebourne, he has restored two

315

exquisite little madrigalian duets, for Ulysses and Eumaeus, which he omitted before. He should also have let poor Pisander and Amphinomus have their invocations back.

The further cuts made by the City Opera are not happy. Since the divine council (or what Mr. Leppard left of it) has been omitted altogether, the early appearances for Neptune and Jove might as well be scrapped, too. Minerva, who seems at times almost an embodiment of Ulysses' resource and daring, a young Brünnhilde of his will, is the only essential Olympian; to bring on other gods for a moment in Scene 2 and then drop them is dramatically ineffective. In fact, since the main force of *Ulisse* lies in the human drama, the allegorical prologue might as well also be junked. Such cuts would diminish the work, but if for practical reasons it has to be shortened, then large clean cuts of complete scenes are preferable to the numerous mid-scene snicks.

The production, first seen in Washington in 1974, is mounted in a simple toy-theater setting, by Douglas W. Schmidt, with wings and backcloth in navy blue, decorated with a silver pattern. Aerial machinery is reduced to a simple chariot that can move from side to side or up and down. (The wondrous baroque elaboration that Peter Hall and John Bury devised for the Glyndebourne première hardly lends itself to repertory use.) Ian Strasfogel's staging moves well. The characters are crisply defined. The menace at court and the mounting tensions are strikingly portrayed. The final tableau—a return to the starry skies in which the opera opened—is a shade cheap, and might be read as Mr. Strasfogel's comment on Mr. Leppard's orchestration. (In a similar vein, Colin Graham showered down golden spangle on the final duet of the Monteverdi-Leppard *Poppea*.) Most of the singing is accomplished. Kathleen Hegierski's charming Melantho and Henry Price's keenly projected Telemachus are outstanding.

As always, after seeing and hearing and enjoying a Leppard "realization" I have mixed feelings. That his edition of *Ulisse* is the most effective available for use in a modern theater, the easiest to bring off without much special study, I have no doubts. In some ways, it is also the most stylish; Harnoncourt, too, scores Monteverdi's arioso passages for singing strings, and he goes further, by composing brilliant trumpet obbligatos around the gods and threading a pastoral oboe line through the music of Eumaeus. But he doesn't make such disfiguring cuts. As an editor, he is not impelled by those imperatives—Keep things moving! Join things together!—which underlie some of what Mr. Leppard does. And he is more scrupulous about rewriting Monteverdi's lines. Yet it is the eminently performable Leppard editions that have brought Monteverdi and Cavalli to the stages of the world. And for that the world must be grateful.

March 15, 1976

GOING TO THE DEVIL

Since music lends itself to the depiction of otherworldly scenes, opera composers have from early days been dealers in magic and spells, in prophecies, witches, and knells. The music of incantation was used to powerful purpose by Cavalli (*Ormindo, Giasone*), Purcell (*Dido and Aeneas*), Handel (*Alcina*), Gluck (*Armide*), Mozart (*Lucio Silla*), Verdi (*Macbeth, Un ballo in maschera*), Busoni (*Doktor Faust*), and many others; the list could easily grow long. The music of demonic possession sounds strongly in Prokofiev's *The Fiery Angel* and Krzysztof Penderecki's *The Devils of Loudun*. Opera's first-class assortment of magic, with effects that are comic or tragic, includes comic conjurations from Sullivan, Humperdinck, and Prokofiev (*The Love of Three Oranges*). The most famous witch-burning in opera takes place before curtain-rise, and is described by Azucena, in *Il trovatore*. The latest witch opera is *Bilby's Doll*, by Carlisle Floyd, which had its première in Houston last month.

The source of the libretto, written by the composer himself, is Esther Forbes's novel "*A Mirror for Witches*, in which is reflected the Life, Machinations, and Death of Famous DOLL BILBY, who, with a more than *feminine perversity*, preferred a Demon to a Mortal Lover. Here is also told how and why a Righteous and Most Awfull JUDGEMENT befell her, destroying both Corporeal Body and Immortal Soul." The book was published in Boston in 1928. It reached the Covent Garden stage in ballet form (with choreography by Andrée Howard) in 1952. The musical version had been shaping in Floyd's mind since, in 1956, two Broadway producers suggested the subject to him as matter for "a serious musical, if not an outright musical drama or opera." But when the time for financing arrived, the producers—Floyd says in a program note—"felt that the book should be re-cast in a more conventional musical comedy mold, and at that point we regretfully went our separate ways." In 1973, he was able to acquire the rights for himself, and *Bilby's Doll* is the result. It is a witch opera with a difference, and the difference can be defined by comparing it with *The Fiery Angel, The Devils of Loudun*, and Robert Ward's *The Crucible*.

Valery Bryusov's novel *The Fiery Angel*, the source of Prokofiev's opera, purports to be a sixteenth-century narrative—"a True Story in which is related of the Devil, not once but often appearing in the image of a Spirit of Light to a Maiden, etc."—and proves to be a piece of thinly veiled autobiography, a study of an unstable, fascinating woman with whom the author had a passionate and desperate love affair—a woman who behaved "as if she were possessed of a devil." The simile is expanded in picturesque historical detail to form a vivid symbolist novel.

Prokofiev, with his wonted dramatic flair, set the surface of the tale—and in the process upset its points of correspondence to a real-life relationship—to form a vivid, theatrical opera. The witchcraft in his *Fiery Angel* has no deeper "meaning"; it is simply a frame for exciting, impressive music.

In Aldous Huxley's *The Devils of Loudun*, the seventeenth-century history of hysterical Loudun nuns and the priest, Grandier, who was burned as their diabolical corruptor, is a stalking-horse for the pursuit of two themes concerned with public and private behavior. In recent years, we have been burning people alive in greater numbers than ever our ancestors did but giving different reasons for doing so. As Huxley puts it:

The charm of history and its enigmatic lesson consist in the fact that, from age to age, nothing changes and yet everything is completely different. In the personages of other times and alien cultures we recognize our all too human selves and yet are aware, as we do so, that the frame of reference within which we do our living has changed, since their day, out of all recognition.

Huxley's other theme is self-transcendence—forms of escape from the ego by means sexual, chemical, artistic, or spiritual. But John Whiting in his play *The Devils* and Penderecki in his opera could make no use of the last (and most interesting) third of Huxley's book, the spiritual adventures of Sister Jeanne and of her confessor, Jean-Joseph Surin, after Grandier has been burned. Penderecki has professed pious and humane intentions for his opera, but it is hard to acquit him of sensationalism. In performance, the audience is invited to join the eager crowds who watched the possessed nuns at their antics, the tearing out of Grandier's fingernails, the administration to Jeanne of a devil-purging enema (holy water given to an accompaniment of screams, then gurgles of pleasure), and Grandier's burning. The text is a sequence of Theater of Cruelty clichés, the music an eclectic (and skillful) sequence of avant-garde devices.

If Huxley's study is at once a history and a parable, Arthur Miller's *The Crucible* is at once a strong play and a parable. About Ward's *Crucible* opera I speak with diffidence, having not heard and seen it in the theater; my impression from the vocal score is of an effective "play-set-to-music" opera, in which the plights of the characters find singing voice but the force of Miller's parable is lessened. In Prokofiev's opera, the supernatural prompts much of the music: little demons whine and mew; mysterious knockings are heard; a Satan theme thunders through the largest ensembles. In Penderecki's opera, the supernatural is used for effects grotesque (as when a deep bass voice sounds from the belly of the possessed Jeanne) or sensational. In Ward's opera, except for an ensemble of mass hysteria in the courtroom scene, manifestations of witchcraft are musically unimportant.

Esther Forbes's *A Mirror for Witches* is a romance. A French orphan whose parents have been burned as witches is adopted by Captain Bilby and brought to New England. Bilby's wife, Hannah, resents her; the townsfolk mistrust her exotic appearance; she herself believes that by her parents she was initiated into witchcraft. The tale is told as if by a seventeenth-century chronicler who believes in witches, and with skillfully handled irony (reflected in the title) the author brings forward, in her narrator's mouth, the evidence that leads to Doll's conviction— evidence to the reader of no more than the unhappy, deluded girl's attempts to find romance. The period is somewhat before the Salem outbreak; Mr. Increase Mather is one of the characters. A link with *The Crucible* is provided by the fact that the accusations of witchcraft are motivated at least in part by malice—from Mrs. Bilby, and from the mother of a youth, Titus, who has courted Doll in vain.

Where Prokofiev would have seized on such episodes as Doll's hallucination, one night in the wood, when before her "a long parade of figures, fiends, witches, warlocks, imps, beasts, familiars, satyrs, and even the beautiful chaste Diana herself, moved in fleshly form: a wicked, most fantastic procession," Carlisle Floyd omits them and eschews any depiction of witchcraft or supposed witchcraft in action (apart from cries from a pair of hysterical children, taught by their mother to fear Doll). But in two scenes he has most delicately mirrored, and with his music enhanced, the irony of the original novel. An escaped pirate, playing upon Doll's credulity, presents himself to her as a demon—and eagerly she welcomes him into her arms. The scenes are consecutive, at the center of the central act. In the first of them, the young pirate, Shad, appears to her lit by the glare of a blazing barn; during the second, in Doll's bedroom, the two enact a childish demonic marriage rite, which Doll recalls from the nonsense with which her head has been stuffed. The action is realistic—nothing supernatural is happening—but the music can suggest to us, as it were, Doll's view of the events and portray her mystic rapture as she surrenders to her demon lover. In these two scenes, Floyd's opera becomes more than a sung play. There are other episodes in which music has more than a merely heightening role; to the "truths" enacted on the stage it adds images of the untruths in which both Doll and her accusers believe. Floyd has altered details of the book. In the third act of the opera—but not in *A Mirror for Witches*— Doll is persuaded that her lover, by whom she is now pregnant, was no more than a human seducer. She is dying in despair—rejected, she feels, by both God and the Devil. The minister, Zelley, determines to give her something to live for; he restores her faith in the demon. The opera reaches its climax in a long duet during which the earnest man of God, deeply troubled, wrings out lie after lie, misdescribing the swarthy real-life Shad by signs—golden hair, blue eyes, a missing finger—that convince Doll her lover was indeed someone else. Her music regains its note of ecstasy: "I am in truth a witch, and my lover a messenger from Satan, a demon from Hell!" She dies, and the curtain falls on Zelley's murmur of "God forgive me."

This is a complicated and effective scene, meet for musical treatment. Both Doll and Zelley are interesting character studies. The others—Bilby, with his more than paternal affection for the girl; the vindictive Hannah, who in Floyd's version has been provided with a final change of heart, too late; the gently romantic Titus—are two-dimensional. I think Floyd claims too much for his work, a Bicentennial commission, when he says, "I believe my opera has a comment to make on our national character and destiny. . . . Can we afford to permit Doll Bilbys to live and flourish among us or, more to the point, can we afford not to? It seems to me that no more crucial question can be asked in this year of celebration." Only in a very loose way can we regard Doll—Floyd's Doll—as a plausible symbol for the artistic imagination, condemned and destroyed by "a world firmly committed to the creation of whatever [is] functional and of practical use." The composer is on firmer ground in declaring that "I choose a subject not for polemical reasons, but because it contains vivid characters in highly charged dramatic situations."

The trouble with *Bilby's Doll* in performance is that for quite long stretches it seems to move rather slowly. On the first night, the opera was deemed long. By the time I saw it—the fifth performance, of six—there had been cuts: nothing very extensive, but several small tucks here and there. If still it hung fire at times, the fault was not of length but of pacing. I said "seems" to move rather slowly because, although examination of the score reveals no particular shortage of passages marked to be played at fairly fast tempi, the apparent gait is slackened by two things: Floyd's fondness for anchoring his harmonic movement on pedal points long sustained, or sometimes over ground basses, and his prevailingly deliberate declamation of the text. The aim, a good one, seems to be that all the words should be apprehended, and it is largely achieved. The word setting is flexible, not tied to the bar lines, natural in its response to what would be the spoken inflections of the text but unnatural, much of the time, in its slowness—sometimes almost Wagnerian in its use of instrumental measures to provide punctuation between sentences, or even phrases. Christopher Keene, who conducted, observed the composer's tempo indications. In some scenes, I felt, he could with advantage have hurried things on a bit. Floyd drops very readily into unhurried, expansive utterance, into arioso declamation with markings like "Lento assai, teneramente." In the last scene of Act II, which reaches its climax as a crowd gathers to see Doll carted off to

Salem jail, there is music that does move fast and can be heard to do so. It is welcome. But it makes one aware of what has been missing.

There are operas (Humphrey Searle's *Hamlet* is an example) that seem to be no more than plays slowed down because the actors are singing instead of speaking; the music adds nothing remarkable (except, in the case of Searle's piece, a powerfully eerie atmosphere for the Ghost scenes). There are operas (the lesser works of Mascagni and Giordano afford examples) that seem to proceed almost entirely in arioso and recitative, aspiring to the condition of lyrical melody but seldom achieving a tune that strikes home with Puccini-like effectiveness. There are operas (Giordano's *Andrea Chénier* is one) where the turnings of the plot lead the characters into situations that demand full-throated lyrical utterance, and obtain it. And operas (like Hans Werner Henze's *The Young Lord*) where the plot itself—concerned with the interaction of different "worlds"—needs music for its manifestation. *Bilby's Doll* falls partly into each of these categories, and precisely into none.

By the Houston Grand Opera the piece was very well performed. Cunningly combining painted backcloths, a two-story saltbox frame, and picturesque detail in the way of furniture and properties, Ming Cho Lee's décor for the six different settings was at once varied, realistic, and romantic. Duane Schuler's lighting was just about the best I have seen on the American operatic stage. David Pountney's direction was dynamic, detailed, unfussy. By the three collaborators the tone of each scene was securely established. Catherine Malfitano, in the title role, was gleaming, vivacious, touching, and credible; her singing spanned a wide range of emotional colors. Act I ends with Doll's version of Azucena's "Stride la vampa"—recalling her parents' death—and Miss Malfitano made much of it. Tom Fox's grave Zelley was impressive, but perhaps a shade light in voice. In a large cast without serious weakness—except for a town crier who had not learned how to cry his news in a way that could be understood—there was especially good work from Joy Davidson as Hannah Bilby, Alan Titus as Titus, and Barrie Smith as his mother. Jack Trussel made a dashing Shad. Mr. Keene was an expert conductor.

March 22, 1976

MUSIC TO ATTENDING EARS

The Celebration of Contemporary Music held this month at the Juilliard School—seven concerts in the course of eight days—was one of the best festivals of modern music I have ever encountered. By "best" I mean most enjoyable, engaging, rewarding, and important for a healthy musical life. True, no new major masterpiece was unveiled; in fact, there were no first performances, though there were some American or New York premières. No particular school or movement was especially favored. There was one piece from the thirties (Roy Harris's Symphony, of 1933, which might as well now be called his First Symphony, since its successors are numbered from two to fourteen) and two from the forties (Carl Ruggles's *Organum* and Wallingford Riegger's *Music for Brass Choir*, both first performed in 1949); for the rest, it was a "celebration" of various musical achievements during the last twenty-odd years. Varèse, whose *Nocturnal* as completed by Chou Wen-chung had its New York première, and Shostakovich, whose Fifteenth String Quartet was given its first professional performance in this country, were the giants from the recent past. Elliott Carter (Third String Quartet and Double Concerto) and Roger Sessions (Third Symphony) were the biggest names among the living. Schoenberg, Stravinsky, Ives, and Copland, having been amply celebrated in recent seasons, were omitted; and the artistic directors of the festival, Peter Mennin and Pierre Boulez, had decided that their own compositions would not be represented.

The New York Philharmonic, the Juilliard School, and the Fromm Music Foundation joined in the venture. The Philharmonic, conducted by Boulez and in one piece by James Levine, gave three concerts—two at full orchestral strength, one in chamber formation. The Juilliard String Quartet, the Juilliard Theater Orchestra, conducted by Walter Hendl, the Juilliard Orchestra, conducted by Sixten Ehrling, and the Juilliard Ensemble, conducted by Richard Dufallo, gave one each. All were held in the Juilliard Theater, which, for everything except late-Romantic music on a very expansive scale, is just about New York's best concert hall. As an opera house it may lack resonance, but when the pit floor is brought up to stage level and the stage is cased in its acoustic shell, when the proscenium opening disappears and it all becomes one room, the sound is bright, warm, open, and immediate. The most delicate tap, tinkle, or whisper can be heard, yet full orchestral climaxes are accommodated without causing pain. (The acoustics were strained to their limits by thirty brass players in the fortissimo climaxes of the Riegger.) Moreover, it is architecturally a pleasing place to be in, not plain or dull. To the Philharmonic and Juilliard Quartet concerts, admission was five dollars. Everything else was free—and "everything else" was more than just the concerts given by the Juilliard student players. Morning and afternoon, rehearsals were open to the public. In Paul Hall, the Juilliard School's recital room (it seats 278), there were afternoon "seminars"—lectures and discussions—on the music to be performed, on musical uses to which computers can be put, and on contemporary musical notation; and on the concertless day there was a "round table" event at which seven of the composers (seated in a row, at a long rectangular table) talked about "Composers in the Twentieth Century." The sharing of work among the four orchestras meant that none was overtaxed; performance levels were kept high.

The last work heard at the Celebration was Carter's Double Concerto. In a program note on the piece, the composer cites as a "literary analog" the close of *The Dunciad*, celebrating the Triumph of Dulness:

> Before her, Fancy's gilded clouds decay,
> And all its varying rain-bows die away.
> Wit shoots in vain its momentary fires,
> The meteor drops and in a flash expires. . . .
> Nor public flame, nor private, dares to shine,
> Nor human spark is left, nor glimpse divine!

Insofar as Carter applies Pope's lines to the close of his own brilliantly animated composition, he commits self-calumny. (But perhaps he intended a wry, oblique comment on the fact that the concerto had its first performance between the papers of a learned international congress.) For many an earlier festival of modern music *The Dunciad* might provide apt texts. The line "See Mystery to Mathematics fly!" could have been printed as an epigraph to programs in the days when total serialization was the mode. Those ordeals devised for critics, in the second book of the poem, to see whether they can listen to the works performed without falling asleep have on occasion been revived during the Warsaw, Palermo, and Royan festivals and at the annual gatherings of the International Society for Contemporary Music—with results similar to those in Pope. But Great Dulness was successfully denied admittance to the New York Celebration. Some of her minions slipped in, it is true, wearing pleasant or ingenious masks to gain initial acceptance. Not every one of the works performed was gripping from beginning to end. But most of them were.

About three-quarters of the music played was written by Americans and one-quarter by Europeans. In an essay for the program book, Mr. Boulez reflected that "solidarity within ethnic groups" had been a phenomenon "strictly the result of local, very temporary necessities"; in another essay, Paul Fromm noted that American music has outgrown any need to be consciously and identifiably American, and that whereas in 1876 a Centennial March was commissioned for the occasion from Wagner, "by now, the flow of musical influence between the United States and Europe has become a two-way street; at times it even seems that more lanes lead away from this country than toward it." An English critic, Bayan Northcott, presented a transatlantic view of American music, and an American critic, Michael Steinberg, a transatlantic view of European music. Among the twenty-three American composers named in Mr. Northcott's essay, ten were played at the festival (Varèse, Cage, Sessions, Carter, Stefan Wolpe, William Schuman, Gunther Schuller, Milton Babbitt, George Crumb, Charles Wuorinen); those he mentioned who were not played include Samuel Barber and Virgil Thomson, Morton Feldman, Arthur Berger, Lejaren Hiller, Steve Reich, Andrew Imbrie, Donald Martino, William Bolcom, Henry Brant, and David Del Tredici. (Composers like Reich, Hiller, and Philip Glass possibly reach a wider, more "central" public in London than they do in New York.) Mr. Steinberg's essay mentioned all the Europeans played except Yannis Xenakis and Aribert Reimann.

From a festival that was by intention a non-doctrinaire general retrospective it is hard to pick any specific "themes" for comment; but at least three of the works played—one by an English, one by an American, and one by a German composer—had traveled Mr. Fromm's two-way street, having been commissioned for performance by a celebrated American soloist with a European ensemble. Peter Maxwell Davies's *Stone Litany: Runes from a House of the Dead* was written for Jan DeGaetani and the Scottish National Orchestra and first heard in Glasgow, at Musica Nova 1973. (Musica Nova, sponsored by the Scottish Orchestra and the University of Glasgow, is another kind of modern-music festival—a week of open rehearsals, lectures, and discussions focused on the single concert of new music that forms its climax. In 1973, the other composers were György Ligeti, Luciano Berio, and Martin Dalby.) *Stone Litany* is a highly organized, picturesque, and very beautiful composition. Its landscape is the prehistoric monuments on Mainland, the largest of the Orkney Islands, where Davies lives, and specifically the great barrow Maeshowe. Vikings broke into the barrow and, probably in the twelfth century, incised graffiti on its stones—phrases like "Lif the Earl's cook carved these runes," "Great treasure is hidden in the northwest," and (aptly and amusingly, the composer, known as Max, uses it to sign off his piece) "Max the Mighty carved these runes." In his setting of these runic inscriptions, our new Max the Mighty says he has "taken liberties . . . assuming that as the texts are in an extinct language (Orkney Norn, a dialect of Old Norse) they will not be readily understood anyway." It seems a fair assumption. The score (published by Boosey & Hawkes at forty-five dollars, which is surely a high price even for a most elegant specimen of musical calligraphy) reveals the precise craftsmanship of the piece. From his early (1957) *St. Michael* Sonata, for seventeen winds (to be given its New York première at a Juilliard School concert this week), Davies has been writing vanguard music—in veins exuberant, irreverent, angry, reflective, poetic —firmly based on such strong things as cantus firmus, canons, and isorhythms, and in recent works he has added to his expressive armory a very delicate control of harmony and a flair for decoration that enhances and does not obscure structure. The ear delights in the sounds of *Stone Litany*, in the "atmospheric" effects suggesting sigh of wind, play of light, and surface movement over grand, ancient stillness. The instrumentation is magical. Davies is not afraid to use that childhood toy the flexatone—a tongue of resonant metal struck by wooden bobbles —or, through the closing pages, wineglasses tuned to E-flat and C, stroked with a damp finger into soft-shining sound. The voice enters as the most colorful and sensitive of all instruments, uttering first the letters of the runic alphabet, and then (as in Harrison Birtwistle's *Nenia*, another piece that Miss DeGaetani does to perfection) singing a duet with itself—one line apparently continuous against the quick flourishes of another. The final inscription is set to a long, seamless melody that starts on the F below the treble staff, climbs to the A above it, and closes on the low F again. By the Philharmonic, under Boulez, and Miss DeGaetani the work was exquisitely performed.

The American transatlantic piece was Earle Brown's *Centering*, for solo violin and ten instruments, commissioned by the London Sinfonietta and first performed by Paul Zukofsky and the Sinfonietta in 1973. It, too, makes delicate, beautiful sounds. The title "refers to the molding of clay on a potter's wheel and to all of the life-things that would be a metaphor of." The form is defined, but how exactly some of its sections are to be filled is left to the violinist and the conductor. In a central cadenza, for example, the composer writes out the soloist's line, indicating its general rhythmic shapes but not the precise timing; the other instruments are allotted various kinds of musical material, from which the conductor selects, cuing in his choices at appropriate moments to accompany the cadenza. Mr. Zukofsky was once more the eloquent soloist, and Boulez was the conductor. The Philharmonic playing was fine-grained; everyone played as if inspired by his responsibilities. The final staff of *Centering* has the indication "Bruno's line"; Bruno Maderna, who for a while had an important part in American musical life, is commemorated. His own *Quadrivium* was played, and also Luciano Berio's *Calmo*, dedicated to his memory.

The German piece, Reimann's *Inane*, was commissioned for Joan Carroll and the Berlin Radio Symphony Orchestra, who gave the first performance, with Lukas Foss as conductor, in Berlin in 1969. The title must presumably be understood in the sense of "empty." It is a long, long monologue, the words by Manuel Thomas, for a woman who wakes from a dream of her baby crying to the realization that the baby was torn from her body before it was born. Remorse, regret for the lost child, and bitter reproach of the father who insisted on the abortion recur in a free rondo form. The instruments provide a kind of "backing" to her agitated declamation. Miss Carroll, a dramatic performer, probably made something of the piece; at the Juilliard, Nadine Herman was a dutiful rather than a moving soloist. *Inane* marked an Expressionist turning point in Reimann's progress from his earlier, somewhat schematic, but pleasing pieces to the freer, wider manner of his opera *Melusine*.

The oldest living composer represented was Roger Sessions, born in 1896. His Third Symphony, of 1957, with its scherzo-fantasy on "Yankee Doodle," Harris's First Symphony, and William Schuman's Seventh Symphony, of 1960, made a general point that could perhaps be made in any country but at festivals of contemporary music seldom is: that while symphony orchestras survive there are likely to be composers who still turn gladly to the traditional four-movement symphonic form and write symphonies worth hearing. At one of the seminars, Boulez remarked that "without new materials we cannot have any new thoughts," and by "materials" he apparently meant the sonic materials of which music is built. Using only traditional materials—the three works were written for the Boston Symphony—Harris, Sessions, and Schuman all seemed to me to have created freshly; and their clear, orderly discourses were good to follow.

The youngest composer represented was Peter Lieberson, born in 1946. His Cello Concerto received its third New York hearing. It was first done at a Group for Contemporary Music concert in 1974, and then, rather less well, at one of the Philharmonic's Prospective Encounters last year. At this third performance, I began to enjoy it, feeling at last that it had shape as well as lively, quicksilver ideas. One of the newest pieces performed was John Cage's "*Score* (40 drawings by Thoreau) *and 23 Parts* (for any instruments and / or voices): *Twelve Haiku* followed by a Recording of the Dawn at Stony Point, New York, August 6, 1974," first played here by the St. Paul Chamber Orchestra during its visit in January. The piece consists of twelve sound flurries, each followed by a silence of equal length; after all that is done, players and audience spend an equivalent time listening in silence to the Stony Point recording (no dawn chorus sang—only one dull, repetitive bird). The piece did not fit well into what Boulez described, in his program essay, as "that benign mode of communication that is called the concert in the form in which we still have it, bequeathed to us at the end of the nineteenth century"; The Kitchen, on Wooster Street, where Cage's *Score* had its first New York performance, is a more suitable ambience. Another piece using tape—not of plain nature sound, however, but carefully composed —was Babbitt's *Correspondences*, in whose performance live string players and synthesized tape combine. (This was also a carry-over from an earlier Prospective Encounters program.) The mathematics of the composition are doubtless formidable; the result, like most of Babbitt's music, is elegant and engaging, both as sound and as structure.

I still have not mentioned all that was done, and should at least record that Jacob Druckman's *Lamia* (see pp. 219–21) was revived, and pleased; and that Charles Wuorinen's glittering *Arabia Felix* (first performed by the Composers Ensemble, conducted by Peter Lieberson, in 1974) can be counted a hit among the works of this prolific, hit-or-miss composer.

The open rehearsals afforded the chance to hear pieces several times over. The audiences could share with the executants the experience of bringing a work to life, finding its shape and sense, and the shirtsleeved working sessions were quite as important as the concerts. The general program book and the daily program leaflets, edited by David Hamilton, were admirable, setting a standard to which other organizations must be held. All the necessary information—basic biography, details of instrumentation and of first performance, publisher, availability of scores and of recordings—was included, along with commentary helpful to the listener. Full texts and translations of any sung words were provided, and the houselights were left up, so that they could be read. The only failing: that curious common American practice of setting out movement headings on one page and the program note on quite another. In the lobby outside, there was a "publishers' table" where scores could at least be examined; next time they should also be on sale, and so should records. The concerts were not broadcast nationally, nor even within the city, as from a comparable European or Australian festival they would have been, increasing the audience of a thousand perhaps tenfold, perhaps a hundredfold. The Juilliard did not open its restaurant as the traditional "festival club" where audience, composers, publishers, and performers gather to drink, eat, and talk before and after concerts and on into the small hours of the morning. Those are also things for next time. That there will be a next time is implied by the legend on the programs: "Inaugural Festival." Perhaps already the other ensembles who could so profitably figure in future celebrations—Speculum Musicae, the Light Fantastic Players, the Composers Ensemble, the Contemporary Chamber Ensemble, the American Brass Quintet, and all the rest— are clamoring to schedule some of their concerts within the framework. In a sense, New York provides a season-long, but scattered and spotty, celebration of contemporary music. The eight-day Juilliard-centered festival brought things into focus, brought people together, and drew full houses for some programs that, if they had been presented in isolation, might have been but thinly attended.

March 29, 1976

EXHUMATIONS

Bellini's last opera, *I puritani*, has beautiful music in it but is perhaps hardly so important a piece as to need production in both of New York's opera houses. The Metropolitan gave it a single performance during the inaugural season, in 1883 (with a very grand cast: Marcella Sembrich, Roberto Stagno, and Giuseppe Kaschmann), and four performances in 1918, and has now revived it in a new production, with Joan Sutherland as its heroine. (The Covent Garden history of the opera is similar; it held the stage there into the 1880s and then disappeared until, in 1964, it was revived for Miss Sutherland.) Meanwhile, the New York City Opera unveiled its version, with Beverly Sills, in 1973. The City Opera production is bold, handsome, and successful. The new Metropolitan production looks old and dusty. It is a late and undistinguished essay in the style the Italians call *riesumazione*. The term was applied first to a repertory—the unfamiliar operas of Donizetti, Bellini, and Rossini—"dug up" for performance in the fifties, and then to a manner of staging devised for their presentation. Just as the singers concerned went back to study early vocal manuals and methods, so the designers and directors went back to study the décors in which the operas had first been performed; then they copied them, or borrowed elements from them, or created designs of their own in a similar style. The masters of *riesumazione* staging were Luchino Visconti and Franco Zeffirelli. Its most literal employment was in the Spoleto production of Donizetti's *Le Duc d'Albe*, in 1959. Donizetti had left the opera unfinished; completed by his pupil Matteo Salvi, it had its first performance in Rome, in Italian translation, in 1882. When Visconti was invited to revive it at Spoleto, he visited Italy's largest theatrical warehouse and asked if there were any old sets in stock for *una piazza, una birreria, un oratorio*, and the other scenes that the opera requires. The stock book was consulted. Yes, he was told, we do have some, but they're *very* old—they were made back in 1882 for something called *Il Duca d'Alba*. Visconti used them.

At its best—in Visconti's Scala production of Donizetti's *Anna Bolena* (with Maria Callas) in 1957; in Zeffirelli's Covent Garden production of *Lucia di Lammermoor* (with Joan Sutherland) two years later—*riesumazione* staging provides beautiful new scenery that looks like beautiful old scenery when it was new: décor that matches the spirit and style of a work, adorning and enhancing its merits without trying to translate them into a modern idiom. Lighting, acting style, stage groupings are at one with the music and the drama, but the result is not simply a meticulous museum reconstruction of a nineteenth-century performance. Artistic imagination and interpretative genius are not fettered by observing the style of a piece as its creators conceived it—any more than a great pianist's are when he plays Schubert sonatas on an instrument that Schubert would have recognized. On the contrary, many things about the work concerned are more likely to make sense, to come to life for modern ears and eyes, than in an anachronistic presentation. But when *riesumazione* is practiced in a dull or routine fashion, as in the Met productions of Rossini's *Le Siège de Corinthe* and now of *I puritani*, the outcome can be deadly—as deadly as a Schubert sonata played by someone who thinks that using the right instrument is enough in itself to insure a living performance. *Le Siège* has scenery by Nicola Benois, derived from the sets that Alessandro Sanquirico designed for the Scala première of the opera, in 1828, and Benois has been prominent in the *riesumazione* movement. His décor for the Visconti *Anna Bolena* already mentioned left its mark on all that followed; his sets for Donizetti's *Poliuto* (with Callas) at La Scala in 1960 and for Rossini's *Semiramide* (with Sutherland) at La Scala in 1962 were closely fashioned after Sanquirico originals. The Met's *Puritani* décor is by Ming Cho Lee: large studies in gray and brown, pretty enough in their way but dispiriting—suggested perhaps by faded illustrations of nineteenth-century scenery rather than by the thought of how such scenery looked when it was fresh. The general effect of dustiness, of old sets hired from a warehouse, is increased by the frequent use of a painted front gauze. (Audiences applauded the moment when the gauze was first removed.) The lighting leaves the singers' eyes in shadow. On the day of the première, Sandro Sequi, who directed the show, was reported in the *Times* as saying, "Let's face it, the plot of *Puritani* is one of the weakest of all operas; it's a *terrible* opera." Dramatically, it *is* rather feeble, but in musical terms the piece holds together. The dramaturgical gaucheness is the direct result of Bellini's shifting numbers about until he achieved the musical sequences he deemed most effective. (For example, a Hymn to Liberty originally intended for the first scene was moved to the end of Act II; in the new position it makes very little verbal sense—but it does bring the curtain down to cheers.) A production should reflect the colors and contrasts of the score. The careful stage directions—and, for that matter, the music itself—suggest clearly enough what Bellini had in mind: a brisk, bright military background played upon by romantic effects of sunrise and of moonlight (the opening horn calls, the composer said, should surge forth "as if from the heart of the mist" while the sun tips the towers of Plymouth citadel), and vigorous political activity as the background to Elvira's unhappy plights. Mr. Lee and Mr. Sequi did not provide an animated spectacle; the chorus trooped on, lined up to sing, and moved about as if by numbers.

To his inexperienced and pliant librettist, Count Carlo Pepoli, Bellini said, "Grave on your mind in adamantine letters: *A musical drama must make people weep, shudder, die through the singing.*" Great singing, which is worthily decked by a good production, can also, of course, triumph over a weak one. Great singing can justify all. But there was little in the Met singing to "make people weep, shudder, die." Foremost among that little must be counted the heroine's long, soaring line in the first-act finale, "Vieni al tempio." Here the full power of Miss Sutherland's voice rang out most splendidly and affectingly. In rapid passage work she did some astonishing and brilliant things. But in slow cantilena, which lies at the heart of Elvira's music, there was cloudiness in the tone. Luciano Pavarotti, as Lord Arthur, was disappointing. The fresh, limpid flow of sweet sound with which he used to delight us now ran jerkily. He broke up the phrases, chopped lines into segments. Giovanni Battista Rubini, the first Arthur, was praised by Henry Chorley for his "honeyed elegance"; Mr. Pavarotti was not elegant, not graceful, in his singing, and handled his solos as if their high notes were what mattered most. (Though he played the only Cavalier of the action, he wore shorter hair than anyone else onstage.) Sherrill Milnes, as Sir Richard, smudged the coloratura of "Ah! per sempre" and was too blunt in "Bel sogno beato." James Morris, as Sir George, was good—even of tone, flexible of line—but he lacked the magnificence of voice and of manner that a *Puritani* bass requires. Richard Bonynge, conducting, accompanied the solo music sensitively but tended to hurry the passages in between.

The *riesumazione* movement (as suggested by several parentheses above) has been closely associated with the tastes and abilities of our star sopranos. Whereas their great predecessors—Giuditta Pasta, Giulia Grisi, Giuseppina Ronzi de Begnis, Carolina Ungher—spent most of their careers singing contemporary music and inspiring the composers of their day to new achievement, Miss Sutherland, Miss Sills, and Montserrat Caballé prefer digging up the past. The latest piece exhumed for Mme Caballé is Donizetti's *Gemma di Vergy*, produced for her in Barcelona and in Naples, and last month given a concert performance, in Carnegie Hall, by the Opera Orchestra of New York. *Gemma*, based on a play by the elder Dumas, has quite an interesting plot. The baritone, the Count of Vergy, has been ordered by Charles VII to divorce his childless wife, Gemma, and get an heir by another marriage. Gemma takes this badly, alternating between grief and rage. The tenor is an Arab slave, Tamas, who loves his mistress (and is on first-name terms with her). The action is violent: in the course of it, Tamas kills three people (Vergy's squire, Vergy, and finally himself), Gemma makes two opportune entrances to prevent earlier murders by Tamas, and Tamas makes one just in time to stop Gemma from stabbing her successor. On the stage, the recurrent bloodthirstiness might seem slightly ridiculous, but it inspired a lively score. The opera dates from 1834; like *Lucrezia Borgia* and *Maria Stuarda*, which came just before it, and *Marino Faliero* and *Lucia di Lammermoor*, which came just after, it belongs to Donizetti's high romantic period, when he did daring and impressive things with form, with orchestration, and with dramatic turns of melody. Two of the duets in *Gemma* are especially striking: in the first the strings carry the lyrical line while the baritone declaims; the second unfolds over a ground bass.

Of the title role Mme Caballé gave a grandly accomplished performance, which reached its artistic climax in the final air: a soft line went looping upward, swelled to a shining fortissimo—and from that peak the soprano dropped precisely, delicately, down into a very soft, exquisitely smooth chest voice for the pianissimo close. Tamas was a new young Spanish tenor, Luís Lima, who has the ring of bright metal in his voice. That metal is not yet refined, but, putting his heart into the delivery of every phrase, declaiming the words with uncommon ardor, he made a winning impression. Louis Quilico sang Vergy's music admirably; though he looked like Mr. Pickwick, he sounded like a grandee. Paul Plishka, as Guido (one of those basses who, like Sir George in *I puritani* and Bide-the-Bent in *Lucia*, are ever on hand for comfort and counsel), was sonorous and secure. Eve Queler conducted with her wonted flair for apt tempi; she never fails to generate excitement. The opera was given in an impure and abridged performing edition by Rubino Profeta. No libretto was on sale. Yet this concert performance of *Gemma* had more life and drama in it than the Met's staged *Puritani*.

The new favorite for exhumation is Jules Massenet. His *Esclarmonde*, with Joan Sutherland, is due at the Met next season; Beverly Sills is to record his *Thaïs* this summer, and a Met production of that, too, is in prospect. Six days before *Gemma*, Miss Queler, also in Carnegie Hall, put on a concert presentation of Massenet's *Le Cid*—a grand, slightly pompous, but very efficiently made opera, whose libretto incorporates many of Corneille's lines. It was given a very loud but stirring performance. In the title role composed for Jean de Reszke's début at the Paris

Opéra, Placido Domingo poured out an unfailing stream of heroic tone, effortless, unforced, and beautiful. As Chimène, Grace Bumbry was, to start with, somewhat hard of timbre at high dynamic levels and somewhat unsteady when the volume dropped, but as the opera progressed her voice became warmer and more even, and in the final scenes she sang nobly. Mr. Plishka, as Don Diègue—originally Édouard de Reszke's role—was commanding. The long opera was cut, but not very much.

April 5, 1976

The Carnegie Hall performances were recorded and published by Columbia, Gemma di Vergy *on M3 3475 and* Le Cid *on M3 34211.*

FESTIVAL CITY

Since a festival is a place and people, not just performances, any account of the Adelaide Festival of Arts must begin with praise of Adelaide, one of the most civilized and agreeable places in the world. The city, the capital of South Australia, was planned in 1837 during the last months of William IV's reign, named for his consort, and built under the young Victoria. Colonel William Light, Surveyor-General to the Colony of South Australia and charged with creating its capital, was a man of nice classical taste. On a coastal plain between the Mount Lofty Ranges and Gulf St. Vincent he laid out a square mile of city, whose principal roads intersect at a central forum; there stand the nineteenth-century equivalents of basilica and temple, with the mercatus close by. On gentle slopes above the city, the Colonel set out long, pleasing lines of residential streets; this is North Adelaide, divided from Adelaide proper by a winding river. No city walls; these two square miles of built-on ground with leafy parks are girdled round (and there are gardens bright with sinuous rills, where blossom many an incense-bearing tree). Beyond the parks, Victorian suburbs; beyond them, the beaches and the mountains. A visitor who judges a city's health by the health and abundance of its trees, the glowing, healthy faces of its citizens, the freshness of the air (and other pleasant features: no tipping; excellent local wines; democratic customs such as sitting beside one's taxi driver) will be happy in Adelaide. The place has not survived into the twentieth century quite unscathed. Though much of it is still only one or two stories high, along King William Street, the principal thoroughfare, and in Victoria Square, the forum, a few tall, crude buildings have been allowed to steal the skyline from spire and civic tower. (Nevertheless, during a busy ten days there I only once had to enter the small prison of an elevator cabin.) The main south road has sprouted shopping complexes and plastic-pennanted automobile lots as beastly as any in America. Only one tramway route survives. But on the whole the impression is of a functioning, alert, and lovable city that has not sacrificed amenity to greedy commerce. It is the perfect place for a festival. In the words of the Beethoven song, one wanders to the events "Mild vom lieblichen Zauberlicht umflossen, Das durch wankende Blütenzweige zittert, Adelaide!"

Festivals celebrated daylong and nightlong through the theaters, halls, museums, galleries, houses, parks, rivers, squares, streets, bars of a town, at some point touching all its residents, are very common, perhaps too common, in Europe; I have not yet encountered one in America. There are other great festival places; York, Amsterdam, and Aix-en-Provence are three that come at once to mind. York, where Constantine was acclaimed emperor, may have nobler buildings, medieval walls, and a history underfoot reaching back nineteen centuries; Amsterdam greater pictures; Aix a more splendid cathedral, the shade of André Campra, and, at festival time, hotter sun than Adelaide. Norwich has its medieval churches; Aldeburgh its Constable skies and, in the concert hall of The Maltings, unrivaled acoustics; Spoleto its spectacular stone-walled vistas and lime-scented streets. But none has anything to compare with the Adelaide Festival Centre. In 1973, the opening of the expensive and extraordinary Sydney Opera House stole the Australian headlines; a few months earlier, without ballyhoo, Adelaide had opened the main theater of its Festival Centre—a building that, roughly speaking, cost a tenth of what the Sydney house did, was built in a tenth of the time, and is ten times as successful. Its individual excellences can be matched elsewhere. There are other theaters that stand in a park beside a river; that are an easy walk from the city center; that have pure sight lines and admirable acoustics, spacious foyers and terraces, well-run restaurants open into the small hours, a well-stocked bookshop, an open box office—not a barred hole in the wall—from which it is a pleasure to buy tickets; that are cordial inside and, outside, sensitively related to their surroundings, with bold planes responsive to changing lights. But the sum of these things—looks, facilities for performance and for the performers, convenience for the audience, setting, climate, and that elusive quality the "feel" of a place, its easy welcome to an audience where neither tiaras nor bare feet cause embarrassment—comes out higher in Adelaide than anywhere else. (Imagine Lincoln Center opening on one side to Central Park while, on the other, lawns slope down to the Hudson; with its subterranean Footlights cafeteria—

which now closes at eight—brought up into the open and turned into a spacious restaurant where, for hours after the various shows are done, Met audiences and Juilliard students mingle.)

The Centre's architects are the Messrs. Hassell & Partners, an Adelaide firm. Plans began with the large auditorium; the festival was already established as a biennial event, but the city lacked a full-scale concert hall and lyric theater. Then the South Australian government decided to enlarge the scheme to include three other performance spaces, and the 1976 Festival, last month, was the first at which they were all in use. The large Festival Theatre seats just under two thousand people in well-raked stalls and two galleries extended down the sides as boxes. The stage is fifty-five feet wide and fifty-two deep, with four times as much wing space. The orchestral pit holds ninety players. For concerts, the pit floor comes up, the proscenium seems to disappear, and (as in the Juilliard Theater) a timbered orchestral enclosure turns stage and auditorium into one resonant hall. I have heard grand opera, full orchestra, and the delicate sounds of solo guitar there, and heard everything well. The Playhouse, home of the South Australian Theatre Company, is a flexible theater that can be used in thrust or proscenium form for drama, chamber opera, recitals, and dance; it seats up to 635 people. The Space is a seventy-foot-square room, galleried round, provided with movable and removable banks of seating, trapdoors, a small orchestral pit, and abundant sound and lighting equipment. New Opera South Australia and Australian Dance Theatre, two Adelaide-based companies, favor it for their more adventurous presentations, and it is much used by children for dramatic activities. Between the Festival Theatre and the Playhouse is a fan-shaped open-air theater, misnamed the Amphitheatre, which can hold about twelve hundred people. Airy foyers, terraces, and walks of interesting shape, open to views of trees, water, and sky, link the four performing sites and are themselves performed in. I'm not alone in my enthusiasm for the place, in finding it superior to other edifices of the kind; let me quote two colleagues who were at the 1976 Festival. Peter Heyworth, of the London *Observer*, remarks that whereas on London's South Bank (where three concert halls, the National Theatre, the National Film Theatre, and the Hayward Gallery are clustered) "the environment is grim and faceless, the arts are acceptable only in so far as they fit preconceived forms, and people are not positively unwelcome so long as they do not sit on window sills or indulge in other unscheduled activities . . . the Adelaide centre seems to open its arms to people and to events. . . . At any hour of the day one is liable to round a corner and stumble on something going on." John Lahr, of *The Village Voice*, declares that "Adelaide's Festival Centre is unlike any of the cultural supermarkets in America which package art like junk food into neat and palatable units to be hastily taken away. The Festival Centre has been built . . . as a place to live in—a space where people come to play, talk, discover, relax. It's an extraordinary building—a vital part of community life." As such, it functions throughout the year. At festival time, there is an influx not of tourist audiences (Adelaide is 10,835 miles from New York, and a few miles farther from London) but of international performers, and activity spreads out from the Centre through the numerous and varied halls and theaters of the city into the parks and gardens. This year, the railway station, in full swing, was taken over for one of Marilyn Wood's cityscape events; at another of them Juliet appeared on the Premier's balcony of Parliament House. At the Art Gallery, there was Fernand Léger, Thai sculpture, and a preview of the collection that is being amassed for the so far unbuilt Australian National Gallery, in Canberra. Parallel to the official program there runs, as at the Edinburgh Festival, the "fringe"; campus troupes and local artists in all mediums display their talents. And so on any day there may be twenty, thirty, even forty events competing for one's attention.

In this Bicentennial Year, American visitors were prominent. The Composers Quartet played Elliott Carter's three string quartets, in successive recitals. Four programs by the Contemporary Chamber Ensemble of New York included Carter's Sonata for flute, oboe, cello, and harpsichord and his Double Concerto, a full evening of George Crumb, and works by Jacob Druckman, Donald Martino, Arthur Berger, and Chou Wen-chung (also those international classics Varèse's *Octandre*, Webern's Concerto, Op. 24, and Boulez's *Marteau sans maître*). A new work had been commissioned for the festival, by two Adelaide patrons, from Charles Wuorinen. It is called *Hyperion*, lasts about fifteen minutes, is for twelve instruments, "proceeds through and is generated by a rotating series of pitches . . . and a reordering/transformation of motivically-treated fragments" (the composer's note), and sounded dense, sometimes sparky, mainly clotted—a satyr to Berger's elegantly wrought Septet, which preceded it on the program. The Ensemble also performed, with chat and explanation, to a hallful of fairly attentive children. Jan DeGaetani captivated all listeners in Crumb's *Ancient Voices* and in *Le Marteau*, and gave two solo recitals as well. Merce Cunningham and Dance Company gave five performances, and brought out a new work, *Squaregame*, which is a sort of company square dance enclosing trios, solos, duos—a happy, sunny invention. All Cunningham's work looked good on the big, open Festival Theatre stage. John Cage gave a solo recital, including *Empty Words*, Part III, which puzzled people, as well it might. Nigel Butterley, an Australian composer and pianist, played, across two recitals, the full set of Cage's Sonatas and Interludes for prepared piano, with mastery. These formed part of a late-afternoon series called "Mozart Plus." Among other plusses of the series were Charles Ives's four violin and piano sonatas, and two Australian string quartets heard for the first time. Colin Brumby's Quartet is not new but dates from 1965, after his study with Alexander Goehr; it is a worthy, well-ordered stretch of serial discourse. Butterley's Second Quartet *is* new—and rapturous, lyrical, joyful. In earlier works—*Laudes, Meditations of Thomas Traherne, In the Head the Fire, First Day Covers, Fire in the Heavens*—this prolific composer has sometimes seemed to me to be so eager in his pursuit of new techniques as to obscure his individual voice. But the Second Quartet is written with serene confidence and is made of beautiful, arresting, eloquent ideas. These chamber recitals were given in Edmund Wright House, once an opulent Victorian bank building, then threatened with demolition and development, and rescued by the South Australian government to serve civic purposes.

As the festival is intended mainly for Adelaide residents, a visitor's disappointment that there should not have been more native music is irrelevant. Australians can hear it the year round; Carter, Crumb, and Cage are more unusual fare. All the same, I think so large a festival could have found a place for a series of all-Australian concerts. There are plenty of pieces worth hearing. Peter Maxwell Davies, after a spell as composer-in-residence at the Adelaide conservatory, wrote that "I dealt with a class of half-a-dozen or so of the most gifted composers I have ever been privileged to teach or learn from." Richard Meale, Peter Sculthorpe, Don Banks, and Malcolm Williamson are the Australian composers internationally known; of the generation born in the forties, Peter Brideoake, Anne Boyd, Barry Conyngham, Alison Bauld, and Ross Edwards are among those whose works and personalities have caught my ear. Only Williamson, whose *Symphony for Voices* was sung by the John Alldis Choir, figured in the festival. There were two new Australian one-act operas, done with spirit by the New Opera troupe: Larry Sitsky's *Fiery Tales* and George Dreyfus's *The Lamentable Reign of King Charles the Last*. But these were lumpen comedies: the first "The Miller's Tale" and a tale from the *Decameron* slung together—a closestool their common feature—and enacted to undistinguished music; the second a ham-fisted political romp. The big operatic production was of Alban Berg's *Wozzeck*, mounted for Adelaide by the Australian Opera. (This is a Sydney-based company, but *Wozzeck* is too big an opera to fit the cramped quarters of the Sydney Opera House.) I missed the show, saw a television tape of it, and feel able to report that by Edward Downes it was wonderfully well conducted, in a performance at once very clear and very lyrical. Lens and microphone revealed finely detailed individual performances, but I am told that in the theater they did not carry strongly. To judge Elijah Moshinsky's production from its showing on the small screen would be unfair.

The chronicle could easily be extended—there was an equally busy theater program, including a clever, lively, affectionate entertainment based on the life of Melba, by Jack Hibberd; rock concerts; films; lectures; an international writers' conference—but perhaps I have said enough to show that the Adelaide Festival, which lasts three weeks, is on the scale of those in Edinburgh and in Holland and has a vigorous character of its own. Two remarkable Australian performers, destined, I guess, for international acclaim, should be noted. One is Reg Livermore, a pop star with a difference. Working with borrowed material—songs by, among others, Billy Joel, Leo Sayer, Charles Aznavour—he assembled it into a new kind of music theater. A protean Pierrot, his white makeup unaltered but everything else—costumes, wigs, personality, stature, sex, voice—mercurial, for nearly three hours, with only a brief interval, he played out aspects of a human comedy. The other is Lyndon Terracini, who took the title role in Hans Werner Henze's "recital for four musicians," *El Cimarrón.* Henze was in Adelaide. With the Saarbrücken Radio Orchestra, he conducted his First Symphony, Second Violin Concerto, *Compases,* and *Kammermusik,* and he coached Mr. Terracini and three young Sydney instrumentalists to give an electrifying performance of *El Cimarrón.* How Mr. Terracini's baritone sounds in straight cantilena I have no idea; as the smoldering, explosive, shrieking, whispering, singing, expansive, fierce, suddenly sly runaway slave he was tremendous. It may be glib but it also is irresistible to see in both Mr. Livermore and Mr. Terracini models of that honest, open vitality and naturalness which make Australian art, and Australians, so invigorating to encounter.

April 12, 1976

THE MATTER OF MEXICO

In Boston, during the three days of a conference convened by the Central Opera Service, three operas were presented whose common theme was the destruction of American civilizations by white invaders: Roger Sessions's *Montezuma,* set in sixteenth-century Mexico, and Robert Selig's *Chocorua* and Paul Earls's *The Death of King Phillip,* both set in seventeenth-century New England. *Montezuma,* while remaining unperformed after its première, at the German Opera in West Berlin in 1964, acquired almost legendary status—as Sessions's magnum opus and, until the Whitman cantata *When Lilacs Last in the Dooryard*

Bloom'd appeared, two years ago, to dispute the claim, his masterpiece. In Berlin, the opera was hardly a success; the *Times* reported that on the first night "whistling and booing partly drowned the fairly enthusiastic applause." Sessions champions explained that it had been poorly performed—insufficiently rehearsed, insensitively cut, and, by Gustav Sellner, directed on the superficial level of a Meyerbeerian spectacle. Present at the première was Sarah Caldwell, and she had no doubts about the merits of *Montezuma*. Twice she announced the American first performance, to be given by her Opera Company of Boston; twice it was canceled. But now she has brought it off.

William H. Prescott's *History of the Conquest of Mexico* is the great American epic, as stirring as the Matter of Arthur or the Matter of Troy, as romantic and adventurous as Ariosto or *The Faerie Queene*, and with the added charm and interest of being true. The Conquest of Peru, as Prescott remarked, "notwithstanding the opportunities it presents for the display of character, strange, romantic incident, and picturesque scenery, does not afford so obvious advantages . . . as the Conquest of Mexico. Indeed, few subjects can present a parallel with that, for the purposes either of the historian or the poet. . . . It is a magnificent epic, in which the unity of interest is complete." Long before Sessions, and long before Prescott, the Matter of Mexico had provided inspiration for the operatic stage; some thirty operas on the subject have been counted. One of the earliest is Carl Heinrich Graun's *Montezuma*, of 1755 (performed in Boston in 1973), with a libretto by Frederick the Great. Cortes is the villain. Frederick, as he told Count Algarotti in a letter, hoped that his opera would serve at once "to reform behavior and destroy superstitions" and to reform operatic abuses such as constant da-capo airs. The most celebrated opera on the theme is Spontini's *Fernand Cortez, ou La Conquête du Mexique*, of 1809; at the Metropolitan, in 1888, it was performed with forces that, according to the critic H. E. Krehbiel, "rivaled in numbers those who constituted the veritable Cortez's army, while the horses came within three of the number that the Spaniards took into Mexico." Sessions's opera is not intended as an exotic spectacular; in a preface to the score, he says, "This work was conceived by both its author [Giuseppe Antonio Borgese] and its composer as a story of human beings as such, rather than in their specific qualities as Aztecs and Spaniards." The libretto is not an epic, and not a historical romance. Nor is it a strong drama of personalities, such as Peter Shaffer, in *The Royal Hunt of the Sun*, fashioned from Prescott's *Conquest of Peru*; as individuals, the operatic Cortes and Montezuma are barely characterized. Rather, it is a series of reflections, shaped in lyric-theater terms, on such themes as the problems of empire, the responsibilities of colonists, the disruption of stable agricultural societies by "modern progress," the impossibility of rival creeds' or cultures' peaceably inhabiting the same terrain, the tragic inability of tolerant rulers to inspire tolerance in their subjects, and the causes of Fascism. The librettist of *Montezuma*, Borgese, was the author of *Freedom and Discipline in a Vital Democracy*, of *Foundations of the World Republic*, and of poems and plays. A visit to Mexico, in the thirties, prompted him to approach Sessions with the idea for an opera; six years later, in 1941, his forty-thousand-word libretto was ready. Sessions began to make sketches at once, but eighteen years passed, he says, before he really got down to work on *Montezuma*. Borgese had died in 1952; the composer and the librettist's widow, Elisabeth Mann Borgese, abridged the text, while the Princeton theater historian Francis Fergusson gave advice on conveying information wordlessly and contributed the second of two pantomime scenes in Act II—the ritual sacrifice of eleven victims. The vocal score is dated 1962, and the orchestration was tackled the following year.

Montezuma is in three short acts, amounting to about two and a half hours of music. The dramatic tableaux are introduced by a narrator, the aged Bernal Díaz, apparently inditing his *True History of the Conquest of New Spain* (one of Prescott's main sources), recalling scenes that then shape themselves on the stage. Each episode is short; elaborate arguments are reduced to a few statements. For example, the moral issues of a pastoral feudal economy are debated in just thirty measures. Pedro de Alvarado, Cortes's fiery lieutenant, interrupts a ritual dance celebrating the maize harvest, snatches an ear of corn from the leading dancer, and cries scornfully, "I saw the hungerers in Tlaxcala with not a sprinkle of salt on the poultice of their lamar dish. The carrier beneath his load would burst rather than roll a wheel. I saw the market in Toluca with itch of lice and squeak of mice, and reek of vomitable fish. Indeed! An Eden. The Golden Age." Montezuma replies, "Much grieves the heart of the ruler that all men are not born equal. Yet patience and prayer lighten the burdens, atoning with the highest the lowest." An Aztec priest, unbidden, adds, "Quarrier pave road. Carrier heave load. Other trim the tree. Other till the soil. That the free be free, slave must toil." And Alvarado says, "And cropper, carrier, slave bear the hoard of gold to sky-high lair. [*To Montezuma*] Share!"

I prepared for *Montezuma* by freshly reading Prescott and Díaz. That makes a start; the action of the opera can hardly be followed by anyone who has not done so. But Borgese's libretto needs advance pondering, too, for it is dense in ideas but laconic in their expression; set by Sessions to an accompaniment that causes many of the words to be inaudible (even when the voices are electrically amplified, as they were in both Berlin and Boston); and so tortured in its syntax, so fancy in its poetic diction, that even when the words are heard, or read, their sense is by no means immediately clear. Some of the points are simply made. Both

339

Cortes and Montezuma have youthful, impetuous lieutenants, Alvarado and Cuauhtemoc (Guatemozin), who precipitate the violence that both conqueror and emperor seek to avoid. Other dramatic correspondences are less straightforward. In Act II, Indian victims (reduced in Boston to a single victim) are ritually sacrificed by Indians; in Act III, Cortes burns an Indian who has killed a Spaniard—whether as a punitive execution or in an auto-da-fé is not made clear, and the ambiguity is deliberate. (The narrator remarks, "Ev'n weren't I old I could not tell what shakes at him the Inquisitor. A club? A hammer? A petronel? Or the holy cross of the Savior?") Between these demonstrations of faith in action, there is a religious discussion. The Spaniards produce a picture of the Madonna, the Aztecs disclose that they, too, worship a virgin goddess, mother of sorrows, and the mild Montezuma attempts reconciliation:

Countless are the gods, and he knows little who, dazzled by one, blinds him to the others' glow. . . . Hence let *no* gods be banned or slighted. . . . You sacrificed a god to man, Him, the Crucified, making death and wail supreme. We offer to the immortals mortal victims, who, since death must be, on Death's flowered bosom with shriek of self-effacing fertility swoon. So justice to each other's cult, armor against the blows of fate.

Malinche, Cortes's Indian mistress, who is baptized Marina, plays an important role, singing duets with both Cortes and Montezuma. In a love duet at the end of Act I, she ecstatically yields to Cortes as if to Quetzalcoatl, the white-faced god awaited from the east; gently questioned by Montezuma about the Spaniard's possible divinity, she answers, "To truth unspeakable the query prods lame tongue. God is in him. . . . My king, listen to their message which they call gospel, the news that won this realm to Heav'n." She describes herself as "the abject maid, for gods to tread a rainbow-bridge." Montezuma describes her as "a Magdalen, and a mixer of seeds, a builder of a new race of men, wherefore I praise her." But the narrator remarks that hers is but a facile, personal, and local reconciliation of racial and religious differences:

Poor girl! No expert Circe she, nor yearning Ariadne, haughty Medea! for all her fleeces and Minotaur, a girl with a girlish idea, that th'earth, less round than goes the story, bears just her country on its pear-nipple, where Eden, risen from the sea-ripple, *must* make each morning a morning-glory.

And so idea is piled upon idea; one observation qualifies another while Cortes and Montezuma move toward central, and Alvarado and Cuauhtemoc take up extreme, positions, and Malinche is the ineffectual mediatrix. In his last utterance, Montezuma addresses his subjects from the roof of the besieged citadel where he is held prisoner by the Spaniards:

Let us share with them our maize, water, the gift of Tlaloc. They can provide us with chariots and wheels, the tame high deer, feather-maned, rampant skyward, to span with cotton-haired harvest the ranges, together with many crafts, until we show them to provinces uninhabited, where they can settle unhurt, unhurtful, for this land is roomy, of bounteous lap, fit to be happy under the custody of all gods! . . . So let us have a compact universal. These, were I soon to die, would be my words: that ye love one another.

The Indians respond by stoning him to death. The opera ends with a long, beautiful invisible chorus of Clouds, uncertain whether to cloak the Spaniards' retreat in blinding sheets of rain or to favor the Aztecs, who "must, by storm unhamper'd, storm the fortress." While prophesying the Aztecs' eventual defeat, they decide for the present to assist them.

Sessions, who will be eighty in December, is revered by most serious American musicians and not much heard by the public. In his teaching, his writing, and his music he has, in Wilfrid Mellers's words, "served as guide and mentor to the young and as guardian (in no pejorative sense) of academic respectability." His principal medium has been the full orchestra; he has composed eight symphonies—all of them, he has said, with the sound of Karl Muck's Boston Symphony in his ears. *Montezuma* uses a large orchestra: triple woodwinds with a fourth clarinet, fourfold brasses that do not simply support the voices but, very often, enter into active contrapuntal dialogue with them. In the prefatory note to the score, the composer says that "the vocal parts of this work constitute always its principal melody"; but the principal melody is sometimes hard to hear. A critic tempted to declare that the instrumental part of an opera is too dense, too elaborate, is inhibited by the thought that the same charge was once brought against Mozart, against Rossini, against Wagner. Time has proved a remarkable clarifier of textures. But, at any rate, it can safely be asserted that Boston's Orpheum Theatre, where there is no pit to contain the orchestra, was unhelpful to the sound of *Montezuma*. Even in the Berlin house, which does have a pit, there were difficulties. According to Peter Maxwell Davies, who reviewed the show for the *Times*, "A magnificent production by the Deutsche Oper did everything possible to make the apparent complexities clear, yet the profusion of musical detail obscured, for many listeners, the basic simplicity of Sessions's musical material." "Simplicity" is an unexpected word, yet a fair one for music that moves essentially in sweeping, full-blooded lyrical gestures of long span. "Except in a very few passages where a declamatory mode of delivery is expressly indicated," says the composer, the vocal lines "are to be sung in an expressive *bel canto* style throughout." They lend themselves to such singing, and in Boston they were for the most part lyrically sung. But the orchestra, even where its function is to define or emphasize the articulation of a long vocal gesture, offers what amounts in performance to stiff competition; and sometimes, in addition, voices obscure one another. Alvarado's speech "I saw the hungerers in Tlaxcala"—whose words are important to the dramatic argument—is simultaneous with a duet from Montezuma's two daughters. The old Díaz's reflections during the burning are simultaneous with singing from Alvarado and from the young Díaz, present at the event. To the difficulty of following Borgese's Wardour Street diction ("Bread and wine needs a man to fight and die"; "Us enchants he, but eke frightens") Sessions adds that of hearing the words. It would matter less if *Montezuma* were a conventional drama of passions and pageantry; then it might be enough to read the libretto in advance, and during the performance simply be swept along by the sound of the music. The score is thoroughly and solidly composed; interesting things happen all the time. But insofar as *Montezuma* is dramatic it presents a very intricate drama of ideas given swift, not expansive, expression; anyone who can't follow them is likely to become bored, since both text and music are insistent, unrelaxed, and reject passive acceptance. They demand close intellectual attention to everything that happens. *Montezuma* is both personal and closely argued, in ways that Pfitzner's *Palestrina*, Busoni's *Doktor Faust*, Hindemith's *Harmonie der Welt*, and Dallapiccola's *Ulisse* are, but less than all but the last of those aspiring works does it make any concessions to the ordinary tenets of the theater—stopping to explain, to amplify, to provide breathing spaces. It would be easy to state that it is dramaturgically incompetent, but wiser and fairer—and certainly more prudent —to suggest that, for all the magnitude of the Boston endeavor, we have not yet properly heard and seen it. Clever critics deemed Berlioz's *Les Troyens* a sorry muddle until at length it was adequately performed.

The Boston staging, by Sarah Caldwell, was plain—plainer than one might have expected from stage directions like "As if by an act of magic, lamps of wax in translucent pottery and resinous torches, fixed to the floor or the walls, are being lit almost simultaneously, as Cortez speaks. A tall candelabrum, of single flame, burns beside the ascetic face of Montezuma. The fumes of copal and liquid ambar are seen rising from glowing braziers." None of that happened. The basic set, by Herbert Senn and Helen Pond, was white, and represented old Díaz's study in Guatemala, invaded by and dissolving into the characters and scenes that he recalled. Some colors were brought in for the tableau during which the Spaniards enter the capital and meet the emperor, but they gave no more than a hint of the "wonderful sights" recalled by Díaz ("like an enchanted vision from the tale of Amadis; indeed, some of our soldiers asked whether it was not all a dream"), so vividly evoked by Prescott, and called for in the stage directions of the score. The Boston company, without a proper opera house, without a full-time chorus, orchestra, and stage crew, is not equipped to provide opera on a fully professional level. That should not be forgotten—though in the past, when carried away by the genial spirit that informs Caldwell productions, by brilliant, inspired performers, and by the joy of hearing great works that are ignored, or less stirringly performed, by other companies, I have found it easy to forget. Miss Caldwell achieved wonders with the forces she had available. The starkness of her presentation, her insistence on the basic issues under discussion rather than on the romance of the locale in which Borgese and Sessions chose to embody them, was perhaps dictated in part by practical limitations and in part by a belief that so earnest an opera should not be glamorized. Her Aztecs did not have burnished bodies; from neck to toe they were zipped into drab body stockings, and this seemed somehow symbolic of the determinedly unsensuous approach.

Musically, both orchestra and cast, conducted by Miss Caldwell, sounded confident. As Cortes, Brent Ellis was decisive, vigorous, commanding of voice and of presence. As Malinche, Phyllis Bryn-Julson sang clearly and truly, but her acting was tentative. (It was her first stage role.) Richard Lewis, who took the title part, has never been much of an actor. The plot may require Montezuma to be somewhat ill at ease both with the conquerors and when addressing his own rebellious subjects, and Mr. Lewis certainly conveyed that impression. But he had no majesty. He did not dominate the opera. Joseph Evans's Alvarado was aptly incisive. Donald Gramm, as old Díaz, told far less strongly than he usually does; he was apparently reading the music from a score concealed on his writing desk, and did not address himself directly to the audience. Those are the five principal roles in a very large cast—so large that the public has difficulty knowing who's who.

This account of the Boston *Montezuma*, though not altogether enthusiastic, should at least close with enthusiastic expressions of gratitude to Miss Caldwell and her colleagues for bringing the work to the American stage, and of appreciation for the immense labors of musical preparation that must have gone into it. Such phrases always sound flat. I had hoped that I would be adding, "and at last the glory of the work was revealed!"

The two operas with Northern Indian subjects—one-acters—were played by the New England Chamber Opera Group in All Saints Church, Brookline. Robert Selig's *Chocorua*, which had its première at Tanglewood in 1972, is a small but touching tale, deftly and economically told in Richard Moore's libretto and a score for small orchestra and six singers (soloists melting in and out of the chorus). Paul Earls's *The Death of King Phillip*, a new piece, with a text taken from a play by Romulus Linney, is a more elaborate work, containing multiple scenes, multiple sound sources, and, in addition to "regular" singing and playing, electronic effects both prerecorded and applied to the living performers. King Phillip, Pometakomet, Sachem of the Wampanoag, was, I learn from the program note, an Indian leader who "barely missed driving the white settlers into the sea." He captured a minister's wife, Mary Rowlandson, and in 1682 the *Narrative of the Captivity of Mrs. Rowlandson* was published. Like Díaz in *Montezuma*, on the stage she is twice impersonated—both in old age, remembering, and as a young woman taking part in the remembered events. I found *King Phillip* an adventurous, exciting, and very accomplished opera, enhanced by astonishing light effects devised by the M.I.T. Center for Advanced Visual Studies—laser-projected images solidifying in the spaces of the church, luminous silhouette snapshots of battle actions lingering onstage after the actors had moved on—and by some excellent performers. Beverly Morgan as the young Mrs. Rowlandson, Kim Scown as her husband, and Thomas Olsen and Jerrold Pope as two warriors deserve special mention. The words were exceptionally clear, even during passages of simultaneous discourse. Rafael de Acha directed, and Philip Morehead conducted.

April 19, 1976

TWO DONNAS AND A DEVIL

Nineteenth-century critics wrote often about prima donnas' eyes. Modern critics have little chance to do so, for nowadays eyes are seldom visible on the operatic stage. The Prologue of Donizetti's *Lucrezia Borgia* reaches its climax on a unison cry of "È la Borgia!," doubled by menacing brass octaves, as a mask is torn from the heroine's face; when Giulia Grisi sang the role, there were disclosed, according to Théophile Gautier, "features pale as if cut in marble, and defiant, flashing eyes." Beverly Sills has been singing the role at the State Theater, and none could tell whether at that moment her eyes flashed defiance or not; they remained in pools of dark shadow beneath a ledge of long, heavy lashes. In common with the Bolshoy Opera, both the City Opera and the Metropolitan favor a form of basic lighting which strikes visitors from abroad as strangely primitive; it consists of pointing white spotlights at the soloists. Hans Sondheimer's lighting plot for *Lucrezia Borgia* touched bottom in the second scene of Act I, when his spotlights scurried around after the three singers, spilling circles of light and hard shadows on the furniture and the walls of the ducal apartment. Electric light has had an important part to play in opera. Eduard Hanslick declared that "Wagner could as little have composed *The Ring* before the invention of electric light as without the harp and the bass tuba." Queen Victoria heard *Lohengrin* for the first time on her eightieth birthday (a command performance at Windsor with a very grand cast: Nordica, Schumann-Heink, Jean and Édouard de Reszke, David Bispham), and noted that "Jean looked so handsome in his white attire, armour, and helmet, and the electric light was turned strong upon him, so that he seemed surrounded by a halo." The production book for Verdi's *Don Carlos* specifies that when Charles V appears at the end, splendid in mantle and imperial crown, "his figure is illumined by a ray of electric light." We take such effects for granted now. It would be a pity if New York audiences took it for granted that opera singers are regularly lit only by hard white beams angled to hit their foreheads, noses, and chins.

That Miss Sills, like Cressida, has language in her eye I know, for I met her once, soon after I had written a distinctly unenthusiastic account of her London début. Although this language was denied her by the City Opera staging of *Lucrezia Borgia*, in other ways she was eloquent. *Lucrezia* is a strong opera, worth exhumation. The libretto, by Felice Romani, reads well. The play that is its source, Victor Hugo's *Lucrèce Borgia*, forms, in the words of Hugo's preface, a "bilogy" with *Le Roi s'amuse* (the source of *Rigoletto*): the one deals with "moral deformity purified by maternal emotion," the other with "physical deformity sanctified by paternal emotion." There is no conventional love interest; the opera's two duets of affection are between mother and son and between that son, Gennaro, and his friend Orsini, a breeches role for a contralto. The score, like that of Verdi's *Un ballo in maschera*, consists of one good number after another; the listener is carried forward on a powerful tide of melodic and dramatic invention. The predominance of lower voices—the tenor, Gennaro, has five companions who function as a semichorus—gives richness and warmth to the texture, and the title role stands out in high relief. It was composed, in 1833, for a prima donna, Henriette Méric-Lalande, at the end of her career, and so devised that great effects could be achieved without prodigies of weighty vocalism. For all the forcefulness of personality revealed in Lucrezia's music, the role does not need the sheer vocal force that an

345

Elizabeth in Donizetti's *Roberto Devereux*, his Fausta, or his Gemma di Vergy (three parts written for Ronzi de Begnis) must command. Of Lucrezia, so tender, so passionate, so wicked and proud, Miss Sills gave an inspired performance, bringing each episode to life with her delivery of the words, her rhythmic control of accent, and her use of the coloratura for dramatic expression. One tiresome trick—flying up to strident, unwritten high notes at the end of numbers—I wish she would drop. Her *acuti* are no longer reliable; instead of adding a final touch of excitement, they merely diverted attention from Lucrezia onto an imperfect singer. In any case, the interpolated high notes are unnecessary, and often inartistic. Donizetti wrote the role up to B-flat, with some passing C's in a final cabaletta that was included only at Méric-Lalande's insistence.

In admiration and advocacy of Donizetti's serious operas I sway to and fro, overinfluenced by impressions the latest performance has left. Sometimes it makes me quite cross that the City Opera should have been playing *Lucia, Anna Bolena, Maria Stuarda, Roberto Devereux*, and now *Lucrezia Borgia* during years when there has been no Rameau, no Handel, no Gluck, no Haydn, and no *Rake's Progress* in its repertory. (But then there has been Monteverdi, Cherubini, Janáček, Delius, and Henze; no one can say that City Opera fare is unadventurous.) And sometimes I come away, as from this *Lucrezia Borgia*, eagerly scanning the billboard to discover when the next performance is due. Winton Dean's paper on "Donizetti's Serious Operas," published in the latest *Proceedings of the Royal Musical Association*, lists three good reasons for looking closely at these works, considered "until recently . . . not respectable enough for musicology": they can be extremely moving in the theater; their composer was "from the first a conscious innovator, eager to expand the range of operatic form"; and he "exercised a more decisive and fruitful influence on Verdi than is commonly recognized." The specifically Verdian things in *Lucrezia* are the finale of the Prologue, echoed in the Act II tenor-baritone duet of Verdi's *Battaglia di Legnano*, and, in the first scene of Act I, a duettino for two rogues—in nefarious dialogue over a flowing orchestral melody—which closely anticipates Rigoletto's encounter with Sparafucile. The formal enterprise shows itself in the setting within a duet of the tenor's only air; in a trio whose final section becomes a duet; generally in the treatment of the semichorus; and most of all in the *finale nuovo* that Donizetti added for an 1840 revival when his Gennaro was Napoleone Moriani, celebrated as the "tenore della bella morte." The composer scrapped Méric-Lalande's cabaletta (which opens well but then becomes trumpery) and wrote instead a "beautiful death" for Moriani, unconventional in form, punctuated by Lucrezia's sad cries of "Figlio mio!" (At the City Opera, we hear *both* pieces—first the death and then the cabaletta.)

The affective power of the opera is fully revealed by Miss Sills and by Julius Rudel, who conducts with feeling for and complete control of its colors and its dramatic pacing.

Gennaro, at the performance I attended, was Gaetano Scano; he was clean and true, and sustained his part well. (Neither of the additional tenor arias—Donizetti wrote one for the Gennaro of Mario, and another for that of Ivanov—was included; they are unwanted unless a second Mario or Ivanov is at hand.) Hilda Harris was a sparkling Orsini. Richard Fredricks, as Duke Alfonso, lacked the large, majestic line implied by Donizetti's basso-cantante writing, but he sang with vigor, and should have been allowed the second verse of his cabaletta. The first and the last of Henry Bardon's scenes are striking: the Venice nocturne of the Prologue he bathes in a rich, dusky red; the transformation of a merry banqueting hall into a death chamber is dramatically achieved. But the proportions of his Ferrara piazza seem awry; the buildings are too small. (The production is borrowed from Dallas; perhaps this décor sat more easily on the Dallas stage.) Details in Tito Capobianco's staging suggest that someone has not been attentive to the text (Gennaro declares that he keeps ever next to his heart a letter from his unknown mother—while drawing it from his cuff), but on the whole it moves surely and strongly. The device of bringing the singers out into the house itself—over bridges that span each flank of the orchestra pit—and in front of the main auditorium wall lent acoustic immediacy to several numbers. *Lucrezia* returns in the fall season, and I look forward to enjoying it again.

For the last weeks of its spring season, the City Opera planned a small flurry of contemporary works—Josef Tal's *Ashmedai* and Douglas Moore's *Ballad of Baby Doe* for three performances each, and Jack Beeson's *Lizzie Borden* for two. *Baby Doe* and *Lizzie Borden* are still to come; *Ashmedai* has been and gone, leaving little impression save of a brilliantly accomplished performance by the company. The piece was one of Rolf Liebermann's many commissions for the Hamburg City Opera and was first performed there in 1971. The libretto, by Israel Eliraz, is a political parable. In Talmudic lore, Ashmedai—Asmodeus, a major devil—took on King Solomon's features, usurped his throne, and was accepted by his people as their ruler. In the opera, the peaceable king of an unspecified country has a lovable but fallacious belief in his subjects' essential goodness; willingly—and in order to enjoy a respite free of regal cares, of his termagant wife, and of his ambitious, bellicose son—for a year he renounces his throne to Ashmedai, convinced that no great harm can result. Great harm results. The curtain falls on a people gone to the devil, spiritually and materially ruined. The old king is killed; his illegitimate daughter, a dreamy girl

347

out of touch with reality, keens for the vanished sunlit world in which she was born.

It's a big theme—the transformation of an easygoing, romantic folk, enjoying their music and poetry and gardens, into murdering brutes following their Führer. A few years earlier, in another Hamburg opera, *Arden muss sterben*, Alexander Goehr had reminded the newly prosperous German burghers that "Wir waren immer dagegen" is easily said and that the guilt remains. (He and his librettist, Erich Fried, were booed for their pains.) The year before that, the chorus in Henze's Salzburg opera *The Bassarids* had sung in a "We were always against it" vein when the madness of mass possession had cooled. None of those operas is a cut-and-dried allegory of the Third Reich. ("Do not forget," Shaw wrote in *The Perfect Wagnerite*, "that an allegory is never quite consistent except when it is written by someone without dramatic faculty.") They have that varied applicability to the thought and experience of audiences which distinguishes drama from didactic spectacle. Eliraz's libretto, which is possibly as much about Israel as about Germany, and not irrelevant to recent American history, contains a warning ("All a poet can do is to warn": Britten set those words of Wilfred Owen as epigraph to his *War Requiem*)—against any easy belief that innate human decency is incorruptible. It's a warning that is needed today. But—with regret I record it—between conception and execution *Ashmedai* seemed to have lost its power. It came across as a cleverly crafted diversion, mildly amusing, mildly touching, and mildly distasteful as, for our entertainment, it flickered lightly over very serious questions. Tal's music is no more than a thoroughly professional job of libretto-setting: the words are clear (the piece was done in an English translation by Alan Marbé), the pace is skillfully controlled. But nothing happens. The music goes in one ear and out the other. Harold Prince's direction was deft, slick. It functioned flawlessly, and left both mind and heart unmoved. Ken Billington's lighting was highly accomplished. So was the large cast, led by John Lankston in the title role, Paul Ukena as the King, Eileen Schauler as the Queen, and Richard Taylor as the Prince. Everyone danced, sang, acted with effortless assurance and address. Gary Bertini, who was in charge of the Hamburg première, was a masterly conductor.

Thomas Pasatieri's *Ines de Castro*, commissioned for the Baltimore Opera Company and performed by it this month, is a "culinary" opera of no interest, cooked up from stale ingredients, weak in its musical and dramatic ideas. The subject, one of the great love stories, could have life in it still, even after so many stage treatments. (The most celebrated is Giuseppe Persiani's opera of 1835, with a libretto by

348

Salvatore Cammarano.) Bernard Stambler's libretto is partly in prose, partly in insipid verse.

> Love is a soaring joy
> That leaps high over the hills.
> Love brings such delight,
> My heart holds nothing more.
> Let my lady treasure me,
> And let the world go by

is a fair specimen, from the first duet of Ines and Dom Pedro. The dramaturgy is neat enough, in a schematic, unimaginative way. Pasatieri's short-breathed music goes through Giordano-like or Cilea-like gestures, without ever capturing the note of full-throated emotion that can bring Giordano's and Cilea's operas to life. Baltimore did the piece proud, having assembled a notable cast: Evelyn Mandac and Richard Stilwell as the lovers, and Lili Chookasian, Sheila Nadler, Lou Ann Lee, William Neill, James Atherton, and James Morris in other roles. Christopher Keene conducted. Tito Capobianco directed. An appreciative audience applauded Mario Vanarelli's set for the Coimbra garden thrice over: each time the curtain rose on it. Robert Brand's expert lighting—without follow spots—both revealed expression and enhanced Mr. Vanarelli's décor. (As Hanslick once said, "the painter of the scenery can account for only a half of the total effect; the other half rests with the lighting, which corresponds to the instrumentation of a musical idea.") But Baltimore's Lyric Theater—not so much an opera house as a concert hall, apparently modeled on the Leipzig Gewandhaus, with a stage added to one end of it—proved too big a place to be set ringing by these voices. In Berlioz's phrase, one heard but one did not vibrate.

April 26, 1976

OPERA PRIMA

Music by the young Mozart, given by the Westchester Chamber Chorus and Orchestra, under Jens Nygaard, made a delectable concert in Alice Tully Hall last week. Music, one should perhaps say (though the program book did not), by the young Mozart and his father, since the autographs of all the works that were performed are partly in Wolfgang's hand, partly in Leopold's. First, there was one of the three piano concertos arranged from sonatas by John Christian Bach. Köchel, in his catalogue, dated them to 1771; Alfred Einstein, in his revision of Köchel, pushed them back six years; and then Wolfgang Plath, noting (in an article in the *Mozart-Jahrbuch 1960–61*) that only the string parts are filled in in Wolfgang's hand, decided from the shape of the clefs and the natural signs that they cannot be earlier than the end of 1770 and are probably later. It is tempting to assign these adaptations to the summer months of 1771, between Mozart's two Italian visits, and realistic to credit Leopold with their simple formal design. (By that date, Wolfgang was a far more enterprising creator.) But in any event J. C. Bach's galant melodies, which so happily influenced the young Mozart, provided a happy introduction to the concert. Mr. Nygaard, who directed the performance from the keyboard, had the right feeling for elegance that is not brittle, charm that is not cloying, and buoyancy that is not boisterous. Throughout the evening, his molding of phrases, his care for the precise weighting of harmonic progressions, and his unfussy attention to any sudden, surprising inner parts, which he made audible but not overemphatic, conspired for our delight. The concerto was followed by "God Is Our Refuge," those twenty-three "learned" measures presented to the British Museum in 1765 by the nine-year-old genius and his father, and the Kyrie, K. 33, of the following year—most of it in Leopold's hand and all of it astonishingly prophetic of Wolfgang's later church style. Then came the Cassation in G, K. 63, for which oboes and horns joined the little string band. Wind and strings were excellently balanced in this performance. Mozart was thirteen when he wrote the score (Leopold's contribution seems to have been only some tidying of tempo and dynamic indications), and yet the word "masterpiece" is justified: the mastery is of harmonic adventure and control; of learned devices used with unobtrusive skill (the first minuet is a canon); of unconventional phrase lengths; and of string textures—combinations of muted against unmuted, cantabile against pizzicato, swift figuration against slow—such as are admired in the mature Haydn. Mr. Nygaard observed many repeats, but not those in the adagio—an exquisite concerto movement that would have been well worth hearing twice. Into the trio sections of both minuets he introduced some quirky but rather attractive articulations of his own, making staccato the slurred bass lines of the first, and slurring some of the staccato scales in the second.

The second half of the concert was devoted to Mozart's first opera, *Apollo et Hyacinthus*, composed when he was eleven—a school opera written for the Salzburg Gymnasium, an intermedium whose acts alternated with those of a Latin play. The original Hyacinth, a treble, was twelve years old. The cast of five contained another treble (aged fifteen), two altos (aged twelve and seventeen; the elder, Joseph Vonderthon, later became Superior of Maria Plain, that beautiful pilgrimage church outside Salzburg), and a tenor (aged twenty-three, a student of moral theology and law). The second treble has the role of Melia, Hyacinth's sister. By introducing her into the tale, a happy ending—her betrothal to Apollo—could be contrived and at the same time, as the latest editor of the score puts it, the tricky subject of Apollo's and Zephyr's love for Hyacinth (thin ice at a boys' school) could be skated over, for in the opera god and swain are rivals for Melia's affections. There is not much action apart from the two metamorphoses: "Zephyrus in ventum mutatus abripitur" and "Subsidens cum funere, tellus Hyacinthos flores germinat." But there is a sequence of ten very shapely and attractive numbers: an overture, a chorus, five arias, two duets, and a final trio for the characters— Apollo, Melia, and her father, Oebalus—who have been left in recognizable form. In true opera-seria fashion, Mozart set out to provide arias in many different manners, accompanied by different kinds of texture. (The band, as in the cassation, is just strings and pairs of oboes and horns.) Oebalus sings a simile aria, "Ut navis in aequore luxuriante, per montes, per valles undarum jactatur," in which the choppy sea is vividly and amusingly depicted by stretches of up to thirty measures at a time in alternate *forte* and *piano*; the first violins set the vessel pitching, the seconds set her rolling, and the vocal line heaves uneasily. The high point of the opera is a duet for Oebalus and Melia, tenor and soprano, "Natus cadit . . . Frater cadit," as they grieve for Hyacinth's death. The movement is more familiar in its abridged form as the andante of the symphony K. 43 but is far more beautiful in the operatic original. First violins, muted, play the flowing melody; cellos and double-basses sound the beats, pizzicato; second violins pluck off-beat three-part chords; divided violas murmur; the horns sustain gently. The voices, when they enter, steal in and out of the first-violin line, and at one ravishing moment they cross. There are movements in Mozart—the andante of the C-major Piano Concerto, K. 467, comes to mind—which hold their listeners rapt from the opening measures, which . . . But words fail me, and instead I think of certain of Vermeer's pictures, not because they are "like" Mozart but because they, too, inspire serene, intense rapture. Pulling down the Britannica to see what words have been found for Vermeer, I read that his "beauty of tone and perfect harmony are conspicuous," and of his "singular completeness and charm," of figures that "seem to move in light and air." For the duet in *Apollo* and the andante of K. 467 those phrases are apt.

In Mr. Nygaard's concert performance, Barbara Hendricks doubled the roles of Hyacinth and Melia, and Jeffrey Gall, a countertenor, those of Apollo and Zephyr; Grayson Hirst sang Oebalus. All three were delightful—fluent and true in division, sweet in timbre, delicate in their phrasing, daring but not reckless in their cadenzas. Were they right to sing the Latin with an Italian, rather than an Austrian, pronunciation? The recitatives were abridged, but not so severely as to jam numbers too close together. A narrator, June LeBell, pleasantly simple in manner, kept us in touch with the plot. One's only regrets were that Mr. Nygaard had not, for the concerto, obtained an instrument better suited to the music than a modern Steinway; that he clumped all his fiddles together on one side, so that antiphonal effects in the first two movements of the cassation and in the accompaniment to the chorus of the opera were obscured; that the program book contained no Latin libretto and English translation (some pretty details of word-painting must have passed unnoticed by anyone without a score, or fluent Latin); and that the wooden shutters at the back of the platform were not pushed aside, so that the organ might serve as a handsome backdrop to a memorable concert.

Three days before, there was Mozart choral music in Avery Fisher Hall—the *Regina coeli*, K. 276, the K. 321 Vespers, and, in the second half, the C-minor Mass, K. 427. There were no program notes at all. Every schoolboy knows that Mozart left the C-minor Mass unfinished; no hint was given about whose edition would be used, and I did not wait to discover—the lackluster singing of the National Chorale, feeble soloists, and Martin Josman's way of beating through the music without shaping the phrases, tending the instrumental textures, or sounding the sense of the harmonies had made the first half of the concert a dismal, un-Mozartian affair.

Leonard Bernstein ended his stint at the Philharmonic this season with a program that included two local premières. The more substantial piece was William Schuman's *Concerto on Old English Rounds*, for viola, women's chorus, and orchestra, first played in Boston in 1974. This is at once a viola concerto in five movements and a suite-*cum*-fantasia on "Amaryllis," Henry Aldrich's "Great Tom Is Cast," "Who'll Buy Mi Roses?," and John Hilton's "Come, Follow, Follow, Follow, Follow, Follow, Follow Me." Good rounds—and these four are all good—are fascinatingly ingenious things, mesmeric as they get under way, but at a certain point monotony of rhythm and harmony sets in and one longs for the singers to stop. Schuman recognizes that point, and before reaching it he cunningly slides his rounds into new keys (no easy task if their progress is to remain smooth), or transforms their rhythms, or does other dexterous, entertaining things. This is a happy, witty score, which often made me smile and nearly made me laugh aloud; the composer's sleight of hand when he starts bringing the different rounds together in a wicked gallimaufry is wonderfully neat. But it is also a poetic piece. The viola begins it, "uttering" the Amaryllis melody and musing on it; and elsewhere the viola is descant commentator on the other tunes. The work, which lasted nearly forty-five minutes, almost outstayed its welcome: at the end of the fourth movement a fugue subject is assembled from elements of all the different rounds, and counterpoint is ground out in a ruthless way that recalls Hindemith at his most insistent; and the coda, more musing on Amaryllis, takes a very long time to reach its conclusion. Donald McInnes, for whom the piece was written, was an eloquent viola soloist, and Abraham Kaplan's Camerata Singers sang with fair, smooth tone and sure pitch.

Before Schuman's concerto, there was Benjamin Britten's *Suite on English Folk Tunes: A Time There Was*, first performed at the Aldeburgh Festival last year. There are five deftly wrought movements, based on songs and dances, of which the most immediately attractive is "Hankin Booby," scored for wind band and percussion, pungent and tangy in tone as a Spanish *cobla*. In the last number, an English horn "declaims" that very beautiful song "Lord Melbourne," handled far more lyrically and less vigorously than it was by Mr. George Wray, the Lincolnshire sailor, brickmaker, and then coal merchant who, when aged eighty, sang the song to Percy Grainger, in Brigg, in 1906, and again in 1908. Britten used Grainger's transcription of the song; recordings of Wray's performances are in the Library of Congress.

The concert ended with an unhappy, incoherent account of Robert Schumann's Piano Concerto, in which Mr. Bernstein seemed to think he was the star and Murray Perahia, the soloist, a kind of continuo player. Since the conductor gets first go at most of the tunes, he can set the paces. They were set slow, and slowed still further by heavily sentimental touches of rubato. Mr. Perahia played along meekly and tidily. If he had taken up the themes at anything like a natural tempo, it would have sounded like a public rebuke to Mr. Bernstein. For all three works there were thorough program notes. A text sheet was provided for the rounds. The only information missing was that the score of the Britten is published by Faber, and of the Schuman by Merion.

May 3, 1976

EARTHBOUND

Spring has brought a crop of American operas. Among those already reviewed in these pages are Roger Sessions's *Montezuma*, Robert Selig's *Chocorua*, and Paul Earls's *The Death of King Phillip* in Boston; Carlisle Floyd's *Bilby's Doll* in Houston; and Thomas Pasatieri's *Ines de Castro* in Baltimore. There have since been revivals of Douglas Moore's *The Ballad of Baby Doe* and Jack Beeson's *Lizzie Borden* at the City Opera, and, most recently, the first performance of Hugo Weisgall's *The Hundred Nights*, put on by the Juilliard American Opera Center. And there are more pieces to come—Dominick Argento's *The Voyage of Edgar Allan Poe* in St. Paul; Gian Carlo Menotti's *The Hero* in Philadelphia; and Alva Henderson's *The Last of the Mohicans* in Wilmington, are three—so any general reflections about the State of Contemporary American Opera should wait. In particular, *The Voyage of Edgar Allan Poe*, commissioned for the Minnesota Opera Company, which has given the first performances of two other Argento pieces, will test a thesis that the most rewarding new work is likely to be done within a community where composer, company, and audience have regular and mutually dependent roles to play.

Works that I should like to see the City Opera revive are Marc Blitzstein's *The Cradle Will Rock* (Mercury Theatre, with the composer at the piano, 1937; Broadway, 1947; City Opera, 1960) and *Regina* (Broadway, 1949; City Opera, 1953), and Kurt Weill's *Street Scene* (Broadway, 1947; City Opera, 1959). *Street Scene* was put on earlier this year at the Manhattan School of Music—not well, but well enough to show that in the hands of an able and committed composer "Broadway opera" (Weill's term for the genre of that piece) has more savor and zest in it than romantic late fruits from Puccinesque or Straussian stock. Moreover, since operatic communities cannot flourish on revivals alone, I should like to see William Bolcom, and perhaps Stanley Silverman, writing pieces to be played on Lincoln Plaza. They are two composers who can use popular idioms to serve more than commercial ends —as Weill and Blitzstein did, and, before them, the Mozart of *The Magic Flute*.

Baby Doe, first performed in Central City, Colorado, in 1956, and two years later taken into the City Opera repertory, is a popular opera in that its score is largely a sequence of square dances, waltzes, polkas, and shamelessly sentimental ballads in blamelessly diatonic idiom. No essential harm in that; what makes *Baby Doe* a bore now is the blandness of its melodies—cliché tunes accompanying, not bringing vividness and particularity to, a play that is itself a series of dramatic clichés. The tunes should at the least be catchy; after two hearings (one in decent

WQXR sound, accompanying Channel 13's live transmission of the show), the only tune that caught and stayed with me was Baby's final "Always through the changing of sun and shadow, time and space"—a cunningly crafted melody in B major whose vocal line avoids any straightforward tonic close but hovers again and again on silvery F-sharps, differently harmonized. I can well believe that in the title role Beverly Sills, the Baby of the first City Opera performances, must have been captivating; and that, in general, subtle, potent performers might lend their own distinction and richness to the kitschy tale of a mining magnate and his tender, loving mistress, wife, then widow. But in the revival these two, played by Richard Fredricks and Ruth Welting, were two-dimensional figures in a pasteboard setting.

Lizzie Borden, on the assumption that she really did take that ax to her stepmother and her father, provides sensational dramatic material—a kind of Electra-cum-Hamlet who really lived, in New England, not so long ago. In their musical treatment, first played at the City Opera in 1965, Beeson and his librettist, Kenward Elmslie, make that assumption and then add further touches—perhaps too many—to the tale. Their Lizzie is the elder, not the younger, Borden daughter, and, in addition to hating her stepmother, Abigail, and being harshly treated by her father, she is secretly jealous of her sister, Margret, and longs for the embraces of Margret's suitor, Captain Jason MacFarlane. The first Mrs. Borden, Evangeline (who, in history, died when Lizzie was only two), remains a vivid presence in her daughters' minds, and her portrait plays an important part in the action. One almost expects it to start singing. Step by step, across two busy days, the thwarted virgin's progress toward parricidal fury is traced. The opera, like *Werther*, begins and ends with voices of children. When the curtain rises, Lizzie is teaching them a hymn. Then events pile up. Mr. Borden refuses to buy Lizzie the new dress she needs; promises to buy Abigail a new piano; deposes Evangeline's portrait; taunts Lizzie by telling Jason that if he will only take not Margret but Lizzie off his hands he'll reward him with the price of a ship. Margret and Jason elope. Lizzie, wearing her mother's bridal dress, which she has brought down from the attic, imagines herself in Jason's arms. Abigail eavesdrops on the fevered fantasy, and jeers at the girl. Lizzie broods, snatches up a handy weapon, and makes for Abigail's room, whence a scream is soon heard. Aegisthus-like, Mr. Borden returns, to be greeted by Lizzie and escorted upstairs. In a coda, we see her, after the trial and acquittal, as mistress of the lonely house; outside, children are singing the familiar jingle.

There is one episode where the music strikes beneath the surface of the action. Father and daughter go through a kind of ritual: "What am I forbidden now?" "To see the preacher." "Must not come here." "Must not come here ever again." "—ever again. What am I forbidden?" "The children's choir." "Must not see them . . . ever again. What else am I forbidden?" "The Captain!" "I must never see him again." It is like a children's game that over the years has become a master-and-slave ceremony necessary to them both. He draws strength from her submission; but she, cringing before him like a whipped bitch, has initiated the exchange. The music is a dark chorale, tensely harmonized; the vocal lines are crooned phrases, evidently familiar to both of them but always capable of being invested with new, wounding turns. The scene has some psychological complexity, and the score defines emotions of which the characters themselves are hardly conscious. Opera, using musical shapes and timbres, here communicates through channels denied to the spoken theater. But elsewhere the music is mainly humdrum. It may have been Beeson's intention to show that the stuff of tragedy can as readily be found in Fall River, Mass., as in the lofty air of Elsinore or Mycenae. What he achieves is not musical tragedy, or even effective musical melodrama, but a kind of drab musical prose that stirs few feelings of excitement, understanding, or compassion. Things go their way, and we watch and listen unmoved. The composer does show great skill in setting both colloquial speech ("Provided it's a sensible investment, I'll buy the grand piano") and the short lines of "free verse" in which most of the libretto is written ("When I hear your voice / the years disappear / and I forget my cares") at speeds that sing naturally; the vocal gait is more efficiently paced than in, say, *Bilby's Doll* or *The Hundred Nights*. Eileen Schauler was strong, dramatic, and—insofar as the score permits—subtle and various in the title role. This Lizzie, and last year's Governess in Britten's *The Turn of the Screw*, revealed a singer who should be an inspiration to future City Opera composers. Edward Pierson lacked the presence to be convincing as her father.

Baby Doe is musical comedy claimed for the opera house. *Lizzie Borden* might be described as an Ibsenesque play set to music. *The Hundred Nights* is an opera of another kind, observing Busoni's precept that enchantment and irreality are the only fit matter for the lyric theater. The base material is Kwanami's Nō drama *Sotoba Komachi*, a very beautiful play. Komachi, once so lovely, once so proud, is now an old woman tormented by the spirit of her lover, Shōshō, whom she bade attend her for a hundred nights before she would yield to him—and who died after the ninety-ninth. In the course of the play, her troubled soul finds peace. There are just three characters: two traveling priests and Komachi, who for a while takes on the form of the faithful Shōshō. Yukio Mishima adapted this as one of his *Five Modern Nō Plays*. In his version, Komachi is a filthy old hag gathering cigarette butts in a Tokyo park. There is a new character, a poet. As the old woman tells him her story, the scene changes to a ballroom eighty years before, when she was at the height of her beauty, and the poet enacts the role of her gallant. Although her own appearance does not change, he now sees her as fair, fresh, and lovely. She warns him that if ever he should *say* she is, he will die. He does say so, and dies. The scene changes back to the park. I am not sure what the point of Mishima's play is—that illusions, once formulated, prove fatal?—and am even more puzzled by the adaptation of it that John Hollander has made to serve as Weisgall's libretto. Mishima recommended that productions of his modern Nō plays should be localized. Hollander has set *Sotoba Komachi* not in modern Central Park and then Delmonico's but in London's Kensington Gardens, in the shade of the Albert Memorial, in 1899, with a flashback to a Regency assembly room. The poet has become another kind of image-maker, a photographer "who specializes in shooting night scenes." Furthermore, at the scene change the old woman herself is transformed. (The rejuvenation is not specified in the score but happened in the Juilliard staging.) This makes the role a more attractive proposition for a young and beautiful soprano (such as Victoria Vergara, who led the Juilliard cast at the performance I saw) but destroys the dramatic irony of the hero's delight, while touching her lousy rags and wrinkled dugs, in her sweet-smelling clothes and seductive body, and markedly alters the theatrical presentation of illusion.

The new work makes the effect of an exercise in musical dramaturgy, carefully planned, neatly executed—and not very interesting. Weisgall has the right ideas about opera; he likes to leave a performance "feeling as if something has happened to me." So do I. But nothing much happened to me during *The Hundred Nights*. I heard lots of notes; much would-be lyrical song along chromatic phrases of wandering, unmemorable line; declamation that proceeded with unnatural slowness, in which short English syllables were unhappily prolonged; dance meters, in the assembly-room scene, that were lively enough in themselves but were clad in harmonies and melodies of hessian. Things perked up when two London bobbies came on with a "Now then, now then. What's all this?"—but by then the opera was almost done.

The Hundred Nights, which lasts something over an hour, was given on a double bill with Goffredo Petrassi's *Il cordovano*, which lasts something under an hour. This is Petrassi's first opera; it was produced at La Scala in 1949 and was revived in Florence earlier this year. Petrassi is an important teacher, and has his place in history among the Alfredo Casella disciples who brought post-Puccini Italian music into the twentieth century. His instrumental scores are dry but, in their severe way, not undistinguished; in Guido Gatti's measured phrases, "less happily conceived and executed are Petrassi's works for the stage, particularly the one-act opera *Il cordovano*, where the composer endeav-

357

oured to try his hand at comic and grotesque expression." The libretto may have a distinguished ancestry—by Eugenio Montale, after Cervantes—but the outcome is a depressingly earnest, busy, but not at all vivacious or sparkling variant on the old matter of the sprightly young woman, the elderly guardian or husband who keeps her locked from the world, and the handsome young man who finds his way to her. Columbine, Pantaloon, and Harlequin. Rosina, Bartolo, and Almaviva; Norina, Don Pasquale, and Ernesto—Rossini and Donizetti handled the traditional comic triangle more deftly. Ravel in *L'Heure espagnole* elaborated it. Lorca in *Dom Perlimplin*, made into a ballet by Luigi Nono and into an opera by Vittorio Rieti, transformed it to romantic tragedy. Molière in *L'École des femmes*, made into an opera by Rolf Liebermann, gave it an amusing twist. Leoncavallo in *Pagliacci* and Puccini in *Il tabarro* recast it as melodrama. And the list could easily be prolonged. (How many different subjects are there? Is not *Tristan* yet another variation?) Petrassi's title presumably refers to a roll of Spanish leather (the translation used by the Juilliard renders it as *The Tapestry*), and maybe a pun is intended; maybe the young man smuggled in inside the roll comes from Cordova. (At the performance, it was hard to catch the words, and no libretto was on sale.)

Students are seldom successful in period comedy, unless they are skillfully and imaginatively directed. The Juilliard's 1973 *Don Pasquale* and its production, earlier this year, of Cimarosa's *Il matrimonio segreto* are unhappy memories, and *Il cordovano*, like those shows, suffered from a staging based on stock comic business (Does anyone in real life ever bite a coin when handed it as a tip? Does anyone on the stage ever *not* do so?) and on fun with props rather than with quiddities of human behavior accurately observed. The nub of Jack O'Brien's direction was an irrelevant bowl of fruit; lewd gestures with a banana, plums popped into mouths, the whole lot spilled, much gathering up again . . . on and on it went. In John Olon-Scrymgeour's staging of the Weisgall opera there was more discretion. Both shows were designed by Robert Yodice and lit by Joe Pacitti—the regular Juilliard team, whose work, over the years I have been seeing it, has maintained a high standard of unobtrusive excellence.

May 10, 1976

The City Opera recorded The Ballad of Baby Doe *in 1958, and the set has been reissued by Deutsche Grammophon on 2709 061.*

358

BY A ROUTE OBSCURE

For the French, Edgar Allan Poe has been an obsession. Baudelaire's lifework was translating Poe. Debussy spent twenty-seven years brooding on his two Poe operas, *The Fall of the House of Usher* and *The Devil in the Belfry*—but got very little music for them down on paper. (See pp. 532–8.) Mallarmé acknowledged Poe as his "great master." For Valéry, Poe was "the only impeccable writer." Musically, his influence has been indirect and has come from France; the direct settings, though very numerous, are almost all undistinguished. (Rachmaninoff's *The Bells* is an exception.) The tales matter more than the poetry. Their atmosphere of mystery and terror, the procession of overwrought images, the recurrent allegorical architecture of rich decay, the evocation of hypnagogic states between dream and waking—these have worked upon poetic minds more finely tuned, more skillful in their command of verbal "music" than Poe's was, and, in turn, the Poe-influenced poets have inspired great music. Poe lies beneath *Pelléas et Mélisande* not only because Debussy came under his spell but because Maeterlinck owed to him, in his own words, "the birth in my work of a sense of mystery and the passion for the beyond." Pierre Boulez's *Pli selon pli* rests on Mallarmé, and much of Mallarmé rests on Poe.

Dominick Argento has now written a Poe opera, *The Voyage of Edgar Allan Poe*, which was given its first performance last month by the Minnesota Opera Company. It was not written out of long obsession with the author. The composer describes its genesis in a series of diary notes, published—along with useful, informative essays, well-chosen pictures, and the complete libretto—in an admirable program book prepared for the Minnesota production. (The book cost five dollars; there was also a program book of the more usual kind distributed free.) Argento was casting about in his mind for a subject. Thornton Wilder's *Heaven's My Destination* had attracted him, but the necessity for a naturalistic handling was a problem there. Then "it occurred to me that perhaps something could be done with the Tales of E. A. Poe, something fantastic and non-realistic." Maybe several tales combined—compare *The Tales of Hoffmann*—with Poe himself as link man . . . These were the steps, and then a reading of Poe's biography suggested a frame for the opera: that last journey of his, its details unaccounted for, which began when Poe boarded a steamer at Richmond and ended in a Baltimore hospital ten days later. Still on the analogy of Offenbach's *Hoffmann*, there might be an Evil Genius dogging the hero's path; he could be Rufus Griswold, Poe's literary executor and earliest biographer, who fired off his first calumnies with an obituary in the New York *Tribune* two days after Poe's death and then maligned him thoroughly in the widely printed memoir. ("Can it be that America has no ordinance prohibiting dogs from entering cemeteries?" said Baudelaire.) A cast of five took shape, in which each real-life personage had a fictional counterpart: Poe (Roderick Usher); Virginia, his cousin and wife (Madeline Usher); Griswold (William Wilson, the *Doppelgänger* in the story of that name); an Annie or Helen, a composite of all the muses Poe apostrophized after Virginia's death (Ligeia); and a narrator (perhaps Auguste Dupin).

This is an attractive scheme with clever correspondences. It was not pursued very closely by Charles Nolte, whom Argento chose as his librettist. Nolte retained the voyage, the packet boat setting for the adventures, but threw far more emphasis onto Poe's real life, less onto his fictions. In Nolte's text, three mother figures loom large: Poe's actual mother; Mrs. Allan, who adopted him (in fact, though not formally) after his mother's death; and his aunt/mother-in-law (with whom Griswold accused him of having "criminal relations"). Poe, Virginia, and Griswold as Evil Genius remain; an added incarnation of the last is Mr. Allan, Poe's unloving foster-father. In the journal, Argento describes frankly his disappointment with each of the two acts as Nolte first brought them to him, and his efforts to reshape the piece along the lines he wanted. "No doubt Charles will accept my views, but will he bring about what I *mean*?" "Good things in [Act II], but all wrong for my purposes . . . I spent the weekend—in the same low spirits I had after seeing the first act draft—trying to salvage the work." But later he interrupts composition "to enter a few words of apology for whatever doubts I've had about Nolte's libretto." And when the revised second act returns he is content with it: "The overall shape and structure are fine now, I think: interesting, varied, several clear levels of meaning."

So they are. Nevertheless, even though it seems a bit unkind to use a composer's candor against him, I shall do so to define some misgivings about *The Voyage of Edgar Allan Poe*. On setting finis to the score (not yet orchestrated but with the orchestration established in mind's ear and indicated in the vocal score), Argento reflected:

On balance, what do *I* think of the work at this moment? It is far and away the most ambitious thing I've done; it is fairly close to what I planned it to be . . . Verdian, lyric, exciting, imaginative and interesting (to me, naturally), *rich*, in short. . . . I suppose it is less fantastic, less strange than I had hoped. Or am I discovering that many of the fanciful things I can contemplate, I simply can't entertain in composition?

The last is what Debussy discovered when he tried for so long, and usually in vain, to find sounds for Poe's imaginative world. Argento *has* found sounds—but the work is indeed less fantastic, less strange than a Poe opera should be. The music *is* lyrical, rich, imaginative, and interesting; however, it is not so extraordinary that it seizes the listener's mind, to lead him into the labyrinthine, tortured mind of the opera's protagonist.

A voyage is Poe's regular symbol for a dream. The opera begins on the Richmond quayside, where Poe boards a spectral vessel peopled by a strange company and leaves with them into the mist. In the ship's saloon, a troupe of actors begins to play out a melodrama in which the writer recognizes scenes from his own life: his mother's death; his adoption; marriage to his thirteen-year-old cousin Virginia; Virginia's death. Hallucination and nightmare spill from the shipboard stage into all the company. The first-act finale is a phantasmagoria: Poe is trying to give a lecture on the poetic principle; characters transformed into those of the "King Pest" tale interrupt him; choruses echo Griswold's charges against him; from the distance, first his mother's voice and then Virginia's sings "Annabel Lee." The curtain falls as Virginia, risen from the tomb like Madeline in "The House of Usher," enters on the scene in bloodstained white garments and falls upon Poe-Usher, the cousin-lover-brother form of the hero. The frame of Act II is a trial, the basic scene still the ship's saloon. The charge is madness, Poe's defense that "I welcome visions! I cast out reason. . . . As others do the light, I choose the pain." The next charge is "You murder for your art! . . . Murder all that you love to make a sacrifice to your muse!" Here Virginia's death is re-enacted; then, Eurydice-like, she returns to life, to be killed again by Poe's insistence on learning, though he has been warned not to ask, about life beyond the grave. Poe pleads guilty to causing her death. After a dramatic dialogue with Griswold as his other self, he stabs his accuser—and so kills himself. In the epilogue, back on the quay of the opening, he expires, while offstage a male chorus is singing "Eldorado."

"Eldorado," "Annabel Lee," and "To Helen" are the poems most extensively used in Nolte's libretto. His action whirls and swirls. His language, a convincing imitation of Poe's, moves easily in and out of actual quotation. Six of the eight principals (Poe and Virginia maintain their identities) slip deftly into their many linked roles. Some of the allusions to the tales will pass unnoticed by a listener to whom they are not familiar. The repetitive Oedipal references will puzzle anyone who does not deem that particular complex among the foremost in Poe's complicated character. (Poe, in a small boat moving over a lake with Virginia, is horrified to see his mother and Griswold in another; in the wedding scene, Griswold-as-Allan embraces Poe's mother-as-slut.) Not everything works out precisely or clearly, but in the theater it proves gripping enough.

In Argento's score there are some touching lyrical passages. The scene with the boats on the lake is one; another, rather surprisingly, is the start of Poe's lecture, in the first-act finale: "And so I ask you then, when is poetry most poetic?" Here Poe makes the impression of being the only lucid, sane person in an otherwise crazy company. For "Annabel Lee" the composer has found a melody of shapely but pleasantly elusive, not quite conventional outline. At its fullest statement, sung by Virginia on her first deathbed, it is unaccompanied except by a recurrent bell stroke: a touch of color, a touch of symbolism, and, on a practical level, a tuning note to guide her through the chromatic shifts of the melody. The use of choruses onstage and offstage, the colors drawn from the orchestra, the variety of textures, the control of pace—all these are notable. So is the sensitive, flexible word setting. The Britten of the chamber operas provides the nearest parallels: in Argento's opera, a harp interlude is like that in *The Rape of Lucretia*; piano-accompanied passages and sudden flowers of melisma are like those in *Death in Venice*; little bursts of ostinato figuration and big, blurry, busy ensembles built by superimpositions recall those of the church parables. And another composer came to mind more than once: Monteverdi, evoked first by the fluid two-tenor duet lines of the opening scene and later by some striking madrigal choruses dramatically used.

The production, given in the O'Shaughnessy Auditorium of the College of St. Catherine, in St. Paul, was a shade tame, and this may have emphasized any lack of sharp, compelling fantasy in Argento's music. H. Wesley Balk was the stage director, Tanya Moiseiwitsch the designer, and Duane Schuler the lighter. One scene was much like another in visual tone. The lighting was not wild or surprising. On all levels, the opera had been very well prepared, and it was ably done; the soberness of presentation was evidently a directorial decision. Poe is a role that calls for someone like Jon Vickers; George Livings, a lyrical tenor, sang keenly and well but could not project the big scenes with full force. Karen Hunt was true and tender as Virginia. Barbara Brandt, as Poe's mother, etc., was vivid. John Brandstetter, who played Griswold, etc., has a baritone of delightfully smooth, pure timbre—almost too poetical and refined for the role. The chorus, the company's and the University of Minnesota Chamber Singers combined, sang admirably, and Philip Brunelle conducted an evidently assured performance. *The Voyage of Edgar Allan Poe* may not set the Mississippi on fire—very few operas do that. It may not rise to the challenge of re-creating in sound Poe's imaginative world—even Debussy found that impossible to achieve. But it is an intelligent, accomplished, imaginative, not at all boring new opera.

May 17, 1976

FLOUR OF WYFLY PATIENCE

Even the most assiduous operagoer is unlikely to have seen more than a handful of pieces by Alessandro Scarlatti. *Mitridate Eupatore* (1707) and *Il trionfo dell' onore* (1718) are the works of his most often staged, since for them modern performing editions—abridged and unsatisfactory, but handy for a director unwilling to prepare his own material—are available. Giuseppe Piccioli's "ricostruzione scenica e strumentale" of *Mitridate* appeared at the Piccola Scala in 1956, with Victoria de los Angeles and Giulietta Simionato as its heroines (the opera reached New York last year), and Virgilio Mortari's "riduzione scenica, elaborazione e adattamento" of *Il trionfo* was published back in 1941. Both works hold the stage easily. During the last decade, there have been revivals, with mixed results, of at least seven other Scarlatti operas, and the trickle may soon swell to a stream now that a careful edition of the scores, under the general editorship of Donald Jay Grout, and published by the Harvard University Press, is under way. Three volumes have appeared so far: *Eraclea* (brought to the stage, by Cornell University, in 1970), *Marco Attilio Regolo*, and *Griselda* (staged this month at Berkeley, California). The first and third were edited by Mr. Grout himself. In addition, Scarlatti's earliest opera, *Gli equivoci nel sembiante*, edited by Frank A. D'Accone, was staged in Los Angeles last year.

Scarlatti is worth hearing. Though he rates only a passing mention in Charles Rosen's *The Classical Style*, he formed the language in which that style could be developed. As Edward Dent put it, in the closing pages of his 1905 study of the composer:

Before 1700, he had gathered up all that was best of the tangled materials produced by that age of transition and experiment, the seventeenth century, to form out of them a musical language, vigorous and flexible as Italian itself, which has been the foundation of all music of the classical period.

And elsewhere:

Thematic development, balance of melodic phrase, chromatic harmony—all the devices which the seventeenth century had tentatively introduced, are by him woven into a smooth and supple texture, which reached its perfection in one who, although he never knew his true master, was yet his best pupil—Mozart.

Scarlatti, it is true, left opera in need of the reforms that Gluck and Mozart were to introduce. In his earliest pieces, we find bold experiment, traces of roughness, and something of the direct quality that makes earlier seventeenth-century opera so fresh to modern ears. His *Statira*, of 1690, is more formal but short-breathed. *Rosaura*, later that year, begins smoothly, almost glibly, and then in its third—so far unpublished —act embarks on brave formal innovations. *Eraclea*, at the turn of the century, sounds to us Handelian in its brisk stride; Bononcini has been proposed as the originator of this vigorous, easily enjoyed manner, varied by melting movements in 6/8 or 12/8, and the little Bononcini I have heard does suggest that he left his mark on both Scarlatti and Handel. *Mitridate Eupatore* is in an altogether grander and more passionate vein. *Griselda*, of 1721, Scarlatti's last surviving opera, represents effortless mastery. Nothing new remains to be "solved." Form, harmonic control, balance of melodic periods, and beauty of expressive line conspire; the delicate intimacy of his chamber cantatas and the emotional force of his earlier dramas are united. But in lesser hands his forms became formula. Anyone could write an opera along his lines, and many did.

"I do not know—there's something in that Rural Cottage of *Griselda*, her forlorn Condition, her Poverty, her Solitude, her Resignation, her Innocent Slumbers, and that lulling *Dolce Sogno* that's sung over her; it had an Effect upon me." Indiana, the heroine of Steele's comedy *The Conscious Lovers*, is talking specifically about Bononcini's *Griselda*, which in 1722 at the King's Theatre ran in competition with Handel's *Floridante*, but the subject seems to have had an effect upon people for six centuries and more. It's an odd tale. The lordly Gualtiero married the shepherdess Griselda, who showed herself in every way worthy of a throne. But then her husband decided to test her: he pretended to have their two children executed; he sent her back to her rural cote; later he recalled her to serve at his forthcoming wedding to a more worthy bride. Patient Griselda bore all her trials without complaint and did not waver in her love for and submission to her lord—whereupon Gualtiero at last embraced her, declared that she had shown herself a model wife, and revealed that his new "bride" was in fact their daughter, not killed after all but brought up at another court in ignorance of her origins. And everyone lived happily.

Most tellers of the tale have felt some qualms about Gualtiero's behavior. Dioneo, introducing it as the last story of the *Decameron*, remarks on the fellow's "senseless brutality." Petrarch retold Boccaccio's version in Latin, and thence it passed into the mouth of Chaucer's Clerk of Oxenford. The Clerk draws a pious moral: "nat . . . that wyves sholde / Folwen Grisilde as in humilitee, / For it were importable [unbearable], though they wolde," but that we should all bear the things God sends to try us with a meekness equal to hers. Chaucer, however, adds his own spirited envoy, urging women to stand up for themselves and let husbands do the wailing. Hans Sachs, Thomas Dekker, Goldoni, and Lope de Vega all made versions of the story. In an operatic treatment by Massenet, it's the Devil (a high-spirited, elegant Devil, originally played by Lucien Fugère) who causes Grisélidis's troubles. In a play by Gerhart Hauptmann, the husband turns nasty because he refuses to share Griselda's love with their newborn child. Some authors point parallels with Abraham and Isaac, and with Job. Others tell it as a kind of Cinderella story in which the shoe pinches very hard before goodness can triumph. Few commentators are as forthright as was Boccaccio's Dioneo, who ends by remarking that while high virtues may on occasion descend into the dwellings of the poor, there are some rulers in palaces who would be better employed as swineherds. Scarlatti's *Griselda*, like Bononcini's, depends from a much-set libretto by Apostolo Zeno, in which an attempt is made to justify Gualtiero's actions. In the cast there is a villain—called Ottone in Scarlatti's opera, Rambaldo in Bononcini's —who desires Griselda for himself and stirs up the populace against their lowborn queen. So Gualtiero devises the trials to make public demonstration of her merits and end the murmurings against her.

The recurrent operatic situations are Gualtiero's public harshness and private pangs; Griselda's tender compliance and, in solitude, her plaints; Ottone's wooing of the cast-off queen and her steadfast refusals of him; and lovers' tiffs between Costanza, the daughter of Griselda and Gualtiero, and Roberto, the prince who won her heart before she was summoned to be Gualtiero's bride. The individual moments of drama, to each of which Scarlatti rises superbly, occur when Griselda, told that Gualtiero has ordered the execution of her infant son and that her acceptance of Ottone's hand alone can save him, is torn—in a vehement aria—between maternal love and wifely submission; when Griselda and Costanza, their relationship still mutually unknown, are drawn by natural affinity to embrace, in duet, as if the one had found the lost daughter, the other the lost mother, she longed for; and when Griselda, catching Costanza in Roberto's arms, chides her for thus betraying the noble Gualtiero. The work reaches its climax in recitative, when Griselda, ordered by Gualtiero to wed Ottone, is driven at last to passionate disobedience. Scarlatti's recitative, said Burney, "is, in general, excellent," and Griselda's long recitative, starting "Mio Re, mio Nume, mio sposo un tempo, e mio diletto ancora," is excellent indeed. It moves most beautifully between string-accompanied and secco (supported only by harpsichord and string bass) declamation, and crowns the drama most movingly. After it, the loose ends are quickly tied, and there is a brief, happy ensemble.

Griselda was written for Rome at a time when women were not allowed to appear there on the stage. So in 1721 it had an all-male cast— five castrato principals, and a tenor in the subaltern role of Corrado (Roberto's brother, privy to Gualtiero's plot). Griselda was sung by Giacinto Fontana, alias Farfallino, the little butterfly. Three of the other performers are well known to Handelians. As Gualtiero, there was Antonio Bernacchi, renowned—also reproved—for his "instrumental" virtuosity; past his prime, the critics tell us, when Handel wrote *Lotario* for him, in 1729; and, according to Mrs. Pendarves, "in person not so good, for he is as big as a Spanish friar." The great Giovanni Carestini, Handel's primo uomo from 1733 to 1735, made his début in *Griselda*, as Costanza; he was then a youth of about sixteen and, as his music makes clear, still a bright soprano, not the deep, noble, heroic mezzo for whom Handel composed Theseus in *Arianna*, the title role of *Ariodante*, and Ruggiero in *Alcina*. Andrea Pacini, Scarlatti's Ottone, was three years later Handel's first Tamerlane. These details are worth recall, since individual singers play a more than ephemeral role in musical history. In all ages, they have helped to determine what kind of music was written. Bernacchi and Carestini left their mark on *Griselda* as decisively as Giuditta Pasta and Giovanni Battista Rubini did on several of Bellini's scores, as Gaetano Fraschini on several of Verdi's, and as Cathy Berberian and Jan DeGaetani have done on many contemporary works. The "vocalità" of individual pieces—the part played in their composition by the timbres, range, technique, and personality of their first interpreters—is a fairly new field of musical study, and the Scarlatti edition will help in its tilling. One's only complaint about Mr. Grout's score of *Griselda* is that, Carestini apart, it makes no mention of the original cast.

Anyone who now revives an eighteenth-century opera seria must choose between using for his heroes women in breeches, countertenors with highly developed falsetto voices, or tenors and baritones who growl out the music an octave or so too low. There had been four modern revivals of *Griselda* before Berkeley's. Franco Zeffirelli directed the opera in Catania in 1960; Rina Gigli was its heroine. In Bielefeld in 1962, and in Kiel two years later, there were productions of an edition by Christoph Bitter. A Naples concert performance in 1970 achieved wide currency through broadcasts; the eminent cast included Mirella Freni, Sesto Bruscantini, Luigi Alva, and Rolando Panerai. All four used women in the two female roles (which seems reasonable enough) but a tenor Roberto and a baritone Gualtiero and Ottone (which involves unacceptable octave transposition). At Berkeley, Roberto was sung by a female soprano, and Gualtiero and Ottone were countertenors. There is no simple right in the matter (though octave transposition can quite simply be deemed wrong); it depends on the singers available. In my experience, alto castrato roles have been most notably filled in our day by dashing female mezzos—Janet Baker, Marilyn Horne, Yvonne Minton. Countertenors who sound comfortable, act convincingly, and do not shriek or hoot their high notes have been rare. When Alan Curtis conducted Cavalli's *Erismena* at the Holland Festival two years ago, he assembled four countertenors of markedly different type: the mellifluous Paul Esswood as his hero; the incisive, fluent, sometimes unpleasantly pungent Daniel Collins as a rival prince; René Jacobs, who has a firm, virile, precise voice of a kind to cure anyone's possible dislike of countertenors, as a young servant; and John Ferrante in the drag-hag role of a bawdy old nurse, making comic capital of his squawks and booms. They were well directed. The result was excellent. At Berkeley, Mr. Collins, as Gualtiero, and William Zukof, as Ottone, hardly seemed to have had any dramatic direction at all. Moreover, they both looked ridiculous. Gualtiero postured in a salmon-pink costume topped by a red wig; Ottone was hangdog in two-color tights, a long cape that he never shed, and a long brown straggle-wig. Neither of them played, or enacted the dialogue, with any theatrical force. This was no way to solve the castrato problem. But Judith Nelson, as Roberto, representing the other solution, was similarly unhelped by director and designer: her slight frame was weighed down by a mane of white powdered curls; she was made to sit on the floor during one of her arias.

The production was a joint effort by the Departments of Music and of Dramatic Art on the Berkeley campus of the University of California. It was disappointing in that the conventions of eighteenth-century staging, and the numerous twentieth-century essays in reproducing, approximating, or finding acceptable alternatives to them, did not seem to have been carefully studied. (Since just about all the possible mistakes have already been made, they need not be made again.) Henry May's décor was a row of lumpy chandeliers hanging from the proscenium, pastel-flecked side panels, some columns of tangled liana, and, suspended in midair at the back, enlargements of some real eighteenth-century scenic sketches. George House's stage direction was fumbling. Movements and stances were gauche. The house curtain came down between scenes. For some arias, the stage was darkened while a follow spot prowled after the singer. The opera was sung in Italian: a bilingual libretto was printed, but the houselights were turned out, so it could not be consulted during the performance. Warren Travis's costumes flattered only Carole Bogard, in the title role. An orchestra of modern instruments, with modern (not gut) strings tuned to modern pitch, and horns an octave too high, was perhaps inevitable. (Berkeley has a Collegium of players trained in baroque practices, but maybe there are not enough of them to make up an orchestra calling for flutes, oboes, horns, and trumpets as well as strings.) Lawrence Moe, who conducted, did not inspire secure playing; every night there were fumbled entries. I make it sound pretty dire, but in fact I went back, and back, and back again, and each time enjoyed the performance more keenly. For mingled reasons.

First, the music itself. Scarlatti's score does not yield all its secrets at once, and there are things in *Griselda* that one can hardly hear too often.

For example, in a trio Gualtiero proposes a two-bar phrase, Costanza sings two bars in balanced reply, leading to the dominant, and then Griselda enters with a six-bar utterance staying the swift impetus of the movement and leading the harmony along a poignant path. Each night, Griselda's entry was a moment one waited for with bated breath. Second, the music was written for singers to shape, and as the performers learned what could be done with it, they became more and more eloquent. Griselda opens the second act with an aria, "Mi rivedi, o selva ombrosa," whose middle section ends with a long-sustained note that must be joined seamlessly to a reprise of the opening melody. Miss Bogard spun the sustained note ever more exquisitely, made the join ever more tenderly, until by the last performance (of six) she inspired her listeners to rapture. In the same act, Griselda has a "sleep" aria, accompanied by strings and flutes (recorders), whose beauty of line depends on an alternation of dropping sixths, small steps, and motifs outlining the harmony; this, too, was something that Miss Bogard sang ever more affectingly. After a performance or two, it was easy to stop minding about the stage production and just enjoy what the singers, and their increasingly confident accompanists, were doing. And easy to understand why eighteenth-century audiences could happily go repeatedly to the same opera, with the same cast. Number after number was brought to fuller life during the run. (Rough luck on those who heard only the first night; it's a pity that critics usually attend only first nights.) Besides, the singers varied their ornaments and cadenzas, so there were always surprising new feats of bravura as well as awaited favorite moments to enjoy.

Miss Bogard is a vivid, appealing performer, with charm in both her timbre and her appearance. Sometimes she let rhythms grow slack; sometimes her tuning strayed; but always she "made something" of the music—and often something wonderful. Costanza was Kari Windingstad, warm and appealing in tone, smooth yet precise in passage, and mistress of a well-turned trill. Miss Nelson provided a good contrast—trim, light, clear, very exact of voice and shapely of phrase. Miss Bogard and Miss Windingstad in one of the two duets, Miss Windingstad and Miss Nelson in the other, produced that happy combination of sounds in which the ingredients match yet keep their distinct characters. Mr. Collins's virtuoso prowess in divisions made him a worthy successor to Bernacchi, and his decorations were the boldest of all. Mr. Zukof was happiest in his Handelian (or Bononcinian?) air "Mi dimostra il tuo bel dono." On the first night, Miss Bogard alone seemed to act, and to utter recitatives as if they meant something. But by the last all three ladies were acting, and the men were at least making sense, not merely sound, of the words.

The opera is long. It has thirty-seven arias (all in da-capo, or ABA, form), two duets, a trio, a quartet, just eleven measures for three-part chorus, and a final "coro" for the principals. At Berkeley, all the ensembles but only twenty-one arias were retained. What numbers were done were done whole; there was no disfiguring recourse to A-section-only. Good. In preparing the abridgment, Joseph Kerman and Gary A. Tomlinson shifted three arias to new positions but otherwise—as far as one can judge without having heard *Griselda* in full—kept violence to a minimum. I was sorry to lose Roberto's rather grand-looking entrance aria, a pompous affair with horns and oboes. Among the numbers omitted were most of those with thin accompaniments (such as Costanza's "Un affetto," where the singer is supported only by violins, generally but not quite all the time in unison with her). By comparison with Handel, or with Bononcini's *Griselda*, Scarlatti's piece lacks variety of instrumental textures—but in fact there is rather more variety than we heard in this Berkeley edition.

Between the acts of the opera seria, a comic intermezzo was played, in true eighteenth-century fashion. I was glad to encounter it; a little sorry that the work chosen should have been, once again, that most familiar of all intermezzi, Pergolesi's *La serva padrona*; and captivated by the sweet, witty, most musical singing of Marlene Rozofsky as the "maid made mistress" of this English-language version.

May 31, 1976

Selections from this Berkeley production—nine arias and all the ensembles—were recorded during the run and are published on Cambridge CRS 2903. But only Miss Windingstad and Mr. Collins are heard at their best.

SEE HOW THEY RUN

Canons—to write of them without becoming technical is hard. First, a definition. Canon, from κανών, a rule; an inscription set above a piece of music indicating how it is to be performed; by extension, the piece of music composed according to that rule. A voice or instrument utters a melody; another voice or instrument takes it up, and others may follow suit. If the original melody is repeated exactly, a simple round (such as "Three Blind Mice" or "Frère Jacques") may result. But the replies may enter at a different pitch level from the original melody; may invert it (moving up where it moved down, and vice versa, to form a mirror image); may reverse it, sing or play it backward; may present it halved, quartered, doubled, quadrupled, or otherwise altered in speed. All or any of the entries may transform the initial melody by any or all of these devices. Canons can be elaborate. William Byrd composed a canon motet, "Diliges Dominum," for eight voices in which four of the voices sing a pair of simultaneous canons while the other four sing the same music backward. The Victorian teacher W. S. Rockstro, on whose *Practical Harmony* generations of British musicians were reared, remarked that "it is scarcely possible to study this complication attentively without feeling one's brain turn giddy; yet, strange to say, the effect produced is less curious than beautiful." Canons can be beautiful, and beautiful canons abound in great music of all ages. One can hardly attend a Carnegie or Fisher Hall concert without hearing some. Canons can be in a strict sense academic: Haydn wrote one such for the University of Oxford when he was doctored there, in 1791 (it can be read with the page turned either way up), and Bach presented another to the Society for the Musical Sciences, in Leipzig, when he became a member, in 1747. Canons can be puzzles, and fifteenth-century composers would give cryptic clues to their interpretation. The sense of Pierre de La Rue's "rule," or inscription, "Vade retro, Sathanas" is plain enough. "Nigra sum, sed formosa" gives a broad hint that black notes are to be sung as if they were white. But Josquin's βάτραχος ἐκ Σερίφου may baffle singers who do not know that—according to the second-century fabulist Aelian—frogs on the island of Seriphos do not croak (hence one voice is to remain silent); at the sight of the Gorgon's head they were struck dumb. Canons, it becomes clear, can easily lead one away from music down mathematical and mythological bypaths. Every third variation in Bach's Goldberg Variations is a canon—the first at the unison, the second at the interval of a second, the third at the interval of a third, and so on up to a ninth. The arrangement, as Charles Rosen has observed, "has its own beauty and gives pleasure, but not a specifically musical pleasure." The pleasure (if any) given by lines like "Roma tibi subito motibus ibit amor," "Odo tenet mulum, madidam mappam tenet Anna,"

```
S A T O R
A R E P O
T E N E T
O P E R A
R O T A S,
```

and "Lewd did I live, evil I did dwel" is not specifically poetic. However, the Goldberg Variations, and a newly discovered canonic parergon to that piece, and a performance of both works that did give specifically musical pleasure, are my main subject.

Research has tended to shrink rather than swell the catalogues of the great masters. The best-known of all "Haydn" movements, the Andante cantabile, or "Serenade," of his string quartet Opus 3, No. 5, has now been attributed to the obscure composer Roman Hofstetter, along with the rest of the Opus 3 set. Bach has lost six of the church cantatas once reckoned his, among them the well-loved *Schlage doch, gewünschte Stunde*, No. 53, and the popular *Uns ist ein Kind geboren*, No. 142. Pergolesi has shed quantities of instrumental music, including everything that Stravinsky used in *Pulcinella*. The Brahms-Haydn variations are now Brahms-A.N.Other. But there have also been some gains. I have heard first performances of far from negligible music by Beethoven (from his unfinished opera *Vestas Feuer*) and by Verdi (the scenes from *Don Carlos* cut from the score before its 1867 première). And last month, in Berkeley, I heard a work of Bach's played for the first time at a public recital.

This was "Divers Canons on the First Eight Bass Notes of the Preceding Aria"—that aria being the sarabande which is the theme of the Goldberg Variations. The Variations were published probably in 1742. Bach's first biographer, J. N. Forkel, noted that in the publication "there are some important errata, which the author has carefully corrected in his copy." That copy—is there a handy English term for *Handexemplar*, by which word the Germans denote the author's own annotated copy of a work?—has survived. It once belonged to Franz Stockhausen, who directed the Strasbourg Conservatoire at the turn of the century, and then to Paul Blumenroeder, a professor at the Conservatoire; now it has been bought by the Bibliothèque Nationale, for about $150,000. On the last page of the volume, on sixteen ruled staves, there are set out the fifteen "Divers Canons." About ten years ago, the Italian organist Luigi Tagliavini suggested that the hand they are written in is Bach's. The French Inspector of Music, Olivier Alain, confirmed it early in 1974, "solved" most of the canons, and brought them to performance at meetings of the Société Française de Musicologie in Strasbourg and in Paris. Christoph Wolff, of Columbia University, who was editing the Goldberg for the *Neue Bach-Ausgabe*, "solved" them all and brought them to performance in Freiburg, in Leipzig during the 1975 Bach Festival, and at a meeting of the American Musicological Society in Los Angeles last fall. In Berkeley, they were played by Alan Curtis and Bruce Brown, on two harpsichords, at a recital in Hertz Hall; a few days later they were played in London, in a different instrumentation, during the English Bach Festival. A performing edition by M. Alain has been published by Salabert, and Mr. Wolff's scholarly edition has been published by Bärenreiter.

Why the talk of "solving"? Because Bach did not write out his canons in full. The first of the set is represented by just the eight notes of the basic theme

$$(\#F, 2/4) ,4G/F E/D ,,B/,C D/,,G$$

superscribed "Canon simplex."* Simple indeed to complete it, either by adding a transposed inversion

$$,4D/E F/G B/A G/'D$$

entering with the fifth note of the theme, or else (as Mr. Wolff, more elegantly and accurately, has done) by supplying the original theme reversed as an accompaniment to itself. Procedures become more complicated as the set continues, until for the last canon Bach writes out only four measures of running melody (an extension of the original theme) and the instruction "Canon à 4. per Augmentationem et Diminutionem." Three other voices are supplied, in Mr. Wolff's solution, by the melody at half speed, transposed and inverted; the melody at quarter speed, differently transposed; and the main theme as bass.

Two of the canons were known before the Goldberg *Handexemplar* turned up. One of them Bach wrote in the album of the Leipzig theology student Johann Gottfried Fulde, in 1747. It was published in 1910, "solved" in 1934, and then again, independently, in 1945 by the authors of *The Bach Reader*. Two chromatic themes are set out over the eight-note bass. Above, Bach writes "Canone doppio sopr'il Soggetto," and below, "Symbolum/Christus Coronabit Crucigeros," with the four capital "C's" prominent. That gives the clue. The canon must be completed with *crossing* parts, and the note C is, so to speak, the mirror plane on either side of which the themes must be reflected. The second is the canon, already referred to, that Bach presented to the Society for the Musical Sciences. In the Elias Gottlieb Haussmann portrait of 1746 he holds it in his hand. Here, three parts have to be increased to six in a "Canon triplex." A neat way of doing so was discovered in 1840. The Bach scholar Friedrich Smend wrote a short book about this canon

---

* I quote the music in Barry S. Brook's easily mastered "Simplified Plaine and Easie Code System for Notating Music," which can be typed directly on an ordinary typewriter, without fidgety subscripts and superscripts, and can be fed into computers. Key signature and time signature are shown in the parentheses. Then the preliminary single comma (,) indicates pitches from the C to the B below middle C; the double comma (,,) the octave below that; and an apostrophe (') pitches from the middle C to the B above. The 4 means quarter-notes. Each pitch and duration sign remains in effect until another appears. The slash (/) represents a bar line. The working of the "Plaine and Easie Code," which, without recourse to music type, can give precise notation of a melody, is summarized on a single page published by the City University of New York.

(*Johann Sebastian Bach bei seinem Namen gerufen*, 1950). If A=1, and B=2, and so on up to Z=24 (I and J count as one letter; so do U and V), then the sum of BACH is 14 and the sum of J. S. BACH is its "retrograde," 41. Those two figures can be counted so often in Bach's music that I fear we must acknowledge his deliberate use of them as a "signature." Between the repeat signs of the portrait canon there are, in the upper voices, fourteen notes. In all, those staves contain nineteen notes, which is the "sum" of 1747, the year in which Bach joined the Society. Handel was an honorary member; the first eight notes of the Goldberg bass, Bach's soggetto, had already been the bass of a "Chacoone" with sixty-two variations published by Handel in 1733. The sum of G. F. HAENDEL (to give him a German spelling) is sixty, and Smend has laid out a solution of Bach's canon in which a group of sixty notes can be counted. Throw into the pot the facts that the tenor voice of the canon also starts the E-major fugue in Book II of the "Forty-eight"; that the theme appears in J. J. Fux's treatise *Gradus ad parnassum*, of which Lorenz Mizler, the founder and moving spirit of the Society for the Musical Sciences, had published an edition; and that Smend counts fourteen silver buttons in the Haussmann Bach portrait (I don't)—and an interesting stew may result. Moreover, though there are fifteen canons in all, they are numbered only from one to fourteen, with two included as No. 10. They fall into groups that give the pattern 4.1.4.1.4—surely not a coincidence, but a play upon Bach's "41+14" signature. Maybe it's too easy to prove things with figures. I started counting this and that in the Fulde canon, to discover why the composer should have chosen this piece for his friend's album. It contains only forty-four notes and the sum of FULDE is forty-six. But wait: J. G. FULDE=62, and 6+2=8; forty-four notes, and 4+4=8. Eight notes in the soggetto, and exactly eighty between the repeat signs of the solution (which may be found on page 405 of *The Bach Reader*). Q.E.D.?

In Berkeley, the newly found canons were played both before and after a complete performance of the Goldberg, given by Mr. Curtis. As prolegomena they passed by quickly and made a rather small effect. The Goldberg itself held one rapt, for Mr. Curtis is an interpreter with a rare instinct for living rhythms, pulses, and inflections, free in his phrasing of the slow melodies—with freedoms that do no violence to, but enhance, the natural flow of the music—and buoyant in fast numbers. His instrument, patterned on a mid-eighteenth-century Flemish harpsichord, was rich but not fierce, full in timbre but not cluttered, distinct but not dry. Moreover, he played from a text corrected as Bach had corrected it. (When one read in the program note of significant changes to measure seventeen of the seventeenth variation and to measure twenty-three of the twenty-third, it seemed that the composer must have been up to his numerological tricks once more.) I won't swear that without marked-up score on knee I would notice all the differences, but certainly the added instruction "al tempo di Giga" to No. 7 and much extra ornament in No. 26 make an audible difference to the music.

What can still be said about the Goldberg which is not summed up in Tovey's observations that until Beethoven wrote the Waldstein there was nothing to compare with it in instrumental brilliance and that, for all the science that went into its making, "Bach has never covered so wide a range of feeling and effect in any other instrumental work"? Bach himself, though he seemed to have said just about everything that could be said over that thirty-two-bar bass, nevertheless found still more to do with its first eight notes when he entered those canons on the last page of his copy. Heard after the great work itself, they formed a moving epilogue: a microcosm of his art, starting so simply, then growing to include bright, buoyant little inventions and strange passages of tense chromatic meditation. Private music, learned music—but affecting music by a composer who wrote in canon as naturally as a poet writes in verse.

June 7, 1976

The "Fulde" canon is reproduced on p. 180 of The Bach Reader *(eds. Hans T. David and Arthur Mendel; Norton Library, revised edition 1966); the "presentation" canon on p. 177; and the Haussmann portrait, in which Bach holds it, opposite p. 192.*

The fourteen newly discovered canons have been recorded by a group of Marlboro musicians, for the Marlboro Recording Society (MRS 12), in a version scored for a small broken consort (strings and wind). Some are done gravely, some gaily, and all are played with a memorable beauty of tone and phrasing. This is a performance to persuade one that the canons are indeed a balanced and ordered set, not a random series of contrapuntal exercises. Rudolf Serkin frames them between two limpid performances of the Goldberg aria, *played on the piano.*

Alan Curtis has also recorded the canons (with Arthur Haas on the second harpsichord) as a coda to his performance of the Goldberg *on (German) EMI 1C 151–3071–11. He plays the temperamental and captivating 1728 instrument, by Christian Zell, in the Hamburg Museum of Art and Craft. And there is another two-harpsichord recording, played by Wolf Junghanns and Bradford Tracey, on Toccata FSM 53 622.*

HOUSEHOLD TALES

Anne Sexton, who died in 1974, became an untidy, self-indulgent poet whose imagery increasingly resembled the uncontrolled—sometimes beautiful—patterns of a kaleidoscope; memories of father, mother, and childhood horrors were fragments of jagged glass in the tube, anguish and madness the confining mirrors within which they were spun. But in *Transformations* (1971) there was other matter—sixteen tales by the brothers Grimm—to be reflected, and Sexton was a good reteller of tales. (Any modern choreographer who tackles Prokofiev's ballet *The Buffoon* might well use the scenario colored as in her version of it, in *The Book of Folly*.) The Grimm tales, it's true, she turned into Sexton tales. Her Sleeping Beauty wakes up crying "Daddy! Daddy!"— and

> It's not the prince at all,
> but my father
> drunkenly bent over my bed,
> circling the abyss like a shark,
> my father thick upon me
> like some sleeping jellyfish.

Mother Gothel, who kept Rapunzel locked in a tower, is a lesbian aunt pressing "Old breast against young breast"; Iron Hans is a lunatic cured "without Thorazine / or benefit of psychotherapy" but by kindness; Rumpelstiltskin is a *Doppelgänger*; and the Wonderful Musician who behaves so cruelly is

> Saved by his gift
> like many of us—
> little Eichmanns,
> little mothers—
> I'd say.

The familiar Sexton horrors are here, but then the Grimms' *Kinder- und Hausmärchen* was filled with horrors, too, and the charm of *Transformations*—it *is* a charming book, for all the pain it enshrines—lies in the revelation of ingenious, unexpected links between folk mythology and private modern hells. Sexton's use of smart similes is liberal, reckless, and eventually tiresome: "Her blood began to boil up / like Coca-Cola"; "The king looked like Munch's *Scream*"; "Just as the Supreme Being drills / holes in our skulls to let / the Boston Symphony through"; "and the princesses sprang out of their beds / and fussed around like a Miss America Contest"; "She was as persistent / as a Jehovah's witness"—every few lines the next simile arrives. But the large similes—each tale as a parable of plights that still exist, though wizards and wicked fairies are no more—are deftly handled. The book, dedicated to the poet's daughter, reads partly as autobiography; the author introduces herself as "a middle-aged witch, me," but it is soon clear that she is not only the witches and cruel mothers but also the variously injured maidens who fill the tales.

Four years ago, at the suggestion of H. Wesley Balk, a director of the Minnesota Opera Company, Conrad Susa made an opera, for that company, of Sexton's *Transformations*. He set verbatim the introduction and nine of the tales, to form "an entertainment in two parts," with five scenes in each part. Eight singers, eight instrumentalists—and staging left to the imagination of the director. After its Minnesota première, the Susa-Sexton *Transformations* was taken up by the University of Wisconsin, in Madison, and the Handel and Haydn Society, in Boston. Next year, it is to be produced by the Netherlands Opera. Last month, it had its New York première, at the Manhattan Theater Club. I trust there will be many more productions, for *Transformations* is one of the brightest and best of recent American operas.

In Minneapolis, the setting was a madhouse. The Manhattan version began in Anne Sexton's attic. The scenic resources of the Theater Club are few—a small open platform at one end of a room, orchestra to the side—but the resourcefulness of David Shookhoff, the director, and his eight vivacious performers was abundant. A few old trunks, which had opened to reveal the characters, were variously disposed to serve as evocations of palace, cottage, tower, enchanted forest, and magic pool. The idea of transformations runs through all the piece. Each singer plays many parts. Karen Clauss began as Anne Sexton, shaded into Wicked Queen (in the tale of "Snow White: Narcissism and the Rivalry Between Mother and Daughter"), became Mother Gothel, the "woman who loves a woman," and later the singer of the long blues to which "Godfather Death" is set. This is basically the dramatic soprano role, and Miss Clauss gave of it a strong, gleaming performance, if sometimes rather strident above the staff. The lyric soprano role compasses Snow White, Rapunzel, Gretel, and sundry put-upon princesses; Carolyn Weber sang it sweetly and played it with a piquant, understated sense of humor. The mezzo is, among other things, the Mirror on the Wall and the mother whose mother love—as she turns into the "Hansel and Gretel" witch—becomes all too literally consuming; in Patricia Deckert, expressive, dancing eyes, elegantly timed words, and a warmly attractive timbre were combined. Tonio Di Paolo, as Iron Hans, etc., was outstanding among the men—a young baritone so eloquent and touching in timbre, so communicative in manner, that if I were a composer I should want to write music for him to sing. Three tenors—Thomas A. Rowe, bonny as an assortment of princes, Jonathan Rigg and John Shackelford, lively in various character parts—and the bass Raymond Sambolin completed the cast.

Susa's score is economical, intelligent, witty, alert: a cunning theater piece, sure in its proportions and its varied gaits, always engaging and inventive. Each of Sexton's tales has an introduction; in her fables the moral is stated first, then comes its exemplification. This gives the composer a chance to practice his own kind of transformations, as music from the preface returns in the tale proper. There are happy allusions to the styles of specific performers—Bing Crosby, the Andrews Sisters. The instrumentalists are also asked to be inventively imitative, to recall now Ethel Smith, now Perez Prado. I like the opera even better than the book of poems; fresh winds from the world blow into it. It inhabits the terrain of Stravinsky's *Reynard* and *Soldier's Tale*, Kurt Weill's *Little Mahagonny* and *Seven Deadly Sins*—not as an imitation of any of those works but in being a 1970s successor in scale, texture, and tunefulness, and in being a delightful entertainment that is not trivial. In a well-ordered society, so gifted an ensemble of singers and players as the musical director, Benton Hess, had gathered for this performance would stay together, exploring the "music theater" repertory and adding to it with commissions of its own. (In England, though the pound may sink, a new opera company has risen to do just this— the English Music Theatre Company, a stable troupe, its members engaged on a full year's contract. It kicked off last month with a new piece, *Tom Jones*, commissioned from the talented young Stephen Oliver (see pp. 412–3). I commend *Transformation* to its attention.) There are lively young troupes in America. Minneapolis and St. Paul have the Minnesota Opera Company—though the singers' contracts run only twenty-six weeks. Texas has the Texas Opera Theater—the Houston Grand Opera's "TOTS"—with thirty-five-week contracts. New York could do with something of the kind.

Gian Carlo Menotti's new opera, *The Hero*, commissioned for the Opera Company of Philadelphia and given just two performances, earlier this month, in Philadelphia's Academy of Music, is a slight, feeble, philistine, and rather common work—essentially a one-act sketch (there is about an hour and ten minutes of music) spun out by two intermissions. The Hero, David Murphy, has been asleep for ten years and six days, and at curtain-rise is within hours of beating the world record for uninterrupted slumber. His wife charges a two-dollar admission to see him; he has become an attraction "only second to Niagara Falls." The next day, a monument will be unveiled to him, "the master-

377

work of the noted artist Randy Cornpone . . . artistic and smart, / the latest example of pop art. / It is an exact replica of David Murphy's bed. . . . / It is worth two million dollars / and it is the donation of the Rockaford Foundation." But David's pretty cousin Barbara kisses his sleeping lips, and—a few hours short of the record—he wakes up. Consternation!

The composer-librettist-director describes his work as "a gentle, good-natured plea for Americans to wake up to reality, to abandon self-congratulatory illusions, to return to their former rugged individualism and to the uncompromising honesty of their ancestors." David Murphy "is the prototype of the 'yes' man, achieving stature by agreeing with everybody's views, and by turning a blind eye to corruption. . . . Barbara stands not only for David's conscience, but also for the new courage and honesty of American youth who dare to challenge the long-standing myths of 'success' as a sine qua non of respectability, and search, instead, for self-respect and inner peace." Fine words. In the last scene, David makes a big speech to the populace:

> This fair land we live in
> was once reclaimed by steadfast pilgrims
> with unswerving souls.
> The hard truth must be faced again
> with sturdier hearts.
> Again our voice must rise
> with blinding candor
> against the naked emperors,
> the charlatans.
> There is no truth too bleak to face,
> no hardship too severe,
> provided that the soul remain unscathed.

Glib words—and set to music of such banality that, however sincere Menotti's own feelings may be, the artistic effect is cheap and unworthy. The rest is a potting at easy targets. Mrs. Murphy enters with her hair in curlers, and people laugh. A guide announces a reception (ten dollars a ticket) at which chicken à la king and American chablis will be served and "the famous soprano Madame Vocestanca of the Metropolitan Opera of New York will sing," and people laugh. There are a few tuneful scraps of sub-Puccini melody, unsustained. Twenty years ago, after *The Saint of Bleecker Street*, Joseph Kerman remarked that "every attitude, every feeling, every response is on Menotti's own special level of banality." True of the new piece, too, which can replace *The Saint* as "of all Menotti's operas . . . the feeblest in purely musical invention, and the most slovenly in dramatic effect." Christopher Keene conducted.

378

The cast was led by Dominic Cossa as David; Diane Curry, very coarse, as his wife; and Nancy Shade as Barbara. Their voices were not quite big enough to fill the Academy.

June 14, 1976

A vocal score of Susa's Transformations *is published by E. C. Schirmer.*

ONLY VERDI

When the critic Henry F. Chorley assembled his *Thirty Years' Musical Recollections,* in 1862, he reflected that "Signor Verdi is . . . the only writer of his country representing, during the last fifteen years, that Maestro of better days [Rossini], whose music was heard from one end of Europe to the other." And not only Europe. Verdi won his first large success with his third opera, *Nabucco.* It was produced at La Scala, Milan, in the spring of 1842 and revived in the autumn season for fifty-seven more performances—a figure unmatched before or since in the Scala annals. Swiftly it carried his name throughout Italy. In 1843, it reached Vienna and Lisbon; in 1844, Barcelona, Berlin, Corfu, Stuttgart, Oporto, and Malta; in 1845, Paris, Hamburg, Marseilles, and Algiers; in 1846, Copenhagen, Constantinople, Budapest, and London; in 1847, Havana and Bucharest; in 1848, New York and Brussels; in 1849, Prague; in 1850, Lemberg and Buenos Aires; in 1851, Zurich and St. Petersburg. Similar accounts could show how rapid and wide was the dissemination of all Verdi's popular operas. And, unlike Rossini's —which, except for *The Barber,* soon disappeared from the central repertory—they continued and continue to be performed. For a century and a quarter, Verdi has dominated the operatic scene in a sustained way unmatched by any other composer except Mozart and Wagner. Donizetti and Meyerbeer, who were deemed giants in their day, came and went (and seem to be coming back again). Puccini and Richard Strauss have arrived, but who can tell if they are here to stay? Mozart, Wagner, and Verdi have stood the test of time, and Verdi's reputation is still growing. In London, Covent Garden has just staged its first production of Verdi's fourth opera, *I lombardi alla prima crociata,* with clamorous success. In the fifties and sixties, *all* his operas were revived on various British stages, and also in Italy. In New York, this season, *La battaglia di Legnano, Giovanna d'Arco,* and *Stiffelio* were given their first American stagings, and an American Institute for Verdi Studies was founded. A large body of works that used to be lumped together as "early Verdi" has become a sequence of distinct operas, each worth individual inspection.

When Alfred Noyes, in a once well-known poem, wrote that "the music's only Verdi"—it was a *Trovatore* tune he heard, ground out by a barrel organ—that "only" was a fair reflection of serious critical opinion early this century. *Otello* and *Falstaff* were respectable; Verdi's other operas formed a progression from crude vigor to that late-reached mastery. Some people think differently now. Gabriele Baldini, a cultivated and scholarly man, translator of Shakespeare, claimed *Il trovatore* as Verdi's masterpiece; the conductor Gianandrea Gavazzeni has dubbed it "the Italian Matthew Passion." Such champions go too far. The general perspective of the old view was more nearly true. Almost at the start of his career, Verdi formulated the articles of operatic belief that guided him along the path to *Otello*, and in the letters of 1843, when *Ernani* was planned, there are ideas, precepts, very phrases that recur constantly during the next forty years. That path began under the shadows of Rossini and Donizetti, composers to whom Verdi's music paid frequent and sometimes, it seems, deliberate and specific tribute. It led him—as Rossini and Donizetti had both been led—to Paris. Verdi's life for the decade after *Ernani* reads like a travel diary, a chronicle of journeys, from a Milan base, to bring new operas to the stage or supervise local premières. He later referred to this time as his "years in the galley"; a long, pretty continuous stay in Paris, from July 1847 to August 1849, provided the only patch of relative stability. *Rigoletto, Il trovatore,* and *La traviata* mark the climax of that busy period; in nine years Verdi had composed fourteen or fifteen operas (depending on how *Jérusalem,* an expanded and extensively revised *I lombardi,* is counted). There followed *Les Vêpres siciliennes* and another long Paris stay, from October 1853 to January 1857; for some thirty years Verdi strove (with results that never quite satisfied him: *Simon Boccanegra, La forza del destino, Don Carlos,* and to some extent *Aida* were all refashioned after their premières) to create a *grand opéra* in which lofty Meyerbeerian subject matter could be brought to life by his own particular kind of Italian "warmth." Those years need not concern us here. *Giovanna d'Arco, La battaglia di Legnano,* and *Stiffelio* all belong to the earlier period.

•

Giovanna, first given at La Scala in 1845, was the third of the four large patriotic operas that Verdi wrote with the poet and patriot Temistocle Solera. (The others are *Nabucco, I lombardi,* and *Attila.*) It is large in scope, not in duration—just under two hours of music. I first saw it staged ten years ago, in a student production at London's Royal Academy of Music, and was bowled over: "There are passages that are naïve in a *banda municipale* way; the supernatural music strikes no depths; but every number in the score is filled with life, with feeling. There is no fluently mechanical writing along approved models for easy effect. All is bold, vigorous, alive, and marked by that response to character which always fired Verdi's musical imagination." Solera protested that he had devised "an entirely original Italian drama," but in fact he took Schiller's play *Die Jungfrau von Orleans* and boiled it down. *Die Jungfrau*, patterned on Shakespeare's histories (there are clear echoes of *Henry IV* and *Henry V*), turns on a situation familiar to every operagoer—a conflict between amorous inclination and patriotic duty. Joan, on the battlefield, feels a sudden attraction toward the handsome young English knight Lionel and spares his life instead of killing him. She feels that the purity of her mission has been sullied by this moment of sensual weakness and so is unable to reply when—before the crowds assembled for the Reims coronation of the Dauphin, Charles —her father charges her with diabolical practices. Dishonored, captured by the English, she recalls Samson and with superhuman strength bursts her bonds, to lead the French to victory, though dying herself on the battlefield. Solera dropped Lionel, along with a dozen or so other characters, and transferred Joan's transitory affection to Charles. At the end, her father, not heavenly power, strikes off her chains. Solera also provided words for Joan's "voices," which in Schiller are imagined. The operatic demons tempt her in a lilting 3/8 chorus, "Tu sei bella, pastorella," whose fresh prettiness has no infernal overtones; but since the temptation is precisely that Joan should continue in pastoral bliss, rather than take up arms, the result is not altogether inappropriate. The character of Joan is simplified but not spoiled. She is still David, the shepherd who rose to lead a people to freedom, and Samson, the champion who yielded to desire but repented and destroyed his foes. And she is the first Verdi heroine to be drawn in depth. As Julian Budden puts it (in *The Operas of Verdi*), "at no point does Giovanna descend to the level of an ordinary prima donna. Almost everything she has to sing carries her own unique blend of simplicity and majesty." Her father, Jacques, a baritone, is also the kind of torn personage Verdi delighted in: a fanatic who sets religious rigor above patriotism and above paternal tenderness, a kind of Azucena rent by loftier emotions. Charles, a tenor, has chivalrous, graceful music. On these three, and much chorus, the opera depends. The bass, Talbot, has a small role— leading the English troops in a rousing chorus rather like "Heart of Oak."

The American première was given last month by the New York Grand Opera, in the Brooklyn Academy of Music. The first performances were said to be rough. By the third, which I attended, everything conspired to produce a rousing event in which any critical reservations were swept away by the energy and excitement that such music generates when it is executed with spirit. Pyramid Sellers, in the title role, sang with feeling, with force, and with some delicacy. Aristides Inchaustegui, a tenor from Santo Domingo, as Charles, had smoothly produced tones and a good sense of phrase. Theodore Lambrinos, as Jacques, was robust, if not subtle. Vincent LaSelva's conducting was passionate yet not uncontrolled. And the Brooklyn Academy itself—New York's only public opera house built on a human scale—played its part in creating the sort of occasion recorded by the nineteenth-century critics: when a Verdi opera "muove all'orgasmo il pubblico."

Verdi's early biographer "Folchetto" (the pen name of Jacopo Caponi) declared that "foreigners will never be able to understand the influence exerted, for a certain period, by the ardent, blazing melodies that Verdi conceived when the situations, or even isolated lines of verse, recalled the unhappy state of Italy, or her memories, or her hopes. The public saw allusions everywhere, but Verdi found them first and shaped to them his inspired music, which often ended by causing a revolution in the theater." Similarly, Luigi Dallapiccola said that in words and music Verdi "formulated a style through which the Italian people found a key to their dramatic plight and vibrated in unison with it." But to some extent foreigners can understand. Beyond any specific "relevance," there was and is the power of Verdi's melodies and strong slow-surging rhythms to generate mass emotion. It is an important element in his works, a reason for their continued as well as their immediate popularity. Even people who have lived comfortable, untroubled lives are moved to "vibrate in unison" with the Hebrews' cry of "Oh mia patria sì bella e perduta," in *Nabucco*, or the Scottish exiles' of "Patria oppressa," in *Macbeth*.

La battaglia di Legnano (1849), composed for performance in a Rome on the point of declaring itself a republic, is the most openly patriotic of all Verdi's operas, a Risorgimento call to arms. (It proved unperformable elsewhere until its political teeth had been drawn.) Paradoxically, it is also the most "French" of his early works. As Budden says, "it could only have been written in Paris, against a background of French opera and above all the French military march. . . . Verdi was reaping the fruits of his first encounter with French opera." Unlike the Roman audience, I have never been bowled over by *La battaglia*. The fault may lie in the performances I've heard (in the Fenice, Venice, with Leyla Gencer as a squally heroine; in a Welsh National Opera version set in Lombardy during the last war—the Italians as partisans, Barbarossa a German commandant; and, in February, in the Great Hall of Cooper Union, where the Amato Opera put on an indifferent production). But Budden suggests a possible failing in the work itself when he describes its accompaniment patterns as "unusually studied," and continues, "Everything is deliberately made 'interesting'; nothing is repeated without harmonic variation wherever possible. Even the scoring is calculated." There are stirring things in *La battaglia*. Much of the third and fourth acts rises high. But it lacks the sweep and naturalness of the best early Verdi. Or so I shall maintain until my mind is changed by some irresistibly splendid presentation. Performances can often cause revaluation; the full merits of Verdi's *I masnadieri* were concealed until the masterly Philips recording of the piece brought them to light.

The domestic scenes of *La battaglia* show Verdi moving into his "second period," in which, it might be said, there is a new care for the delicate, subtle musical presentation of personal predicaments. There followed *Luisa Miller* (1849) and *Stiffelio* (1850), both "bourgeois" dramas. "Among my neglected operas," Verdi once said, "some I abandon because the subjects were a mistake, but there are two which I should not like to be forgotten: *Stiffelio* and *La battaglia di Legnano*." *Stiffelio* was the last of his operas to be revived in our day. In revising it as *Aroldo*, the composer cannibalized the autograph. The original *was* forgotten; a few Italian houses did it, and then it petered out in Barcelona, Corfu, Oporto, and finally Málaga (1862). Only in 1968, after two copy scores had come to light, was it revived, in Parma. In all but two of the early productions, the action had been shifted from nineteenth-century Austria to fifteenth-century Germany, and the piece renamed *Guglielmo Wellingrode*. Then, as *Aroldo*, the action was relocated for three acts in a medieval castle "near Kent," and finally on the banks of Loch Lomond, where all the characters—some presumably took the high road, and some the low—were by preposterous coincidence reunited. *Aroldo* is no substitute for *Stiffelio*. The matrimonial difficulties of a nineteenth-century Protestant pastor sit less pertinently on an English crusader, and *Stiffelio* loses its special interest as being one of the two operas in which Verdi used a "modern" setting. (The other, of course, is *La traviata*.)

At the time of their composition, Verdi was living openly with a woman not yet his wife and already the mother of at least two illegitimate children (not by him). His choice of subjects has a biographical interest. While Stiffelius was away preaching, his wife, Lina, was seduced by Count Raphael. The drama turns on the clergyman's belief in forgiveness and the man's inability to practice what he preaches where his own wife is concerned. There is a striking coup de théâtre in Act II, when Stiffelius is about to fight Raphael: from the church come the voices of the brethren awaiting their minister, and the sword drops from

Stiffelius's hand. In Act III, he decides to let Lina join her lover, draws up a deed of divorce, and, ignoring her tears of repentance, invites her to sign it. She does so, and then turns on him spiritedly—on the man who has coldly regained his honor at the price of his wife's love, since she has always loved him. As for Raphael, she says, "fu tradimento." The scene changes to the chapel. Stiffelius mounts the pulpit and opens the Bible at random. It falls open, conveniently, at John 8, the story of the adulterous woman. With his eyes on Lina, who is ascending the pulpit steps on her knees, Stiffelius reads on: "Neither do I condemn thee"—and the curtain falls as the full congregation cries out, "God declared that she was forgiven!"

An interesting subject, although in Francesco Maria Piave's libretto some of its details are rather clumsily worked. (Besides the deed of divorce, no fewer than five letters are involved.) Verdi rose to it with some of the most adventurous music he had written. Only one number, an aria for Stankar, Lina's father, is cast in conventional form; and since Stankar is a conventional nobleman of the old school, even that makes dramatic sense. (Stankar's cabaletta breaks new ground, how-ever, for, instead of the usual repeat, it collapses into a series of broken exclamations, with a final ferocious rally.) The other pieces are in what has been called Verdi's "dialectical" vein. Form is determined by the verbal and emotional content; when arias are interrupted by the person to whom they are addressed, the music moves off on a new tack. The interview between Stiffelius and his wife is the high point. He addresses her in measured Bellinian phrases; the effect is of someone forcing him-self to contain fierce emotions within formal utterance. When she re-plies, her voice is doubled in octaves by clarinet and solo cello, and accompanied only by hollow fifths—an extraordinarily poignant passage. Then an English-horn melody takes over, to express the intensity of feelings that has reduced her speech to little more than a monotone.

Stiffelius was composed for Verdi's cherished tenor, the ringing and resonant Gaetano Fraschini. In the American première of the opera, given this month by the New York Grand Opera, in the Brooklyn Acad-emy, Richard Taylor did not have the needed weight and force of tone, but he sang with intelligence and ability. Norma French, as Lina, seemed somewhat too cautious; the role calls for more generously energetic singing. The performance, again conducted by Vincent LaSelva, was not as headily exciting as the same company's *Giovanna* had been; nevertheless, it was good enough to make plain the remarkable merits of *Stiffelio*. Both *Giovanna* and *Stiffelio* were simply staged, in settings of painted canvas. At a guess, the castle hall of *Stiffelio* was borrowed from *Rigoletto*, the churchyard from *Don Carlos*, and the chapel from *Ernani*. Martin Platt staged both operas with a careful regard to the composer's instructions. There were some comical moments: as when

Stankar, crying "O sword of honor, which for so many years, girt at the side of the aged warrior, in perils garnered glory for him," drew a battered and buttoned practice foil from the belt of his smart blue suit. But on the whole the intentions were right—which is more than can be said of some of the big, ambitious Verdi productions put on in larger houses.

The formation of the American Institute for Verdi Studies was prompted, in part, by the need to throw a bridge over the gulf between what scholars have discovered about Verdi's intentions and the way his operas are often performed today. The gulf became apparent during the International Verdi Congress held in Chicago in 1974, when the Lyric Opera, host to the *congressisti*, staged a production of *Simon Boccanegra* at odds with much of what the assembled scholars had been saying about the work. (See pp. 7–9.) The congress had been convened by the Institute of Verdi Studies, in Parma. The archives and publications of that organization have revolutionized Verdi research. The exchanges of ideas at its congresses—the cross-fertilization of differing national techniques of music criticism, music history, and musicology; the friendships, rivalries, and shared special interests; the casually dropped clues that led others to discover treasures—have transformed our knowledge, and therefore understanding, of several Verdi operas, of his approaches to form and to the execution of his works, and of many related matters. But performers have failed to take much account of them—and musicology is a sterile exercise until its results are put into performance.

Much of the new work on Verdi is being done in America. After Chicago, Martin Chusid, of New York University, gathered a few enthusiasts together (I was among them) to see if there would be support for a parallel American institute. Mario Medici, the director of the Parma institute, sent his blessing. And support was immediately forthcoming: from scholars; from just about all the opera companies of this country; from conductors, directors, and singers; from the general public. The result is the American Institute for Verdi Studies, which already has an extensive archive—housed in the music division of New York University's Bobst Library, on Washington Square—and a busy program of future activities.

June 21, 1976

"Heart of Oak," words by David Garrick and music by William Boyce, is a well-known British patriotic song. It was first heard in the panto-mime Harlequin's Invasion *(1759). According to* The Oxford Com-

panion to Music, *an American version, "The Liberty Song," was introduced in 1768 and also achieved enormous popularity.*

The American Institute for Verdi Studies has prospered; its address is % Department of Music, New York University, 268 Waverly Building, New York, N.Y. 10003.

GIANT TO THE MIND

Girolamo Frescobaldi was organist of St. Peter's—and had been for some time—when Urban VIII engaged Bernini to give the church new splendor. Knowing that, recalling the scale of Bernini's works for the place, reading of the thirty thousand persons who turned up to hear the young organist's début recital there, and hearing in the mind's ear the resonances of that vast building, we are apt to think of Frescobaldi as a composer of music on a majestic scale—and so, of course, he was. Odd fare, then, for one of the intimate recitals given in the André Mertens Galleries for Musical Instruments, in the Metropolitan Museum? No, not exactly, for the pieces played, all but two of them, were taken from the two volumes of toccatas and other items that Frescobaldi published as being collections of works for harpsichord and for organ. What a title page says isn't always hard evidence. The Moonlight Sonata was first published as being "for harpsichord or piano." Try it on the harpsichord. It works, after a fashion, and the second and third movements are possibly closer in sound to what Beethoven wanted than anything that can be coaxed from a modern concert grand. But plainly it's a piece written for a piano of the late eighteenth or very early nineteenth century, and the mention of an alternative instrument is probably a sales gesture in the direction of still piano-less households. Some of the Frescobaldi toccatas, I think, are plainly organ music, and some of those in the second volume are specifically designated as such. But all of them *can* be played on the harpsichord, and not all of them are thereby diminished.

Someone or other—Pliny? Statius?—records the remark of a guest at a dinner party where a small bronze statue of Hercules decked the board: that, while small to the eye, the figure was a giant to the mind. Majesty *can* be suggested in little space—or with few decibels. On the harpsichord, Gustav Leonhardt has given performances of toccatas that, since they bear liturgical subtitles (such as "to be played during the Elevation"), Frescobaldi must surely have meant for organ performance, and has done so in a manner that makes one feel the full Petrine grandeur of the compositions. At the Met recital, Lionel Party did not quite achieve this. He is a thoughtful and sensitive player. He observed those freedoms of tempo and meter—the slowing down for expressive effect, the pause preceding a determined assault on bravura passages, "in order to exhibit the agility of the hands all the more"— that the composer prescribed. But at this recital he did not show himself to be a man of fiery temperament or huge imagination. He used two instruments from the museum's collection—a harpsichord, dated Rome 1666, ascribed to Girolamo Zenti (who was Charles II's instrument builder about that time), and a virginal said to have been made for Eleonora d'Este, Duchess of Urbino, in 1540. The former is an instrument of firm, clear, pleasing tone. The little virginal is exquisite to look at and surprisingly strong in its attack tones, but the notes are short-lived, and any rapid movements in the bass produced whirr and whine. It sang sweetly in variations on the air "Or chè noi rimena" (a very beautiful melody) but could not sustain the suspended notes in the Twelfth Toccata of the First Book. The program was cunningly fashioned in three groups—played on harpsichord, virginal, harpsichord again—each ending with a masterpiece. Frescobaldi's varied kinds of achievement were juxtaposed, and by the end of the evening we had heard examples of most of his skills and moods. (Not quite all: his playful side—shown by merry capriccios on the cuckoo call or by that ricercar in which the player must be a vocalist as well and, over the four-part music his fingers are sounding, sing out a fifth melody wherever he can make it fit—was represented only by a passing moment or two.) There were grand toccatas, dances, the madrigal by Arcadelt "passagiato" (arranged as a keyboard piece, with passagework for the fingers), a set of variations, capriccios, and three of those works in which Frescobaldi pushed the new resources of baroque chromatic harmony to the limits attainable within mean-tone tuning. Mr. Party's first group ended with the variations on the "Romanesca" melody, a precursor of the Goldberg and the Diabelli; his second with the Eighth Toccata of the Second Book, an essay in "lengths and ligatures"; his third with the magnificent Ninth Toccata from the same book.

Summer is usually deemed a time for musical mass meetings: at Wolf Trap Farm Park, outside Washington, with its audiences of sixty-five hundred; in Philadelphia's new Robin Hood Dell West, which holds sixteen and a half thousand people; in Central Park, where last week a crowd estimated at up to a hundred thousand assembled to hear the Metropolitan Opera's concert performance of *Aida*. At these events, the music is electrically amplified and comes through loudspeakers. At the Metropolitan Museum, there were perhaps fifty listeners—all the gallery can comfortably hold. The air-conditioning was turned off, so that the music could move against a background of silence. And although Mr. Party, as I have suggested, was not the most impulsive of interpreters, he proved a knowledgeable and persuasive guide to a rich musical world where science, skill, proud flourish, passionate intensity of harmony, and quiet, simple, lyrical inventions conspire. It was the kind of recital that sent one to the library to get out the Frescobaldi scores, made one eager to try the pieces under one's own fingers. And eager, too, to hear the grand works on the grandest possible scale. The Cathedral of St. John the Divine holds not thirty thousand but something more like seven thousand. Would a Frescobaldi recital fill it?

June 28, 1976

MUSIC AT THE FALLS

Walter Scott's romances were a rich mine for operatic librettists. It is surprising that "the American Scott," whose books were well known in Europe, should not have been raided more often; I know of only a few operas based on James Fenimore Cooper. In 1834, at the Théâtre-Italien, in Paris, there was Marco Aurelio Marliani's *Il bravo*, launched by Grisi, Rubini, and Tamburini; within a year it had reached Italy, England, Austria, and Bohemia. It turns up in the memoirs of James Robinson Planché, who made an English version entitled *The Red Mask*; at Drury Lane the final decapitation scene was staged with such disconcerting realism that at the second performance a happy ending was substituted. Mercadante's once-popular *Il bravo*, of 1839, is at a further remove from Cooper. In 1856, Luigi Arditi's *La spia* was performed in New York at the Academy of Music. The critic of the *Dispatch* heard a preliminary run-through, and reported:

To the dash and brillancy of Verdi, [Arditi] unites the flowing harmonies of Donizetti, and the *savoir faire* of Meyerbeer's effects. The subject of this opera, as the reader may know, is strictly American; and it is so treated, brilliantly and tellingly so. In the introduction, and sometimes repeated in the course of the opera, is a martial, liberty chorus, for which we predict the most extensive popularity. . . . There are a *finale* to the first act, a mother's malediction, one or two prayers, and some duos, which are perfect gems; and the truly artist-like way in which the melody of "Hail Columbia" is worked in with the last grand *finale* of the opera will, we are sure, create a *furore* on its production.

388

Was he being sarcastic, or is Arditi's *La spia* really a work that some enterprising company—the Minnesota Opera, the Texas Opera Theater —should look into? The "musical gems" printed at the end of the 1856 libretto suggest the former; but in his memoirs Arditi does say that one song from *La spia*, "Colli nativi," became so popular that it was sung by "almost every tenor of note" and was introduced into various other operas. In 1877, Gaston Salvayre's *Le Bravo* appeared at the Théâtre-Lyrique in Paris. (A year later, Richard Genée's *Die letzten Mohikaner* was staged in Munich; but, despite its title, this operetta has nothing to do with Cooper.) In 1916, *L'ultimo dei moicani*, by the Boston composer Paul Allen, was done in Florence. And last month Alva Henderson's *The Last of the Mohicans* had its first performance, in Wilmington, Delaware.

The Spy (1821) and *The Bravo* (1831) are novels about men of principle caught in environments of, respectively, moral disorder (Westchester County in 1780, the "neutral ground" between the British and American forces) and immoral order (Venice ruled by the Secret Council, the Venice of *La Gioconda*). Both books provide good matter for opera, but neither can compare with *The Last of the Mohicans* (1826) in grandeur and richness of content. It is easy to see why a composer might be drawn to *The Mohicans*. In its physical descriptions of upstate New York there is something of *Paradise Lost*; the landscape of forest, lake, and river plays a more than picturesque yet not obtrusively symbolic role. In the final threnody for Uncas and Cora there is something of the great elegiac sequence that closes Handel's *Saul*. It is a tragic love story—of love between Uncas, the beautiful and chivalrous young Indian, and Cora, the beautiful and brave Scottish girl who has black blood. ("The tresses of this lady were shining and black, like the plumage of the raven. Her complexion was not brown, but it rather appeared charged with the color of the rich blood, that seemed ready to burst its bounds. And yet there was neither coarseness nor want of shadowing in a countenance that was exquisitely regular and dignified, and surpassingly beautiful. She smiled . . . discovering by the act a row of teeth that would have shamed the purest ivory." That "yet" and the flash of white teeth in a dark face tell us something about Cooper; but, remember, he was writing in 1826.) Uncas and Cora are both killed; the story ends happily only for Heyward, the rich young Southern officer, and the fair Alice, Cora's half sister. We can presume that they go on to have plenty of fair-haired children—and in that there is a reflection of Cooper's recurrent theme: that the forests, the rivers, the Indians, the animals, the old ways, the old order are doomed to destruction by the conquering white men. It is too late now, and it was already too late then, to expect all the white and all the black people in America to pack up and return to the countries whence their ancestors came or were brought, and to cease exploiting this continent. (It is too late to think of expelling the Angles, the Saxons, the Norsemen, and the Normans from England. Or the Dorians from Greece.) But Cooper's book and Henderson's opera do at least set one reflecting on large matters: on the morality of conquests, and on the reasons that America and Australia have, perhaps irretrievably, been taken over by European invaders, while Asia and most of Africa are retained or regained by races that were there before the white men came. The opera opens long perspectives. It is easy to point out, as Mark Twain did, the infelicities of Cooper's prose and plot; easy to point out, as the *Times* critic did, that Henderson's music is not memorable. All the same, it is work on a different level from stuff like Thomas Pasatieri's *Ines de Castro* or Gian Carlo Menotti's *The Hero*, Baltimore's and Philadelphia's new Bicentennial operas—more imaginative, more romantic, nobler in intention.

Cooper's story is filled with sounds, both of the woods and water and of men's music. In the cave at Glens Falls:

The air [an evening hymn, sung by the company after their first escape] was solemn and slow. At times it rose to the fullest compass of the rich voices of the females . . . and again it sank so low that the rushing of the waters ran through their melody, like a hollow accompaniment. The natural taste and true ear of David governed and modified the sounds to suit the confined cavern, every crevice and cranny of which was filled with the thrilling notes of their flexible voices. . . . The singers were dwelling on one of those low, dying chords, which the ear devours with such greedy rapture, as if conscious that it is about to lose them, when a cry that seemed neither human nor earthly rose in the outward air, penetrating not only the recesses of the cavern, but to the inmost hearts of all who heard it. It was followed by a stillness apparently as deep as if the waters had been checked in their furious progress.

That is white men's music mingled with nature's. The Indian Uncas's battle hymn is a "wild and irregular chant. . . . The notes were in the extremes of human sounds; being sometimes melancholy and exquisitely plaintive, even rivalling the melody of birds—and then, by sudden and startling transitions, causing the auditors to tremble by their depth and energy." Cooper goes on to describe the musical form of the four strophes. Speaking voices are also listened to attentively. When Uncas and his father, Chingachgook, talk, it may be "impossible to describe the music of their language, while thus engaged in laughter and endearments," but the author tries: "The compass of their voices, particularly that of the youth, was wonderful—extending from the deepest bass to tones that were even feminine in softness." The finale of the book is the funeral rite, recounted at length. "A low murmur of voices commenced a sort of chant in honor of the dead. The sounds were those of females, and were thrillingly soft and wailing. The words were connected by no regular continuation, but as one ceased another took up the eulogy or lamentation." There is a long sequence of solos, punctuated with choral outbursts of grief. After the women, the men sing or speak. "Then a low, deep sound was heard, like the suppressed accompaniment of distant music. . . . It was the monody of the father." The last words of all, both in the book and in Henderson's opera, come from the aged chief, Tamenund: "The palefaces are masters of the earth, and the time of the Red Men has not yet come again. My day has been too long. In the morning I saw the sons of Unamis happy and strong; and yet, before the night has come, have I lived to see the last warrior of the wise race of the Mohicans."

Allen's opera, which has a libretto by Carlo Zangarini (a collaborator in Puccini's *La fanciulla del West*), is focused on the double romance, amid adventures, of Cora and Uncas (soprano and tenor) and Alice and Heyward (mezzo and baritone), ending with a duet-in-death for the former pair. A good deal of the book's incident is retained. The music—to judge from the vocal score, which was published by Ricordi—is colorful, patchily effective, and a bit rambly. The piece is possibly worth a radio revival. Henderson's opera, whose "dramatic concept" is by Robert Darling and whose libretto is by Janet Lewis, treats *The Last of the Mohicans* more largely, and in a less conventional way. It *begins* with the funeral rites for Uncas and Cora, who were lovely and pleasant in their lives and in their death not divided; the incidents of the adventure story are then placed within the framework of the threnody. The love theme is not dominant, though it is expressed in a recurrent visual image, of the young man offering drink to the maiden. It is but one strand in a larger tragedy: the destruction of the Mohicans, and of their country, by the white invaders. Even Magua, the villain of the piece, is a fallen prince whose fall was brought about by the white men and their firewater. The effect is almost as of a choral drama with solos, kin to those music dramas of Handel that he called oratorios, though the twentieth century has put them onto the stage with powerful effect. Henderson's handling is unhurried; the three-act opera contains nearly three hours of music. He sets expansively Chingachgook's long lament for the vanished Mohicans, "Where are the blossoms of those summers!" (Much of the libretto is taken directly from the book.) He sets almost in full Hawkeye's long speech in which the wild flurrying of the Hudson at Glens Falls, a temporary turbulence in the long, smooth flow of the river, is a symbol for the transitoriness of men's particular troubles. (It was in the Glens Falls cave that Edward Stanley, later Lord Derby, and translator of Homer, remarked to Cooper, "Here is the very scene for a romance," and planted the seed for *The Last of the Mohicans*.) Offstage choruses echo, amplify, provide a background to thoughts that are voiced and moods that are felt onstage. Henderson's aim seems to have been to find and sustain those "musics" that are never long absent from Cooper's pages, and suggest them in his own neo-Romantic idiom, without essaying any ethnic or exotic authenticity. It is an opera more reflective than active, concerned more with thought than with individual characters. The massacre outside Fort William Henry is eventfully treated. But the dramatic "trial" before Tamenund is slowed down by extended speeches and ensembles; contrariwise, the deaths of Cora, Uncas, and Magua are whisked through in three successive measures, and then at once we re-embark on the threnody. This is not a failing, except to the ears of someone who wants *The Last of the Mohicans* to be quite a different kind of opera. But Henderson's music does fail, I think, to be as communicative as it sets out to be. It has many virtues: lyricism, vocal lines that are flexible and good to sing, liveliness and color in the orchestral writing. But many of the tunes are just not quite good enough. For example, the theme (based on successive triads a tone apart) that rings out, twice, at Chingachgook's "My boy is the last of the Mohicans" is banal for its purpose.

Robert Darling's staging, in his own designs, was very successful. The Wilmington Grand Opera House has no fly tower. With revolving rocks, gauzy curtains on tracks, and clever lighting (by Thomas Watson), the sequence of ever-shifting and cross-fading scenes was smoothly achieved. An accomplished cast of young singers was led by Linda Roark and Peter Van Derick, as Cora and Uncas; Kristine Comendant and William Austin, as Alice and Heyward; Lawrence Cooper, as Magua; Alan Wagner, as Hawkeye; and Cary Smith, as Chingachgook. Ideally, one would demand singers of more glowingly romantic appearance and personality; Cooper stresses the physical beauty of all the young people in his tale. But Wilmington might find it hard to engage, say, Kiri Te Kanawa and José Carreras to lead its cast. The words were sometimes less audible than they should have been; I know not whether to blame the singers, the scoring, or the acoustics of an unfamiliar theater. Christofer Macatsoris conducted. Marvin Keenze had prepared his chorus securely.

The work was commissioned by the Wilmington Opera Society as a Bicentennial event and for the gala reopening of the Grand Opera House. The subject had a double local connection: Chingachgook and Uncas are Delaware Indians, and N. C. Wyeth, who illustrated Cooper's novel, is a local hero. Henderson, a Californian, was chosen as composer on the strength of his *Medea*, produced in San Diego in 1972. The Opera House itself was built in 1871; Wilmington then was a city of only fifty-five thousand, but the Grand's stage was reported as second only to the New York Hippodrome's in size. Edwin Booth, Adelina Patti—all the gang played there. In 1897, an Edison Vidascope was installed, and before very long the place was given over to movies. Warner Brothers relinquished it in 1967. In 1971, it was threatened with destruction. Instead, it is being lovingly restored. The essentials needed for a performance—a stage, stage equipment, and seats—were there for *The Mohicans*, though the foyers were still bare planks and bare plaster. Already, it is a very attractive place; when completed, it will be a jewel. It seats some eleven hundred—a human size for an opera house. A restaurant and a bookshop are planned. One leaves it not into traffic but into a tree-lined pedestrian street, with fountains and sidewalk cafés. I look forward to hearing opera in Wilmington again.

July 5, 1976

SUMMER BOUNTY

New York's summer music is provided mostly by Mozart. Most nights, from now to the end of August, there is a Mostly Mozart concert in Alice Tully Hall. This "festival," which began on June 28, consists of twenty-four programs. There are sixty concerts in all: nine orchestral concerts are given four times each, and each chamber-music program twice; the piano recitals are once-only events, except Alicia de Larrocha's, which is repeated. The orchestra—a pickup group of able players: twenty-one strings, double winds, and drums—will be worked hard, under nine different conductors. The bills are studded with master performers— among them Lili Kraus, Walter Klien, Christoph Eschenbach, Anton Kuerti, and the Guarneri, Cleveland, and Tokyo String Quartets—and with masterpieces. What is not Mozart is mostly Haydn and Beethoven, the former's *Harmoniemesse* and the latter's Diabelli Variations being the largest non-eponymic compositions. Vivaldi, Handel, Bach and sons, Hummel, Friedrich Kuhlau, and Schumann are also represented.

Avery Fisher Hall, for nine previous years the home of this summer series, is being rebuilt; hence the move to Tully. And thence, one might have hoped, a new concern for doing things in a properly Mozartian way —possible now, before audiences of something over a thousand rather than approaching three thousand. Vain hope! It is the old-fashioned mixture as before—modern instruments with the timbre of the late nineteenth and the twentieth century. Inevitable so long as our conservatories concentrate on training performers of the late-Romantic repertory, for whom such instruments are the norm. (They turn their techniques to Bach, to Mozart, to Beethoven, to Schubert, and if they

393

are sensitive they modify their style and clarify their tones when tackling the earlier repertory. But they cannot hope to produce the sounds that those composers had in mind.) Regrettable that not one single concert, not one recital should be performed on the right instruments. But perhaps not inevitable at all if the director, instead of plumping for the eminent, the familiar, and the convenient, had engaged some of the artists who not only play eighteenth-century instruments but are also interpreters of the first rank.

The opening concert, conducted by Alexander Schneider, consisted of a symphony, Haydn's No. 49, and three concertos, in which the soloists were members of the mixed quartet that calls itself Tashi (Tibetan for "good fortune"). Peter Serkin was the soloist in Bach's Harpsichord Concerto No. 4, in A major. The program note called the work a "Concerto for Clavier and String Orchestra" and tactfully refrained from any further explanation; it did, however, point out that for its performance two keyboard instruments are required, one for the soloist and one for the continuo. "Clavier" (which can refer to any keyboard instrument) is ambiguous; the superscription on the manuscript score of the concerto is surely not: "Concerto a Cembalo certato, due Violini, Viola e Cont." Mr. Serkin played his part on a modern Steinway piano, and there was no continuo. I am not a person to make a great fuss about an occasional performance of a Bach harpsichord piece on the piano. For one thing, Edwin Fischer as a piano soloist in the concertos and Rudolf Serkin as a piano soloist in the Fifth Brandenburg have in the past given too much pleasure for me, even now, to find a modern concert grand altogether unacceptable. For another, Peter Serkin's performance of the A major was so lucid, both in conception and in execution, that it was impossible to do anything but enjoy it. The solo writing is two-part throughout (which suggested to the author of the program note—it doesn't to me—that the piece may have been conceived from the start for keyboard rather than derived, like most of the keyboard concertos, from a violin original). Mr. Serkin's right hand maintained a strong singing line, and his left a firm yet discreet accompaniment. It was all just about as good as a piano performance of the concerto can ever be.

Mozart's D-major Violin Concerto, K. 218, followed, with Ida Kavafian as soloist. She has a clear, well-formed, unassertive tone; her playing was poised and lyrical; the phrases were well shaped. Then came the Haydn symphony (or, at any rate, three-quarters of it; the repeats of the first and second movements were not taken). In the preface to his edition of the score, H. C. Robbins Landon remarks that "the presence of a harpsichord (*cembalo*) . . . was a matter of course in the eighteenth century, and a performance of the work without this instrument is unthinkable," for reasons both of harmony and of timbre. But Mr. Schneider found it thinkable enough, and used no harpsichord. (The whole question of whether Haydn's Esterházy symphonies were played with or without harpsichord continuo has recently been reopened—and not answered decisively.) Mr. Schneider also, I suspect, used obsolete instrumental parts, since the first violins did not play Haydn's expressive turn at measure sixty-one of the first movement, and nineteenth-century editions likewise omit it. Not a very important point—unless it indicates a general indifference to performing the music from the best possible texts. Similarly, one could remark that Richard Stoltzman played the next piece, Mozart's Clarinet Concerto, on an ordinary A-clarinet and in the familiar version now regarded as an arrangement of a work that Mozart composed for an extraordinary instrument reaching a few notes lower. (The autograph has disappeared, as has that of the Clarinet Quintet; Mozart's likely original has been deduced from internal evidence.) But—this "but" always recurs when the artistic excellence of a performance outweighs its transgressions against authenticity; Beecham's peerless recordings of Haydn symphonies, from corrupt texts, afford an obvious example—a listener cannot suddenly stop enjoying a score whose notes have delighted audiences since first it was published, early in the nineteenth century. And Mr. Stoltzman gave a bewitching performance. It is a critic's duty to scold when the results of musical research are ignored by artists. (Musicology is a sterile occupation until its discoveries are put into practice.) It is a Mozart-lover's pleasure to praise the almost "creative" way in which Mr. Stoltzman molded the phrases. He produced the effect of extemporizing his role, inspired by and inspiring the orchestral players. It was fresh and free; supple yet rhythmically trim; fanciful in its coloring and inflections; emotional, in the slow movement, without being soppy; dancing in the finale.

Mr. Schneider is a conductor readier to persuade than to dictate. His tempi are sometimes slow—the minuet of the Haydn symphony was slow to the point of heaviness—but, as Casals did when conducting Mozart, he sets easy tempi, it seems, only so that wonderful details of the scores should not be scamped. When all the phrasing can be defined, the result sounds more, not less, energetic. Many years ago, Mr. Schneider, with the Dumbarton Oaks Chamber Orchestra, recorded a performance of Mozart's G-major Piano Concerto, K. 453. I recall the disc (which has long been out of print) for two reasons: because the soloist, Ralph Kirkpatrick, played not a modern concert grand but a modern copy of a late-eighteenth-century instrument, and made an unanswerable case against the big late-nineteenth-century piano in such music; and because the slow tempi adopted for the outer movements, though surprising at first, allowed one to hear—and mark the sense of—so many of the notes, from keyboard, winds, and strings, that most other performances now sound hurried.

The second concert was all Mozart, and of chamber music. The Tashi quartet (its fourth member is the cellist Fred Sherry) was joined by Mr. Schneider, violin now, and Daniel Phillips, viola and violin. It began with a curiosity, Mozart's "other" Clarinet Quintet—not the familiar piece in A major but the allegro movement in B-flat (K. Anh. 91, or 516c in Alfred Einstein's revised numbering), which breaks off at the foot of a page, after ninety-three measures. In 1968, Robert D. Levin added a brief, tactful development section, recapitulation, and coda, and his completion was used. (The exposition, ninety measures long, was repeated, so what we heard was "mostly Mozart.") It is a striking, in places even a dramatic composition; there are some arresting entries for the clarinet, and Mr. Stoltzman handled them boldly. There followed the Second Quartet for piano and strings, K. 493, and the late Divertimento for string trio, K. 563. Both works received promising rather than completely finished performances. It was rewarding to hear these alert, accomplished players engaged together on great music, yet it was evident that not everything had been fully resolved. Mr. Serkin, leading the piano quartet, blurred some of his passagework with pedal, and tended to release chords smudgily. Miss Kavafian, leading the divertimento, scurried through some of the little notes and did not find for the second subject quite the serene, happy touch she had brought to K. 218. Mr. Phillips, who had played second violin in the quintet, was violist in the divertimento. If I were to say that he is a player who stands out in everything he does, it would be a poor compliment to someone I have heard only in chamber music, and always as a responsive and sensitive partner in ensemble. He "stands out" in no unsuitable way. But I have never heard him play a phrase that did not come to life under his fingers; he has a natural instinct for rhythm and for eloquent articulation, for making one listen keenly. And so the lilting first trio of the second minuet, which is the viola's special solo, became the high point of the divertimento.

The program notes for the first two concerts, supplied by an agency, efficiently assembled information about each individual work. There is no general program book for the whole series, with thoughtful essays about Mozart's work in the many genres represented at this festival. There were no illuminating cross-references from program to program— nothing to place Mozart in relation to the Bach, Handel, Haydn, and Beethoven works that are being played. In the foyer of the hall a little shop had been set up. It sold bars of soap with musical notes printed on them, and playing cards, and T-shirts bearing a leering caricature of Mozart, and other unhappy images of composers in plaster statuettes or on plaques. It also sold some books, but only accounts for kiddies of the lives of the great composers. It sold nothing of musical merit—not Charles Rosen's *The Classical Style*, not Stanley Sadie's *Mozart*, not A. Hyatt King's *Mozart Chamber Music* (one of those excellent BBC guides designed to deepen the experience of the ordinary concertgoer, and published over here by the University of Washington Press, at a mere $1.95; for next year's festival *Mozart Wind and String Concertos* and *Mozart Piano Concertos* should also be ready). It did not even sell pocket scores of the works that are being played.

Four further regrets. That no new works should have been commissioned—from, say, William Bolcom and Jacob Druckman—to be played amid the Mozart. That, although Miss Alice Tully has presented the hall with an organ that (quite apart from its sonic merits) provides a beautiful visual background for any performance, it should be screened away out of sight at these concerts. That Jens Nygaard and his Westchester Chamber Chorus and Orchestra should not have been invited to repeat, to the fuller festival audience, the captivating program of very early Mozart that they gave a few months ago. And that the concerts should not be broadcast, so that wide audiences at home could also enjoy them. For the rest, simple gratitude to Mozart and to his devoted interpreters.

July 12, 1976

1976–1977

OPERAS IN ITALY

In summer, Europe's musical season becomes more intense. There may be fewer concerts and recitals each night in the large cities, but everywhere there are festivals; new works, new productions of unfamiliar works, and, for that matter, new productions of familiar works abound. London has year-round opera: Covent Garden's 1975–76 season closed on July 22, and the English National Opera's 1976–77 season opened a week later; the gap was bridged by the London Opera Centre, playing Offenbach's *Robinson Crusoe* and Wolf-Ferrari's *I quattro rusteghi* at Sadler's Wells, and by the nightly performances at Glyndebourne. The Henry Wood Proms (fifty-six different programs of music new and old), the Festival of the City of London, and the festivals in Munich, Bayreuth, Salzburg, Verona, Aix-en-Provence, Edinburgh are but some of the large summer events that claim an earnest music lover's attention; the Lucerne Festival produced a new completion of the important choral work *Atlántida*, left unfinished by Manuel de Falla—again a version by Ernesto Halffter, but different from his 1961 score. Away from all those centers, living quietly for two months in the Tuscan hills between Arezzo and Siena, I nevertheless discovered that, given the readiness to drive an hour or so, I was still within reach of an interesting opera or a concert just about every night (and, in addition, could hear all the Bayreuth productions, all the Salzburg operas, and most of the Salzburg concerts via Italian Radio, and most of the Proms via the BBC's European service). But ears need a rest after a busy New York season, and so, passing up things like Emilio de' Cavalieri's sacred drama *La rappresentazione di anima e di corpo* a mile or two up the road at the Castle of Gargonza, *Pia de' Tolomei* (not Donizetti's opera but a *bruscello*, a form of "folk opera," done by amateurs) a mile or two down the road at Monte San Savino, and Rossini's *Moïse*, grandly cast, over at the Perugia Festival, I limited my live attendance almost entirely to performances of eighteenth-century operas, and heard five—none of them in regular repertory, and three of them quite new to me.

Batignano is a small Tuscan town not far from Grosseto. Some years ago, the Australian designer Adam Pollock bought an abandoned monastery there, and for three years he has presented a brief summer season he calls Musica nel Chiostro, consisting of recitals and an opera. In 1974, the opera was Purcell's *Dido and Aeneas*, last year it was the Leppard-Cavalli *Ormindo*, and this year it was Handel's *Tamerlano*. *Tamerlano* (1724), together with *Giulio Cesare* and *Rodelinda*, which came before and after it, marks a peak in Handel's career. Like them, it is an opera of arresting characters powerfully and consistently drawn.

401

Act II is high drama, in which the conventions of opera seria, so often a mere sequence of coming and going, are given theatrical shape. The princess Asteria, daughter of the captive Bajazet, has declared her readiness to share Tamerlane's throne and bed—to the distress of her father, of her lover, Prince Andronicus, and of Irene, a Trebizond princess, whom Tamerlane has jilted for Asteria. The five principals are assembled. Asteria flings a dagger onto the steps of the throne, declaring that Tamerlane would have received it at his first embrace. The situation explodes in a trio, and the angry Tamerlane leaves. Is she, Asteria asks, an unworthy daughter, a faithless lover, an ambitious rival? Bajazet, Andronicus, and Irene reply in three brief exit arias, each starting with the word "No," and thus Asteria is left alone to sing an extended and noble aria-finale. Act III is tragic; Bajazet takes poison and expires in a long monologue—an eloquent sequence of accompanied recitatives and ariosi, in which his defiance of Tamerlane, his tender affection for his daughter, and an invocation of avenging furies collapse at last into broken, almost incoherent syllables. Asteria sings a Bach-like lament. There is a happy ending of sorts, as Tamerlane ordains a pairing of himself and Irene, and Andronicus and Asteria, but Handel sets the conventionally optimistic final words ("Gloomy night yields to splendid day") to an E-minor chorus that has, in Winton Dean's words, "a flavor almost of Shakespearean tragedy."

At Batignano, these two great sequences were done complete, and they made a great effect. Elsewhere in the opera, there was much cutting; of the twenty-seven arias in the score, ten were omitted and eight reduced to A-section only. Until audiences are prepared to devote to Handel the time they give to Wagner, some abridgment of his operas is no doubt inevitable; but in *Tamerlano* there is nothing that can readily be spared. Alexander Young, who has made the role of Bajazet— one of the few tenor leads in Handel opera—pretty well his own ever since he took part in the first modern revival of *Tamerlano*, in Birmingham in 1962, once again sang it affectingly. Mr. Young is head of vocal studies at the Royal Northern College of Music, in Manchester, and from that college (which might be described as England's Juilliard) came an expert young orchestra (including oboists who doubled on recorders, eighteenth-century fashion) and three of the other singers: two talented countertenors, Christopher Royle and Brian Gordon, for the castrato roles of Tamerlane and Andronicus, and Rachel Gettler, a gleaming and passionate Irene (one of Janet Baker's early roles). Asteria was that experienced Handelian soprano Eiddwen Harrhy. (Two weeks earlier, I had heard her as the heroine of Handel's *Lotario*, at the Festival of the City of London.) Her voice, although not yet quite smooth through its registers, is charged with emotional colors, which she uses with uncommon skill and conviction. She is a singer who makes one listen to everything she does. Jane Glover conducted, with a sure feeling for the pace and character of each number and the dramatic progression of each act.

Between the walled monastery garden and the main building Mr. Pollock had designed a vertiginous open-air setting of gleaming steel scaffolding. Bajazet was caged at stage level; Tamerlane made his entrances high, high above. Patrick Libby's stage direction cunningly harmonized the dramatic talents of the two women and the limited acting prowess of the men. Since the player of Tamerlane was plainly not fierce by nature, Mr. Libby had him stand still while a posse of black-armored guards, stepping forward in silence, silhouetted against the stars, added the touch of menace that Mr. Royle himself lacked. The various levels of the set were used skillfully to define shifting dramatic relationships. The performance began at ten and ended about one, and it was a cold night. (Summer was slow to touch Tuscany this year.) Tamerlane's boy slaves shivered, with only a film of grease between them and the biting air; the audience snuggled into blankets provided by a thoughtful management. After the show, hot soup was served to all; the monastery's chief cook earned a credit in the program.

Viterbo, in the heart of Etruscan Latium, about fifty miles from Rome along the Cassian Way, is in aspect a medieval city, and famous in papal history. In May and June, the newly formed Center for Medieval and Renaissance Theater Studies held its first congress there, and monks from St. Anselm's, the Benedictine seminary in Rome, performed medieval music dramas. In August, however, Viterbo is host to a Festival Barocco, and the main production of this year's festival was of Antonio Caldara's *Ifigenia in Aulide*, written for Vienna in 1718. Caldara is an interesting and important composer—a Venetian who, in his long collaboration with the Vienna court poets Apostolo Zeno and Metastasio, played a dominant role in operatic history but who in our day has been little studied, published, or performed. Like Dr. Burney when he wrote his *History*, I had heard none of Caldara's operas before but "from his other productions which have come to my knowledge" had formed a high opinion of his "harmony, contrivance, great effects, and every species of learning." The Viterbo *Ifigenia*, even though it had been put through the mangle of a modern performing edition, confirmed that opinion.

Zeno's libretto is based partly on Euripides, partly on Racine. To the Greek play he adds two new characters and a new, almost Gilbertian final twist: Elisena, Princess of Lesbos, in love with Achilles and therefore eager for her rival, Iphigenia, to be sacrificed; Teucer, the Greek captain, in love with Elisena; and the last-minute revelation that Elisena's real name is also Iphigenia, so when Elisena/Iphigenia kills herself in a fit of despair, the letter of the oracle (which called for the death of an Iphigenia) is fulfilled, the titular Iphigenia is saved, and the wind sets fair for Troy. Racine's *Iphigénie* has a similar dénouement. Here and there, Zeno's text catches some of the Euripidean freshness and force—particularly in the long speech, close to the original, in which Iphigenia accepts her cruel fate, bids her mother not mourn her, and offers herself as a martyr to the Greek cause. For the rest, he provides a sequence of arias in varied moods: Agamemnon's anguish, Clytemnestra's anger at him and grief for her daughter, Achilles' chivalrous protestations, Teucer's gentle wooing, and so on. Of Handelian music drama there is no trace. But Caldara set these arias to touchingly beautiful, supple, eloquent melodies, excellent in every vein and especially successful in the tender. The melodic beauty, which is the opera's most striking feature, arises from grace of contour and is given an individual quality by Caldara's rhythmic fancy. Some words are set syllabically, to longish notes; others suddenly flower in melismatic divisions, in an unpredictable fashion that banishes regularity, creating delicate tensions between expectation and outcome, and between the verbal and the musical paces. Several arias begin with a tune in the bass which then winds its way, in whole or in part, variously transposed and transformed, through what follows. Caldara, like Niccolò Jommelli, like Richard Strauss, was a master of *Fortspinnung*—never at a loss how to devise delightful new extensions of a motif or a melody. And so, although his and Zeno's *Ifigenia* is opera seria unreformed, and although the clear, sharp lines of the classical drama (which Gluck, fifty-six years later, handled with noble neoclassical simplicity) are embellished with amorous arabesques, the opera held its listeners rapt. A second visit proved as enjoyable as the first.

Whether, as in Caldara's sacred music, there is rich instrumental interest, too, was unrevealed. Marcello Peca, who also conducted, had made his performing edition from what he described, vaguely, as a copy score bearing a few orchestral indications. He scored every aria for full strings (no oboes, no flutes, no bassoons, and in several numbers no continuo), in an unvaried texture. Of the eighteen arias retained in his edition, a few were in binary form, and of the others only five were allotted the necessary da capo. Otherwise, the singer was left high and dry after the B-section. Sometimes the orchestra restored the tonic with a scrap of ritornello, sometimes things broke off abruptly in the wrong key; either way, the result was lopsided. Achilles, the principal castrato role, was dropped an octave, and suffered accordingly, despite the bright singing of Gianni De Angelis, a promising young baritone. Teucer, left at pitch, was attractively taken by Giuseppina Dalle Molle. Gabriella Novielli (Iphigenia), Maria Borgato (Clytemnestra), Silvia Silveri (Elisena), and Massimo Panzironi (Agamemnon) all proved acceptable young artists. The piece was mounted simply on a stage tucked between the wings of the nymphaeum that crowns the great gardens of the Villa Lante, at Bagnaia, outside Viterbo. After the show, the garden walks and the fountains were lit by hundreds of small flares.

Montepulciano, in the words of the Italian Touring Club guide to Tuscany, "is a city of most noble aspect, thanks to the richness of its Renaissance buildings, of markedly Florentine stamp." The place looks patrician. The civic administration, like that of most Tuscan towns, is Communist. And here, for eight days in August, the composer Hans Werner Henze and the dramatist Giuseppe Di Leva set up their Cantiere Internazionale d'Arte, or International Construction Site for the Arts, working in a blaze of publicity from Italian, German, and British television crews. Henze explained in a program note, "The form, content, and character of this little didactic festival are the result of numerous meetings with the citizens and of public debates. Each event has been prepared with the intention of creatively involving the public. Young people collaborate in the shows, artisans have offered their aid . . . schoolchildren have designed costumes and scenery and worked as librettists, children have composed a song about Don Quixote, the town band has studied the Paisiello numbers transcribed for it. . . . Our desire was and is to offer a small example of what the cultural world could be or perhaps one day will be."

Peter Maxwell Davies held a course in composition, and Julian Bream and Aldo Minella one in guitar, and in the piazza the guitar students played pieces written for them by the composition students. Mark Furneaux held a course in mime, and his charges went mopping and mowing through the streets at all hours. The Hinz und Kunst ensemble, fifteen talented graduates of the Hamburg Music Academy, who are champions of politically committed music—a Speculum Musicae of the left—played several new pieces, among them Henze's quintet *Amicizia!*, a set of lyrical and finally resolute instrumental fantasies spun around Hanns Eisler's "Song of the United Front." Montepulciano has a delightful late-eighteenth-century theater, named for the playwright Politian (who took his pen name from the town; the citizens are called Poliziani), and here two operas were produced. One, *The Zoological Palace*, had a libretto written by London schoolchildren, translated into Italian by Politian schoolchildren, and a score by Thomas Jahn, of Hinz und Kunst. It was a childish charade, with sketchy music. The other was Rossini's *Il turco in Italia*, one of his most elegant creations, to a libretto, by Felice Romani, of Pirandellian ingenuity. Sandro Sequi, a director whose usual fault (as in the Metropolitan's *Siège de Corinthe* and *Puritani*) is dull conventionality, destroyed the grace, charm, wit, and character of the piece; he sought to present it as a critical study of

"Italian petite bourgeoisie (1815 as in 1950 or 1976)," and set the mimes scampering through it all to illustrate "a frenzy of movement unjustified by realistico-psychological reasons."

The hit of the week was *Don Chisciotte della Mancia*, Giovanni Paisiello's opera of 1769, "recounted" by Di Leva and Henze. Paisiello's strong point was an ability to write simple, graceful, catchy tunes. Several of them remain in Henze's score, and so do some elements of the original plot, but essentially the piece is a new creation, an opera for modern piazza performance. Borges provided an epigraph: "Why should it be disturbing that Don Quixote might read *Don Quixote*, and Hamlet watch a performance of *Hamlet*?" At Montepulciano, a Don Quixote and Sancho Panza drove into the square in a battered Cinque-cento, and then settled down to watch an opera about their exploits, occasionally intervening. The Countess sang her first phrases from the piano-nobile windows of the Palazzo Nobili Tarugi, an imposing Sangallo pile; windmills ready to whirl stood all around; the action romped through the *piazza grande* in a lively, high-spirited spectacle. Henze had restored not only arias but also recitatives for a modern chamber ensemble, amplified, and had done so with impudence, wit, and affection. At big moments, the massed town bands of Montepulciano and Abbadia San Salvatore broke in as well. There were some extra numbers by Henze himself and by others. Gerald English sang the title role, and the athletic Australian baritone Lyndon Terracini his squire.

As a people's opera, this *Don Chisciotte* was an evident success. All the town seemed to be there enjoying it; it made the effect of a popular celebration, yet there was no question of condescension to a musically unlearned audience. I observed as a visitor; one would have to be a Poliziano, or else one of the young artists, mainly from England, Germany, and Italy, who "gave up their holidays and worked harder than ever"—without any pay, incidentally—"seeking to lessen and maybe one day abolish the gap between the artist and his public," to assess how fully Henze realized his aim of "a *cantiere* for all: artists, peasants, workmen, artisans, old and young alike." The artists, he declared in his program note, "are fighting to help this city in its struggle against reaction, against civil death, in its struggle for a happy future and an improvement in social conditions." In Cuba and in Germany, Henze has sought to take contemporary art to the people. In several of his recent compositions, he has set to notes the musings of an essentially lyrical, personal artist ridden by a quickened social conscience—no longer kin to "The Composer" of Auden's early sonnet, whose notes are "pure contraption," who, unlike a painter or a poet, is "unable to say an existence is wrong," but, rather, a musician who does ask what doubtful deed allows his picnics in the sun. In his grand operas *The Bassarids*, commissioned by the Salzburg Festival, and *We Come to the River*, commissioned by London's Royal Opera, Henze has been "concerned . . . with extending our knowledge of good and evil, perhaps making the necessity for action more urgent and its nature more clear." The quotation is from Auden's introduction to the 1935 anthology *The Poet's Tongue*; the personal field of Henze's artist-and-society struggle was often plotted in the thirties—by Auden, Spender, and Day Lewis, by Brecht and Weill, by Clifford Odets and Marc Blitzstein, among many. But the public field has changed. Whereas those creators worked in the shadow of impending war, Henze and his like-minded colleagues work in a Europe moving erratically but inexorably left. "How should I act?" has been the troubled artists' regular question. By acting in Montepulciano, a Renaissance hill town ringed by agriculture, they retreat from the pressures and cultural problems of industrialized cities and build a model that could hardly be reproduced on a Milan, London, or New York scale. Retreat from the bustling world is traditionally a way to find answers to the hard questions it poses.

The *cantiere* came to a confused close. The Teatro Poliziano was filled by an audience awaiting the second performance of *Il turco*. The mimes came before the curtain and, finding lively tongue as well as eloquent gesture, declared that they would not go on unless their travel expenses to and from Montepulciano were paid. There was perhaps an hour of noisy public argument. The mayor attempted placatory speeches; the mimes were implacable. The well-known music critic Fedele D'Amico mounted the stage to propose that the audience should pay the fares, but only on condition that the mayor should resign. Singers wandered on from the wings; a performance without mimes nearly took place. At length, Henze himself appeared, but only to announce that the orchestra would strike in solidarity with the mimes. The *cantiere* was over—until next year.

Siena also devoted its Musical Week, the thirty-third Settimana Musicale Senese, to revolutionary art this year. The theme of the annual congress promoted by the Chigi Musical Academy and Siena University was "Between Revolution and Restoration: Links Between French and Italian Musical and Theatrical Culture," and the large musical offerings were two Cherubini operas, *Lodoiska* (1791) and *Les Deux Journées* (1800). They are the direct ancestors of *Fidelio*. *Lodoiska*, first played in Vienna in March of 1802, and *Les Deux Journées*, which was given two different Viennese productions later that year, started a wave of enthusiasm, in which Beethoven shared, for energetic, high-minded, by intention elevating music drama. Both pieces are "rescue operas"— dramas in which perils are faced with high valor, wickedness is opposed with constant virtue, and not a deus ex machina but a courageous mortal effects the happy ending. In the first scene of *Lodoiska*, the fierce Tatar

407

chieftain Titzikan says to his band, "Never forget, brave fellows, that one cannot serve one's own interests at the expense of justice and humanity." The final chorus of *Les Deux Journées* proclaims that "the foremost charm of life is to serve humanity." Mendelssohn described the essential features of rescue opera in a letter to the librettist J. R. Planché. A London commission was in prospect, and Mendelssohn said, "A subject between *Fidelio* and *Les Deux Journées* would suit me best, more like the first with regard to the internal plot and the development of passion, and like the second in the historical basis, the activity of the choruses, and the serene atmosphere that breathes through the whole, notwithstanding the perils and narrow escapes. In short, if you could find me a subject in which some virtuous heroical deed was celebrated, which represented the triumph of some noble, aspirant feeling equally known to every one of the hearers who knows any feeling at all, who could then see his own internal life on the stage, but more concentrated, translated into poetry; and if that story happened in a country or time that could provide a lively background to the whole, one which, in reminding us of history, could at the same time remind us of our present day (as in *Les Deux Journées*); and if every act had its own effects, its own poetical point, which come to issue in the finale (again, as in *Les Deux Journées*)— if you could find such a subject, that would be the one I wish for."

Cherubini did not originate the genre—Grétry's *Richard Cœur-de-Lion* (1784) is an evident precedent; Henri Berton's *Les Rigueurs du cloître* (1790) is sometimes claimed as the first true rescue opera—but he filled it with more powerful, vigorous, and extended musical numbers than his predecessors had done. *Lodoiska*, described as a *"comédie héroïque,"* is almost too insistently thorough in its musical working. Everything is clear-cut, sharply defined, emphatic, incisively scored. The plot, set in Poland, is simple. Lodoiska has been imprisoned by the wicked Dourlinski; her faithful Floreski comes to rescue her, but he, too, is captured. Titzikan and his band storm Dourlinski's castle, and, amid scenes of battle and general conflagration, accompanied by a noisy *symphonie guerrière*, Floreski saves Lodoiska from a burning tower and Titzikan saves Floreski from Dourlinski's dagger. Lodoiska, Floreski, and Dourlinski are vocal and dramatic counterparts to Beethoven's Leonore, Florestan, and Pizarro, and are musically characterized, by melodic line and by instrumental texture, in similar ways. However, they bear the sort of relation to Beethoven's figures that the personages of Meyerbeer's *Les Huguenots* do to those of Verdi's *Don Carlos*: in the one case, carefully fashioned embodiments of virtues, vices, and high emotions; in the other, individuals who "live and breathe." Some light relief is provided early on by Varbel, Floreski's squire, who has a hint of Leporello about him. Romance touches the first-act finale, when Lodoiska's voice rings out from a tower in solemn phrases of warning, unaccompanied, punctuated by sonorous wind chords, and Floreski responds eagerly, Varbel apprehensively, and the strings with agitated figuration. All in all, *Lodoiska* is a noble, strenuous, but slightly too schematic composition.

Both *Les Deux Journées* and Pierre Gaveaux's *Léonore* (1798; it provided the material for *Fidelio*) have admirable librettos, by J. N. Bouilly, based upon true incidents—"faits historiques," from the Reign of Terror—and so both are closer to real life than are the adventures of *Lodoiska*. Bouilly reclad the originals of his Léonore and Florestan (who could have been present to watch the opera about them) in seventeenth-century Spanish dress; and the escape from Paris of two aristocrats, the matter of *Les Deux Journées*, he moved back to the time of Cardinal Mazarin. Count Armand, president of the Paris Council, has refused to ratify some of Mazarin's harsh decrees, and there is a price on his head. Mikéli, a water carrier, whose "supreme joy is to help a brother, and succor the innocent," twice saves Armand and his wife, Constance, from arrest. But on the second day they are captured at last; in the nick of time Mikéli runs on with the news that a general amnesty has been declared. That, of course, is a dramatic weakness; it smacks of conventional deus ex machina, or the Royal Messenger who rides on at the end of *The Threepenny Opera* to save Macheath from the gallows. But Mikéli's earlier resourcefulness and his generous spirit, Armand's courage, and Constance's constancy have been strongly enough portrayed to carry the piece through to a happy ending that does seem to be deserved, not merely fortuitous. *Les Deux Journées* has a charm lacking in *Lodoiska*. There are domestic scenes for the water carrier and his family; the last act plays at a country wedding, where Mikéli's son marries a farmer's daughter. Throughout, there is a feeling for ordinary people whose lives are suddenly brushed by great events and who are then forced to decide for the good or the evil side. And Cherubini has learned to relax: in this score, the heroic, the domestic, and the pastoral are easily and effectively blended. Although *Les Deux Journées* has a large cast, none of the roles are exceptionally demanding. It is a piece worth smaller companies' attention.

Les Deux Journées was staged simply and well in Siena's attractive mid-eighteenth-century Teatro dei Rinnuovati (created originally by Antonio Bibiena, within the great council hall of the Palazzo Pubblico). Like nearly all rescue operas, it proceeds variously, in plain speech, melodrama (words spoken over music), and recitative as well as song. With happy results, Luciano Alberti, who directed, had paid especial attention to the pacing and relation of spoken dialogue and music. Emanuele Luzzati had designed simple, satisfactory scenery. The young Chigi Academy singers were on the whole pleasing. *Lodoiska* was given a concert performance, without dialogue, in Santa Maria della Scala, a rectangular church with full, bright acoustics. It was billed as the "first revival in the original edition" but was not that. When La Scala presented *Lodoiska*, in 1951, with Delia Rigal as its heroine, the edition was certainly not original but decked out by Giulio Confalonieri, Cherubini's biographer, with numbers from other Cherubini operas, and with sung recitatives instead of speech; in 1962, however, University College, London, staged the piece in authentic form. In Siena, the principal roles were sung by the American soprano Lynne Strow, a Lodoiska of broad, powerful line; the American tenor Lionel Stubbefield, a strong Floreski with an edge of metal in his tone, which was likened—favorably or not, according to taste—to Aureliano Pertile's; and the Hungarian baritone Lajos Miller, a ringing and forceful Dourlinski. Alessandro Corbelli doubled the roles of Titzikan and Varbel; this meant that numbers in which both characters are prominent were cut, but it was good to hear Mr. Corbelli in two contrasted veins, for he has one of the finest baritone voices I know—pure, precise, and very beautiful in timbre. The Prague Conservatory Orchestra played, none too precisely, for both operas, and both were conducted by Gabriele Ferro. As in Gluck's *Iphigénie en Tauride* in Siena last year, Mr. Ferro combined passion, energy, and intensity of phrasing with firm rhythms and un-hurried, athletic tempi. He is one of Italy's most impressive young conductors.

October 11, 1976

For the various ways of ending Iphigenia in Aulis, *and the classical authorities therefor, see Racine's preface to his* Iphigénie en Aulide. *Edward Bond (see p. 433) had been asked to write a libretto for the new Montepulciano opera; it was at his suggestion that, instead, two prize-winning plays in a competition sponsored by the London* Observer *and the Royal Court Theatre were used: Zoe Everest-Phillips's* Watercress Sandwiches *(about a dragon called Tunkinbutton, tamed by eating sandwiches belonging to Willie Winchbucket) and Conrad Mullineaux's* Zoological Palace. *The authors were both thirteen, and their plays had been performed at the Royal Court.*

ATLANTIC OVERTURES

Last month, in London, the English Music Theatre Company, which looks to the achievements of the late Walter Felsenstein at the Komische Oper in East Berlin as "a beacon for the rest of us to follow," was at Sadler's Wells, playing its current repertory of six productions. The Royal Opera, at Covent Garden, was playing two cycles of a *Ring* directed by Götz Friedrich, one of Felsenstein's two principal disciples; the English National Opera, at the Coliseum, was playing a *Salome* directed by Joachim Herz, the other of them (in addition to *Tosca, The Magic Flute, Poppea,* and new productions of Smetana's *Dalibor* and of *Don Giovanni*). In Cardiff, which is now less than two hours from London by British Rail, the Welsh National Opera's autumn season included new productions of Michael Tippett's *The Midsummer Marriage* and of *Orphée aux enfers,* together with four other pieces, among them a Mussorgsky *Boris,* that should have been revivals but were in effect new productions, too, since most of the company's décor had gone up in smoke a month before the season began. Glyndebourne and Scottish Opera were both on tour up and down the country, the latter with Thomas Wilson's new *Confessions of a Justified Sinner* and a new production of *Macbeth,* conducted by James Conlon. All these companies, with the exception of the Royal Opera, tour widely. Leeds, for example, gets a week of Scottish Opera in September, a week of English Music Theatre in October, and a week of Welsh National Opera in November; earlier this year the English National played *The Ring* and three other operas there—nineteen different productions in all, in a city the size of Atlanta.

The English Music Theatre Company, whose artistic directors are Colin Graham and Steuart Bedford, is a successor to the English Opera Group, founded in 1947 by Benjamin Britten and others to promote a less cumbersome, less costly, and more adventurous kind of opera than that provided by large traditional houses. It differs from the English Opera Group in employing more singers—some fifty of them—and engaging them on a year-round basis. The company, which made its début in April, will by the end of the year have given nearly a hundred performances, in thirty different towns. The repertory to date contains one work from the eighteenth century (Mozart's *La finta giardiniera*), one from the nineteenth (Rossini's *La Cenerentola*), and four from the twentieth (two "classics," Britten's *The Turn of the Screw* and Kurt Weill's *The Threepenny Opera;* the first stage revival of Britten's early operetta *Paul Bunyan;* and a brand-new commission, Stephen Oliver's *Tom Jones*).

Paul Bunyan, which was first performed in 1941 at Columbia University, is an opera about America by two Englishmen, Britten and Auden. It opens in virgin forest, plays in a lumber camp, and closes "as the frontier closes, / Gone the natural disciplines / And the life of choice begins." The theme is responsibility. It's easy to be honest, industrious, cooperative, social when you're a band of brothers together, taming nature; "pioneer" virtues are put to the test once pioneering days are done. The camp cook goes off to manage a mid-Manhattan hotel, the foreman to public-works administration in Washington, and the bookkeeper to be technical adviser for a Hollywood movie about logging, and the opera ends with a litany: "From a Pressure Group that says I am the Constitution . . . From a Tolerance that is really inertia and delusion . . . From the theology of plumbers or the medical profession, From depending on alcohol for self-respect and self-possession, Save animals and men." Once, it was men united in the struggle against nature; now is it to be every man for himself, or man working for men? *Paul Bunyan*, written at the same time that Orwell, in wartime England, was writing *The Lion and the Unicorn*, is a deeply serious work treated with a light touch that justifies the authors' calling it an operetta. On the surface, it is an idyll. The music is deft, charming, filled with captivating tunes; it displays Britten's genius for drawing sonority from a small orchestra, and often adumbrates (in threnody, ballad, and dapper ensemble) his later compositions. The libretto is lightly strung, elliptical, understated, as revuelike in structure as *The Dog Beneath the Skin*. The lack of a clear plot and the conceits of leaving Paul as an offstage voice (but how could one represent onstage a folk hero as tall as the Empire State Building?) and of using Fido, Moppet, and Poppet, a dog and two cats, as commentators may have helped to keep *Paul Bunyan* in obscurity for thirty-five years. But it was a happy Bicentennial revival; its attractions far outweigh the structural weaknesses. The British performance was lively but uncommitted; the subject matter is exotic there. It remains to see whether American productions (one is due in April at the Manhattan School of Music [see p. 569]) can make the political and national points without losing the lightness.

Stephen Oliver, the composer of *Tom Jones*, came to attention when his ninth opera, *The Duchess of Malfi*, was done by the Oxford University Opera Club five years ago. He was twenty-one. *Tom Jones* is his twenty-second opera; few composers since Rossini (who had written most of his operas before he turned twenty-seven) have been so prolific so young. In *Malfi*, Oliver himself sang a leading role, Bosola; for *Tom Jones*, he wrote his own libretto, a trim, clever piece of work. The three acts are set in Somerset, the inn at Upton, and London. The "many strange accidents" at the inn provide, for the second act, an extended finale of the kind Lorenzo da Ponte, in his memoirs, prescribed: "Every-

412

body sings, and every form of singing must be available—the adagio, the allegro, the andante, the intimate, the harmonious, and then—noise, noise, noise, for the finale almost always closes in an uproar. . . . The finale must produce on the stage every singer of the cast, be there three hundred of them . . . and they must have solos, duets, terzets, sixtets, thirteenets, sixtyets; and if the plot of the drama does not permit, the poet must find a way to make it permit, in the face of reason, good sense, Aristotle, and all the powers of heaven or earth." The plot of *Tom Jones* does permit, and Oliver seizes all his chances. Coleridge deemed *Oedipus Rex, The Alchemist*, and *Tom Jones* "the three most perfect plots ever planned." Fielding himself stands by in his novel, expounding his Pelagian ethic, demonstrating his careful plan, drawing the reader's attention to the concinnity of incidents hundreds of pages apart. Hardly possible in an opera—so for the Olympian voice of the novelist Oliver has substituted the Olympians themselves: Jove doubles with Squire Allworthy, Juno with Lady Bellaston, etc. Things begin, Monteverdi fashion, with a divine council: man's virtue is to be put to the test. The device works neatly. The score is a high-spirited amalgam to which Monteverdi, Handel, Mozart, Britten, and Stravinsky have made large contributions. There is rather too much busy scherzando music for my taste, too much ready pastiche, too little lyricism. For all that, *Tom Jones* is a cunningly wrought, lively, and highly intelligent diversion. Oliver has a well-stocked and witty mind, copious technical resource, theater flair, and uncommon skill in writing for particular forces in hand. It was a pleasure to be entertained by someone so confident and so bright.

Mozart was younger, eighteen, when he composed *La finta giardiniera*. It is an opera constructed as Haydn's comedies are: a long sequence of beautiful, delicately worked arias in many veins, spun on a thread of amorous intrigues and mistaken identities, with elaborate, extended finales to the first two acts. For the EMTC, Edmund Tracey had provided a crisp new English translation, and Colin Graham's production of the piece was the best I have encountered. Since outside festival conditions some abridgment is inevitable, he removed five of the twenty-eight numbers, but he left the others largely intact; his staging was founded not on funny "business" but on patterns of human behavior observed with an amused and accurate eye—and with an ear tuned to Mozart's genius for revealing character in the turn of a phrase or the twist of a harmony. And so even this piece of eighteenth-century artifice became "music theater," faithful to Felsenstein's precept that "the performer must not give the effect of being an instrument or a component part of already existing music, or a marionette manipulated by the music, but that of being its creative fashioner." Felsenstein's achievements in Berlin, as Graham remarked in a program note, were supported by almost unlimited time and money. The English Music Theatre received only £425,000 from the Arts Council for its first year's activity; its stagings were simple, economical, and resourceful. Graham and Bedford have molded a team of talented young musicians into a real company.

Joachim Herz and Götz Friedrich, who have divided Felsenstein's mantle between them, are very different kinds of director. Put simply, Herz never seems to get in the way of the work and its performers, while Friedrich makes both the work and its performers subordinate to his own emphatic commentary on what he believes the piece in question can be made to mean. Music theater, Herz wrote in 1960, "opposes the concept of the star stage director. Rather, it establishes the thinking, performing artist who transforms himself into the character he portrays; to him the stage director is only a helper, a mirror to tell him whether his interpretation is sufficiently clear and intelligible to the spectator, an arranger and coordinator who sees the individual in relation to the total effect and puts the details together into a harmonious entity." In this sense Herz has directed *Salome* for the English National Opera, and drawn most arresting performances from those thinking artists Josephine Barstow (Salome), Norman Welsby (Jokanaan), Emile Belcourt (Herod), and Elizabeth Connell (Herodias). It is a very detailed production—in addition to the seventeen singing roles, some forty other characters are individualized and named in the program—and yet "a harmonious entity" that never leads the eye, and therefore the ear, away from *Hauptstimme* at any particular moment. "The main tower of strength in our work," Herz also wrote, "is the conductor. It is in his hands to determine whether the performance will or will not be music theater, and the most beautiful stage direction comes to naught if he has not made the conception his own." At the Coliseum, the young Mark Elder was such a tower of strength; I have never heard the score more eloquently played.

I should like to see Herz's production of *The Ring*, in Leipzig. Friedrich's, at Covent Garden, is the latest in the current series of fashionable, extravagant, perverse "glosses" that diminish the scope and stature of the work by contradicting its composer's clearly expressed intentions. Friedrich began with *Das Rheingold* and *Die Walküre* in 1974, added *Siegfried* last year, and this year *Götterdämmerung*. The setting, designed by Josef Svoboda, is a very large square platform that can rise, revolve, and tilt at any angle, around a central support. Its underside is mirrored; the Rhinebed and Nibelheim's depths are seen in reflection from deep pits below the stage. The top surface is louvered; at the flick of a switch a steep ramp can become one of Svoboda's favorite giant staircases. Gunther's palace is made of Plexiglas panels, and in *Götterdämmerung* huge square lenses hang down, so that the faces of characters behind them can appear in magnified closeup. It is a vastly impressive piece of stage machinery; although the full figures have not yet been published, the cost of the production is commonly reckoned at about a quarter of a million pounds. The Gods are portrayed as a gang of seedy, white-faced, white-robed clowns. (Wotan's face is painted half white, half black, to indicate his split personality.) Froh is a finicky queen, Donner a fuddy-duddy, and Loge a hippie houseboy. The Giants jig through a Tweedledum-Tweedledee comedy routine during Fasolt's "Sanft schloss Schlaf dein Aug'." Siegmund is a shaggy beatnik. The Valkyries are dressed as birds of prey. Black and silver are the dominant colors. Of nature, the constant background to Wagner's drama, there is no trace.

Thousands of words have been written about Friedrich's intentions. In a hundred or two, let me declare them most unmusical. Curtain-rise is invariably composed into Wagner's score, and in every scene Friedrich begins shaping the visual pictures too soon. Even the start of it all, 125 measures of E-flat welling up in darkness before the Rhine becomes visible—one of the high inspirations of music theater—he makes the accompaniment to a light show and a spinning platform. The preludes to Acts I and III of *Die Walküre* and the Rhine Journey he sets as pantomimes; conversely, he ignores Wagner's careful scenario for the start of the Funeral March. In the prologue of *Götterdämmerung* Wagner wrote a radiant, striding entry for Brünnhilde and Siegfried; Friedrich reveals the pair lying on the ground in an amorous clinch. Lest anyone forget that Hagen broods about obtaining the ring, Friedrich leaves him onstage, a brooding excrescence, during Brünnhilde's dialogues with Waltraute and with Siegfried-as-Gunther. There are some high theater-strokes in the production, but, one after another, the big, important symbolic actions—Alberich's rape of gold, the shattering of sword upon spear—are muffed. What Wagner "meant" by the end of *Götterdämmerung* has often been argued, but all agree that it is something serious, important—all except Friedrich, who closes the cycle with the bare wooden platform under working light, as if to say, "Never mind what tremendous things the music is expounding; it was only a play." A cast of well-known Wagnerians—among them Berit Lindholm, Marita Napier, Josephine Veasey, Yvonne Minton, René Kollo, Peter Hofmann, Jean Cox, Donald McIntyre, Norman Bailey—is constricted, not inspired, by the tight, dictatorial direction. On the credit side, Colin Davis, conducting, flowered this year into a *Ring* interpreter who is passionate but not frenzied, sets natural-seeming tempi, and supports the singers without driving them.

415

The Covent Garden *Ring* was carefully prepared, and its performances occupied the company's undivided attention for more than three weeks. Two weeks later, the "regular" season was due to begin with a revival of *Macbeth*, joined two weeks after that by a revival of *Così fan tutte*. This represents the *stagione* system in action—amply rehearsed runs of each opera, with a stable cast—at which James Levine has recently been turning an envious eye. (But Covent Garden seems to be carrying it to extremes this season: for eight weeks in December and January only three operas are billed, two of them with José Carreras as hero; then for two weeks there is no opera, only ballet, while Friedrich rehearses his new *Freischütz*.) Given artists of equal prowess—and between Covent Garden and Metropolitan casting there is probably little to choose now—*stagione* yields a different and, I believe, superior kind of performance. The New York repertory system affords more variety. But it can scarcely be possible for any regular working company, however efficient, to bring five different operas up to a very high performance level for presentation on five consecutive days. (That is how the Metropolitan season opened last week.) Or for any orchestra to give of its best when it must play both the five-and-a-quarter-hour *Meistersinger* and another opera on the same day. (That is what the Met orchestra must do this Saturday and next.)

The Metropolitan season opened with *Il trovatore* and continued with *Aida*. A simple, central criticism of the shows could be that Leonora and Manrico (Renata Scotto and Luciano Pavarotti) did not seem to be very much in love with, or even care very deeply about, one another; nor did Aida and Radamès (Rita Hunter and Carlo Bergonzi). And so from a dramatic point of view both productions must be deemed failures. Not music theater. But there were musical rewards. Although Scotto and Pavarotti are lyric or lirico-spinto singers who have acquired force at the cost of sweetness, both were able, and they sing well enough to make one regret that Scotto cut a verse of "Di tale amor" and of "Tu vedrai che amore in terra," and Pavarotti a verse of "Di quella pira." Shirley Verrett was Azucena; the voice was unsettled (she has been alternating soprano and mezzo roles lately), the interpretation striking. Matteo Manuguerra made a sound Di Luna, though on Met opening night one expects to hear a rather grander, more romantic baritone. Gianandrea Gavazzeni, who has been conducting for nearly fifty years, made a belated Met début and led a capable, traditional performance.

Two things about the *Aida* were outstanding. Carlo Bergonzi's share of the final scene—the thirty-two B's that begin the recitative, the delicate, tender, occasionally heroic phrases in the duet—was voiced with a beauty and eloquence of timbre such as one seldom hears today.

416

Earlier on, he mingled fine singing with some provincial vulgarities of rhythm and inflection. And Elena Obraztsova, the lambent Marina of the Bolshoy's *Boris* at the Metropolitan last year, was an Amneris of uncommon force and authority—decisive, passionate, very powerful, and a tall, commanding actress. The timbre was not velvety—there were flecks of impurity in the texture—but her phrasing was smooth, by turns seductive and formidable. Everything she did told strongly. Miss Hunter was vocally a correct but unremarkable Aida; she wasn't bad but she didn't seem worth the importing. Louis Quilico was an acceptable but not imposing Amonasro. James Morris was a suave and sonorous Ramphis. Kazimierz Kord, conducting, with rare skill gave some shape and direction to a performance made up of largely uncoordinated individual interpretations.

Die Meistersinger, the next night, was far more of an ensemble performance. (It was also an uncut performance, possibly the first in Metropolitan history.) The production, by Nathaniel Merrill, which is fourteen years old, was new to me. It looked fresh, newly rehearsed, sensitive, and unroutined. There were several house débuts, the most notable being Dieter Weller's, as Beckmesser. He was a tall, personable young town clerk, a plausible suitor for Eva's hand, shy and fussy, not spiteful, in manner. He sang both serenade and prize song with beauty of tone. Gerd Brenneis's Walther was less winning; the voice is robust but unlyrical in timbre. Ellen Shade's Eva was delicately played and was most musically sung, if not with the pure shine that an Eva requires. Peter Meven should be an admirable Pogner when someone persuades him to phrase in long, smooth spans, not choppily. From earlier casts there were Thomas Stewart's Sachs, very sure, very skillful, limited only by a lack of rich colors in the voice, and Kenneth Riegel's David, rather too insistently boyish in action but clear and bright. Allan Monk was a new and excellent Kothner. Robert O'Hearn's settings are a little too smart for my taste (the last scene suggests a Hollywood production number), but at least the action is not transferred to the moon or to Manchuria; the Masters do not wear dinner jackets or diving suits. The left-to-right reversal of the traditional sets for Act II and Act III, Scene 1, did no musical harm that I could hear. (Sometimes a composer's stage placing is acoustically important; only an unmusical director stations Fenton, in the first-act finale of *Falstaff*, away from the orchestral horns.) The evening provided a demonstration of how without transgressing stylistic limits implicitly or categorically set by the creator of a masterpiece a director and his artists can still give individual and unconstricted performances. The only directorial sin of commission occurred at the very end of Act II, when Sachs reappeared on what should remain an empty stage; and of omission when the supers failed to open their mouths during the "Wach' auf" chorale, which everybody except Sachs should at least appear to be singing. David Stivender's chorus—as also in *Il trovatore* and *Aida*—made a splendid sound. Sixten Ehrling conducted a performance that moved steadily and confidently forward but was hardly poetic. The evening touched no great heights, as *Aida* had done when Obraztsova and Bergonzi were singing, but was never less than a serious and scrupulous endeavor to do justice to Wagner's work.

Any thoughts about *Dalibor*, a noble and stirring opera that should be more widely heard, I will save to the time of the Carnegie Hall performance promised by Eve Queler in January (p. 490). The English National's *Don Giovanni* and the Met's revival of *Figaro* can perhaps be paired for future discussion (pp. 424–25). But the Welsh National's *The Midsummer Marriage* deserves a word. Tippett's opera first appeared at Covent Garden in 1955; in 1968 there was a new production there, followed by a recording that won widespread acclaim for one of the most joyful, musically and spiritually generous of modern operas. The Welsh production, due to be seen in five cities, showed that the piece—during which an English country scene is transformed into a world of magic, where a staircase leads to heaven, mysterious gates open into the teeming earth, and ritual dances encompass the four seasons—is not beyond the resources of a medium-sized company. Full houses have shown that the public is not afraid of it. The Welsh company began its existence in 1946, with a week of *Cavalleria rusticana* and *Pagliacci*, and *Faust*. Today, it plays twenty-six weeks a year and has an orchestra on full-time contract. *Nabucco, Les Vêpres siciliennes*, and *La battaglia di Legnano* are among the works it has taken through the country; also Rossini's *Moïse* and *Guillaume Tell*; Rimsky-Korsakov's *May Night*; *Billy Budd* and *Lulu*; and some new Welsh operas. To be frank, I thought that the performance of *The Midsummer Marriage* was overrated by most of my British colleagues. Ralph Koltai's set, kept deliberately simple, so that it can tour easily, conveys as little as did the two Covent Garden stagings any sense of a real countryside, peopled by ordinary, everyday people, who are then drawn into visionary adventures. Jill Gomez and John Treleaven in the leading roles (created by Joan Sutherland and Richard Lewis) lacked sharply defined characters. Cardiff's civic-owned New Theatre has had its orchestra pit enlarged this season, but the place is still too small for the music to flower as fully as it should. (The Welsh company seeks an opera house of its own; there is in Cardiff a theater that would serve it well, but it would cost about three million pounds to acquire and convert; for a similar sum, Scottish Opera acquired its own opera house in Glasgow last year.) Richard Armstrong, the company's musical director, conducted buoyantly. I must not underrate the achievement; *The Midsummer Marriage* may still await a fully pleasing produc-

418

tion, but this youthful, enthusiastic, and successful performance should help to bring it nearer.

At Glyndebourne, a new production of *Falstaff* was directed by Jean-Pierre Ponnelle with the proliferation of vulgar detail that marks so much of his work. The end of Act II, Scene 1—the "Prima voi" exchanges of Falstaff and "Master Brook"—became a comedy routine for six, involving the two of them, Pistol and Bardolph, the innkeeper and the page Robin. Robin was present and prominent during Falstaff's wooing of Alice. Children capered about during the enchanted strains of Nannetta's fairy song. Need one say more? On the other hand, Glyndebourne's revival of *Capriccio*, a marvelously accomplished performance, led by the captivating Countess Madeleine of Elisabeth Söderström, showed how, given sufficient skill and taste, and given the right work, a director—in this case, John Cox—*can* play fast and loose with a piece. Glyndebourne had mounted a traditional eighteenth-century *Capriccio* in 1963; ten years later the eighteenth-century Paris room was redecorated in the height of fashion as if by an early-twentieth-century Countess, and since then a Braque and a Vlaminck have hung on her walls. Madeleine has become, as it were, Marie-Laure; a young Cocteau and a young Stravinsky frequent her salon; a Diaghilev expounds the impresario's thoughts on how to astonish the public. It works. The result is entertaining and delightful.

October 25, 1976

The Met Meistersinger *was uncut on the first night, but later performances were abridged.*

SOUNDS THAT GIVE DELIGHT

The new Avery Fisher Hall is a success. "New" because within the outer shell of the old Avery Fisher—*olim* Philharmonic—Hall the auditorium has been from floor to ceiling rebuilt, to a different shape and of different materials. And "a success" because music sounds good in it. That summary approval is based on a hearing in the new hall of no more than two movements of Mahler's Ninth Symphony, Brahms's Violin Concerto, and Stravinsky's *Firebird*, and of only one orchestra, the New York Philharmonic, under one conductor, Pierre Boulez. But, in my

419

experience, first impressions of a hall can generally be trusted. So it proved with Vienna's Grosser Musikvereinssaal, Amsterdam's Concertgebouw, Boston's Symphony Hall, and Glasgow's City Hall when it reopened as the home of the Scottish National Orchestra; their musical excellence was evident at once, and later visits confirmed what one had heard from the start. So it proved with London's Royal Festival Hall and New York's Philharmonic Hall—acoustic failures that one had to learn to live with, since each played a central role in the musical life of its city. The Festival Hall was eventually rendered tolerable when an elaborate system of "electrically assisted resonance" was installed in its ceiling—hundreds of small loudspeakers, each responsive to a single frequency. Repeated tinkering with Philharmonic Hall—in 1963, 1964, 1969, and 1972—effected no more than marginal improvements; now the place has been demolished and replaced.

The good halls just mentioned date from the nineteenth century, and the failures from the twentieth. The latter were built according to carefully determined theories of how musical sounds behave, but the acoustical experts of the twentieth century, for all their scientific calculation, seemed to have lost skills commanded by their predecessors. In the Greek theater of Epidaurus, which seats 12,000 people, I have, sitting in the back row, heard a pin drop onstage. In the Roman arena of Verona, opera is played unamplified to an audience of 22,000. Nineteenth-century concert-hall architects could build for smaller gatherings: the Grosser Musikvereinssaal (1870) holds 1,680, and Leipzig's Neues Gewandhaus (1884; destroyed in 1945) held 1,560. Trouble began when more people had to be packed in; yet Boston was able to make a success of its Symphony Hall (1900), which holds 2,600— much the size of Philharmonic Hall when first it opened. Trouble increased when architects began to abandon the traditional shape for a hall and—starting with the notorious Salle Pleyel (1927), in Paris—to deploy curves, fan forms, funnel forms, suspended reflectors, instead of the plain rectangle of proved acoustical merit. Philharmonic's back wall was a shallow curve; the side walls ran parallel for a while and then stepped in toward the platform. Not every modern hall was a flop; Berlin's Philharmonie (1963), a piece of romantic concrete landscape that seats 2,300 people in terraces grouped picturesquely around an orchestra out in the middle, was not. But many were.

Four years ago, after the last round of modifications to Philharmonic Hall, I described the common characteristics of the good old orchestra halls: rectangular in plan, with a flat floor, a coffered ceiling, wall surfaces broken up by heavy window frames, niches, or something of the kind, and a shallow balcony or balconies carried round three sides of the hall. Last year, I described the pleasure of hearing music in a modern hall—Minneapolis's new Orchestra Hall—built according to those principles. The acoustic consultant for that hall was Cyril Harris—he already had the Metropolitan Opera House and Kennedy Center to his credit—and he is the man who has made Fisher Hall sound so good. Dr. Harris knows all about reverberation times, frequency decays, and initial-time-delay gaps but prefers to talk about proved shapes and proved materials—wood and heavy plaster. His Minneapolis hall seats just under 2,600, and his Fisher Hall just over 2,700. Each is rectangular, with a wooden floor, a heavy plaster ceiling, and three tiers of shallow balcony around three sides. Fisher Hall departs from tradition in having a floor that slopes down gently toward the platform, and a ceiling line approximately parallel to that floor: in vertical long section it is a rhomboid rather than a rectangle. (The Amsterdam floor is flat; the Leipzig floor was; and the Vienna and Boston floors are nearly flat. All four halls were built with horizontal ceilings.) Like Boston, and like Carnegie Hall, Fisher Hall differs from the European model, and from Minneapolis, in housing the band (I use that term only because in discussion of a hall "orchestra" can be ambiguous) behind a kind of proscenium arch, in a tapered box opening into the auditorium proper.

Every listener has acoustical measuring instruments of uncommon sensitivity. (According to the acoustician Llewelyn S. Lloyd, "the loudest sound our ears can bear to hear has an intensity ten million times that of the faintest sound the most acute ear can detect.") He distills his impressions from a host of variables. But he does not have precise words to describe the result, and usually resorts to visual or tactile metaphor—"bright," "dull," "warm," "cold"—once resonance and loudness have been assessed. Moreover, the eye can apparently affect the ear. Navy blue, which dominated one of Philharmonic Hall's earlier decorative schemes, seems to absorb sound; dim lighting can effectively take the shine off a score; and when the ceiling of Boston's Symphony Hall was repainted a few years ago some concertgoers reported a loss of "mellowness," which returned only when the décor had lost its first scrubbed appearance. (But maybe dust on the reflecting surfaces does have acoustic properties; a new ventilation system in Fisher Hall insures that there will be little there.) I'd go further: some old halls even seem to have acquired a sonic "patina," as if they had been tuned and tempered in performance by generations of great performers. Acoustic judgments are highly subjective. A colleague has described Fisher Hall as having "a 'modern' sound," in contrast to Carnegie Hall and Boston's Symphony Hall, where "the listener is enveloped in a warm, velvety sound. In the new Fisher Hall, there seem to be less reverberations; the sound is cooler; the emphasis is on clarity." I don't altogether agree, and am happy that I don't, because "warm" is a term of high praise in my acoustical vocabulary, and "a 'modern' sound" has been the curse of so many orchestra halls where the main fare is still nineteenth-century music and twentieth-century music written for performance in good nineteenth-century acoustics. In his *Music, Acoustics and Architecture*, Leo L. Beranek listed the desirable attributes of a musical building as a musician, rather than a scientist, might try to define them. Dr. Beranek worked on the original Philharmonic Hall, and he certainly did not achieve all of them there (though he claims that he could have if he had been given a freer hand). In Fisher Hall, I find them admirably achieved; although on "ease of hearing among performers" only the players can report, and "uniformity" can be assessed only by someone who has sat in more places than I have yet done.

The first attribute is "intimacy or presence." This is difficult to achieve in a large hall. Essentially, the music and its performers should not seem and sound far away from the listener, as they did in Philharmonic Hall if one sat farther back than about row S (and as they do in London's Festival Hall, similarly) but do not even from the very back row, SS, of Fisher Hall. The players *are* far away, of course—120 feet away —but still one feels in touch with them. Other qualities are "liveliness, warmth, loudness of direct and of reverberant sound, definition or clarity, brilliance, diffusion, balance, blend, immediacy of response, dynamic range." The new hall is lively and quick to speak. The sound is warm. There was plenty of volume in the *Firebird* climaxes; one could feel the music physically, through the soles of one's feet and the palms of one's hands on the armrests. The whole hall was resonant with sound, but it was not an assault on the eardrums; rather, it provided that sense of physical exhilaration on which the composer must have counted. Loudness is important, but so is softness—the ability for a very gentle sound, of low dynamic level, to steal distinctly and eloquently through all the space. Lorne Munroe's cello solos, in the last movement of the Mahler symphony, showed that the hall does have this attribute. Clarity and brilliance it has, too, but not at the expense of warmth, balance, and blend. "Freedom from echo" and "freedom from external noise" are achieved. "Tonal quality"—allowing a beautiful tone to be heard as such—must raise the question of the Philharmonic Orchestra's own tonal quality, which I would prefer to leave aside for a while. There was some beautiful playing, however—again I would cite Mr. Munroe's solos—and it did sound beautiful. In short, unqualified initial approval for the acoustics of the new Fisher Hall. And more detail when I have heard its response to a piano, a singer, and a large chorus, and listened to a wider range of music.

In the lobbies outside, the columns of Max Abramovitz's original building and wall surfaces have been painted chocolate brown. The normal civilized amenities of a metropolitan concert hall—restaurants, buffets, a large, friendly café to gather in afterward, a bookshop where the scores of works to be played and the latest music magazines are on sale—are missing, alas, but there is a bar on the ground floor, and there are drink stands upstairs. The architects for the new auditorium were Philip Johnson and John Burgee, working to Dr. Harris's prescriptions. Their design does not have the exuberant, disciplined boldness and imagination of Hugh Hardy's for Minneapolis's Orchestra Hall. The decoration is off-white and gold—and there is far too much gold for my taste. It covers the semicylindrical tier fronts, which look like fat bolsters, or sections of a gilded pipeline; the players are framed by a broad gold band, echoed in diminution at each step-back of the tapered orchestra house. True, the effect of so much gold is less vulgar than at the Metropolitan Opera, but nevertheless it looks raw and ostentatious, and the new ventilation system will presumably prevent its dulling down to the unobtrusive dusky glint—rich, not gaudy—of gilding in the Vienna State Opera or Covent Garden. Rows of dimmed naked bulbs, lining the tiers penny-arcade fashion, cast their own golden glow through the hall while the music is being played. There is just enough light for reading the program or following a clearly printed score. The seats are comfortable. The shape of the hall feels right. Old Philharmonic Hall was a place I avoided except when the interest of the program made a visit imperative. The approaches to the new Fisher Hall are still pretty bleak, sterile, chilly (very different from the warmly human, welcoming, unpretentious lobbies in Minneapolis). But, once inside the auditorium, one is predisposed toward enjoyment.

At the Metropolitan, James Levine made his first appearance of the season conducting a revival of Puccini's *Trittico*. Cornell MacNeil repeated his powerful Michele in *Il tabarro* and his resourceful Gianni Schicchi; otherwise the major roles were newly cast, and there were several debutants. None of the three heroines seemed well suited to her part. Hildegard Behrens, a straightforward, well-schooled German soprano, lists Giorgetta in *Il tabarro* among her roles in the newly published *Who's Who in Opera* (a fat, fascinating compilation, edited by Maria F. Rich, and compulsive reading for all opera fans; $65, from the Arno Press), but it was as Leonore in *Fidelio* that she came to international attention, and as Puccini's lustrous heroine she seemed dowdy and awkward. Josella Ligi lists Aida, Amelia in *Un ballo in maschera*, and Leonora in *La forza del destino*, and she describes her voice as "spinto." She sounded too full and mature in the young-lyric role of Lauretta in *Gianni Schicchi*; either Giorgetta or Suor Angelica would surely have been a happier choice for her Met début. Angelica was Teresa Zylis-Gara, an admirable singer but one who, effectively restrained at first, continued to eschew sentimentality to the point of being colorless and unmoving.

Gianfranco Cecchele made an unimpressive Met début as Luigi in

Il tabarro; the voice did not seem to break free. Neil Shicoff's Rinuccio in *Gianni Schicchi* was ardent, a little too insistently athletic in manner. Two veterans had joined the cast. Italo Tajo was perfect, and richly unobtrusive, in the small role of Talpa in *Il tabarro*. Fedora Barbieri as Angelica's aunt boomed out mightily on her remaining good notes and struggled for higher reaches of the role. Both of them overplayed as Simone and Zita in *Gianni Schicchi*. The Met production of *Il tabarro* will pass muster; its *Suor Angelica* is arid (the convent does not even have a garden), and its *Gianni Schicchi* coarse. Fabrizio Melano's direction misses the fine, delicate details that should inform the staging of all three operas, and Mr. Levine's conducting made little of the Straussian and Debussian instrumental finesses that give charm to Puccini's piece. *Il trittico* should be at once three bewitchingly scored tone poems, cunningly decorated for both ear and eye, and a good old wallow in passion, then pathos, followed by light-fingered comedy. At the Met it was none of these.

The English National Opera's new production of *Don Giovanni* and the Met's revival of *Figaro* made an interesting contrast. *Don Giovanni* was not particularly well sung, except by Felicity Palmer, as Elvira, and by Noel Davies it was clumsily conducted. But the cast missed none of Mozart's dramatic points. The staging was by the director-designer team of Anthony Besch and John Stoddart, already renowned in Britain for Scottish Opera's *Così fan tutte*, Covent Garden's *La clemenza di Tito*, and the English National's *Magic Flute*. Mr. Besch gives the impression of having thought not "What new things can I do in this familiar work?" but "What did Mozart have in mind when he wrote those notes to those words?" The Met's *Figaro* staging was done last season by Günther Rennert and has been revived by Phebe Berkowitz and Bruce Donnell. Its only novelty lay in investing the Countess with a nymphomaniac streak, in her scene with Cherubino in Act II, and that, fortunately, has now been toned down. The staging was not otherwise eccentric, but it lacked, and still lacks, freshness. In *Don Giovanni* one was caught up anew, both simply and intricately, in Mozart's drama; watching *Figaro* was more like paging through a familiar and well-loved masterpiece with unquickened eyes. Except—and it is a large exception —when Judith Blegen was on the stage. Each of Susanna's phrases came from her lips as if new-minted, and she listened to what the other characters were saying as if she had never heard the lines before. Maria Ewing made her Met début as Cherubino; she is a promising young mezzo with a dark, attractive timbre. Richard Stilwell's Count still bore traces of the cheerful, plebeian manners imposed on him by Götz Friedrich's farmyard production of the opera at the 1974 Holland Festival. Justino Díaz was an equally cheerful, easygoing Figaro. Leopold Hager, from Salzburg, made his Met début conducting a light, bland account of the score. Where, last season, Steuart Bedford had driven unfeelingly straight through the musical marvels of the work, Mr. Hager slipped over them.

November 1, 1976

MAHLEREI

To open the Philharmonic's regular concert series in the rebuilt Avery Fisher Hall, Pierre Boulez conducted Mahler's Third Symphony. Four days later, the same work brought to an end the Philharmonic's "Mahler-month" in Carnegie Hall—a series of concerts at which his nine symphonies, the first movement of the unfinished Tenth Symphony, and some of the songs with orchestra were done. Deryck Cooke's new performing version of the whole Tenth, published this year by Associated Music Publishers and Faber, awaits a New York première. (Mr. Cooke's death last week will be lamented by Mahlerians, Brucknerians, and Wagnerians everywhere.) Erich Leinsdorf conducted No. 5, Boulez Nos. 3, 7, and 9, and James Levine the rest. The performances were very well attended. The public appetite for Mahler, which historians chronicling taste and fashion will note as a striking sixties and seventies phenomenon, shows no signs of growing less. "Now it's Sibelius," Delius once remarked, "and when they're tired of him, they'll boost up Mahler and Bruckner." That was in the early thirties. Outside Germany, Austria, and Holland, Bruckner and Mahler were often lumped together as two long-winded Teutons. As late as 1955, they had to share between them a single volume of the "Master Musicians" series. Any distinction was commonly made along lines suggested by the tale of a traveler on a mountain path who, plucking a daisy, remarked to his companion, "That is Mahler," and then, indicating the distant peaks, "and there is Bruckner." Mahler's skill as a conductor was unforgotten and his command of the orchestra was not unacknowledged; in 1950 Vaughan Williams wrote that "intimate acquaintance with the executive side of music in orchestra, chorus, and opera made even Mahler into a very tolerable imitation of a composer."

Things began to change, and Delius's prophecy to be fulfilled, during the centenary celebrations of 1960; thenceforward both performances and recordings of his music grew more and more frequent. Five conductors—Maurice Abravanel, Leonard Bernstein, Bernard Haitink, Rafael Kubelik, and Georg Solti—have now recorded all nine sym-

425

phonies; there are many, many other versions available, and most months add to their number. But when I began listening to music in earnest, twenty-five years ago, four of the symphonies were not available on disc. The Bruno Walter sets of Nos. 4 (on twelve sides) and 5 (on sixteen), made with the New York Philharmonic-Symphony, and of No. 9 (on twenty sides) and *Das Lied von der Erde* (on fourteen), recorded at Viennese public performances in, respectively, 1938 and 1936, were treasured possessions. So was Ormandy's Minneapolis performance of No. 2, and—available to Britons only as an import—the Mitropoulos album of No. 1. To anyone who cared about Mahler the records were essential, since live performances of anything but the Fourth Symphony were rare. Over twenty years ago, I crossed the North Sea to hear the Sixth Symphony for the first time; there was a performance at the Holland Festival, and any performance of the Sixth was then a "festival event." But in New York's 1972–73 season the work was played by three different orchestras, six times in all.

"Mahler is not for every day," said the authors of *The Record Guide*, in 1951. "To hear Mahler's Eighth Symphony in the flesh is an experience as rare as it is tremendous," Deryck Cooke wrote nine years later, in a program note for what was only the fourth London performance of a work fifty years old. But today Mahler *has* become pretty well an everyday composer. Hearing the Eighth Symphony in the flesh is no longer a rare experience. Has it therefore become one less tremendous? I find that the answer is yes—and yes to a similar question about any other of the symphonies—except when it is conducted by a conductor who seems to be not so much in command of the work as commanded by it, a conductor in disciplined surrender to the flow and surge and swell of the music and to its emotional dictates. Such conductors, in my experience, have been Bruno Walter (the Second and Ninth Symphonies, *Das Lied*), Jascha Horenstein (the First, Fifth, and Eighth), William Steinberg (the Sixth), and Leopold Stokowski (the Second). Dimitri Mitropoulos and Otto Klemperer gave vastly impressive but less "transcendental" interpretations; mingled with Mahler's music there was too much sense of the conductor's own forceful personality. After a performance of the Sixth Symphony conducted by Steinberg, in 1960, I tried to jot down some impressions: "Sometimes— perhaps more often to ordinary human concertgoers than to music critics—there comes a performance which, for as long as it lasts, transforms the world and transforms the listener. The concert hall, the people around him, the platform and players disappear. He is listening, moving, breathing, and seeing in a new world where forms and feelings and thoughts have all become sounds. Scriabin and Busoni sought to provide this mystical experience. But Mahler, who once declared that a symphony should contain all the world, is the composer whose music

426

can most completely engulf the listener." And so on. It is gush, not music criticism. But how does one find words to relate adventures of the spirit? Musical notes are a better medium. What Mahler's music has meant to composers as disparate as Kurt Weill, Shostakovich, and Britten, to Hans Werner Henze and Peter Maxwell Davies, they have expressed in their own scores.

"Mehr Ausdruck der Empfindung als Mahlerei," Beethoven said of his Pastoral Symphony. Twisting the phrase, I would suggest that "Mahlerei," in the sense of revealing what Mahler's music has to offer, is above all "the expression of feelings." It is not a fashionable view. Modern Mahler scholarship has been concerned to demonstrate careful structure, and a modern Mahler conductor is usually praised for revealing that structure, rather than for dissolving us into ecstasies and bringing all heaven—or hell—before our eyes. Boulez has written that "the more [an interpreter] gives in to imprudent ecstasy, even in the hysteria of the moment, the more the original motivation is disturbed. One destroys the multilayered ambiguity which is the essence of this music—in so doing one makes it uncommonly trivial and squanders its deep content; what is more, one hurts the subliminal structure which keeps all the moments of development in balance; one permits this development to degenerate into the confused, chaotic, disorientated motions of an oaf!" (To say that Boulez wrote that is perhaps unfair; at any rate, he has been thus translated from the German in the opening chapter of *Gustav Mahler in Vienna*, an album of essays and pictures published this month by Rizzoli. A tidied-up version of his contribution appeared in *The New York Review of Books*.) "Imprudent ecstasy" and "hysteria of the moment" are loaded phrases, which do not apply to the Mahler conducting of Walter, Horenstein, or Steinberg. (My phrase was *"disciplined* surrender.") Were their interpretations different in kind from those of Boulez and Levine, or do I hear them in memory's ear through a cloud of romanticizing nostalgia? Thanks to the phonograph, it is sometimes easy to check. Unmoved by Boulez's performance of the Ninth, I bought the next day a copy of Walter's 1938 performance, the recording through which I first learned to love the symphony. (Walter conducted the première of the Ninth, in 1912.) I soon found that memory had played odd tricks. Boulez's tempo for the final adagio had seemed to me too fast—but Walter's, remembered as ideal, proved to be no slower. Nevertheless, there are in that Viennese reading a sense of long-breathed singing and an emotional intensity, expressed in tone color and by accent and rubato within the phrases, that were missing in the Philharmonic performance. But the largest differences between the two interpretations occur in the scherzo. "Etwas täppisch und sehr derb" ("Rather clumsy and very sturdy") is the first marking. Walter's handling is heavier, sturdier. The accents are more emphatic.

All the contrasts are stronger. The distinctions in rhythmic lilt between the Ländlers and the waltz are sharper. The movement is not meant to be pleasant. Mahler, says Cooke, is "presenting the 'dance of life' as something utterly tawdry, stupid, and empty." "A tragic undertone," wrote Walter, "sounds in the joy." But there *is* charm in it—charm in the simple, Schubertian melodies—and by sounding this charm, by encouraging his instrumentalists to play with a kind of joyful zest, as if unaware that soon their C-major security and cheerful, regular rhythms will be shattered, Walter, far more potently than Boulez, brings out the "ambiguity" that the latter prizes so highly. In a new book—Joan Peyser's *Boulez: Composer, Conductor, Enigma*, a readable mixture of gossip, chronicle, and criticism (Schirmer)—a Philharmonic player is reported as saying that Boulez "requires only that we play the right notes at the right time. He asks for no sweat, blood, guts, or tone quality. . . . There is no robustness in the sound, never any dance feeling in the dances, never any joy in making music." It is a hard indictment, but if to "joy" we add "awe," even "terror," it begins to explain why Boulez's Mahler proves so unaffecting.

Two technical points can be added. Boulez, like Levine, eschews the portamento that was standard—recordings survive to prove it—in the string playing of Mahler's day. Even when a portamento is specifically marked in the score—by a straight line, indicating a more prominent "swoop" to the next note than the portamento implied by an ordinary curved slur—the sign gets no more than token observance. And thus the music is delivered, as it were, in a clipped modern accent rather than with the warmer inflections its composer must have intended. Boulez also, like Levine, and like most conductors now, ranges his orchestra on the platform in the modern lopsided manner: all the violins bunched on the left, cellos on the right, and basses strung out in a line on the far right. This not only destroys clearly planned antiphonies between first violins and seconds but also, I believe, produces an unbalanced sound. Mahler had his first violins on the left, his seconds on the right, and his double-basses and cellos center: that much at least is evident in the rather blurry photographs of him conducting the Eighth Symphony which appear both in *Gustav Mahler in Vienna* and in *Mahler: A Documentary Study*, compiled and edited by Kurt Blaukopf (Oxford).

Levine's performances—I heard the Fourth and the Eighth Symphonies—were straightforward, agreeably enthusiastic, and unmemorable. (An unmemorable Eighth? Something must be wrong.) Boulez's, of the Seventh, Ninth, and Third Symphonies, left a stronger impression; although unmoving, and unidiomatic both in timbre and in the use of rubato (which Boulez seems to apply in a cosmetic fashion, and not because he feels the music that way), they were exceptionally lucid. The performance of the Third could serve as illustration to the analytic points made in Donald Mitchell's new *Gustav Mahler: The Wunderhorn Years* (Westview Press). But what of the symphonic program? Mahler once described the opening of the work thus:

It has almost ceased to be music; it is hardly anything but sounds of nature. I could equally well have called the movement "What the Mountain tells me"—it's eerie, the way life gradually breaks through, out of soul-less, rigid matter. And, as this life rises from stage to stage, it takes on ever more highly developed forms: flowers, beasts, man, up to the sphere of the spirits, the "angels." Over the introduction to this movement, there lies again that atmosphere of brooding summer midday heat; not a breath stirs, all life is suspended, and the sun-drenched air trembles and vibrates. At intervals there come the moans of the youth—that is, captive life—struggling for release from the clutches of lifeless, rigid Nature. At last he breaks through and triumphs.

Does Boulez consider such things? Or ask his players to? I found little sign of it in his performance. (Almost the only moments of romance were provided by the posthorn solos of John Ware, which were tenderly and exquisitely played.) About these programs Mahler himself was ambivalent; he hoped that his music would "speak for itself," he withdrew the "scenarios," and yet he saw to it that at least some knowledge of them was disseminated. And, as Mitchell remarks, "the enormous importance of the dramatic programme for his early symphonies cannot be gainsaid: the symphonies *are* the programmes, embodied and transcended, it is true, but unthinkable without them, and also partly incomprehensible without them."

In the final paragraph of the essay already cited, Boulez tries to explain what in his view draws modern audiences to Mahler's music:

That such a work needed time before it became convincing does not seem unreasonable today. The exuberance and the lushness are more attractive now than in former times, they call back to memory the luxuriance which for many years had been forgotten or damned as superfluous and lascivious. But this somewhat primitive reaction would not in itself suffice to explain the attraction which has established itself more and more toward a work that had first been repudiated because of its ambiguity but whose very ambiguity establishes its value today.

Mahler, he argues, can be claimed neither as "a revolutionary who unleashed an irreversible process of radical innovation" nor, since he manipulated old material in so many new ways, as "the end product of a line of generations." But because

the sources of his inspiration . . . hardly exist any longer we can regard them benignly, as valuable testimonies which we cannot understand any longer directly. This material has taken on documentary value and instead of refuting it we prefer to look at it as the first step of invention. That makes it possible to give our attention from there on almost exclusively to its transformation and transmutation.

That "almost exclusively" suggests a bleak and unemotional approach. And is it Mahler's musical sources (Mozart, Beethoven, Schubert; bird-call, fanfare, and popular tune) or his philosophical sources (those "tremendous questions" about life and death, transience and recurrence, beauty and decay, tragedy and consolation with which he wrestled) that Boulez thinks have passed into history? To modern audiences, I would say, both are living. And it is because Mahler uses this familiar material so vividly, so picturesquely, so adventurously, and, above all, so emotionally that he has been able to take in the public's affection the place once held by Tchaikovsky.

A word about the Mahler books mentioned in passing. Mitchell's is the second installment of a long Mahler study in progress. (His *Gustav Mahler: The Early Years* appeared in 1958.) It is a leisurely, discursive, and thorough meditation on the first four symphonies and the songs with which they are inextricably linked. The author, as he puts it, employs both microscope and telescope "to seize on what I take to be some of the principal and unique features of a given work and look at these in close detail, both in the narrow context of the isolated work and in the broader perspectives of Mahler's art as a whole." The book is wordy; deliberately discursive; awkwardly organized; packed with information, acute observation, and stimulating surmise. Mitchell is a Mahler interpreter to my taste; he shows his love for the music. *Mahler: A Documentary Study* is a volume in large format with 128 pages of illustrations and another 128 pages close-packed, in double column, with documents of various kinds—letters, reviews, memoirs; recommended. The nine essays collected in *Gustav Mahler in Vienna* contain some interesting matter but are awkward to read, being printed in very long lines stretching two thirds of the way across large oblong pages. The book is "designed" to the hilt. Some of the numerous but unindexed illustrations are valuable, others are mere decoration, and many are fuzzy. One full page is devoted to an enlarged snippet of score saying just "V. Finale," another to two notes dying away *pppp*, a third to a page of torn, blank music paper.

November 8, 1976

CROSSING THE RIVER

Hans Werner Henze was fifty this year, and in most countries where Western music is played Henze celebrations have mingled with the Bicentennial observance that has otherwise made American music and American artists dominant in festival programs. Festivals feed on new works, and Henze, always a fertile and fluent composer, has been providing them to a point where it has been hard to keep track of all the premières. At the Brighton Festival in May, he conducted the first performance of a suite drawn from his music for the Volker Schlöndorff film *Katarina Blum*. In London, on July 12 Covent Garden gave his latest opera, *We Come to the River*, its first staging. Two days later, for the City of London Festival, he conducted his new orchestration of Carissimi's oratorio *Jephte*. In August, he was in Montepulciano, directing the Cantiere Internazionale d'Arte for students and citizens; two Henze premières there, the quintet *Amicizia!* and the recomposition of Paisiello's opera *Don Chisciotte*, were noted in these pages last month (pp. 405–6). In September, he went to West Berlin to conduct the Berlin Philharmonic in two concerts of his music during the Berliner Festwochen; those festival weeks also saw the German première of *We Come to the River* and the world premières of his Third String Quartet, written for the Concord Quartet, and his *Royal Winter Musick*, for solo guitar, written for Julian Bream. The last of these pieces had its second performance, in Town Hall, last month, as the most substantial item in Mr. Bream's lute and guitar recital.

Prolificness is commonly viewed with suspicion—today, if not in earlier centuries—and Henze has not escaped the charge of composing without due care and attention. Within works as well as with works, he has been copious; into such scores as the opera *König Hirsch*, the cello concerto *Ode to the Westwind*, the cantata *Novae de infinito laudes* he poured so much ready invention and wove such richly intricate textures that he was often recommended to try for a simpler, less efflorescent manner. Most of his later compositions are certainly leaner, less lushly embroidered, but neither in thought nor in workmanship are they thin. *Royal Winter Musick* is a substantial six-movement "Sonata on Shakespearean Characters" lasting about twenty-six minutes. In a spoken introduction to his Town Hall performance, Mr. Bream explained that the "Gloucester" whose name heads the first movement is not the Earl in *King Lear* but the future Richard III, and that the winter of the title is a "winter of discontent" not yet made glorious by any sun. ("My music," Henze said in 1972, "has been and is now more than ever the analysis of the amount of mental sadness that is present now.") The movement is in sonata form and has a drum rhythm on the body of the instrument as one of its themes. "Romeo and Juliet" is a reverie, and "Ariel" a quicksilver fantasy. "Ophelia" is made of a gentle, plaintive melody above a flowing accompaniment, and "Audrey, Touchstone, and William" is a scherzo-and-trio in which the scherzo sounds like the transformation of an Elizabethan galliard. "Oberon" provides a rondo finale. Henze is a master of modern guitar writing: the 1958 *Kammermusik*, a reflection on a Hölderlin poem for tenor, guitar, and instrumental octet, includes three eloquent guitar solos headed by phrases of Hölderlin (it has recently been recorded on Oiseau-Lyre); a guitarist is one of the four musicians who perform *El Cimarrón. Royal Winter Musick,* Mr. Bream said, results from his request to the composer ten years ago for a guitarist's *Hammerklavier*—a work that would extend both technique and expressive powers to the utmost. The new piece does.

Lutenists—for the first half of his recital Mr. Bream played the lute—need no special inducement to play John Dowland, who wrote for the instrument with a Lisztian combination of poetry and virtuosity. But since this year is the three-hundred-and-fiftieth anniversary of Dowland's death, Mr. Bream's large Dowland group could be considered a part of the 1976 Dowland commemoration. One of the works he chose was "My Lady Hunsdon's Puffe," a piece that Henze uses in his Second Violin Concerto. (It is not the only piece of Dowland that reappears in Henze.) Mr. Bream must have played it in public hundreds of times before, yet he played it again with no trace of staleness; the large, mainly young audience hung intent on his delicate inflections—the subtle rhythmic nuances and small, bewitching changes of tone color. I have often praised the ambience and acoustics of Town Hall; hearing so well, as if in a room, this most intimate of all instruments gave new proof of their excellence.

We Come to the River is Henze's seventh full-scale opera. Ten years separate it from the sixth, *The Bassarids*, a work that plays for two and a half hours without intermission, and is shaped as a huge Mahlerian symphony, plus action. *The Bassarids* closed a chapter in Henze's career. After it, he turned to "music theater" for the concert platform, in such scores as the oratorio *The Raft of the "Medusa,"* the "recital for four musicians" *El Cimarrón*, and the "show with seventeen" *Der langwierige Weg in die Wohnung der Natascha Ungeheuer.* The soloist of his Second Violin Concerto hurries onto the stage after the music has begun and, wearing a plumed tricorne and a red opera cloak, "enacts" Baron Münchhausen as he fiddles away in a musical counterpart to the Baron's celebrated feat of pulling himself out of the mire by his own hair. The concerto has a text, recited by the soloist and by "a gentleman in the audience"; it is a poem based on the famous theorem that Kurt Gödel, the Princeton mathematician-philosopher, formulated in a 1931 issue of the *Monatshefte für Mathematik und Physik*. Given Henze's concern for words, ideas, actions, and music in communicative interplay, that he would sooner or later return to opera was predictable. Given the importance of a text or, at least, a "program" in just about all his compositions, his choice of literary collaborators reflects both his musical and his political development. Words—by Shelley, Hölderlin, Giordano Bruno—had inspired him to music; but words had also to be found, or commissioned, to express his latest ideas and match the kinds of music he now wanted to write.

W. H. Auden and Chester Kallman were the librettists of Henze's operas *Elegy for Young Lovers* and *The Bassarids*; they worked for him in the tradition of Hofmannsthal. But the texts of *El Cimarrón*, of the Second Violin Concerto, and of *La Cubana* (1972), the "vaudeville" commissioned by WNET, are by Hans Magnus Enzensberger, a poet with whom the post-*Bassarids* Henze had much in common—as a Marxist artist repudiating the orthodoxy of most Communist art; as a thoroughly German artist repelled by the New Germany (Enzensberger's poem *man spricht deutsch* could be the text for Henze's ambivalent feelings about his cultural patrimony); as one who would work for "the people" but most readily expressed himself in "élitist" idioms; as a lyricist who felt he should also be a lecturer; and as a creator who made these dilemmas the subject matter of his art. Michael Hamburger, introducing the Penguin anthology of Enzensberger in translation, writes of the poet's "moral purpose at variance with his personal needs and perceptions" and of "the antagonism between public purpose and personal impulse." Similar conflicts prompted Henze's *Versuch über Schweine, Natascha Ungeheuer*, the Second Violin Concerto, and the viola concerto *Compases para preguntas ensimismadas*. In music of great precision—lyrical, nostalgic, peremptory, aggressive; Mahlerian in its brusque oppositions—he plotted his uncertainties about the roles a troubled artist and his work can play in a world of social injustice. A decade of (musically fruitful) self-questioning seems to have ended with *We Come to the River*. The librettist of the new piece is Edward Bond, a dramatist who in his play does not ask questions about the nature of art (those are reserved for, and answered in, his uncommonly interesting prefaces) but considers it his job "to create public images, literal or figurative, in sight, sound, and movement, of the human condition." Bond is England's major living playwright: a visionary, a clear-eyed observer of human nature and of forces that can shape and misshape it. His comedy *Saved* (1965) achieved notoriety because during it five men, more or less as a lark, stone to death a baby in its pram. ("A typical English understatement," said Bond. "Compared to the 'strategic' bombing of German towns it is a negligible atrocity, compared to the cultural and emotional deprivation of most of our children its conse-

433

quences are insignificant.") The preface to his *Lear* (1971) begins, "I write about violence as naturally as Jane Austen wrote about manners. Violence shapes and obsesses our society, and if we do not stop being violent we have no future." Violence done to men's spirit and imagination as well as to men's flesh is his theme: long, slow violation ("The English slums [of the nineteenth century] were like slow-motion concentration camps—death takes longer in slums") as well as sudden, sensational brutality. The protagonist of *The Fool* (1975), a play published together with *We Come to the River*, is the poet John Clare; in an introduction Bond writes of capitalism as a system that can lead to Fascism (which "would work *if* we were prepared and able to behave permanently worse than animals") and can lead to an affluence that "isn't well-being but a form of aggression." Capitalist affluence, he argues, creates no culture—first, because it thrives by destroying the natural resources of a limited world, and, second,

because the more wealth that's put into the business of feverishly creating and stoking-up private dissatisfaction, the less there is to spend on the public fundamentals of culture or of any human society. The richer our organization becomes, the more impoverished are our schools, hospitals, and welfare and social services. We abandon the old, we can't afford to socialize our children, our cities decay, and our streets become the playground of violence, because we have neglected the necessities and decencies of life for the trivializing and ultimately despairing consumption of ersatz satisfactions.

Bond is neither resigned nor pessimistic. He believes in the possibility of change and in an artist's ability to help bring about that change, not by inventing a utopia in abstract opposition to the present but by showing, whether realistically or in symbol, an accurate and critical picture of the present. His Lear

is blind till they take his eyes away, and by then he has begun to see, to understand. (Blindness is a dramatic metaphor for insight, that is why Gloucester, Oedipus, and Tiresias are blind.) Lear's new world is strange and so at first he can only grope painfully and awkwardly. Lear is old by then, but most of the play's audiences will be younger. It might seem to them that the truth is always ground for pessimism when it is discovered, but one soon comes to see it as an opportunity. Then you don't have to go on doing things that never work in the hope that they might one day—because now you know why they *can't*.

The central character of *We Come to the River*, the General, begins after a victorious and bloody campaign to see the truth of what he is doing—and is told he is going blind. Later, on his emperor's orders, he is actually blinded. *Lear* and *We Come to the River* have much in common, beyond the scene of deoculating the straitjacketed protagonist: images of brutality, executions, and jubilation; of soldiers starting to question their orders ("They make you do things no one should even have to dream of and cheer you when you've done it"); of suffering; and—fleeting yet powerful in both works—of a peaceful family life in which children's questions are asked and answered about the marvels of the natural world, not about hardships and unhappiness. The opera ends with a chorus of affirmation, in which the victims—men, women, and children—rise again and sing, "We stand by the river. If there is no bridge, we will wade. If the water is deep, we will swim. . . . We have learnt to march so well that we cannot drown." It comes dangerously close to the obligatory optimistic finale practiced in orthodox Communist compositions. One critic declared that it "emerges not as an expression of faith but as unmotivated gush." Critical reaction to *We Come to the River* ranged from "Marxism, Schmarxism, what does it matter so long as he can write for the theater?" through "I doubt whether anyone in the audience would dissent from the view expressed about the futility of war, the suffering that results from it, and the inequalities that exist in many societies (East and West)" to the shrill denunciation "Hans Werner Henze, you will not teach me anything: I have been more a victim of Nazism than you have, and I have experienced the Communist corruption of basic human values at closer quarters than you have, as a member of one of their musical juries. . . . There is no substitute for individual conscience."

But, it seems to me, the action of "individual conscience" is precisely what Bond's and Henze's opera is about. As individuals, the General, the Deserter, the Soldier driven to assassinate the Governor, the Young Woman, and the Old Woman make their protests. (Those generic titles suggest a piece more schematic than in effect *We Come to the River* is; the personal characterizations are sharp.) It is the rulers and their wives, and such of their servants as have been dulled into mindless obedience, who show unthinking acceptance of a collective ethos. Because the soldiers of the Covent Garden production wore modern British battle dress and the civilians Edwardian costumes, the first critic quoted concluded that the object of the authors' attack, instead of being "the régime that shuts sane men in a madhouse [and] Nazism (which blighted Henze's youth), Stalinism, Aminism, the hijacking and murder of innocent travellers," was "the British social system . . . not the most potent symbol of violent oppression." Bond's and Henze's concern is with nothing so narrow or specific. (Several productions of the opera in Germany, one in Zurich, and one in Turin are scheduled, and presumably the soldiers in them will not be attired as Tommies. In Volker Schlöndorff's Berlin production, where most of the principals were American, the General is reported to have looked like General MacArthur.) There are, it is true, some points of local British reference. For example, the officers celebrate their victory in a public copulation scene ("it suggests romantic pictures of officers listening to girls playing the piano") to the strains of the Eton Boating Song. But then the work *was* commissioned by the Royal Opera House; in the unlikely event of the Met's having commissioned it, the melody in that scene might have been "Semper Fidelis," and "Hail to the Chief" could have worked its way into the band music that greets the Governor. When Beethoven set *Fidelio* in Spain, he did not mean to suggest that only there were upright men imprisoned.

"The opera houses exist," Henze said, "and their facilities are the best available. They have good stage equipment, and good acoustics. So instead of saying let's blow them all up, as Mr. Boulez suggested, I say let's *use* them." In *We Come to the River*, he has written large-scale music theater rather than traditional opera. Like Ives in the Fourth Symphony, he uses three orchestras (and, in addition, a large military band), and, like Bernd Alois Zimmermann in *Die Soldaten*, he divides the stage into three sectors on which scenes are played simultaneously. The orchestra pit is covered over and the stage advances into the house. Two of the orchestras (one of eight players, the other of thirteen) are clustered one at each foot of the proscenium arch, and the third (of twelve) sits in a gallery at the back of the stage. Onstage there is also an organ, and many percussion instruments are built into the resonant structure of the large, wooden, barnlike basic set by Jürgen Henze, the composer's brother. Thus, all the musicians are out in the open. The piece, which is subtitled "actions for music," brings together techniques Henze has pursued in recent compositions. There are parodies (a coloratura song, "Hail Liberator," with chorus from the patriotic daughters of the nation), quotations, variations (a set for organ, on the chorale "Herzlich tut mich verlangen," during the Deserter's court-martial; more chorale variations when the General is blinded), and improvisations, both vocal and instrumental, within carefully defined limits. There are tonal passages, bitonal passages (the chorus's last, triumphant cry is a C-major triad superimposed on a D-minor), twelve-note passages, and two virtuoso sequences for the onstage percussionist. The music, filled with contrasts and oppositions of rhythms, colors, and musical styles, is eclectic in Henze's personal and distinctive manner. One orchestra contains viols; the string quartet in another alternates on hyoshigi, pandereta, sistrum, and cabaça. One of the most beautiful passages is a long, lyrical aria for the ruthless, exquisitely civilized Emperor (a mezzo role, *en travesti*), gently accompanied by the three orchestras working together and the softly melodious clonking of an angklung, or Javanese bamboo tubular chime. In such episodes, Henze honestly avows the seductive charm of the life led by the rich. In the next scene, the General is neatly and elegantly blinded.

Bond, writing of the artist's task, says that "the complexity is usually in the skill, the vision should be simple." *We Come to the River* enshrines a simple and stirring vision in intricate musico-dramatic forms. It is at once clear and complicated. The simultaneity of scenes and the resulting counterpoint of musics and actions mean that at any single visit much is bound to be missed. A prior reading of the libretto is essential, and several hearings are needed before, having concentrated now on one set of events, now on another, one begins to "assemble" all that is going on, to be able to hear and see it all at once. The Covent Garden performance was one of superlative accomplishment. About eighty solo singers took part (there are more roles than that, but much doubling is possible), several of the principals being borrowed from the English National Opera. Josephine Barstow, Anne Wilkens, Josephine Veasey, Deborah Cook, Valerie Masterson, Norman Welsby (as the General, the central character), Gerald English, Robert Tear, and Raimund Herincx form a short-list of the most remarkable, while the whole cast afforded a panorama of singers by whom—after Royal Opera productions of *Moses and Aaron*, Michael Tippett's three operas, and Peter Maxwell Davies's *Taverner*, and the English National Opera productions of Krzysztof Penderecki's *The Devils* and Henze's *The Bassarids* —difficult new music is performed with assurance and eloquence. *We Come to the River* had a special difficulty—that of coordinating three far-flung orchestras—but a single conductor, David Atherton, held things together (via television screens) in masterly fashion. The instrumentalists, each of whose parts is solo, were drawn from both the London Sinfonietta and the house orchestra. Henze himself directed the staging. Five performances were given, to full houses.

When it was new, in 1864, Offenbach's *La Belle Hélène* contained sharp satire of Second Empire mores. The topical references mean little now except to a historian, but the score, surely Offenbach's most captivating, remains a delight. The City Opera production, directed by Jack Eddleman, designed by Lloyd Evans, has style—a style which seems not to have been to all tastes, but which I found deft and attractively diverting. I caught up with the show after the company, strikebound for two weeks, had resumed its performances. It was conducted, by John Miner, with not quite enough verve (puny cymbal clashes for the entry of the heroes!) but with full appreciation of the Mozartian grace and beauty that distinguish much of the music. (Not only Rossini, with his "the Mozart of the Champs-Élysées," but also Wagner acknowledged an affinity between Mozart and Offenbach.) Karan Armstrong was a voluptuous Helen, and Joseph Evans a passable Paris. It was a mistake to drop Orestes' music by an octave; the role was written for a sparky young lady in chiton and monocle.

La Belle Hélène is the only one of the three new productions of the City Opera season to which I would gladly return. *Der fliegende Holländer* has been directed and designed by Robert E. Darling in weak imitation of Wieland Wagner's Bayreuth staging. Richard Wagner's own detailed, almost move-by-move, measure-by-measure instructions were ignored, and there was none of his grandson's genius for creating an alternative dramatic treatment such as at Bayreuth in 1959 held audiences spellbound. On the first night, the singing was poor, and the principals' use of words provided no justification for doing the opera in German rather than in English. There were many romantic and poetic musical moments in Julius Rudel's conducting, but both his orchestra and his chorus sounded too small for the large house. It was probably the fault of the house itself. Can anything be done about its acoustics, short of demolishing the auditorium and rebuilding it to Cyril Harris's prescriptions? Yet it is a good theater for ballet. I look at that space where the Lincoln Center band shell stands bleak and empty most nights of the year and wonder whether it is extensive enough to hold the opera house that the City Opera and New York deserve—a place where both voices and words would carry, and the orchestra would well out to support them.

Sitting in a seat closer to the stage, I heard *Il barbiere* more strongly, and admired very much the finesses and the admirable tones of Donald Gramm's Don Bartolo and Samuel Ramey's Don Basilio. But Sarah Caldwell's production was gross, based on the idea that a piece of business that might be funny once would be six times as funny on the fifth repetition. A similar overelaboration marked Helen Pond's and Herbert Senn's scenery. Jan Skalicky, the costume designer, had dressed Mr. Gramm in a crinoline festooned with big bunches of keys, and the others with similar heaviness. Beverly Sills played Rosina as a grinning doll. The Almaviva, William Harness, lumbered through his divisions. The Figaro, Alan Titus, relied on his all-purpose boyish charm. No one had character; all was rude farce. A Sarah Caldwell of different stamp conducted, one who brought rare insight to the rhythms and colors of Rossini's score (even when the ensemble went awry). But her directing altera ego destroyed the conductor's good work and smothered the music with scenic japes.

November 15, 1976

RHAPSODY IN BLUE

Lohengrin is not a difficult opera to stage. There is a firm historical background to the action: Henry the Fowler's visit to Antwerp in 932 to enlist Brabantine allies in his forthcoming war with Hungary; the nine-year truce with that country is drawing to an end. In the foreground there are two linked dramas. One is of human relations, about a woman's unquestioning faith in her husband, and the undermining of that faith by a woman who has established an unnatural dominance over *her* husband. The other is the legend of the pure chivalrous knight who comes to the rescue of a damsel in distress. Wagner combined them in a clear and effective play, against which little more can be objected—except by fierce feminists—than that it moves at a majestic, unhurried gait. *Lohengrin* is not an opera for anyone who grows impatient with long, stately processions or large-scale repetitions. The composer insisted that it should be given uncut (apart from the final paragraph of Lohengrin's narration in Act III; he removed that himself); music, poem, and stage action were indissoluble; an opera house that could not manage all of it should attempt none of it. Bernard Shaw, in an account of the first Bayreuth production (1894), related how an apparently needless and oft-omitted repetition in the Act I finale became, when properly staged, "a dramatic effect, a scenic effect, and a musical effect" the total effect of which was tremendous. Ernest Newman once told me that in Heinz Tietjen's Bayreuth production of 1936 the long Act II procession to the minster and Ortrud's sudden interruption of it provided one of the most thrilling theater experiences he had ever had. My own first *Lohengrin*, at Covent Garden, was traditional—a postwar revival by Otto Erhardt of the production he had mounted for Beecham in 1935. It followed the scandal of a perverse *Salome* designed by Salvador Dali and directed by Peter Brook, and the standard history of the house records the wise comment of the critic Eric Blom: "Here was something like a return to the old, proud standards, opera on a grand scale . . . and produced by Otto Erhardt with discretion and a sense of responsibility towards the music."

Wolfgang Wagner's first production at Bayreuth, in 1953, was of *Lohengrin*, and it was an arresting and successful attempt to combine the traditional staging of the opera with simplified, stripped-down décor such as his brother Wieland had been using. Everything was in its hallowed place, where the composer had located it in the stage plans and scenic designs he sent Liszt before the première, in Weimar in 1850: the Scheldt flowing across the back of the stage; the great oak tree on the left with King Henry's dais at its foot; Elsa's balcony on the left, in Act II, the Palas (knights' quarters) center back, and the minster steps rising on the right. But the leafy river bank of earlier décors had been reduced to a single tree; when Elsa descended to Ortrud in Act II no real door opened but a shaft of light as if from an opening door was thrown across the stage.

Five years later, Wieland Wagner produced the opera at Bayreuth. The curtain rose on a dense, luminous blue dusk where land melted imperceptibly into sky. (Has the secret of Wieland's dense lighting been lost? In Act II of his 1956 *Meistersinger* the heavy, scented midsummer air seemed to be so solid that one could cut and carry away blue cubes of it.) On a tiered semicircle the chorus was ranged motionless while on a central platform the actors sang their parts, moving little but powerfully. The processions were solemn, symmetrical, and stylized. Confrontations were not realistic: the swan, a large and beautiful gauzy white apparition, came on at the back while the chorus, exclaiming at its arrival, sang straight out front; in Act II, Ortrud did not bar Elsa's way but suddenly appeared at the top of a flight of steps Elsa had been descending. This act was played as formally as a game of chess: Black Knight and Black Queen threatened the White Queen; White Knight moved forward from beside the White King to save her. We were no longer in Antwerp. The King was no historical Henry the Fowler. Lohengrin was Perseus or St. George, and Elsa was Semele or Psyche, the mortal woman beloved of a god, who destroys herself by wishing to look on divinity. Two things were lost: the historical color and pageantry, on which Richard Wagner set such importance that when horses were not available for an 1867 Munich production (Henry's cavalry played a major role in routing the Hungarians in 933) he said that in that case the music for the martial assembly in Act III might as well be omitted, too; and the tender, personalized warmth of an opera that can seem to be about human beings rather than figures of myth. Wieland appeared to agree with Newman that the lovers are "a pair of operatic puppets," and Ortrud and Telramund "for the most part mere figures of melodrama." In the first scene of Act II, Elsa was radiant in white, high on a pulpitlike balcony, center stage. Ortrud and Telramund prowled about below in greenish shadows, and then closed in on the foot of the tower. The scenic symbolism could not have been simpler. *Lohengrin* was illumined in a series of Wieland's "magic pictures," and his great Ortrud, Astrid Varnay, recalled in a memoir that for him the opera was "a fairytale in blue," and that after this great production he had nothing more to say about it. Instead, the production was re-created on several other stages—Hamburg, Stuttgart, Berlin, and, posthumously, at the Met in 1966. Small variations were introduced to suit local circumstances. As long as Wieland's stamp remained fresh upon any particular version, it remained strong and beautiful, but when it was re-enacted by singers with whom he had not worked, under lighting that he had not supervised, it lost much of its force and beauty.

At Bayreuth in 1967, Wolfgang undertook another production. It was technically of great interest. The first and last scenes were flanked by tall screens of, apparently, foliage in beaten metalwork—details from the door of San Zeno, in Verona, immensely enlarged; for Palas and Kemenate (women's quarters), in Act II, walls of gleaming ceramic tile reached into the flies; the bridal pavilion of Act III was modeled on the east portal of Pisa Cathedral. It all looked immense and very solidly built; I watched one performance from a lighting tower backstage and was amazed to see this massive scenery rolled up in sections like carpets, hoisted up or down and carried on or off in a jiffy. Wolfgang had also perfected a new lighting device—bright rays traveling not at the speed of light but slowly, like a jet trail through the sky. In *Das Rheingold* they had flowered upward from the solid earth, emanating from Erda; in the last scene of *Lohengrin* they descended in glory upon the knight. Some historical elements were reintroduced— a costume distinction was made between Henry's Saxons and the Flemings—and, in contrast to Wieland's precision-drilled rituals, the chorus indulged in some naturalistic scuffling. According to Wolfgang, "the eventual conflict lies not between Elsa and Ortrud, or Elsa and Telramund, but in Lohengrin's collision with a world to which he longs to join himself." All details of the production were to be subordinated to this conflict. The visual key to it was the vast expanse of blue sky between the leafy screens, a magic casement opening, from a solid Belgium racked by political strife, on a world glowing with A-major incandescence as the swan (made of some translucent white substance, back-lit by powerful xenon lamps) materialized against it.

Directly or indirectly, by imitation or by reaction, all recent *Lohengrin* stagings of any importance have been influenced by those Bayreuth productions. The new Metropolitan Opera version, which opened this month, is by August Everding (who has directed *Der fliegende Holländer* and *Tristan* at Bayreuth and *Tristan* at the Met). With Wieland's production it shares at least the introduction of an unwritten scene change into Act II, the clustering of Ortrud and Telramund below Elsa's balcony during her Song to the Breezes (at the Met, where Elsa pops out through an archway just large enough to admit her, the three look like figures on a mechanical clock), and an ambiguity of setting (are we inside or outside the minster?) during the closing stages of the act. With Wolfgang's second production it shares the mistake of allowing Lohengrin to fell Telramund with a gesture (at the Met he merely reverses his sword, presenting the hilt as a cross) instead of "with a mighty stroke"—thus diminishing the hero's valor and spoiling the story. Mr. Everding says he is against "concepts," but in a preliminary interview he outlined a concept of Lohengrin as a savior from a better world, "offering us through his championship of Elsa a chance for our dirty planet. She fails him and us simply because she is human, and so Lohengrin must leave." According to Wagner himself, we shouldn't lay all the blame on Elsa. Lohengrin is in need of redemption, too. He also transgresses:

> When first I saw you on that river bank
> I felt my heart at once ablaze with love,
> Deflected from the chaste service of the Grail;
> And now I must forever make atonement
> Because I turned from God and longed for you.

The lines, it is true, were rejected, and not set to music. But soon after the première of *Lohengrin* Wagner wrote, in the *Communication to My Friends*, of

Elsa, the Unconscious, the Undeliberate, into which Lohengrin's conscious, deliberate being yearns to be redeemed. . . . This woman who, by the very outburst of her jealousy, wakes first from the thrill of worship into the full reality of Love, and by her wreck reveals its essence to him who had not yet fathomed it; this glorious woman, before whom Lohengrin must vanish, because his own specific nature could not understand her . . . *True Womanhood*, which would one day bring to me and to all the world redemption, after mankind's egoism, even in its noblest form, had shivered into self-crushed dust before her—Elsa, the woman—woman hitherto un-understood by me, and understood at last . . . made me a revolutionary at one blow. She was the Spirit of the Folk for whose redeeming hand I too, as artist-man, was yearning.

Tall talk, remarked Newman, and "Well, who, in the name of heaven, takes Lohengrin and Elsa quite so seriously as that?" Wagner did, and, at the least, his words suggest that Elsa is more than a little goose who can't hold her tongue, and a heroine less passive than a first glance at the story might suggest. At the Met, Pilar Lorengar played her with a pleasing spontaneity and directness. She was impulsive: the first solo moved from reverie to animation as she recounted the details of her dream; her eyes began to sparkle. In the bedroom scene, her mounting importunity had an almost veristic inflection. She was an Elsa who recalled Victoria de los Angeles in the role—sweet and limpid of timbre, most musical and natural in her phrasing, and totally unaffected. There was very little grandeur in her manner, and this can perhaps be deemed a fault; Elsa, I believe, needs a touch of grandeur both musically and in her demeanor. (From photographs and records of Emma Eames and

442

Olive Fremstad I built up my idea of what a Met Elsa should be.) More seriously, Miss Lorengar's voice lacked the body and volume to dominate so large a house. There was a slight feeling that a Mimì had with great charm and accomplishment mounted the throne of Brabant.

Lohengrin was René Kollo, making his Met début. "I see Lohengrin as a very human person, despite his otherworld origins," he has said. "He really loves Elsa—he wants to settle down, and even raise a family." In this, Mr. Kollo echoes Wolfgang Wagner, in whose production of *Lohengrin* he played in 1972. But his interpretation was curiously bland, almost noncommittal. The voice was beautiful—sweet, lyrical, true, excellently in tune most of the time, and so purely focused that, although not especially powerful, it carried in a way that more evidently robust and heroic but less cleanly projected tenors often fail to do. He looked like a Holman Hunt chevalier; the puppy charm of his 1972 Lohengrin had been disciplined into correct and dignified behavior. As ardent an Elsa as Miss Lorengar could never have been happy for long with this cool, self-contained embodiment of English public-school virtues. The two interpretations conspired to suggest that Elsa did right to pose the forbidden question. Wagner himself implies as much in the "tall talk" quoted above. Such a Lohengrin needed such an Elsa to wake him to realities of earthly life.

The regular Telramund of Wolfgang's production, Donald McIntyre, repeated his forthright, virile performance. His first utterance, and the proud, powerful "Ja!" with which he accepted the king's challenge to back the charge against Elsa in a fight to the death, rang out most imposingly. But something odd is happening to his voice; sometimes it sounded as if it were coming through a megaphone, loud but distorted in timbre. Ortrud was Mignon Dunn. Wagner wrote eloquently about this character:

A political *man* is repulsive, but a political *woman* is horrible. . . . There is a kind of love in this woman, the love of the past, of dead generations, the terribly insane love of ancestral pride which finds its expression in the hatred of everything living and actually existing. . . . She is terribly grand.

Miss Dunn was terribly grand, menacing, gleaming with evil power. Praise of her performance would be almost unqualified had she elected to sing instead of scream the invocation "Entweihte Götter!"

Wagner wanted *Lohengrin* to be staged without too much courtly ceremony. It was Henry's son Otto I (Wagner pointed out in a letter to Ferdinand Heine, with whom he planned to publish a production book of the opera) who introduced pomp and circumstance to the German court; in Henry's day, "no one does anything out of mere routine and court custom, but in every encounter the participants take a direct and personal part. . . . Look at my Herald: how the fellow sings as if everything concerned him personally!" Allan Monk, at the Met, was an excellent Herald, crying every phrase with the proper eager enthusiasm, and in clear, telling tones. Bonaldo Giaiotti's Henry was bluff and benevolent, but both words and phrasing could have been more sharply cut. Mr. Everding in his handling of the chorus did suggest the "noble, naïve simplicity of that time" which Wagner wanted, but he mishandled the bridal procession, by trying to improve on the composer's own staging. Elsa came last, unattended except by Ortrud, who had been enlisted as train-bearer; Wagner intended Ortrud to thrust her way suddenly forward from among a group of women forming the rear guard, to bar Elsa's way.

The sets are by Ming Cho Lee. The two principal scenes, the river bank and the citadel, employ the emphatic built-up diagonals that Mr. Everding favors. There are no trees in the first of them, only a bare mast topped by a circle, suggesting something between a Maypole and a gibbet. Acoustically, the scene may not be well planned; it was noticeable that both Mr. Monk and Mr. Giaiotti sounded stronger and firmer when they descended from the elevated pier that dominates the left side and sang with stage floor beneath their feet. The Scheldt is assumed to flow through the orchestra pit. The swan—a swan shape in outline, made of tubing, almost hidden by a bank of reeds—came up like a submarine, behind the footlights. It did not reappear in the final scene; Gottfried walked up out of the river, and Lohengrin walked down into it. Not very successful. There was no dove. The first part of Act II is played before a drop curtain painted as a wall, pierced by the small arch leading out onto Elsa's tiny balcony. The rest of the act presents a large confusion of steps, arcades, modern columns (cylinders without bases or capitals), and a pulpit. It is hard to make any topographical sense of it; presumably the proscenium arch represents the minster portal, since Elsa and Lohengrin are advancing to the footlights as the curtain falls. The bridal chamber of Act III is department-store Gothick. The attendants deck the bedposts with tight little bunches of flowers, and a beautiful image is lost when Lohengrin, instead of drawing Elsa's attention to the fragrant gardens beyond their window, uses these nosegays to illustrate his simile about enchantment that should be enjoyed without being investigated. The costumes, by Peter J. Hall, are satisfactory, on the whole. Ortrud's are striking. But Elsa's white bridal gown looks modern bourgeoise, and when, just before the love duet, Lohengrin, in a long white coat, turns to her, the effect is irresistibly of doctor and nurse before an operation.

Keys and colors have often been associated, though not with much consistency. (Rimsky-Korsakov thought that F major was green; Scriabin declared it to be red.) *Lohengrin*, however, is an opera in A major that has long been considered intensely blue. "Blausilberne Schönheit" was Thomas Mann's phrase for it. "Out of the clear blue ether of the sky . . ." begins Wagner's account of the shimmering A-major prelude. If the Met *Lohengrin*, a carefully prepared and costly production ($350,000 is the figure quoted), lacks something of the expected magic, the main reason for that, I believe, is that it has been staged largely in gray scenery against a black background. Acts I and III are played behind a scrim. An electric-blue swirl is turned on the backcloth for a while when the swan is due to appear, and white light streams down on the spot where it surfaces. But when, in Act I, Henry remarks that the noonday sun is at its height, nothing in the lighting plot seconds his observation; dawn in Act II is very slow to arrive. Wagner in black and gray is à la mode; it is a dreary mode, and I hope it soon passes.

James Levine's conducting confirmed what his *Tannhäuser* in Cincinnati last year had shown: that he is a first-rate Wagnerian, with an instinctive feeling for pace, for the placing of a climax, for rhythms that are lively yet responsive to the dramatic inflections of individual singers. Wagner once said that a conductor has mastered his task only when an audience is no longer aware of his existence. Mr. Levine was never obtrusive. *Lohengrin* did not seem to last long: it never dragged or became tedious, even in the long passages of recitative; nor did it seem to be driven ahead with any unseemly haste. Not everything was right at the first performance: chorus and orchestra sometimes got out of step; the very lightly accompanied C-major ensemble in Act II went out of tune, so that the woodwind chords of its coda entered like a correction. But, musically speaking, everything was right in intention, and most things were right in execution. With more light on it—and blue skies kindling into incandescence—the production should serve well for many a season to come.

November 23, 1976

Wagner's stage designs and production notes for Lohengrin *are now in the Burrell Collection, in the Curtis Institute, Philadelphia (No. 156). The Met* Lohengrin *was almost uncut, but from the final scene the long passage beginning with Lohengrin's "O Elsa! was hast du mir angetan?" and ending with his prophecy that Germany would not be overrun by victorious Eastern hordes was removed.*

PILING IT ON

The new Avery Fisher Hall has passed every test so far put it. The second of the Philharmonic's subscription programs pushed its sonic capacity to the utmost with the shattering sonorities of Olivier Messiaen's *Et exspecto resurrectionem mortuorum*, a memorial to the fallen of two world wars commissioned by André Malraux when he was French Minister of Culture. *Et exspecto*, its composer says, was "destined for large spaces: churches, cathedrals, even the open air and mountain heights." The first performance was given in 1965 in the Sainte-Chapelle, in Paris, "where light breaks into a radiance of blues, reds, golds, and extraordinary purples," and the second in Chartres Cathedral, where again the light from great windows fills resonant space with colors. Messiaen expressed the hope that one day the piece would also be done "opposite the glacier of Meije, amid those powerful, solemn landscapes that are my true homeland. There, through the play of the sun on the whiteness of the ice, I shall obtain visually the second symbol that is present in my music, the principal quality of the Glorious Host, the 'gift of brightness.' " Ambience spiritual as well as acoustical is important to the piece: Messiaen recalls, when speaking about it, that the Sainte-Chapelle was built by St. Louis to house the Crown of Thorns, and that Chartres is also one of the high places of Christianity. Avery Fisher Hall is expensively gilded but not exactly numinous. It was intelligent to leave the lights full on during the performance. (It might have helped further to introduce a whiff of good strong thick stupefying incense smoke into the ventilation system.) But the music had to stand on its own, to play upon the listeners' souls without assistance from architecture, sacred associations, or tremendous nature. Its timbres and rhythms, its massively formalized plainchants and heavily stylized birdsongs had to evoke Messiaen's apocalyptic visions. *Et exspecto* is a "Resurrection Symphony" in five movements, which begins with an "Out of the depths have I cried unto thee," reaches its climax in the fourth movement with "They shall be raised in glory, with a new name— when all the morning stars sing together, and the sons of God shout for joy," and closes with "As it were the voice of a great multitude, and as the voice of many waters, and as the voice of mighty thunderings." The texts are set as headings to the movements. The music is for an orchestra of eighteen woodwinds, sixteen brasses, and—originally—the magnificently tempered percussion instruments of the Strasbourg Battery, that virtuoso ensemble which also provided inspiration for Messiaen's previous pieces *Seven Haiku* and *Colors of the Celestial City*. To the fifth Haiku and through the score of the *Celestial City* Messiaen affixed color indications, to enable the conductor and players to realize his visions more completely. (Last week, when writing about *Lohengrin* and color associations, I should have remembered the A-major song of Messiaen's *The Blue Thrush,* caroling over the blue Mediterranean, "un timbre lumineux, irisé, auréolé de bleu," and the A-major blue dominating the "carillon of light" that seems to play upon his *Visions of the Amen,* for two pianos.) In any discussion of Messiaen it is hard to stick to musical facts. The second movements of *Et exspecto* is based on an Indian rhythm whose count of fifteen is divided into a 2.2.2.1.3.2.3 pattern. That is a musical fact. But Messiaen goes on to remind us that fifteen is the product of three (the Trinity) and five (the number of Shiva, who "represents the death of death" and is therefore a symbol of Christ), and to tell us that the Indian name for this rhythm, *simhavikrama,* means "the power of the lion" and that it comprehends another rhythm, called *vijaya,* or "victory." Thus the rhythmic basis of his movement symbolizes the victory of the Lion of Judah. As if that were not enough, he likens a trumpet melody bursting through some complex woodwind colors to "the resurrected Christ of Matthias Grünewald, who appears to take flight in a rainbow generated by his own light."

How much do all these associations matter to the listener? (One cannot call them extramusical; they are composed into the score.) Messiaen sets store by them. He thought it would be helpful to the players of his *Exotic Birds* to know the appearance and action of the birds they mimic—without, of course, actually expecting the percussionist to flick his tail and cock his head to one side before pattering out a call on the xylophone. Messiaen's music poses in extreme form the old, often debated questions about "program music." The second item in his *Bird Catalogue,* "The Oriole," is a rapturous piece of piano writing by any standard. Yet a listener may well respond to it with added emotion when he bears in mind its written preface:

Gardépée toward 5:30 A.M. Orgeval toward 6. Les Maremberts in the full midday sun. The oriole, a beautiful golden bird with black wings, whistles in the oaks. Its song, fluent, golden, like the smile of a foreign prince, evokes Africa and Asia, or some unknown planet filled with light and rainbows, filled with Leonardo da Vinci smiles. In the gardens, in the woods, other birds: the rapid, resolute strophe of the wren, the robin's confiding caress, the blackbird's brio, the amphimacer [long-short-long] of the redstart, with its white breast and black throat, the incantatory repetitions of the thrush. For a long while, the garden warblers tirelessly pour out their sweet virtuosity. The chiffchaff adds his jerky waterdrops. Untroubled, carefree memories of gold and of rainbow. The sun seems to be a golden emanation from the oriole's song.

Any answer to the question of associations can only be personal. To the Philharmonic performance of *Et exspecto,* under Pierre Boulez, I

447

brought memories of colored light streaming through the windows of the Sainte-Chapelle and of Chartres, and of the way music sounds in those two places; of a morning spent among the mountains of the Dauphiné (the smell of the crisp air, the color of rocks and rushing water come back to me as I write); and of a performance of the piece at an Albert Hall prom (where the British percussion sounded dry, since the brave, bright blaze of the Strasbourg Battery, heard a week or two earlier, was still in my ears), of another, more impressive, in West-minster Abbey, given by a French orchestra, and of the best-played of all, on the Columbia recording conducted by Boulez. Of the Grünewald panel I retained a vague impression rather than any sharp visual image, but the texts from the Book of Job and from Revelations played their part in stimulating the imagination; one need not be a credent to re-spond to that prose, that imagery. And so, not in any purely musical way, I "surrendered" to the Philharmonic performance, and found it a tre-mendous experience, even while my critical ear remained detached enough to note, first, that the hall accepts "mighty thunderings" without causing pain, and, second, that the Philharmonic's three giant gongs did not provide the well-matched sequence of sounds—medium, low, and extremely low—that the Strasbourg instruments do.

The third Philharmonic program began with the New York première of John Cage's *Renga with Apartment House 1776*, one of six works jointly commissioned, from six different composers, by the main orches-tras of Boston, Chicago, Cleveland, Los Angeles, New York, and Phila-delphia, each to be played by all of them. Cage's piece is in fact two works that are played at the same time. A renga, I learn from the com-poser's note, is a sequence of at least thirty-six wakas, and a waka is a haiku (a poem of five-seven-five syllables) that has grown two more seven-syllable limbs. The score of Cage's *Renga* is made from 361 Thoreau drawings "literally taken apart" and reassembled to form seventy-eight instrumental parts. Not choice but casts of the I Ching determined which drawings were taken, how they were redisposed, and by how many instruments and how loudly each drawing is to be played. No part is allotted to any particular instrument, and no instruments are named; "this absence of specification permits the use of instruments from other cultures and times, from eighteenth-century America, for in-stance." So choice presumably enters there. Tempo and duration are decided by the conductor, who "may introduce silences at the ends of most of the lines." Meanwhile, *Apartment House 1776* consists of "sixty-four pieces, any number of which may be performed in any se-quence and any superimpositions," distributed between four small en-sembles. Four vocalists, individual representatives of eighteenth-century Protestants, Sephardim, American Indians, and Negro slaves, sing their own songs, not composed by Cage. The instrumental pieces are derived

448

from eighteenth-century American music, some of it directly transcribed, most of it modified as the I Ching dictated. The conductor, having decided how long his account of *Renga* will be, and whether or not he wants *Apartment House* to overlap it at either end, tells the *Apartment House* performers how long their individual programs should last, and then everything gets going.

Mahler once remarked that a Sunday walk was enough to produce all the materials for a symphony: songs, dances, bands, barrel organs, puppet shows, each with its distinct rhythm and melody. It was the composer's task to "adapt, order, and unite them into a harmonious whole." Cage, like Ives, doesn't bother about precise musical fit but heaps everything together in a splendid old jumble, letting the listener pick out what he can and will. For perhaps fifteen minutes, *Renga with Apartment House 1776* could be enjoyed as a colorful pageant of bits and pieces from the past heard against a background of bright, fragmentary noises from the main, *Renga* orchestra. But it lasted twice as long as that, and became tedious. The texture was unvaried. All the points had long since been made. Although each component moved at a different pace, the superimposition of all those paces made the general progress seem a trudge—a slow-moving parade, despite the individual capering and animation of those taking part. The ear seized for relief on incidents: Chief Swift Eagle, one of the vocalists, started smacking his stomach, broke into peals of hearty laughter, began to play a wooden flute, was quickly drowned by fife-and-drum signals from the other side of the platform. Boulez presided over it all with imperturbable aplomb.

At the first of these two concerts, the Messiaen was preceded by Handel's Double Concerto in F, given a clean-cut performance, and by Berg's Violin Concerto, given an awkward performance, in which Leonid Kogan, the soloist, and Boulez seemed to have different ideas about the piece: Boulez was supple and sensitive; Kogan just played the notes. At the next, the Cage was followed by Martinů's First Cello Concerto and a Ravel group—the *Shéhérazade* overture, the delicate little fanfare for *L'Éventail de Jeanne*, and the *Rapsodie espagnole*. The Martinů, in which Pierre Fournier was soloist, is an empty piece, an odd work for Boulez to choose to promote. (A long program note told us that it exists in three versions but failed to say that it was the second of these, the 1939 revision, which was played.) The next Philharmonic concert, conducted by Rafael Kubelik, began with Hindemith's *Der Schwanendreher* (Sol Greitzer an undistinguished soloist), that estimable if rather dour fantasy on old German folk tunes, and then, with Bruckner's Fourth Symphony, brought the first return to the Romantic nineteenth century since Mahler's Third was done at the opening concert of the series.

Kubelik chose the 1886 version of the score, which Anton Seidl

449

brought to New York and played here in 1888; it differs little, and in ways scarcely audible during performance, from the 1880 version, which most Brucknerians prefer. Listening to familiar music in the fine new acoustics, one heard the Philharmonic's playing with sharpened ears; the same week, at Carnegie Hall, the Chicago Symphony and the Berlin Philharmonic provided two models of what orchestral playing at its highest can be. The Philharmonic's woodwind chorus seems weak at the moment: oboes and clarinets have firmness and character, but the top and bottom lines, from flutes and bassoons, are not strongly drawn. (Odd that Julius Baker, who can be so decisive a soloist, allows so much flute detail in orchestral textures to recede.) There has been criticism of the brasses' forcefulness. ("Never look at the brasses" was Strauss's advice to a young conductor. "It only encourages them.") But in this symphony I found them bright and bold in exactly the way that Bruckner's score seems to require, well balanced, and not violent. The upper strings are athletic. The violin tone is keen and focused. In Bruckner one would like more charm both of timbre and of manner: the "zizibee" (titmouse) melodies of the second subject were unsmilingly and strictly uttered; they sounded more like military signals than like birdsong. Violists seem to be born with poetic souls; and the Philharmonic cellos are the orchestra's special glory: the long theme of the andante was most movingly sung.

When it comes to assessing the full ensemble sound, I mount my old hobbyhorse for a brief trot round the subject of platform placing. Seidl's 1897 seating plan for the Philharmonic survives. Clockwise from the left, he stationed the first violns, the violas, the cellos, and then, balancing the firsts opposite, the second violins. Woodwinds were centrally grouped, behind them the brasses, behind them the drums and percussion. The double-basses provided a solid foundation extending all the way round the back. This arrangement was normal in the nineteenth century, and, for the performance of nineteenth-century music, experience tells me that it provides the finest sound. Klemperer used it; Boult still does. But Kubelik, like most conductors now, adopted the modern lopsided arrangement, with *all* the violins on his left, the cellos right, and the double-basses far right. On one level, this plan destroys antiphonies between the first violins and the seconds which figure largely in so much nineteenth-century music (the "zizibee" calls are an example); on another, it seems to unbalance the full broad sound of climaxes. Has anyone written well about the subject? A conductor who has tried both seating methods? The usual defense of the modern arrangement is that since all the violinists play with their instruments facing "forward," a more brilliant sound results. In practice, I find that second-violin parts lose prominence by the arrangement, and that throwing the double-basses way off center leads to unsupported tuttis.

450

The finale of Tchaikovsky's Sixth Symphony, the Pathétique, opens with an *adagio lamentoso* melody whose notes are played alternately by second and first violins. Each group has its own continuous line, but the ear connects the top notes into a single theme drawn from crossing parts. This is a complicated and interesting device, but for its full effect to be heard the first violins and the seconds must be separated. Sir Georg Solti conducted the work as the second half of a Russian concert with the Chicago Symphony in Carnegie Hall. (The first half was a dapper account of Shostakovich's Ninth.) He used the modern seating plan, violins all left, and if the passage had been rewritten with the melody given entirely to the firsts and the lower notes to the seconds I don't believe a listener would have detected the difference. It was an impassioned and emotional performance of the symphony—superlatively well played and powerfully affecting. Nevertheless, it was Tchaikovsky in the modern manner, and therefore to my ears less satisfying, and less stylistically true to the piece, than the kind of performance my old teacher Albert Coates used to give. Coates was not a master of all styles. When I played organ continuo for him in massively romantic performances of the B-minor Mass, he encouraged me to draw a thirty-two-foot reed to underline the striding bass line of the Sanctus. (How severely I would review such a performance today!) He was further from Bach than we are now—but closer to Tchaikovsky. In his Pathétique there was more rubato, a sharper sense of vivid, personal utterance, and encouragement for each player to be an individual character, contributing to the progress of the piece with the utmost possible romanticism and eloquence. This is not imagination or mere nostalgia for the past at work. The Rodgers and Hammerstein collection of the New York Public Library provides the chance of once again hearing Coates conduct the Pathétique —a recording made before I was born but very like the performances I remember—and the style and manner *are* different. The Chicago violas did not break in in the fourth and tenth bars, or the horn enter in the twelfth, with anything like the passionate concern for expression that Coates's players do. Nor did Solti's violas begin the allegro non troppo with the same quick, nervous intensity.

Herbert von Karajan seats the Berlin Philharmonic slightly differently. He has the violas at the front, on his right, and the cellos more or less central. The row of double-basses begins far right, beyond the violas, but then curves inward toward the cellos, providing a foundation more central than usual, if not quite central. As a result, at last week's Carnegie Hall concert the antiphonies in the slow movement of Beethoven's Ninth Symphony, where second violins and violas in unison provide one line and first violins provide the other, *could* be heard as such, although it was the violas that dominated one voice of the dialogue. (The second violins were tucked behind the firsts in the usual modern way.) Karajan had brought both the Berlin Philharmonic and the Vienna Singverein, a choir 150 strong, to New York to give four concerts on four consecutive nights; besides Beethoven's Ninth, there were the Requiems of Brahms, of Mozart (in a program together with Bruckner's Te Deum), and of Verdi. Is there anything new to be said about Karajan? These were all superbly efficient performances, smoothly and just about flawlessly executed. If you've heard the records, you'll know what they were like. The Berlin Philharmonic is a precision instrument, tuned and tempered in every department. The choir, which sang without scores, proved a shade less impressive; soprano tone grew thinner as it rose. (Can the curtain that fills half the proscenium opening and the low-slung panels overhead—reminiscent of pre-Harris acoustical devices —really be helpful to voices placed at the back of the Carnegie platform? They don't appear in old photographs of the hall.) One instrument in these performances made a horrid noise; it did not come from Berlin but was the hall's own electronic organ, disagreeable to hear in the Brahms and the Mozart and disastrous to the timbre of the climax of the Te Deum.

Distinguished vocalists had been engaged, and something can be said about them. They at least showed human strength and weaknesses. At each of the four concerts, the bass-baritone José van Dam was a noble soloist whose precisely focused, cleanly projected voice was a joy to hear. Leontyne Price sang her first Brahms Requiem in a direct, pleasingly unaffected way. The Elsa and Lohengrin of Karajan's *Lohengrin* at Salzburg last Easter, Anna Tomowa-Sintow and Karl-Walter Boehm, made their New York débuts in the Ninth Symphony. Mr. Boehm was rough. Miss Tomowa-Sintow, later heard more extensively in the Mozart, is an interesting soprano with a complicated timbre not quite schooled to smoothness. Werner Krenn was an elegant tenor in the Mozart and the Bruckner. Ever since Agnes Baltsa sang Carmen in Houston five years ago, the international reputation of this young Greek mezzo has been growing, and her first New York appearances (in the Beethoven, the Mozart, and the Bruckner) showed that it is well deserved. None of the alto parts concerned are large, but everything that she did gave evidence of a very beautiful, firm, even voice of distinctive character. We must hear more of her. Although Verdi wrote the soprano solos in his Requiem for an Aida, pure lyric sopranos have succeeded in the work, and I believe that Mirella Freni would succeed if she approached it as a pure lyric soprano. But at the Carnegie performance she essayed a dramatic Aida way and was not altogether happy—despite some exquisite phrases, particularly in melting downward curves. Fiorenza Cossotto, the mezzo, almost resisted her usual temptation to boom. Luciano Pavarotti, the tenor, sounded cautious in his soft singing but free and splendid when loud. Mr. van Dam was magnificent; what a fine Philip II in *Don Carlos* he should be.

The choir and soloists sang all the Latin as if it were Italian. This is right for Verdi. Is it right for Mozart? Is that how Latin was pronounced in eighteenth-century Vienna? And what of late-nineteenth-century Vienna? Was Bruckner brought up on Italianized pronunciation of Latin? If so, when did "German Latin"—"rekviem," "kvi," "kvis," etc. —become standard in Germany and Austria? What sounds did Bruckner have in mind when he composed? Or Mahler, in the Eighth Symphony? One might as well use historically authentic pronunciation when performing these works.

Discussion of the soloists and questions about the Latin pronunciation adopted are peripheral, I know, to any serious discussion of the Karajan performances. I skirt the main issues because I still cannot find words to explain why in concerts—less regularly in the opera house, where many personalities come into play—Karajan's interpretations leave me admiring but unstirred. How can I be so grudging? Why do I not simply cheer executions more polished than any others I am likely to hear? Is it that I hear only Karajan's relaxed mastery of orchestral timbres, effortlessly powerful sonorities, suave, smooth phrasing, disciplined rhythmic flow—and not the voices of Mozart, Beethoven, Brahms, Bruckner, and Verdi? (The Karajan performances I have admired without reservation were of *La Bohème* and *Lucia di Lammermoor*.) The reason is not any perverse resistance to the "star" reputation. Toscanini had such a reputation—but at the thought of Toscanini and Beethoven's Ninth, or Toscanini and Verdi's Requiem, the Karajan readings dwindle to beautiful hollow shells, mere sounds. Toscanini took one to the heart of the work; Karajan presents an immaculate surface.

November 29, 1976

Several scholars wrote to support my suggestion that it was at best affected, and at worst unmusical, for an Austrian choir, when singing Mozart and Bruckner, to have unlearned the Austrian pronunciation of Latin that Mozart and Bruckner would have expected. When the Chicago Symphony Chorus came to Carnegie Hall to sing Beethoven's Missa Solemnis *(p. 599), it pronounced the text in the German way.*

PETIT BAYREUTH

The first edition of Massenet's *Esclarmonde* is one of the prettiest vocal scores ever published. Three separate title pages in blues, buffs, and gilt, five pages of dramatis personae and contents, delicately bordered with art-nouveau scrolls, beasts, and flowers, and a final emblem of a fretful porpentine in white against blues, with a golden crown—even by the very high decorative level of other Massenet scores, these make *Esclarmonde* outstanding. In bygone days when bargains could still be found on the quais, and the banks of the Seine had not yet been turned into motorways, I began to collect early Massenet scores as attractive objects, little dreaming that one day I should actually find a use for them— that *Marie-Magdeleine, Cendrillon*, and *Sapho* would be produced, *Le Cid* and (twice over) *La Navarraise* recorded, and *Esclarmonde* brought to the stage of the Metropolitan Opera. Who knows only *Manon, Werther, Thaïs*, and *Don Quichotte* knows the best of Massenet but not all the genres that he attempted. *La Navarraise* and *Sapho* are verismo operas. *Le Cid* is heroic. *Cendrillon* is a delicate blend of faery and sentiment. *Grisélidis* and *Le Jongleur de Notre-Dame*, to judge by the vocal scores, are medieval tales retold with a warmth and wit that point toward *Don Quichotte*. (Once that lovable singer Lucien Fugère began to appear in Massenet's casts, a new vein of mature tenderness entered his music; he became more than a purveyor of what Vincent d'Indy called "discreet and semi-religious eroticism." Fugère was the elderly des Grieux in *Le Portrait de Manon*; Cendrillon's loving father; the jaunty Devil of *Grisélidis*; and—in the first Paris casts—the dear old cook in *Le Jongleur*, and Sancho Panza. He lived until 1935, and made some excellent records.) What of *Esclarmonde*? The composer styled it "opéra romanesque." The plot is drawn from the twelfth- or thirteenth-century *roman d'aventure Partonopeus de Blois*, a variant of the *Mélusine* story—a kind of reversed Cupid and Psyche, in which Partonopeus, transported to a magic castle, enjoys the love of Melior, princess of Constantinople, on condition that he does not attempt to see her face. One night, he turns a lantern on her; the ensuing misfortunes do, however, reach a happy ending. In Alfred Blau and Louis de Gramont's libretto much of the *roman* is changed, including the names. There are anticipations of *Turandot* in the first scene, where Esclarmonde "appears in her radiant beauty" but does not sing, and in the final reunion *coram publico* of Esclarmonde and Roland. The action of the opera, which moves between Byzantium, an enchanted island, Blois, and the Ardennes, suggests a mixture of Handel's *Rinaldo*, Weber's *Oberon*, and *Lohengrin*. The music is harder to place. It was composed during those years—the 1880s—that Fantin-Latour characterized by entitling a group portrait of French artists and musicians "Petit Bayreuth." Wagner is the large influence playing upon Massenet's individual manner of lyrical utterance suggested by the contours of the text. The young Californian soprano Sibyl Sanderson was the composer's particular muse. The autograph vocal score of *Esclarmonde*, which turned up for sale at Sotheby Parke Bernet two years ago, carries in its margins a running record of time spent with "S.," and notes whether the composer worked on any passage in the Sanderson apartment or "*seul chez moi—triste.*" Esclarmonde is an amazing role to have been written for a twenty-three-year-old débutante. The heroine appears in seven of the eight scenes, and sings extensively in all but the first and the last. She sings low; she sings very high (a sustained Queen-of-Night F and a sustained G above it appear in the score); and she needs weight and power in addition to range and agility. Last year, the Bel Canto Opera's production of the piece showed much of what Massenet must have had in mind. The role, bravely and brilliantly sung by a young soprano, Marilyn Brustadt, made a great effect. That small, simple, clever production, piano-accompanied, raised hopes for the work which were not quite fulfilled by the full-scale version put on by the Metropolitan Opera last month. Writ large, *Esclarmonde* proved to be an inflated, pretentious, and unmemorable score.

The opera was due at the Met in 1891, but the season had already brought three contemporary operas and the public had had enough: *Esclarmonde* (along with Lalo's *Le Roi d'Ys*) was canceled and Wagner took the place of Wagnérisme. Eighty-five years later, *Esclarmonde* can fulfill a public's desire for novelty without contemporaneity. The Met production, borrowed from San Francisco, is very pretty to look at. The traditional settings that Handelians know so well—enchanted island, beleaguered city, royal apartment, forest glade—are redrawn by Beni Montresor in a large romantic manner that perfectly matches Massenet's large romantic handling of the traditional matter. The costumes are picturesque and becoming. The colorings suggest a deliquescent, softened Klimt. The stage pictures melt and reassemble before our eyes as painted gauzes rise and descend. But it is a mistake to play everything behind a painted *front* gauze. The device, if it is not to put a barrier between an opera and its listeners, needs more skillful lighting than the Met seems able to provide. (In the duet of Act IV, the lovers strove, often in vain, to have light on their faces while they sang.) And though a gauze may in fact absorb little sound, it *seems* to act as an acoustic baffle—to haze the voices as well as the view. Things were made worse by a play of restless lights across the front gauze itself.

The singing on the first night was less strong than in the London recording made by the same principals. Some clouds had gathered around Joan Sutherland's voice. When it broke through them—notably

455

in the ringing phrases at the end of Act II, while Esclarmonde invests Roland with the sword of St. George—all the old power and brilliance were heard. But much of the time the sound was veiled, and in the first act sustained notes were unsteady. Her manner had majesty. She sang the love music with a tenderness and the incantatory episodes with an authority that recalled her early triumph as Handel's amorous sorceress Alcina, in 1957. By vocal standards other than those she herself has set, or in a less enormous house than the Met, she might be found magnificent. At his best, Giacomo Aragall, the Roland, was as good as in the recording—virile, imposing, and sensitive—and he made a handsome hero. But then suddenly, sometimes in mid-phrase, the metal in the voice disappeared when the volume dropped, and the core of the tone became mushy. Clifford Grant, in the *basse-chantante* role of Phorcas, Esclarmonde's father, began the opera nobly and continued well, though not quite on the same level. Louis Quilico as the Bishop of Blois and John Macurdy as King Cléomer were both unwontedly bumbly. Huguette Tourangeau as Parséïs, Esclarmonde's sister, was splendidly firm, focused, and true, and she alone made anything of the words. Parséïs's betrothed, Énéas, was portrayed by John Carpenter as a chevalier fresh from the campus. Lotfi Mansouri's direction was certain and stylish. Richard Bonynge's conducting was vivid and assured. But the organ, which is important in this score, sounded almost as nasty as the Carnegie Hall instrument.

Esclarmonde first appeared at the Opéra-Comique in 1889. The year before, there had been *Le Roi d'Ys*, a more successful product of Petit Bayreuth. And the year before that there had been Emmanuel Chabrier's *Le Roi malgré lui*, one of its most felicitous products. The day before *Esclarmonde* opened at the Met, *Le Roi malgré lui* opened in the Juilliard Theater, for a run of four performances given by the Juilliard American Opera Center. This was its American première. By the invention, the zest, the individuality and freedom of rhythm, form, and scoring—by the sheer distinction—of Chabrier's delightful music, Massenet's meticulously ambitious opera was almost eclipsed. A few years before *Le Roi*, in *Gwendoline*, Chabrier had got a full-blooded Wagnerian tragedy out of his system. He was neither a solemn idolater (the quadrille on themes from *Tristan, Souvenirs de Munich*, makes that plain) nor a follower of fashion. He loved and understood Wagner's music, but his own music was tempered by admiration and affection for Weber and for Berlioz. Moreover, he said, "My first concern is to do what pleases me while trying above all to express my personality; and my second is not to be a bore." (Massenet's first concern, like Meyerbeer's, was to do what pleases the public.) In his little book on

456

Chabrier, Poulenc asserts that *Gwendoline* is a masterpiece that would bear revival. *Le Roi* certainly bears revival. It is not exactly a masterpiece, for the libretto is a mess. (D'Indy told the composer that, although he adored the piece, "I can't understand the plot. . . . People go in and out, arriving when they ought to depart, or departing when they ought to stay.") In brief, *Le Roi* concerns the future Henri III (brother of Elizabeth in Verdi's *Don Carlos*), his reluctance to mount the Polish throne, two romances, and some mistaken identities. It is an opéra comique with some buffo elements. I glance down the contents page of the score, wondering which of the twenty numbers to pick for special praise, and recall bewitching touches in all of them. Ravel declared that "the first performance of *Le Roi malgré lui* changed the whole direction of French harmony." Wagner is now thoroughly assimilated. The path from *Le Roi* points directly toward Ravel and Debussy; the paths that lead to it come equally from Wagner, Berlioz, Bizet, and Offenbach.

By its second performance, the Juilliard production was a happy one. The piece was done in a lively, witty new English translation, by Maurice Valency, as *The Reluctant King*. Robert Yodice's scenery provided Berman-type richness with a minimum of fuss (though black backcloths to each act lent an unsuitably somber note to the comedy), and there seemed to be an endless supply of handsome costumes. Bliss Hebert's direction was at once entertaining and musically sensitive. Manuel Rosenthal's conducting, leaden on the first night, took wing on the second. The School of American Ballet gave an enthusiastic, if unpolished, account of the *Fête Polonaise*, which opens the second act, choreographed by Balanchine. (It is the finale of his Chabrier ballet *Bourrée fantasque*.) The ordering of the numbers within acts had been altered; in so loosely constructed a plot it makes little difference.

The title role was taken by Tonio Di Paolo, who has one of the most beautiful baritone voices—in timbre, in focus, in the way it moves from note to note and spans the phrases—to be heard in this country. James Schwisow, the Nangis, has a clear, bright, steady, but still unsupple tenor. Gilbert Price, the Fritelli, was overanimated; he both acted and hit his music too hard. (Had he studied the record of the two solos made by Fugère, who created the role?) Susan Peterson, an imprecise Alexina on the first night, had found a more secure form by the second. Sheila Barnes was a touching Minka most of the time; her voice is pure and true, but there were moments when she was too composed, unspontaneous. The opera is a happy choice for student production since it has many small roles. Five of Henri's mignons are named and have solo lines; Minka has six sisters who cluster round her, Valkyrie-like, when she is in distress.

Chabrier, Mussorgsky, and Palestrina—in that order—were the composers Debussy said he loved. Ravel declared he would be prouder to have written *Le Roi malgré lui* than *The Ring*.

The first solo recital given in the rebuilt Avery Fisher Hall was Elena Obraztsova's. It was not a success, except as measured by noisy acclaim from a public many of whom evidently felt that she could do nothing wrong. I thought that in a short program (nine Rachmaninoff songs formed the first half, the *Seven Spanish Popular Songs* of Falla and Delilah's "Amour, viens aider" and "Mon cœur s'ouvre" the second) she did very little right, and that it was distressing to hear a compatriot of Nadezhda Obukhova adopt, and the townsmen of the late Jennie Tourel applaud, so broad and coarse an approach to Rachmaninoff's delicate music. That she enacted the songs with the same large, theatrical gestures that made her Metropolitan Amneris so powerful did not really matter; there was no need to watch. But it did matter that the vocal equivalent of these gestures entered the musical line. The songs took a walloping. Miss Obraztsova's early records display a voice more even, purer in timbre, and less fiercely vigorous than the one she uses now. In the theater, she is so passionate, so commanding, and, to put it simply, so excitingly *loud* that she triumphs. The lieder platform calls for artistry of a finer grain. One of her encores, Fauré's "Après un rêve," elicited smoothly controlled, carefully scaled tones. So did "Asturiana," in the Falla collection. The Delilah arias, foretaste of the Met *Samson* due in April, held promise of a voluptuous and temperamental performance.

In Carnegie Hall, three days later, Dietrich Fischer-Dieskau, with Jörg Demus as pianist, gave a model lieder recital, the most consummately accomplished that even from him I have ever heard. His occasional failings are well known: a tendency to exaggerate climaxes; to hit accents too hard, bumpily; to overdo crescendos and overdo diminuendos; to indulge in overinflecting words and vocal lines to the point of preciousness. None of these was in evidence, but all his virtues were: beauty of tone and line, range of expressive colors, perfect scaling, and sensitivity to the weight and shape and meaning of the words. The program was sixteen of Hugo Wolf's Goethe settings. The second part, after an exquisite account of "Anakreons Grab," reached a climax with an overwhelming performance of "Prometheus." One felt wrung, exhausted. After this blasphemous, hurtled defiance of the gods, this proud, magnificent assertion of human self-sufficiency, what could follow? The singer brought us back gently to everyday life with "Genialisch Treiben" and the two Coptic Songs. The audience would not let him go. As encores, he sang two more Goethe settings, from the *Westöstlicher Divan*, then moved to Mörike (I have never heard him voice and utter "Verborgenheit" and "Gesang Weylas" more beautifully), and finally bade farewell with the traditional, rueful "Ich kann nicht länger singen." The program book contained texts and translations—something one should be able to take for granted, but can't.

December 6, 1976

MANY-COLORED GLASS

The Metropolitan Opera's commitment to contemporary music is probably slighter than that of any other major house. It was not always so. During Gatti-Casazza's twenty-seven seasons, he kept the New York public abreast of what was being composed elsewhere, producing significant operas from Germany and Italy while they were still new, and he introduced some fifteen American pieces, often starrily cast. It is true that none of the latter have lasted; the wastage rate in new operas is high. *Mona, The King's Henchman, Peter Ibbetson, The Emperor Jones,* and *Merry Mount* are titles remembered; who but a historian can name the composers of *Shanewis, Cleopatra's Night,* and *In the Pasha's Garden?* The premières of *La Fanciulla del West* (1910) and *Il trittico* (1918)—and, to a lesser extent, of Humperdinck's *Königskinder* (1910) and Giordano's *Madame Sans-Gêne* (1915)—have secured for the Met a modest place in the history of operatic creation, but it is a long time since the eyes of the world were turned on it to discover the outcome of a commission from a leading composer—something like a new score from Sessions, Henze, Tippett, or Berio. Since the move to Lincoln Center, only two new operas have been baptized by the company— Barber's *Antony and Cleopatra* (1966) and Marvin David Levy's *Mourning Becomes Electra* (1967). If James Levine and John Dexter have placed some exciting commissions for future seasons—if, say, Carter, Crumb, Druckman, or Bolcom is even now working on a Metropolitan opera—the public has still to learn of it. Even local premières of works whose merit has been tested elsewhere have become few. None of Thomson's operas have been taken up by the Met, although his *Lord Byron* was written for it, and his *Mother of Us All* could surely have been a Bicentennial hit. The reasons for doing Massenet's *Esclarmonde* rather than Sessions's *Montezuma,* for doing Meyerbeer's *Le Prophète* rather than Bernd Alois Zimmermann's *Die Soldaten* or Henze's *We Come to the River,* are obvious. But one of those reasons—that the public stays away from contemporary operas—was challenged last month when two performances of Philip Glass's *Einstein on the Beach* were both sold out. And yet the most adventurous intendant in the world might think twice before billing *Einstein*. It is a four-act opera that lasts for nearly five hours without an intermission. It has no plot in any conventional sense. The "libretto" consists for the most part of numerals sung or spoken (counting out the rhythmic patterns of the score) and sol-fa syllables (do, re mi, etc., naming the notes sung). The music is in essence a series of extended moto perpetuos, each of them lasting longer than Ravel's *Bolero*.

Einstein on the Beach was not part of the regular season but was presented on two Sunday evenings by the Byrd Hoffman Foundation in cooperation with the Met. It lends itself to guest appearances, being a self-contained "two-truck show" (scenery and sound equipment pack into two forty-foot containers) that has already toured widely in Europe. *Einstein* opened in Avignon last July, and visited Venice for the Biennale, Belgrade for the International Theater Festival, Paris for the Autumn Festival, Brussels, Hamburg, Rotterdam, and Amsterdam. Since it arrived at the Met prepared and complete, it was a practical as well as an exciting addition to the fare in a theater whose resident troupe is unaccustomed to tackling contemporary scores. The orchestra is the Philip Glass Ensemble (five instrumentalists and a sound engineer), plus a singer and a solo violinist who takes the role of Einstein. A versatile company of twenty-one sings, acts, and dances; one of the leading singers joins the ensemble to play, with effortless mastery, a long organ cadenza that is the music for a scene in the last act.

Einstein is described as an opera "by Robert Wilson–Philip Glass." The two planned the work together, plotted the time it was to occupy, and determined its large structure. Music and lyrics are credited to Glass, direction and décor to Wilson. There are three basic images: a train, a courtroom that dissolves into a prison, and a field of dancers with a spaceship in the sky above them. If these are called A, B, and C, then Act I consists of A and B, Act II of C and A, and Act III of B and C. Act IV presents developments of all three images: the train has become a building; from the prison only the bed remains (a rectangle of light, it moves on an empty stage); the spaceship is no longer a model overhead but a large cellular structure filled with people. Five episodes for a couple on the stage and varied musical forces form prologue, entr'actes, and epilogue. At first, these seem to function like the intermezzi that were played between the acts of an opera seria, or the *kyogen* interludes between the plays of a nō cycle, but they carry so much musical (and, at the last, emotional) weight that they can be regarded as the main matter of the opera, and the acts themselves as extended intermezzi or developments. Although *Einstein* has been generally treated as if it were a work by Wilson with incidental music by Glass, it is very different—in tone, structure, pace, and appearance—from Wilson's earlier pieces. To describe it as a characteristic Glass score with scenic accompaniment by Wilson (and choreographic accompaniment by Andrew deGroat) would be nearer the mark but still not quite accurate. It is a *Gesamtkunstwerk* in which Wilson's romantic profusion, allusiveness, and collage techniques are tempered by Glass's sharp-focus insistence on pure structure.

The opera can be compared and contrasted with Wilson's *Deafman Glance*, which when I saw it in Amsterdam five years ago had grown by accretion into a six-hour theater piece. The cast of *Deafman* was enormous. At one point, coal-black mammies came dancing on in greater profusion than Bolshoy bayadères. The company picked up new players as it went along. The blind people were really blind. The cripples were crippled. To find an actor for the role of Sigmund Freud, a photograph of the psychoanalyst was taken to an Amsterdam old folks' home; yes, said its caretaker, he lives here—and the old man joined the company. Amassing people and properties, Wilson composed a series of richly picturesque dream images, usually very slow-moving, then suddenly galvanized into activity: by the mammies; by Bugs Bunny, eight feet tall, dancing on; by the startling leap of a large frog that for perhaps two hours had been sitting motionless, host at a dinner table. Act I was set on a beach (the stage deep in real sand), Act II in a drawing room; Acts III and IV were magic sites, several places at once. There was a little spoken dialogue (a pianist chatted pleasantly to a walrus) and some music (the first movement of the Moonlight Sonata and the first prelude of Bach's Forty-eight were played through a dozen times or so in succession), but most of the time several independent, mysterious dramas were enacted simultaneously in silence and at different paces. A tortoise took an hour to cross from one side of the stage to the other, and a lonely long-distance runner a few seconds. *Deafman Glance* acted on the spirit through the eyes. It was a drama of surrealist pictures. The form appeared to be elastic. Episodes and incidents could be, and were, added, removed, extended, abridged between one performance and the next.

Einstein, on the other hand, is precisely organized, tautly patterned, economical in its forces, and austere in its décor. Instead of the rich colors and textures and the visual elaboration of *Deafman Glance*, there are simple, largely geometrical scenes in a muted color range. If pressed, I suppose I could concoct some sort of scenario that emerged during the presentation. The images cohere. In the first scene, a child throws paper airplanes from a high platform; in the last, a toy rocket ship zooms up into space. Einstein fiddles while a drop curtain behind him spells out statistics on destruction caused by a nuclear explosion. A man involved in ceaseless mathematical calculation is a recurrent symbol. The images of motion also invoke ideas of relativity. ("Does Oxford stop at this train?" asked the professor of physics, embarking at Paddington.) But what *Einstein* was "about" for me was much what Glass's *Music with Changing Parts* is about: the effect of rhythmic patterns and short melodic motifs endlessly repeated but slowly altering; of bright, insistent timbres whose colors gradually shift as one instrument, then another cuts into or drops from the texture; of simple harmonic progressions rooted in laws of acoustics (one of the main themes of *Einstein* is a IV-V-I sequence) underpinning moto-perpetuo activity. In his *Music in Twelve Parts*, Glass asked for "another mode of listening—one in which neither memory nor anticipation (the usual psychological devices of programmatic music, whether Baroque, Classical, Romantic, or Modernistic) has a place in sustaining the texture, quality, or reality of the musical experience." A listener to his music usually reaches a point, quite early on, of rebellion at the needle-stuck-in-the-groove quality, but a minute or two later he realizes that the needle has not stuck: something has happened. Once that point is passed, Glass's music—or so I find—becomes easy to listen to for hours on end. The mind may wander now and again, but it wanders within a new sound world that the composer has created. The simple harmonic foundations induce a feeling of security. Lively incident soon recaptures one's full attention. A listener's memory, it should be added, does play a part in *Einstein*, since there are recurrent themes, picked up in one scene from another and sometimes reflecting, sometimes in counterpoint to, the recurrent visual imagery. Another source of listeners' rebellion, however, may be the sheer loudness of the music. *Einstein* is scored for two electric organs and three saxophones, alternating with flute or clarinet, all heavily amplified, as are the voices. Twice, during the first performance, I felt that at sustained climaxes the level of noise emerging from the tall banks of loudspeakers on either side of the proscenium arch was not merely painful but probably perilous, too. For the second performance, I found a seat not directly in the line of sonic crossfire.

In common, Wilson and Glass require a suspension of the usual time scale observed in Western theaters and concert halls. In this—but in this alone—their works are akin to nō cycles that last from dawn to dusk, and *kathakali* cycles that last from dusk to dawn. In an age when Erik Satie's *Vexations*, a few bars for solo piano, *très lent*, played over and over again for twenty-four hours, can find performances, when Stockhausen begins his *Piano Piece IX* with the same chord sounded 227 times and builds his *Stimmung* on one chord sustained for seventy-five minutes, audiences are readier than their fathers were to sit and savor slow-shifting, chronic experiences—hypnotized by repetition, stimulated by the observance of tiny changes, not bored. *Einstein* is busier, more active, than those pieces. Glass's score may be incantatory, but it is not lulling.

Wilson and Glass also share an ability to obtain dedicated, amazingly accomplished, unflagging performances from the artists they work with. Instrumentalists, actors, and singers had *Einstein* by heart. How, without the aid of rosaries, they knew when to repeat and when to move on I cannot guess.

December 13, 1976

Glass's Music with Changing Parts *is recorded on Chatham Square LP 1001–2.*

MASTERY

A master class held in public sometimes becomes a kind of recital at which the instructor is the star and pupils provide the performance material. I never heard Elena Gerhardt or Lotte Lehmann sing a full program, but at public master classes I certainly heard and saw them perform. (Gerhardt, short of breath but still sure in her shaping of word and phrase, sang parts of the *Winterreise* with wonderful intensity; Lehmann suddenly, in full voice, set the Wigmore Hall ringing with the Marschallin's "Heut' oder Morgen"—just five notes, producing sound and sentiments never to be forgotten.) There was no suggestion of public performance, however, about the three public master classes given at the Juilliard School last month by Herbert von Karajan or the three given last month and this by Elisabeth Schwarzkopf and Walter Legge. Karajan worked with a group of student conductors on Strauss's *Don Juan*, Brahms's First Symphony, and *The Rite of Spring*; Schwarzkopf and Legge worked with young singers on Schubert, Brahms, and Wolf lieder and Mozart arias. They ignored the audiences. Karajan sat below the podium, among the players of the Juilliard Orchestra, and, scorning a microphone, conversed in unraised voice with the students, not caring whether his comments reached the visitors or not. Schwarzkopf and Legge sat, backs to the audience, on the edge of the Juilliard Theater platform. They used microphones, so all that they said could be heard. But they turned to the audience only to chide it when it was noisy.

Karajan concentrated on the techniques of rehearsing. He tried to persuade flamboyant young men not to mime their excitable interpretations, not to "perform," but to beat time simply and clearly while using their ears as if they were "two microscopes" to discern whatever was wrong, and then correct any mistakes of pitch, timing, or dynamics in the fewest possible words. A handful of terms, he said—loud/soft, fast/slow, early/late, long/short, sharp/flat—were all a conductor needed to do his work. Trust the orchestra was the burden of his advice. Put everything right in rehearsal; repeat passages, first slowly and then up to speed, until every note from every player is rhythmically and dynamically in place—this was the practice he enjoined on his pupils. Then, on the night, a performance will flow as if of its own accord. Relax, he often said; use your ears, not your arms and body. A jerky, jittery young firebrand was told to stop flashing his baton about as if it were a wizard's wand and made to summon the orchestral surges of *Don Juan* by moving no more than an index finger. (The second of Richard Strauss's Ten Golden Rules for a young conductor was "Never sweat; only the audience should get warm.") Karajan recalled his apprehension, as a child, that he would never be able to lift his huge, heavy horse over a fence, and his discovery that one had merely to get the pace and place right and the horse would do the rest. So with an orchestra approaching a climax. All this told us much about a man who, with a technique as calm and unflashy as Sir Adrian Boult's, elicits virtuoso playing of effortless smoothness and power. His remark that if the presence of bar lines is ever felt, lyricism is lost perhaps helps to explain why his performances can be overfluent, gritless to a fault.

Walter Legge, although unmentioned in Grove's Dictionary of Music and Musicians, has probably done more than anyone else alive to raise standards of musical performance—not just in Britain, where he founded and directed the Philharmonia Orchestra and engaged Karajan, Cantelli, Klemperer, Giulini, and, for two memorable Brahms concerts, Toscanini to conduct it, but internationally, through many, many recordings of performances executed to his exacting requirements. He was the man behind many HMV and Columbia records—matching artists to repertory, casting, coaching, coaxing, and, at recording sessions, commending or criticizing until he was satisfied: "I was determined to put onto disc the best that artists could do under the best possible conditions." Before the war, he produced all Beecham's recordings and the influential Hugo Wolf Society albums; after it, symphonic albums by those Philharmonia conductors, the Callas series of operas, Mozart operas under Karajan, Böhm, and Giulini, *Fidelio* under Klemperer, shining Richard Strauss, captivating Johann Strauss, great lieder recitals by

Schwarzkopf and Fischer-Dieskau, piano recitals by Dinu Lipatti, and much else. Legge's genius was, and is, for recognizing and remembering in detail what constitutes greatness in musical execution, for perceiving potential greatness, and for inspiring new interpreters to learn from and emulate—not merely ape—the best achievements of their predecessors. I owe him a personal debt, for he persuaded my first employer that a music critic should be sent wherever in the world there was something or someone worth hearing. The world owes him a debt for having sought out, sifted, promulgated, and preserved for posterity the best in mid-twentieth-century musical performance.

When Legge married Schwarzkopf, two perfectionists joined forces. In their master classes, they instilled the attention to detail that has been the hallmark of Legge-directed and of Schwarzkopf-executed interpretations. Many minutes were spent working with a student on the single word "graust" in Schubert's "Der Doppelgänger"—on the timbre, the attack, the volume, the pronunciation of the *gr*, the pronunciation of the *s*, and then on all these together in the context of the whole phrase. The quality stressed was line—musical line—above all. Like Peter Pears last year, like Karajan, and like, I am told, Maria Callas in her Juilliard classes, they constantly urged their pupils to have a whole line in view before embarking on its first note. Schwarzkopf insisted on pure, precise German; allowed no disruptive North German *r*'s—especially final *r*'s in such a line as "Immer leiser wird mein Schlummer"—to break the legato, except for some special expressive effect; urged an aristocratic Viennese pronunciation as the most musical. Consonants should be distinctly but rapidly and unobtrusively sounded; no spitting, no buzzing, hissing, *rr*rolling, or humming (except, again, for a rare special effect); vowels, fully sustained throughout the length of a note, are the creators and carriers of a musical line. Legge's bugbear was the insertion of an *h* between notes slurred to a single syllable, and often he stopped singers to complain of a lifeless note or word—here an anacrusis not already instinct with sense, there a final note that died into blankness when it should have pointed, across a rest, to what was coming. Both instructors refused to pass unsteadiness or uncertainties of pitch. Students were not allowed to "swim" with their hands, or "swim" in that other sense of moving vaguely through a phrase. Divisions and ornaments had to be sounded clearly, not scurried, and not merely "indicated" by little shakes of the head. There were many things of many kinds to be learned. George Szell and his advice were several times invoked. So was Lotte Lehmann's magical way of breathing out an initial *j*. I hope that the students felt they were being made heirs to great traditions that Schwarzkopf and Legge have both absorbed and extended—and that they were given a listening list for further study. In the early days of their collaboration, Legge made Schwarzkopf listen to records as challenges. In an *Opera News* article about his wife, he recalled how he "set out to widen by recorded examples her imaginative concept of the possibilities of vocal sound." Among the examples were Rosa Ponselle's creamy timbre and noble line; the Slavic brilliance of Nina Koshetz; some insinuating phrases from Geraldine Farrar's Carmen; a single word from Melba, "Bada," in Mimì's farewell; some Elisabeth Rethberg and much Meta Seinemeyer, "to show how essentially Teutonic voices can produce brilliant Italianate sound"; Lotte Lehmann for generosity, warmth, and impulsiveness; Elisabeth Schumann for charm and lightness; Frida Leider for dramatic tension. And there were instrumentalists, too: "Fritz Kreisler for the dark beauty of his tone, his nobility and elegance, his vitality in upbeats, his rubato and cavalier nonchalance; Schnabel for concentrated thinking over long musical periods, firmly rhythmical, seemingly oblivious to bar lines. From the analysis in these diverse models we made our own synthesis."

In his *Life of Rossini*, published in 1824, Stendhal indulged in a flight of fancy—that one day a device would be invented to preserve for successive generations of students and opera lovers the sound and style of great singers. Edison turned fancy into fact, but I sometimes wonder whether singers of today profit from his invention as fully as they could. If Lenus Carlson, a young baritone of abundant natural gifts, had listened attentively to records by Mattia Battistini, Giuseppe De Luca, and Pablo Casals, could he have turned the long spans of Valentin's "Avant de quitter ces lieux" into a set of unjoined notes, as he did in the Metropolitan Opera's revival of *Faust* this month? If Paul Plishka, the Mephistopheles of that performance, knew how Pol Plançon sang the arias, would he not have striven for aristocratic elegance, greater lightness and delicacy of inflection? I cannot believe that Maria Ewing, heroine of the Houston Grand Opera's new production of *Il barbiere di Siviglia*, knew what Conchita Supervia—and a dozen other singers besides—did with the single word "ma" in Rosina's cavatina, since she made nothing of what should be a bewitching moment. I have met singers who grew indignant at the suggestion that they should seek instruction from old records: "I want to do *my* Norma, *my* Almaviva, *my* Carlo, not a copy of Rosa Ponselle's, Fernando De Lucia's, Battistini's." [A few days after this piece appeared, Renata Scotto spoke out in similar vein to a *Times* interviewer; see p. 479.] Strange, and not sensible, the failure to realize that many great artists began by imitating the best of their predecessors and then, challenged and inspired by a full knowledge of what others had achieved, developed and refined a personal interpretation in the light of individual temperament and technique. Henry Chorley praised Giulia Grisi, London's and Paris's fa-

466

vorite prima donna in the mid-nineteenth century, for "her cleverness in adopting the effects and ideas of others more thoughtful and originally inventive than herself." "Her most popular personations," he added, "followed those of other actresses. Her Norma, doubtless her grandest performance, was modeled on that of Madame Pasta—perhaps, in some points, was an improvement on the model, because there was more of animal passion in it," and because Grisi had the more beautiful voice. As a modern instance of not straight imitation but the realization that at a particular moment something special is needed, I would cite Frederica von Stade's singing of Rosina's "ma" on a new Philips disc of Rossini and Mozart arias. It is not like Supervia's "ma," nor like Callas's, but like theirs, and especially in the repeat verse, it twinkles delightfully.

One day, I hope to see *Il barbiere* played as a high-spirited, elegant comedy of situation and character, not as a low, vulgar romp. The Houston version, directed by Anthony Besch, began promisingly but fell to pieces in the first-act finale. When the officer, about to arrest Almaviva, came to attention, he stamped on Figaro's foot, Figaro went hopping around the stage, and the start of the *quadro di stupore*, "Fredda ed immobile," was drowned by belly laughter. Then the soldiers raided Bartolo's cellar; they drank and diced while Figaro applied leeches to Bartolo's calf and Almaviva flung Berta's washing—frilly undergarments—all over the stage. As the curtain fell, Berta was being carried off to a bedroom by a drunken crew. In Act II, Almaviva-as-Alonso clowned broadly during the lesson scene and had evidently forgotten the plot of the opera altogether. The "Buona sera" quintet was "enlivened" by nonsensical added business: at each successive entry, someone prevented Basilio from picking up a guinea he had dropped, thus keeping him onstage during a scene the sense of which is that everyone is eager to hasten his departure. Anything for an easy laugh!

Still, things were less frenzied than in Sarah Caldwell's production for the City Opera, and Donald Gramm could make a substantial character, not a caricature, of Dr. Bartolo. Paolo Montarsolo's Basilio routines have become polished with years of practice. Hermann Prey's Figaro bounced about in a conventional, exuberant way. Edoardo Gimenez could not manage the trickier divisions of Almaviva's role. Maria Ewing's Rosina was attractive but lacked piquancy. Besch and Charles Mackerras, who conducted, are men who usually think out a performance afresh, using score and libretto as their starting point and testing later "traditions" by their aptness to the work the creators conceived. It was disappointing to find that here they had assembled a routine modern *Barbiere*.

Houston does its operas in two versions: with an international cast, in the original language, and with an American cast, in English. The American cast, inadequately directed by David Gately and tamely conducted by Chris Nance, did not realize its potential. There were good voices—Stephen Dickson's in the title role, Scott Reeve's as Basilio—but they were not used to create lively personages. Ruth and Thomas Martin's translation is drab; it sounded doubly so because the recitatives were chopped into separate phrases, served out like sections from a presliced factory loaf. But there was merit in Linda Kowalski's Rosina —dark in timbre, vivacious, and sparkly in the upper reaches. And as Almaviva there was the young tenor Rockwell Blake, who seems to be what the world has been waiting for ever since the Rossini revival began. Several modern sopranos and mezzos have shown themselves able to get through Rossini's fiendish runs and roulades with fair accuracy; modern tenors have usually sketched them, smudged them, or cut them. But Mr. Blake sings coloratura with the freedom and accuracy of a young Sutherland, and he sings it in full voice. He is not a *tenorino* but a manly lyric tenor with the kind of agility seldom heard since Hermann Jadlowker recorded "Ecco ridente in cielo" in 1912—and with more grace and charm of musical manner than Jadlowker showed. A cadenza in Almaviva's first aria took Mr. Blake to the high F; the final aria ("Cessa di più resistere. . . . Ah, il più lieto, il più felice," better known in the mezzo version that ends *La Cenerentola*) revealed all his abilities. The number was slightly shortened, which was a pity. It brought the house down. (In the international performance, Mr. Gimenez struggled through it, and was received in silence.) If Mr. Blake fulfills his promise, Rossini's *Otello* and *Semiramide* can return to the stage as more than shows for a prima donna and supporting cast.

Faust went on being done at the Met while most other major houses abandoned it. (Covent Garden's 1974 production, gift of an American foundation, was the first performance there in nearly forty years.) I was brought up to believe that unless Melba or Eames and the de Reszke brothers were to come again, *Faust* could not be accepted by a modern audience. Not so. In the long run, the public is always right, and *Faust* has had a long enough run to be proof against critical attack and passing fashions: at Covent Garden, from 1863 to 1924 it played every season but one before falling from favor; it was the first opera ever done by the Met, and most subsequent seasons have included it. This season's revival was not well sung; in fact, by Melba and Eames standards it was wretchedly sung. But Jean-Louis Barrault's 1965 production, set out now by Bodo Igesz, moves well. Jacques Dupont's simple décor, though monotonously brown or gray, changes with a swiftness that removes cumbersomeness from the piece. The scale is grand, the chorus and dancers are abundant, and the effects are picturesque without being heavy. Much is missing—colors, trees, walls—but not much is flatly contradicted. This is a serious and honest attempt to stage Gounod's *Faust*, not a clever director's modish, unmusical commentary on it.

The shortcomings of the principals can be described by negatives. Jeannette Pilou, Marguerite, was not limpid in timbre. Stuart Burrows, Faust, was not romantic. Lenus Carlson was not legato. Paul Plishka was not elegant. On the credit side, Miss Pilou is an actress and musician of charm, character, and intelligence. Mr. Burrows is reliable and never strident. Mr. Carlson is promising. Mr. Plishka is powerful. All of them knew what they were about. Georges Prêtre, the conductor, also has ideas about the score. The romantic fluctuations in his tempi were generally convincing, but the duet and trio of the last scene, I felt, needed broader, less excitable handling. There was new choreography, by Stuart Sebastian, for the Brocken ballet. His divertissement—part Balanchinesque, part Las Vegas—was chic, civilized, and, although rather uncertainly danced, less ridiculous than most Walpurgisnacht dances.

Of recent New York recitals, one that stays with me is Raymond Dudley's, in Alice Tully Hall, of six Haydn piano sonatas, played on the instrument that we call a fortepiano to distinguish it from the powerful modern pianoforte. Mr. Dudley used a replica of a Viennese instrument now in the Smithsonian Institution, of light construction (it weighs about a tenth as much as a modern concert grand) and light, clear, sweet tone—the kind of piano for which Haydn and Mozart wrote. Hearing the right instrument is not enough in itself to insure a fine musical experience. As Cyril Ehrlich remarks in his newly published *The Piano: A History* (Dent/Rowman & Littlefield), "comparisons between old and new instruments have little meaning without reference to methods and standards of performance. For example, it is said that early pianos 'speak' more easily and clearly, particularly in the bass, where individual notes of a chord are heard with a clarity denied to the 'woolly' modern instrument. Yet . . . in Schubert's posthumous B-flat Sonata the low bass trills are executed with perfect clarity [on a modern instrument] by Brendel or Serkin, and the textures of his 'Wanderer' fantasy never sound muddled in the hands of a Richter or Pollini." True enough—yet anyone who gets to know the sound of the pianos Schubert knew is likely to wish that Brendel, Serkin, Richter, and Pollini would turn to such instruments, and add to their interpretative artistry the extra delight of authentic timbre. In a Bicentennial gesture, Mr. Dudley played six sonatas composed in 1776, and gave fluent, thoughtful performances distinguished by naturalness and by freedoms that did not become un-disciplined. Haydn's piano sonatas are strong and surprising; the sur-prises sounded just as impressive on the intimate scale as they do on Horowitz's Steinway.

December 20, 1976

A JOYFUL NOISE

The Boston Symphony performance of *Messiah* in Carnegie Hall, con-ducted by Colin Davis, was exhilarating. It was a *Messiah* in the modern manner—not by any means a historical reconstruction of an eighteenth-century performance but closer to that in spirit and in sound than were the massive *Messiahs* of the nineteenth and the first half of the twentieth century. Many a long-familiar work, and perhaps *Messiah* most of all, has recently changed its character—or, more precisely, the assumed character under which, decade after decade, it appeared before audiences —as a result of musicological research, scholarly-minded criticism, and the wide dissemination, on phonograph records, of modern perform-ances undertaken with the aim of re-creating as accurately as possible the sounds that a composer of the past would have expected to hear. Such records are already legion; to their number let me welcome the first release in this country of the German SEON series, published here on a new label, ABC Classics. A sample disc, CLS-67001, is enough in itself to justify the company's claim of "exemplary performances on period instruments." Listening to a Haydn string quartet done by such an en-semble as the Guarneri Quartet or the Quartetto Italiano, played with modern bows and instruments that, even if their bodies are old, probably have new necks, bass-bars, and bridges, and some metal strings screwed up to modern pitch—instruments that are tenser, louder, and more bril-liant than those Haydn knew—can, of course, still be a profoundly moving experience. Yet why should anyone cross the road to hear such an ensemble play Haydn's Opus 20 Nos. 2 and 4 when he could stay at home and listen to those works played (on ABCL-67011, in the SEON series) by the Quartetto Esterházy, four very accomplished Dutch musicians who use the right instruments and have studied the techniques and musical style of Haydn's day? And who wants to hear Bach church cantatas with women's voices in the boys' parts and nineteenth- or twentieth-century instruments, possibly underrehearsed and ill-balanced as well, when the Alte Werk series of Bach cantata recordings can pro-

470

vide performances whose timbres and phrasing make most other accounts of those pieces, however accomplished, sound like transcriptions?

To those questions there is an easy answer: The pull of the live event is strong. I attend the Sunday-afternoon Bach cantata series in Holy Trinity Church, on Central Park West, not expecting anything on the Alte Werk level but because—quite apart from the illuminating "contextual" presentation of each cantata, heard along with a chorale prelude, psalm, lesson, and hymn related to it—assisting at a performance (the old phrase for attending seems apt) is something different from listening to one on records. Which proves more rewarding depends mainly on the level of the respective performances—but not only on that. Better a very fine recording than a very poorly executed live concert. Better good clear sound from loudspeakers than dry or muddled sound in acoustically unsatisfactory surroundings. Better to be alone and undistracted than seated near a chatterbox or a persistent cougher. Better to be at home under a lamp than in a darkened hall if following a printed score or text is likely to enhance one's enjoyment of the music. But the choice is not always so sharply defined. Admirable live performances, acoustically excellent and adequately lit halls, and attentive, congenial audiences exist. The presence of such an audience can make a difference to both listeners and performers. Walter Legge believes that, by and large, artists are able to scale greater interpretative and technical heights in the "ideal conditions" of a studio than on the public platform, and many of the records he produced in that belief bear him out. But perhaps not all. Under Legge's supervision, Maria Callas made two recordings of *Lucia di Lammermoor*, in 1953 and 1959. Both are magnificent representations of her art. Yet if anyone asked me to demonstrate why Callas's Lucia was deemed great I would choose to play, first of all, the "live" performance in Berlin in 1955, conducted by Herbert von Karajan, which was captured and has been circulated on a pirate recording. Before the public, Callas is even more vivid and inspired, and she dares more. A similar comparison obtains between the two published albums of *The Ring* conducted by Wilhelm Furtwängler. One was recorded in 1953, an act a day, for Italian radio, before only a small invited audience, the other during live performances of the cycle at La Scala, in 1950. Both are magnificent representations of Furtwängler's art. But the Scala version is the greater; a few coughs from the large audience and a few wrong entries are a small price to pay.

There are no rules about this matter. Some artists seem to need an audience to give of their best; others— Clifford Curzon and Glenn Gould come to mind—are happier in a recording studio. Nor, fortunately, are there mutually exclusive alternatives. One can hear Beverly Sills and Joan Sutherland "live" before an audience at La Scala (thanks to the pirates) and "live" before an audience at the Met (thanks to Texaco),

471

hear them in polished studio recordings—and, of course, also hear them really live, by going to the theaters where they sing. But when it comes to the eighteenth- and early-nineteenth-century classics—Bach, Handel, Mozart, Haydn, Beethoven, Schubert—then, since most performers stick to the modern instruments and methods on which they were trained, one usually has to turn to studio performances, on records, to hear the music played with historically accurate sound and style.

The Boston Symphony used modern instruments for its *Messiah*, but in other ways the performance took heed of scholars' researches. The instrumental numbers employed were not very different from those of Handel's day. For a *Messiah* at the Foundling Hospital in 1754, Handel had fifteen violins, five violas, three cellos, and two double-basses; four oboes and four bassoons; pairs of horns and trumpets (the horns presumably doubled the trumpets in jubilant choruses, for there are no horn parts in the score); a drummer; and probably two continuo players. In Carnegie Hall, Davis had eighteen violins, eight violas, six cellos, and three double-basses; two oboes and two bassoons; two trumpets (no horns); a drummer; and two continuo players. By Handelian standards, the winds were understrength in relation to the strings, and they sounded so; in oboe/violin and bassoon/string-bass doublings, the oboes and bassoons were not very audible. But the sound was light, clear, and alert. Although it did not lack force in those numbers where force is called for, it never thickened. That the score used contained Handel's notes and did not contain Mozart's and Ebenezer Prout's additions to them can perhaps pass without comment in our day; not long ago Handel-Mozart-Prout was the norm and pure Handel the exception, but things have changed. Not *only* Handel's notes were heard, of course; that would be unstylish. There was a small amount of the unwritten variation and adornment of melodies expected once by eighteenth-century and now by 1970s ears. There was not quite enough for my taste—it came as a shock when the tenor soloist declined Handel's invitation to a cadenza in the eighth bar of "Comfort ye"—but too little ornament is preferable to too much. (Sir Adrian Boult once tartly suggested the publication of a Joan Sutherland record entitled "Mad Scenes from *Messiah*.") Similarly with the harpsichord continuo: constant twiddles, cunning divisions, and ingenious imitations can become maddening, but Davis's player erred on the side of sedateness—if we can rely on Sir George Macfarren's recollection of Sir George Smart's recollection of Joah Bates's recollection of Handel's own continuo playing: "The harpsichord part of the songs was contrapuntal. It was not merely the filling up of the harmony, but improvisation . . . of an interesting florid contrapuntal part." One Victorian mannerism Davis retained: delaying the dominant-and-tonic cadence of a recitative until the voice has closed, instead of letting it clash in as the vocal phrase reaches its end. But the fact that Handel expected these cadences to be played more or less as he wrote them is a fairly recent assertion of scholarship. Respected editions of *Messiah*—J. M. Coopersmith's, Alfred Mann's, Watkins Shaw's, John Tobin's—all imply, by the placing of the notes on the page, the familiar timing of, for example, "a highway for our God . . . *plink-plonk*" rather than the crisp close that we are now told was Handel's intention. The bold authentic cadences would suit Davis's bold approach very well, and I imagine he will need little persuasion to adopt them.

At that Foundling Hospital performance, Handel had a choir of five or six trebles and thirteen lower voices. Davis had the Tanglewood Festival Chorus, sixty-five strong, with female sopranos and altos. Good boy sopranos are hard to come by today (St. Thomas, on Fifth Avenue, has them); women sopranos as accomplished as those of the Tanglewood Festival Chorus are a very acceptable substitute. Their tone was fresh, light, and even. Following the first violins, they touched an easy high C (which boys find hard to compass) toward the end of "He trusted in God." The note is unwritten but makes better musical sense than the repeated G's of the autograph: Handel kept the compass down only by docking the fugue subject of its true climax. The choir was excellent in all its departments—balanced; fluent and distinct but not mannered in runs; buoyant in rhythms; athletic, incisive in entries; clear in diction. It was natural, unexaggerated in all it did.

In 1754, Handel divided the songs among five soloists, and in 1758 among six. Davis used four. Susan Davenny Wyner, the soprano, seemed nervous. Her timbre was limpid, but her phrasing and intonation were often insecure. Florence Quivar, the alto, was arrestingly unpredictable. I suppose her sudden register switches and the sudden changes of style, even in mid-phrase, should be deplored, but I found them oddly attractive—especially by contrast with the blandness of so many *Messiah* contraltos. When Miss Quivar cried "Arise, shine," the imperatives rang out so incisively that people sat up in astonishment. There was a touch of blandness about Neil Rosenshein, the tenor. He was lyrical; his voice and his phrasing were cultivated; but he seemed so evidently on his best behavior. John Shirley-Quirk, veteran of many *Messiahs*, brought unflagging ardor, nobility, and energy to the bass songs.

In his *Handel's Dramatic Oratorios and Masques*, Winton Dean quotes with approval some sentences from Robert Manson Myers's *Handel's Messiah, a Touchstone of Taste:*

When composing the Hallelujah Chorus he "did think" he "did see" God seated on His throne, just as when he composed *Semele* he probably imagined he saw Jupiter on his throne, and the fact only proves his intense imaginative powers and his relative freedom from the genuinely devotional mood. . . . As an operatic composer Handel sought never to reveal his own personality, but always to depict some object or to render some dramatic scene. Never did he cling with greater resolution to this laudable intention than in *Messiah*. Never therefore did he compose a work more fundamentally secular in spirit.

Devout people were shocked when *Messiah* was first put on at Covent Garden, in 1743. The Victorians made the work respectable by performing it in a piously devout—and un-Handelian—manner. There may have been some in Carnegie Hall who were shocked by Davis's secular, undevout—and thoroughly Handelian—approach. Much of the work danced along, not skittishly, not irreverently, but with that uninhibited and quite unmystical joy which is never long absent from Handel's music: even amid the Passion choruses of Part II—which were sung with tender, humane feeling—those irresistibly high-spirited sheep come capering on, plainly delighted to have gone astray. In this performance which had so much variety of mood, the grandeur and glory of the big choruses shone more brightly than ever. Ten years ago, Davis recorded a *Messiah* for Philips, in much the same spirit. Nine years ago, Charles Mackerras made a recording for Angel, also with modern instruments but with a tangier reed-string balance and greater boldness in melodic adornment. I would not be without either set; nor would I have missed assisting, in the flesh, at this *Messiah* in Carnegie Hall, and sharing in happiness that seemed to flow from the platform and fill the hall.

December 27, 1976

C MAJOR AT THE CLOSE

The sight of Leonard Bernstein dancing and prancing all over the podium, leaping into the air, leaning over like a lover to shape every last nuance of a cello solo, makes it hard to take him seriously as a conductor. If one averts one's eyes, one hears something less extraordinary than the performance he mimes. I have not seen him at work in a recording studio and wonder whether he puts on a similar show there— and whether the Philharmonic players need such carryings-on to induce them to play with passion. Last month, with the Philharmonic, Bernstein conducted Shostakovich's Fourteenth Symphony, for soprano, bass, nineteen strings, and percussion, and Saint-Saëns's Third Symphony,

"for orchestra with organ," in a series of five concerts. The Shostakovich, the night I attended, was prefaced by a little homily. Bernstein told
his audience that, since the symphony is dedicated to Benjamin Britten
(who conducted its Western première), the Philharmonic performance
could be regarded as a joint memorial to the two composers. Quite correctly, he pointed out—as the program note did not—that, while death
is the common subject of the eleven poems (by Lorca, Apollinaire,
W. K. Küchelbecker, and Rilke) making up the text of the symphony, in
sum they amount to a barely concealed denunciation of Soviet tyranny.
(It is indeed surprising that the symphony was played openly in Leningrad
and Moscow, and has twice been recorded in Russia.) But Bernstein
also said that Shostakovich's piece was an exception amid "the feeble
works of his declining years"—thus writing off the Fifteenth Symphony,
the Thirteenth, Fourteenth, and Fifteenth String Quartets, and the final
Sonata for Viola and Piano, all of them later than the Fourteenth
Symphony and none of them feeble—and he warned us to follow the
text sheet provided if we were not to find the work "a sleepy-making fifty
minutes of droning in Russian." That suggests something less than confidence in the purely musical merits of Shostakovich's score. Bernstein
was right, however, to stress the importance of the words, even if his
way of putting it was unfortunate. Comprehension of the text is as
necessary as in the Thirteenth Symphony, a setting of Yevtushenko
poems beginning with "Babi Yar" and ending with "Careers" and its
declaration that "Genius will conquer, regardless of the charges brought
against it." (After three performances in Russia, the Thirteenth *was*
banned for some years.)

Both Britten's music and Shostakovich's often owed a debt to Mahler,
and in their later works the composers drew closer to one another—
Britten in the Cello Symphony and Cello Sonata, Shostakovich in his
last two symphonies. Shostakovich's choice of an "anthology" text
(comparable to Britten's in the *Serenade*, the *Spring Symphony*, and the
Nocturne), his free use of twelve-note melodies within a diatonic context, and the intent, delicate working of small motifs suggest a parallel;
in the Fourteenth Symphony some of the string writing clearly recalls
that of Britten's early *Variations on a Theme of Frank Bridge*. The
opening of the symphony—a slow-moving, long-breathed unaccompanied
violin line with rhythmic and melodic patterns repeated, but not quite
exactly, in the gentle sequences of its progress—is very characteristic of
the composer. Like so many Shostakovich openings, this one seems to
be a deep, somber thought made manifest in sound. Motifs from it
recur throughout the work, and the theme itself returns to start the tenth
song, "The Poet's Death." The sixth and seventh measures present, in
transposition, the four-note motto (D–E-flat–C–B) that forms the
composer's "monogram." (Д.Ш. is "D.Sch." in German transliteration;

and in German musical spelling S is Es, or our E-flat, and H is our B.)
Four variations on the motif continue the line, and the second violins
steal in with another version, in long notes. (Moreover, since B in German musical spelling is our note B-flat, the recurrent B-flats of the
opening may possibly have been suggested by the dedicatee's initials.)
Spotting the composer's initials is not merely a trivial exercise. The chromatic four-note motif carries an emotional charge, and in several earlier
works Shostakovich invested it with musical significance. But it is only a
small detail in a work whose large "message" can hardly be missed. In
late Shostakovich there is little comfort. At official congresses he spoke
of music as a "weapon" in the ideological struggle; in his last three
symphonies that weapon was turned against the rulers of his country.
("A hundred times more wicked than Barabbas . . . rotten cancer . . .
mad butcher" runs the invective in one of the Fourteenth Symphony's
songs.) In the Thirteenth there are some notes of hope; in the Fourteenth and Fifteenth, disillusion, bitterness, and ultimately despair. But
not that alone. As in Mahler's most disquieting movements, one can find
charm—even when that charm turns to horror. ("On the Alert," in the
Fourteenth Symphony, is a companion piece to Mahler's "Der Tamboursg'sell.") And heroism—the courage of a man who went on telling
the truth as he saw it.

For all Bernstein's extravagantly mimed eloquence, the Philharmonic
performance seemed to me insufficiently communicative. The soloists,
Teresa Kubiak and Isser Bushkin, sang the notes as if to display the
ability and power of their voices. The conductor was too rhetorical. The
Fourteenth Symphony is intimate chamber music, and needs to be
treated as such.

The Saint-Saëns that followed was a curious choice of work to perform in Avery Fisher Hall, a place that has no real organ, only an
electronic substitute. And it is hardly a work of such value as to justify
six performances this season (five from the Philharmonic, a sixth from
the visiting Orchestre de Paris, under Barenboim, given in Carnegie Hall
—another place that has no true pipe organ except when, as happened
for the Boston Symphony *Messiah*, a small portable instrument is
brought onto the platform). But it does deserve better than this. One
hears high claims for electronic organs, and in their own right—as they
are used, for example, by Philip Glass in his *Einstein on the Beach* and
other compositions—they can make music of merit. But for the Saint-
Saëns the Fisher Hall machine was a horror. Its low notes produced
an artificial pulsing effect quite unlike that from the pedal pipes of an
organ, and in sustained chords one could hear the sound being switched
on and off, not entering and dying away, or blending with the orchestra,
as chords from a real organ do. The American Guild of Organists is
fighting a battle against the acceptance of electric imitations; in me they

have an ally. Next time Saint-Saëns's Third Symphony, Elgar's *Enigma Variations* or *Cockaigne*, or Strauss's *Also sprach Zarathustra* is played here, let it be in Tully Hall, which has a handsome organ.

Shostakovich's last composition, the Sonata for viola and piano, Opus 147, had its first performance in Leningrad two months after the composer's death, in 1975; its Western première at the 1976 Aldeburgh Festival; and its New York première in December at a concert of the Chamber Music Society of Lincoln Center. It lasts about half an hour. It is dedicated to Fyodor Druzhinin, the violist of the Beethoven Quartet, long associated with Shostakovich's music. (Four of his quartets are dedicated to members of the ensemble.) Until about 1960, Shostakovich made public political statements in his symphonies and expressed private doubts in his chamber music (although there are exceptions—the String Quartet No. 8, composed after a visit to ruined Dresden, is an individual's protest against a public event). The Eleventh Symphony ("The Year 1905") and the Twelfth ("The Year 1917") celebrate triumphs of Revolution; then the Thirteenth, the Yevtushenko cycle, deals with subsequent miseries, as do its successors. Meanwhile, the String Quartet No. 13 enshrines private anguish, and No. 14 a more serene acceptance of mortality. If No. 15, whose first movement is subtitled "Elegy," and fifth "Funeral March," is Shostakovich's farewell to the world, the final Viola Sonata is a coda in which his musical mind still spins beautiful thoughts. Its contents, it seems to me, can be discussed only in musical terms: the sound of fourths and fifths; the effect of repeating a motif with one note altered, or of repeating it note for note with rhythmic displacements, so that the stress falls differently; the dissonances set up when, while everything else remains the same, a bass note shifts from D-flat to C. Like Quartet No. 15, the sonata has a lean, exposed texture. Much of it is in two parts, and very little of it in more than three. This is musical discourse pared down to the essential notes; some pages of the score resemble those schematic representations of, say, a Beethoven sonata reduced to its structural elements. There is Beethoven in the last of the three movements—reflections on the arpeggiated figuration, on the repeated-note theme, and on the harmonic movement of the Moonlight Sonata—and Beethoven elsewhere, I think, in the nature of the thematic metamorphoses. The central movement, an allegretto, set between a moderato and an adagio, recalls the open fourths and fifths of the scherzo in Shostakovich's Fifteenth Symphony, but while there the intervals created a harmonic prison against which solo strains beat their wings in vain, here they suggest contemplation of the unaltering, basic acoustical facts on which all Western music has been built.

It is difficult to maintain tension in meditative music so linear and spare. Walter Trampler, viola, and Richard Goode, piano, did so with complete success, in a thoughtful and uncommonly moving performance. Like Saint-Saëns's Third Symphony, the sonata closes in C major. But while the symphony ends with an affirmative blare, long sustained, Shostakovich's final C major seems more like a gentle sigh, neither sad nor ironic, but welcoming of peace.

January 3, 1977

The Chamber Music Society performance of Shostakovich's Viola Sonata, on December 17, 1976, was billed in good faith as the American première. *In fact, the work was already in print, and on November 12 it had been played, by Herbert Levinson and George Robert, in the Keller Hall concert series of the University of New Mexico, Albuquerque. Although billed only as a "first performance in Albuquerque," this seems to have been the American première of the sonata. The piece has been recorded by Fyodor Druzhinin, its dedicatee and Mikhail Muntyan on (British) Angel/Melodiya HQS 1369, where it is coupled with Shostakovich's Violin Sonata, Opus 134, recorded at a live 1969 performance by David Oistrakh and Sviatoslav Richter. Another, less desirable recording of the Viola Sonata, by Milan Telechý and Lýdia Mailingová, on Rediffusion Aurora, spreads the work across both sides.*

VISIONS BEATIFIC

The Sacred Music Society of America, inaugurated last season by a performance of Massenet's *Marie-Magdeleine*, this season gave a concert performance, in Avery Fisher Hall, of Licinio Refice's *Cecilia*. The work was first performed at the Rome Opera in 1934; this was its North American première. *Cecilia,* described by its composer as an "azione sacra," is a music drama about a saint. In Act I, Cecilia, a secret Christian, is married by ancient Roman rites to Valerian but resists her husband's embraces; when he pursues her ardently, "an angel of God appears, flaming in light, on the pagan altar, defending Cecilia's purity. . . . A silvery cloud surrounds the angel, the altar, and Cecilia." In Act II, Cecilia takes Valerian to a Christian gathering in the catacombs; St. Paul appears, in a blinding vision, and Valerian is converted. At curtain-fall, an angel is seen, as in the Domenichino painting, holding garlands of lilies and roses above Cecilia and Valerian while they kneel at the altar. In Act III, Cecilia is condemned to death by being thrust into an overheated hypocaust. From the heart of the furnace her song pours out, and from above a shower of dewy rose petals pours down upon her, keeping her from harm. A soldier stabs her, and she falls to the ground "in the position in which Stefano Maderno sculpted her." The scene dissolves into a vision of the Saint "surrounded by the heavenly host, in a garden of blazing golden light."

It is an opera of miracles, and it could look marvelous on the stage. Emidio Mucci's libretto carefully describes the richly picturesque settings, filled with historical detail lovingly observed. (An edition of it with English translation was specially printed for this performance and distributed gratis.) The imagery of his verse is D'Annunzian: flowers fill the first act, blazes of mystic light the second, and sweet heavenly songs the third. The effect is perfumed and luxurious, as of a pious counterpart to Wilde's *Salomé*. There is some Strauss in Refice's score—Strauss softened and sweetened as he was by Puccini, Cilea, and Zandonai. The music, although cloying and unmemorable, is effective while it lasts. Refice uses Gregorian chant to underpin his rich textures, but the love strains his heroine sings to God differ little in idiom from the love strains Cilea's and Zandonai's sopranos sing to their tenors. Similar things, of course, could be said of much eighteenth- and nineteenth-century sacred music. The trio from Verdi's *Attila* was easily converted (by William Jones, organist of St. Alban's, Blackburn) into a three-voice anthem, "O sacrum convivium."

The heroine of the Sacred Music Society performance was Renata Scotto. When asked if she had listened to Claudia Muzio's recordings of two numbers from *Cecilia*, Miss Scotto replied, "No, I have not. I make it a practice never to listen to recordings of roles which I am singing. The role must be completely my own. . . . I want to give the work everything that I have of my deep self." Since the opera was composed for Muzio, and the recordings are conducted by Refice himself, that is rather like, say, proudly refusing the chance of a coaching session from Jenny Lind and Verdi while learning the role of Amalia in *I masnadieri*. (Do singers who take this curious stand believe themselves to be incapable of being taught anything by others, or are they so insecure that they fear to have their own personalities swamped?) In any event, Miss Scotto sang the role with tenderness, warmth, and passion, and although at climaxes her tone became hard and squealy as she forced more volume into her high notes than they could comfortably bear, her soft and mezzo-forte phrases were very beautiful. In smaller roles, the contralto Gwynn Cornell and the Greek bass Dimitri Kavrakos made favorable impressions. Harry Theyard was Valerian, and Clamma Dale the Voice from Heaven. Angelo Campori conducted an able pickup orchestra with enthusiasm but without subtlety; "louder, louder" seemed to be the sense of his highly animated podium demeanor.

479

The Opera Society of Washington began its 1976–77 season with a new production of *Attila*, a work that, while not the most neglected of Verdi's operas—there has been a sprinkling of productions round the world since the first postwar staging, in Florence in 1962—has proved just about the hardest to carry off successfully. Operas of his once dismissed as failures—*Alzira, Il corsaro, Stiffelio*—have been brought back to life on the stage and on disc to greater acclaim than has *Attila*, which pursued a triumphant career for some decades after its première in 1846. What is wrong with the piece? The usual answer is the libretto, which Verdi himself admired—"Oh what a fine subject! And the critics can say what they wish, but I shall say: Oh, what a fine, musicable libretto!" Its source was the five-act romantic tragedy *Attila, König der Hunnen*, by the playwright-preacher Zacharias Werner, whom Beethoven admired. (He crops up several times in the Beethoven conversation books; Beethoven thought of using his *Wanda* and possibly his *Attila* as opera subjects.) Werner's play mingles Nordic and Teutonic myth (Attila is Etzel in the *Nibelungenlied*, Atli in the *Volsunga Saga*), Italian history, and cloudy notions of Redemption through Love. The apparatus is Wagnerian. Offstage, the Norns spin their fateful rope. Wotan has sent Attila to be the scourge of a degenerate Europe. When thousands of Attila's men are killed in battle, he remarks, "They drink now in Valhalla with their fathers, Refresh themselves at Wotan's cheerful feast." The heroine is derived from the Norse Gudrun, who, brooding on her beloved Sigurd's murder, stabs her husband Atli and then herself. Two years before Wagner produced his first sketch for *The Ring*, Verdi had brushed against some of the same material. But he brought it into the clear Italian light. In his opera, the mythology is reduced to frequent invocations of Wotan and Valhalla by Attila and his followers, and, apart from a vision of two airborne saints, there are no mystical overtones in his tale. His Attila is a ruthless but greathearted giant ambushed and killed by three treacherous Italians. The soprano, Odabella, takes Judith, the least endearing of Old Testament heroines, as her exemplar. The tenor, Foresto, tries to poison his host at a peace banquet. The baritone, the Roman general Ezio, whose cry of "You may have the universe, if Italy remains to me!" roused Risorgimento enthusiasm, proposes in those lines to betray his emperor to the Hun. Attila, the bass, emerges in barbaric splendor, cruel yet magnificent, incapable of meanness or betrayal. At the end, instead of feeling that devoted Italian patriots have triumphed, we watch a lion netted by pygmies. That an ostensible villain should turn out to be the hero is not necessarily a dramatic flaw: Milton's Satan, Borodin's Khan Konchak (in *Prince Igor*), and perhaps Mussorgsky's Boris Godunov afford proof to the contrary.

480

It does matter that Odabella's and Foresto's musical characters—Verdi sets them singing in the tones of romantic and patriotic heroes—should be hopelessly at odds with their odious and dishonorable behavior.

The verses of the libretto are by Temistocle Solera and—in the final trio and quartet—Francesco Maria Piave, but the poets worked closely to Verdi's instructions: the responsibility for the sequence of numbers and for the dramatic action is his. Before any details had been settled, Verdi had been drawn to Werner's play partly by the personalities of the inflexible warrior, of the heroine nursing revenge in her heart, and of the ambitious general (Foresto was an addition to Werner's dramatis personae; an opera needs a tenor), but chiefly by the thought of two very effective scenes that he longed to compose: curtain-rise on the smoking ruins of Aquileia, with cowed populace and strutting conquerors; and the solemn appearance of Pope Leo the Great on the Aventine, checking the barbarian advance at the very gates of Rome, while above him in the sky gigantic figures of St. Peter and St. Paul appear, with flaming swords, to bring the Scourge of God to his knees. (Raphael's Vatican fresco was at the back of Verdi's mind; toward the time of the première he sent to Rome for details of the costumes.) Later, he added another striking scene: a storm in the Adriatic lagoon; hermits emerging from wooden huts to pray; refugees from Aquileia arriving over the waters and founding the city of Venice. The desire for stage pageantry of an arresting, unconventional kind is often expressed in Verdi's letters. (The coronation and skating scenes of the Scribe-Meyerbeer *Prophète* were models that he more than once held up to his librettists; the camp scenes of *La forza del destino* and the auto-da-fé ceremonies of *Don Carlos* were added to those works at his request; and the lagoon scene of *Attila* recalls the celebrated gathering of the cantons in Act II of Rossini's *Guillaume Tell*.) It may be that what *Attila* needs first of all is a more bravely picturesque and colorful kind of production than is fashionable today. James de Blasis's staging in Washington, like a 1963 Sadler's Wells staging, played in near-perpetual darkness. Spotlights traipsed after the principals, and there seemed to be not quite enough of them to go around: in the fuller ensembles, some of the soloists were lit and others not. The general effect was of murk and gloom—enough to destroy a stronger work than *Attila*, and particularly ill-suited to an opera that depends so largely on bold color contrasts and scenic splendor. Robert E. Darling's décor looked striking enough when it could be seen.

But staging cannot solve all the problems. Even if the Aquileia, Venice, and Aventine scenes come off superbly, they only get one through the prologue and the first of the three acts. Moreover, by then the best solo numbers—Foresto's cavatina, Odabella's romanza, and

Attila's dream—have already been sung. The finale to Act II is strongly shaped, but of trite materials. Act III begins with a conventional tenor romanza. Verdi twice replaced it before the year was out, composing arias tailored to the individual gifts of Nicholas Ivanov (the score, in private hands, is unpublished) and of Napoleone Moriani (a sentimental but beautiful piece). The rest of the act, a duet that becomes a trio and leads to a final quartet, is good music but poor drama, and inadequate to close an opera laid out on so public a scale. Solera had intended a choral close, a solemn hymn, as at the end of *I lombardi*. Verdi wanted to try something more unusual, but it was not until the revised *Forza* that he learned how to end a grand opera—as opposed to a personal drama—with only the soloists on the stage. Solera remarked fairly that the new dénouement made nonsense of the characters as he had conceived them.

Reluctantly, I echo Julian Budden's summing up in *The Operas of Verdi*: Despite the "fitful gleams of a *Nabucco*-like solemnity" and the "moments of tenderness and beauty," the opera is "blunt in style, daubed in thick garish colors; full of theatrical effects with no depth to them and containing more than its fair share of brash cabalettas." Yet I still hope to encounter, one day, a performance that will make me change my mind. The singing in Washington was but moderately effective. Marisa Galvany was the Odabella. Usually, she is exciting on the stage, but on this occasion she seemed to be under a cloud, vocally and dramatically. As Foresto, Harry Theyard sounded raw and stringy. Antonio Salvadori made his American début, as Ezio, revealing a full, burly baritone, bluntly used. Justino Díaz, in the title role, lacked the necessary weight and grandeur. Anton Guadagno conducted in routine fashion. Foresto's and Attila's brash cabalettas were not improved by being reduced to a single verse each. *Attila* is already a short opera (a hundred and two and a half minutes in the uncut Philips recording); cuts can make what, if brash, is vigorously so seem merely perfunctory.

January 10, 1977

THE MEMORY OF BYRON

Virgil Thomson was eighty last November. As one of the birthday tributes of the season, WNYC broadcast last month a recording of Thomson's third opera, *Lord Byron*, which was first performed at the Juilliard School in April 1972 (a climax to the composer's seventy-fifth-birthday celebrations) and has not been performed since. The recording, made at one of the three Juilliard performances, was of poor quality— dry and hard in timbre, cramped, narrow in range—yet clear enough, all the same, to provide a welcome rehearing of an opera that I felt was generally underrated at the time of its première. *Lord Byron* must inevitably disappoint anyone expecting a redly romantic, heart-on-sleeve, conventionally "Byronic" opera; it has nothing in common with Berlioz's *Le Corsaire* or *Harold en Italie*, Verdi's *Il corsaro* or *I due Foscari*, Schumann's or Tchaikovsky's *Manfred*, or any of the other numerous nineteenth-century compositions that Byron's poetry inspired. Thomson and his librettist, Jack Larson, have not dramatized the poet as the poet dramatized himself. Their opera, an elegant and cultivated piece, affords pleasures kin to those of witty, lively, precise, shapely conversation on an interesting subject. Thomas Hardy's "A Refusal" could have been set as an epigraph to the piece:

Said the grave Dean of Westminster:
Mine is the best minster
Seen in Great Britain,
As many have written:
So therefore I cannot
Rule here if I ban not
Such liberty-taking
As movements for making
Its greyness environ
The memory of Byron,
Which some are demanding. . . .
And passed is my patience
That such a creed-scorner
(Not mentioning horner)
Should claim Poets' Corner.

Dean Ireland's refusal to allow Byron an Abbey burial provides the framework for the opera. Instead of an overture, there is an elegiac chorus sung by the people of London, mourning the poet-hero whose body has just been returned from Greece; then, in Poets' Corner, the shades of Spenser, Milton, Dryden, Thomson, Johnson, and Gray prepare to welcome their colleague. But more than Byron's body has come to London: also the Thorwaldsen statue of him; his last attachment, Teresa Guiccioli; and, more embarrassing still, his memoirs. In life, a council of six gathered in the office of John Murray, the publisher, to decide what to do with the memoirs, and the fireplace in which they were burned is still to be seen. (The present John Murray regrets that his great-great-great-grandfather did not first take a secret copy.) In the opera, John Hobhouse calls a similar conference in Poets' Corner:

Tom Moore, Murray, Lady Byron, and Byron's sister Augusta Leigh join him to discuss what must be done, and the texture builds skillfully from duet to quintet. The Thorwaldsen statue, crated, is wheeled in by sailors, accompanied by the Countess Guiccioli, her brother Count Gamba, and an eager crowd. When the statue is revealed, the people fall silent—and the shade of Byron strolls on to sing a mocking apostrophe to London and its society.

That forms Act I. In Acts II and III, the discussion continues, before and after five "memory scenes." The first three are social gatherings: at Lady Melbourne's, Byron meets Annabella Milbanke; at a Waterloo victory ball, he proposes to her; in a divided scene, he spends the wedding eve drinking with his cronies and Miss Milbanke spends it with Augusta and Lady Melbourne. The next scene contains the only dramatic confrontation of the opera: Lady Byron surprises her husband and his sister embracing. The final "memory scene" is a dance divertissement that whisks through the last eight years of Byron's life. Back in the Abbey, the memoirs are thrust, unread, into a brazier—Moore, as he did in Murray's office, demurring at but not preventing their destruction. The Dean catches the company at the task, and declares that a man whose life is unfit to print can never be honored in his precincts; the statue (it's now in the library of Trinity College, Cambridge) is wheeled out. In the darkling Abbey, the semichorus of poets grieve—but the shade of Shelley leads on the shade of Byron, and as the curtain falls to a C-major fortissimo the poets welcome Byron to their midst. (In the last strophe of Hardy's poem, the grave Dean says:

> 'Twill next be expected
> That I get erected
> To Shelley a tablet
> In some niche or gablet.

In fact, a tablet shared by Shelley and Keats was added to Poets' Corner in 1952; one to Byron followed in 1969.)

Clearly, this is not a work of fiery romanticism. Thomson and Larson play it cool. The piece is a series of urbane, intelligent comments—none of them particularly surprising or searching—on Byron's character and reputation. There is none of the identification with artistic genius and its struggles which marks Pfitzner's *Palestrina*, Hindemith's *Mathis der Maler*, or even Henze's *Elegy for Young Lovers*. There is no passion in the piece. It is not that kind of opera. Most of the text is polished conversation, not emotional declaration. Byron's own verses drift in and out of the libretto, but Larson has used mainly playful lines—jingles from letters to friends:

My boat is on the shore,
    And my bark is on the sea;
    But, before I go, Tom Moore,
    Here's a double health to thee!

And a few things more bitter, like the quatrain to Lady Byron that accompanied the deed of separation:

A year ago you swore, fond she!
    "To love, to honour," and so forth.
    Such was the vow you pledged to me.
    And here's exactly what 'tis worth.

"She walks in beauty" is adapted and paraphrased as a duet for Byron and Augusta. Annabella, declaring that "the soul is worth saving that writes of love and death so nobly," begins to quote one of the Thyrza elegies, and Byron brings her down to earth brutally with "Fool! . . . Those lines were to a boy." (Larson then has him identify the boy as his page Rushton, rather than the chorister Edleston.) Lady Byron's response represents Larson's worst lapse from literary discretion: "Oh God!" she sings. "You *are* mad, bad, and dangerous to know."

Thomson's score limns sentiments with sure, easy strokes and does not aim to stir emotion in the listeners. The music is distinguished, above all, by the peculiar justness of word setting found also in *Four Saints in Three Acts* and *The Mother of Us All*, his earlier operas. Like Purcell and Britten, Thomson has the gift to declaim English lines in melodies that not merely are fitting in rhythm and pitch inflections but make a music in which words and musical contour seem indissolubly joined. Yet *Lord Byron* is not just the mixture as before: the rhythmic interplay between the delicately paced, free-flowing conversation and regular musical meters is more intricate and even subtler than in those earlier works. Many of the other devices are familiar—the clear, spare orchestration in unmixed colors, the citation of well-known ditties, the fondness for Scotch-snap cadences. No matter: by new combination, known materials make a new whole, and *Lord Byron* is a new combination of Thomson's previous operatic manners with robust elements found in his choral and orchestral music. The harmonies are much of the time less limpidly diatonic than in *Four Saints* and *Mother*: a little tertonal canon on "O, du lieber Augustin" is a piquant microcosm of harmonic effects used elsewhere. Act II closes with another canon, on "Auld lang syne," accompanied by "O, du lieber Augustin." Tom Moore, coming before the curtain to cover a scene change, sings the Irish melody to which he in real life added the text "Believe me if all those endearing young charms," but not to those words, and the flowing 6/8 of the eighteenth-century

485

tune is provided with a harp accompaniment in 3/4. The simple device, while teasing and pleasing the ear, gives cunning expression to Moore's anxiety about the disposal of the memoirs. His words are confident ("What those thousands would give to read of his life"); the harmony is a stable I-IV-V-I over a ground bass; and in the second verse a warm counter-subject from solo cello flows out as if from Moore's generous, affectionate spirit. But the 3/4 cross-accents add a dash of uncertainty and uneasiness. What might have been too bland and sweet an episode makes a dramatic point.

Thomson has the gift to be simple; his notes come down where they ought to be, in the place just right. But his simplicity is that of a master, not a naïf. The music is not artless but careful, refined and purified by a process that has not destroyed its zest. *Lord Byron*, while decorous and controlled, is also lively; Thomson's evident joy in setting down a witty musical idea as neatly as possible proves infectious. The opera may lack the fresh, free lyric inspiration of *The Mother of Us All*, his masterpiece, and it is certainly a less moving work. It is hard to perform, for two reasons: voices are kept cruelly long in their upper ranges; and the acting has to be very polished. A plain, realistic manner is not enough. (The Juilliard cast managed the notes with accomplishment, the style less securely.) But it does not deserve neglect.

Any company wishing to mount it, however, must look beyond the vocal score that was published, by Southern, in 1975. As done at the Juilliard, *Lord Byron* was a fairly long opera. For publication, the composer cut it. Overinfluenced, perhaps, by the largely unfriendly reception of his piece, he cut it far too severely, snipping and snicking on page after page, removing much that ought to remain; and in the process he stunted his work. Reading the score, I thought this was probably so; after rehearing the full Juilliard performance, I am sure of it. The only cut that seems justified is the large, clean one of the whole danced scene. To the opera that scene was an afterthought, and its music does not really belong, being an orchestrated version of Thomson's Second String Quartet, of 1932. In orchestral dress, the music has now been published as his Third Symphony. The New York première was given in Carnegie Hall by the American Symphony Orchestra on St. Stephen's Day.

January 17, 1977

The Mother of Us All *was performed by the Santa Fe Opera in summer 1976, and the production was recorded by New World Records (NW 288–9, distributed by Peters International).*

ALL FOR OUR DELIGHT

On the lyric stage, the story of Jason and Medea has usually been treated seriously (notably by Cherubini and by Simon Mayr), not merrily, but the earliest opera on the subject, Francesco Cavalli's *Giasone*, is a romantic comedy. It had its première in Venice in 1649. Last summer, the Clarion Opera Group of New York presented some performances in Castelfranco (northwest of Venice) and Crema (northwest of Cremona), and it followed them this month with a concert performance—the American première of the piece—in Alice Tully Hall. *Giasone*, Cavalli's big hit, was widely produced in the seventeenth century. Giacinto Andrea Cicognini, its librettist, was an established comic dramatist. He prefaced his text with a little note to readers and spectators explaining that he had written *Giasone* for fun, and that his true intent was all for our delight: if it succeeded, well and good; if not, he would have wasted several days' work, and we but a few hours of our time. The Clarion performance contained a little over three hours of music, and they were hours well spent.

On the way to Colchis and the Golden Fleece, the Argo put in at Lemnos, that island with an all-female population (since the women had recently killed all the men on the place). The Argonauts met with a warm reception. Jason sired twins by Queen Hypsipyle, and if Hercules had not reminded the crew of their quest they might never have sailed on. On arriving at Colchis, Jason fell in love again and—in this operatic version—put off his attempt at the Fleece for a year and spent most of his nights with an unknown beauty. She, too, bore him twins. All that happens before curtain-rise. After an allegorical prologue—an entertaining exchange between Helios, Medea's grandfather, and Amor —the opera begins with a dialogue between Hercules and Bessus, one of Jason's men, outside Medea's palace. They discuss their chief's philandery in terms that recall the first scene of Monteverdi's *Poppea* (1642) and anticipate the first scene of *Don Giovanni*. Medea reveals that she herself was the beauty Jason held in his arms. With the aid of her magic spells, Jason wins the Fleece at last, and the pair set sail with the prize. But a storm drives them to the shore where Hypsipyle has found refuge. "How happy could I be with either, Were t'other dear charmer away!" is Jason's burden in Act II. In Act III, he decides to get rid of Hypsipyle, but the impetuous Medea walks into the ambush he has prepared and is tossed into the sea. She is rescued, however, by Aegeus, King of Athens, who has been following her like a faithful spaniel. By this deed, Aegeus wins Medea's heart. By singing a poignant lament, Hypsipyle, who has learned of her narrow escape, regains Jason's. And all ends happily.

There is a large cast of subaltern characters. (It could have been larger still, since not only Hercules, who joined the expedition after capturing the Erymanthian Boar, but also Castor and Pollux, and Orpheus—how readily *he* might prompt a composer to a cue for song —were on the muster roll of the Argo.) Orestes turns up, presumably— forget chronology!—on his way to Iphigenia in Tauris. (Thoas, King of Tauris, was Hypsipyle's father.) Here Orestes plays the role of Hypsi- pyle's babysitter, and amusingly recounts his vain attempts to keep her twins quiet with songs and stories. For the rest, Cicognini contents him- self with an elderly nurse, a young lady-in-waiting, soldiers, sailors, and the cowardly, comic, stuttering servant Demus, a new incarnation of Irus in Monteverdi's *Il ritorno d'Ulisse* (1641). The attendant gang sing, often bawdily, of loves new, old, faded, or fresh, in seventeenth- century Venetian manners familiar now that Monteverdi and Cavalli have become current repertory.

Cavalli composed with a light hand. The libretto trips out in a run of lively recitative, passing into measured arioso and then, at emo- tional climaxes, into full-throated song. He had found a ready formula— but he also had something like genius. In melodic turns of phrase and in sudden twists of harmony he reveals the gift of the born opera com- poser, able through his music to move his listeners to tears or to laughter. *Giasone* contains two great numbers. The first is Medea's in- cantation: tracing triads of E minor and C major, in powerful outlines that seem to call for the dramatic declamation of a Callas, the sorceress summons infernal powers to aid her lover in his rape of the Fleece. The other is Hypsipyle's lament: recitative leads into an aria accompanied by full strings, which continue a measured movement when the voice breaks back into free recitative; the last section is a chromatic arioso mounting by semitones to its accusatory climax, then tumbling down into a final confession—"Jason, though thou art a murderer, I love thee." These two numbers illustrate a difference between Monteverdi's and Cavalli's dramatic manners—not only because Hypsipyle's lament in- cludes two of those plangent cadences, with a flat sixth added to the dominant chord, which form a Cavalli fingerprint at moments of high emotion (cf. the aria "Amara servitù," from "Mutio Scevola," which Raymond Leppard added to his performing edition of *Calisto*). By comparison with the great monologues for Penelope and Ulysses in *Il ritorno d'Ulisse*, the Cavalli scenes are more patently theatrical, and plainer in musical structure. The charming occasional duets for Medea and Jason and the careful patterns of balanced duets in *Ulisse* afford a similar contrast. Cavalli sets a text to striking effect; Monteverdi, in addition, creates musical forms that mirror the characters' inner emo- tions. A work by Cavalli—in this he is closer to the ideas of opera's inventors—is a play declaimed to fluent, vivid, variously paced, and very effective music. The older master enriched opera with all the devices of non-dramatic music, capturing them for the theater in the process, and set up tensions between straight-line theatrical narrative and closed musical forms that—in Mozart, Beethoven, Rossini, Wagner, Verdi, Berg, Henze—have held operagoers' attention ever since.

And since a Cavalli opera is essentially a sung play, it must be brought to life by the words. Clarion's *Giasone*, first announced in English, was in the event sung in Italian, but the loss in vivacity was minimized by the distribution of a witty English translation for the audience to follow. The houselights were left up. The singers, on a bare stage, made entrances and exits, while the accompanying players were at pit level. Royal men wore white ties, and their officers black ties. Demus wore a checked suit. A little more might have been done to suggest the action; for example, if there had been a sofa, characters would not have had to pretend to be asleep on their feet. (There are three sleep scenes in *Giasone*.) And there were enough little verbal slips ("diletto" for "delitto," some wrong genders) to suggest that the cast was not fully at home with the language or the text; only three of the company had played their roles in the Italian stage production. All the same, a good deal of the humor came across.

Cavalli does not need much conducting. He needs actors and continuo accompanists who know the lines so well that the piece flows along, sometimes at speech tempo, sometimes in metrical periods, as if of its own accord. But in this performance the conductor, Newell Jenkins, not the cast, set most of the tempi, and he laid rather a heavy hand on some of the triple-time numbers. His two harpsichordists, Kenneth Cooper and Frederick Hammond, tended to doodle away at their own overfanciful and often unrhythmical inventions when they should have been supporting the singers. Nevertheless, Mr. Jenkins and his company effectively communicated the high spirits and the romantic beauty of Cavalli's score. As Medea, Susan von Reichenbach sang with evenness and assurance, commanding a role whose range of sentiments and range of notes are wide. Susan Davenny Wyner's timbre, as Hypsipyle, was sweet, but her pitch was not always true. In the title role, John Angelo Messana's alto voice came and went in disconcerting fashion. Elaine Bonazzi, Diana Hoagland, Robert White, Douglas Perry, Raymond Murcell, Andrew Foldi, and Ronald Corrado completed the cast, and each of them had entertaining contributions to make.

Other revivals of *Giasone* in recent years have been in an unsatisfactory performing edition by Marcello Panni. For Clarion, Ellen Rosand had prepared a satisfactory and stylish performing edition. Not all of it was done—it seems that New York concert life imposes Procrustean conditions—but the cutting was skillful and sensitive. Besides the harpsichords (and their attendant cellos and double-bass), a lute and an archlute provided continuo. Mrs. Rosand suggested which instruments should play where but did not, Leppard-wise, compose elaborate parts for them. There were moments when I felt that a touch of cornett or brass was called for (although whether they were really employed in Venetian theaters is a matter of dispute); and the Tully organ, if discreetly used, could surely have added grandeur and solemnity to the incantation scene. Mrs. Rosand's score has the necessary flexibility to allow other conductors to take their own decisions about cuts and accompaniments; and, particularly if an English singing translation is provided, *Giasone* could embark on a second successful career.

What Mr. Jenkins and Clarion do for opera of the seventeenth and eighteenth centuries, Eve Queler and her Opera Orchestra of New York do for that of the nineteenth. Last week, in Carnegie Hall, they gave, if not the American première of Smetana's *Dalibor* (that occurred in Chicago's Národní Divadlo, alias Sokol Hall, in 1924), a stirring concert performance of that great opera, which has been too long neglected outside Czechoslovakia. *Dalibor* is apt to provoke intemperate, well-nigh incoherent enthusiasm. The Czech poet Jan Neruda wrote:

Heaven knows what strange enchantment there is in Smetana's music! Tears come to the eyes during the tender passages; at others, one starts from one's seat without knowing one has risen. That happened to me during the finale of the second act of *Dalibor*. . . . Genius has spread its mighty wings, and the overpowering music of the spheres sounds and throbs. When all had suddenly come to an end I was standing in my box, my body stretching forward, my eyes fixed somewhere in space, and every nerve vibrating with untold delight.

When *Dalibor* was produced by the English National Opera, earlier this season, the critic of the London *Times* declared that it ranks as far above *The Bartered Bride* as does *Don Giovanni* above *Bastien und Bastienne*. That is unfair to *The Bartered Bride* (I would substitute *Figaro* for *Bastien*, and suggest that the difference is one of kind rather than of merit), but it does show the devotion that *Dalibor* can inspire. Why is the piece not in the Met repertory? Is the Czech language an obstacle? There are at least two English translations available (though neither of them is altogether happy), and there can be no very serious objection—except on the ground of common sense—to a performance in German, since the composer worked with both Josef Wenzig's original German libretto and a Czech translation of it before him. Is that libretto a problem? It is. Smetana himself had initial misgivings about the text, which disappeared only when the music began to flow. Then he made of the piece what he wanted to write—a heroic national opera. Reading the words alone will not show why the Czechs regard Dalibor as the type of a patriotic hero, the embodiment of chivalry, fighter for freedom. The knight is motivated solely by love for his murdered friend Zdeněk (to whom most of the love music in the opera is addressed) and by his desire for vengeance. The king against whom he rebels is no tyrant but a wise and reasonable monarch. Yet in this libretto Smetana found several themes that moved him deeply: Dalibor greeting the Day of Freedom (even though it be only his own personal escape from prison); the heroic Milada venturing her life to save the man she loves; popular feelings roused against authority; and that deep love of music which every true Czech must feel. These drew from him music of such eloquence that the libretto is transfigured and its episodes take on a shining, symbolic quality. On one level, *Dalibor* is a dramatic tale of high events in fifteenth-century Prague. On another, it hymns friendship, freedom, and heroic self-sacrifice. Above all, it is an unfailing stream of lyrical music, spontaneous yet finely organized, whose inventive power places Smetana in the line of Mozart, Schubert, Weber, and the early Wagner. A handful of motifs is made to bear a great deal of repetition—but what in a lesser composer might amount to working an idea to death becomes in Smetana finding ever new inspiration and life in it. The operatic structure of *Dalibor*, with its numerous processions and long stretches of entrance music or action music, is simple, even naïve; the treatment of the musical material is masterly in its supple transformations and effortless extensions.

All the same, those processions, entrances, etc., are difficult to stage, and the English National director, John Blatchley, was moved to invent uncalled-for and ineffective extra business. A Prague production that I saw in the early sixties, directed by Václav Kašlik and designed by Josef Svoboda, had more dignity and purposiveness but did not avoid squareness. (Anyone who knows only Kašlik's and Svoboda's recent work may find it hard to believe that they once sought to subordinate their own ideas to a composer's.) Moreover, the dramatic line—like a string on Dalibor's fiddle when he is about to give the signal of his escape—snaps after his "freedom" aria, and the remaining episodes are an anticlimax. *Dalibor* is not an unflawed masterpiece. But that it is a masterpiece I have no doubt.

Stage difficulties disappear in a concert performance, and in Carnegie Hall we could sit back—or, like Neruda, strain forward—and enjoy the music. Libretto difficulties were masked by Miss Queler's decision to perform the opera in Czech. Inside each program was a Czech-English libretto, with Jindřich Elbl's rhymed English words. This was not the vintage version, prized by collectors of translation curiosities, that accompanied the first Supraphon recording (it begins by telling us that "the story of Dalibor resembles an overflowing kettle of passions, emotions, sympathies, and hatreds" and ends with the furious exclamation of the commander of the castle guards: "By golly! Surrender Dalibor!") but the revised version that accompanies the later recording. The thoughtful request "Please turn pianissimo!!" had been added to the foot of each right-hand page. Most, but not quite all, of the brief cuts that were made were indicated. (They were unexceptionable, all but one. I regretted losing most of the little duet for Milada and Beneš: "Plenty of sausage, of juicy meat, bread, butter, cheese, and plenty of beer!") The lights were dimmed a shade too low to make following easy, but in every other respect this was a model presentation of an unfamiliar opera.

Dalibor needs much the same cast as *Fidelio*. Milada and Dalibor, the heroine and hero, have roles similar to those of Leonore and Florestan. Beneš, the jailer, is another Rocco. Jitka and Vítek are a sparkier Marzelline and Jaquino. Budivoj, commander of the guard, is like a reduced Pizarro, and King Vladislav is like an enlarged Don Fernando (although his role is to imprison, not to free, the hero). At the Carnegie performance, Teresa Kubiak—a singer whom I first encountered in Cavalli, as Juno in *Calisto*—sang Milada in strong, gleaming tones. She was more telling in fiery passages than as a jailer's lad or in the tender duet in Dalibor's cell. Gabriela Benackova, a Leonore in her own right, was billed for Jitka, but she was ill. Nada Sormova, from the Prague Opera, took over. She has an intense, "channeled" Slav soprano, and in the opening scene she was unsteady, but then the voice firmed up and she became bright and pleasing. Nicolai Gedda had the title role, which proved heavy for him. Dalibor's voice must be able to flash out like a keen sword and then melt into strains suffused with tenderness. (Shortly after the war, Beno Blachut made memorable 78-r.p.m records of the principal scenes which show exactly what the part calls for; when he recorded the complete opera, about ten years later, some of the old brilliance had been lost.) Mr. Gedda's singing was effortful. Lacking the reserves of heroic power to launch ringing lines, he tended to hit each note separately. But he was secure, reliable, and suave in the lyrical episodes. Paul Plishka, Beneš, was grandly sonorous, if sometimes louder than he needed to be. Harlan Foss, Budivoj, was incisive. Allan Monk, Vladislav, sounded noble. John Carpenter, Vítek, sounded husky, but not unattractively so, in middle ranges, and cleared above into a sweet lyric tenor. There was strong chorus singing from the New York Choral Society, trained by Robert DeCormier.

Eve Queler has the ability to make an opera go, to set phrases surging and singing out so that listeners are stirred, excited, elevated. She communicates love and warmth and enjoyment—more fully than any of the conductors I have heard at the Met this season. She imposes nothing on the score: the composer's will alone is done. Her performances have the increasingly rare quality of naturalness. Everything seems to move at the right tempo. The singers are neither held back nor driven onward; she seems to breathe with their breath. There was a good orchestra. The important violin, cello, and horn solos were eloquently played by Raymond Gniewek, Jascha Silberstein, and William Hamilton.

Dalibor was first performed in 1868, the same year as *Die Meistersinger*, Boito's *Mefistofele*, and Ambroise Thomas's *Hamlet*. Its acceptance into international repertory is overdue. The English of the preface to Elbl's translation may be quaint, but what is said of *Dalibor* is true: "There is no trace of halfheartedness in its entire score; with unique strength and liveliness human qualities and sentiments are rendered captivating and sharply chiseled into true symbols and types." The passions in that overflowing kettle "are musically expressed with a marvelous assurance and compelling dramatic force by Smetana's score. There is no falsity, no search for empty effect."

January 24, 1977

CHANCE, DEATH, AND MUTABILITY

When Pierre Boulez relinquishes the Philharmonic, at the end of this season, and people try to draw up balance sheets of what he brought to New York and what he failed to bring, the second column can be headed by performances of his own music. For Boulez is above all a great composer, and in most of his later works the act of composition continues during his conducting of them. With the Philharmonic he has not done *Pli selon pli*, that towering orchestral masterpiece of our day, or *Domaines*, or the early cantata *Le Soleil des eaux*, or *Le Marteau sans maître*. In fact, at subscription—or, for that matter, at Rug and at Prospective Encounter—concerts he had conducted none of his own music, except for two "Improvisations sur Mallarmé" (movements from *Pli selon pli*), until, this month, he introduced his *Rituel* to New York. During the four years that he was chief conductor of the BBC Symphony, Boulez performances of Boulez were frequent. He explains that of the BBC he was not music director, and that BBC concerts are not sold by subscription; at the Philharmonic, of which he *is* music director, he is unwilling to impose his own music on subscription audiences. It is an understandable decision. But as a result Philharmonic audiences have been cut off from a mainstream of contemporary music, and Boulez has wasted much of his and our time on routine and worse

493

than routine executions of standard classics. Earlier this month, he conducted a deplorable performance of Beethoven's Fifth Symphony (and, before it, Toru Takemitsu's *Arc*, a work that was not worth adding to the Philharmonic repertory). A week later, with *Rituel*, he led us to the heights.

It is true that by means of phonograph records and sneak tapes of foreign performances an enthusiast can create his own Boulez performances. Yet where Boulez is concerned a recorded performance is likely to be in the nature of a snapshot of a work at just one stage of its life—better than nothing, but a poor substitute for living with, observing, being inspired by the progress of that marvelous musical mind, made manifest in individual compositions that themselves develop and grow from year to year, fold upon fold, and are so closely related one to the next that they seem to be parts of a single magnum opus in progress. Ideas from Boulez's Second Piano Sonata were reworked in his *Livre pour quatuor*, and that quartet, in turn, was reworked for string orchestra as *Livre pour cordes*. At the 1960 ISCM Festival, in Cologne, I heard him play a piano solo that was then a new addition to *Pli selon pli*, while *Pli* itself was still a work for chamber forces, not the great full-orchestra piece it is now. Four years later, that piano solo had grown into *Éclat*, for a glittery chamber ensemble, and was played by the BBC Symphony. The following year, there was a "world première" of *Éclat* in Los Angeles, in the form that excited Stravinsky's admiration (recounted in his *Themes and Episodes*: "*Éclat* is not only creative music but creative conducting as well, which is unique"). *Éclat* continued to expand, into *Éclat-Multiples*, a work now about thrice as long as the *Éclat* of 1964, and still open-ended. In rather similar fashion, Boulez's . . . *explosante / fixe* . . . began life, in 1972, as a page of musical ideas, clusters of instrumental monodies, followed by six pages of suggestions about how they might be assembled. It was one of seventeen "Canons and Epitaphs: In Memoriam Igor Stravinsky," by different composers, published in the magazine *Tempo*. That year, London heard a ten-minute version for flute, clarinet, and trumpet. Early in 1973, the Chamber Music Society of Lincoln Center presented a half-hour version, more elaborately scored, and intricately equipped with electronic spatial effects. Later that year, in Rome, members of the BBC Symphony under Boulez played a revised, longer version, and a few months after that, in London, they played one longer still.

From which it should be clear that a Boulez score as first set down contains ideas and possibilities that are then explored in performance, and that from such exploration there may result new ideas, for additional or more interesting and exciting ways of handling the original material. And that from a germ in one work another work may grow.

Such practices are common enough in musical history. Stravinsky remarked that Beethoven in his piano sonatas "discovers and sometimes maps out the different territories of several future composers, including himself." Joseph Kerman, in *The Beethoven Quartets*, noted how a cadence in Beethoven's B-flat Quartet, of 1825, "helped clarify what, in 1812 [in the allegretto of the Eighth Symphony], had been dimly and much less beautifully present in his mind." Irving Kolodin's *The Interior Beethoven* is largely concerned with such matters. But few great composers—at any rate, since the days of the composer-executants who improvised in public the thoughts that they later set down on paper —have kept pieces "open" for so long. What Handel could do with one of his recurrent melodies, making it flower afresh in new forms through work after work, Boulez does with an "idea"—a structural device, a generative procedure, a way of organizing time or timbre. There is a parallel with Balanchine, who builds one work upon another, and is likely to change "finished" work, rethink passages of it, as he revives it in the living medium of performing artists.

Rituel, commissioned by the BBC, was performed by the BBC Symphony under the composer first in April 1975 and again in November 1976. (Second-season reprises are important for the understanding of a major new work, both by the players and by the listeners; I wish the Philharmonic did more of them.) The American première was given by the Berkshire Music Center Orchestra, under Gunther Schuller, at Tanglewood in August 1975. The piece bears the subtitle "In memoriam Maderna," and commemorates Bruno Maderna, the Venetian composer and conductor, who died in 1973. Boulez has described it as music "for an imaginary ceremony" that is at once a "ceremony of remembrance" in its constant return to the same ideas and a "ceremony of extinction, ritual of disappearance and survival" in its constant alterations of those ideas, which change as memories are apt to change. Like . . . *explosante / fixe* . . . , *Rituel* is a memorial composition. The two works have other things in common, including a precedent in Stravinsky's *Symphonies of Wind Instruments*, his memorial to Debussy. Like . . . *explosante / fixe* . . . , the *Symphonies* grew from a brief obituary tribute published in a magazine. (Stravinsky's was a two-page chorale, which appeared in the Debussy number of the *Revue Musicale* in 1920). *Symphonies* is a work that Boulez is close to (he conducted it at his first concert with the BBC Symphony, and has several times conducted it with the Philharmonic), and in an introductory talk he gave about *Rituel* he explained that Stravinsky's block structure—and, in particular, the "idea" of long, complicated sounds followed by short ones—provided one stimulus for his own composition. The influence of *Symphonies* on *Rituel* is both sonic and formal, and it was not by chance that works by Debussy and Stravinsky completed the bill at the Philharmonic. . . .

explosante/fixe . . . and *Rituel* also share a fixed point of reference—the note E-flat (which in German is Es, or S, Stravinsky's initial). In the score of the former, it sits at the center of the page, with an archipelago of six monody clusters scattered around it; alternative routes for moving about the page are provided. In the latter, a unison E-flat is the note of resolution for the chordal progressions that make up seven of the work's fifteen sections. This E-flat, on the first line of the treble staff, limns a kind of "horizon" above, below, or across which the events of the work can be heard to take place.

As a creator-performer, Boulez has long been concerned with the opposed claims of chance and predetermination; with controlling instinct by intelligence; with giving order and lucidity to, while not clipping the wings of, imagination in full flight. Toward the end of his elegant but difficult Darmstadt lectures, published as *Boulez on Music Today*, he cites Baudelaire's attempted reconciliation of "lucidity" and "genius," and continues, "Imagination must stimulate intelligence and intelligence must anchor imagination." A thoroughly mastered modern technique is "an exalting mirror which the imagination forges for itself, and in which its discoveries are reflected." Once possessed of it, a musician can act freely and rationally. In the early fifties, Boulez began work on *Structures*, for two pianos, and the three pieces of Book I constitute perhaps the most rigidly controlled large composition of our day, in which the sequence of notes, their durations, their dynamics, and their modes of attack are determined by a set of rules and tables drawn up in advance. (The composer left himself free to choose as he went along in which octave to place any note.) Twelve pieces were planned; two more of them, making up Book II, appeared in 1961, and in these there are passages where the tempo and spacing of events are now left to the performers to decide. He had entered his freer period. As an epigraph to the score of *Pli selon pli* he set a line of Mallarmé: "A throw of the dice will not abolish chance." Boulez has never been an *aleator*, a dice roller. His aim of "deducing multiple consequences from a certain number of rational points of departure" suggests something closer to chess. And . . . *explosante/fixe* . . . and *Rituel* are like games played with similar pieces but according to quite different sets of rules. The composer has compared the score of . . . *explosante/fixe* . . . to a city map: the journey from A to B can be made by many different routes, and each traveler can choose his own, but along the way there are signs—one way, no entry, no right turn—that must be obeyed in the interests of an orderly, controlled ensemble flow. *Rituel* is set out on the page in a more conventional fashion. The program note for the London performance last November said that "nothing is left to choice; the work is immutable." The New York program note, on the other hand, said of seven of the fifteen sections that it was "unlikely . . . that even in a thousand successive performances these sections would ever turn out exactly the same." The second statement is correct. *Rituel*, at this stage of its life, contains both an element of choice for the conductor and an element of chance—but choice and chance alike are held within narrow limits. On *this* map, everyone's route has been carefully plotted in advance. All that can happen is that along certain stretches members of the company may break step: some may straggle behind, others forge ahead and then wait at the next corner until the rest have caught up.

Rituel lasts about twenty-seven minutes. Seven is the recurrent number in its making. Seven odd-numbered sections are the chordal progressions with the final resolution on E-flat. In the first of them, there is one chord; in the second, two; and so on to seven in the seventh. The seven even-numbered sections, alternating with the chordal passages, are played by one or more of seven instrumental "groups," widely spaced on the platform. These groups are: one oboe, two clarinets, three flutes, four violins, five woodwinds, six strings, and seven woodwinds. The music they play is either elegiac lament or flickering, rapid figuration. The chordal sections are given out by a centrally stationed brass ensemble of twice-seven players, joined, after the first section, by whichever of the groups have been playing in the preceding section. This sounds schematic, and so it is: a well-planned, firm, and easily apprehended framework, on which Boulez has composed music of eloquence and beauty. A few sentences from one of my more lyrical London colleagues, written after last November's performance, may help to dispel any notion that *Rituel* is a dryly manufactured or unemotional work:

This odd, austere orchestral essay once again conjured, at second hearing, in a way that no other Boulez work seems to conjure, a multitude of references, echoes of other music faintly perceived: a swirl of instruments heard through the pink veil of Stockhausen's *Trans*; a sudden priestly cadence of Messiaen; delicate bubbles of Italianate texture, quickly punctured. And many insinuating moments: the dying-ember tones of gongs, woodblocks and dark-muted strings; nervous riffs of scraped and shaken percussion; the sudden shriek in pain of brass and clarinet.

I have not yet mentioned the percussion. At the back of the platform, two players, provided with seven gongs and seven tam-tams, introduce each chordal section with a gong stroke and continue during it with a knell-like tolling rhythmically independent of the chords. Seven other percussionists, each of them with seven instruments (many of them exotic), are allotted one apiece to the seven groups, where they function as sub-conductors, giving the beat with tap, clack, tinkle, or tock. The element of chance enters here: Although the rhythmic notation is precise, the meters are so tricky and the players so widely separated that at each performance the lapping of the different groups is bound to vary. The main conductor gives the signal to start the even-numbered sections and then leaves it to the individual percussion-conductors to carry on. He conducts the odd-numbered, chordal sections himself. When seven of one have alternated with seven of the other, all the forces unite in a long, elegiac final section, built on motifs that have been heard before. Then, one by one, the groups fall from the ensemble. The last note is a soft unison E-flat, over the tolling of a gong.

What else? Boulez gave his introductory talk at one of the informal Pre-Philharmonic Concert Lectures, which are held in the choral room of Avery Fisher Hall on Friday mornings. (Elliott Carter, David Del Tredici, Morton Subotnick, and George Crumb are others billed to talk in the series this season, at the time their new works join the Philharmonic repertory.) There he disclosed that practical considerations went into the making of *Rituel*. A work that calls for an unusual platform disposition, he decided, should be long enough, as well as good enough, to justify the disturbance it causes: an audience grows impatient when the reseating of an orchestra lasts almost as long as the music that follows. The idea of the seven solo percussionists came to him as he considered the difficulties his seven groups would have if there was no one to give them a beat; a single conductor would need seven arms. The element of choice was introduced at a late stage, because it proved difficult to secure unanimous attack on the chords. So now the conductor is invited to "spread" them, bringing in at will each group of instruments in turn until the full sonority is built up. The percussion is an integral and beautiful part of the piece; its manifold colors and the effect of clocks ticking away at different speeds are major expressive elements. But whether the spreading of the chords is a good idea I am unsure. Since most of these chords are prefaced by a brief appoggiatura-like anacrusis, a restless rat-a-tat of successive entries disturbs the grand solemnity of the original idea. However, the composer opined that the "analytical" effect of hearing timbre laid upon timbre was interesting. And so it was.

The traditional devices of funeral music are here: bell harmonies produced (as in the *Symphonies of Wind Instruments*) by sustained and complicated chords, the knell of the gong strokes, alternations as of versicle and response. After the very soft opening chord, the first sound heard is the solo oboe in lament. (The melody is close to the main theme of . . . *explosante / fixe* . . .) Gradually, the sections grow longer, and the textures denser, until a climax is reached. Then the long coda begins—solemn utterances broken by pauses during which the percussions, representing the varied ticks of time, become prominent. On all levels, *Rituel* seems to me a major work. It relates to earlier musical experience (Stravinsky; Messiaen; possibly the slow pageant of Harrison

Birtwistle's *The Triumph of Time*, a work that Boulez has championed; Boulez's own *Domaines* and *Éclat* as well as . . . *explosante / fixe* . . .). It is at once complicated and lucid. The scoring is beautiful. After being stirred by this grave, passionate, and precisely ordered work, no one could call Boulez unemotional.

In most musical cities, successful orchestral concerts can be devoted to the work of a single composer. In 1972, the BBC Symphony gave a concert the first half of which was Stockhausen's *Carré*, and the second half another performance of *Carré*; the Albert Hall was packed. In New York, the Coliseum, Madison Square Garden, or the Cathedral of St. John the Divine would surely be similarly packed. (The four orchestras and four choirs of *Carré* could hardly be fitted into Fisher or Carnegie Hall.) In Paris, during the annual Journées de Musique Contemporaine, days on end are devoted to going through the complete works of a single composer. Such extravagant jamborees can be somewhat indigestible, and even inartistic. But well-chosen all-Carter, all-Stockhausen, all-Tippett, and all-Boulez concerts at the Philharmonic would be welcome. Perhaps the four could be put on a special subscription series. New music, it is true, is not being neglected this season, as that list of Friday-morning lecturers indicates. (Franco Donatoni's Concertino and Britten's Cello Symphony are also on the bills.) But there is still much catching up to be done. I hope that Zubin Mehta, the Philharmonic's music director-elect, will be able to persuade Boulez, when he is no longer responsible for planning the weekly fare, to come back often, and conduct not only *Rituel* but also the works he has so far felt obliged to withhold from his Philharmonic audience.

January 31, 1977

PROPHETIC STRAIN

When Longfellow saw *Le Prophète* in Boston in 1856, he noted in his journal that "it is a grand opera, with startling, splendid passages, and an air of power all through it." And those who see it now at the Metropolitan, where it is being played for the first time since 1928, are likely to agree. The world needed a major new production of *Le Prophète*. The three other works that Meyerbeer and Scribe devised for the Paris Opera had already been revived with strong casts: *Les Huguenots* at La Scala in 1962, *Robert le Diable* in Florence in 1968, and *L'Africaine* in San

Francisco in 1972. The Met *Prophète*, which has Marilyn Horne, Renata Scotto, and James McCracken in the leading roles, completes the picture. There have been other productions of these pieces during the last twenty years, but those are the four big landmarks of the Meyerbeer revival.

Each of them showed a different approach to nineteenth-century grand opera, and *Les Huguenots* alone was staged in a style that Meyerbeer would have recognized. Nicola Benois had designed large, grand scenery of painted canvas; the queen entered Act III on a white horse; Franco Enriquez, directing, got his cast to do what the stage directions ask them to. It was all carried out on a vast scale and with the wonted Scala efficiency, if without any particular distinction. *Les Huguenots* is probably the best constructed of Meyerbeer's grand-opera tetrad, and the staging preserved the carefully plotted sequence of indoor and outdoor scenes. The score, however, was heavily cut. The show lasted about four and a half hours, of which about an hour and a half was interval.

Les Huguenots was first produced at the Opéra in 1836. *Robert le Diable* preceded it there, in 1831; four years earlier it had been announced as an opéra comique but was then remodeled for the big house as a very grand opera indeed. *Robert* is a rum work, at once picturesque, popular, and mystic—as if a *Faust* had been superimposed on a *Freischütz*, with the second act of *Giselle* and the pomp of some Spontini spectacular thrown in. The plot is lively. The opera became one of the great successes of all time and held the stage into the last decade of the century. Its imagery left a mark on *Tannhäuser* and *Parsifal*. Wagner, who conducted it in Würzburg, relates in *Mein Leben* how his initial contempt for the music yielded to fascination at its ability to elicit applause. To Italy *Robert* was first introduced as a work that had caused a great stir "through the splendor of its décors and for Meyerbeer's lovely music"—in that order. But in Florence Margherita Wallmann, who directed, had decided "to eliminate all that is purely decorative . . . to present the romantic theme in a dimension accessible to the way of life of modern man." There were stark, abstract settings by Josef Svoboda, dun costumes, and a "formalized" production. Scribe describes his convent scene with romantic relish: moonlit arcades, overgrown tombs, will-o'-the-wisps flickering toward the tombs, rusty iron lanterns starting to glow with devilish light, nuns rising at the bass's command (Taglioni led the way) and stripping off their habits to dance more freely. In Florence, the nuns popped up as if on automatic deck chairs, and were dressed in pink body stockings painted to simulate nudity. A scene that could be enchanting, if inevitably a little absurd, became both risible and ugly. Large crowds of chorus, corps de ballet, and extras had been engaged, but by the second performance, which was when I arrived, the running time had been cut down as if for some provincial repertory house. Less than three hours of music was left; an hour had been taken out since the dress rehearsal. Nevertheless, something came across. The big numbers had not lost their show-stopping power. As a drama, it would be hard to take *Robert* seriously; Miss Wallmann's endeavor to stage it so as to "throw light on the predicament of modern man" was doomed from the start. But as a theatrical spectacle thoroughly and brilliantly composed, as a feast of many courses in cunningly planned sequence, the opera could again be a hit, I believe, if it were done on the scale and in the manner that its creators intended.

Robert and *Les Huguenots* were both so successful—Michelangelo and Beethoven were names mentioned in a breath with Meyerbeer— that the composer pondered long before approaching the public with a new work. He would not venture anything less than another triumph. Soon after *Les Huguenots*, he had received the librettos of both *Le Prophète* and *L'Africaine*. He began work on the latter, and then set it aside to compose *Le Prophète*, whose first version was finished in 1841. But the Opéra did not have the cast for it—Meyerbeer wanted Pauline Viardot to be engaged for the leading role, and Léon Pillet, the director of the Opéra, wanted to use Rosine Stoltz, his resident prima donna and mistress—and the composer said he "would rather wait twenty years than risk a cast that did not satisfy me at every point." Eventually, he agreed to Stoltz—but then no suitable tenor was available. In 1845, he completed a version of *L'Africaine* for Stoltz. In 1847, she and Pillet left the Opéra. In 1848, Meyerbeer revised *Le Prophète*, and it was put on—with Viardot, after all—the following year. *L'Africaine* was remodeled in or about 1852 but did not reach the stage until 1865, a year after Meyerbeer's death. This intricate chronology is being brought to light by the publication of Meyerbeer's correspondence and diaries, of which three fat volumes have so far appeared. They, taken in conjunction with the evidence of the scores and the memoirs of contemporaries, reveal that Meyerbeer was at once a rapid and fluent composer, an inveterate tinkerer and reviser, and a last-minute improviser prepared to make spur-of-the-moment changes to a work that may have occupied him on and off for some twenty-five years. His artistic exigence is oddly at variance with sudden capitulations to singers' demands once the works got into rehearsal. It was a poor idea to supply Jeanne Castellan, the first Berthe of *Le Prophète*, with the added entrance air she asked for; Meyerbeer acknowledged as much by omitting the number from his first published score. (In fact, he supplied two airs, and Castellan chose the more florid; Miss Scotto sings it at the Met.) It was possibly a bad idea to omit the tenor's air in Act III; it's hard to say without having seen the music (which is presumably lurking in the Opéra archives). Gustave Roger, an opéra-comique tenor promoted to create the title role, was finding it burdensome, and Mme Roger insisted on its being lightened.

Without the air, there is an uncharacteristic bump in the action and a hole in the presentation of the hero's character. After Meyerbeer's death, the process continued when the great baritone Jean-Baptiste Faure transferred a passage from Act III of *L'Africaine* to Act V so that he, and not the prima donna, would have the last word.

The San Francisco *Africaine*, directed by Lotfi Mansouri, designed by Wolfram and Amrei Skalicki, was the most satisfying of the four revivals—more imaginative and energetic in style than the Scala *Huguenots*, closer to the spirit of Meyerbeer than the Florence *Robert* or the Met *Prophète*. If one is going to reject a careful "re-creation" of the original, based on the surviving production books and scene designs, in favor of something more modern, then this is the way to go about it. (I'm not recommending such a rejection; I believe that an *Otello* carefully and intelligently based on Verdi's production of 1887, which is notated in detail, and done in scenery painted and built from Carlo Ferrario's original designs would be a revelation.) With lighter and presumably less costly modern materials, the San Francisco staging hinted at Manueline splendors in the first two acts; the shipwreck of Act III, as the great vessel grinds on the reef, was effective; and the Malagasy paradise looked exotic and attractive. Scribe's and Meyerbeer's instructions were not fulfilled to the letter, but they were not flatly contradicted. The score was cut, when I heard it, to something under three hours of music.

After *Robert*, Scribe and Meyerbeer turned to history for their subjects, but not in any very serious or precise way—only to provide novel and picturesque scenes. The hero of *L'Africaine* happens to be Vasco da Gama, and his voyage takes him to Madagascar, but in the first version of the opera he is a Spaniard who sails to "the center of Africa, near the source of the Niger." In *Les Huguenots*, a conventional love-versus-loyalty story is played out against the background of the St. Bartholomew's Day Massacre. *Le Prophète* takes up the theme of religious fanaticism. The Prophet is John of Leiden, described by Dr. F. C. Conybeare (the eleventh Britannica's authority on ablution, baptism, Anabaptism, and such things) as the Brigham Young of the mid-sixteenth century: "Giving himself out as the successor of David, he claimed royal honours and absolute power in the new 'Zion' "—which was Münster, a city that under John and his Anabaptist followers became "for twelve months a scene of unbridled profligacy." (Another number cut from Meyerbeer's score during rehearsals was the "Choix des Reines": John's henchmen chose the ten prettiest girls in the town to be wives to the Prophet. Some profligacy survives in the *bacchanale* and *couplets bachiques* of the final scene.) In Act I of the opera, three Anabaptists incite a band of happy peasants against their masters with communist promises; the reformers' chant of "Ad nos, ad salutarem undam" punctuates the score in the way Luther's chorale does that of *Les Huguenots*. The wicked Count Oberthal refuses to allow the pretty young Berthe, his vassal, to go off and marry John. In Act II, John tells the Anabaptists of a dream of being crowned, while they observe that he's just the man to make a popular leader. Berthe runs in, fleeing from Oberthal, who tells John to yield Berthe or see his mother, Fidès, killed. John yields Berthe, and Fidès blesses him (the famous "Ah, mon fils!"). The three Anabaptists tell John they can make his dream come true, and, although reluctant to leave his mother, he goes off with them. In Act III, Zacharias, one of the three, sings some rousing *couplets*, "joyfully brandishing his battle-axe." Across the representation of a frozen lake, dancers—originally on roller skates—glide in, and then take off their skates to dance an extended divertissement. In a *trio bouffe*, Oberthal, caught wandering about the camp but unrecognized, swears to join the Anabaptists and hang Oberthal when he is caught; there is more grim humor when he is recognized and ordered off to execution. (This curious form of light relief was a Meyerbeer specialty; the Valentine/Marcel duet in *Les Huguenots* has something of the same quality.) John arrives, sickened of his mission and longing only to see his mother again, but when he learns that Berthe is in Münster he rallies his army with a prayer and a triumphal hymn, and leads them against the city. An electric sun blazes out—the first use of electricity at the Opéra.

Act IV contains the coronation scene whose structure and situations Verdi so much admired. It is dominated by Fidès. Reduced to penury, she sings in the street her *complainte de la mendiante* (strikingly accompanied by two bassoons) and then a duo (of poor quality) with Berthe. The scene changes to the cathedral, and the well-known march is heard. There is a band of twenty-two on stage; the organ plays; Fidès hurls imprecations on the Prophet; children sing of his divine origin. John appears, murmuring to himself that it is true, he is indeed the son of God—and comes face to face with his mortal mother. It is a strong scene. One of the Anabaptist trio whispers to John that if he acknowledges his mother she will be killed, so he denies her: "Who is this woman?" John then makes it plain to her that if she persists in claiming him *he* will be killed, so she pretends that she was mistaken. On a verbal level, the motivation is quite rational. But on a musical and theatrical level it is played out in New Testament terms, with echoes of Christ's cool question to his mother "Woman, what have I to do with thee?" and of Peter's denial, and with a "miracle"—a section of the score headed "L'Exorcisme," in which the desperate woman is made calm by the Prophet's gentle, persuasive voice. One of Meyerbeer's earliest comments on the libretto was "How would it be if John really believed in his mission?" Does he? In Act V, both mother and son implicitly own that the miracle was a fraud. In the vaults of Münster castle Fidès sings her grand air of parade ("A musical aberration," said Berlioz). John comes to seek forgiveness. Berthe arrives, intent on blowing up the castle, discovers her John, plans to return to the country with him and his mother, then learns to her horror that he is the Prophet, and stabs herself. (An extended death scene, saxophone-accompanied, was cut before the first performance; Berthe is now polished off in a few perfunctory measures.) John joins the carousal in the great hall, having apparently, though this is not explained, set a slow fuse to the castle magazine. There is an explosion, Fidès, disheveled and bloody, runs in. Mother and son strike up the drinking song together, changing its words from "Versez! que tout respire l'ivresse" to "Ah! viens, divine flamme," and the castle collapses in flames about them and all the company.

This story certainly contains novel and piquant situations. It was something quite different from *Les Huguenots*, being a grand-opera plot with common people, not nobles, in the principal roles. Meyerbeer had initial misgivings about monotony of color and predominance of males, but saw how diversions could be introduced. John Dexter, who directed the Met production, has made the mistake, I believe, of taking the play in one way too seriously and in another not seriously enough. Scribe's characters do not really bear close inspection; consistency is regularly and ruthlessly sacrificed to passing theatrical effects. In terms of the text alone, Fidès is a selfish and possessive old woman. John, as Bernard Shaw wrote, "is at the disadvantage of being a hero without having anything heroic to do, and of having finally to degrade himself by shouting a vile drinking song amid a pack of absurd nautch-girls." He is also an Albert Herring who does not succeed in untying the apron strings. Berthe is pasteboard. The rabble-rousing music of the Anabaptists has a kind of dark, sinister power, but elsewhere the text and the buffo elements make it clear that they are not dedicated fanatics but hypocrites with an eye to the main chance. It is just possible that the composer was attracted subconsciously to the subject by parallels between his own position and John's. Heine once remarked that Meyerbeer's mother was the second woman in history to see her son accepted as divine; like the Prophet, Meyerbeer himself may have had clear-sighted moments when he realized the world rated him too high. But such speculation is irrelevant to the opera as it was composed. "People often dismiss *Prophète*," Mr. Dexter has said, "as a *pièce de théâtre*, but I think the work exists on a much more profound level. . . . [Meyerbeer] tried to capture, musically and dramatically, the explosive atmosphere of Northern Europe in the 1530s—a time when the movement for a populist, instinctive religion had reached the boiling point." The Metropolitan set, designed by Peter Wexler, "began as a half-built cathedral, but it has become a kind of Gothic cage, because that's what Northern

Europe was at the time; the Church was a cage, and everybody was trapped inside it. I first thought of staging the opera as a morality play." That "profound level" Mr. Dexter speaks of does not exist. *Le Prophète is* a very skillfully made *pièce de théâtre*—and to be valued, not dismissed, as such. What Mr. Dexter *has* dismissed—by running scenes and acts together without clear punctuation; by playing everything, indoor or outdoor, in the same somber set and in costumes uniformly brown, gray, or white, with touches of red—is the scenic power of Meyerbeer's opera, based on carefully planned contrasts of moods, colors, décor, depths and densities of setting. He has achieved the visual monotony the composer sought to avoid. The curtain should rise on the Dutch countryside: "In the background, the Meuse. Right, a fortified castle with drawbridges and turrets. Left, the castle farms and mills; on the same side, in the foreground, sacks of wheat, rustic tables, benches, etc." When we enter the Met, the curtain is already up on a Gothic apse run up in wood, which remains there throughout the evening.

On a practical level, there is much to admire. The production cost only three-fifths of its allotted half-million-dollar budget. No time is spent on scene-shifting, and so a good deal of music can be packed into a four-hour show with only two intermissions—after Acts III and IV. (A rousing, bloodthirsty chorus that should open Act III is omitted; so are the *trio bouffe*, a good deal of the ballet, a verse of John's pastorale in Act II, and some less significant passages. On the other hand, the prayer of Act III and the duo-reprise of the drinking song, both cut in 1849, are reinstated.) Yet even a *Prophète* mounted on the cheap could, I believe, be mounted in a more picturesque and appropriate fashion. It is a matter of intention, not of cost. When the musical historian Georges Servières assessed the reasons for the opera's success, high among them he listed the electric sunrise, the skaters, the Sax band onstage, and the explosion of the palace. At the Met, a projection of a rose window onto the backcloth pays token observance to the sunrise. What is left of the ballet, choreographed in rustic style by Stuart Sebastian, is quite fun. But the band is invisible, and the explosion is a feeble affair of ribbons fluttering to the ground.

On the first night, Marilyn Horne sang the principal role with energy, power, and prowess. In 1841, Meyerbeer wrote that Fidès was "all gentleness," that she had only one energetic moment; that was why he wanted Viardot with her "broad, sweet, smooth singing," and not the fiery Stoltz. But the Fidès of 1849 needs a good deal of fire—in the *imprécation*, in the fourth-act finale, and in the trumpery cabaletta of her last air. Miss Horne provided it. She was highly dramatic in the threefold utterance of "Qui je suis?" after John has denied her—marked to be sung the first time "d'une voix tremblante," the second "avec indignation," the third "avec une douloureuse tendresse, et en pleurant." In tender moments, her singing was "broad, sweet, smooth." The role is written across the same range as Brünnhilde's, from the G below the staff to the C above it. Alternatives are given so that singers without Viardot's exceptional diapason can avoid the extremes, but Miss Horne had no need of them.

John is also a difficult role. Meyerbeer composed it first for Gilbert Duprez, and when Duprez's voice declined thought of Gaetano Fraschini, Verdi's favorite tenor, and of the great Mario. Both Roger, who created the part, and Mario, who sang it in London a few months later, found it heavy, and omitted portions—Roger the Act III prayer, and Mario some of the triumphal hymn that follows it. Mr. McCracken has the weight, force, and stamina for the heroic episodes. (He sang both the prayer and the hymn.) The head voice he employed in several gentle passages marked "pianissimo" and "très doux" was criticized, but unjustly in my view: the sound had the right touch of strangeness, suggestive of visionary delusion. His performance was noble, poetic, and convincing.

Miss Scotto seemed to have confused Berthe with Mad Margaret. She turned her four appearances into four mad scenes of increasing wildness, and, although there were some sweet, beautiful phrases to be heard, she tended increasingly to scream out anything loud and high. But then Berthe is a thankless role; I have come across no warm praise for any of the Berthes in history, not even for Claudia Muzio's, at the Met in 1918. Zacharias is the only other character with a solo. Nicolas Levasseur came out of virtual retirement, at the age of fifty-eight, to create the part. At the Met, Jerome Hines sounded a little rusty in timbre, but he had authority, grandeur, and a fine rhythmic verve.

From Berlioz onward, critics have noted the Handelian cut of the roulades in Zacharias's *couplets*. I think that Handel may be a general influence on *Le Prophète*. Meyerbeer knew many of Handel's dramatic oratorios, and he read and admired *Jephtha* while composing his opera. The influence is not (except during those *couplets*) in musical details but in the general layout, in the disposition and cumulative effects of choruses, solos, ensembles, and in the flair for capturing a mood and a movement in music. Consider the coronation scene. This is Henry Chorley's account of it:

The march is gorgeous in its opening beyond precedent of stage marches, choicely rich in the melody of the trio. Then comes the organ behind the scenes, with the church anthem . . . broken by the imprecations of the distracted woman, who hears the praises of the false Prophet . . . Next follows the chant of the children with their censers . . . all wrought up, with consummate art of climax, to the instant at which the false Prophet, having quelled a revolt, intoxicated, self-deluded, crowned, conceives himself—*is* to himself—divinely inspired. The thunderbolt falls, in the moment of terrible recognition. The wild appeal of the mother, bewildered by surprise and horror, and the weary, wearing yearning of months of pilgrimage; the more fearful struggle still in the heart of the impostor, with the knives of the fanatic fiends who have goaded him into the blasphemous crime close at hand; all this is treated by M. Meyerbeer with the grasp of a giant, able to control the surge of the most tremendous and unlooked-for emotions. . . . There can be nothing grander in combination than the sweep of the procession from the cathedral, after the false miracle has been accomplished, with the "Dominum salvum fac" pealing behind the scenes from the organ, and the people shouting almost in adoration. It is a moment of pomp and splendour, never outdone in stage-music.

Some of the great dramatic sequences in Handel's oratorios have been described in similar terms. Not all Meyerbeer's music is good. Some of it is labored, and some of it cheap. But two of his cheapest tunes— Fidès's outburst at her son, later blared out in unison by the full ensemble, and pushed through key after key, and the "vile drinking song" at the end—are two of the catchiest and most theatrically effective in the piece. One cannot help being stirred by them.

Bernard Shaw once declared that all sorts of excellent qualities in the conductor of a French grand opera went for nothing unless to them was added "the vulgar little gift . . . called 'go.' " Henry Lewis, who conducted the Met performance, occasionally rushed things. Both triumphal hymn and coronation march were taken noticeably faster than the composer's metronome markings indicate. (So they are in the Columbia recording of the opera made in London by the same three principals and conductor; the album is a valuable and rousing supplement to the Met performances, and it contains some passages—the opening chorus of Act III, the *trio bouffe*—omitted in the theater.) But Mr. Lewis certainly had "go." And the players gave full value to curious instrumental inventions whose novelty and merit even Meyerbeer's sternest detractors have never denied.

February 7, 1977

Giacomo Meyerbeer: Briefwechsel und Tagebücher, *edited by Heinz and Gudrun Becker, is being published in increasingly expensive volumes (Volume III cost $127) by Walter de Gruyter, Berlin. The plot of Act V would make better sense if Berthe herself before her entrance had already set slow fire to the castle magazine and if John then learned that she had done so. That is how* Kobbé *tells it. But the dialogue and stage directions of the score, from the first edition onward, give no warrant for such a reading.*

BRAVE, NOBLE,
AFTER THE HIGH ROMAN FASHION

No one, not even Wagner, seems to have been quite sure just how good, or how bad, Wagner's first three operas are. The composer never saw *Die Feen*, written in 1833, the year of Marschner's *Hans Heiling* and Donizetti's *Lucrezia Borgia*; it was neither performed nor published until 1888. He directed a single, unfortunate performance of *Das Liebesverbot* in Magdeburg in 1836, the year of Meyerbeer's *Les Huguenots* and Donizetti's *Belisario*; the opera was not published until 1922 and not revived until 1923, in Munich. *Rienzi* was more successful. First produced in Dresden in 1842, the year of Verdi's *Nabucco* and Donizetti's *Linda di Chamounix*, it held the stage there throughout the nineteenth century and into the twentieth; in 1844 both a full score and a vocal score were published. But *Der fliegende Holländer* had appeared in 1843, and thereafter Wagner (except when revising *Tannhäuser* for Paris) followed his own advice: "Good people, do something *new, new, and once again new.*" That injunction—often quoted out of context to excuse the modish aberrations of modern Wagner stage directors—occurs in an 1852 letter to Liszt deploring the fact that Berlioz should be reworking his fourteen-year-old *Benvenuto Cellini* for Weimar instead of embarking on something completely different; he himself would never think of reworking his superannuated *Rienzi* or allowing it to be revived. (A few years later, as it happened, Wagner was eager for *Rienzi* revivals, but that was because he needed money.)

No one, not even Wagner, seems to have heard Wagner's first three operas performed in full—until last year, when the BBC mounted uncut studio productions of all three. I missed those, and hope that the reported plans of an American record company to issue them on disc comes off. Some earlier, variously unsatisfactory accounts of the works (brave, exhilarating essays by enthusiastic students or young professionals, and cut-to-the-bone versions by regular opera companies) had pretty well convinced me that *Die Feen, Das Liebesverbot*, and *Rienzi* are all three worth performing—as operas rewarding in their own right, not merely as interesting precursors of later Wagner—and that they are all three better, more important works than several to which our major companies currently devote attention. That growing conviction had still to be put to the test of large-scale, stylish theater productions. When the music society of University College, London, gave the British première of *Das Liebesverbot*, in 1965, I wrote that an age that welcomes Donizetti would certainly welcome Wagner's opera; three years later a performance by Nottingham University students led me to urge the piece (so far without result) on Glyndebourne and Sadler's Wells. After performances of *Die Feen* by Bayreuth students in 1967 and in the town hall of a London borough six years later, I declared that neither Covent Garden nor Sadler's Wells need hesitate to stage the piece. The references are British because no American performances of either opera have come my way. But America has just produced what I believe to be the first large-scale, stylish *Rienzi* staging of our day. It was presented by the San Antonio Symphony for two performances at the end of last month. Much work has been done on *Rienzi* recently: a new —and very expensive—critical edition is under way (three of its five volumes and a supplementary volume of documents and texts have so far appeared); for that BBC performance, a version of the score with more music in it than in any ever published or performed before was prepared; Angel has issued the first commercial recording of the opera; and a monograph, *Wagner's Rienzi: a reappraisal based on a study of the sketches and drafts*, by John Deathridge, has appeared from the Oxford University Press. Musicology is a sterile pursuit until its discoveries are put into performance. John Mauceri, who conducted the San Antonio *Rienzi*, and Robert Darling, who directed and designed it, took note of new researches and used them to enrich an imaginative and impassioned presentation of the opera. They achieved the kind of performance that causes the stock judgments of musical histories to be rewritten.

Die Feen (*The Fairies*) is a German opera with its roots in Weber and Marschner. It is the link between *Oberon* and *Tannhäuser*: both music and action point more clearly than those of *Das Liebesverbot* and *Rienzi* toward later Wagner. The plot, freely adapted from Gozzi's *La donna serpente*, is kin to that of *Die Frau ohne Schatten* and may have influenced it. (Strauss prepared the Munich première of *Die Feen*.) *Das Liebesverbot* (*The Ban on Love*) is Wagner's Italianate piece, composed at a time when Italian opera—and, above all, Wilhelmine Schröder-Devrient as Bellini's Romeo—broke over him and provoked what he diagnosed as "a pert fancy for the turmoil of the senses, a defiant exuberance of glee." He, too, would write a Shakespearean opera filled with delightful melodies. Being Wagner, he introduced serious autobiographical elements into the sources. It was his idea, not Gozzi's, that the hero of *Die Feen* should attain immortality through the power and beauty of his music making. (In terms of the tale, the tenor's song literally melts a heart of stone.) When moving *Measure for Measure* to Sicily, as *Das Liebesverbot*, Wagner changed Angelo into a German governor who, in familiar German fashion, feels at once irresistibly attracted by and earnestly censorious of a license and frivolity considered typically Mediterranean. Much of the *Liebesverbot* music is merry and uncomplicated, but the harmonies point toward *Tristan* in a powerful monologue where that governor struggles—in vain—to resist the Latin sensuality that has intoxicated him.

In Wagner's own case, such intoxication did not last long. His next hero, Cola di Rienzi, is a grandiose visionary whose tremendous plan to restore a decadent folk to the dignity and glory of their ancestors is thwarted by the intrigues of his enemies and the malice and obtuseness of the common people. To see what drew Wagner to Rienzi one must read his source, Bulwer's novel *Rienzi: The Last of the Roman Tribunes* (1835). After Bulwer's expansive pages, the blunt verse and foreshortened action of Wagner's libretto come as a surprise: Rienzi's seven months of rule, seven years of exile, and seven weeks of return are collapsed into a few scenes; his death (1354) follows hard on his excommunication (1347). In a preface to the novel, Bulwer notes the distinction between his epic and Mary Russell Mitford's dramatic treatment of the subject (1828): "The slender space permitted to the Dramatist does not *allow* Miss Mitford to be very faithful to facts;— to distinguish betweeen Rienzi's earlier and his later period of power, or to detail the true but somewhat intricate causes of his rise, his splendor, and his fall." I wonder if Wagner knew Miss Mitford's *Rienzi* (it was published in Berlin in 1837); his drama depends quite largely on what Bulwer called "a love-intrigue between a relative of Rienzi and one of the antagonist party, which makes the plot of Miss Mitford's Tragedy, and is little more than an episode in my Romance, having slight effect on the conduct and none on the fate of the hero." Bulwer's book is concerned mainly with Rienzi as popular politician and hero, and when introducing the 1848 edition he remarked with a little pride that the novel seemed to have played a part in stimulating Italy's political regeneration. Verdi certainly contemplated a *Rienzi* in 1843 (but decided the censors would never pass it; Bulwer's book was banned in some Italian states) and again five years later (but his librettist found the story intractable). Wagner reduced the principal actors to three : Rienzi, tenor; Adriano, mezzo-soprano, who combines the roles played by Bulwer's Adrian Colonna (an enlightened young patrician torn between family loyalty, his sympathy with Rienzi's ideals, and his love for Irene, the tribune's sister) and Angelo Villani (Rienzi's trusted secretary, who finally turns traitor); and Irene, soprano, who similarly "doubles," as sister and as Nina Raselli, Rienzi's wife, his sole support when all Rome has turned against him. Wagner's *Rienzi*, despite its length, has quite a short, simple libretto and a plot without subtleties. There are only two arias. The ensembles and choruses, the processions and marches and hymns, and a long sequence of a pantomime followed by a ballet make it huge. Of the Meyerbeer-Scribe grand operas, only *Le Prophète* has

510

so uncomplicated an action. Hans von Bülow once described *Rienzi* as Meyerbeer's best opera, and his mots (in similar vein, he dubbed the Requiem Verdi's best opera) have a way of being thoughtlessly repeated: *Rienzi* is often called Meyerbeerian. Insofar as that implies Meyerbeer influence on it, it is nothing of the kind, in either its musical or its dramatic manners. The superficial similarities are due to a common ancestry in Spontini's *Fernand Cortez*, that grand opera which had also left its mark on Rossini, and in Halévy's *La Juive*, itself Spontini-descended. Yet to compare *Le Prophète* and *Rienzi* is irresistible. They were composed at almost the same time, on the same scale, and for the same solo forces of tenor, mezzo, and soprano. (Soon after *Le Prophète* appeared at the Opéra, Liszt urged Wagner to pay court to Gustave Roger and Pauline Viardot, singers of the Prophet and his mother, and thus pave the way for an Opéra performance of *Rienzi*.) In addition, topically, the San Antonio *Rienzi*, following hard on the Met *Prophète*, illustrated a strikingly different approach to the twentieth-century revival of a nineteenth-century grand opera.

If there was any influence, it was of Wagner's work on Meyerbeer's. Wagner drafted his libretto in 1837 and composed the music between 1838 and 1840. Meyerbeer received his libretto from Scribe in 1839 (though there had been some earlier discussion of the subject) and had barely begun composition when Wagner showed him the first two acts of *Rienzi*. Meyerbeer's recommendation helped to achieve its acceptance by Dresden. In 1844, Meyerbeer (along with Spontini) went to Dresden to hear it. His own opera did not reach the stage until 1849. The main point that emerges from any comparison is already implicit in Wagner's own account of the *Prophète* Act III finale. He uses the episode to exemplify his oft-quoted charge against Meyerbeer of "effects without causes":

Let us assume that a poet has been inspired with the idea of a hero, a champion of light and freedom, in whose breast there flames a mighty love for his downtrod brother men. . . . He wishes to depict this hero at the zenith of his career, in the full radiance of his deeds of glory, and chooses as image the following supreme moment. . . . The hero has arrived before a fortified city, which must be bloodily stormed by his unpracticed mob if the work of freedom is to have a victorious issue. . . . At his mighty voice, the folk assemble. . . . They feel themselves uplifted and ennobled, and their inspiration in turn uplifts the hero to still loftier heights: from inspiration he presses on to deed. He seizes the standard and waves it high toward those fearful walls, the embattled city of the foe, who, so long as they lie secure behind their trenches, make impossible a better future for mankind. "Onward! Death or victory!" . . . The scene must now become for us the stage of all the world; Nature must declare herself a sharer in this exaltation.

511

. . . Lo! sacred need compels the poet: he parts the cloudy curtains of the morn, and at his word the streaming sun mounts high above the city. . . . Here is the flower of all-puissant art, and this miracle only the art of drama can achieve.

The *externals* of such a scene, Wagner continues, are found in Meyerbeer's opera. The ear notes a popular hymnlike melody, thunderously swelled, the eye a sun that is a masterstroke of stage mechanics, nothing more. No inspired hero stands before us, but a costumed tenor playing "a poor devil who through weakness has taken on the role of a charlatan, and finally bewails not an error, a fanatical delusion, which at a pinch might still have justified that sunburst, but his weakness and mendacity." Compare that, Wagner might have continued, with the tribune's battle muster of a popular army in Act III of my *Rienzi*—stirring, elevated, dramatic but not stagy, charged with honest, lofty idealism. Note that after the battle and before the victory chorus there is a tender threnody for the fallen. Compare Meyerbeer's entertaining but quite irrelevant ballet of skaters with my ballet—a symbolic representation, ordered by the tribune, of tyrants overthrown and ancient and modern Rome united beneath the blessing of Peace. Compare the admittedly effective *coup de théâtre* that interrupts the Prophet's coronation procession with Adriano's interruption of Rienzi's progress: the noble youth runs forward, seizes the bridle of Rienzi's charger, and pleads for negotiation, not bloodshed. Note that Rienzi dies as a tragic hero, not bawling a brindisi.

Wagner, hugely ambitious, aimed to write an extra-grand opera that would triumph in Paris and rescue him from the chores of a provincial conductor's life. Like Verdi in *Don Carlos*, he accepted the form— " 'grand opera' with all its scenic and musical splendor, its massive, vehement effects, was my objective"—but he made no concessions to frivolous Parisian taste. "The material itself truly filled me with enthusiasm, and I included nothing unconnected with this enthusiasm"— nothing for mere, unmotivated effect. *Le Prophète* is a carefully worked, cunningly assembled score by an experienced, very skillful, and technically conscientious composer. *Rienzi* is different—an outpouring of copious and passionately felt music by a young genius who wished to inspire his listeners, not just excite them to pleasure and admiration. Wagner's musical means are simpler and more spontaneous than Meyerbeer's, and his stagecraft is more direct, more honest in intention. (Just how good it is I did not realize until I saw the San Antonio production.) What keeps *Rienzi* from the stage is its very copiousness. It is impractically long and large for modern repertory use, and by much cutting it is spoiled. The same is true of *Die Feen* and *Das Liebesverbot*. But it is precisely the vigor, the melodic exuberance, the youthful, unfettered, overflowing invention of all three works which make them so attractive.

Bowing to the exigencies of theatrical life, Wagner shortened *Rienzi* before its Dresden première, and again after it. (The bill had announced a performance beginning at six and ending at ten; the show ran until nearly midnight.) The 1844 vocal score was abridged, the 1844 full score still more so, and the tale of subsequent editions is too tangled to be set out here. The complete original work is possibly lost forever. *Rienzi* was Hitler's favorite opera; he owned the autograph, and, it has been said, it perished with him. The Dresden theater copy was apparently destroyed by bombs. But Wagner's composition draft, in short score, survives. Working from that, and from the early vocal score, Ernest Warburton and Edward Downes, the producer and conductor of the BBC performance, themselves orchestrated the passages missing in full score. Their reconstruction of *Rienzi* contained four hours and forty-seven minutes of music. The San Antonio text was not nearly so long; there was about three hours and ten minutes of music in it. But it was a longer and more impressive version than any I had heard before. My first *Rienzi* was in Augsburg, in the open air. The flames at the end for the burning of the Capitol were real; they leaped into the night from kerosene poured over actual masonry. That was striking. But the company did not have the necessary choral forces; offstage choruses, prerecorded, were piped in over loudspeakers. And there was much cutting. A Munich Festival production in 1967, done with just one long interval, lasted less than three hours in all, and Adriano, that role inspired by Wagner's memories of Schröder-Devrient in Romeo's and Leonore's breeches, was allotted to a tenor; his aria, "Gerechter Gott!," was omitted. Three years earlier, a Scala performance with Giuseppe di Stefano in the title part also had a tenor Adriano, and was abridged to a point where it was reviewed as "Highlights from *Rienzi*." When the ensembles are cut to short statements, the majesty and the contrasts are destroyed. The chorus seems to troop on and off, on and off, to sing one brief number after another. Act III suffers especially. Excitement in the Forum at the impending patrician attack; drums summoning the army; "Gerechter Gott!"; the huge muster of army, populace, and priests, with a large military band marching across the stage; the battle hymn launched by Rienzi, interrupted by Adriano's plea; the offstage alarums while onstage the women, led by Irene, are praying; the triumphant processional return; the threnody; Adriano's fierce outburst over his father's corpse; the final victory chorus—in San Antonio all this was done just about complete, and was tremendous.

There were about 250 people on the stage. The brass band turned up in force (at the Met, the *Prophète* band is relegated to the wings), and the rousing effect produced by a marching, uniformed band is something composers counted on. Rienzi, as in the well-known picture of the Dresden production, rode a white charger. There is a good deal of evidence

513

about the way Wagner intended *Rienzi* to be staged; Robert Darling either followed the composer's instructions or devised actions in their spirit which could be accomplished by local forces. For example, Rienzi's festival dancers (the Red Beret Drill Team from Lackland Air Force Base and the Churchill High School Band Flag Corps) deftly medieval-ized a halftime banner-waving routine—apter, far, than any awkward ballet—and it was a nice nominal touch to cast Irene as Peace. Mr. Darling's settings were built from two quadrants of tall, classical colon-nade, variously grouped and added to in ways that evoked palace, piazza, or church portal without monotony. Space could be deep or shallow. The materials used vividly suggested the decayed grandeur that was fourteenth-century Rome. Through hundreds and hundreds of hired cos-tumes, period precision was not entirely maintained, but the general effect was richly and colorfully medieval, and the dress of the principals recalled the original Dresden designs, themselves drawn from detailed descriptions in Bulwer. Patricia Collins's lighting was imaginative, but not bright enough in the scenes of splendor.

John Mauceri's conducting was notable for its broad, sustained grasp of the huge spans, for the sureness of tempo relations, for stylish, dra-matic rubato, and for eloquent detail. His reading had both passion and grandeur. He was energetic, buoyant but not hectic, ample but never heavy. His large, balanced, shapely handling of the score came to me as a revelation of its merit, and banished doubts that Heinrich Hollreiser's performance on the Angel recording had raised. (Many of Mr. Holl-reiser's tempi are demonstrably wrong, and the general effect of that ill-cast set is of a routine read-through.) Each of the many marches, taken at the composer's prescribed tempo, showed an individual mood and character, which were reflected in Mr. Darling's staging. The San Antonio Symphony was admirable: warm strings, playing in smooth, full lines; woodwinds firm in tone, flexible in phrase; brass that was bright and clear but not searing. The massed choirs, prepared by Dorothy Randall, were amateur but accomplished: boys, women, and men sang with a spirit that could put some professional choruses to shame.

The five-act opera was given with only two intermissions, after Acts I and II. The long stretch of Acts III, IV, and V on end puts a tre-mendous strain on the protagonist, and also on the audience, kept at high tension for an hour and a half. A good deal of the solo music in Act V was cut: all but a snatch of Rienzi's cavatina (after his prayer) and all of the Rienzi-Irene duet. I regretted this—it diminishes the portrait of a great man progressively deprived of support until only a loving sister remains (Irene is the third of the six loving sisters to be found in Wagner's operas), it leaves all the emphasis on Rienzi's public appearances, and it makes Irene's role very small—but I understood the

514

reasons for it. Elsewhere, some ensemble music was cut (far less than in most *Rienzi* performances), some recitative (which is the most primitive part of Wagner's score), all of the pantomime, and some of the ballet. Three of the four ambassadorial greetings in Act II were reinstated, from the critical edition, and lent interest to the E-major ceremonial march; eight bars more and we could have had the fourth of them.

James McCray, the Seattle Siegfried, was Rienzi. He made little of the text (the opera was sung in English), broke the line of phrases ("Accept this humble. Fervent prayer"), and sang recitatives as written—instead of adjusting length and stress to the sense of the words—in a way that often made noble sentiments sound perfunctory. He is worth being thus harsh to, since potentially he is a most valuable heldentenor. His voice was strong, firm, untiring, still clear and vigorous as a long evening of heavy, heroic utterance drew to its close. RoseMarie Freni, the Adriano, has one of those complicated mezzo timbres which are not limpid or conventionally beautiful but are arresting in their dramatic colors. And she also has temperament: her performance held the ear and the eye. Janet Price, a Welsh soprano associated with such roles as Mercadante's Virginia, Meyerbeer's Palmide (*Il crociato*), and Donizetti's Eleanora d'Este (*Torquato Tasso*), made her American stage début as Irene, showing both that bel canto is the right road by which to approach Wagner and that her voice has the weight to sail out over big ensembles. The smaller roles were strongly cast: among the company were Douglas Perry and Thomas Paul as Rienzi's henchmen, Philip Steele as Colonna, and Ara Berberian as the Papal Legate.

San Antonio, a pleasing town, exotic to an Easterner, has most of the attributes of a festival place. As in Venice, one can walk beside water between hotels, restaurants, and the theater without meeting motorcars. (There *are* cars, all too many of them, but river and roads are on different levels.) There is history underfoot within the town (the Alamo) and a short, level bicycle ride away (the Spanish missions) to occupy the visitor's days. There is local architecture (notably in the nineteenth-century German quarter) worth exploring. The Theatre for the Performing Arts, where *Rienzi* was done, has a good auditorium, seating 2,800, and airy, agreeable lobbies; there are halls, churches, galleries, and other theaters in the city which could help to give San Antonio a festival comparable to Adelaide's or York's—provided federal, state, and city funds were generously forthcoming. (Art costs very little in terms of a national budget.) In nineteenth-century Dresden, *Rienzi* was played a hundred times in thirty years, and people came from all over Europe to see it. Although San Antonio may prefer to turn next to "something new," it would be a pity if its *Rienzi* disappeared after just two showings. If *Rienzi* could be kept in the repertory and *Die Feen* and *Das Liebesver-*

bot added in subsequent years, San Antonio would be able to mount an opera festival unparalleled elsewhere. In time, early Wagner could be varied by the works that Wagner conducted or was influenced by in his formative years. *Fidelio* has already been done, and *Norma* is due this season. (In such a context as I am suggesting, it would be enriched by the extra bass air that Wagner composed for it.) But I am thinking of fare less common—of Weber's *Euryanthe*, Spontini's *Cortez*, Méhul's *Joseph*, Auber's *La Muette de Portici*, Meyerbeer's *Robert le Diable*, Spohr's *Jessonda*, Halévy's *La Juive*, and Marschner's *Der Vampyr*. *Rienzi* has proved that San Antonio has the ability to make a success of such pieces.

February 14, 1977

On August 8, 1977, the Daily Telegraph *carried a report of an anonymous telephone call to the mayor of Bayreuth from an Austrian who claimed he had seen the Wagner autographs "in the possession of a librarian who was cataloguing Hitler's private property for the American occupation forces."*

A PECULIAR GRACE

Francis Poulenc's opera *Dialogues des Carmélites* appeared at La Scala in 1957, swiftly made its way round the world, and is still revived from time to time—most often now, perhaps, in opera schools attracted by the abundance of female roles it offers. There was a production at the New York City Opera in 1966. This month, the Met has taken up the piece, and has done well by it.

In 1794, a group of Carmelite nuns from Compiègne defied the secularization decrees of the Revolution, and went to the scaffold for doing so. One of the community survived, and wrote her memoirs. On them, the Catholic-convert author Gertrud von Le Fort based her novella *Die Letzte am Schafott* (1931), which in somewhat sensational fashion embodies her chosen themes of redemption through suffering and of self-sacrificing love. A movie scenario was prepared from it by Father Raymond Brückberger and Philippe Agostini, and the Catholic writer Georges Bernanos was invited to write the dialogue. The movie wasn't made until 1960, and then only part of Bernanos's script was used, but his *Dialogues des Carmélites* was published in 1949, the year

516

after his death—the same year that Emmet Lavery's play *Song at the Scaffold*, also drawn from the Le Fort novella, was produced in Los Angeles. In Lavery's play, which calls for considerable use of music, the conventual scenes are punctuated by brief mob scenes, and horrors are not avoided: Blanche, the protagonist, is forced to drink from a goblet containing the blood of her slaughtered father. Bernanos's text—which was staged as a play in 1951—is partly movie script and mainly measured dialogue, some of it rather chop-logical:

"Great trials await you, my daughter."
"No matter, if God gives me the strength."
"What He wishes to test in you is not your strength, but your weakness . . ."

And:

"You believe me kept here by fear?"
"Or by fear of fear. That fear, after all, is no more honorable than any other fear. One must know how to risk fear as one risks death, and true courage lies in that risk."

Both works turn on the paradox that Blanche ("I was born in fear, I have lived in it, I live in it still") at the last goes freely and fearlessly to her death on the scaffold, while Mother Marie of the Incarnation, the brave subprioress, who in her zeal for martyrdom has bound all the nuns by vow to seek it, is herself deprived of a martyr's crown. (At the time of the nuns' arrest, she is in quest of the fugitive Blanche. Blanche finally rejoins her sisters; Mother Marie is made to understand that her own sacrifice must be to embrace life, not death.)

In the early fifties, Poulenc was commissioned by Ricordi to write a ballet about St. Catherine of Siena, couldn't hit on a suitable scenario, and said he'd prefer to compose an opera for La Scala. Bernanos's *Dialogues* was suggested as a subject, and appealed to him. As a sort of test, he chose the opening words of the prioress, when Blanche first visits the convent:

Do not believe that this armchair is a privilege of my rank, like the footstool of a duchess! Alas! through charity to my dear daughters, who set great store by it, I wish I could feel at ease in it. But it is not easy to resume old habits too long abandoned, and I see clearly that what should be a pleasure will never again be more than a humiliating necessity for me.

Having chosen that speech, "apparently simple but pregnant with meanings," Poulenc said, "I told myself that if I could succeed in keeping its spirit intact in a musical setting, I would have written the opera." He set it, with a flowing Moonlight Sonata figure as accompaniment, to a graceful line that is at once rhythmically patterned and sensitive to natural speech timing. The inflections of the sentences as they might be spoken are widened into lyricism: though the line has the easy spontaneity of "word melody," it spans a surprisingly wide range. When Blanche replies, she, the soprano, does so across smaller intervals than the contralto prioress has used, going less high and less low—one of the many ways in which Poulenc's music throughout the opera delicately limns character and situation. The G-minor harmonic progression is borrowed from "How dark and dreadful is this place," in the cemetery scene of Stravinsky's *The Rake's Progress*. The ostinato bass oscillates across a minor third; the finale of the opera is founded on a similar bass, and there its derivation from the opening and close of Stravinsky's *Oedipus Rex* has often been noted. Poulenc inscribed his score "to the memory of my mother, who revealed music to me; of Claude Debussy, who gave me the taste to write some; and of Claudio Monteverdi; Giuseppe Verdi, and Modest Mussorgsky, who served here as my models." The eclecticism is proclaimed; perhaps the name of Franck should be added, of Gounod, of Prokofiev (for the "white-note" opening of the first interlude in Act III, recalling the cloister scene of *The Fiery Angel*, which was performed in Paris in 1954, and for the *marche macabre* that introduces the final scene), and, above all, of Stravinsky, through whom the most Mussorgskian passages (such as the start of Act III, Scene 1) seem to have been filtered, and whose *Symphonies of Wind Instruments* probably suggested the big harmonies near the start of Act II.

Wherever one looks and listens, there is fine, careful working, and other men's devices become Poulenc's own, because they are put to unexpected uses. *Dialogues* is an opera that happens to be about religion; it is not religious music. The composer made it clear that what attracted him to the subject was the passionate vehemence of the characters and the "terrestrial conflict" they wage against fear. He set perhaps a third of Bernanos's text. The characters will not seem rounded to anyone who has not read the whole of it; nor will the subtleties of the character drawing in music be fully apparent. But the dramatic ellipses here provide the sort of check that, in one form or another, Poulenc regularly imposed upon himself. Essentially, he was a romantic and sentimental composer who never quite let himself go. (It is not a failing, but the source of that ambiguity which gives his music its piquancy and distinctive tone.) In early years, the check was provided by containing impulses within forms and manners of composers less romantic, less sentimental than he was. Then, in his first opera, *Les Mamelles de Tirésias*, he could let himself go more freely, within a framework that allowed him a jester's license; it is hard in the exuberant *Tirésias* to tell the ironic from the serious. But when, in the *Dialogues*, Mother Marie proposes the vow of martyrdom over a squashy chord sequence that could well be that of a Gershwin song, what are we to make of it? "Disarming simplicity"? David Drew, an acute critic of Poulenc's music, asked the question nearly twenty years ago, and continued with others: "Can we be sure of who is being disarmed, and of what? Is it the sophisticated Poulenc of yesterday, the unsophisticated nuns of the story, or the adamant theology of Bernanos' text?" The almost buffo tone of the exchanges between Mother Marie and the officer who comes to expel the nuns from their convent prompts similar questions. And what could be more stagy than the finale: a "Salve Regina" started by fifteen voices, punctuated by the thud of the guillotine, and reduced voice by voice until only one is left? Is this a tasteless musical *coup de théâtre* that Puccini might have flinched from? It does not seem so in the theater. Throughout the *Dialogues*, there are tensions between theatricality and reticence, effusion and understatement. Swift surges of emotion are suddenly cut short. Secure in the discipline that his text imposes, Poulenc can indulge in romantic gestures freely; Bernanos insures that they do not get out of control.

Poulenc cast his opera in three acts, each of four scenes, some of them divided by "interludes," or brief dialogues played before a drop curtain. The act curtains define three stages in Blanche's quest for a refuge from fear. At the end of Act I, the prioress who received her into the convent dies a "bad," fearful death, almost blaspheming; the convent brings no assurance of spiritual calm. At the end of Act II, revolutionary shouts of "Ça ira" break into the sacristy, and Blanche in alarm drops *le Petit Roi*, a figure of the Christ-child, which shatters; her physical safety is threatened even here. At the end of the opera— through some mysterious working of grace—Blanche suddenly conquers her fear and goes steadfastly to a "good" death. This pattern is somewhat obscured in the Metropolitan production, where John Dexter, its director, has reshaped the opera in two acts, each of six scenes. His production is a disciplined and successful essay in what might be termed the post-Piscator or early-Rennert manner—the lean, simple, black-and-white method of staging widely practiced in postwar Germany, when there was not much money available for scenery, and directors made a theatrical virtue of economy, seeking to reduce the "clutter" and trappings of traditionally opulent opera. David Reppa's set for the *Dialogues* is a large black box, with a raked cruciform platform as its floor. Abstracts from what the realistic scenery would be—a fireplace and doorway, the grille of the convent *parloir*, a row of arches sketched in aluminum tubing—drop down to suggest the different localities, and are seconded by Gil Wechsler's deftly accomplished lighting. On the open stage, scene follows scene without a break; Mr. Dexter has invented pantomimes to accompany the instrumental passages that Poulenc composed for the practical purpose of covering scene shifts and the more important musical purpose of varying the dramatic mode by throwing all attention for a while on the orchestra. With increasing frequency, opera directors refuse to allow opera composers to make any of their points unaided: overtures are "choreographed," the *Ring* preludes are turned into action scenes, orchestral interludes are mimed. Mr. Dexter's pantomimes are inoffensive—indeed, rather impressive—examples of the practice, but the listener will probably get a better idea of Poulenc's intention by looking away from the stage and just listening between scenes; the composer's moment for curtain-rise can nearly always be heard in the music itself. The staging is lucidly conceived, cleanly and cogently executed. On the first night, something went wrong at the very end: the climactic moment when Blanche steps forward from the crowd to join her companions in death was no more than a vague scuffle at the back of the stage; one critic even had the impression that she went "silently" to her death—whereas the musical point is that, marching to the scaffold, she continues the singing that, voice by voice, the guillotine has cut short. This was put right in later performances.

The casting of the Met production is almost perverse in that the two principal soprano roles are assigned to mezzos: Maria Ewing is Blanche, and Shirley Verrett is the second prioress (a role Joan Sutherland used to sing). Both of them can get the notes: the question is one not of range but of vocal color. In phrases that call for the clear, floating sound of a soprano we hear the complicated, rich, intense timbre of a mezzo in her upper ranges. The only soprano left us is Sister Constance, latest avatar of the innocent, merry, carefree companion to a troubled heroine. (Aennchen in *Der Freischütz*, Sophie in *Werther*, and Barbara in *Kat'a Kabanová* are among her ancestors.) Betsy Norden sang the part prettily, even if her tone was a shade thin. Miss Ewing's Blanche was touching, and surely sung. The portrayal of outward composure broken by sudden, uncontrolled surrender to the promptings of her constant inner fear was skillfully achieved. She did not quite solve the problem that Poulenc, largely by his abridgment of the Bernanos text, had set her: revealing to us why the tiresome, selfish girl should be the object of so much loving care from the two prioresses and Mother Marie and Sister Constance.

In an otherwise very consistent, integrated production, Miss Verrett alone seemed to have resisted the force of Mr. Dexter's harmonizing hand. There was almost a touch of Josephine Baker in her portrayal of a nun. (She crossed herself not naturally but with high operatic flamboyance.) The point about the second prioress is that she is a strong woman of sound common sense, not prey to the passions that flare both in her predecessor and in Mother Marie; and, unlike them, she is a bourgeoise—a cattle dealer's daughter—not an aristocrat. Her two solos are the closest things to arias to be found in the *Dialogues*. Miss Verrett sang them in lustrous timbres but did not make much of the words. (All that I caught in the first piece was the phrase "many kinds of porridge"; that can't be right.) The opera was done in Joseph Machlis's English version, which is fluent and musical (even if here and there one itched to tinker with details of inflection) but calls for singers ready to adjust the strict musical notation to English stresses. From this point of view, it was the Frenchwoman in the cast, Régine Crespin, as the first prioress, who provided a model of how to sing English words on the operatic stage. Each vowel was given its distinct color. Meter was modified by sense. The words were laid along the music, or vice versa, with the mastery of someone who knows how to declaim. There was none of the unnaturalness that, for example, William Dooley, as Blanche's father, brought to such a phrase as "when wine is plen-ti-ful and cheap" by giving each syllable the same length and weight. Mme Crespin, who played the second prioress at the Paris première of the *Dialogues*, in 1957, and does so in the Angel recording of the opera, was in her new role most powerful, dramatic, and affecting. So was Mignon Dunn in the role of Mother Marie. In a subtly controlled portrayal, by a stance, a gesture, a glance, a telling verbal emphasis, she revealed in detail the proud subprioress's feelings about her successive superiors, about Blanche, about her own duties as a Carmelite. Mother Marie is in effect the tragic heroine of the tale. Miss Dunn's performance was of the kind that made not only her own role but everyone else's more vivid.

Michel Plasson conducted, admirably, as a supple interpreter of Poulenc's phrases, quick to reveal the expressive colors of the orchestral writing, and as an accompanist who refused to allow his players to drown the voices. His blend of delicacy, reticence, and sudden, full-throated emotion, of sentiment tempered by discretion, of charm and intelligence combined, was exactly what Poulenc's score requires.

February 21, 1977

David Drew's "The Simplicity of Poulenc," an introduction to a BBC broadcast of the Dialogues, *appeared in* The Listener *for January 16, 1968, p. 137.*

SONG IN GREEN

A sad tale's best for winter. At least twice this winter we were invited
in—by Benjamin Luxon and Yehudi Wyner at Town Hall, and, six days
later, by Richard Dyer-Bennet and Nancy Garniez at Alice Tully Hall—
to hear the sad tale of a miller lad who loved a miller's daughter, lost
her to a huntsman, and drowned himself for grief. Wilhelm Müller wrote
the words. The action passes in spring, but Müller headed his verses
with the direction "Im Winter zu lesen." He speaks a prologue, which
might be rendered as:

> Fair ladies, clever gentlemen. draw near,
> And something worth your while you'll see and hear:
> Today I offer you a brand-new play
> Recounted in an extra-brand-new way,
> Plainly constructed, fashioned without guile,
> Decked in the noble, simple German style,
> Cocky as a soldier-boy with gay cockade,
> Yet by a pious touch or two o'erlaid.
> I do not ask that I should be applauded;
> Just step inside—by that I'll feel rewarded.
>
> I hope, since icy winter rules outside,
> An hour or so in green you'll gladly bide;
> For know you this: that in my songs today
> Fair spring and all her flowers are on display.
> Out in the open air I lay my scene,
> Far from the city, where the air is clean.
> Through woods and fields, through dales and hills we'll roam,
> And any indoor action, played at home,
> Will through an open window be observed;
> Thus Art and you alike are fitly served.
>
> You ask about the persons in the play?
> Well—blame the Muses!—all that I can say
> Is that there's only one. It's not too bad,
> For he's a blond and youthful miller lad.
> (Although a brook may sing the final word,
> To dub that brook a person is absurd.)
> A Monodrama—that's the term I seek;
> A Monodrama: one alone will speak.
>
> One moment, while I set a fitting scene:
> Our stage is richly carpeted in green;
> A thousand colored flowers bedeck the ground,
> And tracks and paths are trampled all around;
> Above our heads the glorious sun appears;

Below, it sparkles bright on dew—or tears!
Ere long, the silvery moon through clouds will smile,
Most melancholy—in the modern style.
A lofty forest forms my hinterground,
Where dogs are barking, hunters' horns resound,
And from the crags a crystal fountain gushes.
Down to the vale, a silver brooklet rushes.
There mill wheels roar, machinery clatters round,
Till birdsong in the neighboring grove is drowned.
Good people, if my songs seem rude or lame,
The simple rustic setting is to blame.
Yet mill wheels have a charm some can't resist;
What is it?—Ask my monodramatist;
If I revealed it, I might spoil his play.
Farewell, good friends! enjoy yourselves today!

There follow twenty-three poems—twenty-one from the young miller, a dialogue between him and the brook, a final lullaby from the brook alone—and then an epilogue from the poet. Müller's *Die schöne Müllerin* was published in 1821. Shortly before his death, six years later, he wrote to a friend, "Perhaps a kindred spirit will someday be found whose ear will catch the melodies from my words, and who will give me back my own." It's a puzzling thing to have said. Schubert's setting of *Die schöne Müllerin* had been published in Vienna, in five volumes, in 1824. Did no one draw Müller's attention to it? Could he have known the songs and not perceived that in Schubert the kindred spirit he sought had already been found?

Many eloquent words have been written about Schubert's cycle. To read Lotte Lehmann's pages on it, in her *More Than Singing*, is almost to hear an ideal interpretation. And to see one, too: to see not only the singer—who at the start of "Am Feierabend" should "stand very erect, with flashing eyes, as if really to struggle and determined to win"—but also what he (or possibly she, but it is really a man's cycle; Lehmann herself and Inez Matthews are the only women to have recorded it) is singing of. Lehmann blends scenic description, emotion, and practical advice. About "Thränenregen":

You see the deep blue heaven with its brilliant stars reflected in the brook. Heaven and water seem mysteriously interwoven, the earth seems extinguished. . . . This vision grips your thirsty, impressionable, vulnerable, poet's soul. Confusion sweeps over you—the beauty of this moment is too great, too much for you. You lean down toward the brook and see its waters, like a luminous veil, rippling on over the image of your beloved. . . . Sing mysteriously, calling and yet listening. . . . Lift out the two words "Geselle, Geselle" like a call, sing them separated from the continuing musical phrase.

523

It was Lehmann who first revealed to me the character of the eponymous *Müllerin*. "Das Mühlenleben," one of the three poems that Schubert left unset, tells us something about her: when the hands are at work, she occasionally visits them, prattling prettily but also checking on their industry with a sidelong glance; "judiciously she praises one lad so that another will notice and consider how he can do better and earn her thanks." In "Thränenregen," a sentence of hers is quoted. The boy has been so deeply affected by the beauty of the scene that his eyes fill with tears. And *she* says, "It's beginning to rain, goodbye, I'm going in." "In this one sentence," Lehmann tells her reader, "you must convey the picture of the girl: an unromantic, commonplace nature, coquettish, a little superior, scornful but at the same time almost superstitiously fearful of anything which is at all foreign to her. . . . In the postlude, slowly bow your head as if you, the miller boy, withdraw into yourself."

The singer of Schubert's second Müller cycle, *Winterreise*, has no human company—snarling dogs, a sinister crow, a will-o'-the-wisp, a withered leaf are his companions—until in the final song he meets the hurdy-gurdy man. He must be a skillful scene painter, but he himself is the only character who crosses the scenes. *Winterreise* is a series of linked wintry images and reflections. But *Die schöne Müllerin* is a drama. Although the monodramatist begins and ends in solitude (except for his constant companion the brook), the central scenes are played out in company: his master the miller, the fair daughter of the mill, his fellow workers, his rival the huntsman from the wooded hill—all these must be evoked. Schubert spent a great part of his brief life writing ambitious operas, and had no success with them. *Die schöne Müllerin* is a kind of one-man, one-piano domestic opera. A successful performance requires that it should be more than a sequence of beautiful songs, and more even than a dramatic narrative: it must be a drama, just such a drama as Müller promises in his prologue. And this drama the two performers must create by fine imaginative strokes, by touches of emphasis and color which depict and then people their scenes without the aid of set designer and stage director.

Mr. Luxon, a Cornishman, sang the cycle in German to an American audience, and it is hard to be dramatic in a foreign language. (At the Vivian Beaumont, Joseph Papp is not presenting *The Cherry Orchard* in Russian.) But there are things to be said in favor of singing songs in the original language—I won't plow through that well-tilled field again— and there are ways to diminish the loss of communication which results when the language is not that of the audience. Mr. Luxon forwent the simplest of them: providing listeners with a text and a line-by-line translation. His program book contained only a close-set, run-on prose translation of the poems. For those not fluent in German it would have been better than nothing—if it had not been rendered useless by the turning out of the lights in the hall. Another way is to use words so vividly that some of the sense and a good deal of the feeling come through; purely formed, distinctly sounded vowels and subtly timed, carefully placed consonants can be expressive in their own right. But Mr. Luxon's German was not especially expressive or eloquent. As if in an endeavor to get at least something across, he sacrificed fine detail and concentrated on broadly emotional effects, laying on colors with a wide brush, in energetic strokes, and underlining them with altogether too vigorously active a platform demeanor. Physically and vocally, he lurched into phrases. After what seemed to be an attempt to raise the roof with "Mein!" I felt I had had enough, and left in the pause that preceded "Pause." Time could be better spent with Aksel Schiøtz and Gerald Moore, or with Peter Pears and Benjamin Britten. I choose two tenors from the long list of the singers who have recorded *Die schöne Müllerin* because it is essentially a tenor cycle. Baritone timbre (Mr. Luxon is a baritone) darkens its springtime freshness, and downward transpositions to accommodate the lower voice inevitably cumber the sonorities of the piano part. (Nevertheless, the baritones Gerhard Hüsch, Dietrich Fischer-Dieskau, and Gérard Souzay have put memorable interpretations of the cycle on record.) And I choose the two pianists who have played it with art unrivaled since recorded musical history began.

Mr. Moore has also written about the cycle. To read his pages on *Die schöne Müllerin*, in *The Schubert Song Cycles*, is again to hear an ideal interpretation—and this time, if one happens to be a pianist, also to feel it through one's fingers. Of the miller maid's unfeeling remark at the end of "Thränenregen" Mr. Moore says:

This blow is delivered so carelessly and unfeelingly, and with such unexpectedness that it must be thrown away by the singer: lightly sung in the most matter-of-fact way. He will be helped if the quaver passage in the pianoforte trips down without delaying. . . . That the boy is hurt is clearly shown in the postlude. Once again our Schubert comes up with a telling stroke in the final bars. Hope and despair are in those four bars. Hope in [the first two]: despairing realization in [the next two]. The pianist allows us to hear this dramatic change by a distinct hesitation before the minor chord, as if reluctant to accept the inevitable.

Anyone who loves Schubertian detail, and can play the piano at all, must surely be impelled by that to go to the keyboard and try the effect of the distinct hesitation; and also, if he has a record collection that allows it, to listen to Mr. Moore's own rendering of the passage. (He has recorded *Die schöne Müllerin* at least five times, with Schiøtz, with Rudolf Schock, and thrice with Fischer-Dieskau as his vocal partner, across a period of some thirty years.) And then, perhaps, to hear next how Britten handled it—for Britten played Schubert as if he had *become* Schubert; there was no sense of someone "interpreting" another's notes. The imagery of the final *Müllerin* songs ("Ah, down below, cooling rest!" "Hither, hither; whatever can cradle will lull and rock the boy to rest") is the recurrent imagery of Britten's own oeuvre: Peter Grimes, Billy Budd, the Little Sweep in Charles Kingsley's version of that tale, the cabin boy in *The Golden Vanity*, Aschenbach as in imagination he follows Tadzio out to sea—all find peace at last in the cradle of the deep. Tarquin's seeking to cool his wild blood in the Tiber and then in Lucretia is a variant of the theme. So, if less directly, is the encounter of the two soldiers in the finale of the *War Requiem*. The E major of "Des Baches Wiegenlied" found its way into *Death in Venice*. In several Britten works, its cradling water rhythms answer the question "What harbour shelters peace?" posed by Grimes and taken up (often with the same motif of a rising ninth) in later compositions. Another *Müllerin* song, "Die liebe Farbe," is the basis of a scene in Michael Tippett's opera *The Knot Garden*. I doubt whether any composer could know *Die schöne Müllerin* without finding that some currents from Schubert's stream—nature as an ever-changing reflection of men's feelings, and all turned into music—have flowed into his own musical personality. That stream lives in the piano part. I have still to hear it played on such a piano as Schubert himself knew, light, silvery, and clear; Britten comes closest to making a modern concert grand sound right. Though Mr. Luxon had a most musical, imaginative pianist in Yehudi Wyner, it was too often big, round, modern sound that we heard from his Baldwin.

It is hard on modern performers that they should be measured against not only their contemporaries but also the greatest of their predecessors. Yet since the phonograph became our most abundant provider of musical experiences it has been inevitable. Why brave winter's snow and ice to attend a recital less rewarding than one that can be enjoyed in comfort at home? Because, of course, the live performance may well have something to offer which cannot be caught by the phonograph. Richard Dyer-Bennet's recital had. He presented the cycle as the little play that Wilhelm Müller had in mind, and drew his listeners with him into the drama. He introduced and ended it by speaking an English version of Müller's prologue and epilogue. And he sang the songs in English, too, so that the audience could follow the action scene by scene, line by line, without a language barrier between them and the work, and without having to scan parallel columns of German and English. *Die schöne Müllerin* has been many times translated; versions by A. H. Fox Strangways and Steuart Wilson, in their *Schubert's Songs Translated*, and by Richard Capell are notable. But in any version a singer may find things that lie uncomfortably for him, and Mr. Dyer-

Bennet has made his own translation, under the title *The Lovely Milleress.* (The Oxford English Dictionary records the unusual word in Aubrey's *Letters Written by Eminent Persons*: "O God! Woe is me miserable, my father was a Miller, and my mother a Milleresse, and I am now a Ladie"—referring to an early, unequal match in the Herbert family.) The new translation, which is published by Schirmer, sings easily and naturally. I do not have Fox Strangways-Wilson or Capell at hand for comparison, but Dyer-Bennet is certainly a cut above Theodore Baker, Henry S. Drinker, and Robert Randolph Garran—three earlier versions that I pulled from the Public Library shelves. If anyone doubt that lieder can successfully be sung in English translation, let him listen —if he can find a copy—to Harry Plunket Greene's record of "The Hurdy-Gurdy Man," and study Plunket Greene's *Interpretation in Song* and Dorothy Uris's *To Sing in English.* Mr. Dyer-Bennet provided further proof that it can be done—even though his recital was not quite all one had hoped for. As a ballad singer he made his name, and as a ballad singer he is adept at adjusting strict meter to words and their sense in a way that most young lieder singers, especially outside their own tongue, neglect. But to sing Schubert's "art songs" he donned a suit and tie not just in fact but, so to speak, in his art as well. His phrasing lacked the verbal freedom and vividness he brings to "Lord Rendal" or "Barbara Allen." His tenor was small—too small for so large and so unresonant a hall as Tully—but still clear. Mrs. Garniez, at a Steinway, subdued the piano part to a point where often it ceased to sparkle as it should. (She could have hit a Schubertian fortepiano harder without fear of drowning the singer.) All the same, it was a *Schöne Müllerin* that came to life. At the age of sixty-three, Mr. Dyer-Bennet may be tempted to view the miller lad's eager joys and swift despairs with the eyes of experience, but his presentation of the drama was unfailingly fresh, youthful, and enthusiastic.

February 28, 1977

GREAT BRIDGE, OUR MYTH

Much American imagery is drawn together in Elliott Carter's latest composition, *A Symphony of Three Orchestras*, dedicated to the New York Philharmonic and its music director, Pierre Boulez, and first performed by them last month. The opening can be heard as an evocation in picturesque sound of the Brooklyn Bridge. High on the violins, as one thin, shining, open-textured chord is laid upon another, in shifting aeolian strains, it seems as if the cradle of wires overhead may be sounding: "Sibylline voices flicker, waveringly stream, As though a god were issue of the strings." The violins span the stage from side to side. Between them, three piccolos then break in with keen, bright bird cries, given added sharpness by small, high hammer beats from piano and xylophone; clarinets and oboes swell the shrill chorus to a brief tumult. In a program note, the composer quotes the beginning of Hart Crane's *The Bridge*:

> How many dawns, chill from his rippling rest
> The seagull's wings shall dip and pivot him,
> Shedding white rings of tumult, building high
> Over the chained bay waters Liberty—

And then a single trumpet wings out in long solo flight. Wheeling through the faint, ethereal violin chords, it mounts, hovers, circles down, soars again, swiftly plummets, stays for a moment poised low, traces a final, sudden ascent and fall before coming to rest. A series of emphatic descending figures from each orchestra in turn ends the introduction (in the Crane opening, "elevators drop us from our day"), and the symphonic argument begins in earnest with a huge span of sixths softly sustained by the strings of one orchestra and *giocoso* chattering from two bassoons of another.

The piece lasts fifteen minutes. Orchestra I, on the left of the platform, consists of brasses, strings, and kettledrums. Orchestra III, on the right of the platform, consists of triple woodwinds (without clarinets), two horns, strings (no cellos), and unpitched percussion, mainly metallic. Orchestra II, central, is a smaller ensemble: three clarinets, piano, vibraphone, xylophone, marimba, chimes, long drum, tomtom, and a handful of strings. The violins of Orchestra I and of Orchestra III, arranged across the front of the platform, provide a sonic balance like that of the first and second violins of a traditional orchestra traditionally seated; the differing wind and percussion complements give to each orchestra its distinctive timbre and character. Orchestra II is a band of soloists, a concertante group set against the twin-ripieno of the rest, and it is invited to phrase with rubato.

The work plays without break but is not exactly a "one-movement symphony." Between the introduction and an extended coda there are twelve brief movements, four for each orchestra, and each orchestra plays its four movements twice, not in regular order. Each movement is altered when it returns. Each is based on a different three-note chord. Between movements, each orchestra falls silent for a few measures, and the silences and the lapping are so arranged that, for some moments at least, each movement can be heard by itself. But most of the time

528

two or three movements are being played simultaneously. "The listener, of course," says Carter, "is not meant, on first hearing, to identify the details of this continually shifting web of sound . . . but rather to hear and grasp the character of this kaleidoscope of musical themes as they are presented in varying contexts." At fourth and fifth hearing, much of the detail still remained elusive. The movements most easily recognized are those of clear harmonic character: the piled-up sixths already mentioned, which form the first movement of Orchestra I; the pure, open fifths of Orchestra II's first movement; the 6-4 major and 6-3 minor triads (result of putting a major third above a perfect fourth, or vice versa) in the second movement of Orchestra III. Each of the twelve movements proceeds at its own distinct speed. The general effect, the "character of this kaleidoscope," is easy to enjoy. One kind of music breaks in upon another, comes to the fore, then recedes at the advance of yet another kind of music. Harmonic colors, instrumental timbres, varied textures, speeds, and kinds of figuration lap, clash, combine, cohere, then part. Perspectives shift. Foreground becomes middle or background. Image crowds upon image. It might have been chaos, but it is a disciplined dance of clearly formed ideas, defined in space by the siting of the three orchestras and defined in time by the composer's carefully balanced structure.

The structure recalls that of Carter's Third String Quartet, which is two independent, patterned duologues, one of four episodes each heard thrice, the other of six episodes each heard twice, concurrent but not synchronous, and so distributed that at some point each of the four episodes encounters and overlaps with each of the six. But the symphony is an "easier" work for the listener than the quartet, because its ideas are so colorful. Well before his ear has learned to spot and recognize the recurrent movements, he will have learned to find his way through the piece by sonic landmarks—besides those already mentioned, two rhapsodic violin solos; a peal of bells, clanging open fifths; a poignant melody from the bass clarinet; a sudden, insistent reiteration of G minor. Carter, as I have often remarked, is a "graphic" composer. To find words to describe the music of his Third Quartet and his Duo for Violin and Piano I turned to similes from nature. But the words for the symphony have already been written by Hart Crane. Since student days, Carter says, he has dreamed of making a musical work from Crane's *The Bridge*, and he calls the symphony in some sense a sketch for that work. Behind the jocund two-bassoon episode lies the Rip Van Winkle section of the poem. The pealing bells are partly a response to Columbus's prayer in *The Bridge*, partly an image from a later poem: "The bells, I say, the bells break down their tower; / And swing I know not where. Their tongues engrave / Membrane through marrow, my long-scattered score / Of broken intervals."

Anyone brought up, as I was, in the English choral tradition is brought up with Walt Whitman—set to music by Gustav Holst (Carter's teacher at Harvard), Delius, and Vaughan Williams—and comes to America prepared for long democratic vistas, primed with the poetic imagery of the New World, and ready for Crane. Long before I read *The Bridge*, I had walked to Brooklyn along that "path amid the stars crossed by the seagull's wing" and had ridden to Brooklyn on the IRT subway—had discovered with eyes and feet and feelings two of the most potent symbols in this city of romantic symbols. Some of them, such as Whitman's ferry to Brooklyn, have gone. Others, once visions, have become everyday sights: Whitman's view of the earth as a "vast Rondure swimming in space," which I sang of as a treble and have now seen through eyes transported by television's magic far out into space; Crane's day when "The soul, by naphtha fledged into new reaches, / Already knows the closer grasp of Mars." The new monuments have their own meanings. Since man is not allowed to set foot on the Verrazano-Narrows Bridge, it stands as a huge symbol of his slavery to the motorcar, while the Brooklyn Bridge continues to be celebrated. Alan Trachtenberg, in his monograph *Brooklyn Bridge: Fact and Symbol*, took the tale of what it has inspired up to 1965. Since then, Marianne Moore has hymned the "Caged Circe of steel and stone" (Elizabeth Bishop had invited Miss Marianne Moore over Brooklyn Bridge to come flying into Manhattan, "mounting the sky with natural heroism"), and now Elliott Carter has set sounding not only the "arching strands of song," the "humming spars," but Crane's transcendent vision of the bridge extending to span not just the East River but all America from east to west. Far below the river runs the bridge's dark shadow, the subway—path amid the stars and swift passage tunneled through the earth. With Columbus, Cortés, and Pizarro, the poet voyages west, meets Pocahontas, dances with her, merges with the land and with the great flowing river. He travels now with the gait of a dreamer, lingering on the bridge itself while his mind voyages out in the clippers below to distant shores; then rushes swiftly by iron road across this huge land; then moves with the Mississippi, slow. Finally, he rides the subway home to Brooklyn—and Poe, his eyes like agate lanterns, is companion on that journey.

Carter's symphony is in no sense a musical "transcription" of *The Bridge*, but its different kinds of movement and its rich superimposition of image upon image produce something of the effect of that poem. And, because it compasses so much in fifteen minutes, other visions are recalled, other feelings stirred, while one listens—sights and sensations familiar to Carter's contemporaries but not to Crane's: the view of Manhattan from an airplane that has climbed steeply from La Guardia, when the huge, populous city shrinks to a small island in the river and its towers become play blocks heaped by a child; the sense, while flying west, that one is actually tracing through air and traversing the mythic span of Crane's bridge. Whitman hymned the linked Union Pacific and Central Pacific as "Bridging the three or four thousand miles of land travel, / Tying the Eastern to the Western sea . . . (Ah Genoese thy dream! thy dream! / Centuries after thou art laid in thy grave, / The shore thou foundest verifies thy dream)," but flight has added a swifter metaphor-made-concrete to his vision. New York might be a hard city to live in were it not for the poets, painters, and musicians who teach us to see, to feel, and to dream here. Without them, a subway ride might be no more than a dirty, noisy, possibly dangerous way of getting from place to place—instead of a romantic adventure, symbolism experienced as fact. Without them, we might not see Hector, Orestes and the Furies, Faust, Don Quixote as through Manhattan's streets we saunter pondering. Pale, impassioned Norma, crazed Lucia, John of Leiden would stay locked inside the Met, and the vocalism of sun-bright Italy and German organ majestic not sound forth in the bold American day. Crane placed a sentence from Job at the start of *The Bridge*—"From going to and fro in the earth, and from walking up and down in it"—but it is not only Satan who stalks the city with him and with us. Columbus, Cortés, and Pizarro, Pocahontas, Rip Van Winkle, and Poe have been mentioned. Walt Whitman is ever at hand, a Virgil to Crane's Dante. Marlowe, Blake, Melville, Isadora Duncan, and Emily Dickinson appear, and Plato prefaces the final section with his "Music is then the knowledge of that which relates to love in harmony and system." That Carter should have found *The Bridge* an intractable text to set as an oratorio is not surprising: Crane struggled for lucid utterance; in Waldo Frank's words, "his attempt, with sound materials, to achieve poetic form was ever close to chaos." That Carter should have been moved by the ideas and imagery of the poem to compose this ordered symphony is not surprising, either. The techniques of time flow and overlapping discourse pursued in his earlier works prepared him for the handling of so rich a theme.

We can praise *A Symphony of Three Orchestras* for its visionary aspiration. We can praise it for its refined, very delicate, and subtle workmanship. (Even the notation, designed to catch the differing tempi within a single set of bar lines, so that one conductor can keep time for all three orchestras, represents a triumph of musico-mathematical ingenuity.) On the simplest but not least important level, we can praise the expressive quality of the melodies and of the instrumental colors (shimmering touches from a bell tree, warm cello cantilenas, brass notes climbing one upon another like the courses of some cyclopean wall—or of the "twin monoliths" that carry the bridge). The symphony is of all Carter's scores the richest in sound. But not aspiration, or good con-

531

struction, or vivid orchestration is in itself enough to produce a composition so moving and memorable as this. All three combine. In a series of performances, Boulez and the Philharmonic played it with ever-increasing mastery. They have also recorded it, for release by Columbia.

March 7, 1977

FRAGMENTS OF THE HOUSE OF USHER

One of Giulio Gatti-Casazza's earliest acts on being appointed general manager of the Met, in 1908, was to obtain for his house the first-performance rights to a Poe double bill that Debussy was working on. He paid the composer two thousand francs for those rights; ten thousand more was due on delivery of the score. But, according to Gatti's memoirs, Debussy said, "It is a piece of bad business you are doing. I have some remorse in taking these few dollars. Yes, because I do not believe that I will ever finish any part of all this." Gatti continued to encourage him. Years passed. But "Alas! I never saw even a note of the operas of which the Metropolitan had been so proud to secure the rights. Debussy left nothing but a few scraps of music, insufficient and incomplete."

The most substantial of these scraps, the first two hundred bars or so of *The Fall of the House of Usher* sketched out in a particella (vocal lines, with the orchestral part indicated in condensed form on two, three, or four staves), was published, in facsimile, in 1962, and since then many people must have tried their hand at salvaging something performable from it. That year, excerpts from the opera were broadcast by the BBC and by the French radio. A more thoroughgoing reconstruction was staged last month in the Great Hall of Jonathan Edwards College, Yale. The particella, transcribed by Carolyn Abbate, a Yale student, had been orchestrated by Robert Kyr, a former Yale student. When the music ended, after twenty minutes, the remainder of Debussy's libretto was played out as a spoken drama. Its dénouement was accompanied by orchestral music built from a sketchy seven-bar fragment on a page the composer inscribed "Pour la fin de la m[aison] u[sher]," adding a large question mark.

A large question mark, I think, must also be set over Miss Abbate's and Mr. Kyr's work. At any rate, I penciled several small question marks beside preliminary claims that were made for it, and, mentally, several more over details heard in the performance and later checked against the facsimile of the original, when I was able to borrow a score. Gatti-Casazza called the surviving fragments "insufficient and incomplete." The Debussy scholar Robert Orledge, who has examined the *Usher* material and describes it in the latest issue of *The Musical Quarterly*, concludes that "it is impossible that anything approaching a complete version of *The Fall of the House of Usher* could ever be accurately reconstructed for performance, even with piano accompaniment only." Miss Abbate, in a program note, declares that the particella "has received little attention, often being erroneously dismissed as too confusing and incomplete to construct a rigorous and accurate performance." She also says that it represents about half the text. It doesn't. Debussy's libretto as printed in 1962 contains some three hundred lines of dialogue, and only some sixty-five of these appear before the particella peters out. The composer describes his work as "a progressive expression of anguish" but was unable to get beyond the first step of that progress. What Miss Abbate means by "rigorous" I am unsure; the implication that the Abbate-Kyr version can afford a strictly "accurate" representation of Debussy's intentions is unfounded. The particella's indications for scoring are scant; there are no tempo, dynamic, or expression marks; and other sources provide no more than a few hints of what the composer may have had in mind. What one heard at Yale was a freely inventive—and skillful—orchestration in a Debussian manner incorporating such definite instrumental cues as are specified. But even the actual notes—let alone their timbre and tempo—are not always certain. Short passages transcribed by Mr. Orledge differ from their counterparts in the Yale score, and when I consulted the facsimile I sometimes came up with yet a third reading (but tentatively, for the facsimile is of very poor quality and the original is far away in Paris, in the Bibliothèque Nationale). A question mark is likely to hang over *any* transcription of this music, and an attempt to complete it in full score can only be speculative. The show was billed as the world première of a one-act opera by Claude Debussy. More decently, it could have been described as a bold student endeavor to give sound and context to an important, extended sketch for an unfinished work. As such, it was an occasion of the highest interest, and deserves extended discussion.

In 1890, Debussy was reported to be composing "a symphony on psychologically developed themes drawn from various Poe tales, particularly 'The Fall of the House of Usher.'" (That year, he named Poe and his translator, Baudelaire, among his favorite writers.) Miss Abbate, on what strikes me as rather flimsy evidence, dates Debussy's first work on an *Usher* opera to 1903. There is abundant evidence that between 1908 and 1911 he was immersed in the piece, dreaming of new, strange sounds, sketching music for the opening scenes, and shaping, from numerous drafts that have survived, the libretto now in the possession of his stepdaughter. For relief, he turned to Poe's "The Devil in the Belfry" (the sketches for which do go back to 1903). Other work was set aside: "I have reached the point of having entirely sacrificed the *Images* to Monsieur E. A. Poe. Although dead, this personage exercises an almost agonizing tyranny over me. I forget the normal rules of courtesy and shut myself up like a wild beast in the house of Usher, unless I am keeping company with the Devil in the belfry." In May 1910, the pieces were announced for the Opéra Comique (presumably after a Metropolitan première). But in February 1911, they were "postponed until I don't know when. . . . I am not very sorry, since there are many points of expression with which I am still unsatisfied; moreover, the scheme of things [mise en place] is insufficiently clear in my mind." *The Devil* was to contain choral writing of a kind that would make that of *Boris Godunov* and *Die Meistersinger* seem primitive; Debussy's account of his intentions suggests a vocal counterpart to the texture of *La Mer*. In *Usher*, the "naked flesh of emotion" would be laid bare; the phrase suggests that Debussy had been reading Poe's *Marginalia*, in which *My Heart Laid Bare* is described as a book no man *could* write, even if he dared. Debussy found that he could not write it. At the end of December 1911, he confessed that "everything [about the two Poe operas] strikes me as deadly dull. For a single bar I write which may be free or alive there are twenty stifled by the weight of what is known as tradition"—and it doesn't make it any better, he adds, that the tradition in question may well be his own. The powerful influence of Poe on Maeterlinck, on Debussy, and on *Pelléas* has often been observed. But what Debussy set store by was the difference between *Pelléas* and his new project. To a correspondent of *Harper's Weekly* he said in 1908 that "the inspiration I have found in Poe is totally different from that which I have experienced in Maeterlinck." Two years later, he told an interviewer in Budapest that, having had a success with *Pelléas*, he would "never again write a work in which its subject or atmosphere is recalled." But how could an opera set in an ancient castle where the air seems stifling, where the action passes into subterranean vaults, where a pale, mysterious maiden suffers fail to recall *Pelléas* in subject or atmosphere? And that, I suggest, is one reason that he found he could not get on with *The House of Usher*, and set it aside.

In 1916, he returned to the opera. He shortened and reordered the libretto, made a few more sketches, and ordered his earlier ideas in the form of the particella. A prelude, the Lady Madeline's song, a conversation between the Friend and the Family Doctor, and the first section of Roderick Usher's monologue were set down. But the particella breaks off inconclusively, with alternative settings of Roderick's cry to the

534

"vieilles pierres" of his house. Once again, Debussy could get no further. That, it seems to me, is what must have happened, though others may draw a different conclusion from the confusion of fragments and the numerous scattered references to the opera in Debussy's letters. All accounts may have to be modified when more of the *Usher* material—apparently there is more of it—comes to light. Maybe the composer did find some music for more than the opening scenes.

During his last bout with the opera, Debussy was dying. I have suggested one possible reason that, in the earlier period, the struggle to set it defeated him. Perhaps there is another and more cogent reason: in refashioning Poe's tale for the stage, the composer destroyed its essential character, and on some level he may have realized this. The "quaint and equivocal appellation of the 'House of Usher,' " as Poe makes clear, includes both the family and the family mansion; Roderick Usher and his house are described in similar terms. From the eaves of the building, moss hangs "in a fine tangled webwork," and from Roderick's head there hangs "hair of a more than weblike softness and tenuity," which "had been suffered to grow all unheeded." The aspects both of the house and of its master are beautiful in their features yet suggestive of decay within. A fissure, actual in the masonry, mental in the man, destroys them both together. Roderick's song, "The Haunted Palace," spells out the metaphor. Roderick Usher is central to the story; everything in it is about him. What did Debussy make of this? He invested Roderick with a guilty Byronic passion for his sister, which plays no part in Poe's story. He transferred the singing of "The Haunted Palace" to the Lady Madeline. By implication, he applied the Béranger couplet set over Poe's story—

> Son cœur est un luth suspendu
> Sitôt qu'on le touche il résonne—

to Madeline, not Roderick, by making the Doctor exclaim angrily that Usher plays upon his sister as if she were a lute. The sinister Doctor is a major new character, developed from a passing mention in Poe ("On one of the staircases, I met the physician of the family. His countenance, I thought, wore a mingled expression of low cunning and perplexity"). This Doctor also loves Madeline. In Debussy's version, it is he, not Roderick, who buries her alive—and that change in itself is enough to destroy the sense of Poe's carefully constructed tale.

Debussy compressed Poe's two weeks or so into about an hour of stage time. His opera starts with Madeline singing a verse of "The Haunted Palace," begun and ended offstage; in mid-song she crosses the scene. The Friend arrives and has a conversation with the Doctor. Roderick enters and soliloquizes. The Friend makes his presence known.

They talk; Roderick describes his plight and rushes abruptly from the room. The Doctor returns to say that meanwhile Madeline has died and has by him been interred in a vault, closed by a massive iron door, directly beneath the room they are in. Roderick re-enters, and the final scene follows Poe—except that it is for seven or eight minutes, not seven or eight days, that Roderick hears Madeline's struggles to escape from her tomb.

This is not a very good libretto, but it *is* Debussy's, and it is a pity that the Yale stage director, Graf Mouen, did not choose to stage it. Mr. Mouen decided to do something different. In his version, Roderick and Madeline share a bed-sitting-room, to which the Doctor comes with his early-morning tea. (He leaves pot and cup behind; later both Roderick and his Friend take swigs of what must by then be a very nasty stewed, cold brew.) Madeline wakes up, finds that her pet canary or budgie has died (or maybe she squeezes it to death—it was hard to be sure), and, closely observed by the Doctor, sings a verse of "The Haunted Palace" over it. She wanders out. The Friend arrives, and he and the Doctor sit down on Madeline's bed. Roderick slumbers on through their far from quiet conversation. During what should be *his* entrance music, Madeline returns to retrieve the corpse of the bird. Later, while Roderick and his Friend are talking, we *watch* her interment and her struggles to escape; these take place in an upper room, behind a gauze, and so of course Debussy's stage directions, for Roderick prone on the floor, listening with horror to the sounds from below, have to be scrapped. When the bloodstained Madeline makes her final appearance, instead of tottering for an instant on the threshold and then falling upon her brother, she first chases him round the room. This was not merely a very bad staging in its own right (Mr. Mouen set his actors to business that not even a Gielgud could make convincing); even if it had been effective, it would be no way to present a work being performed for the first time, before an audience that had come to see what Debussy had in mind.

Musically, things went rather better. Since there is not much space in the hall, Mr. Kyr had prepared a reduced, double-wind version of his score, without trombones, for this performance. [His full version, with a *Pelléas*-sized orchestra, was heard at a concert performance in Woolsey Hall on April 23.] The band—members of the Yale Symphony under their admirable young conductor, C. William Harwood—played well. Sheila Barnes delivered Madeline's song in clear, flexible tones, very beautifully. John Cimino as Roderick, John Ostendorf as the Friend, and Rinde Eckert as the Doctor were passable singers, but only the last was any kind of actor—and half the piece is spoken drama. The music was sung in French; the rest, for some curious reason, was spoken in a mixture of English and French. To translate the spoken text was

536

sensible. But if the House of Usher is to be assigned a more than symbolic location, it must surely be in some remote part of Britain, where the family physician would be likely to speak English, not French.

The vocal music—apart from the lyricism of Madeline's song—suggests the recitative style of *Pelléas* made still more urgent and intense. The motifs in the orchestra are often those found throughout Debussy's music—melodies poised for a moment on a sustained or repeated note, then breaking into a shapely tendril of sound, usually falling but sometimes ascending. The harmonies are held over pedal chords more often, perhaps, than in *Pelléas*, with the effect of a somber, persistent anchoring from which dissonant progressions struggle in vain to break free. Against the word "peur" in Debussy's copy of the Poe tale, Miss Abbate tells us, she found an annotation for violas "sur la touche" and a "léger coup de cymbale," and with this sound Mr. Kyr begins the opera. In 1909, Debussy told his publisher that the music he had devised for Roderick's monologue "has an attractive mustiness obtained by mixing the low notes of the oboe with violin harmonics. . . . I am rather proud of it." Mr. Kyr uses violin harmonics in what seem to be the right places, but, rather surprisingly, he places the oboe there in its highest register. He draws largely on the dark colors of alto flute, English horn, and bass clarinet. One would have to hear his full-orchestra version before judging the score; the general impression, of gloom, mystery, and murky passion, was effectively conveyed.

All in all—and despite the ridiculous staging—this *Fall of the House of Usher* was an adventurous and thoroughly worthwhile enterprise. Student musicology can come to life in performance; operatic history can take on shape and sound. I gratefully recall university productions of Georg Benda's melodrama *Ariadne* and of François Philidor's *Tom Jones* directed by scholars whose dissertation subjects they were. *The Fall of the House of Usher* obviously has no future in the regular operatic round, but this performance of its largest surviving fragment gave me a clearer idea of what Debussy was striving for—and also of why he could not achieve it—than long poring over the scattered sketches could do.

March 14, 1977

Debussy's libretto of The Fall of the House of Usher *and the facsimile of the particella were published in Edward Lockspeiser's* Debussy et Edgar Poe *(Monaco, 1962). See also Robert Orledge's articles "De-bussy's Musical Gifts to Emma Bardac," in* The Musical Quarterly, *60 (1974), pp. 544–56, and "Debussy's* House of Usher *Revisited," in* The Musical Quarterly, *62 (1976), pp. 536–53. A further page of* Usher *sketch is reproduced in Lockspeiser's* Debussy *(London, third edition, 1963), facing p. 111, there is a little more in the British Library, and some further pages have been traced; see* The New Yorker *for May 8, 1978, pp. 129–31.*

CATCHING UP

An all-Penderecki concert in Carnegie Hall, given by the Philharmonia Orchestra of Yale, the Westminster Choir, and the Trinity Choristers, conducted by the composer, provided a chance of catching up with two of Penderecki's fairly recent (1974) compositions—*Als Jakob erwachte . . .* and the Magnificat—in live sound. (Both have been recorded.) The full title of the first is, in translation, "And Jacob awaked out of his sleep, and he said, Surely the Lord is in this place; and I knew it not." It is a solemn, striking composition for large orchestra, made, like most of Penderecki's music, not of notes but of sounds—of evocative sonorities and timbres carefully laid out in time. Twelve ocarinas are used. "No composers," said Grove, "take the instrument seriously, or write music for a consort of ocarinas," but now Penderecki has done so. The soft, steady, pure, yet mysteriously undefined whistle of the ocarina duodecet makes an apt musical symbol for awe. The piece opens with a sequence of full, heavy, but pianissimo brass chords. In the printed score, they carry no expression marks and look quite plain; it was interesting to hear the composer himself treat each of them expressively, with a soft attack, a swelling to mezzo forte, and then a dying away. The massed sliding up and down that begins later presumably represents Jacob's re-calling his dream—angels of God ascending and descending a ladder from earth to Heaven.

The Magnificat was commissioned for the twelve-hundredth anniversary of Salzburg Cathedral and was first sung there during the 1974 Salzburg Festival. It is the 1966 *Luke Passion* mixture as before, except that drama is omitted and the gait is slower, more ceremonial. Again there are broad bands of background sound, gestures in the foreground, unisons that swell into clusters, common chords that thicken into dissonance, dense dissonances that clarify and resolve into triads or unisons, massed choral glissando that turns into caterwauling, massed sighs, whispers, and shouts. Rolling round a huge, resonant cathedral, and colored by a historical imagination roaming the centuries, the work would probably be very impressive; in the concert hall I began to get the fidgets before the forty-five minutes it lasts were done. The effect is of fluent and by now familiar formula, applicable to any pious text—

of generalized impressiveness in an all-purpose vanguard idiom. Penderecki's Magnificat is not a joyful song. Its most memorable episode is the bass solo insisting sternly that "he hath showed strength"—"potentiam, potentiam, potentiam"—"with his arm."

The program was completed by the Capriccio for Violin and Orchestra (1967), a compendium of fashionable orchestral effects, in which Syoko Aki was a brilliant soloist, and *Polymorphia* (1961), for forty-eight strings, whose score is made largely of encephalographs of mental patients recorded while they listened to Penderecki's earlier composition *Threnody*, and rounded off by a chord of C major. In this score, the duration of each "sound event" is measured out in seconds, but when the composer conducted his own piece he did not seem to be counting, and interpreted his own notation very freely. Maybe he has changed his mind about relative durations. But the result was to confirm any suspicions of a free, throwing-things-together method of composition, aiming at a general effect in which the details need not be precise. Pictures have been painted, sculptures assembled, dramas staged, and ballets choreographed in a similar way. Penderecki is a talented and imaginative musician, challenging to perform, and very easy to listen to. But there are few Penderecki compositions I find worth hearing more than once or twice.

Ian Strasfogel's New Opera Theatre at the Brooklyn Academy of Music, began operations last month by staging a triple bill of music mostly not intended for dramatic representation. That "mostly" allows for the two exceptions: Monteverdi's *Lamento della ninfa* and his *Combattimento di Tancredi e Clorinda*, which appeared in the Eighth Book of Madrigals as works "in genere rappresentativo"—dramatic episodes to insert into an evening of madrigals "senza gesto." (How the *Lamento* might be staged is a puzzle; *Tancredi* has both rudimentary and vivid cues for action in the music itself.) These formed the last two numbers of a Monteverdi anthology assembled under the title *Guerramore* and sung by four singers in costume, *con gesto*. Then came Leoš Janáček's song cycle *The Diary of One Who Disappeared*. A "scenic" presentation of the cycle was given, in Ljubljana, as early as 1926, but it gains as little—and loses as much—by staging as *Die schöne Müllerin* would. The third item was György Ligeti's *Aventures* and *Nouvelles Aventures*—nonsense music for vocal trio and instrumental ensemble, written for concert use but quite often treated as full-blown music theater.

There was no skimping. A baroque ensemble had been engaged for the Monteverdi, and the Speculum Musicae, under David Gilbert, for the Ligeti. There was no doubling of roles, except for the distant trio of women's voices in the Janáček; that was sung by principals of the two other pieces. Karl Eigsti's décors made the Lepercq Space of the

Academy look good. (Even without décor, it is one of New York's most congenial performance places.) But there was nothing quite first-rate, except Ursula Oppens's playing of the piano part in the *Diary*, and Susan Kay Peterson and Phyllis Hunter as the soprano and mezzo of the *Aventures*. New York needs a small, lively, adventurous opera company; I hope I can report with enthusiasm on the next production, due in May (p. 602).

Joan Morris is just about my favorite American singer—the one whose records I play and play and play again. Sometimes when I've been grumbling on about a recitalist who doesn't bring the words to life, who sings without rubato, straitjacketing a text and its sense to the written values of the notes, who thinks more about rounded tone production than about expressive timbres, I've asked, "Well, who does get everything right?" From recorded history, it's easy to answer: Adelina Patti, Alma Gluck, John McCormack, Conchita Supervia, Elisabeth Schumann are among the first names that come to mind. "But they're all dead; is it a lost art?" "No, there's Joan Morris; listen to two Nonesuch records she's made—'After the Ball' and 'Vaudeville.' They show exactly what I have in mind, what I've been missing."

This month, Miss Morris, with her husband and regular pianist, William Bolcom, gave a song recital in Alice Tully Hall; and Miss Morris in life is even more delightful than on disc. The voice is small; I had wondered whether it might be lost in that large, unresonant hall, which only a full orchestra can set ringing. In fact, it carried beautifully, for Miss Morris's projection is precise, her tone pure, and her intonation true. A sparkle like Alma Gluck's can enter the sound (it did so at the words "the sun came shining down," in Harry Von Tilzer's "Wait Till the Sun Shines, Nellie"). Basically the tone is sweet, limpid, and tender; in Sir Henry Bishop's "Home, Sweet Home" it was exquisite. She can warm it for the sentiment of Paul Dresser's "On the Banks of the Wabash," bleach it for the understated tragedy of Richard Rodgers's "Ten Cents a Dance," thicken it for the music-hall gusto of Henry Pether's "Waiting at the Church." She can bubble. She can sing risqué songs, such as Eubie Blake's "My Handy Man Ain't Handy No More," with a choirboy innocence that removes any taint of vulgarity but loses none of the humor. She knows when to join notes and when to separate them. She makes Charles Harris's "After the Ball" as moving as "Der Leiermann." She has the true lieder singer's genius for creating scene, character, and emotion with small, vivid, perfectly scaled strokes. There are records—Supervia's of Delibes's "Les Filles de Cadiz" is one—that it is hard to play through just once; something about them demands an immediate encore. Many of the tracks on Miss Morris's two Nonesuch LPs have this quality; her coloring or placing of a particular word is so enchanting that one needs to hear it again at once. Walter Legge set Elisabeth Schwarzkopf to study the single word "Bada" as it is sung by Nellie Melba on her disc of Mimì's Farewell. There is something in the way Miss Morris enunciates the single word "oh" in John Flynn's "Yip-I-Addy-I-Ay," the word "elephants" in Maurice Scott's "I've Got Rings on My Fingers," and the words "Fifth Avenue" in Alfred Solman's "The Bird on Nellie's Hat" which is magical. If I taught a lieder class, I would set it to study Miss Morris's and Mr. Bolcom's command of tempo and rubato in those songs, in James Thornton's "When You Were Sweet Sixteen," and in Rosamond Johnson's "My Castle on the Nile." Anyone who can manage "The Bird on Nellie's Hat" as she does should have no difficulty with the "Erlkönig." Copying—whether of pictures, compositions, or interpretations—is a good way of learning, a first step toward the acquiring of techniques that any artist of personality then uses for individual purposes. When Miss Morris sings songs associated with Adelina Patti, Blanche Ring, Ruth Etting, or Peggy Lee, she makes them all her own. She is a complete artist, and I hope one day to hear her sing Schubert, Loewe, Wolf, and Schoenberg's *Pierrot Lunaire*—in English translation, of course. Mr. Bolcom, with his rare command of rhythm, of textures, and of wide dynamics that support yet never drown the singer, is her ideal partner; his playing is at once witty, buoyant, and poetic.

Earlier this season, Jan DeGaetani gave three recitals in the Grace Rainey Rogers Auditorium of the Metropolitan Museum. The second of them included Schoenberg's *Buch der hängenden Gärten*. The program book had been slipped with a text of Stefan George's poems and an English translation, but the lights in the hall were turned out. As Miss DeGaetani took her place for the cycle, there was a cry from the darkness, Let there be light. And there was light, and it was good. But when the singer saw the light, she remarked, not altogether graciously, "Now that you can see the words, I hope you enjoy them." She herself did not make the words very enjoyable. She is an artist who works with sounds, timbres, and phrases, with melodies but not with words—an exquisite and precious musician who does very beautiful and expressive things with her voice, "playing" on it like an instrumental virtuoso. Of vocal writing by George Crumb, Peter Maxwell Davies, and Jacob Druckman she is an incomparable interpreter. But Crumb's *Madrigals* (the third book of which she sang at this recital), Davies's *Stone Litany* (which she sang so memorably at the Celebration of Contemporary Music festival a year ago), and Druckman's *Animus II* (which she sang at the third Metropolitan recital, and has recorded for CRI) do not employ words in any traditional way. The Crumb is based on fragments of Lorca —brief, vivid images that one can scan quickly in the program and remember during the songs. The Davies text, transcribed from stone-carved runes, is in Orkney Norn, an Old Norse dialect, and, in the composer's words, "the voice part can be regarded as a coloured vocalise." The Druckman "text" is made of alluring noises notated in phonetic symbols. In all three compositions, the voice is one strand in an instrumental ensemble. And no one can color a vocalise so expressively as Miss DeGaetani or put so much "meaning" into the sheer sound of a vocal line. With the arabesques of four old Sephardic songs, at this recital, she ravished the ear. But when she turns to Schubert (which she has recorded on a Nonesuch disc, along with *Das Buch der hängenden Gärten*) and Schoenberg, to Stephen Foster and Charles Ives (which she sang at the recital, and has recorded for Nonesuch), she is disappointing. The sounds are still beautiful, but the poetry does not come to life.

Crumb's third and fourth books of *Madrigals* are dedicated to Elizabeth Suderburg, who has recorded them, along with Books I and II, for Turnabout. She sings them well but without the special enchantment that Miss DeGaetani brings to them. Mrs. Suderburg gave an Alice Tully Hall recital in January, all of Bartók: the Opus 15 and Opus 16 songs, the *Village Scenes*, and the set of Hungarian Folk Songs (1907–17)—a program that, with the same pianist, Béla Siki, she had already recorded on a Turnabout disc. The ten songs that make up Opus 15 and Opus 16—composed in 1916, and Bartók's only mature "art songs"—are difficult on many counts. The vocal demands are extravagant, both in terms of range and expression and on the singer's pitching; through Expressionist harmonies the voice often clashes with the piano. Hungarian prosody, it seems, resists a singing translation into any Indo-European language, and so direct experience of the songs is possible only to Hungarian-speakers. In straight translation, the poems seem rather awful. Mrs. Suderburg, who has a clear and well-schooled soprano, sang the music securely. I cannot comment on her command of the Hungarian. She showed an admirable reluctance to force her voice beyond its natural scale, but this meant that Bartók's big, passionate climaxes did not ring out. Without the text leaflet, no one could have guessed that the calm, composed recitalist was saying, "Kissing! My lips cry out for a kiss! My blood is a river of fire tonight, In a passion I fling open my naked arms, The coverlet falls away from my body. On the night of such a ripened lust, It were well to be kissing, embracing." But Mr. Siki's contribution was passionate. His playing has always united crispness and lyricism, elegance and emotion. It was good to hear him again, and in such good form.

Some three years ago, when I encountered *Louise* for the first time, I thought it an opera that no serious house would dream of reviving. Yet here it is back at the State Theater, with Beverly Sills as its heroine and

Julius Rudel in the double role of director and conductor. Charpentier to my generation meant Marc-Antoine (1634–1704), the composer of *Médée*, not Gustave (1860–1956), the composer of *Louise*. And *Louise* meant one aria, "Depuis le jour," recorded by sopranos from Mary Garden, Melba, and Dorothy Maynor to Callas and Caballé, and otherwise a title that was important in operatic history because the piece chalked up its hundredth, five-hundredth, and thousandth performance at the Opéra-Comique in record time. The only recording available, with Ninon Vallin and Georges Thill, was old and heavily abridged; the composer even in his ninety-fifth year was reported to be sticking out tenaciously for higher terms than any record company was prepared to offer for a modern, complete version. But the story was familiar from Kobbé and from Abel Gance's 1938 movie, in which most of the dialogue is spoken against background music and only the principal numbers are sung, even though Grace Moore and Thill play the leading roles. The story told of a Parisian seamstress who prefers free love with a poet to a decent life with her industrious, God-fearing parents. *Louise*, subtitled "a musical novel," was celebrated in its day (1900) as the last word in verismo. There is a little orchestral interlude that accompanies the drinking of soup. Act I ends with the heroine reading the newspaper aloud to her father. Where Wagner began a scene with the "Summ und Brumm" of spinning wheels, Charpentier began one with the clickety-clack of sewing machines, notated in 6/8.

But when at last I saw *Louise*, in a spectacular student production at the London Opera Centre, it seemed to be quite a different sort of opera from what one had been led to believe—to be not verismo but a full-blown example of Symbolist art. The stage was a glittering symbolical representation of Paris, dominated by the Klingsor figure of the Noctambule ("Je suis le Plaisir de Paris!"). The audience sat only in the balcony; the orchestra was out of sight below, and the main theater floor was bare. Onto it the realistic scenes—the Montmartre garret, the sewing shop, the lovers' garden—were trucked out on large floats, from below the balcony, to meet the allurements and menace of the mingled Paradise and Inferno that made up this Paris. The Montmartre carnival advanced through the proscenium to swallow up Louise and Julien and fill all the acting space. The director brought out links with *Parsifal*, and stressed the piquancy of up-to-date props against Charpentier's pretentious, mystical background. Stage directions such as "Dans une apothéose de lumière, Paris semble fêter les amants" and "Louise s'est transfigurée; elle écoute avidement les voix de son désir auxquelles la Ville de Plaisir semble répondre" provided the general tone of the production.

As a rule, I believe operas are best performed in the way their creators intended them to be done. There is a move-by-move, thought-by-thought, bar-by-bar production book for *Otello* which represents the opera Verdi wrote far more closely than any actual production of it I have ever seen. It provides for the staging what the score does for the singing, and to observe it should be no more "inhibiting" to artists than it is to observe the composer's musical notes. The rule is often broken by directors who think that they know better than a creator or who have not bothered to discover what he had in mind. It is broken with impunity only by those few who really do know better—or, on occasion, when a creator's flawed execution needs mending, when the original text is in doubt, or when the work in question scarcely merits serious handling anyway. *The Tales of Hoffmann*, for example, has always seemed to me fair game for an inventive director's fancies. (That view may have to be modified once Fritz Oeser's reconstruction of Offenbach's original—it had its première at the Vienna Volksoper last December—becomes available for study.) And although there exist very precise instructions for the staging of *Louise* (Sarah Caldwell drew on them for her 1971 production of the opera, in Boston), one could hardly mind that they were ignored in the London version. *Louise* is not a work that needs to be treated as scrupulously as *The Ring*, *Otello*, or *The Barber of Seville*. The music does not bear much listening to in its own right. The drama does not stand up to scrutiny. But the multitude of roles does make the piece an attractive proposition for opera schools, and the staging described above provided an attractive, entertaining show. I wondered whether a realistic *Louise* might not prove mawkish.

The City Opera *Louise*, staged in a refurbishing of the scenery for its 1962 production, is not altogether realistic. In Act III, the lovers lie down to spoon on bare planks, carefully avoiding a strip of synthetic lawn that is waiting for them. In Act II, the sewing girls ignore the cries of the ragman, offering to buy, and then throw bundles of stuffs into a *poubelle*. The lighting, even when the action is set within one small room, is achieved by follow spots trailing round after the characters. But these seem to be miscalculations rather than planned touches of unreality. The basic style is of naturalistic acting within "painterly," not realistic, scenery. The sets are made to look like enlarged pictures of Paris. (At the Opéra-Comique, when, after fifty years of hard service, the original production was replaced, Maurice Utrillo provided similar painterly décor.) The designer, Gordon Micunis, has redone his Act III; the new panorama-of-Paris backdrop, well executed, cunningly catches the effect of evening light on the Seine.

Charpentier's first Louise, Marthe Rioton, was fresh from the Conservatoire. His second, a young Mary Garden, had never been on a stage before she stepped into Act III one night when Rioton was taken ill, and (as she relates in "I Start at the Top in Louise," a chapter of her lively autobiography) brought the house down with "Depuis le jour." The role calls for a candid, clear, fearless young soprano, and at the City

Opera Miss Sills convincingly became one, singing and playing without artifice, directly, intently. There was some unsteadiness on sustained notes, but there were also many pretty phrases, and a touchingly romantic, girlish manner that seemed natural, not assumed. John Alexander was a reliable but unromantic Julien. Frances Bible was an impressive Mother. Robert Hale sang the Father's music very clearly. Charpentier had a gift for musical scene painting, also shown in his early *Impressions d'Italie*. At the New York première of *Louise*, in 1908, the dawn scene of Parisian street life was, according to H. E. Krehbiel, simply eliminated, "with much else of the local color rubbish." But Mr. Rudel showed it to contain some of the best-written passages of the score, and its numerous small roles were ably taken. It was a mistake to try to sing the opera in French instead of in English translation; many theatrically important lines—the street urchin's comments, the ragman's song at the end of Act III—were incomprehensible.

Paul Dukas, writing enthusiastically about *Louise* in the *Revue Hebdomadaire,* regretted its mystical passages and drew an interesting distinction between German music drama, essentially a musical affair, and the French tradition of operatic music arising specifically from the dramatic action. But he also had some questions to ask about this particular action: "Does M. Charpentier side with this Julien, so little concerned with the grief he is causing the parents of his beloved? Does he side with the father, so jealous of his daughter's honor? Does he side with the daughter, so avid for her freedom? One hardly knows." Much of the success of *Louise*, I suspect, was due to the fact that everyone could find in it a moral to his or her liking. Pious parents deploring errant children and their talk of "l'amour libre"; rebellious children impatient with parental control; working girls dreaming of a Prince Charming who would sweep them away to happiness; feminists deploring that there was no other escape route from drudgery; social reformers deploring the system that made life, for people like Louise's parents, a narrow round of hard work, producing for others; conservatives hardened to the acceptance of such a system—all could read in *Louise* a confirmation of their beliefs and aspirations. Krehbiel, in 1911, reported with distaste that in Paris "funds are raised to send the working girls of the city to the opera in droves, there to hear the alluring call to harlotry, under the pretense that the agonies of the father will preach a moral lesson." "L'égoïsme appelle l'égoïsme!" Julien cries in Act III, correctly formulating the central dramatic situation. Charpentier does not take sides. Whether a composer should take sides is a question that can be argued. If opera is to be an instrument of social change, of course he should; if it is a mere diversion, it hardly matters. But even if we do not blame Charpentier for putting every point of view in turn, we can blame him for exploiting each sentiment for maximum titillation, like a sensational reporter. There is something unwholesome, something opportunist, about *Louise*—something Puccinian unredeemed by Puccini's musical genius. In his great book on French music, Martin Cooper put it roundly: Charpentier "had neither taste nor distinction." The final twist comes when the Father reveals the patently sexual basis of his paternal care. (At the State Theater, Mr. Hale did not actually cuddle Miss Sills on his lap, as the stage directions require.) There are more worthy ways for Miss Sills, Mr. Rudel, and the City Opera to spend their—and our—time. (Mounting the other Charpentier's *Médée* could be one of them.) Nevertheless, Gustave Charpentier's *Louise* is part of operatic history, and I am glad to have seen it—once—in a traditional production.

March 21, 1977

"After the Ball" is Nonesuch H-71304, "Vaudeville" H-71330. Several readers asked why I had not mentioned a third Nonesuch record, "Who Shall Rule the American Nation: Songs of the Civil War Era by Henry Clay Work" (H-71317). The reason was that I like it less well; there are fine moments—and some magical individual words—from Joan Morris, and her performance of "Come Home, Father" is in itself worth the price of the record, but she shares the program with a veteran baritone and with a chorus. "Wild About Eubie" (Columbia M 34504) is also unrecommended as a first introduction to Miss Morris's wonderful art.

Martin Cooper's book is French Music from the Death of Berlioz to the Death of Fauré *(Oxford University Press, 1951).*

ADVENTURES

In his two operas, *A Life for the Tsar* (1836) and *Russlan and Lyudmila* (1842), Glinka laid the foundations for, first, the historical epics (*Boris Godunov, Prince Igor, War and Peace*) and, second, the glittering fairy tales (*The Golden Cockerel, The Firebird, The Stone Flower*) that have been Russia's special contribution to the lyric theater. All the history books stress Glinka's importance. Outside Russia, companies seldom perform him. Yet the few times that I have caught productions of *A Life for the Tsar* and *Russlan*—usually as brave student or opera-club ventures—I have felt that they have a stronger claim to be in the repertory than many operas that do get done. The Opera Company of Boston opened its season this month with a bewitching presentation of *Russlan,* and that feeling turned into certainty as far as *Russlan* is concerned. A simple reaction to the show was "Why does the Met waste its time on dull rubbish like *Esclarmonde* when it might be doing *Russlan*?"

Championship must be careful. Glinka's latest biographer, David Brown, remarks, "The saddest thing for the Western student of Glinka is that he knows, for all his commendation of the riches in *Russlan and Lyudmila,* that what he writes is less likely to prove a testimonial that will gain the work's admission to the opera houses of the West than an obituary." He admires the music but calls the piece "a dramatic disaster . . . so flawed dramatically that there is no hope that it will ever become a repertoire piece outside Russia." Nevertheless, with Sarah Caldwell as its director—she both staged and conducted the Boston performance—*Russlan* became a dramatic as well as a musical delight. Miss Caldwell revealed a "quest opera" and "rescue opera" whose situations are more colorfully fantastic but no sillier than those of *The Magic Flute, Siegfried,* and *Die Frau ohne Schatten.*

With the verse fairy tale *Russlan and Lyudmila* (1820) the young Pushkin established his reputation; his death in 1837 dashed Glinka's hope that the poet himself would adapt the tale as a libretto for him. In the opera, three suitors set out from Kiev in search of Lyudmila, who has been abducted by the wicked magician Chernomor. One is Farlaf, the bass, a Varangian warrior and blustering braggart. (His brilliantly energetic and catchy rondo was made famous in a recording by Chaliapin.) He allies himself to the witch Naina, behaves very badly, carries off Lyudmila after Russlan has rescued her, but is unable to wake her from an enchanted sleep. Another is Ratmir, the mezzo, an Eastern prince. A fickle and susceptible youth, he is deflected from his quest by the charms of Naina's Persian attendants when, like Klingsor's flower maidens, they surround him as he enters Naina's castle. The third is Russlan, the baritone, who wins Lyudmila in the end, partly through his own perseverance and valor, partly through the help of the good magician Finn. When Russlan shows sign of falling for Gorislava, a former flame of Ratmir's, Finn recalls him to his mission (and reunites Gorislava and Ratmir); Finn provides the magic ring that wakens Lyudmila from her sleep.

A seeker after symbolic meanings could no doubt discover some significant allegory in all this. But there is no need to. It is an eventful, diverting, and sometimes touching tale, told in music of uncommon brilliance and beauty, and that is enough. One scene makes a profound and disturbing impression: Russlan comes upon an ancient battlefield, strewn with bones, and sings an aria that Mr. Brown rightly describes as "noble heroic music of Beethovenian strength." When mists lift in the background, a gigantic head is revealed, which addresses Russlan

547

solemnly in a voice represented by a unison male-voice choir concealed within it. Victor Braun, the Russlan of the Boston performance, excels in a vein of romantic yet virile melancholy (as shown by his Hamlet, in Humphrey Searle's opera, and his Orestes, in Krenek's opera), and he made much of this scene. Lyudmila was Jeanette Scovotti, delicate, precise, and appealing in the first aria (when, before the abduction, Lyudmila bubbles with joy and playfulness), and affecting in the long, passionate spans and tricky, extended chromatic arabesques of the second. (Antonina Nezhdanova recorded a great performance of this aria in 1907.) Ratmir was Eunice Alberts; she did not efface my memories of Yvonne Minton (who made her mark in London, twelve years ago, in this role), but she was pleasing, direct, and musical. The choreographer was Ben Stevenson, who also played Chernomor (a non-singing part), doing so with a wicked glee reminiscent of Sir Frederick Ashton in the cognate role of Kashchey in *The Firebird*. John Moulson, from the Berlin Comic Opera, was charmingly rueful and narratively graphic in Finn's fine ballad (which is based on a Finnish melody). Joseph Evans was lyrical and winning as the Poet, who introduces the action to the audience. Marianna Christos (Gorislava), Edith Evans (Naina), Giorgio Tozzi (Farlaf), and William Fleck (Svyetozar, Lyudmila's father) completed the large cast. The opera was sung in English.

Of course, by Imperial Russian standards the singing lacked smoothness and sweetness of timbre. But it was good enough to show that *Russlan* contains marvelous music, of considerable variety. Gerald Abraham, that acute critic of Russian opera, once remarked that Glinka's thought is "always simple, usually individual, and often extremely beautiful," and spoke of the light that seems to shine through his work. It was this beauty and luminosity of thought, not merely of execution, that Miss Caldwell's direction revealed. She gets under the surface of a work. All the colors—the exotic melodies, timbres, harmonies, and rhythms that Glinka brought together from many lands and made his own—were there: all the grace, the verve, and the lyricism of the score. But the Boston production also seemed to convey some "inner sense," of an imaginative voyage through fantastic and romantic adventures, which makes the opera more than a diversion and prompts thoughts of *The Magic Flute*. This was a poetic performance. Rimsky-Korsakov's fairy operas are glittering, and delectable in their melodies, their instrumentation, and their spectacle; so is *Russlan*—and something more besides.

The staging was an enchantment. Herbert Senn and Helen Pond had designed scenery and Carrie F. Robbins had designed costumes in the style of Palekh paintings—those richly colored, finely detailed, captivating folk images. The action soon got off the ground; the duel in midair between Russlan and Chernomor, high above the palace rooftops, was very exciting. Boston productions at their best carry all before them. The limitations and discomfort of the Orpheum Theatre, the pickup nature of the orchestra and chorus (admirable players and some good singers but not regular year-round ensembles)—everything is forgotten except the exhilaration of being rapt in an opera brought to life in all its details. This is the Caldwell miracle. She doesn't work a miracle every time, but in *Russlan* she did.

Half-German, half-Italian, Ermanno Wolf-Ferrari established his reputation in Munich with two Goldoni-based comedies, *Le donne curiose* (1903) and *I quattro rusteghi* (1906), translated into German and decked in music of the most delicate and delightful charm. Josef Rheinberger trained him; study under that composer of substantial, solidly made organ sonatas seems an odd preparation for operatic soufflés, but perhaps it accounts for the excellence of Wolf-Ferrari's craftsmanship. Among his musical ancestors we can discern on the German side Mozart and Schubert and on the Italian Rossini (for high-spirited invention), Bellini (for purity of lyric melody), and the Verdi who wrote the minuet in the final scene of *Falstaff*. This is not to say that Wolf-Ferrari is in all things their equal—only to suggest a kind of felicity that was his. And, in the words of *The Record Guide*, he "wrote for the voice with a Mozartian delicacy unknown to the rest of the modern Italian school."

Yet his operas have no sure hold on the repertory. Are the comedies too finely worked, not red-blooded enough, for those whose taste is Italianate, and too slender in both manner and matter for those whose taste is Teutonic? Is it just that modern singers—and modern stage directors—are too coarse to do them anything like justice? I don't know. I do know that I have never encountered one without being ravished by its deftness and wit, without marveling at the composer's ability to go on spinning new, pretty surprises from his tuneful material. Wolf-Ferrari is a composer who makes one happy; and the Manhattan School of Music's production of *I quattro rusteghi*, this month, was a happy occasion.

The piece was done in Edward J. Dent's English translation but not in the setting of eighteenth-century London whither Dent had transferred it, from Venice. The title—as at the City Opera in 1951—was rendered *The Four Ruffians*, and "ruffians" is not really right for *rusteghi* (curmudgeons, boors). Dent called his version *The School for Fathers* and suggested their characters by the names he devised for them: Mr. Crusty, Mr. Hardstone, Mr. Gruff, and Sir James Pinchbeck. Louis Galterio directed the Manhattan performance. Once or twice, he allowed his actors to overstep the bounds of permissible eighteenth-century behavior (whether Venetian or British), but on the whole his sense of style, of fun produced by quiddities of character, not by imposed "business," was sure. Imre Pallo conducted, lightly and exactly, in the Giulini rather than the Beecham manner—which means that his tempi and textures were elegant and the effect of the whole was refined, but that occasionally one missed a (Beechamesque) lilt and "smile" in the phrasing. The student cast was pleasing, and its use of words bore testimony to Dorothy Uris's coaching. This was the school's first operatic production since John Crosby (founder and director of the Santa Fe Opera, and president of Opera America) became its president. One looks forward to subsequent shows. Opportunities for hearing opera on this level in a house of human scale (the school's auditorium seats under a thousand) are not common in New York.

March 28, 1977

LULU AND HELENE
AND ALBAN AND ALWA

The Metropolitan Opera has mounted an important and successful new production of Alban Berg's second opera, *Lulu*, conducted by James Levine and directed by John Dexter. More precisely, it has mounted as much of the opera as is at present available: the first two of its three acts and some fragments of Act III. The rest has not yet been published. But for the first time, I believe, a production of *Lulu* has been based on as full a knowledge as possible of the *whole* opera that Berg composed, not merely on the (faulty) printed score and the two consecutive plays by Frank Wedekind, *Erdgeist* and *Die Büchse der Pandora*, from which Berg drew his libretto. Two celebrated and much-traveled earlier productions were those of Günther Rennert for the Hamburg Opera and of Wieland Wagner for the Stuttgart Opera. (The former was seen in New York in 1967.) Both were undertaken in the spirit of the prescription that introduces the current score:

The opera is to be performed only as a fragment: Berg completed the orchestration of only the first two acts. Of Act III only the two pieces "Variations" and "Adagio," which Berg prepared for the *Lulu* Suite, are available in full orchestration. They are included as an appendix to this score, and are to be played after the two acts. The "Adagio," which should represent the close of the opera, can be given in scenic form.

550

The two directors differed in their handling of the Act III fragments. To the accompaniment of the available music, Rennert added some spoken dialogue and more pantomime, and Wagner some pantomime and more spoken dialogue, drawn from *Pandora's Box*. But neither of them matched the extra action and extra words to Berg's musical intentions: that was apparent from accounts of the third act written by men who had seen all the music for it. (The earliest account, Willi Reich's in his *Alban Berg*, appeared in 1937, and the fullest, George Perle's in an article for the *Journal of the American Musicological Society*, in 1964.)

Both productions made a great impression, and deservedly so, for even as a fragment—even as a fragment in which the composer's intentions were in some important ways misrepresented—*Lulu* was revealed as a powerful and beautiful opera. Berg's masterpiece? Knowing only two-thirds and a bit of it. how could one tell? Dramatically and musically, the opera is very carefully constructed in a balanced span. The first act and a half, corresponding to Wedekind's *Earth Spirit*, shows Lulu's ascent—as the wife of a respected doctor, of a fashionable painter, and then of the powerful newspaper proprietor Dr. Schön, "the only man I loved." At the center of the opera there is a palindromic orchestral interlude that Berg intended to be accompanied by a film whose images, while narrative (they tell of Lulu's trial for the murder of Dr. Schön, her imprisonment, and her escape), have a matching palindromic pattern. The second half of Act II and the last act, corresponding to *Pandora's Box*, trace Lulu's descent. In the unpublished Act III there is, first, a long and important scene in the demimonde of a Paris casino, involving a large company of minor characters whose ensembles frame three duets: for Lulu with, in turn, the Marquis (a procurer who tries to blackmail her into accepting a position in a high-class Cairo brothel), the Athlete, and Schigolch (two characters from the first part). Dr. Perle, in a lecture for the International Alban Berg Society last month, described this as the greatest operatic scene ever written! Then there is the "Variations" interlude, familiar from the *Lulu* suite, and to its final barrel-organ strains the curtain rises on a London attic. Lulu has become a streetwalker. Three customers are played by the performers who played, in the first part, the three husbands whom she brought to their deaths. Now she has become their victim. The last of them is Jack the Ripper.

The music of Act III consists largely of recapitulations of passages heard earlier in the opera, passages whose full significance (we are told) becomes apparent only at their later statements. The technique has been likened to Wagner's wonderful recapitulation of a long stretch of Act II of *Tristan* as Isolde's Liebestod, the finale of his opera; but Berg's use of reminiscences, correspondences, and cross-references—as revealed by the descriptions of Act III—is far more elaborate. Musically, the published score of *Lulu* might be likened to the score of an extended Mahler movement from which someone had torn the pages where the themes are brought into relationship, leaving behind only the exposition and a few bars of coda. Dramatically, it is rather like a *Hamlet* with everything missing between the end of the play scene and "O! I die, Horatio." Such a *Hamlet* fragment, if it were all that survived of the play, would be well worth performing, and rightly admired. So is the *Lulu* fragment. But it is not all that survives of Berg's opera.

Although the facts about Act III of *Lulu* have been set out several times during the forty years since the composer's death, it is worth setting them out once again, for two reasons: first, they are still contradicted in print; and, second, Helene Berg, the composer's widow, who opposed the publication of the full Act III, died last year, and now it seems likely that the music may at last be made public. On the first count: a new bilingual libretto was published for the Met production, and on its last page the Met audience reads, about Act III, that "only a few words of [the] final scene have been set to music by the composer." In fact, Berg set every word of the scene—and of the preceding, Paris scene. He began *Lulu* in 1929 and completed it in particella, or short score, in 1934. Then he began to set out the opera in full score—first the passages comprised in the *Lulu* suite, and then consecutively from the beginning. Work on this was interrupted by the composition of the Violin Concerto. He died on Christmas Eve, 1935, of blood poisoning, having got as far as the second ensemble of the Paris scene. So of Act III he completed in full score not just the suite passages but the introduction and first ensemble; Lulu's long duet with the Marquis (a set of twelve variations, with episodes bringing in new material and reminiscences and recapitulations of former passages); and the second ensemble. A voice-and-piano score of the whole opera was made by Berg's pupil Erwin Stein. Of this, Acts I and II and about half of Act III were engraved for publication, but then work on the engraving broke off. Only two acts of this vocal score were published, in 1936, with a prefatory note saying that Berg had completed the opera shortly before his death, and promising the rest later. But in postwar printings that promise was withdrawn. Meanwhile, in 1936, Willi Reich, the composer's biographer, wrote, "Berg left a complete and very carefully worked out preliminary score of *Lulu*. Only the instrumentation of a few places in the middle of the last act was not finished and this could easily be carried out from the given material by some friend familiar with Berg's work." That was confirmed in 1957 by H. F. Redlich, in his *Alban Berg: Versuch einer Würdigung*: "In my own opinion (shared by a good many *cognoscenti*) the task of orchestrating the rest of Act

III on the basis of the surviving sketch in short score is not beyond the capacity of a musician thoroughly familiar with Berg's style and methods of composition." And when Perle saw the material in 1963, he reported that one should not talk of another person's "completing *Lulu*, for in every essential respect this has already been done by Alban Berg."

It is understandable that in the politically troubled time before the Anschluss and during the war no further work was done on *Lulu*. After the war, as interest in the opera grew, a new difficulty arose: Mrs. Berg decided that she did not want any more of the music to be made public. Act III of Stein's piano score was not published. Berg's libretto was not published. (If it had been, Rennert might not, when adding dialogue from Wedekind, have "selected those lines that Berg chose to *omit* from his libretto, and omitted those that Berg chose to retain"—as Perle noted in a review of the Hamburg production.) No one was invited to edit a complete full score of *Lulu* from Berg's particella, although Hamburg, it was reported, proposed Pierre Boulez for the job, and the Santa Fe Opera—with Stravinsky's enthusiastic support—had proposed George Perle. The vocal score was republished in 1953, with its new prefatory note ("The opera is to be performed as a fragment"). Mrs. Berg's ban was officially announced when Alfred Schlee, then the head of Universal Edition, Berg's publishers, proclaimed it in the booklet that accompanied the Deutsche Grammophon recording of the (truncated) opera.

To what extent is a composer's private life any concern of the world's? The question has been variously answered. It probably admits of no general answer. My own feeling is that when the knowledge of a "secret program" can enhance a listener's enjoyment and understanding of a piece of music that embodies it, the secret should be revealed—provided that no one who might be hurt by the knowledge is alive. In the forthcoming issue of the International Alban Berg Society's newsletter the "secret program" of Berg's Lyric Suite is disclosed. The Suite is dedicated—not in the printed score but in an annotated copy thereof —to the woman Berg loved during the last ten years of his life, who was not Frau Helene but Hanna Fuchs-Robettin, the sister of Franz Werfel and the sister-in-law of Alma Mahler, Helene's closest friend. Janáček declared that all his later compositions were inspired by his love for Kamila Stösslova. Schumann wove a musical encipherment of his beloved's name, Clara, into composition after composition. Berg's Lyric Suite is woven with the initials H.F. and A.B. (German musical spelling for the notes B, F and A, B-flat). His and Hanna's personal "numbers," 23 and 10, determine the bar counts of the episodes and the movements, and also the metronome markings. The second movement is a rondo dedicated "to you and your children." Hanna's daughter

Dorothea was known as Dodo; she enters the music with the notes C-C (or, in solfeggio, do-do). Hanna's son Munzo had been attending a Czech elementary school (the family lived in Prague); at the entry of his theme, the direction "mit einem leisen czechischen Einschlag" ("with a slight Czech inflection") appears in the annotated score. The last movement is a "secret" setting of Baudelaire's "De profundis clamavi," in Stefan George's translation; in the annotated copy of the score, which Berg gave to Mrs. Fuchs-Robettin, the words are written in. The numerological correspondences of the Lyric Suite have long been noted. The verbal content of musical quotations from an Alexander Zemlinsky song ("Du bist mein Eigen, mein Eigen") and from *Tristan* have been pondered. Redlich spoke of the work's "concealed vocality." T. W. Adorno called it "a latent opera," and cited in connection with it a line of Stefan George's, "Take love from me, give me your happiness." Perle, six years ago, wrote of its musical cross-references as being "not—no more than they are in *Wozzeck*—simply a means of assuring the musical unity of the whole. They are, like the musical cross-references in *Wozzeck* and later in *Lulu*, *Leitmotive* and *Leitsektionen*. The six movements are six acts in . . . a wholly subjective psychological drama."

The details of this Lyric Suite discovery can be discovered in the Berg newsletter article, which is written by Perle. The discovery bears upon *Lulu* in three, related ways. First, it stresses that in Berg's music nothing is insignificant: all details—the number of bars, and the precise choice of wording for some tempo or expression indication, the self-quotations, whether fleeting or extended—form part of a carefully worked musical whole. (In the annotated Lyric Suite, some of the printed directions—"drohend," "dolciss."—are linked into complete sentences.) Second—here we are on delicate ground—a possible reason or contributory reason for Mrs. Berg's animosity toward the opera cannot but suggest itself, since, third, it becomes evident that Berg's "authorized" biography needs rewriting. In a letter to Hanna dated October 1931, the composer writes:

Everything you may hear of me, and perhaps read about me, pertains, insofar as it is not completely false—as, for example, this, which I read today by chance in a Zurich program: "A completely happy domesticity, with which his wife has surrounded him, allows him to create without disturbance" [the sentence reappears in Reich's biography]—pertains to what is only peripheral . . . to a person who constitutes only a completely exterior layer of myself, to a part of me which in the course of recent years has separated itself (ah, how painfully separated) from my real existence. . . . But believe me, Hanna (and now I can finally address you properly: *one and only eternal love*), all this pertains only to this *exterior* person . . . who would never be able to compose *Lulu*. That I am, however, doing so may be proof to you that the other person . . . that *I* still exist.

To publish now this moving and intensely private letter is justifiable, since the autobiographical element in Berg's later music is strong. There is no question, of course, of any crude projection of a *Lulu* drama into Berg's own life; but *one* of the themes of his *Lulu* is that of a creative artist's attempt to stand back and shape a work of art from feelings in which he is at the same time deeply enmeshed. In Wedekind's plays, Dr. Schön's son, Alwa, is a writer. Berg made him a composer, and identified him by quoting the first notes of *Wozzeck* at Alwa's observation "One might write an interesting opera [Wedekind said "play"] about her. Scene 1, the Doctor. . . . Scene 2, the Painter. . . . Scene 3 . . ."—but we are *in* Scene 3 at this moment! The opera we are watching is, in a sense, an opera that Alwa has written. In the second scene of Act II, Alwa says to Lulu, "Through this dress I feel your form like music. These ankles—a Grazioso; these lovely swelling calves —a Cantabile; this knee—a Misterioso; and then the powerful Andante of voluptuousness." The musical terms are altered from those in Wedekind and are brought closer to the movement headings of the Lyric Suite.

This demonstrates one of the kinds of complication within *Lulu*. Berg seems to have been destined to write the opera. He first saw *Pandora's Box* when Karl Kraus produced it in Vienna in 1905, and he noted passages of Kraus's prefatory address. Some of Kraus's remarks can stand in the opera's defense today, should anyone still object to its subject matter:

It is impossible to believe in earnest that anyone could be so shortsighted as to mistake, because of the "painful" matter, the greatness of its treatment and the inner necessity for the choice of it; or overlook—blinded by the truncheons, revolvers, and knives—that this sex-murder is like a doom drawn up from the deepest depths of woman's nature; or forget—because of the lesbian disposition of the Countess Geschwitz—that she embodies greatness and is not just any pathological creature.

Life seemed to take a hand in preparing Berg for the opera he embarked on nearly twenty-five years later. His own sister's lesbian disposition was a source of concern to him. Richard Gerstl, a painter in his and Schoenberg's circle, committed suicide in a spectacular and messy fashion, just as Wedekind's painter does. Wedekind sought to reveal the truth behind things, the split between an appearance maintained before the world and the "real" person beneath. All things Bergian seem to come together in this opera—biographical, emotional, and musical. His technique never functioned more precisely than it does in what we have so far been vouchsafed of the score. A popular music encyclopedia published in 1968 says of *Lulu*, "As the work has been heard more frequently—in the incomplete version and in the version orchestrated by the American composer George Perle—music lovers have found it to be equally disturbing and fascinating." The second part of the parenthesis was premature; music lovers can now hope that the way is open for Universal Edition to make it come true.

When the complete *Lulu* is available, the Met production is ready for it. Earlier versions leaned too heavily on Wedekind. Both Rennert and Wagner set all the action within the circus ring of the prologue (as several other directors have done). They stressed the deliberate crudity, the abruptness, the almost comic-strip directness, and the French-farce episodes of Wedekind's plays, and paid too little attention to Berg's personal transformation of his source. The composer moved the action into the twentieth century. More important, he gave added depth and personality to his principal characters: Lulu, Dr. Schön, Alwa, and the Countess Geschwitz. They—and Schigolch, a timeless old man who threads his way through Lulu's life and is the only principal to survive the tragedy—are named in Berg's dramatis personae, as opposed to the Doctor, the Painter, the Athlete, and so on. The Met production is the first to respect all the doublings of role (Dr. Schön reappearing as Jack the Ripper, etc.) that Berg himself introduced. The sets, by Jocelyn Herbert, are both beautiful and apt. John Dexter's direction is sensitive and precise, exact in its details and true to Berg in its dramatic perspectives, its delineation of relationships, and its feeling for the visual equivalents of the music's *Hauptstimmen* and *Nebenstimmen*. He does not overlook, but does not exaggerate, the jokes. Nothing is distorted to make an easy, vivid effect—and as a result the whole is marvelously vivid and effective. In James Levine's conducting, love for the work, understanding of its formal details and their relationships, and sure technical control of the complicated score are combined.

The cast is strong. In the title role, Carole Farley embodies more completely than any previous Lulu of my experience both the "mythic" qualities of Lulu the Earth Spirit and Berg's humanization of Lulu as a particular woman. Vocally, the role seems to have been written with a Maria Ivogün in mind—a lyric soprano ascending high above the staff, with the ease in *acuti* of Strauss's Zerbinetta and the dramatic accents of Mozart's Constanze. Miss Farley's high notes are not easy, but she reaches them, and her performance is convincing on all counts. Donald Gramm's Dr. Schön, very well sung and acted, eloquently conveys the man's power in the world of affairs and the weakness that binds him to Lulu—the mingled love, cruelty, and despair in his complicated personality. William Lewis's Alwa is an alert and intelligent portrayal, credible, telling in detail, if not quite romantic enough in vocal timbre. Tatiana Troyanos plays Geschwitz nobly and with great discretion. She and the Athlete represent the opposite poles of love for Lulu: com-

556

pletely selfless and able to rise to heroic sacrifice, and completely selfish. Lenus Carlson is a splendid Athlete (and also Ringmaster, his doubled role). Andrew Foldi (an outstanding Schigolch), Raymond Gibbs (the Painter), Nico Castel (the Prince, who wishes to take Lulu to Africa; the Manservant; and, briefly, in a mimed fragment representing the Paris scene, the Marquis), Cynthia Munzer (the Wardrobe Mistress and the Schoolboy, Lulu's adolescent admirer), Richard Best (the Stage Manager), Peter Sliker (the Doctor)—all are excellent.

There are some little things wrong that can easily be put right. Irrelevant projections during the interludes distract attention from music that the composer intended to be heard without visual accompaniment, and lessen the effect of the narrative projections during the Act II interlude (at the Met, a series of slides, instead of a film, is used), which Berg did specify. Mr. Dexter breaks the dramatic mode when, to the interlude that should divide the two scenes of Act III, he sets a Jooss-like pantomime of Lulu's degradation at the hands of men. By an all-American cast, to an American audience, the opera is sung in German, and this mistake (if it be counted as such; I certainly think it one) will take rather more time to correct. *Lulu* has one of the most transparent of all opera scores. Much of its dialogue is spoken. Berg plainly intended the words to be heard—and understood.

April 4, 1977

A list of George Perle's principal writings about Lulu *will be useful to anyone who wishes to pursue the subject:*
"The Music of Lulu: *A New Analysis,"* Journal of the American Musicological Society, *12 (1959), pp. 185–200.*
"A Note on Act III of Lulu," Perspectives of New Music *(Spring–Summer 1964), pp. 8–13.*
"Lulu: *The Formal Design,"* JAMS, *17 (1964), pp. 179–92.*
The Character of Lulu: A Sequel," Music Review *(November 1964), pp. 311–19.*
"Die Personen in Bergs Lulu," Archiv für Musikwissenschaft *(1964), pp. 283ff.*
"The Score of Lulu" [review of the Universal study score], Perspectives of New Music *(Spring–Summer 1965), pp. 127–32.*
"Lulu: *Thematic Material and Pitch Organization,"* Music Review *(November 1965), pp. 269–302.*
"Die Reihe als Symbol in Bergs Lulu," Oesterreichische Musikzeitschrift *(October 1967), pp. 589–93.*

"What They Did to Berg's Lulu" [review of Rennert and Sarah Caldwell productions], Saturday Review (December 30, 1967), pp. 43–5.

"Three Views of Berg's Lulu" [review of the Columbia, Angel, and Deutsche Grammophon recordings], Saturday Review (May 25, 1968), pp. 47–9.

[Review of Wieland Wagner production], The Musical Quarterly, 53 (1967), pp. 101–8.

"Erwiderung auf Willi Reichs Aufsatz 'Drei Notizenblätter zu Alban Bergs Lulu,'" Schweizerische Musikzeitung (May–June 1969), pp. 163–5.

"The Tireless Seductress," synopsis (including Act III), and program notes in Stagebill, 4 (March 1977), the program book of the Met performance.

See also Robert Offergeld's "Some Questions about Lulu" in Hi Fi/ Stereo Review (October 1964) pp. 58–76. The terms of Helene Berg's will, in which her opposition to any completion of Lulu was reiterated, were published in the Oesterreichische Musikzeitschrift, 32 (1977), pp. 169–79. On April 27, 1977, the Paris Opera announced that it had acquired the first rights to a completed Lulu and would produce it in February 1979. The edition has been made by the Viennese composer Friedrich Cerha; Boulez is to conduct and Patrice Chéreau, who staged Bayreuth's 1976 Ring extravaganza, to direct.

Perle's "The Secret Program of the Lyric Suite" appeared in Newsletter No. 5 of the International Alban Berg Society (c/o the Ph.D. Program in Music, Graduate Center of the City University of New York, 33 West 42nd Street, New York, N.Y. 10036) and, in an expanded version, in The Musical Times for August, September, and October 1977 (Vol. 118). See also Walter Szmolyan's "Zum III. Akt von Alban Bergs Lulu" in Oesterreichische Musikzeitschrift, 32 (September 1977), pp. 396–401.

Robert Craft, who esteems Lulu less highly than I do, took exception to several points in my review in "Lulu at the Met," The New York Review of Books, May 12, 1977, pp. 41–5.

ALL ABOUT ALICE

Alice's Adventures in Wonderland and Through the Looking-Glass have moved many composers to music, but few earlier composers can have devoted quite so much of their output to Alice as has David Del Tredici. After a James Joyce period (Four Songs in 1959, I Hear an Army in 1964, Night Conjure-Verse in 1965, Syzygy in 1966), Del Tredici turned to Lewis Carroll, to explore Wonderland in a series of large-scale compositions which began in 1968 with *Pop-Pourri* ("Turtle Soup," together with "Jabberwocky," the Litany of the Blessed Virgin Mary, and "Es ist genug," provided its text), and has not yet ended. An *Alice Symphony* came out in parts—"The Lobster-Quadrille," "A Scene with Lobsters," "Illustrated Alice"—between 1969 and 1975. *Vintage Alice,* based on the Mad Tea-Party, appeared in 1972, and *Adventures Underground* ("The Pool of Tears" and "The Mouse's Tale") in 1975. *Final Alice* was Del Tredici's response to the Bicentennial commission for works from six American composers, each of them to be played by six leading orchestras. Since then, another lobster soufflé, *Annotated Alice,* has been announced; and there may be more of this Alicead to come.

Most of the verse in *Wonderland* and *Through the Looking-Glass* is recited, but some of it is sung. In the earlier book, we meet the Duchess "singing a sort of lullaby" with the words "Speak roughly to your little boy." (The baby and the cook join in the chorus.) "Twinkle, twinkle, little bat!" is a song. The Mock Turtle sings the Lobster-Quadrille "very slowly and sadly," and "Turtle Soup" "in a voice choked with sobs." In *Through the Looking-Glass,* instrumental music strikes up for the round dance of Alice with Tweedledum and Tweedledee: "It seemed to come from the tree under which they were dancing, and it was done (as well as she could make it out) by the branches rubbing one across the other, like fiddles and fiddle-sticks." At the Coronation party, a shrill voice sings the verses, and hundreds of voices join in the chorus, of Scott's "Bonnie Dundee" reworded for the occasion. And, of course, there is the "melancholy music" of the White Knight's song "A-Sitting on a Gate"; the tune, he said, was all his own invention, but Alice recognized it as "I give thee all, I can no more" (which Sir Henry Bishop composed). Perhaps some doctoral student is already at work on a dissertation about "The Music in *Alice.*" ("Turtle Soup," for example, is derived from a song by James M. Sayles, "Star of the Evening"; the Lobster-Quadrille has its origin in a song by Mary Howitt.) By the time Del Tredici is done, his compositions alone will provide matter enough for a thesis. All of them after *Pop-Pourri* are written for amplified solo soprano, "folk group" (two saxophones, mandolin, banjo, and accordion), and orchestra (in *Vintage Alice,* a chamber orchestra). To what extent Del Tredici uses the melodies that Carroll knew, and what thematic relationships and overlaps there may be between the different works, I cannot say, since *Final Alice* is the point at which I came in. It was given its first performance, by the Chicago Symphony under Sir Georg Solti, in October last year; and last month it was introduced to New York by the Philharmonic under Erich Leinsdorf.

Final Alice, although not the last piece to be composed, is presumably intended to hold the final position in a completed *Alice* cycle. It is based on the last two chapters of *Wonderland*—the trial scene. As a coda, there is a setting of the acrostic poem "A boat, beneath a sunny sky" (the envoy of *Through the Looking-Glass*)—and then, as a coda to that, the composer's "signature" in the form of a count to thirteen in Italian, from *uno* to *tredici*. The piece lasts perhaps an hour and ten minutes, but in all performances so far a large section has been cut, bringing it down to about an hour. The soprano is the narrator and takes all the roles: Del Tredici has designated his work a "Grand Concerto for Voice and Orchestra"; alternatively, an "Opera, written in Concert Form." There are five "arias" ("songs" might be a better word) set within scenas. The White Rabbit sings the first four, presenting them as evidence during the trial, and Lewis Carroll the last. Spoken narration ("The King and Queen of Hearts were seated on their throne . . .") begins the piece; it is joined by a measured orchestral simulation of tuning: the oboe's A, the open notes of the strings, shrill flurries from the woodwinds, a thick barrage of warmup sounds from the brasses. Del Tredici uses a very large orchestra—quadruple woodwinds, six horns, four trumpets—and soon the hubbub is immense. The narrator, despite her amplification, has to bawl over it. Finally, she quells the tumult with the White Rabbit's "Silence in the court!" He blows his threefold blast on the trumpet, preliminary to reading the accusation. *Tristan* appeared in the same year as *Alice in Wonderland*, 1865, but it had been composed six years earlier. Del Tredici's White Rabbit evidently knew it, for he models his trumpet call on the Shepherd's that, in the last act of Wagner's opera, signals the arrival of Isolde's ship with a rising sixth, sol to mi. There Kurwenal sings the motif as "O Wonne!" and in more than one of Mozart's operas it figures as a joy motif—the Count's "O gioia," Tamino's "Dies Bildnis," Pamina's "Tamino mein! O welch' ein Glück!" This rising sixth, which has been sounding from the saxophones during the preliminary racket, plays an important role in *Final Alice*. The accusation—"The Queen of Hearts, she made some tarts"—is set to a diatonic tune of simple outline (mi-re-re-do, fa-mi-re; fa-mi-mi-re, sol-fa-mi), each note of which, except the last two, is preceded by the sixth below, in a "Tea for Two" rhythm. The same melody serves for the first aria, "They told me you had been to her," and is rhythmically varied in successive verses. Before and after it, there is the music of Alice's growing, a noisy crescendo in which glissando screams from the theremin play a large part.

For his texts, both here and in the other Alice pieces, Del Tredici has gone beyond the *Wonderland* verses to the originals that Carroll parodied, to earlier versions of the Carroll poems, and to other Victorian parodies of the originals. The words of the second aria are "She's all my fancy painted him," a nonsense precursor, by Carroll, of "They told me you had been to her." Behind it lies an early-nineteenth-century song, "Alice Gray":

She's all my fancy painted her,
    She's lovely, she's divine,
But her heart it is another's,
    She never can be mine.

Yet loved I as man never loved,
    A love without decay,
O, my heart, my heart is breaking
    For the love of Alice Gray.

The second aria is set to a flowing diatonic melody, in which the sol-mi motif is again prominent, and then the theme of Aria I joins it. The following episodes, "The King Muses" and "Aria III: Contradictory Evidence," were omitted. From the score, one discovers that the King's musing is on the evidence thus far presented, superimposed in different keys and at different tempos. Aria III juxtaposes "Alice Gray" and a Victorian parody of it, "Disillusioned" ("I painted her a gushing thing, / With years perhaps a score; / I little thought to find they were / At least a dozen more"). The two poems jostle in violent musical contrast, one set to sweet tonal strains, the other in strident atonal mockery.

"Alice Gray," unalloyed, forms Aria IV, and Del Tredici calls it "the 'heart' of the piece." There were at least two early-Victorian settings of these verses. Both adopt what I called the "Tea for Two" rhythm; C. A. Hodson's starts with the sol-mi motif, and Mrs. P. Millard's sets the line "She never can be mine" to the same phrase that Del Tredici uses. But Del Tredici's melody, a smoothed and extended transformation of the Aria I theme, is more beautiful than either.

Then there is an orchestral fugue, subtitled "Arguments in the Jury-Chamber." (Del Tredici breaks with Carroll by depicting a scene at which Alice is not present.) At the Lizard's request, the White Rabbit repeats some of the evidence ("Alice Gray," sung to the melody of Aria I). The trial ends in uproar, and Alice wakes. The envoy, "A boat, beneath a sunny sky," is set to a long, limpid melody, marked by gently rocking thirds; the lines "In a Wonderland they lie, / Dreaming as the days go by" pick up the traditional strains of "Up above the world you fly, / Like a tea-tray in the sky," with the sixth note charmingly altered. When I read about the "final coda," I thought it would be like the gentle stroke of midnight—counted out loud, perhaps, as in Verdi's *Falstaff*— with an unexpected thirteenth stroke to say "Tredici." (*Pop-Pourri* ends with three bells, at different pitches and tempos, each striking thirteen.) But it proved to be simply a verbal count, underlined by a harp chord, over a sustained A that grows ever softer until it fades on the "tuning A" of the oboe with which the music began.

Final Alice is pleasing and enjoyable music. But there are things that can be said against it. To start with the least important: Carrollians will be distressed by alterations of the hallowed text. That Del Tredici changes the first word of "Everybody looked at Alice" to "Everyone" is unimportant; it was probably just a slip. When he adds the words "quite triumphantly" to " 'Then it ought to be Number One,' said Alice," he perhaps goes too far. That his guinea pig is "suppressed" in "a large paper [instead of canvas] bag, which tied up at the mouth with strings" is ridiculous. And when he changes the first line of the acrostic poem to "A boat beneath a sky" (omitting "sunny," and prolonging "A," because his chosen melody starts with a strong beat) he certainly goes too far. More serious is the question of noisiness. There are some loud exclamations during Carroll's trial scene. (" 'Stupid things!' Alice began in a loud indignant voice"; and " 'Stuff and nonsense!' said Alice loudly. . . . 'Off with her head!' the Queen shouted at the top of her voice.") But one cannot believe that Carroll, as he told the tale in "a boat, beneath a sunny sky, lingering onward dreamily," shouted these things at the top of his voice. There was an awful lot of shouting—not merely the suggestion of raised voices—in *Final Alice*. The matter of scale also causes some uneasiness. To bring a full Mahlerian apparatus, deployed at Mahlerian length, to *Alice* seems—well, somewhat inappropriate. (So does subjecting thematic material like that of Victorian ballads—however pretty, however catchy—to such elaborate and extended development.) There were passages when a listener felt tempted to emulate Alice in Tenniel's drawing at the end of the Lion and the Unicorn chapter in *Through the Looking-Glass* as she "put her hands over her ears, vainly trying to shut out the dreadful uproar." It is true that during the trial scene Carroll's Alice comes close to forgetting her manners (though she never goes as far as Del Tredici's Alice, who indulges in two slanging matches with the King). But otherwise she is sweetly reasonable, curious, intelligent, tidy-minded, and well behaved—"an adequate symbol for what every human being should try to be like," as W. H. Auden put it. (Flora, the heroine of Stella Gibbons's *Cold Comfort Farm*, is her adult incarnation.) I can't feel that Del Tredici's tone is always just. But then the Philharmonic performance was quite coarsely played; it was easy to imagine a more refined, more poetical execution of the score. Barbara Hendricks, in the solo role, showed stamina, and she flew above the staff (much of the music is written very high) with ease and sweetness. Sometimes she was careless about sounding short notes. Someone with a more beautiful speaking voice, and with more wit, intelligence, and literary sensitivity in her inflections, might bring the piece closer to Carroll. Del Tredici requires his soloist to shout; and the harsh amplification to which Miss Hendricks was subjected made her shouting ugly.

On the credit side, *Final Alice* is a large, generous, romantic, and melodious score, inspired by love for the book and sensitive to unwritten feelings that lie beneath it. In a sense, the "evidence" Del Tredici submits is of the Reverend Charles Dodgson's real-life love for Alice Pleasance Liddell. Of Aria IV, "Alice Gray," the composer writes, "With the fullest intensity I try to express Carroll's love of the real Alice. I think of the three variations as the three moods of love: love's first ecstasy, love lost, love regained." Is this *Final Alice*—and the whole huge Alicead that it crowns—impressive, touching, profound, or slightly absurd? Maybe all four at once.

April 11, 1977

SCENES OF BOHEMIAN LIFE

The Metropolitan Opera has a new *Bohème*, directed by Fabrizio Melano, in décor, by Pier Luigi Pizzi, borrowed from Chicago. The sets are less attractive and apt than those Chicago used to have; those were built and painted to nineteenth-century designs by Adolfo Hohenstein, supplied by the publisher of the opera, and so they had the composer's approval. (For some seventy-five years, similar scenery did hard and good service at Covent Garden, and there may still be other versions of it around. Those sets match Puccini's intentions and the style of his opera, and make possible the precise actions prescribed in his score.) At the Met, the loft studio of Acts I and IV is uncomfortably vast for the intimate exchanges between Mimì and Rodolfo; the Statue of Liberty looms over the Latin Quarter of Act II; and otherwise everything is much as usual. For big-house *Bohèmes*, the Zeffirelli-Karajan production that opened at La Scala in 1963 set a standard by which all others are judged. Perhaps it is unfair to judge them so: maybe we shall never again see a *Bohème* so expensive and so beautiful. In Act II, where the stage stretched back from a Seine-side Café Momus across a tree-lined boulevard to house-sized houses, Zeffirelli used three hundred people, all of them carefully rehearsed. The Scala has kept the show in its repertory —a revival came to Washington last year—but has not been able to keep its magical details intact. The Courbet effects of changing lights in the studio, and of dim figures glimpsed through the snowscape of Act III, which reached not to a visible backcloth but through gradations of light to a point beyond which the eye could not penetrate—these are no longer what they were. The Met has settled for a conventional *Bohème* writ large. The sets are serviceable, if not particularly pretty. The staging is routine, which is preferable to tasteless invention but not the same thing as bringing an opera to life in the way that its composer intended.

In this somewhat disappointing but at least unobtrusive frame, individual singers come and go and give their individual performances.

On the first night, Luciano Pavarotti played Rodolfo for laughs, not romance. He destroyed the tender moment of Mimì's first entrance by sprucing up after the exclamation "Una donna!" Later, like an ill-bred provincial tenor, he deliberately blew out his own candle instead of running so eagerly to light hers that his goes out, too. His singing was large and lyrical but not youthfully ardent. Renata Scotto's Mimì was carefully studied and delicately executed, and the vocal weight of the role is just right for her. If she could find a Visconti or Zeffirelli and a Serafin or Giulini to collaborate with, she could surely become a great singer; as it is, neither the dramatic nor the musical focus is quite sure. She has worked out everything for herself, with intelligence and artistry, but now she needs guidance. She made a self-centered impression: what she did took no colors from and shed no lights on the performances around her. James Levine conducted as if he despised the opera and had never listened to Beecham's recording of it. He slammed roughly into the ensembles, allowed much coarse bray and bang from the orchestra, and then would suddenly let the star soloists do more or less what they liked. What Miss Scotto liked was to drag out phrases—lingering here, fading into inaudibility there—until any rhythmic impetus disappeared. But before the final duet, ignoring the stage directions, she struggled painfully and slowly to her feet, to embrace Rodolfo once more, and this was something new (new to me, at any rate), true, and touching.

Three weeks later, in a televised performance of the opera, things went rather better. But it was the second Mimì of the season, Ileana Cotrubas, who brought some emotion to the production. The drama came to life with her entrance, and she held one's attention—not on herself but on Mimì—whenever she was on the stage. For Miss Cotrubas, who was making her Met début, is an extraordinarily touching stage figure, the kind of personality to whom an audience's heart goes out at once. One seemed to listen to Rodolfo's "Che gelida manina" through Mimì's ears and to watch Rodolfo through her admiring eyes. The Rodolfo was now José Carreras, and although in truth his aria was sung neither particularly well nor particularly badly, merely fluently and agreeably, Miss Cotrubas hung on each phrase of it in a way to persuade us that it *was* something wonderful. The Met is far too big a house for her subtle art and for a voice that is not rich and full, although it is attractive, very well schooled, individual, and delicately shaded. And Mimì is not the ideal role for her; as Mélisande, as Susanna, and in the title role of Cavalli's *Calisto*, in smaller houses, her uncommon blend of intelligence, distinction, wit, precision, charm, and youthful vulnerability is more rewardingly revealed. But she is so delightful a singer that the Met audience deserves to hear her, even if it cannot hear her to full advantage.

At this performance, Miss Scotto appeared as Musetta. She chewed up the scenery in Act II, in an exuberant and rather awful display of high spirits, but in Act IV she had some moving moments. Another important soprano, Josephine Barstow, made her Met début a few days later, as Musetta. She, too, is not a "natural" for the Met, and anyone who was hearing her for the first time may have wondered why she is Britain's admired Violetta, Leonore, Octavian, Elizabeth of Valois, and Salome—besides being an incomparable performer in Prokofiev's *War and Peace*, Tippett's *The Knot Garden*, Henze's *The Bassarids* and *We Come to the River*. Anyone sitting near the front, however, must have noticed that the unusual, heavily shaded voice is used with rare dramatic eloquence; that Miss Barstow commands the art of joining notes—or separating them—expressively; and that she is a skillful and potent actress even when, as a flighty, excitable Musetta, she plays against the natural grain. Miss Cotrubas and Miss Barstow, like Elisabeth Söderström (who has not sung for the Met for several years now, although her triumphs in such roles as Janáček's Jenůfa and Strauss's Christine and Countess Madeleine are regularly reported from abroad), are rare, precious, and wonderful artists who shine most brightly in the setting of a carefully rehearsed ensemble production, given in a house whose scale allows every fine detail to tell.

On the first night of *Bohème*, Maralin Niska was a somewhat harsh Musetta. The other main roles have been strongly cast: Ingvar Wixell as Marcello; Paul Plishka, and later Justino Díaz, as Colline; and Allan Monk as a bonny Schaunard, ready for promotion to Marcello. Italo Tajo, in the small role of Benoit, tried to make too much of it. The production began badly—Rodolfo was seated at a table looking out front, although he informed us that he was looking out of the window at Paris's smoking chimneys—and it ended badly, with a prominent tableau for Musetta and Marcello at a moment when all attention, theirs and ours, should be on Rodolfo and the dead Mimì. But presumably these details will change when other singers take over.

That other *Bohème*, Leoncavallo's, was put on by the New York Grand Opera for a single performance in the large Beacon Theater, but the execution was below a tolerable level, and after two acts I fled. The pleasures of opera in a small theater were demonstrated by a bewitching performance of Tchaikovsky's *Iolanta*, given by the Mannes College of Music in the Marymount Manhattan Theater, on East Seventy-first Street. This is a gem of an opera house—a 250-seater, built two years ago, raked like a miniature Bayreuth, with a pit, reaching back under the stage, that held fifty-five players and allowed them to play out without drowning the student cast. *Iolanta,* Tchaikovsky's last opera, about a blind princess who, with love to help her, gains her sight, is a sweet and beautiful composition, exquisitely scored, filled with captivating melodies and tender sentiment. I wish the City Opera would take it up. It is short, and needs a companion piece on the bill; Tchaikovsky wrote it to be done along with *The Nutcracker*. (I last heard it—with Miss Barstow, as it happens, in the title role—accompanied by Rimsky-Korsakov's *Mozart and Salieri*, and the two made a good Russian pair.) The Mannes performance was very prettily designed by Robert Joel Schwartz, warmly and sensitively conducted by Semyon Bychkov, and ably directed by Harvey Vincent. Young-Soon Kook's singing in the title role was true and pure, and she looked delightful. The opera was done in English; although the translation was not a happy one, it at least provided a medium of communication between the cast and the audience. This poignant student *Iolanta*, I thought, afforded keener pleasures than a slew of star-cast Metropolitan *Bohèmes*.

April 18, 1977

CITY OPERAS

I'd been warned off the City Opera's *Ariadne auf Naxos*: too much of a romp, people had said, and too little romance. But when I dropped in to see it the other day, I enjoyed it from beginning to end. How a company with two new productions (Leon Kirchner's *Lily* and a triple bill) in rehearsal and a new production (*The Pirates of Penzance*) and two big revivals (*Mefistofele* and a Stravinsky-Carl Orff double bill) just staged could have found time to prepare so deft and dapper a performance of Strauss's tricky ensemble opera I can't imagine. But it had. Julius Rudel conducted with delicacy, spirit, and affection. Sarah Caldwell's production revealed subtleties in the piece which had escaped me before. The performers understood clearly what they were about. (It helped, of course, that most of the work—all but the opera-seria scenes of Ariadne and Bacchus—was played in English.) Two performers were exceptional: Johanna Meier in the title role and David Holloway as the Music Master. After a curiously cautious "Ein schönes war," Miss Meier's voice began to flow in a stream of warm, beautiful sound. Her phrasing was eloquent; so were her appearance and demeanor. Mr. Holloway's baritone was so clear and true and his utterance so polished that one wished he had been assigned the role of Harlequin as well. (The doubling was practiced at the Vienna première of *Ariadne*, in 1916: in the prologue Hans Duhan played the Music Master and a Mr. Neuber played Harlequin, who has nothing to sing there; in the opera proper, where Harlequin has a good deal to sing, Duhan took over.) Thomas Jamerson, the City Opera Harlequin, was not at all bad—but Mr. Holloway has a voice in a thousand. Gianna Rolandi's Zerbinetta lacked softness and sweetness of timbre to start with, but as the music became more difficult her singing became gentler, more prettily and captivatingly playful. The big aria was exquisitely done. There was much to admire in the trios of nymphs (Gwenlynn Little, Glenys Fowles, Jane Shaulis) and of subsidiary comedians (John Lankston, Richard McKee, Melvin Lowery). John Alexander's Bacchus was reliable but unromantic (epithets attached to his performances with almost Homeric regularity). Not everything was right. The second set is a hideous tinsel confection. Hans Sondheimer's lighting is rudimentary. Maralin Niska's Composer was sometimes tough and sometimes edgy in timbre; the role did not suit her at all. But the pleasures of the production carried the day.

The Pirates of Penzance is an opera that would be well cast with Joan Sutherland as Mabel, Marilyn Horne as Ruth, Placido Domingo as Frederic, and Sherrill Milnes as Major-General Stanley. Or maybe Montserrat Caballé, Fiorenza Cossotto, José Carreras, and Piero Cappuccilli; if that quartet tackled the work in Italian translation, with the spoken dialogues musicked, we might find ourselves praising the dramatic verity with which the composer had expressed the characters' predicaments. In an age when *Lucia di Lammermoor* and *Il trovatore* are once again taken seriously, the graceful or brilliant melodies of *The Pirates*, its elaborate cadenzas, high rhetorical recitatives, and striking orchestral gestures to underline dramatic moments acquire a new charm. Sullivan did not have to write parody music. His joke is in the form itself: that a heroine should announce her arrival in a burst of brilliant coloratura; that a conspiratorial chorus should (like Di Luna's men in *Il trovatore*) steal upon their prey with catlike tread, volubly declaring their intentions the while; that all action should cease for an unaccompanied ensemble; that a hurried farewell (as in *Rigoletto*) should take several pages to achieve; that for no urgent reason a baritone should suddenly decide to apostrophize the breezes in a mellifluous cavatina. But in the City Opera *Pirates* the touch of the director, Jack Eddleman, is uncertain. Some of his staging is neat and witty, some of it crass and routine. He has a heroine, Miss Rolandi, whose coloratura is good enough to glitter in its own right; he should not have encouraged her to mime it as well, fluttering a hand to indicate a trill when by an accomplished vocal trill Sullivan's point has already been made. Henry Price was a romantic and musical Frederic, and he alone pronounced the text in a straightforward, sensible manner. The lower orders, led by Muriel Costa-Greenspon's Ruth and Irwin Densen's Sergeant, adopted a strange stage dialect in which "late" was "loyte" but "fate" was "fite." The others often affected those pinched, "refained" vowels that have long been the bane of D'Oyly Carte G.&.S. productions. "Gö, ye heroes, gö to glory!" Mabel cried, and, a little later, something like "Stä, Frederic, stä!" (Miss Rolandi does not pronounce Zerbinetta's lines in this ridiculous way.) Penzance has become "Penzahnce." Do the performers imagine they are adding an authentic British touch? *The Pirates* was less exhilarating than it should be, partly because Judith Somogi was a dull conductor, partly because the company has the habit of delivering spoken dialogue at dictation pace; its *H.M.S. Pinafore* and *La Belle Hélène* suffered similarly.

Mefistofele is a large spectacular production created in 1969 by Tito Capobianco around the Mephisto of Norman Treigle and revived now with Samuel Ramey in the title role. It is a serious, ambitious presentation of a serious, ambitious opera. Chorus and orchestra, under Mr. Rudel, are at their strongest. Miss Meier makes a pleasing Margherita and a luscious Helen of Troy. Ermanno Mauro is a passable Faust, despite his failure to suggest any quick, keen, questing intelligence. Mr. Ramey endows the Fiend with both brains and voice but does not have the huge histrionic flair to make one overlook how dull the music is. This Devil does not have the best tunes. I found no reason to disagree with the opinion of my old mentor Ernest Newman: that Boito's libretto, a compound of Goethe's *Faust* with the Book of Job, is a sorry mess, and that his score reveals "a semi-musical gift that rarely rises above the mediocre and generally dips a point or two below it." Three short arias— Margherita's "L'altra notte," Faust's "Dai campi, dai prati" and "Giunto sul passo estremo"—represent just about all of *Mefistofele* that is worth listening to.

In the City Opera's *Oedipus Rex*, a revival of a 1959 production, the narrator, Charles Roe, struck exactly the right tone and was the least fancy, most convincing interpreter of the part I have heard—and that despite the fact that he mispronounced every proper name except Tiresias. Both *Oedipus* and *Carmina Burana*, which accompanied it on this double bill, seemed somewhat underrehearsed: the chorus movements needed discipline, and in productions as formal as these straggle is impermissible. Manuel Rosenthal conducted tastefully but weakly, without rhythmic energy or force of accent. This was his début with the company; it was odd to have invited him in for two works of a kind that buoyant young Americans could be expected to shine in. *Oedipus* was capably sung, by Richard Taylor in the title role, RoseMarie Freni as Jocasta, Edward Pierson as Creon, Will Roy as Tiresias, and William Ledbetter as the Messenger. David Hicks's direction is on the right lines but was not incisively executed. Paul Sylbert's classical set would look better under harder, brighter light than Mr. Sondheimer provided. *Carmina Burana* is done as a ballet, on a bare black-shrouded stage, with the chorus on benches at the back. John Butler's choreography, executed by Dennis Wayne's Dancers, bears little relation to the sense of the words or of Orff's music. Elizabeth Haley was sweet and true in the Korngold-like cantilena of "In trutina." In Abram Morales the company has a new tenor who can soar into the very high tessitura of the roast swan's song. Mr. Roe sang the baritone solos as firmly as he had spoken the *Oedipus* narration.

April 25, 1977

OF THEE THEY SING

Benjamin Britten's first opera, *Paul Bunyan*, was written between 1939 and 1941 and first performed in 1941, by the Columbia Theater Associates of Columbia University; Britten was twenty-seven. Leon Kirchner's first opera, *Lily*, was written between 1959 and 1977 and first performed this month, by the New York City Opera; Kirchner is fifty-eight. The two pieces were brought into proximity by a revival of *Paul Bunyan* by the Preparatory Division of the Manhattan School of Music; on Sunday last week they could be seen consecutively. They have more in common than just being first operas: each takes America as its subject and handles that subject in terms of dramatic myth. *Paul Bunyan* has a libretto by W. H. Auden, based on the tales of the giant boss logger, his clerk Johnny Inkslinger, and his cook Hot Biscuit Slim. In two acts, it traces the progress of this country from primeval forest to poisoned rivers, polluted air, and PWA projects. It is a moral fable for an age when "the aggressive will is no longer pure." Bunyan takes his farewell saying:

> Other kinds of deserts call
> Other forests whisper Paul,
> I must hasten in reply
> To that low instinctive cry
> There to make a way again
> For the conscious lives of men.

Lily, whose libretto was fashioned by Kirchner himself from Saul Bellow's *Henderson the Rain King*, opens in an African forest; by the end of the opera that forest has been turned into a kind of desert by the blundering, destructive, would-be beneficent action of Henderson, the

569

American protagonist. The opera was at one time provisionally entitled *America,* and subtitles considered were "The Johnson Years" and "Why We Were in Vietnam." In a sense, *Lily,* continues where *Paul Bunyan* left off: Henderson is a product of the forces from which, in a final litany, the characters of *Bunyan* pray to be delivered. He is a violent, impulsive man of great physical strength, a millionaire, a pig farmer, and a questing, unsatisfied spirit, aware that he is wasting his life and seeking a new way to live. *Henderson the Rain King* tells of his African odyssey. Kirchner has based *Lily* on an episode from it, rather as earlier composers would base a *Nausicaä,* a *Circe,* or a *Return of Ulysses* on episodes from that other Odyssey, and he has named it for the Penelope of Bellow's story.

Henderson the Rain King is cast in the form of a long monologue. It opens with a question: "What made me take this trip to Africa?" As the narrator ponders it, "a disorderly rush begins—my parents, my wives, my girls, my children, my farm, my animals, my habits, my money, my music lessons, my drunkenness, my prejudices, my brutality, my teeth, my face, my soul!" Three hundred and twenty-five pages later, we have learned much about all these things, revealed fragment by fragment in the course of a main narrative that seems to flow spontaneously but is as cunningly and consciously constructed as a late Mahler symphony. In musical simile, the book could be likened to a long narrative tone poem dominated by a questioning "motto" theme, a recurrent "Who? What? Why? How? Where?" of an individual human existence. Within the single sweep of the structure, divisions into a prelude, three movements, and a coda can be discerned. The prelude concerns Henderson's pre-African life. Its material is picked up and amplified throughout the work; an important extra scrap of it is even reserved for statement in the coda, where it makes a powerful effect. The first movement is a pastoral. Henderson is among cow people, comforted by the motherly old Queen Willatale, who senses his "will to live"; sought as a bridegroom by her voluptuously fat sister, Mtalba; cheered by the friendship of their nephew Itelo, champion wrestler of the village until Henderson, using commando techniques learned at Camp Blanding, defeats him. Henderson, wishing to do something for them, aims to rid their water supply of a plague of frogs. (Their cows are dying, because "Mus' be no ahnimal in drink wattah" and "Nevah touch ahnimal in drink wattah" are two tribal tenets—expounded to him by Itelo.) His homemade bomb destroys the frogs, all right, but it destroys the whole cistern as well. The movement ends with an explosion and a sad farewell. "I demanded, 'Why for once, just once!, couldn't I get my heart's desire? I have to be doomed always to bungle.' And I thought my life-pattern stood revealed, and after such a revelation death might as well ensue as not."

But life goes on, and Henderson ("thinking about the burial of Oedipus at Colonus—but he at least brought people luck after he was dead") goes on to the lion people, ruled by King Dahfu. The second movement is a vigorous, brilliant, very colorful scherzo, which comes to a climax of ritual festivity: in an arena the massive hero carries a massive idol of the cloud goddess—too heavy for any of the natives to lift—across to an idol of the mountain god, the heavens open, and Dionysian celebrations break out. Henderson is appointed Rain King. The third movement is a double-concerto discourse in which Henderson and Dahfu are the soloists against a background mainly picturesque but disturbed by a menacing mutter. Their dialogues are at once serious and very funny. Montesquieu, Descartes, and Lamarck pass in review; Dahfu, leading Henderson into the den of his tame lioness, quotes Blake. He wishes to invest Henderson with leonine qualities. "Much can be changed. By no means all, but very very much. You can have a new poise, which will be your own poise. It will resemble the voice of Caruso, which I have heard on records, never tired because the function is as natural as to the birds." So Henderson, pretending to be a lion, each day goes down on all fours and roars, "and certain words crept into my roars, like 'God,' 'Help,' 'Lord have mercy' . . . plus snatches from the *Messiah* . . . So I would roar and the king would sit with his arm about his lioness, as though they were attending an opera performance." But Dahfu is killed by a wild lion when, in accordance with tribal custom, he sets out to capture it single-handed. (Tribal treachery probably plays a part in his death; the lion-catching equipment fails him.) The movement comes to an exciting and tragic climax.

Homeric echoes begin to sound more strongly in the later sections. Recurrent epithets are suggested by the repetitive descriptive phrases attached to characters at each appearance; Dahfu rides beneath his lioness much as Ulysses rode beneath the Cyclops' ram; references to Lily waiting at home for the wanderer's return become more frequent. The brief coda, lyrical and serene, traces the journey back to America. There are stopovers in Athens, Rome, Paris, and London—the cradles of modern civilization. "I thought I should see the Acropolis. . . . I saw something on the heights, which was yellow, bonelike, rose-colored. I realized it must be very beautiful. But I couldn't get out of the automobile." The other cities are quite ignored. On the transatlantic flight, passengers read. (Today, they draw down the blinds and watch a movie, instead of being stirred by visions Leonardo dreamed of but never saw, by views of the world which make Milton's images reality.) "How can you sit in a plane and be so indifferent?" Henderson reflects. "Of course, they weren't coming from mid-Africa like me; they weren't discontinuous with civilization." With him he has a lion cub, invested by the

Africans with Dahfu's soul and spirit; at Idlewild Lily will be waiting. But Henderson has not really been all that discontinuous with civilization. Through the tragicomic adventures in an Africa part symbolic, part fantastic, yet described in sharply realistic strokes, he has carried his Western civilization. The lion people took away his guns, his camera, all his trappings, but lines of Tennyson, Béranger, and Whitman still turn up in his conversation, snatches of Handel and Mozart in his singing, and memories of Chartres and Vézelay in his mind's eye. The Africa and its inhabitants among which they reappear are themselves a brilliant, controlled product of a Western literary imagination, one in which exotic appearances, sounds, scents, and tactile suggestions are vividly conveyed. The monologue reaches a fuel stop in Newfoundland, and ends there. Will Henderson continue to grow as a lion, revert to pigdom, or crumble into a tamed, shabby old bear? He is optimistic: the icy air, the trust of an orphan child he has befriended, and the thought of Lily conspire to fill him with "pure happiness." "And the lion? He was in it, too."

I found *Henderson the Rain King* a very difficult book to get into and a rich, exhilarating book once I had persevered and reached a point where the recurrent imagery began to cohere and the larger pattern to emerge. The clear organization into scenes; the alternation of narrative and reflection; the suggestions of solos, duets, ensembles, and immense choral tuttis; the sharply defined climaxes "orchestrated" in prose of carefully controlled pace and texture; the elaborate network of motivic cross-references—all these give the book an operatic quality. One can understand why Kirchner was drawn to it. He has been a long time making *Lily*. In 1969, his *Music for Orchestra*, commissioned by the New York Philharmonic for its hundred-and-twenty-fifth anniversary, was fashioned from music intended for the opera; the first forty-three bars are used as a prelude to the stage piece. Then, in 1973, there appeared a work for high soprano, chamber ensemble, speaker, and electronic tape, called *Lily*. The soprano doubles the roles of Mtalba and Lily, the speaker is Henderson, and the music makes contrast between the mysterious magic of the jungle and the cheap, chattering world that Henderson has left. Mtalba sings a love song in an invented, incomprehensible language; Lily, to the accompaniment of cocktail-time piano music, sings "Meet me in my orgone box, / With a double bourbon on the rocks"; Henderson speaks of his self-disgust. In the opera, most of this beautiful and imaginative stretch of chamber music follows the prelude, and then there is perhaps some seventy minutes more of music in which the contrasting veins are developed: winding enchanted melismas, the delicate patter of open-air night music, and exotic electronic evocations for the African scenes; parody music (including a mocking snatch of Menotti) for three flashbacks—to Henderson's and Lily's first lovemaking, to a

Paris encounter, to a domestic squabble after their marriage. When the frogs and the cistern have been destroyed, the opera ends: Henderson speaks—and simultaneously Lily, as if reading a letter from him, sings—some lines from the bridge passage that in the book takes Henderson on to the lion people. Kirchner breaks off just before Henderson's reflection that his American life, when recalled in Africa, seems more exotic and fantastic than anything around him.

And so to anyone who has read *Henderson the Rain King*, Kirchner's *Lily* seems but the first act of an unfinished *Henderson* opera. The hero has learned his first lesson; the more colorful, entertaining, and interesting part is still to come. I hope Kirchner goes on to complete a *Henderson* opera—and at the same time to revise the existing *Lily* in the light of what these City Opera performances of it must have taught him. To anyone who has not read *Henderson the Rain King* the drama of *Lily* may well seem baffling, incoherent, even inept. Kirchner's libretto has the usual failings of an opera text that has been hacked more or less verbatim from—instead of being a *dramma per musica* newly fashioned from the matter of—a long novel. (Prokofiev's *Story of a Real Man*, hacked from the Boris Polevoy novel, shows one approach, and Ponchielli's *I promessi sposi*, freely drawn from Manzoni, the other.) In *Lily*, important sentences—the "key statements"—from Bellow's *Henderson* are pulled out of context, strung together, deprived of explanation and qualification, spoken to or by the wrong character, cried aloud when they should be interior monologues. One simple example: Mtalba is described as "the woman of Bittahness . . . Bittah and very beautiful." "Water," remember, has been pronounced "wattah," so how can the listener possibly guess that Mtalba is not "bitter" but (as is carefully explained in the novel) a "*Bittah*," a "person of real substance"? On a less obvious but more serious level, there is a good deal of one-sentence blurting ("I've had a great affection for certain pigs myself") that becomes meaningless or misleading when all the related and contributory sentences, which in the book may be many pages away, are unuttered. It should be easy to revise the libretto, since, although the opera contains several passages that are beautiful to sing (and they were beautifully sung at the City Opera), many—perhaps even most—of its important lines are spoken. It is not primarily a vocal opera in any conventional way. A colleague described its music as "of more interest to musicians than to the opera-going public," and one sees what he means. But, I trust, some operagoers are also musicians, and they can hardly fail to respond to Kirchner's music. The opera is a series of linked, related movements—some melismatic, some built mainly from carefully arranged sounds and rhythms—contrasted in texture, timbre, pace, and emotional tone. *Lily* does not reveal its merits at once. I own that at a first hearing I thought it confused, awkwardly assembled, and lacking in simple theatrical savoir-faire. In fact, I still think it so. But at a third hearing I was drawn into Kirchner's vision of Henderson's adventure, perceived and understood the intentions of his music more clearly, and could discount—having already noted—the obvious theatrical miscalculations in order to concentrate on the power of his musical imagination.

Lily was very well sung, above all by Geanie Faulkner, as Mtalba, who revealed a sweet, pure, high soprano, both flexible and full, warm in timbre even when it rose to high F. Miss Faulkner is young and attractive, a Lakmé, a Nannetta; Bellow's Mtalba is obese, sparkling with fat and moisture, and broad as a sofa across her hips. Joy Blackett was a commanding, generous, and secure Willatale, though she, too, seemed far too young, not monumental enough to play the massive old earthmotherly queen. Benjamin Matthews, the Itelo, is a young baritone with gleaming presence both in his voice and in his bearing. Lily in Bellow's novel is "a big broad," a woman built on a scale to match Henderson's; in the opera Susan Belling's Lily is a svelte coloratura. What Kirchner had in mind I am unsure; in fact, Lily, both in the book and in the opera, remains to me curiously undefined. But in Kirchner's piece it would make musical and theatrical sense if she and Mtalba could be doubled by a very large, energetic soprano with a very large and beautiful coloratura voice. Miss Belling's voice was true but small, and her words were inaudible—sometimes her fault, sometimes the composer's, for setting them high above the staff. These four singers were City Opera debutants. As Romilayu, Henderson's faithful guide, Sancho to his Quixote, George Shirley gave a perfect performance, and one regretted that Kirchner had made this a comprimario role; Romilayu has little to do but, as interpreter, add a subsidiary voice to another's utterance. As Henderson, Ara Berberian, carrying the main weight of the opera, was powerful and convincing, physically and vocally right, forceful, funny, and eloquent. The company was strong all through, and Kirchner, his own conductor, seemed to be obtaining almost exactly what he wanted from a musical point of view.

But the staging, by Tom O'Horgan, left something to be desired. The libretto of *Lily* was made available, in typescript, only to the press. (The public was presumably expected to prepare itself by reading *Henderson the Rain King*. Indeed, it should have been urged to do so—but I saw no stacks of the book on the City Opera sales counters during the weeks preceding the première.) In this libretto, Kirchner puts formidable, well-nigh impossible demands to his director and designer. Mr. O'Horgan and his team did not go far to meet them; they responded, for the most part, with glib professional clichés. While my admiration for the cast grew at each performance, so did my feeling that this staging had failed to give imaginative form to more than the superficies of Kirchner's work. The uses made of a cinema screen downstage, descending and ascending, and of three lantern-slide screens upstage were crude. The lighting (Henderson was generally tracked by a circus-type follow spot) was unromantic.

Lily is the first American opera in six years to have been created by one of New York's two regular companies—the first since Menotti's *The Most Important Man*, done by the City Opera in 1971. (Before that, there was Hugo Weisgall's *Nine Rivers from Jordan*, at the City Opera in 1968; the previous year brought Vittorio Giannini's *The Servant of Two Masters* at the City Opera and Marvin David Levy's *Mourning Becomes Electra* at the Met. A poor record for an operatic decade in a major city.) *Lily* got a bad press—but then more new operas than not get a bad press to start with. And if I had had to review *Lily* overnight, I would have written with small enthusiasm; it was only at the second—and much stronger—public performance that its virtues began to seem far, far more important than its faults. Operas of merit, even of mixed merit, are not killed by an initially unfavorable reception. (Although many London critics wrote obituaries of Britten's *Gloriana* and Tippett's *The Midsummer Marriage* after their premières, some years later both of them became popular successes.) *Lily* is an opera I shall recall, and enjoy recalling, when more featly tailored, more readily acclaimed works have faded from memory. But I hope that it will not merely become a memory: that at least it will be recorded; that at best it will be revised, amplified, and expanded into a complete *Henderson* to be enjoyed, both here and abroad, by musicianly operagoers who are prepared to put in a few hours of preliminary work before attending an unfamiliar piece.

Paul Bunyan also got a bad press when it was first done here—so bad that the opera remained on the shelf for thirty-six years. Its faults were evident: Auden's libretto, clever, often slick and tiresomely "literary," was at once too simple and schematic in its ground plan and too diffuse in its decorative details. The faults were pointed out in reviews not so much untrue as incomplete. (Some of them also implied that it was impertinent of two brilliant young Englishmen to tackle an all-American subject; they should be put in their place.) But when, last year, the BBC and then the English Music Theatre Company (see p. 411) revived *Paul Bunyan*, it became apparent that this "choral operetta" (so its authors styled it) is one of those early works of genius—like Mozart's *Idomeneo*, Verdi's *Nabucco*—whose youthful freshness and abundance of invention set an audience's spirits soaring. The faults remain—there are still lines at which one flinches—but have been lessened by the removal of two of the most "literary" numbers: a love song *cum* rhyming game ("Appendectomy / 's a pain in the neck to me. . . . Psycho-kinesia / Never gets easier") and a sophisticated chorus of film stars

575

and models who materialize while the lumberjacks dream. The specific social criticism in *Paul Bunyan* does not cut deep, and so it can be taken lightly. What matters is the general vision of unspoiled nature and men harnessing (and spoiling) that nature, of first love and first grief, of dreams, ambitions, and the compromises that life imposes. And what matters most of all is the world of lyrical, joy-giving music that Britten creates, a world one can go on living in for days after hearing the opera, and then later, through memory's ear, re-enter at will.

Britten and Auden were not novices or strangers to one another when they created *Paul Bunyan*; the piece is not prentice work. From *Our Hunting Fathers*, in 1936, they had been collaborating on cantatas, songs, films, and plays; the *Variations on a Theme of Frank Bridge*, first heard at the Salzburg Festival of 1937, had already made Britten's international reputation. His felicitous mastery is apparent in every number of *Paul Bunyan*. There is a simple phrase in the prologue, "Once in a while the odd thing happens," set in a way that makes the heavens open (not with a deluge, as they open in *Henderson*, but onto glorious visions of strangeness and splendor). The effect is achieved by a leaping octave taken up by voice after voice, through the four-part writing, in a concealed canon; by an inspired control of diatonic dissonance and resolution; and by the sure, unconventional spacing of the choral chords. On paper, the passage looks simple—as simple as the wonderful bars that open Mozart's Clarinet Quintet. The sound of it defies analytical description. Reading *Henderson*, I came across the words "once in a while" in a very different context, and suddenly the phrase sang out from the page as Britten had set it—to prompt reflections on the difference between a composer whose music seems to break forth with heaven-sent spontaneity and inevitableness, and one who must struggle to set down in sounds his elusive visions. *Paul Bunyan* is a lyrical and vocal opera in a way that *Lily* is not. (Yet its orchestration is also marvelously deft, exact, and colorful; the spontaneous singer—Mozart, Schubert, Rossini —is often a very skillful technician as well.) Other inspirations are the poignant lament of Tiny, Paul's daughter, for her mother; Slim's song to the effect that, as Pinkerton puts in the old translation of *Butterfly*, "the whole-world over the Yankee is a rover" (here Britten uses hemiolia— six beats divided now into twos, now into threes—as buoyantly as if the device had just been discovered); and the large ensemble "O great day of discovery," in which the great globe itself seems slowly to begin turning.

Paul Bunyan was written to be technically accessible to high schools. By the young soloists of the Manhattan School's Preparatory Division— most of them aged sixteen, but some younger—it was attractively sung. Since the School's Borden Auditorium is really too large for small, young voices (it seats nearly two hundred people more than Glyndebourne, where I first heard Birgit Nilsson and Montserrat Caballé), one needed to be very near the front. The littlest children of the chorus set a standard of uninhibited but not undisciplined singing and acting which made their immediate seniors seem at times a shade constrained, too much on their best behavior. A few students from the School's College Division were brought in for some of the more taxing roles; notable among them were Jeffrey Thomas as Slim, Vincent Arnone as Johnny Inkslinger, and David Kline as Helson. Bunyan himself—he is represented only by a voice, for how can one put a giant, taller than the Empire State Building, onto the stage?—was spoken by Harlan Foss. He chuckled too often but spoke very well. In the orchestra, Preparatory and College Division students mingled. The décor, like that for *Lily*, used three screens on which slides were projected. Those that were scenic worked well; those that attempted specific commentary (Lindbergh and Jesse Owens during Slim's "Round the world and back, I must hunt my shadow"; the Yalta Conference and Nixon with Mao Tse-tung during Bunyan's "Often thoughts of hate conceal / Love we are ashamed to feel") did not. In general it was a good staging, and in many points of dramatic and musical detail an exceptionally sensitive one. Cynthia Auerbach was the diversely gifted deviser, director, conductor, and general inspiratrix of a show whose enthusiasm, joyousness, dedication, and feeling of communal accomplishment would have delighted Britten's heart. *Paul Bunyan* was composed to be done in just this way.

May 2, 1977

Kirchner's chamber piece called Lily *was recorded on Columbia M 32740. The record is out of print but worth hunting for.*

WHAT THE COMPOSERS WANTED

The Federal Music Society Orchestra and Wind Band, conducted by John Baldon, made its formal New York début in Town Hall last month. The wind band numbered a baker's dozen (pairs of flutes, clarinets, oboes, horns, bassoons, and trumpets, and a serpent); a dozen strings, drums, and a continuo keyboard joined them to form the full orchestra. They played music, mainly American, of the eighteenth and early nineteenth centuries on instruments of the same date. There were many marches. Most of the native music, by such composers as Benjamin

577

Carr, Samuel Holyoke, Oliver Shaw, and Victor Pelissier, was agreeable and melodious in no very striking way; the overture to John Christian Bach's *Lucio Silla* stood out as a composition of substance. But it was the sounds rather than the scores which gave distinction to the concert: the gentle clarity of the gut-stringed fiddles; the sweet, true timbre of the woodwinds; above all, the purity and freshness of the natural horns, and the easy blend of the whole. While listening, one was persuaded that modern instruments are gross and overpowered, too tensely strung, too fierce and shiny—fit for such stuff as *Salome* and the *Leningrad* Symphony. Of course, one would not want to hear even gentle music by, say, Debussy, Webern, or Elliott Carter tackled by the Federal Orchestra, but—given the same conductor—I certainly would rather listen to it than to the Chicago Symphony in Haydn and Mozart. For this concert made clear on an orchestral scale what many soloists and chamber ensembles who use instruments and techniques contemporary with the music they play have demonstrated: that gentleness is not incompatible with vigor and brightness; that musicians can show strength without being aggressive.

In the second part of the program, the players were joined by solo singers and a small chorus, the Columbian Singers. Two excerpts from Arne's *Artaxerxes*—the overture and the bravura air "The soldier tir'd" —were done. (Whether they were played in Arne's own orchestration or in the rescoring by Charles Edward Horn used at the New York première of the opera, in 1828, was not stated.) They made me eager to hear the whole of *Artaxerxes* again. (Last time I heard it, it was accompanied by a twentieth-century band.) The work goes well in the theater. Let us hope that the Federal Orchestra finds full employment, both symphonic and operatic. Its sound is needed. Two small, connected points: the string section, seven fiddles at the top and only one double-bass at the bottom, seemed top-heavy; and the platform arrangement, with that bass way over on the right, suggested the twentieth century. The addition of a second bass, over on the left, might provide a more authentic eighteenth-century balance.

Concert performances and student productions do much to fill gaps in an operagoer's experience. Puccini's second opera, *Edgar*, which Eve Queler's Opera Orchestra of New York presented in concert in Carnegie Hall last month, was not new to me; ten years ago, the Hammersmith Municipal Opera mounted it as its first production (Hammersmith is a London borough), and five years later there was a BBC studio performance. But I had not heard it grandly cast, as it was by Miss Queler, with Renata Scotto and Carlo Bergonzi in two of the leading roles. *Edgar* is an arresting piece. It does not sound like prentice work. Nor is it, in the third (and briefest) version of the score, which Miss Queler used. This was prepared in 1905, after *Tosca*, after *Butterfly*, and comparison with the earlier vocal scores, of 1889 and 1892, shows how considerably Puccini reworked the piece in his maturity. The libretto is—well, peculiar. Ferdinando Fontana drew it from Musset's play *La Coupe et les lèvres*, cut all the reflective passages, and shaped it as an abrupt, violent, existentialist, and curiously modern drama—formal and symbolic, not veristic. Nothing is explained; actions are shown, not motivated. The libretto is prefaced by a highfalutin poem: "Edgar are we all, for Fate leads everyone to the crossroads—shadow and light, love and death. . . . Woe if, to the light of serene love, which can on mighty pinions lift souls aloft, we prefer the obscene flame that kindles the senses, etc." Fontana's aim seems to have been a kind of *Carmen* ennobled by copious draughts of *Tannhäuser*. The irresolute Edgar, the faithful Fidelia, and the tigerish Tigrana are three type-figures enacting a drama of small credibility but, on a non-realistic plane, of high poetic power. *Edgar* first appeared, at La Scala, on Easter Sunday, 1889. Fidelia was Aurelia Cataneo, Italy's first Isolde. Tigrana was Romilda Pantaleoni, Verdi's first Desdemona. In later revivals of the piece, Francesco Tamagno and Giovanni Zenatello, the first Otello and his most famous successor, played Edgar. That shows the sort of scale Puccini had in mind. It is easy to understand why he was reluctant to abandon the work and repeatedly tried to give it currency. By intention, at least, it represents opera of a different kind from that of his popular successes—more ambitious, more elevated.

The music is enjoyable. There are influences from Verdi, Wagner, Ponchielli, Berlioz, and Meyerbeer; shadows are thrown forward to *Turandot*, to which *Edgar* is closer in tone than to the other Puccini operas. The scoring is filled with interesting and characteristic ideas, and the vocal writing with memorable turns of phrase. The music becomes jaunty, raises a smile, when Edgar—disguised as a monk, assisting at what purports to be his own funeral—and his friend Frank tempt Tigrana, with jewels, to dishonor the memory of the supposedly dead hero. Fidelia's aria in the last act, "Nel villaggio d'Edgar son nata anch'io," can rank among Puccini's happiest lyric inventions. When I saw *Edgar* on the stage, it was treated as a dramatic fable, presented formally, almost as a series of illustrations in a frieze, and this is probably the way to save it from absurdity. In an age disenchanted with *verismo*, *Edgar* may have a future.

In the Micaëla-Elisabeth role of Fidelia, Renata Scotto sang with warmth and intensity, and in tones that were pure and lovely except when the line was both loud and high. To the Carmen-Venus role of Tigrana, Gwendolyn Killebrew brought appropriate fire, though the focus of her voice was not always sharp. As the hero, Mr. Bergonzi produced a splendid stream of effortless, beautiful tone. Vicente Sardinero, as Frank, showed a fresh and well-founded baritone. There was good choral work from the Schola Cantorum of New York. Miss Queler, though not quite as cogent an interpreter of Puccini as she is of Donizetti and Verdi, directed a vivid performance. The show was recorded for future release by Columbia. An Italian-English libretto, printed expressly for the occasion, was supplied gratis.

The April issue of *The Musical Times* reports on university productions of Handel's *Giulio Cesare* (uncut), Schubert's *Alfonso und Estrella*, Auber's *La Muette de Portici*, Verdi's *Giovanna d'Arco*, and Carl Nielsen's *Saul og David*, all done within the span of a month and within a radius of two hours, by British Rail, from London. In March, Sadler's Wells (a state- and city-supported opera house, now maintained as a London showplace for interesting companies both British and foreign) put on a season of student opera which included Lully's *Alceste*, Gluck's *Le Cinesi*, Ib Nørholm's *The Garden Wall*, and Brian Hughes's *Stars and Shadows* (composed, to a libretto by Ursula Vaughan Williams, to make a double bill with V.W.'s *Riders to the Sea*); the troupes came from the opera schools of London, Manchester, and Copenhagen. I wish New York could afford something of the kind—perhaps at the Brooklyn Academy of Music, which is the city's showplace closest in spirit, in friendliness, and in fare to Sadler's Wells. [I drop in a second lament for the Harkness Theater, now destroyed, which the city could have acquired for a mere million dollars; see p. 112. It is across the road from Lincoln Center. It was the right size for student opera, for the Mini-Met, for Met or City Opera productions of Mozart, for visiting troupes such as Glyndebourne.] Campus productions I have valued in this country have included Busoni's *Doktor Faust* (Bloomington, Indiana), Alessandro Scarlatti's *Griselda* (Berkeley), Robert Kurka's *The Good Soldier Schweik* (San Diego), Marc Blitzstein's *Regina* (San Jose), Debussy's *Fall of the House of Usher* (New Haven), and Richard Strauss's *Intermezzo* (Philadelphia). Seeing those required travel. In New York, this season, there have been Chabrier's *Le Roi malgré lui* (Juilliard), Wolf-Ferrari's *I quattro rusteghi* and Britten's *Paul Bunyan* (Manhattan School), and Tchaikovsky's *Iolanta* (Mannes College). From past seasons, Bloch's *Macbeth* (Juilliard) and the world première of Robert Starer's *Pantagleize* (Brooklyn College) stand out. According to statistics gathered by the Central Opera Service, about one of every three opera performances given in this country is done at a university (about 2,400 of the 7,109 performances tallied in 1975–76).

Juilliard's latest production is of Verdi's *Falstaff*—no rarity, but an understandable choice, since Tito Gobbi, a celebrated Italian Falstaff, was on hand to direct it. And, that being so, it was forgivable to essay a performance in Italian. But Mr. Gobbi did some unforgivable things. Perhaps because most of the audience would miss the wit of the Italian

580

text and the way Verdi set it, the director set about amusing them in other ways. In Act I, Falstaff pinched the hostess's bottom. (The start of his "So che se andiam, la notte" was drowned in laughter.) In Act II, he had a merry time trying to poke a long-stemmed rose down the front of Alice Ford's dress. (Anything to do with bosoms seems to strike audiences as hilarious.) The close of Act III, Scene 1—the magical episode of distant voices calling from side to side across an empty, darkling scene—was treated as a pantomime for Ford and Dr. Caius. By then, the audience was in a mood to crash into the start of the next scene—far-off horn calls and delicate woodwind replies stealing through Windsor Forest, introducing Verdi's most exquisite love music—with the noise of their own applause for Robert Yodice's décor. As modern *Falstaff* productions go, this one was not in fact among the worst. By comparison with Götz Friedrich's at the Holland Festival, or Jean-Pierre Ponnelle's for Glyndebourne, it can be counted a marvel of sensitivity. There was nonsense in it—the host and hostess (an invented character), undisguised, pressed bills upon Falstaff during the scene when he should think a supernatural rout has beset him—but basically the characters were correctly conceived and presented. And Mr. Gobbi had coached his protagonist, Ronald Hedlund, into producing a Falstaff at times uncannily close to his own; "Quand'ero paggio" seemed to be a carbon copy, inflection by inflection—a good copy of something good. In general, however, a feeling that the players had got up their roles by rote took some of the edge off the fun. The show lacked spontaneity and natural buoyancy. (Sixten Ehrling's cautious conducting did not help.) But it did not lack accomplishment.

Ricordi assigned a publication number to a production book of *Falstaff* based on the Scala première, which the composer himself supervised. If it is as detailed as that for *Otello* (which leaves no movement and no motivation in doubt; each character, down to the last chorus member, has his actions and positions assigned—yet is told to remember that he is an individual and to act as one), it should be a revelation. But no copy has been traced. Nevertheless, we do have Verdi's own stage plans for the second and fourth scenes, and several of his observations about how *Falstaff* should be mounted: "Nothing easier and simpler than this *mise en scène*, if the designer produces a set in accord with what I kept in my mind's eye while I was composing the music." "At the finale of Act II, the stage should be almost bare, so that the action of the principal groups—at the screen, the basket, and the window—remains distinct and clearly visible." "As for lighting effects, all that's needed is a bit of darkness in the forest scene—but, let it be clearly understood, a *darkness* that allows the players' faces to be seen." By and large, opera directors pay too little attention to what composers wanted. To the detriment of both music and drama, they often ignore or contradict even the clear instructions in the libretto and score. There is no reason why singers should not learn to make the right moves—then fashion personal, spontaneous-seeming interpretations on that basis. After all, we expect them to learn and to sing the right notes.

The Opera Company of Boston's *Rigoletto*, which opened last week, had several interesting features. It was done in a text based on a new critical score that H. C. Robbins Landon is preparing for the complete Verdi edition announced by Ricordi and the University of Chicago Press. It was uncut (the first uncut *Rigoletto* I've encountered in the theater since Solti's at Covent Garden in 1964). Indeed, it was even "more than complete," in that it included Maddalena's aria. The instrumentation was reduced. The wind bass was supplied not by a tuba or a bass trombone but by a genuine cimbasso. And Beverly Sills sang the first stage Gilda of her career.

Mr. Landon's score purges the familiar text of wrong articulations, accents, and dynamics—and of some wrong notes—which have crept in over the years. Maddalena's aria was brought to prominence recently by Patric Schmid, a director of Opera Rara (a London-based company celebrated for its revivals of Mercadante and the rarer pieces of Rossini, Meyerbeer, Donizetti, and Offenbach). The aria appears in an early French vocal score (Escudier, Plate No. L.E. 1764) of 1857–58, and in all French librettos up to the one sold today. In Act III, after the Duke has gone to sleep upstairs, and before Gilda has returned in man's attire, Maddalena sings "Prends pitié de sa jeunesse"—four quatrains of plea to her brother to spare the life of the handsome young stranger: "Une sœur ou bien sa mère / Doit l'attendre en ce moment." It is a suave, attractive piece of music (and in Boston it was poignantly sung, in Italian translation, by Susanne Marsee), but it is undramatic. It was concocted, perhaps, for the French-language première of *Rigoletto* (Brussels, 1858); I say "concocted" because in fact it is merely Verdi's song "Il poveretto" provided with a new text. The aria was dropped from all later editions of the French score. Although it proved interesting to hear the piece in context, I doubt whether "Prends pitié" deserves to become a regular part of *Rigoletto*: once the storm has begun, it should proceed without lyrical interruption to the climax of the trio and the stabbing of Gilda.

For *Rigoletto*, Verdi did not have a sunken orchestra pit; the ordinary Italian term for one is "golfo mistico"—and that "mystic chasm" devised by the magician of Bayreuth did not reach Italy for a long while. In 1871, Verdi regretted that Wagner's admirable idea had not been adopted at La Scala, where, in the spectator's eye, white ties and tails still mingled with costumes Egyptian, Assyrian, or Druidical, and the tops of double-basses and harps formed part of the décor. (It is said that Toscanini was the first to sink the pit at La Scala.) The Orpheum, where the Boston *Rigoletto* was done, has no pit, either. This makes for an "authentic" balance—provided that the orchestra does not produce an overpowering, twentieth-century volume and intensity of sound. Sarah Caldwell's orchestra did not, since her score was stripped of second oboe, second bassoon, third and fourth horns, and second and third trombones. Their essential notes were so cunningly cued in that the average listener probably noticed nothing amiss—only that he could hear the singers uncommonly well. By using an unauthentic score, a nineteenth-century balance more authentic than usual was achieved.

The mysterious cimbasso, defined in reference books as a narrow-bore tuba, proved to be something more like a valved bass trombone, cylindrical for most of its length, then flaring into a big bell that rises over the player's shoulder but points horizontally—not, like a tuba's, upward. Its tone—the instrument used was an American one made on the Italian model—was smooth, and refined, less fat than a tuba's, less brazen than a bass trombone's. (Verdi, incidentally, would have expected valved trombones in his orchestra, not the more fiery slide trombones used today.)

Miss Sills, it was announced, was singing despite a fever and a heavy cold. One would not have guessed it (except, perhaps, when the trill at the end of "Caro nome" slipped down to the lower note), for her voice moved freely, and there was plenty of power in the climaxes. Her interpretation, strongly and richly conceived, was often very moving—especially in the revelatory asides of the last act. Verdi once recalled how Adelina Patti, by her declamation of the three notes of Gilda's "Io l'amo," produced "a sublime effect that no words can describe." Miss Sills was not yet sublime there, but she does have the gift of investing apparently simple phrases with rare eloquence. The role suits her. It is astonishing that she has not undertaken it before. Joseph Evans was a young, fresh-voiced, mellifluous Duke, graceful and buoyant in his phrasing. Richard Fredericks's Rigoletto lacked weight and grandeur, both of tone and of personality, but his singing was clear and often ringing. Miss Caldwell's conducting was dramatic and colorful, her pacing purposive and exciting. Her staging included some needless novelty. Monterone's daughter (Diane de Poitiers in the Hugo play, *Le Roi s'amuse*, on which *Rigoletto* is based) made a mute appearance in the first scene. At the start of Act II, we were still outside Rigoletto's house, where the Duke enacted his narrative recitative ("Inner premonition prompted me to retrace my steps; the gate was open, the house deserted"). To sing the aria, he then stepped into a downstage pool of light while, behind him, the garden scene dissolved into the palace. Quite unnecessary—but not, as it happened, ineffective or destructive of the music. Especially striking was the sharp definition of the courtiers' feelings about their duke and his jester. Too many of the solos, I felt, were sung from the upper levels—the balconies and terraces—of Douglas W. Schmidt's sets; the device began to seem like a mannerism. Gilbert Hemsley's lighting was dramatic—a sharp play of light and shadows which did not depend upon follow spots.

May 9, 1977

AN AMERICAN REQUIEM

In the central episode of *Alexander's Feast; or The Power of Musique*, Dryden celebrates music's threnodial power: the composer Timotheus, seeing Alexander grow flushed and proud at the memory of his battles, chooses a mournful muse, soft pity to infuse, and soon the conqueror is moved to weep for his slaughtered foe, Darius great and good, fallen, fallen, fallen from his high estate. The sounds of mourning—the slow strong beat of a funeral march; the thud of muffled drums; full, solemn minor harmonies; the falling melodic motifs eloquent of grief—have often been shaped into noble music. Requiems usually rank high in their composer's oeuvre, whether the text is liturgical (Victoria, Cherubini, Berlioz, Verdi, Bruckner, Fauré), Biblical (Brahms), secular (Delius), or both liturgical and secular (Britten).

Whitman's *When Lilacs Last in the Dooryard Bloom'd* was written as an elegy for Lincoln. In 1946, Hindemith set it to music as an elegy for Franklin D. Roosevelt and for those who had fallen in the war; he entitled it *A Requiem "for those we love,"* making plural the "for him I love" refrain of Whitman's first, tenth, and eleventh strophes (or sections). In 1970, Roger Sessions completed another setting of the poem, as a cantata dedicated "to the memory of Martin Luther King, Jr., and Robert F. Kennedy." The work, commissioned by the University of California, Berkeley, in commemoration of the hundredth anniversary of its founding, was first performed on the Berkeley campus in 1971, conducted by Michael Senturia. In 1975, there were two performances at Harvard, conducted by Senturia. In 1976, Solti did it in Chicago. Last month, the Boston Symphony, under Seiji Ozawa, performed it. Next year, the San Francisco Symphony, also under Ozawa, will do so. It has not yet been heard in New York.

I attended two of the Boston performances. (It was done there four times in all.) Friends who had heard and got to know the piece at earlier

584

performances had told me it was a major American composition, not to be missed. And they proved to be right. Some added that it is probably Sessions's masterpiece, and probably they are right in that, too: I do not know all of his late music well enough to say. At any rate, *When Lilacs Last in the Dooryard Bloom'd* is an inspired and stirring composition, one to set beside Delius's *Sea-Drift* (1903) and Vaughan Williams's *Sea Symphony* (1910) for its large, visionary presentation, with large forces, of Whitman's thought, and one to set above them for the way it makes music of the sounds and the movement of Whitman's actual lines. In Sessions's cantata we find the rapture, tenderness, and poignancy of *Sea-Drift* and the energy, grandeur, and mystical, contemplative calm of the *Sea Symphony* together with a quality that can be more easily described than analytically defined as American. In part, at least, and especially to a British listener, the Americanness arises from the melodic inflections of the word setting. On the simplest level, it is a matter of pronunciation. Hindemith presumably learned British English as a boy: in his Requiem he scans the word "recesses," at the start of Whitman's fourth strophe, in the British way, with the accent on the second syllable, while Sessions puts the accent on the first; Hindemith gives "missiles" a long, and Sessions gives it a short, second syllable. (Musical setting throws such transatlantic differences into prominence. In the recent Manhattan School production of *Paul Bunyan* one heard Auden's "began / Cézanne" and "farmer / melodrama" failing to rhyme, as in British productions they did; "later / theater" in *The Rake's Progress* and "myrtle / fertile" in *The Bassarids* point to a Chester Kallman, not an Auden, attribution for the relevant lines of those collaborative librettos.) But pronunciation is only a small part of it. National characteristics in melody have their origin in the intonations, inflections, and rhythms of national speech, which make Mussorgsky's tunes Russian, Janáček's Czech, and Sessions's American. *When Lilacs Last in the Dooryard Bloom'd* calls for three soloists: soprano, contralto, and baritone. From a purely sonic point of view, the voices of Gundula Janowitz, Janet Baker, and Dietrich Fischer-Dieskau would provide an ideal cast. And yet those three beautiful singers would not be convincing interpreters of the work unless they had carefully studied American speech patterns. (Fischer-Dieskau's British English is good, as can be heard in Britten's *War Requiem*; his American English is unidiomatic, as can be heard in his record of Ives songs.) In an introductory note to the score, the composer instructs soloists to

interpret the RHYTHMIC DETAIL in terms of the unforced inflections of the English language, which the composer has used as the basis of his vocal conception. [The singer] should, therefore, on no account force himself into

585

a mechanical rendition of the exact note-values as written, but rather interpret them freely in terms of natural English diction, respecting the subtleties of rhythm and stress which are inherent in the words themselves. In this manner he will best realize the composer's intentions.

Whitman's lines spoken as a good American speaker might speak them form Sessions's starting point, and any discussion of his cantata can well begin by looking at the melody to which the first two of those lines are set. The work is above all a lyrical piece. The music, Sessions says, "is always to be sung in a full-voiced and lyrical manner; it contains no passages in which a preponderantly declamatory style is appropriate." And the music is always grateful, though often difficult, to sing. The first three bars present, in three-part wind writing, a gently insistent rocking figure, alternating between a consonant and a dissonant chord. Then the soprano soloist sings the opening lines ("When lilacs last in the dooryard bloom'd, / And the great star early droop'd in the western sky in the night") to a melody whose first ten moves are of either a third or a step; the eleventh move is a leap of a tritone, to sound the twelfth note of a note row. Without music type one would not venture on even the most perfunctory analysis of any two bars of the cantata. Perhaps not even with it, for Sessions does not compose schematic music. Forty years ago, he wrote of his antipathy toward "an intellectually determined basis for music," opposing to such a basis "the response of the human ear and spirit to the simplest acoustic facts," since music's "human meaning . . . lies ultimately in the fact that such elementary phenomena as the fifth, and the measurably qualitative distinction between consonance and dissonance, are psychological as well as physical facts, out of which a whole language has grown, and which in music based on the twelve-tone system seem often more powerful binding forces than those inherent in the system itself." Some of the elementary musical phenomena in the opening melody of the cantata are readily perceivable; some of their simpler consequents became aurally apprehensible, as binding forces, at later hearings. The first nine notes are F-sharp, A; B-flat, D; E, C, A-flat; G, E-flat—a chain of adjacent or linked thirds, the first of them minor, the others major. The "tonal" implications are evident: notes one to four outline a D-major triad with an added note; notes five to eight, C major with an added note; notes six to nine, both A-flat major and C minor with an added note. The ear, even against contradictory harmonies from the rocking accompaniment, hears this, but enough else is happening to insure that (as Sessions remarks in his textbook *Harmonic Practice*) "such quasi-tonal sensations are simply evidence that the ear has grasped the relationships between the tones, and has absorbed and ordered them." And "it is a mistake to regard such

sensations as connected exclusively with the tonal system as such."
Similarly, it would be a mistake to regard the end of the cantata as exclusively a D-major cadence (E and C; D and B-flat; then D, A, F-sharp
—the first part of the row reversed, in pairs) over a dissonant pedal. The
shape of this melody, thirds and steps (or, by inversion or octave displacements, sixths and steps), makes it both singable and memorable;
so one can hear a form of it return at the penultimate line, "Lilac and
star and bird," and perhaps even hear the reversal of its first five notes
at the very last words, "and the cedars dusk and dim." F-sharp and A
seem to provide a recurrent still point, emphasized at the close of the
first movement and at the very end. Thirds and sixths followed by a
step often sound in the melodic line. In the first of his Juilliard lectures
published, in 1950, as *The Musical Experience*, Sessions laid it down
that "a melodic motif or phrase is in essence and origin a vocal gesture,"
and proposed that "the basic ingredient of music is not so much sound
as movement." The start of his cantata is a shapely gesture, and its
movement is precise. The first five notes of the row, to which Whitman's
opening line is set, rise. The next seven would fall did not an octave
displacement convert a falling third to a rising sixth, leaping up to the
words "great star," as the climax of this initial span. "Great" is on the
A-flat above the staff; then the line droops, with a final plunge to the
B-flat below it. Spoken in the rhythm of the music, and given a similar
(though necessarily narrower) pitch contour, the words sound utterly
natural. Not so in Hindemith's setting, where the first syllable of "lilacs"
and of "western" and the last "in" are prolonged, and "star" is set to a
higher note than "great."

Whitman, reviewing his own *Leaves of Grass* in the *Saturday Press*,
wrote that "Walt Whitman's method in the construction of his songs is
strictly the method of the Italian Opera." He was reported as saying in
late years:

My younger life was so saturated with the emotions, raptures, uplifts,
of . . . musical experiences that it would be surprising indeed if all my
future work had not been colored by them. A real musician running through
Leaves of Grass—a philosopher-musician—could put his finger on this and
that anywhere in the text no doubt as indicating the activity of the influences.

The "musical" structure of *Lilacs*, as of *Out of the Cradle Endlessly
Rocking* (from which Delius drew the text of his *Sea-Drift*), has often
been noted. Robert D. Faner's attempt to make *Lilacs* fit into sonata
form breaks down, I think, but in a general—and sometimes in quite
a specific—way one can discern equivalents of recitative, aria, and

chords. The pace and texture of the verse change as those of music might. Not surprisingly, Sessions and Hindemith have allotted Whitman's lines between soloists and chorus in much the same way. Both first bring in the chorus at "O powerful, western, fallen star!"; both set the questions of the tenth and eleventh strophes for solo voice, and the answers for chorus. The main difference is that in Sessions the Death Carol, "Come, lovely and soothing Death," is a long contralto solo, at the heart of the work, while Hindemith—rather unsuitably for the song of "A shy and hidden bird . . . Solitary . . . The hermit"—gives it to his chorus.

In musical terms, there are three "themes" in *Lilacs*: the Star, representing Lincoln; the Lilac, representing spring and perpetual renewal; and the Bird, the reconciler, singing of death with a beauty that makes death "lovely and soothing." In a lecture on Lincoln's death, delivered fourteen years after it, Whitman recalled that the season seemed to reflect the new-won peace:

Early herbage, early flowers, were out. (I remember where I was stopping at the time, the season being advanced, there were many lilacs in full bloom. By one of those caprices that enter and give tinge to events without being at all a part of them, I find myself always reminded of the great tragedy of that day by the sight and odor of these blossoms. It never fails.)

The first, introductory strophe of his poem says the same thing—prophetically, since it was written in 1865 before the lilacs had bloomed again. The next three strophes form an "exposition" of the three principal themes, each of them stated independently. Sessions's cantata is in three movements, and these strophes form the first of them. The chorus sings of the Star, the baritone of the Lilac, and the soprano of the Bird. (Similarly in Hindemith, though he has only two soloists and his mezzo sings of the Bird.) Now Whitman moves into his "development section," where the themes are brought together. (Thus far, Mr. Faner's "sonata form" parallel works.) Like the Star, Lincoln's coffin moves westward, moves from Washington to its resting place in Springfield, moves through the bright burgeoning of Lilac and spring and through the somber dirges and knells of mourning. The Bird is singing, but the poet's attention is still on the national funeral. These strophes, five to thirteen, form Sessions's second movement—part funeral cortège; part hymn to Lincoln; part vision of broad-spreading America, peaceful now and plentiful. In the remaining strophes, which form Sessions's third, and longest, movement, the poet finds his "knowledge of death" and his "thought of death" beside him like two companions. The Bird begins its Death Carol, "with pure, deliberate notes, spreading, filling the night." And during the long,

588

lovely song, the poet's eyes are unclosed to a vision of all those who fell in the war. They suffer not; only those who remain suffer. Hindemith, in his setting, inserts after this vision an orchestral interlude with a bugle playing "Taps." But in the poem something stranger happens. Vision, companions of death, the Bird's song, the Lilac, even the Star—all are left behind. Yet in some way they all form part of a transcendental experience: "Lilac and star and bird, twined with the chant of my soul, / There in the fragrant pines, and the cedars dusk and dim." Sessions's music for this coda does seem to move into "a spiritual world in which 'the unattainable' in Goethe's words 'becomes event' and the fragments achieve a unity impossible in the real world." That, the composer said nearly forty years ago, is what art should strive to do.

Hindemith's setting, which is divided into eleven numbers, lasts an hour. Sessions's lasts about forty-two minutes. He has omitted a few lines, some with a recapitulatory function that the music itself can undertake, and others that describe what the music has already made manifest ("Varying, ever-altering song. As low and wailing, yet clear the notes, rising and falling"). Hindemith sets the poem complete—and, incidentally, both composers use the earlier, *Drum-Taps* text, not the revised version found in later editions of *Leaves of Grass*—but that does not wholly account for his greater length; it is due also to the subordination of the words to his musical designs. Hindemith's Requiem opens with a slow instrumental prelude, a four-note tolling ostinato over a pedal point. Whitman's twelfth strophe is expanded as a choral fugue, with much word repetition and an insensitive forcing of the lines into a jigging 12/8 meter ("Mighty Man / háttan with / spíres— / ánd the / spárkling and / húrrying / tídes"). The imitative entries, one voice after another breaking in with the tune, suddenly shift Whitman into the traditional world of the Three Choirs Festival; the same thing happens in passages of the *Sea Symphony*. There is nothing like that in Sessions's cantata: it is remarkable for being a completely natural setting of the words and yet a span of music so shapely and satisfying that those words might have been written expressly to fit the structure of the score. It has what Sessions has ever sought: a long line, a "total and indivisible musical flow—the *song*." The composer Andrew Imbrie once concluded a close, subtle analysis of thirty bars of Sessions's Quintet with words equally apt to the cantata:

It is true that all the details of line manipulation are not consciously seized by the listener: but the broad design is apprehended, and a sense of the rightness of the details in relation to this design cannot but be intuitively felt. In listening to this music, one is immediately made aware of the presence of a forceful musical personality at work, who has full command over

589

his resources. Here is unconventional music in the great tradition; here is pattern made to sing; here is movement in sound, expressing that which is noble.

I found the cantata, like all Sessions's later music except the Concertino (which comes out to make friends at once [see *A Musical Season*, pp. 277–8]), difficult to embrace at first acquaintance. Besides attending the two concert performances, I had the chance of hearing the piece in the close-up of recording sessions. (Bostonians were lucky, too; three of the concerts were broadcast.) I think that the execution became better and better as the singers, players, and conductor grew together into their interpretation; I am sure that I became a better listener. Only after the harmonies of a late Sessions score have been heard several times, I find, do they begin to make proper sense. What sounded like self-defeating density of texture is revealed as an energetic, lucid progress of lines, in which the movement of the main themes is clearly perceptible. Even the full-throated lyricism of the melodies is not evident from the start. It takes time to sort out background and foreground, to get one's bearings. When that is done, the scores disclose their merits—so clearly that one is amazed they could ever have been imperfectly perceived. But perseverance is needed; and champions are needed, too, to provide the opportunity for it. Sessions's music is not played as often as it should be; the public gets little chance of overcoming its possible first bafflement. Sessions's Third Symphony, completed in 1957, was played in New York that year, by the Boston Symphony, and then nineteen years passed before New York heard it again. His Sixth, completed in 1966, had to wait eleven years for a New York première; it was done last March, by the Juilliard Orchestra. The Eighth, a Philharmonic commission, was played by the orchestra in 1968, and not again. (It was a hit at an Albert Hall Prom last year, in a program with Sessions's Double Concerto, of 1971. Would that the forthcoming Fisher Hall Proms had concerts of that kind.) Still, a recording of the Eighth Symphony is available. [And so is one of *When Lilacs Last in the Dooryard Bloom'd*; the Boston performance has appeared on New World Records NW 296.]

I have described the cantata as I finally heard it, and will do the same for its execution. By the third public performance, and after a long recording session (which gives artists a chance of hearing exactly what they do), the soloists had become precise, focused their tones, refined their pitches, and got the lines surely into their voices. They were now able to sing expressively. Esther Hinds, the soprano, had just the kind of rapt, tender phrasing her music requires. Dominic Cossa, the baritone, sang his lyrical narratives clearly and firmly and his reflective passages with feeling. Florence Quivar, the contralto, made something wonderful of her long solo; the voice is unconventional, not equalized, but her use of it was affecting. The Tanglewood Festival Chorus, trained by John Oliver, sounded strong and confident. The orchestral colors, which at first encounter I had thought rather dense and dull, began to shine. Under Ozawa's baton, the work stood revealed.

May 16, 1977

Robert D. Faner's Walt Whitman and Opera *was published by the Southern Illinois University Press in 1972. Andrew Imbrie's "Roger Sessions: in Honor of His Sixty-fifth Birthday" appeared in a 1962 issue of* Perspectives of New Music *and is reprinted in* Perspectives on American Composers *(Norton Library, 1971). Sessions's Eighth Symphony is recorded by the New Philharmonia Orchestra, under Frederick Prausnitz, on Argo ZRG-702.*

Between November 13 and 24, 1976, the Nash Ensemble played Roger Sessions's Concertino at nine public concerts in Britain, and recorded a studio performance for transmission by the BBC.

CHILDREN OF THE LIGHT

George Crumb's *Star-Child*, which was given its first performances in the penultimate program of the Philharmonic season, is a composition on a large scale. It lasts about thirty-five minutes. It is subtitled "A Parable for Soprano, Antiphonal Children's Voices, and Large Orchestra." That orchestra includes quadruple woodwinds, six horns, seven trumpets, three trombones, tuba, and an immense percussion battery in the charge of eight players. In addition, the composer uses an organ and a peal of twenty handbells. The services of four conductors are required. Most of these forces are assembled in clearly defined cohorts on the concert platform, but three trumpeters, three violinists, and a percussion player are stationed at the back of the hall, on the topmost balcony, and two trumpeters stand at midpoint down the sides. The designation "parable" may bring Britten's "church parables" to mind; those works also make use of music in space. But closer parallels can be drawn to Britten's miracle play *Noye's Fludde*, with its children's choruses, bugle fanfares, and bright ring of handbells. *Star-Child* has even more in common with John Tavener's even larger *Ultimos Ritos*, performed in Haarlem's Grote Kerk in 1974. In that composition, as in Crumb's, trumpet calls ring out from on high, choirs chant antipho-

591

nally in chordal blocks, drums mutter or thunder from far-flung outposts, and a soloist sings mellifluous cantilena. In that composition, as in Crumb's, fairly simple musical ideas are set out and juxtaposed in patterns of high elaboration. In both works, it is hard to separate the "actual music" from the "sound effects"—and perhaps it is wrong to try: the effects in space are an almost inseparable part of the musical idea, as in pieces by Mahler, Berlioz (the Requiem and the Te Deum), Beethoven (*Leonore* overtures), Schütz, and many another composer. It is hard, too, to feel sure that the result really justifies so lavish an expenditure of means.

Star-Child is a progress from darkness to light—"a conception," as the composer says in his program note, "that is at the same time medieval and romantic." It moves from sounds dark, low, and dense to sounds high, pure, and shining. There are three main sections: "Vox clamans in deserto," "Musica apocalyptica," and "Adventus puerorum luminis" leading to "Hymnus pro novo tempore." The voice crying in the wilderness cries the responsory of the Requiem, "Libera me." In fact, two voices are there: one is of the soprano and one of a solo trombone, which "vocalizes" a kind of free commentary on the singer's phrases. The Apocalyptic section is chiefly instrumental, but it includes some snatches of the "Dies irae" marked to be rhythmically shouted "*fff, tutta forza!*" by the wind players. In the final section, the soprano declaims the text of a twelfth-century conductus sometimes attributed to Pérotin, "Vetus abit littera," while the children add exclamations of "Jubilate in Domino!," "Gloria in excelsis!," etc. Finally, the soprano sings John 12:36, in Latin ("While ye have light, believe in the light, that ye may be the children of light"). "There is no particular philosophical basis to *Star-Child*," Crumb says. "It is simply a work within the tradition of music having a finale which expresses the hope that, after a struggle or after dark implications, there is something beyond." In most Western music, such struggles are waged—as by Beethoven, Mahler, Carl Nielsen—on a field of tonal conflict and thematic oppositions, and are won by harmonic resolution and thematic affirmation. In *Star-Child*, it is a matter of timbres and textures. The melodies are of indefinite, drifting outline, and they are not so much harmonized as doubled in parallel at various intervals.

After a long-sustained, very soft cluster chord from the low strings and soft, low percussion sounds, the strings of the orchestra embark on a five-bar sequence of stacked open fifths, moving in parallel, shifting up or down by a tone or semitone, and accompanied by some gentle percussion sounds, one of them being the jingle of sleigh bells. These slow-moving bars (given a characteristic Crumb expression mark, "With serene majesty, like a cosmic rhythm") are, in the score, set out in a circle, and they are played continuously, throughout the work, as a kind of serene drone, which is brought to the forefront of the listener's attention only when the other performers fall silent. After perhaps three minutes of this string music (to which restless audiences on Thursday and Saturday added an obbligato of coughing; the Friday-matinée audience listened more attentively), the trombone and the soprano begin their duet. After it, the "Dies irae" breaks out from winds and percussions in force. The Seven Trumpets of the Apocalypse sound from all round the listeners. Before their summons, the Four Horsemen of the Apocalypse are, in the composer's words, "represented, not quite so literally, by four drummers playing sixteen tomtoms." They beat them in the galloping rhythms of a wild cowboys-and-Indians movie chase. The trumpet calls are dominated by a ululating figure. To mark the "Advent of the Children of Light," the children's chorus takes up the same call and cries it "joyously." The "Hymn for a New Age" is an antiphonal chant given out by the children in organum fourths, accompanied by oboes and English horn. It alternates with free phrases for the soprano, accompanied by four bassoons that "chant" in a dissonant organum. Then three more "circles"—sequences repeated over and over again—begin to revolve: one for brass, with tubular bells; one for flutes and clarinets, with vibraphone; one for organ. The first two are again lapped antiphonal chants, and all three move steadily in parallel chords. So now there are four circles in motion, and each turns at a different speed; meanwhile, the music for the children, the soprano, and the remaining woodwinds grows denser and more elaborate, until it reaches a climax on consonant cries of "Gloria," underlined by handbells. Gradually, all movement then dies down except that of the strings' initial circle. Going off at a tangent, at last, these strings climb higher and higher. The three violins and a vibraphone in the back balcony join them, and then take over the ascent, while the orchestral string players whisper "Libera me!" The piece ends on a single, very high G from a solo violin, over two *pppp* touches on a suspended cymbal.

Stars in their courses, light in the darkness, the voices of children, chants, bells—these have been the main matter of Crumb's recent music: *Ancient Voices of Children* (1970); *Lux Aeterna* (1971), whose text is from the Requiem responsory; the three volumes of *Makrokosmos* (1972, 1973, 1974). The fourth number of *Makrokosmos II* is subtitled "Hymn for the Advent of the Star-Child"; its music is elaborated in the third number of *Makrokosmos III*, entitled "The Advent," which ends with a "Hymn for the Nativity of the Star-Child." The seventh number of *Makrokosmos II* is a "Cadenza Apocalittica," and the eleventh a "Litany of the Galactic Bells." Several of the *Makrokosmos* pieces are set out on circular staves. Those pieces are chamber works:

Makrokosmos I and *Makrokosmos II* are for a solo pianist; *Makrokosmos III* calls for four musicians, *Lux Aeterna* for five, *Ancient Voices* for nine. In performance, they seem to cast a spell; listeners are held hushed, intent on the tiny, delicate differentiations of timbre. Each player is rapt in the music, and the fine concentration needed for its execution communicates itself to the audience. In *Star-Child*, a similar kind of music is writ large. "It seems to me," says Crumb, "that when a Latin text is involved, a large, monolithic quality is suggested, and this fact accounts for the increased orchestra." In the score, the directions to the performers (some of them appeals to the imagination, others exact technical instructions for creating a particular sound) are as detailed as ever, but among so populous an ensemble the intentness is lost. Enlargement has brought about what I fear must be deemed a coarsening. Instead of small, precise statements in which every note, every inflection seems significant, and able to suggest immensities, one hears big, broad, generalized washes of sound. Instead of individual interpreters—such as the singer Jan DeGaetani, the pianists Robert Miller, Gilbert Kalish, and James Freeman—who invest what may be quite a simple musical idea with incantatory power and eloquence, there are massed forces. If *Star-Child* were composed in a new, bold manner, if the musical ideas were conceived for large forces as grandly as those of Berlioz's Requiem and *Symphonie funèbre et triomphale* are, all would be well. But the ideas of *Star-Child* are still those of a miniaturist, an understater. Crumb's music is reflective, illustrative, and seldom active in itself as Beethoven's or Berlioz's is: in *Star-Child* one finds a vivid picturing but not the musical enactment of the "struggle." The composer invites listeners to share his poetic thoughts and visions, to enter a private world of marvels; his method is essentially intimate. It also depends much on extra-musical associations, both literary and visual: Pascal and Rilke provide some of the background for the *Makrokosmos* pieces; *Lux Aeterna* is performed by musicians in masks, on a dim-lit stage at the center of which a single candle burns. *Star-Child* might be more moving in a cathedral performance where architecture, acoustics, and ambience conspired to create a numinous atmosphere.

The Philharmonic performance, it seemed, did musical justice to the piece. Pierre Boulez was the principal conductor. The solo singer was Irene Gubrud, whose pure, true soprano was electrically amplified. The children's voices came from the Boys Choirs of the Little Church Around the Corner and Trinity School and the Brooklyn Boys Chorus, and the bell ringers were from Trinity School. But perhaps less than justice was done. *Star-Child* is a romantic, picturesque score of a kind ill suited to Boulez's coldly correct musical manners. In the first half of the program, he had conducted an unphrased and therefore unpoetic account of the Italian Symphony. A week later, at his final concert as music director of the Philharmonic, he conducted an unemotional, prosaic account of *La Damnation de Faust*. If the light and lilt can be taken out of Mendelssohn and Berlioz, there may be more enchantment in the Crumb than was revealed.

May 23, 1977

LIVING MASTERS

In the second week of May, from Sunday to Sunday, Carnegie Hall housed festival fare—three concerts by a great orchestra, the Chicago Symphony, under a great conductor, Sir Georg Solti, at the peak of his powers; and two Beethoven recitals by a great pianist, Alfred Brendel. These were events I would not have swapped even for the Salzburg Easter Festival, which this year consisted of Mahler's Sixth Symphony, Bruckner's Fifth, the *Matthew Passion*, and *Il trovatore*, done by the Berlin Philharmonic under Herbert von Karajan. Both Solti and Brendel are artists known the world over for their recorded performances; they are "well documented." So is Karajan. But whereas Karajan's concerts in recent years have often seemed like trailers for or live demonstrations of his exquisitely finished records, these Solti and Brendel concerts provided reassurance that in a concert hall more wonderful things can happen than are possible in a recording studio. I am not one to underrate the importance or the musical rewards of the phonograph. Life would be poorer if we could not still listen to Schnabel, Toscanini, Furtwängler, and the great singers from Adelina Patti onward. But this is hard on today's executants. Earlier artists could be weighed only against living memories. (They were commonly found wanting, since the memory of sounds heard in youth tends to acquire a patina of gold.) Today's artists are assessed against precise aural evidence collected from all over the world since recording began. In the nineteenth century, Stendhal and Henry Chorley could bewail in words the decline of vocal accomplishment; in the twentieth, critics like Desmond Shawe-Taylor and John B. Steane can demonstrate it. What Maria Mikhailova did in St. Petersburg in 1900 may be held up as a model for some Mary Michaels in St. Pancras or St. Paul to follow.

However, I do not intend now to compare, movement by movement, section by section, bar by bar, Solti's performances of the Brahms Second Symphony with Mengelberg's, Weingartner's, Toscanini's, and Furtwängler's; or Brendel's of the last Beethoven sonatas with Backhaus's,

595

Schnabel's, Solomon's, and Kempff's. If someone taped the Carnegie performances, that could be done—and it would be worth doing. But each of these five concerts—it was their particular glory—was on a level to make one forget other readings, other interpreters, and respond only to the sound and sense of the great music that was being so vividly played. And if, afterward, any discs came to mind, they were likely to be of the same works recorded by the same artists, remembered only as steps on the way toward the live performances one had heard.

Nearly thirty years ago, at a time when records went round seventy-eight times a minute, Solti recorded Haydn's Symphony No. 103, the "Drumroll," with the London Philharmonic Orchestra. About sixteen years ago, he recorded *Tristan und Isolde* with the Vienna Philharmonic. About seven years ago, he recorded Mahler's Fifth Symphony with the Chicago Symphony. The "Drumroll," the Prelude and Liebestod from *Tristan*, and Mahler's Fifth all figured on the Carnegie bills. The recorded and live performances that were closest in spirit were those farthest from one another in time—those of the Haydn symphony. The young Solti was a classical conductor of rare excellence. His sense of proportion and balance was almost unfailing. Tempi were right. Energy and lyricism were in equilibrium. A *Zauberflöte* he conducted in Frankfurt in the early fifties remains for me a model of Mozart opera conducting. And although memory may have gilded the impression that that performance made—of buoyancy without hard driving, jollity without hecticness, and nobility without pompousness—the early "Drumroll" remains to show similar virtues. In the sixties, when, after a decade at the Frankfurt Opera, Solti spent a decade as musical director of Covent Garden, there was often a critical note mingled with the praise of his powerful, high-tension performances. His declared ambition was to make Covent Garden the best opera company in the world, and he pushed hard. His work was often found obtrusively dynamic, over-assertive—sometimes too fierce, bright, and insistent, sometimes "emotional" in so obvious a way as to be schmalzy. A recent review of his *Meistersinger* recording, which was issued last year, sums up what used to be, and still is, said: "Solti cannot escape the compulsion to spend much of his rostrum career in one extreme or another. If accelerandos start too soon, if the entry of the masters in Act I is hustled, if we go too slowly into the quintet, all is the fault of a demon which will not allow the music its natural flow. Wagner was a master of transition; Solti is not." Nevertheless, having said that, the reviewer continues, "Yet one does ill to carp. The noble work is presented with . . . power and conviction." Ill doing or no, when reviewing a Solti performance one did carp, despite the power, the excitement, and the brilliant technical execution. Sometimes the demon was dormant. Sometimes, especially in Richard Strauss works, it was tamed, harnessed to the service of a score.

But not until this series of Carnegie concerts did I feel it had been exorcised. In them there was nothing—well, almost nothing—to carp at. Everything did flow naturally. And to this natural flow were united the superlative playing, the fine details, the liveliness, and the enthusiasm that have always marked Solti's performances.

Solti and the Chicago Symphony have become a combination such as Szell and the Clevelanders were and Karajan and the Berlin Philharmonic are, in that one feels nothing can go wrong when they make music together. Yet there seems to be a difference. Where Szell enforced discipline, Solti inspires cooperative confidence. It is rather as if, where Szell's first horn, say, would not have *dared* to make a mistake, Solti's first horn simply cannot. (Dale Clevenger's big horn solos in the Mahler symphony were bold and glorious.) On the other hand, there is not the prepackaged smoothness that can remove all savor from Berlin Philharmonic concerts—when all difficulties have been so thoroughly solved in rehearsal that giving the first beat is rather like lowering the needle into the first groove of a record. Although Solti is a more relaxed conductor than he was, he is keen and alert as ever. Busoni once wrote to his wife after a recital in Amsterdam, "The concert was one of those rarely fortunate ones when every bar is successful in the way one wishes, new ideas come as one plays and immediately sound right, and the instrument is responsive. I may be wrong, but from beginning to end it seemed to me perfect and effortless in technique and at the same time free and full of swing." I may be wrong—only Solti can say whether "new ideas" did indeed come while he conducted—but it seemed to me that, reading "orchestra" for "instrument," his three concerts can be described in the same way.

The first of them opened with the "Drumroll" and ended with Brahms's Second Symphony. They were both rich performances, and both perfectly in style. For Haydn, the string forces were reduced, though not by very much; their tone was light and lithe, their articulation clear. The woodwinds played without romantic vibrato, cleanly and classically. Ideally, perhaps, Solti should have breached the row of unbroken strings that spanned the front of the platform, to let his woodwinds stand out even more—but that would have been largely a matter of improving the "visual" acoustics; the balance to the ear was good. For Brahms, the orchestra found that glowing, "saturated" tone associated with the Vienna Philharmonic at its best, full but not fatty, smooth but still muscled. As the cellos played the theme of the adagio, using portamento of a kind that most modern orchestras have forgotten about, the great days of the nineteenth century seemed to have come again. Between the symphonies came the *Tristan* Prelude and Liebestod. The Prelude was overwhelming, and Solti was neither overbearing nor injudiciously excitable. Wieland Wagner once remarked that Solti's Wagner would come to a climax every few bars; but in this performance of the Prelude everything led securely to the single, tremendous, but unexaggerated climax. To hear the Liebestod without an Isolde, the accompaniment without the vocal line, is disconcerting in these days when *Tristan* has become a familiar opera. (I recalled that six years have passed since I last heard Solti conduct a *Tristan* in the theater, and I felt a yearning to do so again.) Beckmesser himself could have found no more than two faults in these executions: in the *Tristan* excerpts the harp was placed forward, out of the proscenium arch, on the left of the platform, and its sound did not blend into the texture of the final pages; in the Brahms the exposition of the first movement was not repeated.

The second concert began with the Jupiter Symphony, performed in the poised, alert way that the Haydn was—a little more grandly, as befits the work, but not at all heavily. Then came Mahler's Fifth Symphony—its seventh New York performance, at least, of the season. (Leinsdorf conducted it in the Philharmonic's Mahler cycle, David Gilbert conducted it four times in the subscription series, and Bernard Haitink conducted it with the London Philharmonic.) Mahler quickly shows up any shortage of romanticism in a conductor's personality, and, equally quickly, any tendency to excess. "Supercharged," "overblown," "persistent whipped-up frenzy," "little more than sonic splendor, and energy rather too lavishly expended" are words that were used of earlier Mahler performances by Solti and the Chicago Symphony. They did not apply to this one. On the simplest level: the brass did not leap out of the frame, to scorch listeners' ears, whenever the music became loud. On a subtler level: a score that falls apart if the constantly changing tempi are not coherently related flowed as if in a single impulse—except in the adagietto. There a basic pulse failed to establish itself, and the harp accompaniment trickled uneasily.

The third concert was devoted to Beethoven's Missa Solemnis. It is unlikely that anyone will ever hear the great Mass in the context for which it was initially conceived—liturgically performed at the installation of a Royal Cardinal Archbishop. I have in fact once heard it at Mass, in Westminster Abbey; the office was carried out with much ceremony, but it was Beethoven who stole the show. Perhaps the piece is best left in the concert hall; as Willy Hess remarks in the preface to his edition of the miniature score, "the insertion of liturgical units . . . must have the effect of implanting foreign bodies into a unified organic work of art, and as such they will impair the overall musical and artistic impression." Carnegie acoustics are better than those of most cathedrals, and Beethoven's music is grander, and to an unbeliever possibly more inspiring, than any ritual, which must inevitably become its accompaniment

At the end of Solti's performance, there was an awed silence; just a few people began to clap, and then stopped short. The silence was tribute to a performance that had transcended mere proficiency of execution. Applause began only when people returned to earth. It is easier to declare a performance ineffable than to find words to describe it. Perhaps a few things can be accurately said. Beethoven's score is made of contrasts: the splendor of royal ceremony, and a kneeling individual worshipper; omnipotence and eternity, and our fleeting, insignificant life. After the blaze of "gloria in excelsis," the composer's gaze drops to earth with the soft, low "et in terra pax." After another spacious climax at "filius patris," there is the descent to "qui tollis peccata mundi." Solti neither exaggerated nor understated these contrasts. His soloists gave just the right intensity to the recitative pleas—marked "timidamente"—of the Agnus Dei, set against the fanfares of gathering inward and outward strife. If they are sung too operatically, these phrases draw attention away from the work and onto the particular soloist. But if they are under-characterized, the effect of Beethoven's shift from corporate to personal prayer is lost.

The performance was noble and classical—"classical" in the sense of attaining to power, eloquence, and beauty through balance, proportion, and contrast of parts, not through rhetorical emphasis on particular phrases. The tenor, Mallory Walker, was not quite on the level of the other soloists—Lucia Popp, Yvonne Minton, and Gwynne Howell completing the vocal quartet, Victor Aitay as violinist in the Benedictus. The Chicago Symphony Chorus, trained by Margaret Hillis, is a choir worthy of the great orchestra. The Latin text was not italianized but pronounced with the hard German consonants that Beethoven knew. All that was missing was, in the Praeludium, what Tovey called "the miraculous depth of one of those thirty-two-foot pedal notes which only the organ itself can produce." Carnegie Hall now has no pipe organ, only an electronic substitute.

For five years, Alfred Brendel has been coming to New York to give a series of Carnegie Hall recitals. In 1973, they were of Beethoven, Schubert, and Liszt; in 1974, Beethoven, Haydn, and Schumann; in 1975, of Beethoven, Mozart, and Schubert; last year, of Beethoven, Bach, and Liszt; this year, of Beethoven. Between 1958 and 1964, Brendel recorded all Beethoven's piano sonatas for Vox, and he is now just over halfway through recording a second cycle, for Philips. This winter, in London, he played all the sonatas in the course of seven Elizabeth Hall recitals. For New York, he distilled three programs, devoted to early, middle, and late periods.

Each generation has its particular Beethoven pianist. I never heard Artur Schnabel in the flesh, but his records represented, and represent, what might be called the standard interpretations were not "standard" far too prosaic a word for Beethoven playing inspired and unsurpassed. In recitals, there was Wilhelm Backhaus, who seemed to embody some great survival of a more openly romantic, pre-Schnabel era; there was Edwin Fischer, poetic, unselfconscious, an ideal middle-period player; there was, and is, Wilhelm Kempff, blending charm, caprice, and profundity in unpredictable fashion. And today there is Brendel. (Lest champions of Arrau, Ashkenazy, Barenboim, Bishop, Gieseking, Gould, Serkin, Solomon, and a dozen or two more be reaching for their pens, I should add that the list is not intended to be encyclopedic.) Brendel is a pupil of Fischer, whose style and personality he writes about in *Musical Thoughts and Afterthoughts*, a collection of essays and occasional pieces just published by Princeton. Other thoughts are about recorded versus live performances, about Liszt and Busoni, about pianos (with technical advice on how to voice them), and about Ur-texts. Brendel is a thinking pianist. But in the second sentence of an essay entitled "Form and Psychology in Beethoven's Piano Sonatas," he says, "Although I find it necessary and refreshing to *think* about music, I am always conscious of the fact that *feeling* must remain the Alpha and Omega of a musician; therefore my remarks proceed from feeling and return to it." He wrote that seven years ago. The year before, after hearing him, at the York Festival, play Beethoven's last three sonatas in a single program (he did so again last week, at his third Carnegie recital), I wrote of his performances as "intellectual, certainly—and yet ablaze with feeling." The fires of feeling burned lower—at any rate, their warmth did not always reach the public—during the early seventies, when he seemed to be playing, and thinking, his way through a period of speculation and experiment. Then, sometimes, his performances sounded like propositions, even hypotheses, about the way a particular work might go. But today his playing has regained all its old confident spontaneity, and his readings are more richly engrossing than ever.

I missed the first recital. The middle-period program consisted of Op. 31 Nos. 1 and 2, and then Op. 54, 79, and 81a, with the minuet of Op. 49 No. 2 and the scherzo of Op. 31 No. 3 as encores. Brendel stressed the middle-period variety of textures, devices, and forms, by giving to each movement a very sharply defined character—or characters, as in the minuet of Op. 54. The allegro vivace of Op. 31 No. 1 poured out at a speed too vivacious for the sixteenth-notes to be clearly heard; the swift dashing and tumbling of the torrent was Brendel's concern, not any dainty, detailed plotting of its channel. In the adagio grazioso of the same sonata, tune and "plucked" accompaniment were sounded in boldly, even fiercely different timbres. In his book, Brendel says of pianos, "The rounder . . . the tone, the less chance one has to color it, to mix timbres, to detach one layer of sound from another. Faced with the choice between a concert grand with an inherently beautiful but invariable tone and a less noble but more colorful instrument, the pianist will usually prefer the more colorful one." His care is for sense rather than for sonic charm. There can be charm in his playing, but it is likely to be some delightful point of rhythm or phrasing, not of pure sound. Declaiming a line, he is a Scofield, not a Gielgud, making his subtle and powerful effects by timing and inflection, unenhanced by sheer beauty of timbre. Yet he does have an exceptional command of chiaroscuro, pierced by sudden flashes of hard-edged light.

Brendel is still growing. One cannot yet say of him, as Edward Dent said of Busoni, in the last sonatas:

Never for a moment, even in the most thundering passages or in the intricacies of the fugue, did he lose sight of his unique beauty of tone-quality. To hear him play these sonatas was an almost terrifying experience; dynamic and rhythmical relations were treated with such vast breadth and freedom that one seemed taken up to heights of perilous dizziness and made, as it were, to gaze steadily into the depths until one's vision became serene.

That suggests a combination of Schnabel, Solomon, Backhaus, Ernst Lévy, and Kempff at their greatest. In Beethoven's last sonatas there are summits of lofty grandeur and serene, sublime spiritual realms to which Brendel has not yet led me. But, as pianists go, at forty-six he is still young. It was only in Busoni's later years, Dent said, that "his interpretations had that indescribable dignity and beauty of which he alone . . . possessed the secret." Schnabel was fifty when he began recording his sonata cycle, and sixty when he rerecorded Op. 109 and 111 (published only last year, by RCA). In any case, while Brendel played, one did not measure his achievement against others'. His own intentness, his power, his tenderness, his fingers (and feet) schooled by practice and pondering to give shape to feelings and form—these cast a spell. After Op. 111, he, too, won the tribute of brief, rapt silence.

May 30, 1977

Ernst Lévy's great recordings of Beethoven sonatas, on the now-defunct, Boston-based Unicorn label (not to be confused wtih British Unicorn), have become collectors' items; they should be reissued.

A LECTURE AND A PARABLE

The second production of Ian Strasfogel's New Opera Theatre, given in the Lepercq Space of the Brooklyn Academy of Music, was a double bill of Dominick Argento's *A Water Bird Talk* and Viktor Ullmann's *The Emperor of Atlantis*. *A Water Bird Talk* was completed in vocal score in 1974, between Argento's song cycle *From the Diary of Virginia Woolf* (p. 292) and his full-length opera *The Voyage of Edgar Allan Poe* (p. 359), and was "previewed" in Minneapolis, with two-piano accompaniment, the following year. The full score, dated September 1976, had its première at these Brooklyn performances. The libretto, by the composer, is a free adaptation and expansion of Chekhov's monologue "On the Harmfulness of Tobacco." (This is Argento's second Chekhov opera; in 1957 there appeared his musical version of *The Boor*, the short play that William Walton, ten years later, set as *The Bear*.) Chekhov's protagonist is lecturing at a provincial club. He announces his subject, and sticks to it just long enough to say that if you put a fly in a snuffbox it will die and that tobacco is, essentially, a plant. Then one aside leads to another. We learn of his nagging, bullying wife; of his seven unmarried daughters; of his wretched existence as an usher in the school run by his wife. The "lecture" reaches a climax of despair:

If only I could escape from this rotten, vulgar, tawdry existence that's turned me into a pathetic old clown and imbecile! Escape from this stupid, petty, vicious, nasty, spiteful, mean old cow of a wife who's made my life a misery for thirty-three years! . . . Once I was young and clever and went to college. I had dreams and I felt like a human being. Now I want nothing—nothing but a bit of peace and quiet.

He notices that his wife has turned up in the wings and is waiting for him, pulls himself together, and pronounces a dignified peroration, ending, "I shall therefore venture to hope that some benefit may accrue from this lecture. . . . *Dixi et animam levavi!*"

Chekhov, it seems, first wrote the piece in purely buffo vein, and then in a series of revisions added the infusions of despair which make it at once funny and a tragedy. In Argento's version, which is based on Chekhov's final recension, the scene is a lecture hall in a small Maryland town in the 1880s. The lecturer's subject is now not the perils of smoking but "Water birds, and the human significance of our feathered neighbors." The talk is illustrated by tinted magic-lantern slides derived from Audubon's *Birds of America*. Chekhov's paragraphs are punctuated by snatches of bird lore, also derived from Audubon, which provide a poignant, poetic, and entertaining commentary upon them. The first of the five birds discussed is the cormorant, whose children, even when fully grown, remain in the nest, "virtually crowding the parents out of their own house." The last is the grebe, "the lowest form of bird life," which "dislikes swift-running water, keeps to the gentle eddies near the banks," and, although it does no harm to anyone, is nevertheless preyed upon by many enemies. Chekhov and Audubon make a convincing match. The courtship rituals of the cormorant; the domesticity of the demure little male phalarope, keeping house while the brightly colored females "all gather together as though they had organized women's clubs"; the orderliness of the grotesque, clumsy puffin, which, once mated, remains mated for life; the grebe's habit of sinking unobtrusively out of sight when confronted by a threat—as the lecturer tells of them, he tells of himself. Argento has found a way of expanding the Chekhov play which gives it color and richness and lends itself to musical treatment. Instead of the swift single curve of the spoken monologue we have a dramatic character study in eight linked paragraphs. As in all musical settings of pre-existing plays, something is lost and something gained.

The musical form of *A Water Bird Talk* is theme, six variations, and coda. The orchestra is an ensemble of twelve players. The theme and the coda are played by a string quintet. In five bird variations—Nos. 1, 2, 3, 5, and 6—an instrumental duo provides the principal accompaniment (clarinet and marimba for the cormorant, harp and glockenspiel for the roseate tern, horn and timpani for the puffin, etc.). The subject of the remaining variation, No. 4, is not a bird but the lecturer himself, and he accompanies it on the piano. He has gone to the keyboard to illustrate the call of the phalarope and remains there, improvising happily: "Ah, how I love music! . . . She doesn't. . . . No birds ever sang for her. . . . She won't even sing hymns in church." He breaks into James Russell Lowell's "Once to every man and nation comes the moment to decide." (Much later in the drama, after his big outbursts of despair, he quietly and sadly sings, "And the choice goes by forever.") One idea leads in an unforced way to another. Some of the jokes are obvious (an upside-down slide is accompanied by a musical inversion of the theme heard when it is righted), but none are labored. The work is at once a tragicomedy, a scena that provides a tour de force for its singer, and a shapely, attractive suite. The six variations are entitled Romanza (the cormorant), Barcarolle (the roseate tern), Spinning-Song (the phalarope), Consolation (the lecturer), Marcia all'italiana (the puffin), and Elegy (the grebe). The theme is a flowing twelve-note melody that, since it traces several common triads and makes nine of its eleven moves by third or by sixth, is easily remembered and recognized. In a diary published in the program book of *The Voyage of Edgar Allan Poe*, Argento wrote, "The [Chekhov] monodrama has turned out well, I think. It was a very concentrated two or three months of work and, as a result, seems very tight to me—compact and rich, highly organized and yet free-ranging." And I think so, too. The instrumental bird music is very pretty. (There are also some effectively placed passages of real bird song, piped in on tape.) The scoring, colorful, varied, and skillful, never obscured the voice. The vocal line is lyrical; it has and expresses character. The formal structure, unobtrusive but satisfying, provides a "justification" for elaborating a one-man show into something using so many performers. (By comparison, Poulenc's large musical setting of Cocteau's one-woman show *La Voix humaine* adds nothing to, maybe even diminishes, the force, effectiveness, and economy of the original.) *A Water Bird Talk*, which lasts about forty-five minutes, should have a future on the concert platform as well as in the theater; magic lantern, slides, and screen are the only props required, and, at a pinch, even they could be left to the listeners' imagination. The lecturer's role can be compassed by a tenor or a baritone. The Brooklyn production had a resourceful and endearing protagonist in Vern Sutton, a leading tenor of the Minnesota Opera. His words were very clear. He also sang in the Minneapolis preview; one of the pianos on that occasion was played by Philip Brunelle, the music director of the Minnesota company, who conducted the deft and dramatic Brooklyn performance.

The Emperor of Atlantis was composed in 1944 in Theresienstadt (Terezín), that garrison town in northern Bohemia which the Nazis converted into a "model" prison camp. Visiting Red Cross officials could see that art, drama, and music flourished there—and need not know that Theresienstadt was also a staging post for the labor camps and death camps. Mirko Tuma, a Czech poet who spent three and a half years in Theresienstadt, has written of a performance there of the Verdi Requiem at which three-quarters of the chorus knew they would be shipped to Auschwitz the following day. Viktor Ullmann and Peter Kien, the composer and the librettist of *The Emperor of Atlantis*, both died in Auschwitz. Their opera had been rehearsed in Theresienstadt but was refused performance. The score survived. The piece was first mounted in Holland in 1975; the same production was given the following year in Brussels and Spoleto, and last April it was re-created by the San Francisco Spring Opera Theater.

The plot is no cut-and-dried allegory but an elusive, death-welcoming parable about a mad, murderous ruler, possibly redeemed at last, who says farewell to the world in a mock-Faustian vision of a natural paradise no longer spoiled by men; had his dream come true, all men would be dead. The Emperor of Atlantis, ruler over much of the world, proclaims universal war and declares that his old ally Death will lead the campaign. Death, offended by the Emperor's presumption, breaks his saber; henceforth men will not die. Confusion results: a Soldier and a Girl-

Soldier from opposite sides sing a love duet instead of fighting; the sick and suffering find no release. Death offers to return to men on one condition—that the Emperor be the first to die. He accepts, and sings his farewell. The work ends with Luther's chorale "Ein' feste Burg," to the text "Come, Death, who art our worthy guest." The other characters are Pierrot, weary of life; a Drummer, who unthinkingly proclaims the Emperor's decrees; and an Announcer, heard through a loudspeaker (the part was doubled by Death in the Brooklyn production). The score is cast in twenty short numbers, only three of which, after two hearings, fixed themselves with any firmness in my memory: the prelude, based on a figure of teasingly ambiguous harmony and rhythm; the love duet; and the final chorale, which is punctuated by figuration from the prelude. Ullmann was a pupil of Schoenberg. His style here seems to be a compound of neoclassicisms practiced by the Strauss of *Ariadne*, by Hindemith, and by Stravinsky. The music is strongest in its passages of chunky neo-Bachian counterpoint. But the Brooklyn performance was not strong. Although the music was securely shaped by Kerry Woodward, who edited the score and has conducted all performances of it so far, several of the singers were vague, among them the veterans Chester Ludgin (the Emperor) and Herbert Beattie (Death). Nancy Williams made nothing of the Drummer's music; a little allegro marziale that in the score looks dapper and pointed left no impression. Janet Pranschke sang the Girl in unfocused tones. Douglas Perry, as Pierrot, was rather better, but Tonio Di Paolo, as the Soldier, provided the only good voice of the evening—and his clear, beautiful baritone was taxed by the upper reaches of a role written in the tenor clef. (I hope this uncommonly promising singer is not risking his timbre by premature tenor aspirations.) The opera was sung in English translation. Most of the words were inaudible, and although the text was printed in the program, that was useful only to people who arrived early enough to read it.

The Lepercq Space, a big bare room above the foyer of the Academy, long and lofty, has a good feel and lends itself to informal, adventurous music making, but it does not seem to lend itself to opera. None of the New Opera Theatre productions there has projected with much force. (It's best to sit in the front row.) There is no suitable place for the orchestra. For this bill, it was way off to one side, and, while such an arrangement works well enough in, for example, the more intimate surroundings of the Manhattan Theater Club, where everything tells strongly, the Space is too large for the result to be acoustically cohesive. Next season, the company moves downstairs, into the Academy's Carey Playhouse, and there things should be better. Meanwhile, it seems only fair to give *The Emperor of Atlantis* the benefit of doubts that arose. It is probably a less scrappy and more impressive composition than it seemed to be. A recording is due to be made this summer.

The opera lasts about fifty minutes. The orchestra is an ensemble of thirteen. The earlier production, one reads, was staged as if in the hut of a prison camp, in a manner recalling accounts of the Buchenwald and Auschwitz cabarets rather than the more ambitious Theresienstadt presentations. Mr. Strasfogel's production was surrounded by cutout figures of prisoners, white-clad, stenciled with numbers; the ground was strewn with skull-size white pebbles. It was a somber and beautiful design, by Franco Colavecchia. It, too, compelled one to consider the opera not, so to speak, solely in its own right but in relation to the circumstances of its composition. And such special pleading is probably inevitable. One can hardly view the piece with unclouded critical eyes.

The evening as a whole was more successful than the New Opera Theatre's first presentation—the triple bill of Monteverdi, Janáček, and Ligeti, last February (p. 539). (And it was a great deal more successful than the City Opera's triple bill of Mozart's *Der Schauspieldirektor*, Poulenc's *La Voix humaine*, and Stravinsky's *A Soldier's Tale*, directed by Frank Corsaro, in which the first and last were overblown travesties of their composer's intentions and the central panel, despite a virtuoso performance by Maralin Niska, seemed much ado about little.) So far, in the New Opera Theatre's work one can note consistent imagination and technical competence on the scenic side; excellent lighting, by William Mintzer; first-rate accompaniment by Ursula Oppens in the Janáček, the Speculum Musicae in the Ligeti, and the New Opera Theatre Ensemble in the Argento-Ullmann bill; direction, by Mr. Strasfogel, in which ideas usually adventurous and apt have sometimes been unclearly or unskillfully executed; and casting less than careful in its choice among the numerous good young singers to be found in and around New York.

June 6, 1977

LOW-COUNTRY FESTIVAL

To Charleston, South Carolina, Gian Carlo Menotti has brought what seems to be America's first full festival modeled after a common European pattern: densely packed days of music, drama, and dance in the principal theaters, churches, halls, parks, and gardens of an attractive and interesting city; of important premières and new productions; of exhibitions, lectures, pageants, and parties; of sunshine and celebration shared by the inhabitants and their visitors, and showers easily endured because there is plenty to see and hear indoors. It is the kind of event found on the largest scale in Salzburg, Edinburgh, Holland (where for three weeks in summer the whole country holds a festival), and Adelaide, and on a large scale in York, Aldeburgh, Bath, Brighton, Harrogate, Leeds, the City of London, and many other British towns. Britons seem to be especially fond of festivals.

The twelve-day festival in Charleston is entitled "Spoleto Festival U.S.A."—which is hard on Charleston. But presumably no neat title could be devised to indicate that this is at once a Charleston festival and an American edition of the Festival of Two Worlds, which Menotti founded in Spoleto, an Umbrian hill town, in 1958. It is not a simple copy or a direct translation, but it does borrow many of the ingredients that have made the Spoleto festival so successful. The two towns are very different. Spoleto (like Montepulciano; see p. 405) has a center, a meeting place—the Piazza del Duomo, on which stand the cathedral, a theater, palaces, cafés, restaurants, and the festival offices. The aspect of the city is part Etruscan, part medieval, with Roman and Renaissance elements. The streets are steep and irregular. Down vistas framed by buildings of sun-baked stone or from terraces and belvederes one looks to the beautiful countryside below. At festival time, the night air is lime-scented. In the words of the eleventh Britannica, "there are . . . few medieval towns with so picturesque an appearance." In 217 B.C., Spoleto repulsed an attack by Hannibal; it recalls the incident in the name of one of its gates. In 1670, Charleston was founded under and named for Charles II, but most of its older buildings are Georgian. It is a pretty town, unlike any other, as individual as Aldeburgh, Wexford, or Aix-en-Provence, and therefore, like them, a good festival place. On the southern tip, at least, of the flat, river-girt peninsula on which Charleston stands, the description in that old Britannica still holds: "The streets are shaded with the live oak and the linden, and are ornamented with the palmetto; and the quaint specimens of colonial architecture, numerous pillared porticoes, spacious verandas—both upper and lower—and flower gardens made beautiful with magnolias, palmettoes, azaleas, jessamines, camellias and roses, give the city a peculiarly picturesque character." That is south of Broad Street. There, one still walks on stone or brick sidewalks, along streets of houses where people live. North of Broad Street, where the hotels, restaurants, and shops are, where visitors stay, and where most of the festival events take place, the city has been less lovingly cared for. The sidewalks are often of concrete. Although many fine churches, temples, halls, and houses from Charleston's brilliant past remain here, too—Georgian, neoclassical, occasionally Gothic —they are punctuated by weedy wastelands. One looks for parks and sees parking lots. Here, the place resembles a once beautiful town badly bombed in a war and not yet restored. Charleston *was* badly damaged in the Civil War, and again, in 1886, by an earthquake, but some of the

607

destruction is modern. The grand neoclassical Charleston Hotel, designed in the manner of Schinkel—possibly by a pupil of his—and admired by Thackeray, was not long ago pulled down and replaced by a motel whose architecture compels no admiration. Still, other cities have fared worse. The Charleston skyline is still dominated by spires, and the picturesqueness remains. I was there for only four days, fully occupied, and cannot report on the beaches, plantations, manors, and gardens, reached easily only by car, not by bus. Bikes can readily be rented, but the ride to Middleton Place or Drayton Hall is a long one to tackle in hot weather. The churches, halls, and theaters are within walking distance of one another, as in a festival town they should be.

Spoleto uses two theaters—the Teatro Nuovo, seating less than nine hundred, for the big productions, and the Teatro Caio Melisso, seating about four hundred, for smaller operas, recitals, and plays. Charleston also uses two theaters. Its "Teatro Nuovo" is a huge place—the Gaillard Municipal Auditorium, built in 1967, and seating over twenty-seven hundred. The stage is a little larger than that of the Teatro Nuovo, but the wing space is less and the pit is small. It is an ugly, graceless building with lobbies as bleak and "institutional" as those of Avery Fisher Hall (though during the festival they were cheered by a bright show of contemporary South Carolina quilts). The auditorium within, not unpleasing to the eye, has lively, clear acoustics; nevertheless, it is hard for opera to make a strong impact in so large a space, and Menotti announced that he is seeking a smaller house to use in future years. Charleston's "Caio Melisso," the city-owned Dock Street Theater, has a closer correspondence to its Spoleto counterpart. It seats 463 people. But where the Caio Melisso is in the traditional horseshoe shape, tiered high with boxes, the Dock Street Theater, built in 1937 as a WPA venture, follows the lines of a Georgian playhouse. Its façade and foyers remain from an early-nineteenth-century hotel that once filled the site; before the hotel, there was a playhouse, which opened in 1736. (Kean, Macready, and Junius and Edwin Booth all used to play seasons in Charleston.) The new Dock Street Theater is intimate, handsome, and convenient. Within the pews there are not hard benches but comfortable modern seats. Auditorium and proscenium are richly paneled with black cypress rubbed until it looks smooth and warm.

In the Gaillard Auditorium two operas were done: Tchaikovsky's *The Queen of Spades*, billed for five performances, and Menotti's *The Consul*, billed for three. *The Queen of Spades* was a restaging of a production given at Spoleto last year. The three principals—Patricia Craig as Lisa, Jack Trussel as Hermann, and Magda Olivero as the Countess— were the same, and so was the conductor, Guido Ajmone-Marsan, but whereas in Spoleto the work was sung in an Italian translation, in Charleston it was sung in an English one (uncredited; apparently a local revision of Boris Goldovsky's). Miss Craig was clear and efficient, but her bearing, her timbre, and her pronunciation were not cultivated. Mr. Trussel was very clear; he has the kind of *voce fissa* that Italian audiences dislike and Anglo-Saxon audiences admire (Martinelli exemplified it)—strongly projected and precisely focused, not vibrant or voluptuous. If he learns to be gentle and caressing (as Martinelli could be) as well as incisive, he should be a notable interpreter of such roles as Don Alvaro, Don Carlos, possibly Tannhäuser. Though handicapped by a blond principal-boy wig—Hermann is surely a Byronic hero in the raven-locked line of Rochester, Heathcliff, and Edgar of Ravenswood—his acting was impassioned and interesting. Miss Olivero's voice was threadbare and her performance ridiculously histrionic; in the bedroom scene she flung Hermann halfway across the stage. Mr. Ajmone-Marsan was a flamboyant, impassioned young conductor, readier to whip up excitement than to shape long, supple lines of unhurried cantabile. He should study the way Medea Mei-Figner, Tchaikovsky's Lisa, phrased the second aria. (So should Miss Craig.) But he is promising, and if he seemed rather often to impose himself between the work and its audience, the lighting was partly to blame: he was raised high; two spotlights played upon him throughout the evening; he was more brightly lit than anyone on the stage. But the sum of this *Queen of Spades* was in fact far more enjoyable than an account of its main ingredients might suggest. Filippo Sanjust designed and directed an intelligent, unfussy production. His sets—largely high, blank walls with tall doors and windows—were simple, almost stark, but impressive. Each of the scenes had a distinct character, but they composed into a gripping sequence. Dominant colors were subtly chosen for dramatic effect. The St. Petersburg Summer Garden of the start was a sepia print animated; gradually the individual characters took shape within it. The mingling of naturalism and hallucination was skillfully achieved, except at the Countess's ghostly appearance in Hermann's barrack room; that was feebly done. Above all, the tone of the production was right. Narrative, sentiment, spectacle, and melodrama were in balance. The director never drew attention to his own cleverness; imaginatively yet unobtrusively he served the composer. The Westminster Choir, from Princeton, was an excellent chorus. Mariana Paunova brought a rich contralto to the role of Pauline, and Charles Long was a resonant but insufficiently silken Yeletsky. Most of the words were clear; they were not always well shaped. (Hermann sang "desire" as three distinct syllables, and "fire" as two.) The long, beautiful opera was given almost uncut, and seemed short.

For ten years, Menotti kept his own works off the Spoleto bills, but then *The Saint of Bleecker Street*, in 1968, was followed by *The Medium, The Unicorn, the Gorgon, and the Manticore, The Consul, Tamu-Tamu,*

The Telephone, and *The Old Maid and the Thief.* Many festivals have grown up around composer-directors—Bayreuth around Wagner, Aldeburgh around Britten, Montepulciano around Hans Werner Henze. (The latest in the series, remote in the Orkneys, where Peter Maxwell Davies lives, is the St. Magnus Festival; this month, Davies's new opera, *The Martyrdom of St. Magnus,* has its première there). Menotti believes in his music, and makes a good case for it. Even a critic who finds much of *The Consul* tawdry and facile also finds, willy-nilly, that some of it remains emotionally affecting. The Charleston production was expertly directed by the composer, in scenery, by Carey Wong, borrowed from the Portland Opera. Marvellee Cariaga was a powerful Magda Sorel, and Sandra Walker a charmingly dapper Secretary. Christopher Keene—not spotlit—conducted with spirit.

Menotti is artistic director of the festival. Mr. Keene is its musical director. The Spoleto Festival Orchestra, like the Westminster Choir, is student—expert young players gathered from all over the country. (They go on to perform at Spoleto itself in June and July.) The choir was worked hard: besides singing in *The Queen of Spades* and *The Creation,* it gave two church concerts. The orchestra was worked even harder: it played for both of the operas, for the Eliot Feld Ballet, for *The Creation,* and in orchestral concerts. From this orchestra is drawn the Spoleto Festival Ensemble, which gave four afternoon concerts. The Spoleto Festival Brass Quintet gave twelve recitals, in various locations. Thirteen afternoon concerts, at three or five o'clock, formed a series called "Intermezzi"; besides the choir, the ensemble, and the brass quintet, the University of South Carolina Trio, organists, and a mandolinist took part in them. Most mornings, at eleven, there was a lecture on some aspect of the festivities. There were ten informal chamber-music concerts at midday, given in the Dock Street Theater. The midday concerts in the Caio Melisso, devised by Charles Wadsworth, who is also their beaming compère, have long been a hit of the parent festival. And the Charleston series, co-directed by Mr. Wadsworth and Peter Serkin, was a hit, too. Although there were no new discoveries to be made—at Spoleto concerts Jessye Norman, Pinchas Zukerman, Christoph Eschenbach, and Robert Szidon first came to international attention—young artists of known excellence played never less than agreeably and often with distinction. There was a pool of eleven instrumentalists and one soprano, topped up with occasional guests, such as Gerard Schwarz, who laid down his baton (he was in Charleston as conductor of the Feld Ballet) to take up his trumpet. On nine of the afternoons, there were also "mini-festivals," admission free, which took various forms: Greek food, dances, and music on the grounds of the College of Charleston; puppets, a parade, and storytellers in a grassy city square; Low Country cooking and music, and more storytelling, in a city park. The first mini-festival spread through thirteen Charleston churches; I took the chance to go organ-hopping, and heard recitals on two good modern instruments and on the Henry Erben organ (1845) in the Huguenot Church. (Charleston once had sixteen Erben organs; two survive, but one is in the restorer's hands.)

There was plenty to do. Dance was presented by the Feld company in the Auditorium and by the Ohio Ballet on the Cistern of the College of Charleston. This Cistern is the principal open-air stage of the festival—a very large filled-in tank set before a giant portico built in 1850 and designed by the versatile Edward Brickell White (whose work greets one at every turn in Charleston) as an addition to an 1828 college building by William Strickland (the architect of Philadelphia's Custom House and Merchants' Exchange). A broad, tree-shaded lawn stretches in front. It is a pleasant spot but not a good stage for dance. Feet were invisible. Trees and lighting towers impeded the view. The music was coarsely amplified to carry in the open air. I caught up with Feld's *A Footstep of Air*, which I had missed in New York (such catching up is another pleasure that festivals often provide), enjoyed again his slight, elegant *Harbinger*, and also enjoyed the Ohio Ballet's buoyant account of Paul Taylor's *Aureole*. A galaxy of new dances (by Balanchine, Ashton, Tetley, and others) and revivals (Duncan, Shawn, the young Ninette de Valois) to music by Scriabin, with eminent performers from all over, was due on the penultimate day—Scriabin Day—with three concerts of his music, too: chamber music, piano music, and, at midnight, the music-and-light composition *Prometheus*, lit by Thomas Skelton. Mr. Skelton lit almost all the Charleston shows, maintaining a poetic and imaginative level that puts Lincoln Center's follow-spot brigade to shame.

At the Dock Street Theater, there was a new play, Simon Gray's *Molly*—not really new, however, but a refashioning for the stage of his early television play *Death of a Teddy Bear*. Four characters hard to believe in are roughed out in dialogue of *Mousetrap* banality; they are données of the plot rather than personages—though Tom Waites, a young actor of forceful personality, made his role almost credible. *Black Medea*, a play by Ernest Ferlita, was due to follow. There were eleven big-band jazz concerts featuring the North Texas State University 1:00 O'Clock Lab Jazz Band. There were ten afternoon film shows. Over on Kiawah Island, *Green Pond*, a musical show, was played eight times. There were many art exhibitions—notable among them one of theatrical drawings from the Janos Scholz collection and another of designs for Diaghilev ballets from the Serge Lifar collection.

By Spoleto standards, the fare was perhaps unadventurous. The first Spoleto festival included a Verdi *Macbeth* directed by Visconti, two operatic world premières, new ballets by Jerome Robbins and John

611

Butler, and a production of Daudet's *L'Arlésienne* with Bizet's music. At the second festival, there was Prokofiev's *The Fiery Angel* (a little-known opera at the time), Donizetti's *Le Duc d'Albe*, and new plays by Tennessee Williams and William Inge. In 1962, Shirley Verrett sang her first Carmen. The list of Spoleto firsts is long. The Charleston fare, if less novel than Spoleto's, was nevertheless abundant, varied, and nourishing; and in any case a festival in its first year is not fairly weighed against the remembered highlights of another nearly twenty years old. Charleston was a success. No one could doubt that who saw and became a part of the happy, interested audiences thronging the shows. This cis-atlantic Spoleto will surely go from strength to strength, and if the city-festival idea takes root and flourishes here as it has in Europe, no doubt Columbia, Charlotte, Charlottesville, and many other places will be wanting a similar festival, too.

June 13, 1977

LOUISAN OPERAS

St. Louis, founded under Louis XV, is a substantial city. When the lights were shining at the 1904 World's Fair, it was the fourth-largest city in the land. There are still plenty of reasons for visiting it—residential streets as handsome as any in the world, an abundance of fine trees, James Eads's great bridge over the Mississippi, a grandly romantic railroad station, a famous art museum, buildings by Louis Sullivan, and the Arch by Eero Saarinen—but until recently opera has not been among them. The St. Louis Symphony Orchestra was founded in 1880 (which makes it younger than the New York Philharmonic and older than the Boston Symphony); it prospers, and plays in a very splendid concert hall, built, in 1926, in the spirit of Versailles. St. Louis opera has led a checkered career. The great touring companies—Mapleson's, and then the Met—used to pass through, but the Met has not been there for ten years. The St. Louis Municipal Opera plays not opera but musicals, in a twelve-thousand-seat open-air auditorium. Local opera companies foundered. Local singers—Marion Telva, Helen Traubel, Grace Bumbry, Richard Stilwell—made their careers elsewhere. But now St. Louis has an opera company that seems to be well planned, well supported, and well received by the public. It is called the Opera Theatre of St. Louis. A predecessor of the same name, which came to an end in 1971, was described by a local critic as "a sort of club in which the board was the chorus, and board members on their travels doubled as provincial talent scouts." The new troupe, managed by Richard Gaddes, is run to high professional standards. Instead of *stagione* (or one isolated production after another), there is a brief repertory season: a company chosen from among America's best young performers comes together and works together, and a visitor can see all its productions on successive days. All operas are done in English. All singers are paid the same fee. The first season, last year, consisted of *Don Pasquale*, Britten's *Albert Herring*, and a double bill of *The Impresario* and Menotti's *The Medium*. This season, the fare was more adventurous—Rossini's *Le Comte Ory*, a double bill of Rameau's *Pygmalion* and *Gianni Schicchi*, and *Così fan tutte*. Last year, there were ten performances in all; this year, fifteen.

Of all the great composers, Jean-Philippe Rameau is the most neglected. The keen *ramoneur* must be prepared to travel, to catch performances where he can. The Paris Opera mounted a spectacular—but musically unstylish—revival of *Les Indes galantes* in 1952, and played it nearly 250 times, through ten seasons, but since then, as far as I know, there has been no Rameau in the repertory of the world's major houses. Rameau is not easy to perform; there are practical reasons for the neglect. He needs singers who have mastered the French declamatory style, players who have studied French baroque practice (and, ideally, who play on eighteenth-century instruments), specialist choreographers and dancers, and in his bigger pieces a large chorus, elaborate staging, and a copious wardrobe. He also needs listeners prepared to give unremitting attention to everything that happens—the notes, the words, and the movements. (The dancing, one of Rameau's librettists wrote, should be even more precisely communicative than the verbal discourse.) One cannot just sit back and enjoy Rameau's music, as one can the music of many of his contemporaries. Around him there raged the *guerre de bouffons*. Jean-Jacques Rousseau, a leader of the frivolous faction that preferred the pretty tunes of Pergolesi's *La serva padrona* to Rameau's noble, carefully chiseled passions, remarked, "It is very tiring for me to follow scores that are rather heavily laden . . . where one hears several simultaneous themes." Rameau *is* tiring. Tiring to performers, since, as Pierre Lalo once wrote:

There are few notes, but each one has a meaning, and must be given it; each fiddle, each flute, each oboe needs an execution that follows and adapts itself to every movement of the musical line, one that can mold and so to speak sculpt itself on the clear, precise, supple, and tight outline, without overlooking any inflection, accent, or intention, on pain of losing touch with the thought and the feeling.

Tiring—but wonderfully rewarding—to listeners who follow him with the needed intentness. And dull to listeners who don't.

Pygmalion is a subject that has attracted many treatments. During Louis XV's reign, Rameau and Rousseau each produced one. Rousseau's, which appeared in 1770 and quickly made the rounds of Europe, is a *scène lyrique*—a spoken monodrama punctuated and heightened by musical interludes, some of them composed by the philosopher himself. His text was translated into several languages, variously adapted, and often set. Cherubini's *Pimmalione* (1809), a striking and inventive opera, deserving to be done more often than it is, is based on an Italian elaboration of Rousseau's scene. In both Rousseau's and Cherubini's pieces, the Pygmalion myth becomes an allegory of an artist's striving for unattainable perfection—unattainable save through divine intervention. In both pieces, some commentators have detected a hint of something more: a rationalist suggestion that to think perfection has been attained is a delusion. By this reading, when Galatea's marble form seems to quiver beneath the sculptor's touch, he is delirious; when in Cherubini's finale Pygmalion and Galatea are welcomed, in an apotheosis, to the court of Venus, a "real" Pygmalion lies dying, in delirium, on his studio floor. I would not stage the work in that "realistic" way, but do think there is more to it than just a musical illustration of Ovid. Cherubini's imagination was evidently stirred by the idea of the artist's being driven nearly mad by an inability to give warmth, life, and breath to even his greatest work. His own music often was—and often is—called marmoreal and cold.

Rameau's libretto is freely adapted from the fifth entrée, "La Sculpture," of *Le Triomphe des Arts*, a work presented at the Opéra in 1700. It, too, goes beyond Ovid—just. A mite of extra drama is introduced in the person of Céphise, who loves Pygmalion and is very cross that he should love a statue. But little is made of her; after a few reproachful phrases she disappears. Very little happens, in fact. Pygmalion sings an air, "Fatal Amour, cruel vainqueur." The Statue, brushed by Cupid's flame, comes to life; in tender dialogue with Pygmalion—three tiny airs and a brief recitative—she tells him that she loves him; and thereafter she is silent. The drama is done; the rest is a ballet, punctuated by three airs. Cupid in a lively air summons the Graces, who teach the Statue the steps of various dances. Pygmalion sings another air, "L'Amour triomphe," echoed by the people who have come to see the miracle. More dance; a brilliant air for Pygmalion, "Règne, Amour"; and some final dances. The work, described as an *acte de ballet* (it lasts about forty-five minutes), appeared at the Opéra in 1748 and was often revived in subsequent decades. It is not one of Rameau's major pieces—not to be compared, except in delicacy of detail, with the great *tragédies lyriques*. But it is beautiful. Pygmalion's first air, marked by a dropping seventh in the accompaniment and by a vocal line that rises in a chromatic outburst of passion and pain, is very affecting. The spare, mysterious sounds that accompany the Statue's animation—two flutes answered by two violas— are magical. All the dialogue is marvelously expressive, eloquent in the precise, telling style that Rameau commanded. The suite of dances that the Graces teach to the Statue—a gavotte *gracieuse*, a minuet, a gavotte *gaie*, a chaconne *vive*, a loure *très grave*, a passepied *vif*, a rigaudon, a majestic sarabande, a final tambourin—forms an exquisite little catalogue of Ramellian dance music: tender, graceful, spirited, always strongly made.

The St. Louis production was simple—there was a corps of six dancers and very little scenery—but deft. Naima Prevots had devised choreography based freely rather than strictly on eighteenth-century steps. The staging, not quite formal enough for my taste, was by Anthony Besch; it seemed curiously extravagant to have imported the eminent British director for a work that has so little dramatic action. Raymond Leppard conducted. He had coached his cast to the right style, to shapely, very clear phrasing, with (in the words of his program note) "ornamentation . . . of a quite different order from the comparatively simple, though showy, divisions, trills, and cadenzas of the Italians. The French singers and players 'graced' their melodic lines with brilliant, fanciful decorations superimposed upon the music, like jewels on a dress." John Aler was Pygmalion. He was good, but on the night I heard him the voice was not so evenly sweet and clear of timbre as it had been when he sang Rameau's Dardanus for the Juilliard. With his orchestra, Mr. Leppard was less successful; its playing was often murky. In general, the orchestra was the weakest point of the St. Louis presentations.

I would suggest a triple bill for next year: a revival of this *Pygmalion* (which I long to hear again), followed by Cherubini's *Pimmalione* and then Donizetti's *Pigmalione* (an early work but a delightful one). Rameau, Cherubini, and Donizetti treated the subject in three very different manners; the trilogy would certainly provide an evening of enjoyable and contrasted music. As a sideshow, the Opera Studio, which is run by Webster College in association with the Opera Theatre, might essay the Pygmalion settings of Rousseau, Georg Benda (1779), and Giambattista Cimadoro (1790, and performed all over Europe during the next thirty years). Then the Midwest chapter of the American Musicological Society might ask to be let in on the act, and provide some learned papers on Pygmalion through eighteenth-century ears. The St. Louis season could become a rival of Siena's Settimana Musicale.

"What musical riches! A wealth of felicitous airs throughout, new schemes of accompaniment, refinement in the harmonies, admirable orchestral effects. . . . All this forms a collection of diverse beauties that, ingeniously divided up, could make the fortune of, not one, but two or three operas!" This is Berlioz on *Le Comte Ory*, Rossini's penultimate opera, and in his enthusiasm Berlioz did not exaggerate. From the first, Rossini had been an entrancing operatic craftsman. Apt modulations, a miraculous orchestral touch, melodies caressing or hilarious, suave or sparkling, were always at his command. In 1824, he settled in Paris. For the first time in his life, he had financial security, a stable company, a good orchestra, and plenty of rehearsal time. He could now afford to work out fully ideas and ideals imperfectly realized in the Italian pieces, when, pressed for money, pressed by impresarios and by prima donnas, he composed and brought operas to the stage at high speed. He revised two of his Neapolitan operas—*Mosè in Egitto* as *Moïse*, and *Maometto II* as *Le Siège de Corinthe*—on the grand French scale. Then, in 1828, he tackled a new comedy, *Le Comte Ory*. The libretto, by Scribe and Charles-Gaspard Delestre-Poirson, tells of Ory's two attempts to seduce the Countess Adèle. Disguised in Act I as a pious hermit, in Act II as the superior of a band of nuns (his rowdy companions), Ory besieges the castle to which Adèle has decided no men may be admitted until her brother has returned from the Crusades. (There are anticipations of Tennyson's *The Princess* and Gilbert's *Princess Ida*.) Each time, he is frustrated. The plot is slight, but the working is neat and witty. And Rossini's music is bewitching. A Mozartian refinement and a Berlioz-like imagination inform it. The old high spirits and the gay spontaneity are still there in abundance, joined by a new delicacy and exquisiteness, which reach their high point in the trio "À la faveur de cette nuit obscure." There the Mozart of *Così fan tutte* and the Berlioz of the *Troyens* garden scene and the duo-nocturne in *Béatrice et Bénédict* seem to join hands.

In St. Louis, the leading roles were taken by the 1976 and 1977 winners of the Metropolitan Opera National Council auditions: Ashley Putnam, as the Countess, and Vinson Cole, as the Count. Miss Putnam is a singer of exceptional promise. The voice is big, bright, flexible, and sure, and it becomes fuller, opens out and flowers, when it rises. But she must work on pronunciation, for some of her vowels were pinched and mean. She is young, tall, slim, and attractive. Offstage, I saw that she was a merry, vivacious person. Onstage, she played Adèle with an expression of unrelieved crossness and sulkiness; she moved not with easy aristocratic grace but like a hoyden. Her singing was elegant; her acting was charmless, and appeared to be deliberately so. Either she or the director, Christopher Alden, had got the character—and the character of the work—quite wrong. All the same, it was a pleasure to encounter a singer who seems to be destined for great things. Mr. Cole has a tenor whose timbre is sweet and compact. In coloratura it lost its sheen; Ory is not really the right role for him, yet. He showed a sense of fun but not the needed lightness and brio; again, the director's somewhat heavy hand may have been to blame. Evelyn Petros sparkled delightfully in the role of Isolier, Ory's page. All *Ory* productions I have seen have used a toy castle onstage. In St. Louis, Paul Steinberg had built an endearing, cuddly castle, a colorful piece of "soft" art in Claes Oldenburg idiom. Mr. Leppard's conducting was both lively and delicate. And, though not everything was quite right, one left the theater humming the refrain of the nuns' chorus: "C'est charmant! c'est divin!"

Così fan tutte was given a nicely balanced, pleasing performance, raised to distinction by the charming, merry, excellently well voiced Despina of Sheri Greenawald, a winning singer who made recitative as enjoyable as aria, and by the wise, ripe, precise, resourceful, but unexaggerated Don Alfonso of Gimi Beni. Linda Roark and Martha Williford were the sisters, Jon Garrison and Stephen Dickson their suitors. Both *Così* and *Gianni Schicchi* were ably conducted by John Moriarty, ably designed by John Kavelin, and admirably directed by Louis Galterio. *Schicchi* had the best performance of all; in fact, I have never seen a better production of the piece. *All* the characters were personalities. There was lots of fun, and no crude clowning. No grossness disturbed the Haydnesque delicacy and wit of Puccini's score. Mr. Galterio—as in his Schubert-Offenbach double bill for the Bronx Opera and his recent *I quattro rusteghi* for the Manhattan School—revealed himself as one of America's most stylish and musical directors. Heinz Blankenburg, who played Schicchi, is a vivid and brilliant artist incapable of a wrong or dull inflection, glance, or gesture. He is a master of timbre and of timing, someone whose performances are to be collected and prized. He and Mr. Beni were the two veterans in the otherwise youthful company. All four shows were sensitively and expertly lit by Stephen Ross.

The Opera Theatre of St. Louis plays in the Loretto-Hilton Theatre, in the suburb of Webster Groves, on the campus of Webster College, some eight miles from downtown. It is a pleasant, attractive, informal house, seating about 950, and thus somewhat larger than Glyndebourne. It is not really ideal for opera: the acoustics, although clear, are unresonant; voices are not flattered: sounds end in an unreverberant deadness. A thrust stage is surrounded by the audience on three sides, and the pit is at the front of it; this means that sight lines and acoustic balance can be poor for those in the side sections, behind the orchestra and sometimes behind the singers. Nevertheless, the theater has the right "feel" for an adventurous young company. There are lawns around it. A step away there is a friendly tavern that functions as a club where performers and audience meet afterward; the atmosphere there resembles that of the Glyndebourne bar. Mr. Gaddes, in fashioning this company specifically for St. Louis, seems to have borrowed good ideas from Glyndebourne, from Santa Fe, and perhaps from Wexford. Adapting them and adding his own, he has produced a season that already has its distinct character, and one whose spirit, like theirs, is fresh, welcoming, artistically serious, and quite unpompous. I enjoyed my visit to St. Louis.

June 20, 1977

ORPHEUS AT THE ORPHEUM

The tale of Orpheus celebrates the affecting power of song: no wonder it plays so large a part in the annals of opera. Charles Burney, in his *History*, calls Politian's *Orfeo* (given in Mantua in 1472, with music by Germi) "certainly the first attempt at the musical drama." The first operas whose music survives are the settings by Giulio Caccini and Jacopo Peri of Ottavio Rinuccini's *Euridice* (1600). The first opera still performed with any frequency is Monteverdi's *Orfeo* (1607). The first opera with words and music by the same pen is Stefano Landi's *La morte d'Orfeo* (1619). The first opera written for Paris was Luigi Rossi's *Orfeo* (1647). Gluck's first reform opera was *Orfeo* (1762). The list could easily be prolonged, to Darius Milhaud's *Les Malheurs d'Orphée* and Ernst Krenek's *Orpheus und Eurydike* (both 1926), and beyond.

For the final productions of its season, at the Orpheum, the Opera Company of Boston mounted two Orpheus operas, played in the same scenery and pretty well in alternation: Gluck's *Orpheus* and Offenbach's *Orphée aux enfers*. I use an English title for the Gluck because neither the Italian nor the French will quite do; the music heard in Boston was largely that of Gluck's French opera *Orphée et Eurydice* (Paris, 1774), but it was sung in Italian, and the role of Orpheus was transposed to the alto pitches that Gluck had used in his Italian opera *Orfeo ed Euridice* (Vienna, 1762). The role is tackled in our day by contraltos, mezzo-sopranos, tenors, and even baritones. Gluck himself prepared three versions of the piece—for alto, for soprano, and for tenor. His first Orpheus was the male alto Gaetano Guadagni. Handel composed for him. Garrick taught him to act, and "as an actor," Burney tells us, "he seems to have had no equal on any stage in Europe: his figure was uncommonly elegant and noble; his countenance replete with beauty, intelligence, and dignity; and his attitudes and gestures were so full of grace and propriety, that they would have been excellent studies for a statuary." He was a serious artist, prepared to offend the public by "his determined spirit of supporting the dignity and propriety of his dramatic character, by not

618

bowing acknowledgment, when applauded, or destroying all theatrical illusion by returning to repeat an air, if encored at the termination of an interesting scene." Gluck's *Orfeo* is nearly a monodrama; the protagonist is offstage only for a moment, at the start of Act II. It is likely that Guadagni's name should be added to those of Gluck and of his librettist, Raniero de' Calzabigi, in the roll call of operatic reformers.

Gluck's *Orfeo* is a short opera, planned to be part of a larger bill. The first performance, on the Emperor Francis I's name day, was preceded by a French comedy and followed by a ball. Seven years later, *Orfeo* was but one act in an entertainment, *Le feste d'Apollo*, staged in Parma to celebrate the marriage of the Infante Don Ferdinando to the Archduchess Maria Amalia. It was preceded by a prologue and by operas about Philemon and Baucis and about Aristaeus (the beekeeper responsible for Eurydice's first death; in headlong flight from him she trod on the serpent that stung her). The Parma libretto—there is a copy in the New York Public Library—is an exquisite piece of printing, a pleasure to handle and to read. In Parma, Orpheus was the male soprano Giuseppe Millico. I have long wanted—but so far in vain—to hear the strong, concise, swift-moving *Orfeo* of Gluck's original intention, played through without intermission. It is something the City Opera might add to its repertory of one-acters. (The Swedish Opera has a production, which it brought to the Brighton Festival a few years ago; last year in London there was a concert performance and broadcast, with a countertenor, John Angelo Messana, as Orpheus.) And I have long wondered why noble, classical sopranos do not undertake the title role, seeing that there is a version for them which has the composer's authority.

The alto and the soprano versions of *Orfeo* made their way through Europe. But then, it seems, as now, full-length works were often preferred to short ones, and so *Orfeo* was amplified. Guadagni introduced it to London in 1770, and the libretto for that performance stated that "in order to make the Performance of a necessary length for an evening's entertainment, Signor [John Christian] Bach has very kindly condescended to add of his own composition . . . chorusses, airs, and recitatives." New characters—Orpheus' father, Eurydice's sister, Pluto—were added. There was also extra music by Pietro Guglielmi, for his wife, who sang Eurydice. And there was even—I regret to report it—an air by Guadagni himself, a bland F-major piece replacing Gluck's F-minor setting of Orpheus' final appeal to the Furies. Guadagni's reputation for seriousness is redeemed by the preface he wrote for this Italian-English libretto. After noting that the work's "excellent composition, added to the classical merit of the drama, would afford something beyond what is usually seen," he said, "The original Composer made himself a perfect master of his author's meaning; and infused the genius of poetry into his music: in which he followed the example of my great master, Handel.

. . . In order to [insure] the more immediate observation of this beauty, resulting from a happy coalition between the writer and composer of an Opera, I most earnestly wish that such Ladies and Gentlemen, as propose to honour the exhibition of this drama with their presence, would read the piece, before they see it performed."

The extended, Gluck-Bach *Orfeo* achieved some currency before Gluck undertook his own full-length version, recomposing the piece for the Paris Opera, in French, in 1774. This *Orphée* has a tenor protagonist. There are many more dances, several of them borrowed from earlier works. Act I ends with a bravura air for Orpheus, "L'espoir renaît dans mon âme," taken from the 1769 *Aristeo*. The Elysian Fields scene of Act II is much expanded, notably by the famous instrumental air with flute solo and by Eurydice's "Cet asile." In Act III, Eurydice sings a trio with Orpheus and Cupid. Recitative is newly composed, some accompaniments are more delicately wrought, and some of the numbers are arranged in a new sequence. This *Orphée* is *Orfeo* padded out. It is a majestic and powerful piece, but less direct, less cogent, than the original. "L'espoir renaît dans mon âme" and the trio hold up the drama with music that is not Gluck at his best, although in the former a brilliant singer can not only win an ovation but also (as the critic Henry Chorley wrote after hearing Pauline Viardot's Orpheus) "convert what is essentially a commonplace piece of parade into one of those displays of passionate enthusiasm to which nothing less florid could give scope." Intermissions break the tension. The added dances are not integral to the work in the way that Rameau's dances are to his operas. Yet it would be a stern purist who could throw out the flute air and "Cet asile." Back in 1781—under Gluck's eye, so to speak—there was an attempt to combine the best of *Orfeo* and *Orphée*, in a Vienna production. It was sung in Italian (the numbers specific to *Orphée* were translated); Orpheus was a tenor, Valentin Adamberger, soon to be the first Belmonte in Mozart's *Die Entführung*. In 1859, Berlioz prepared an edition that is essentially an abridgment of *Orphée* with the title role lifted to alto pitch. It was sung by Viardot. Later nineteenth-century editors added to it some of the *Orphée* music that Berlioz had dropped, and provided an Italian text —Calzabigi's original from *Orfeo* where it fitted and various translations of Pierre Louis Moline's French where it didn't or where the numbers were French in the first place. Occasionally, a pure *Orphée*, with a tenor hero, was given. Usually, these late-nineteenth-century bastard scores held, and hold, the stage.

Sarah Caldwell, who directed and conducted the Boston *Orpheus*, has not shown herself a musician content to settle for the first or the most convenient performance material that comes to hand. Her 1969 *Macbeth* and her 1973 *Don Carlos* represented Verdi's unfamiliar first thoughts about those operas, and her recent *Rigoletto* contained an afterthought (probably not Verdi's) in the form of Maddalena's aria; her 1971 *Norma* included an aria for Oroveso which was composed by Richard Wagner. So one went off to the Boston *Orpheus* not knowing quite what to expect but confident that it would be something new. *Orfeo/Orphée* gives plenty of scope for adventurous textual decisions, and Miss Caldwell delights in putting scholarly speculation to the test of theater performance. Since Shirley Verrett was billed in the title role, it obviously could not be a pure Paris *Orphée*. But perhaps it would be a pure Vienna *Orfeo*. Or perhaps the Parma *Orfeo*, since Miss Verrett has lately been tackling soprano as well as contralto and mezzo-soprano roles. Perhaps the orchestra, as in *Don Carlos*, would be playing from facsimiles of original instrumental parts. Maybe it would be the Berlioz version, complete with Viardot's tremendous cadenzas, which are printed in the Berlioz score. Or maybe Miss Verrett would essay some of Guadagni's own embellishments, which were published in 1788. She did not, and it was none of those editions we heard but only another mixture of Vienna and Paris.

This was disappointing. So was the performance. *Orpheus*, like *Alceste* and *Iphigénie en Tauride* but unlike *Iphigénie en Aulide, Armide*, and *Paride ed Elena*, stands or falls by its protagonist, and Miss Verrett was in poor voice. The lower reaches were furry and unfocused when soft, and harsh under pressure; above, the tone became strident and impure. Like Pauline Viardot, Miss Verrett sings both Azucena and Norma, both Orpheus and Lady Macbeth. But where Viardot eased Lady Macbeth's music downward—the first aria by a third, the brindisi and the sleepwalking scene by a tone—Miss Verrett sings it at pitch. An amazing extension of three octaves and a fourth, from the C below middle C to the Queen of Night F, was claimed for Viardot, but it was generally agreed—she herself admitted as much—that by imposing her musical will on her "real" voice, a limited mezzo-soprano, she had compromised its quality. Yet when she sang Orpheus, then, according to Chorley,

the peculiar quality of Madame Viardot's voice—its unevenness, its occasional harshness and feebleness, consistent with tones of the gentlest sweetness—was turned by her to account with a rare felicity, as giving the variety of light and shade to every word of soliloquy, to every appeal of dialogue. A more perfect and honeyed voice might have recalled the woman too often to fit with the idea of the youth.

Miss Verrett did not make dramatic or musical virtue of the unevenness, harshness, and feebleness that spoiled her tones. The voice simply sounded as if it had taken a beating while being pushed so promiscuously through its recent repertory of vocally incompatible roles. Even in her unclouded mezzo days, Miss Verrett was a dull Orpheus, unable to achieve the needed combination of passionate declamation and firmly molded line. Gluck is not easy to sing. The most moving Orpheus I have ever heard was a young Yvonne Minton, guest star of a Cambridge student performance, in English. She cried the words from her heart yet phrased with noble smoothness. Five years later, at a Covent Garden performance, in Italian, Miss Minton's voice was larger, fuller, and richer, but one heard in it only beautiful sound, not emotions. In memory, I reach back to Kathleen Ferrier, at Covent Garden, in those poignant last performances of her life, and to Elisabeth Höngen, at Salzburg, bringing to the German translation that vividness of utterance which can also be heard in recordings by Margarete Klose. On records, I listen to Alice Raveau, pure, classical, moving, and beautiful, chaste and passionate at once, in the great French tradition; at the Opéra-Comique in the first quarter of this century, Raveau shared the role with the tenor Fernand Ansseau. In imagination, I hear and see Guadagni as his contemporaries recalled him, Viardot as described by Chorley:

The supple and statuesque grace of her figure gave interest and meaning to every step and every attitude. Yet, after the first scene (which recalled Poussin's well-known picture of "I too in Arcadia"), there was not a single effect that might be called a *pose* or a prepared gesture. The slight, yet not childish, youth, with the yearning that maketh the heart sick, questioning the white groups of shadows that moved slowly through the Elysian Fields, without finding his beloved one; the wondrous thrill of ecstasy which spoke in every fibre of the frame, in the lip quivering with a smile of rapture too great to bear, in the eye humid with delight, as it had been wet with grief, at the moment of recognition and of granted prayer.

And Giulia Ravogli as described by Bernard Shaw:

Ah, that heart-searching pantomime, saturated with feeling beyond all possibility of shortcoming in grace, as Orfeo came into those Elysian Fields, and stole from shade to shade, trying to identify by his sense of touch the one whom he was forbidden to seek with his eyes! Flagrant ballet-girls all those shades were; but it did not matter. . . . Even the *première danseuse* was transfigured to a possible Euridice as Giulia's hand, trembling with a restrained caress, passed over her eyes!

There was nothing in the Boston production to add fresh details to that composite, opalescent dream performance of a much-loved and oft-performed masterpiece which an operagoer assembles, over the years, in mind's ear and eye. Most *Orpheus* performances add something. Wieland Wagner's production, in Munich, was willful. Gluck's happy ending was removed: after Eurydice's second death there was a reprise of the opening threnody, and a bewildered audience discovered that the evening was over. But Wieland's vision of the Elysian shades, circling in endless calm, has proved unforgettable, and so has the powerful orchestral playing, massive yet not ponderous, under Robert Heger. Gluck, at the Paris Opera, had six double-basses and eight bassoons; the Boston band was founded on just one double-bass and a single bassoon. Miss Caldwell's reading lacked force, accent, and firmness. The Furies were unferocious, unmenacing almost before Orpheus had sung to them. Everything was curiously soft-grained. The chorus of twenty-one (Gluck had forty-seven in Paris), lined up between the orchestra and the stage, sounded weak. The Eurydice of Benita Valente and the Cupid of Marianna Christos were unremarkable. So was the dancing.

Miss Caldwell's staging was criticized, perhaps unfairly, for its baroque elaboration. In his preface to the original libretto, Calzabigi directed his readers' attention not only to the fourth book of the *Georgics*, where the tale of Orpheus and Eurydice is told, but also to the sixth book of the *Aeneid*, which contains elaborate scenic descriptions of the Underworld—the fearsome gates, the dreadful river, the Elysian Fields beyond —and of its habitants. Virgil notes that at the sound of Orpheus' song Ixion's whirling wheel hung motionless; Ovid says the same in his version of the story, and adds that Tantalus ceased for a while to be tantalized. So I did not feel that Miss Caldwell's introduction of Ixion, Tantalus, Charon, Pluto, and Proserpine as mute background characters compromised the noble simplicity of Gluck's drama. I just wished that the sets had been nicer to look at. After the very first performance of *Orfeo*, there was debate in Princess Esterházy's salon about the precise color of the Elysian Fields. They should surely be green, with an unearthly blue sky overhead. Virgil speaks of "green pleasances" where "an ampler air clothes the meadows in lustrous sheen, and they know their own sun and a starlight of their own." Calzabigi prescribes "a pleasance of verdant groves, flowers that carpet the meadows, shady retreats, rivers and brooklets." In Boston, Herbert Senn and Helen Pond provided a basically black scene flanked by tinseled Corinthian columns. The Parma libretto specifies Corinthian columns for the final transformation scene, to the Temple of Love. Miss Caldwell omitted this transformation, and also the "gloomy cave, forming a tortuous labyrinth," in which Orpheus should turn to look at Eurydice. The last two of the five scenes were played in the grove, back where the drama began.

A year before the Berlioz version of *Orphée* appeared, at the Théâtre-

Lyrique, Offenbach brought out his *Orphée aux enfers*, at the Bouffes-Parisiens. It had not been playing long when Jules Janin, a Jupiter among critics, launched a thunderbolt in the *Journal des Débats:* antiquity was being profaned; the spirit of irreverence bordered on blasphemy. There was plenty of precedent for making fun of the Orpheus legend. Garrick produced an Orpheus burletta in 1767; Cerberus sings a trio with himself, his heads being treble, tenor, and bass, and the piece ends with a dance of shepherds, cows, and trees. In Paris, Gluck's *Orphée* was soon followed by *Roger-Bontems et Javotte, parodie d'Orphée et Eurydice.* Nevertheless, Janin had a point, though he obscured it; it was not antiquity that was being mocked but—as later in *La Belle Hélène* and *La Vie parisienne*—Second Empire personal and public morality. Even then, the satire seems to have been rendered harmless by the high spirits; today only the lively plot and the fizz—and grace and delicacy—of Offenbach's excellent music remain. Miss Caldwell's production (in English, as *Orpheus in the Underworld*) was a romp, but not a crude or clumsy one. Except by Donald Gramm, in the title role, the operetta was not well sung. Maralin Niska was a vocally coarse, strident Eurydice; her trills and coloratura were so hideous that the audience laughed at them, thinking she intended a Florence Foster-Jenkins-type joke. Maybe she did—but Offenbach didn't. The only touching episode, John Styx's spoken recollection of the decent old days, when he was King of the Boeotians, was omitted, and his sad little song was played for straight comedy, without the underlying nostalgia and seriousness. (Alan Crofoot, the Jupiter of this production, used to be a most moving John Styx at Sadler's Wells years ago.) Names were given a pronunciation in which Aristaeus rhymed with "slay us" and Actaeon with "play on." The final set was too somber to reflect the hilarity of the cancan. Despite all that, Offenbach—and Miss Caldwell—triumphed. The evening had the energy, vivacity, and imaginative force that were missing in *Orpheus*. One will remember its merry moments when the Gluck production has been forgotten.

June 27, 1977

MUSIC AT HIGH MALL

Vancouver, British Columbia, an agreeable city set on wide waters against a background of mountains, has a new concert hall—a new-old hall, the Orpheum, built fifty years ago as a Western outpost of the Chicago-based Orpheum circuit, refashioned and refurbished this year as the home of the Vancouver Symphony Orchestra. It was once the largest theater on the West Coast. Charlie Chaplin played there. Beecham and Klemperer conducted there. Margot Fonteyn danced there. But when Vancouver's Queen Elizabeth Theatre, a multipurpose 2,800-seat house, opened in 1959, and became the home of the Vancouver Symphony and the Vancouver Opera, it seemed that the Orpheum's days might be over. The owners planned to convert the grand old house into a "complex" of "mini-theaters"—a fate that has befallen many large places of entertainment. A yet more common fate is demolition: New York lost the Paramount and the Roxy, which should have been protected national monuments; the splendors of the Albee, in Brooklyn, are even now being ground into rubble. Vancouver decided not to repeat mistakes that were made by New York and London. (I am glad I lived early enough to have known McKim, Mead & White's Pennsylvania Station, in the former, and the Coal Exchange, St. James's Theatre, and Philip Hardwick's Euston Station, in the latter.) In Vancouver, the grand Canadian Pacific Railway station still stands, awaiting some new use. So does a noble courthouse. The Orpheum has found its new use. It was saved by a combination of two things: community realization that the world is finite and what is old and good should not be destroyed for short-term profit; and the city's need for two large auditoriums, unforeseen at the time the Queen Elizabeth opened. So the city of Vancouver bought the Orpheum and turned it into a hall for music, at a cost of just over seven million dollars. (The city produced four and a half million, the federal government of Canada two million, and the province of British Columbia a third of a million; the rest is still being raised.) The Vancouver Symphony was not happy in the Queen Elizabeth, which has clear but dry acoustics; as in New York's Avery Fisher Hall before last year's reconstruction, an orchestra had to force its tone if it was to produce a big sound. The CPR station and the abandoned spaces of a big department store that had moved its business into a Miesian monolith were considered as possible new homes. The Orpheum was chosen.

Happy choice. The main entrance of the Orpheum is on a mall—a word that in America has recovered its eighteenth-century connotation of a place for pleasant promenade. (London's Mall is traffic-free only on Sundays.) "High mall," the Anglo-Saxon equivalent of the Mediterranean *passeggiata*, flows past the Orpheum at concert time; the hall takes its place in city life. And it is welcoming, not a forbidding monument to culture. Orpheum theaters come in many styles. The entrance to Boston's, where Sarah Caldwell presents her opera, seems to have been inspired by memories of Nero's Golden House. St. Louis's, now named Powell Symphony Hall, and the home of the St. Louis Symphony, is a Palace of Versailles for the people. Vancouver's was described by its architect, B. Marcus Priteca, as "conservative Spanish Renaissance." Twenties Hispano-Mauresque and M-G-M Spanish are other possible terms. The building is lavish, exotic, and glittering. Colonnaded stairs, balconies, and landings provide the approaches to the auditorium. The frames over doors and niches follow an elaborate ogee curve suggesting memories of Bristol Cathedral and St. Mary Redcliffe. The plasterwork inside the hall itself blossoms with Manueline exuberance. As in St. Louis, the actual detail is coarse, but the effect of the whole is splendid. There was precedent for adapting an existing theater rather than building a new hall: in St. Louis; in Pittsburgh, where the former Loew's Penn Theatre is now Heinz Hall, home of the Symphony; and in Oakland, where the Symphony plays in the Paramount Theatre, an Art Deco movie palace recently designated a National Historic Landmark. Such schemes save handsome buildings. They also save money. Powell Hall, in 1968, cost about two million instead of the fifteen to twenty million estimated for a new building; a year later, Pittsburgh spent only ten million on Heinz Hall.

The acoustical consultant for Powell Hall was Cyril Harris, working, for once, with curved walls and a domed ceiling, not a rectangle, and, by all accounts (I have not heard music in the hall), producing excellent results all the same. The acoustical consultant for Heinz Hall was Heinrich Keilholz; the sound there is also reported to be good. The acoustical consultant for the Vancouver Orpheum was Theodore Schultz, of Bolt, Beranek & Newman, and at the inaugural concert, in April, I could hear that the sound there is good. As in Powell Hall, the stage tower has been blocked off and turned into offices or rooms for the orchestra. The former stage has been solidly walled and roofed to make a concert platform that seems to be part of the hall itself, not an opening out of one end of it. In the Orpheum, the roofline of the new platform continues that of the hall; the platform has been extended forward well beyond the proscenium arch; orchestra and audience are effectively in the same room. It is a big place, with 2,788 seats, but because in basic plan it is, like Carnegie Hall, essentially a cube, not a long cuboid, the back rows do not feel too uncomfortably far from the platform. There is a large balcony. I listened to some of the concert from deep beneath its overhang; the sound was still strong, bright, and full.

The growth of the Vancouver Symphony in recent years is a success story. To the 1968–69 season there were 3,500 subscribers; to the 1975–76 season, over 27,000; to this season, almost 40,000, which must be a world record. (The Israel Philharmonic has 32,000.) Some of the subscriptions are for short series, not for the full run of the main concerts (thirteen of them next season, each played three times). Even so, the figure is impressive and bears witness to community support for the orchestra. Actual attendance at the symphony concerts rose from 119,270 in 1968–69 to 282,486 in 1975–76. Next season's programs are not exactly adventurous. Tchaikovsky looms large (the Second and Sixth Symphonies, *Manfred*, the First Piano Concerto). But there is a sprinkling of twentieth-century orchestral classics (Debussy, Ravel, Falla, Stravinsky, Bartók, Hindemith); and there are five contemporary works, four of them by Canadian composers.

Since 1972, Kazuyoshi Akiyama has been resident conductor and music director of the Vancouver Symphony. (Vancouver is his home, though he is also permanent conductor of the Tokyo Symphony, principal conductor of the Osaka Philharmonic, principal guest conductor of the New Japan Philharmonic, and music director of the American Symphony, in New York; he is billed to conduct nine of the thirteen Vancouver programs next season.) At the Orpheum inaugural concert, he conducted Pierre Mercure's *Triptyque* (composed for the Vancouver International Festival in 1959), Ravel's *Shéhérazade* (with Maureen Forrester as soloist), and Mahler's First Symphony. The Mercure, an exercise in after-Stravinsky timbres and rhythms, showed off the dapper playing of the orchestra and the clean, spacious acoustics of the hall. The Ravel demonstrated that the place welcomes and responds to a voice. The climaxes of the Mahler filled it with big romantic sound, well supported through all the pitch range; the delicate solo writing proved that its acoustics remain warm and immediate throughout the dynamic range—and it brought forward some eloquent woodwind players. Mr. Akiyama is not a "star" conductor but an unobtrusive and thorough musician. As often when listening to his work with the American Symphony, I felt at first that his readings lacked strong character and then that his clear, honest, sensitive intentions were very satisfying. And he has certainly produced an admirably balanced, lively yet lyrical orchestra.

The Vancouver Orpheum is not yet quite finished. Those romantic lobbies and landings, picturesque though they are, are too small to hold a full house during the intermission. There is no place for a convenient bar or café, let alone the restaurant and the bookshop that a modern concert hall needs. But the city has bought the property next door and intends to provide these things. Cinema-organ enthusiasts will be pleased to learn that the Orpheum still houses its mighty Wurlitzer. From Powell and Heinz Halls, the organs are gone.

Baltimore has a new civic theater, the New Mechanic, at the heart of the town. The building stood desolate. There was talk of turning it into a movie house. Instead, the city took it over and spent half a million dollars restoring it. Work was not confined to the auditorium. Baltimore does not believe that going to a concert or a play or a ballet should be a penitential experience or that places of entertainment should open at eight in the evening and close at eleven. So in the flanks of the New Mechanic, giving onto the "high mall" of Charles Center, Baltimore's place of pedestrian throng, three restaurants were installed—French, English, and tetralemmatic in cuisine. (The last has four counters selling health food, junk food, Italian food, and yoghurt.) In the theater itself there is an art gallery, serving coffee, and open all day. The New Mechanic began operations last November. So far, the shows have been mainly Broadway plays and musicals, some on their way to New York, some from it, but this month the Minnesota Opera was invited to bring to Baltimore, a city where Poe associations still linger, its production of Dominick Argento's opera *The Voyage of Edgar Allan Poe*. Four well-attended performances were given in the New Mechanic.

I reviewed the opera at length after its première, in St. Paul, last year (see pp. 359–62). It was enjoyable to hear it again, for it is a romantic, imaginative, lyrical score, rich and various, often exciting, although the action is sometimes confusing. Even after a fresh reading of the libretto, it was hard to sort out, onstage, Poe's mother, foster mother, mother-in-law, grandmother, and Aunt Nancy; their roles are shared by three singers, who in addition play many other parts. But such confusion is essential to the work; the plot is a whirl of episodes from Poe's life, his stories, and his poems presented as if in a vivid, incoherent, delirious dream that fills his final days. That one character should blur into another was part of the composer's original idea. The Minnesota production, with most of the same singers as in St. Paul, had gained a new precision of focus; it was very confident. The orchestra was the Baltimore Symphony, the chorus that of Morgan State University, and both were stronger, more colorful, than those of the original show. The New Mechanic makes a fair-sized opera house, seating nearly sixteen hundred. Even the singers' lightest utterances could be heard so clearly that I suspected an amplification system was in use (I was assured afterward it was not), yet there was space for the "sonic perspectives" created by important offstage choruses to be distinctly drawn. The opera seemed to grow and flower. Its cunning variety of textures, and its kinship with Monteverdi—in fine-drawn duet writing and in madrigalesque interludes—were more apparent than ever.

There should be more such visits. Both the adventurous work of the Minnesota company and Argento's adventurous opera deserved this

East Coast showing. The common practice of allowing an opera production to die after four or five performances, after it has satisfied local demand, is sadly wasteful. Things like the St. Louis *Comte Ory* should be seen in Brooklyn; Brooklyn's production of Argento's *Water Bird Talk* would fit well into the St. Louis season. There are difficulties. This *Poe* venture, which was supported by the National Opera Institute, proved that they can be overcome.

July 4, 1977

INDEX

Index

Compositions and writings are indexed under composer or author. Boldface figures indicate extended discussions or, in long entries, distinguish reviews of the work in question from passing references to it. Musical organizations outside New York based in a particular city are listed under that city; so are concert halls, theaters, etc.

627; Hungarian Folk Songs, 542; *Mikrokosmos*, 37; *Miraculous Mandarin*, 35; Sonata for Two Pianos and Percussion, 77, 187–8; Songs, Opus 15 and 16, **542;** *Village Scenes*, 542; Violin Sonata No. 1, 12
Bartoletti, Bruno, 9
Barzun, Jacques, 262
Basbas, Louise, 111
Bates, Joah, 472
Batignano: Musica nel Chiostro, 211, 401
Battistini, Mattia, 466
Baudelaire, Charles, 359–60, 496, 533–4
Bauld, Alison, 238, 336
Baumann, Kurt, 144
Bayreuth, 240–2, 244, 259, 401, 438–41, 582, 610
Bazelon, Irwin, *Propulsions*, 161
Bazzini, Antonio, *Ronde des lutins*, 276
Beach, Mrs. H. H. A., "Gaelic" Symphony, Quintet in F-sharp minor, Piano Trio, **239**
Beardslee, Bethany, 265
Beaton, Cecil, 115, 283
Beattie, Herbert, 605
Beaumarchais, Caron de, *Mariage de Figaro*, 252–3; *Mère coupable*, 255
Becker, Heinz and Gudrun (eds.), *Giacomo Meyerbeer: Briefwechsel und Tagebücher*, 507
Beckett, John, 181
Beckett, Samuel, 78
Bedford, Steuart, 18, 255, 411, 414, 425
Beecham, Sir Thomas, 82, 188, 241–2, 258, 267, 302, 395, 439, 464, 564, 625
Beerbohm, Max, *Seven Men*, 41
Beeson, Jack, *Lizzie Borden*, 347, **354–6**
Beethoven, Ludwig von, 14, 21, 39, 57, 80, 82–3, 139, 152, 158, 188, 268, 299–300, 333, 393, 396, 430, 472, 477, 480, 489, 495, 501, 592, 594–5, 599–600; Diabelli Variations, 393; *Egmont*, 232; *Fidelio/Leonore*, 67, 123, 149, 187, 232, 240, **272–5, 305–6**, 407–9, 423, 436, 464, 492, 516; *Leonore* overtures, 592; Piano Concertos: No. 3, 299; No. 5, **257;** Piano Sonatas: Op. 27, No. 2 (Moonlight), 386, 477; Op. 53 (Waldstein), 299, 374; Op. 106 (Hammerklavier), 76; Op. 110, **299–300;** last sonatas, **600–1;** *Missa Solemnis*, 453, **598–9;** Septet, 113; String Quartet Op. 133, 495; Symphonies: No. 1, 5, 25, 268, **494;** No. 6, 427; No. 8, 495; No. 9, 158,

208, 267–8, **451–3;** *Vestas Feuer*, 371; Violin Concerto, 274
Beethoven Quartet, 477
Begg, Heather, 207
Behrens, Hildegard, 423
Beier, Carl, 31, 34
Béjart, Maurice, 208
Bekker, Paul, 247, *Wandlungen der Oper*, 131
Bel Canto Opera, 63, 85, 111–12, 132, 186, 279, 455
Belcourt, Émile, 414
Bellincioni, Gemma, 183, 280
Belling, Susan, 287, 574
Bellini, Vincenzo, 175, 293, 328–9, 366, 509, 549; *Adelson e Salvini*, 176; *Capuleti e i Montecchi*, **175–9**, 305; *Norma*, 83, 177, 256, 516, 621; *Pirata*, 177; *Puritani*, 116, 176–7, 240, **307, 328–31**, 405; *Sonnambula*, 150, 177, 185; *Straniera*, 177; *Zaira*, 97, 176
Bellow, Saul, *Henderson the Rain King*, **569–76**
Benackova, Gabriela, 492
Benda, Georg, *Ariadne auf Naxos*, **232**, 537; *Pygmalion*, 615
Bender, David, 261
Beni, Gimi, 169, 617
Benois, Nicola, 141–2, 329, 500
Beowulf, 75
Beranek, Leo L., *Music, Acoustics and Architecture*, 422
Berberian, Ara, 515, 574
Berberian, Cathy, 366
Beregani, Niccolò, 231
Berg, Alban, 11, 131, 139, 213, 246, 489; Four Pieces for clarinet and piano, 129; International Alban Berg Society, 551, 553; *Lulu*, 418, **550–8;** Lyric Suite, **553–5;** Quartet, **139;** Violin Concerto, **449**, 552; *Wozzeck*, **12**, 56, 132, 224, 246, 336, 554–5
Berg, Helene, 552–4, 558
Berg Quartet, 139
Berganza, Teresa, 205
Berger, Arthur, 324, 335, Five Pieces for Piano, 38–9; Septet, 335
Bergonzi, Carlo, 209, 416–18, 578–9
Berio, Luciano, 94, 324, 459, *Calmo*, 325; *Circles*, 187–8
Berkeley: University of California, 363, 366–7, 369, 371, 373, 584
Berkowitz, Phebe, 424
Berkshire Music Center Orchestra, 495
Berlin (East): Komische Oper, 411
Berlin (West): German Opera, 55, 101, 337, 341; Philharmonic, **39–40**, 136, 152, 216, 257, 267, 431, **450–2,**

Carroll, Lewis, *Alice's Adventures in Wonderland* and *Through the Looking-Glass,* 558–63
Carter, Elliott, 21, 24–7, 94, 152, 166, 306–7, 324, 336, 459, 498–9, 578; Brass Quintet, 28, **63, 127;** Concerto for Orchestra, 188; Double Concerto for harpsichord and piano, etc., **26–7,** 322–**3,** 335; Duo for Violin and Piano, **127–9,** 130, 529; Four Pieces for Kettledrums, **160–1;** *Mirror on Which to Dwell,* **306–9;** Sonata for cello and piano, 26, **27;** Sonata for flute, oboe, cello, and harpsichord, 335; String Quartets, 74, 335; No. 3, 26, **27,** 322, 529; *Symphony of Three Orchestras,* **527–32;** "Voyage," **167;** "Warble for Lilac-Time," 167
Caruso, Enrico, 85, 97, 108
Casals, Pablo, 70, 148, 395, 466
Casei, Nedda, 86
Casella, Alfredo, 357
Casellato, Renzo, 53
Casellato-Lamberti, Giorgio, 230
Castel, Nico, 174, 557
Castellan, Jeanne, 501
Cataneo, Aurelia, 579
Cathedral of St. John the Divine, New York, 303, 388
Cavaillé-Coll, Aristide, 144
Cavalieri, Emilio de', *Rappresentazione di anima e di corpo,* 401
Cavalieri, Lina, 95, 106
Cavalli, Francesco, 164, 316; *Calisto,* 492, 564; *Didone,* 310; *Erismena,* 73, 366–7; *Giasone,* 220, 317, **487–90;** *Musiche Sacre,* **72–3,** 303; *Orimonte,* 293; *Ormindo,* **211,** 317; *Serse,* 293
Cecchele, Gianfranco, 423–4
Celebration of Contemporary Music, 79, 322–8
Central Opera Service, 84, 337, 580
Central Park, 387
Central Presbyterian Church, New York, 20, 23, 153
Cerha, Friedrich, 558
Cesti, Marc'Antonio, *Tito,* 231
Chabrier, Emmanuel, 458; *Bourée fantasque,* 457; *Gwendoline,* 456–7; "Little Ducks," 150; *Roi malgré lui,* **456–8,** 580; *Souvenirs de Munich,* 456
Chalia, Rosalia, 79
Chaliapin, Feodor, 60, 62, 282, 547
Chamber Music Society of Lincoln Center, 11, 63, 78, 113, 222–3, 239, 477–8, 494
Chambers, James, 189
Chapin, Schuyler, 43, 138
Chaplin, Charlie, 625

Charles II of England, 387
Charles V of Spain, 164
Charleston, S.C.: Spoleto Festival U.S.A., **606–12**
Charpentier, Gustave, *Impressions d'Italie,* 545; *Louise,* 259, **542–6**
Charpentier, Marc-Antoine, *Médée,* 543, 546
Chartres Cathedral, 446, 448
Chase, Ronald, 134
Chaucer, Geoffrey, 364
Chausson, Ernest, 150; Piano Quartet, 231, **234;** *Viviane,* 235
Chekhov, Anton, *Boor,* 602; "On the Harmfulness of Tobacco," 602–3
Chéreau, Patrice, 558
Cherubini, Maria Luigi, 163, 218–19, 346, 584; *Deux Journées,* **407–10;** *Lodoiska,* **407–10;** *Médée,* **7,** 109, 487; *Pimmalione,* **614,** 615
Chicago: Lyric Opera, 7, 9, 124, 385; Symphony Chorus, 161, 453, 599; Symphony Orchestra, 69, 90, 114, 161, 265, 267, 450–1, 559, 578, 584, 595–9
Chigiana, 213
Chookasian, Lili, 54, 137, 349
Chopin, Frédéric, 22, 37, 41–2, 152; A-flat Ballade, **299**
Choral Society of New York, 492
Chorley, Henry, 141, 330, 466–7, 506–7, 595, 620–2; *Thirty Years' Musical Recollections,* 379
Chou Wen-chung, 322, 335; *Yün,* **265**
Christie, George, 205
Christie, John, 205
Christoff, Boris, 61
Christopher, Russell, 5, 46
Christos, Marianna, 548, 623
Church of St. Paul the Apostle, New York, 301–3
Churchill, Winston, 148
Churgin, Bathia, 80, 213
Chusid, Martin, 385
Cicognini, Giacinto Andrea, 220, 487–8
Cilca, Francesco, 479
Cillario, Carlo Felice, 256
Cimadoro, Giambattista, *Pygmalion,* 615
Cimarosa, Domenico, *Matrimonio segreto,* 358
Cimino, John, 536
Cincinnati: May Festival, **170–4;** Music Hall, 174
Clare, John, 434
Clarion Concerts, 72–3, 80, 82, 110–12
Clarion Opera Group, 487, 489–90
Clatworthy, David, 8
Clauss, Karen, 376

Di Leva, Giuseppe, 405; *Don Chisciotte della Mancha,* **406**

d'Indy, Vincent, 106, 278, 314, 454, 457

DiPaolo, Tonio, 376–7, 457, 605

Dispatch, 388

Di Stefano, Giuseppe, 208, 513

Dlugozewski, Lucia, *Abyss and Caress,* 129

Doernberg, Erwin, 268

Domenichino, 478

Domingo, Placido, 10, 45, 217, 332, 567

Donatello, 214

Donatoni, Franco, Concertino, 499; *Lumen,* **213**

Donizetti, Gaetano, 163, 175, 177, 218, 272, 293, 328, 358, 379–80, 388, 580, 582; *Anna Bolena,* 149–**50, 263–4,** 329, 346; *Belisario,* 508; *Convenienze ed inconvenienze teatrali,* 85; *Dom Sébastien,* 108–10, 123; *Don Pasquale,* 108, 135, 211, 358, 613; *Duc d'Albe,* 328, 612; *Elisir d'amore,* 182, 184–5; *Favorite,* **10, 108–10,** 261; *Fille du Régiment,* 85, 108–9; *Gemma di Vergy,* **330–1,** 332, 346; *Linda di Chamounix,* 508; *Lucia di Lammermoor,* **6–7,** 45, 109, 185, **329,** 331, 346, 453, 471, 567; *Lucrezia Borgia,* 331, **344–7,** 508; *Maria Stuarda,* 331, 346; *Marino Faliero,* 331; *Pia de' Tolmei,* 110; *Pigmalione,* 615; *Poliuto,* 329; *Roberto Devereux,* 346

Donnell, Bruce, 424

Dooley, William, 521

Dorati, Antal, 59, 119

Doria, Renée, 107

Dostoyevsky, Fyodor, 23, 195; *Gambler,* 196–7; *Stranger and Her Lover,* 196

Doussant, Herbert, 305

Dowland, John, 432; "My Lady Hansdon's Puffe," **432**

Dowling, Paul, 189–90

Downes, Edward, 43, 336, 513

D'Oyly Carte Company, 568

Dresden Symphony, 267

Dresser, Paul, "On the Banks of the Wabash," 540

Drew, David, 519, 521

Dreyfus, George, *Garni Sands,* 186; *Lamentable Reign of King Charles the Last,* **336**

Drinker, Henry S., 527

Drucker, Stanley, 12, 129, 235, 237

Druckman, Jacob, 335, 397, 459; *Animus II,* **91, 161, 220, 541–2;** *Animus III,* 91; *Dark Upon the Harp,* **90–1,** 93; *Lamia,* **219–21,** 233, 327; *Synapse,* 91; *Valentine,* **91–2,** 187; *Windows,* **90–2,** 94, 187

Druzhinin, Fyodor, 477–8

Dryden, John, 158; *Alexander's Feast, etc.,* 584

Dubœuf, Estelle, 262

Ducloux, Walter, 261

Dudley, Raymond, 469–70

Dufalle, Richard, 165, 322

Duhan, Hans, 566–7

Dukas, Paul, 545; *Ariane et Barbe-Bleue,* 131

Dumas, Alexandre, père, 331

Dumbarton Oaks Chamber Orchestra, 395

Dunbar, William, *Lament for the Makaris,* 103

Duncan, Isadora, 611

Dunn, Mignon, 62, 137, 171, 230, 443, 521

Duparc, Henri, 150

Dupont, Jacques, 468–9

Duprez, Gilbert, 506

Dürr, Alfred, 153; *Kantaten von Johann Sebastian Bach,* 157

Dürr, Joannes Martin, *Jenůfa,* 44

Dvořák, Antonín, 42; *Devil and Kate,* 261; Peasant Rogue, 185; Piano Quintet, 223; *Rusalka,* **258–61;** Serenade for Strings, **189;** Sonatina, **276**

Dworchak, Harry, 46

Dwyer, Doriot Anthony, 28

Dyer-Bennet, Richard, 522, 526–7

Eads, James, 612

Eames, Emma, 171, 442, 468

Earhardt, Peter, 228

Earls, Paul, *Death of King Phillip,* 337, **344,** 354

Early Music Consort, 181

Eastern Opera Theatre, 112

Easton, Florence, 149, 246

Ebert, Carl, 206

Eckert, Rinde, 536

Eddleman, Jack, 437, 567

Eddlemon, Scott, 160

Edinburgh Festival, 335, 401

Edwards, Ross, 336

Edwards, Ryan, 106–7

Ehrlich, Cyril, *Piano: A History,* 469

Ehrling, Sixten, 136–7, 146, 303, 322, 418, 581

Eigsti, Karl, 539–40

Einem, Gottfried von, *Visit of the Old Lady,* 206

Einstein, Alfred, 350, 396

Eisenstadt, Bergkirche, 284

Eisenstein, Judith, *Binding of Isaac,* 179

Giordano, Umberto, 321; *Andrea Chénier*, 321; *Madame Sans-Gêne*, 459
Giulini, Carlo Maria, 267–8, 464, 564
Giusti, Giuseppe, 67
Glasgow: City Hall, 420
Glass, Philip, 324; *Einstein on the Beach*, **460–3**, 476; Ensemble, 460; *Music with Changing Parts*, 462–3; *Music in Twelve Parts*, 462
Glaz, Herta, 233
Glaze, Gary, 42, 126, 242–3
Glazunov, Alexander, 195
Glinka, Mikhail, *Life for the Tsar*, 546; *Russlan and Lyudmila*, **546–9**
Glossop, Peter, 5, 6, 12
Glover, Jane, 403
Gluck, Alma, 45, 540
Gluck, Christoph, 80, 82, 110, 126, 152, 213–14, 218–19, 346, 363; *Alceste*, 122, 621; *Aristeo*, 620; *Armide*, 106, 317, 621; *Cinesi*, 580; *Don Juan*, 213; *Iphigénie en Aulide*, 106, 122, 404, 621; *Iphigénie en Tauride*, 106, **212**, 277, 307, 410, 621; *Orfeo*, 101, 123, 212, 224, 273, **618–24**; *Paride ed Elena*, 213, 621; *Semiramide*, 213
Glyndebourne Festival, 122, 124, 163, 205–8, 211, 253, 312–16, 401, 411, 419, 581; Touring Opera, 206
Gniewek, Raymond, 493
Gobbi, Tito, 580–1
"God Save the Queen," 24
Gödel, Kurt, 432
Goehr, Alexander, 336; *Arden muss sterben*, 348
Goeke, Leo, 206
Goethe, Johann Wolfgang von, 214, 261, 589; *Faust*, 51, 56–7, 259, 568; *Wilhelm Meisters Lehrjahre*, 51–2, 57
Göhler, Georg, 88
Goldmark, Karl, *Königin von Saba*, 69
Goldoni, Carlo, 364
Goldovsky, Boris, 182, 609
Goldsmith, Harris, 78, 113
Golub, David, 102–3
Gomez, Jill, 45, 206–7, 418
Goodall, Reginald, 135, 137, 240–1, 243
Goodall, Valorie, 31, 34
Goode, Richard, 12, 477–8
Goodloe, Robert, 283
Goodman, Saul, 159; *Ballad for the Dance*, 160
Gordon, Brian, 402
Gorin, David, 305
Gossett, Philip, 124
Gottlieb, Gordon, 286
Gouda: St. John's, 284
Gould, Glenn, 233, 471

Gounod, Charles, 175, 518; *Faust*, **30**, 50, 55, 418, 466, **468–9**
Gozzi, Carlo, *Donna serpente*, 509
Graf, Herbert, 88, 95
Graham, Colin, 18, 316, 411, 413–14
Grainger, Percy, 353
Gramm, Donald, 62, 68, 151, 169, 205–6, 306, 343, 438, 467, 556, 624
Gramont, Louis de, 454
Granados, Enrique, 23
Granata, Dona, 84
Grandi, Alessandro, *Salmi*, 73
Grant, Clifford, 456
Graun, Carl Heinrich, *Montezuma*, 63, 338
Gray, Cecil, 34
Gray, Simon, *Death of a Teddy Bear*, 611; *Molly*, **611**
Green, Curtis, 117
Greenawald, Sheri, 617
Greenberg, Noah, 103–4
Greitzer, Sol, 449
Grétry, André, *Richard Coeur-de-Lion*, 408
Grierson, Mary, 72
Griffin, Ralph, 169
Grigorieva, Nina, 194
Grimm brothers, 375
Grisi, Giuditta, 141
Grisi, Giulia, 330, 344, 388, 466–7
Griswold, Rufus, 359–61
Grossi, Pasquale, 102
Group for Contemporary Music, 129, 162, 190, 265–6, 326
Grout, Donald Jay, 363, 366; *History of Western Music*, 38
Grove, Sir George, *Dictionary of Music and Musicians*, 38, 41, 113, 538
Gruenberg, Louis, *Emperor Jones*, 459
Grümmer, Elisabeth, 242
Grünewald, Matthias, 447–8
Guadagni, Gaetano, 273, 618–22
Guadagno, Anton, 482
Guarneri String Quartet, 393, 470
Guarrera, Frank, 304
Gubrud, Irene, 594
Gueymard, Pauline, 277
Guglielmi, Pietro, 212–13, 619
Gui, Vittorio, 206
Guido d'Arezzo, 211
Guinness Book of World Records, 240
Gullino, Frank, 188
Günther, Ursula, 216
Gutman, John, 230, 240, 242

Haas, Arthur, 374
Haas, Robert, 268–9
Habunek, Vlado, 42
Haddon, Judith, 261

Mahler, Gustav (*cont.*)
Erde, 76, 274, 426; Rückert songs, **13;** Symphonies, **425–9:** No. 1, 36, **627;** No. 2, 173; No. 3, **428–9,** 449; No. 4, 13; No. 5, 172, **596–8;** No. 6, 595; No. 8, 172, 453; No. 9, **13,** 221, 419, 422, **427;** "Tamboursg'sell," 476
Mailingová, Lýdia, 478
Malas, Spiro, 260
Malchenko, Vladimir, 201
Malfitano, Catherine, 149–51, 321
Malibran, Maria, 175, 183
Malipiero, Gian Francesco, *Antonio e Cleopatra,* **99–100**
Mallarmé, Stéphane, 130, 359, 496
Malraux, André, 446
Malvezzi, Cristofano, *Amico fido,* 210
Manchester, Eng., Royal Northern College of Music, 402
Mandac, Evelyn, 44–5, 205, 207, 225–6, 228, 304, 349
Manhattan School of Music, 354, 549–50, 569, 576–7, 585, 617
Manhattan Theater Club, 64, 376, 605
Mann, Alfred, 473
Mann, Robert, 139–40
Mann, Thomas, 14–19, 70, 213–14, 445; *Death in Venice,* **14–17,** 19, 58, 78; *Doktor Faustus,* 57; "Geist und Kunst," 16; "Schwere Stunde," 17
Mannes College of Music, 565–6
Manning, Jane, 265
Mansouri, Lotfi, 456, 502
Mansurov, Fuat, 202
Manuguerra, Matteo, 104–5, 230, 416
Manzoni, Alessandro, 573
Mapleson, James Henry, 612
Marbé, Alan, 348
Marchal, André, 143
Marie Antoinette, 253
Mariette, Auguste, 294–6
Mario, Giuseppe, 506
Mark, Peter, 183–4
Marliani, Marco Aurelio, *Bravo,* 388
Marlowe, Christopher, 56–7
Marmontel, Jean François, 110–11
Marschner, Heinrich, *Hans Heiling,* 508; *Vampyr,* 516
Marsee, Susanne, 582
Marshall, Dennis, 26
Martelli, Luigi, 7
Martin, Barbara, 160
Martin, Ruth and Thomas, 116, 134, 261, 468
Martinelli, Giovanni, 609
Martini, Johann Paul, 213
Martino, Donald, 93–4, 324, 335
Martinů, Bohuslav, Cello Concerto No. 1, **449**

Martirano, Salvatore, Octet, 265
Marymount Manhattan Theater, 565
Mascagni, Pietro, 321; *Cavalleria rusticana,* 150, 418
Masini, Gianfranco, 256
M.I.T. Center for Advanced Visual Studies, 344
Massard, Robert, 219
Massé, Victor, *Paul et Virginie,* 3
Masselos, William, 20
Massenet, Jules, 365, 456; *Cendrillon,* 454; *Cid,* 277, **331–2,** 454; *Don Quichotte,* 454; *Esclarmonde,* 107, 277, **279,** 331, **454–6,** 459, 547; *Ève,* 278; *Grisélidis,* 454; *Hérodiade,* 278; *Jongleur de Notre-Dame,* 454; *Manon,* **4,** 454; *Marie-Magdeleine,* 107, **277– 9,** 454, 478; *Navarraise,* 454; *Portrait de Manon,* 454; *Sapho,* 454; *Thaïs,* **106–7,** 180, 277, 331, 454; *Vierge,* 278; *Werther,* 355, 454, 520
Masterson, Valerie, 437
Materna, Amalie, 171
Mathes, Rachel, 115–16
Matthews, Benjamin, 574
Matthews, Inez, 523
Matzenauer, Margarete, 42
Mauceri, John, 24, 30, 275, 509, 514
Maupassant, Guy de, 3
Mauro, Ermanno, 115, 568
Maw, Nicholas, *Rising of the Moon,* 206; *Scenes and Arias,* 13
May, Henry, 367
Maynor, Dorothy, 543
Mayr, Giovanni Simone, *Medea in Corinto,* 7, 487
Mayr, Richard, 134
Mazurok, Yury, 194, 201
Meale, Richard, 336
Medici, Mario, 7, 385
Mehta, Zubin, 13, 216, 256, 499
Méhul, Érienne, *Joseph,* 516
Mei-Figner, *Medea,* 609
Meier, Johanna, 243, 566, 568
Meiningen Orchestra, 93
Mekeel, Joyce, *Hommages,* **285**
Melano, Fabrizio, 230, 283, 303, 305, 424, 563
Melba, Nellie, 183, 280–1, 337, 466, 468, 541, 543
Mellers, Wilfrid, 341
Memling, Hans, 131
Mendelssohn, Felix, 147, 179, 224, 408; *Hebrides* overture, 257; Piano Trio in C minor, 78; Symphony No. 4, **13,** 594–5
Mengelberg, Willem, 595
Mennin, Peter, 322; Eighth Symphony, **47,** 90

653

Nowak, Leopold, 268–9
Noyes, Alfred, 380
Nygaard, Jens, 64–5, 70–1, 349–52, 397

Obadiah the Proselyte, 179
Obraztsova, Elena, 194, 417–18, 458
O'Brien, Jack, 358
O'Brien, Timothy, 207
Obukhova, Nadezhda, 458
Odets, Clifford, 407
Oeser, Fritz, 544
Oestvig, Karl, 133
Offenbach, Jacques, 151, 249, 457, 582;
    Ba-Ta-Clan, **84;** *Belle Hélène*, **437–8,**
    568, 624; *Contes d'Hoffmann*, 88, 132,
    359, 544; *Orphée aux enfers*, 411,
    618, **624;** *Robinson Crusoe*, 401; *Vie
    parisienne*, 624
Offergeld, Robert, 558
Ogniotsev, Alexander, 197, 200
O'Hearn, Robert, 254–5, 417
Ohio Ballet, 611
O'Horgan, Tom, 574
Oistrakh, David, 478
Old St. Patrick's Church, New York,
    303
Oldenburg, Claes, 617
Olghina, Olga, 5, 95
Oliver, John, 591
Oliver, Stephen, *Duchess of Malfi,* 412;
    Tom Jones, 377, **411–13**
Olivero, Magda, 271, 608–9
Olon-Scrymgeour, John, 358
Olsen, Thomas, 155, 344
Ommerle, Stephen, 84
Opera, 227
Opera Buffa Company, New York, 64
Opera News, 245, 466
Opera Orchestra, New York, 104, 108,
    261, 330–1, 490, 578
Oppens, Ursula, 12, 27, 540, 606
Orenstein, Arbie, *Ravel: Man and Mu-
    sician,* 223
Orff, Carl, 215, 224, 566; *Antigonae,*
    214–15; *Carmina Burana,* 568–9
Organs, 143–7
Orkney Festival, 610
Orledge, Robert, 533, 537
Orloff, Penny, 108
Ormandy, Eugene, 13, 119, 267, 276,
    426
O'Rourke, Jeremiah, 301
Orwell, George, *Lion and the Unicorn,*
    412
Ostendorf, John, 536
Ouseley, Sir Frederick Arthur Gore,
    Martyrdom of St. Polycarp, 279
Ovid, 220, 614, 623

Owen, Wilfred, 348
Ozawa, Seiji, 216, 302–3, 584, 590–1

Pabst, G. W., 209–10
Pacini, Andrea, 366
Pacini, Giovanni, 176
Pacitti, Joe, 107, 259, 358
Paderewski, Ignace, 148
Paganini, Niccolò, *Centone,* 284
Pagliughi, Lina, 6
Paik, Nam June, 162
Paisiello, Giovanni, 212–13, 405; *Don
    Chisciotte della Mancia,* **406,** 431
Palay, Elliot, 243
Palestrina, Giovanni, 152, 458
Pallo, Imre, 134, 550
Palmer, Felicity, 424
Panerai, Rolando, 366
Panni, Marcello, 489
Pantaleoni, Romilda, 579
Panzironi, Massimo, 404
Paris: Bibliothèque Nationale, 52, 371;
    Journées de Musique Contemporaine,
    499; Opéra, 50, 60, 85, 88, 106, 108,
    110, 121, 163, 168–70, 212, 218, 295,
    331–2, 501, 511, 558; Opéra-Comique,
    50–1, 53, 168, 544; Orchestre de
    Paris, 302; Sainte-Chapelle, 446, 448;
    Salle Pleyel, 420; Théâtre-Lyrique,
    168
Parker, Horatio, 24–6; *Mona,* 459
Parma: Teatro Nuovo, 97
Parnas, Leslie, 12
Parry, Hubert, *Judith,* 279
Party, Lionel, 387
Pasatieri, Thomas, *Ines de Castro,* **348–
    9,** 354, 390; *Signor Deluso,* **64**
Pascal, Blaise, 37, 77, 594
Paskalis, Kostas, 54
Pasta, Giuditta, 175, 330, 366, 467
Patanè, Giuseppe, 179
Pater, Walter, 172
Patti, Adelina, 150, 279–80, 392, 540–1,
    583, 595
Paul, Thomas, 515
Paunova, Mariana, 609
Pavarotti, Luciano, 109, 126, 161, 175–
    6, 178, 205, 330, 416, 452–3, 564
Pavlick, Elaine, 260
Pearlston, Steven, 107–8
Pears, Peter, 18, 19, 108, 205, 224, 239–
    40, 465, 525
Peca, Marcello, 404
Pelissier, Victor, 578
Penco, Rosina, 279, 281
Pendarves, Mrs., 366
Penderecki, Krzysztof, *Als Jakob er-
    wachte . . . ,* **538;** Capriccio for Vio-

656

657

Rubinstein, Anton, 234; *Demon,* 69
Rubinstein, Artur, 301
Rudel, Julius, 12, 29, 30, 114–16, 125, 156, 243, 305, 347, 438, 543, 545–6, 566, 568
Rudiakov, Michael, 27
Rue, Robert, 59–60
Ruggles, Carl, 11, 12, 21; *Organum,* 322; *Portals,* **12**
Ruk-Focic, Bozena, 59
Rumyantsev, Pavel, *Stanislavsky on Opera,* 195, 200–1
Rundgren, Bengt, 137
Runge, Philipp Otto, 259
Rusconi, Carlo, 105
Rutgers University Chamber Ensemble, 31

Saarbrücken Radio Orchestra, 337
Saarinen, Eero, 612
Sachs, Hans, 364
Sackville-West, Edward, 58, 299, 301
Sacred Music Society of America, 277–9, 478–9
Sadie, Stanley, *Mozart,* 396
St. Louis: Loretto-Hilton Theatre, 617; Municipal Opera, 612; Opera Studio, of Webster College, 615; Opera Theatre of, **612–18;** Powell Hall, 626–7; Symphony Orchestra, 612, 626
Saint-Maximin, Provence, 284
St. Paul: Chamber Orchestra, 265, 289–90, 294, 326; Schubert Club, 288
Saint-Saëns, Camille, 302; *Samson* arias, 458; "Tarantelle," 231; Third Symphony, **146,** 474–5, **476–8**
Sakharov, Vadim, 299
Salerno, Mario, 213
Salieri, Antonio, *Oxur, Re d'Ormus,* 113
Salta, Anita, 250
Salvadori, Antonio, 482
Salvayre, Gaston, *Bravo,* 389
Salvi, Matteo, 328
Salvini-Donatelli, Fanny, 279
Salzburg: Cathedral, 538; Festivals, 39, 60, 135–6, 215–16, 218, 252–3, 255, 401, 538, **595**
Sambolin, Raymond, 377
Sammarco, Mario, 97
Sammartini, Giovanni Battista, 72, 79–82, 213; E-flat String Quintet, G-minor Symphony, **81;** *Tears of the Magdalen at the Sepulcher,* **81–2**
Sammartini, Giuseppe, 80
Samuelsen, Roy, 58
San Antonio: Symphony, **509–16;** Theatre for the Performing Arts, 515

San Diego: Civic Theater, 261; Opera, 258–61
San Francisco: Opera, 218, 499–500, 502; Symphony, 584
Sanders, Samuel, 276–7
Sanderson, Sibyl, 106, 279, 455
Sanjust, Filippo, 609
Sanquirico, Alessandro, 142, 329
Santa Fe Opera, 205, 486, 553
Sardinero, Vicente, 579
Sargo, Merja, 79
Sarti, Giuseppe, 212–13
Satie, Erik, 211; *Gymnopédies,* **35;** *Vexations,* **462**
Sauguet, Henri, 35
Sauter, Ed, *Eight Random Thoughts,* **287**
Sayer, Leo, 337
Sayles, James M., "Star of the Evening," 559
Scano, Gaetano, 347
Scarlatti, Alessandro, 152, 363; operas, **363–4;** *Griselda,* **363–9,** 580; *Mitridate Eupatore,* **111–12,** 363–4; *Trionfo dell' onore,* 211, 363
Schalk, Josef, 268
Schauler, Eileen, 348, 356
Schenk, Otto, 5, 216, 275
Scherman, Thomas, 42–3
Schiller, Friedrich, 14, 17, 104–5, 198, 293; *Jungfrau von Orleans,* 105, 381; *Räuber,* 104–5, 122, 293; *Wallensteins Lager,* 86
Schindler, Allan, *Cirrus, and Beyond,* **265**
Schinkel, Karl Friedrich, 608
Schiøtz, Aksel, 525
Schipa, Tito, 281
Schippers, Thomas, 62, 141–2, 147
Schlee, Alfred, 553
Schlegel, A. W., 105
Schlöndorff, Volker, 435; *Katarina Blum,* 431
Schmid, Patric, 582
Schmidt, Douglas W., 115, 316, 584
Schmidt, Franz, 69
Schmidt, Jacob, 146
Schnabel, Artur, 148, 300, 466, 595–6, 599–601
Schneider, Alexander, 394–6
Schneider-Siemssen, Günther, 43, 60, 136, 217
Schock, Rudolf, 525
Schoeck, Othmar, 224
Schoeffler, Paul, 241
Schoenberg, Arnold, 11, 69, 83, 131, 138–9, 147, 166, 212–13, 233, 246, 322, 542, 605; *Buch der hängenden Gärten,* 266, 541–2; Five Pieces for

665

Wechsler, Gil, 8, 519
Wedekind, Frank, *Erdgeist* and *Buchse der Pandora,* 550–1, 553, 555–6
Weill, Kurt, 67, 246, 249, 407, 427; *Aufstieg und Fall der Stadt Mahagonny,* 133, 246; *Bürgschaft,* 133; *Dreigroschenoper,* 246, 409, 411; *Jasager,* **246;** "Kleine Mahagonny," 377; *Sieben Todessünden,* 377; *Street Scene,* **354**
Weimar, 168, 170, 246
Weinberger, Jaromir, *Švanda the Bagpiper,* 258
Weingartner, Felix, 595
Weisberg, Arthur, 265, 287
Weisgall, Hugo, *Hundred Nights,* 354, **356–8;** *Nine Rivers from Jordan,* 575
Welitch, Ljuba, 69, 114–15
Weller, Dieter, 417
Wells, Patricia, 54, 116, 169
Welsby, Norman, 414, 437
Welting, Ruth, 6, 53, 355
Wenzig, Josef, 490
Werfel, Franz, 88, 553
Werner, Eric, 179
Werner, Zacharias, 480–1
Wernick, Richard, 77
Westchester Chamber Chorus and Orchestra, 349, 397
Westenburg, Richard, 153
Westminster Choir, 301, 303, 538, 609–10
Westrup, Sir Jack, 111
Wexford Festival, 42, 211
Wexler, Peter, 304, 504
Wexler, Stanley, 155
White, Edward Brickell, 611
White, Robert, 73, 489
White, Stanford, 302–3
White, Willard, 115, 261
Whiting, John, *Devils,* 318
Whitman, Walt, 530–1, 588; *Leaves of Grass,* 587, 589; *Out of the Cradle Endlessly Rocking,* 587; *When Lilacs Last in the Dooryard Bloom'd,* 265, 337–8, 584–6, 588–9
Whitney Museum, 26–8, 74
Widdoes, Lawrence, "Love Song," **190**
Wilde, Oscar, 479
Wilder, Thornton, 359
Wildermann, William, 250
Wilkens, Anne, 437
Williams, Nancy, 53, 169, 605
Williams, Peter, 201
Williams, Tennessee, 612
Williamson, Malcolm, *Symphony for Voices,* 336
Williford, Martha, 617
Willis, Henry, 144–5

Wilmington: Grand Opera House, **392–3;** Opera Society, 392
Wilson, George Balch, *Concatenations,* **94**
Wilson, Robert, *Deafman Glance,* **461;** *Einstein on the Beach,* **460–3**
Wilson, Sir Stewart, 526–7
Wilson, Thomas, *Confessions of a Justified Sinner,* 411
Windingstad, Kari, 368–9
Winkelmann, Hermann, 171
Winston, Lee, 63–4
Wixell, Ingvar, 283, 565
Wohlers, Rudiger, 207
Wolf, Hugo, 52, 224, 264, 462, 541; Goethe settings, 458; Society, 464
Wolf-Ferrari, Ermanno, *Donne Curiose,* 185, 549; *Gioielli della Madonna,* 180, **186;** *Quattro rusteghi,* 401, **549–50,** 573, 617
Wolff, Beverly, 173
Wolff, Christoph, 371–2
Wolpe, Stefan, 324; *Form and Form IV: Broken Sequences,* 38, 41; *Piece in Two Parts,* 38; Sonata for oboe and piano, **163**
Wong, Carey Gordon, 250, 610
Wood, Marilyn, 335
Woodward, Kerry, 605
Woolf, Virginia, *Writer's Diary,* 292
Wordsworth, William 172–3
Work, Henry Clay, "Who Shall Rule the American Nation," etc., 546
Wray, George, 353
Wright, Maurice, Chamber Symphony, **163**
Wuorinen, Charles, 92, 190, 324; *Arabia Felix,* **326;** *Hyperion,* **335;** *Making Ends Meet,* **163;** *On Alligators,* **93;** Piano Variations, **93;** Second Piano Concerto, 90, **92–3;** *W. of Babylon,* 266
Wyeth, N. C., 392
Wyner, Susan Davenny, 157, 307, 309, 473, 489
Wyner, Yehudi, 522, 526

Xenakis, Iannis, 157, 237, 324; *Achorripsis,* 237

Yakim, Moni, 260
Yale Review, 24–5
Yamasaki, Minoru, 120
Yamash'ta, Stomu, 157, 189–90
"Yankee Doodle," 23, 276
Yannopoulos, Dino, 115
Yevtushenko, Yevgeny, 475, 477
Yockey, Joann, 68
Yockey, Ross, 54